S0-AIP-952

How To Write A Nothing Down Offer

HOW TO WRITE A NOTHING DOWN OFFER

SO THAT EVERYONE WINS

A CASEBOOK OF ALTERNATIVE REAL ESTATE INVESTING

BY RICHARD J. ALLEN, Ph.D.

THE ALLEN GROUP INC., PROVO, UTAH

Please Note:

This manual has been prepared as an expression of the author's opinion concerning the subject matter covered. The information is from resources deemed reliable but not guaranteed. If legal advice or other expert professional service is required, the readers are urged to consult competent professionals, attorneys, accountants, etc. The author and publishers specifically disclaim any liability or risk whatsoever in the event any loss is incurred as a result of the application of any advice or information offered herein, whether directly or indirectly used.

All rights reserved.
Copyright © 1982 by The Allen Group, Inc.
This book may not be reproduced in whole or in part, by photocopying or any other means, without permission.
For information write to The Allen Group, Inc., 145 East Center Street, Provo, Utah 84601.
Printed in the United States of America
Fifth Printing October 1984

10 9 8 7 6 5 4

ISBN 0-943402-00-X

*For my wife Carol
And my children Stephanie,
Adrienne, Nathan, and
Matthew, the five best friends I
could ever hope to have.*

Contents

Introduction

"That some should be rich, shows that others may become rich, and hence is just encouragement to industry and enterprise."
—Abraham Lincoln

"For the power is in them, wherein they are agents unto themselves."
—Doctrine and Covenants 58:28

This book is about people who are doers, people who are not afraid to act on their principles when presented with a choice.

I recall an experience from my younger years that has proven to be an indelible emblem for the principle of choice. Perhaps it will strike a responsive chord in the reader and serve to communicate one of the principal themes of this book.

To earn money for college, I made it a practice in my undergraduate days to conduct tours for the visitors who had come to admire nature's wonders in the Canadian national parks of Alberta and British Columbia. Few people were immune to the spell cast by the serene beauty of Lake Louise, the awesome white expanse of the Columbia Ice Fields, the majesty of Takakkaw Falls, or the rugged mountain grandeur along the Valley of the Giants. Being there was for most an exercise in the sublime.

But for those not blinded by nature's highest-order wonders, there was an additional treat too easily overlooked—one that provided less a feast for the eyes than a message for the soul. A few miles west of Lake Louise, at a spot where the highway crosses the Great Divide, a nondescript little stream bubbles down the mountainside toward the valley far below. It is nothing special as streams go, just a foot-wide ribbon of water winding its way towards the same goal that all streams aim for—the ocean.

A few hundred yards below the highway, at a spot where the stream has to traverse a broad treeless meadow, a clump of boulders offers resistance and forces the stream to divide. It is just that simple. One-half of the water continues its journey by turning north-

ward where it joins the Bow River and makes its way via the South Saskatchewan toward the great waterways leading to the Hudson Bay and eventually to the North Atlantic Ocean. The other half of the stream turns southward and finds its way via the Kicking Horse Valley to the Columbia River and eventually into the Pacific Ocean.

That's all there is to it. A stream divides. And yet the tourists gather by the hundreds to watch the little miracle. They park their cars and buses in the parking lot provided for the curious and trudge down to the place where it all happens. They forget Lake Louise and the Athabaska Glacier for a moment and stare as if in a trance at the ugly little stream that all of a sudden becomes two and parts company with itself at the Great Divide. They watch one half head for the Atlantic and the other half head for the Pacific. And they think about that—sometimes for a solid half hour or more—before leaving. For some reason they are temporarily in an altered state of consciousness. Many are forever changed.

Why? What's so significant about a stream that divides? One lady to whom I related this story several years ago in Texas had the answer. She hit the nail on the head. "The reason people stare at the stream," she said, "is that they see in it a reflection of life. In a word: 'That's life!'"

It is true. There are moments in all our lives where we find ourselves at a crossroad, standing before a Great Divide where a decision has to be made. Life is full of decisions—many small, many great. But on occasion we face a choice where the consequences take on the aura of being ultimate. If we decide to move one particular way, our course—like that of a branch of the divided stream—may take us many thousands of miles into the distance and many hours or years into the future before we may again have the opportunity to redirect our energies in a major way. There are important choices in life that will, perhaps forever, change the course of events that will befall us. A choice of a mate is one. A choice of world view—Lebensanschauung—is another. In the commercial realm, a choice of occupation is yet another.

This book is about people who have made and are making choices concerning financial independence—a state of affairs where they will be able to realize their ultimate goals in life. The purpose of the book is to present evidence of action—not helter-skelter action—but rather action of a particular kind, involving a carefully orchestrated program of steps leading to specific outcomes. The arena of action in this case is the world of investments, in particular the world of real estate investments. The events used to illustrate the principles underlying the book are true. Everything, with the exception of proper names and addresses (invented to protect the privacy of contributors), is authentic. Great pains were taken to present the case studies precisely as they occurred. The admirable aspects are celebrated; the problematic aspects are uncovered as teaching opportunities.

Very few of the case studies treated in this book involve buyers who are professional Realtors, brokers, or master investors. Most involve people who very recently stood before a Great Divide and said to themselves, "I have got to do something about my financial future. It's a new world for me to get into, but here are some creative ideas. I must act now." And they did. For better or worse, they took some definitive steps in the direction of financial independence. In doing so, they have enriched their own lives—and those who are trying to follow their example—not only financially, but through the patterns of courage and forthrightness that characterize their efforts.

The immediate theme of this book, as the title indicates, is how to write a nothing down real estate offer so that everyone wins. But the substance of the book is how to seize the initiative when it comes to making important choices—choices that will have profound consequences in the lives of those involved.

The reader can approach the book from a variety of perspectives: how to locate real estate bargains, how to negotiate deals, how to decide which techniques to use in specific situations, how to manage cash flows, how to prepare the documentation with a minimum of risk. The book is organized to accommodate all of these needs. It can be used, also, as a review manual for the Robert Allen Nothing Down System of Real Estate Investing, which underlies all of the case studies. The reader can even use the book for entertainment—each case study is a story unto itself.

Whatever the reader's purpose, I hope the overarching theme will never be entirely obscured by the mass of detail provided, i.e., the power of the individual to take effective steps toward the realization of personal financial goals.

Good luck and happy investing.

Richard J. Allen
Provo, Utah

Acknowledgements

This book would not have been possible without the contributions and accomplishments of Robert G. Allen, whose system of "Nothing Down Creative Financing" underlies the fifty case studies assembled here.

We are equally indebted to the many hundreds of graduates of the Robert Allen Nothing Down Seminar across the nation who shared with us the details of their recent creative real estate transactions. The task of selecting the most instructive and interesting case studies was not simplified by the fact that the amount of valuable material available far exceeded the boundaries of this book.

To those whose contributions were selected for inclusion here, we extend a special thanks. They have demonstrated that creative ability and courage are still very much alive throughout the land. At a time in the nation's history when doomsayers and advocates of economic futility are attempting to drown out those who celebrate the resilient national qualities of hope, initiative, and self-reliance, it is good to know that many people out there are quietly proving that appropriate education and effective action can still lead to the realization of dreams.

We take this opportunity, also, to acknowledge the unflagging efforts of many dozens of R.A.N.D. leaders across the country who voluntarily contribute their time in organizing and conducting the monthly meetings of R.A.N.D. graduates in most major cities. Their help in identifying the most successful investors in the network and facilitating the submission of case studies is much appreciated.

Finally, we express thanks to colleagues and staff for assistance in producing this work: to Charlotte Colley as typesetter, to Grant White as production manager and design artist, to Ruth Ann Fronk for assistance in the collating of materials and the preparation of the documentation, to Jay Mitton for legal advice, to Wade Cook for his suggestions in the early phase of planning, and to David McDougal and Stan Balfour for ongoing assistance in structuring the materials and distributing the final product.

In advance, we thank our readers who will study this work carefully and give us the benefit of their suggestions in how to improve it for future printings.

The following list contains the names of the contributors of materials used in the case studies of this book:

Harvey P. Allan	William G. Kelley
Gilbert R. Andress	Douglas Kinzy
Gary Bohn	Lincoln C. Klabo
Richard S. Casselberry	Charles H. Kram
Laura B. Caswell	Ernest R. Lewis
Bruce L. Congdon	Dr. Jim Loftus
Russell Davis	William J. Martin
LaMarr M. Dell	James Medley
Joseph B. Dixon	Irene V. Milin
Eric Dorsee	Michael J. Milin
Robert & Nancy Eberhardy	Karon Olinghouse
Gary L. Foster	Gil Ortiz
Jeff Gerber	Glenn R. Pollock
Richard E. Goldsby	Frank Scott
R. C. Gunther	David Vincent
Michael Halloran	Paul D. Weinstein
Glenn R. Harrison	Alan S. Wilson
Michael Q. Hesser	William Winkel
Glenn Hottenstein	William A. Wood
Stu and Judy Houston	Jack Wright
R. B. Kavinoky	John Zarrella

Real Estate Investing — Done Right

"In no country in the world is the love of property more active and more anxious than in the United States."

—Alexis de Tocqueville,
Democracy in America

"Upon equal, or nearly equal profits, most men will choose to employ their capitals rather in the improvement and cultivation of land than either in manufactures or in foreign trade."

—Adam Smith, *Wealth of Nations*

R.A.N.D.: The "Robert Allen Nothing Down" System of Creative Real Estate Investing

"Don't wait to buy real estate; buy real estate right and wait."
—Robert G. Allen

In his slender book *New Think*, Edward de Bono makes the statement: "It may be so difficult to escape from a dominant idea that it becomes impossible without outside help" (New York: Basic Books, 1968, p. 33).

The world of real estate has been governed for years by one dominant strain of thought, i.e., in order to buy and hold property successfully, the average person must have excellent credit, a strong financial statement, good income, lots of money for a substantial down payment, and strong collaborative support from the hard-money lenders. With the coming of the days of economic austerity, those who agreed that income property was the finest of all investments found they could not hope to participate in owning a larger piece of America under the dominant rules that had obtained hitherto. New patterns were needed if the cash-poor but creative individual was to break into the world of property ownership.

High-orbit investors had long been aware of creative techniques for acquiring property with minimum capital of their own. Out of the exchange movement of the fifties and sixties—especially in California—formulas for nothing down purchases became the rule of thumb. But such alternative approaches to buying real estate were mostly confined to the private circles of the highly sophisticated investor or real estate professional. The average Joe was still burdened with the dominant ideas of high down, hard money, and heavy credit. How could he hope to participate in America's most beneficial investment?

How, except through outside help? There had to be a way to escape from the domination of conventional ideas. One of the most important popular contributors to that escape—and perhaps the most important—was Robert G. Allen, whose book *Nothing Down* (Simon and Schuster, 1980) remained on the prestigious New York Times Best-Seller List longer in 1981 than any other hard-cover non-fiction work except for Milton

Friedman's *Free to Choose.* Over 300,000 copies of *Nothing Down* have been sold to date. Some 300,000 people nationwide have attended the widely advertised free lectures on the Nothing Down System, and over 30,000 are graduates of the famous two-day Robert Allen Nothing Down Seminar. It would be hard to estimate how many hundreds of thousands, perhaps millions, have taken note of Robert Allen's famous line: "Fly me to any city. Take away my wallet. Give me $100 for living expenses. And in 72 hours I'll buy an excellent piece of real estate for nothing down."

What accounts for the rather phenomenal success of the Nothing Down movement nationwide? From its humble beginnings in August of 1977, the Nothing Down Seminar has grown to be America's most popular educational offering on the subject of creative finance in real estate. The only explanation for this success is the fact that the R.A.N.D. System offered deliverance from the strictures of conventional approaches. At last the general public had access to techniques and formulas that would permit the acquisition of a real estate portfolio under the cashless conditions that prevailed toward the end of the seventies and into the eighties.

Robert Allen became, in effect, the major force for popularizing creative financing in America. It was my good fortune to become associated with this movement in 1979, when my brother Robert invited me to leave the academic world of meditative serenity and venture with him into the world of educational entrepreneurship on a grand scale. My task would be to assure the educational and organizational quality of the nothing down product and to assist in the program for "taking the message" to the American public.

If there was something of the missionary spirit at work in the way we went about our task, it was a conscious effort to place the program in the context of values that had contributed fundamentally to the American way of life—initiative, self-reliance, creative thought, mutual support—values that would strike a familiar chord in the minds of the cross-sectional audience we wanted to reach. The response was overwhelming. What came to be known as the "win/win" approach to real estate investing had immediate appeal to readers and seminar attendees. The nation-wide network of R.A.N.D. graduates organized into "R.A.N.D. Groups" continued the task of expanding awareness of new techniques and practicing principles of peer support and creative problem-solving. Additional seminars, books, tapes, newsletters, and hot-line advisory opportunities were introduced for those with specialized needs. The objective of the movement was to make it possible for anyone—anyone, that is, with the desire and the will—to become successful as income-property investors. As of this writing, some measure of success has been realized. Graduates are acquiring nothing down property at the rate of over one billion dollars worth per year—and climbing. As the case studies in this volume will show, the acquisitions program in general is progressing without undue burdens of negative cash flows and balloons. Here is a program that works!

The organizational framework that I recommended for the Nothing Down System—the one that was eventually adopted—is summarized in the chart below. Details are available in the seminar manual for the Nothing Down Seminar. The basic task of laying the foundation consists in appropriating an open and creative mind-set, establishing realistic goals, targeting "bread and butter" properties in good condition, identifying "don't wanter" (i.e., flexible) sellers, and doing one's homework in analyzing all important aspects of the property. The transaction is then completed by means of the appropriate win/win strategies of negotiation, financial problem-solving using the nothing down system of fifty basic creative techniques (organized according to the nine flexible sources of down payment capital), and seeing to it that the closing is accomplished in as risk-free and professional a manner as possible. The "harvesting of the money crop" can proceed in a variety of ways depending on one's goals and circumstances. Whatever the individual patterns decided upon, all must of course proceed on the basis of action—"Mastering the Art of Becoming a Doer." The entire program is summarized in Bob Allen's formula: "Don't wait to buy real estate; buy real estate right and wait."

Section Two of this volume provides brief vignettes of all fifty of the Nothing Down techniques of the program categorized by sources of capital. The case studies are organized to reflect the coherence and integrity of the Nothing Down approach as a system of action steps proceeding in a logical order. The whole exercise of going through this book is intended as one way the reader can escape a dominant conventional idea and replace it with a new gestalt—one that is more in tune with the needs of our modern age.

Robert G. Allen's
Nothing Down System
of Creative Real Estate Investing

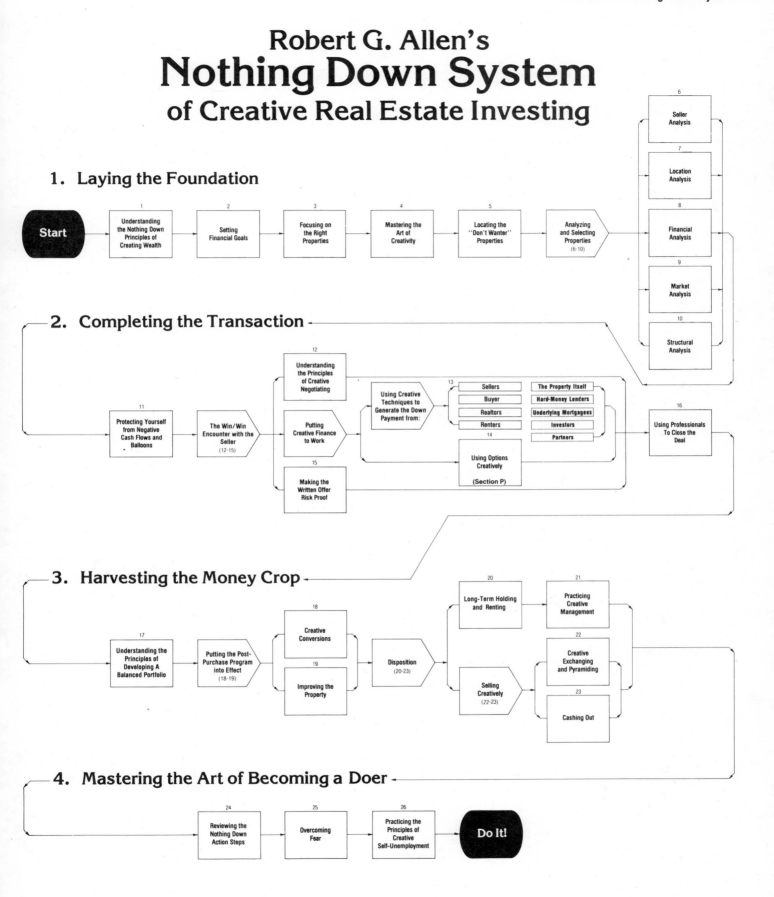

1. Laying the Foundation

Start → 1. Understanding the Nothing Down Principles of Creating Wealth → 2. Setting Financial Goals → 3. Focusing on the Right Properties → 4. Mastering the Art of Creativity → 5. Locating the "Don't Wanter" Properties → Analyzing and Selecting Properties (6-10)

6. Seller Analysis
7. Location Analysis
8. Financial Analysis
9. Market Analysis
10. Structural Analysis

2. Completing the Transaction

11. Protecting Yourself from Negative Cash Flows and Balloons → The Win/Win Encounter with the Seller (12-15)

12. Understanding the Principles of Creative Negotiating
Putting Creative Finance to Work
15. Making the Written Offer Risk Proof

Using Creative Techniques to Generate the Down Payment from:

13. Sellers, Buyer, Realtors, Renters — The Property Itself, Hard-Money Lenders, Underlying Mortgagees, Investors, Partners

14. Using Options Creatively (Section P)

16. Using Professionals To Close the Deal

3. Harvesting the Money Crop

17. Understanding the Principles of Developing A Balanced Portfolio → Putting the Post-Purchase Program into Effect (18-19)

18. Creative Conversions
19. Improving the Property

Disposition (20-23)

20. Long-Term Holding and Renting → 21. Practicing Creative Management

Selling Creatively (22-23)

22. Creative Exchanging and Pyramiding
23. Cashing Out

4. Mastering the Art of Becoming a Doer

24. Reviewing the Nothing Down Action Steps → 25. Overcoming Fear → 26. Practicing the Principles of Creative Self-Unemployment → **Do It!**

"I Agree/You Agree": How to Write Risk-Free Formal Offers

In our research with the graduates of the now famous Robert Allen Nothing Down Seminar, we have learned that the average Nothing Down investor will have to make five formal offers — usually on five different properties — before achieving one purchase. If the purchase is truly a nothing down purchase where 5% or less of the buyer's own funds are used as a down payment, it takes more like ten formal offers to hit pay dirt. One young man from Southern California who acquired over $800,000 worth of real estate within two months of taking the seminar (all with nothing down) had to make 50 formal offers to attain his goal.

There is a lesson there. No offers. No purchases. Many offers. Many purchases. Simple! But naturally it is more than just a numbers game. The offers have to be skillful offers, based on careful analysis and astute use of creative finance principles. The buyer and seller have to agree on terms that will lead to win/win outcomes and then find the language to preserve and formalize their agreement accurately.

For some, the challenge of putting their signature to paper is very nearly an insurmountable barrier. There is something awesome and forbidding about that little dotted line just daring you to scrawl your signature along it — daring you to state irreversibly the commitment: "I do!" For those who cannot bring themselves to formalize their commitments, goals will ever remain fantasy. Such people will have to content themselves with dreams of financial independence. The actuality will always remain out of reach.

This book is about people who were willing to say: "I do." The fifty case studies recorded here would never have occurred without a formal commitment to action on the part of both buyer and seller. At some point in the process of fact-finding, analysis, and negotiation, both parties saw things fall in place and signed on the dotted line. For better or worse, they initiated the process by which real property changes hands. Some deals will no doubt turn out to be more successful for

the buyer than others. But at least there was action — action based on the best information available and the most skillful planning for the future possible under the circumstances.

Graduates of the Nothing Down Program are currently buying real estate at a rate of around $20,000,000 worth per week — over $1 billion worth per year. At an average purchase price of $100,000 per property (as validated by an independent university study on the program), that amounts to 200 properties per week. Based on the offers-per-purchase formula mentioned earlier, it would take between 1,000 and 2,000 offers weekly to achieve that level of success in buying. That means that your colleagues in the Nothing Down Network will be making from 125 to 250 formal offers TODAY (based on an eight-hour work schedule) and between 15 and 30 offers during the HOUR it takes you to peruse this book. In fact, chances are that some wiseguy "nothing downer" made a spectacular offer during the minute or two it has taken you to read this section of the book. His chances are one in five to achieve success and one in ten to achieve a true nothing down deal. Without making the formal offer, his chances of achieving anything are exactly zero.

The same as yours. It's all a matter of making good offers — many good offers — enough offers to achieve your explicit goal. If you want to buy one excellent nothing down property per year, then somewhere along the line you will probably have to make around ten good offers, around one per month. If you want to buy four excellent nothing down properties per year, then get ready to sharpen your pencil at least once a week. It will take that many formal offers to achieve your goal. If you decide to go for broke and buy one million dollars worth of single family homes during the next year without using your own money (around one per month), then you can expect to make a good offer every three days. Of course, if you have the fortune of stumbling across that spectacular multi-million dollar package of homes just ready for the asking, you can take care of your goal with a single successful offer (have a look at Case No. 34 in this book). However, such luck is rare and is usually the result of countless hours of preparation and searching.

Once the Nothing Down Practitioner is persuaded that there is no alternative but action, that offers HAVE to be made on a regular basis, then the next step is to examine the principles of how to make the offers as risk-free as possible. That is the purpose of this chapter. If we could set up a few safety nets below the cliff, then maybe more people would get up the courage to jump off. It doesn't take much instruction in the art of contingency planning before even the most risk-averse begin to come out of hiding.

The notorious document at the heart of the issue is the Earnest Money Receipt and Offer to Purchase. It has various aliases in different areas of the country, among others: Purchase Agreement for Real Estate, Purchase Contract and Receipt for Deposit, Deposit Receipt and Contract for Sale, Preliminary Purchase Agreement, Sales Agreement and Receipt for Earnest Money, Deposit Receipt and Agreement, Agreement for the Sale of Real Estate, Sale Agreement and Receipt for Earnest Money, Earnest Money Receipt and Sales Contract, Commercial Purchase and Sale Agreement, Deposit Receipt and Purchase and Sale Agreement, etc., etc.

It all boils down to the same thing — a legally binding written agreement signed by both buyer and seller committing them to the sale of a specific piece (or pieces) of real estate according to specific terms. To show good faith in entering the transaction, the buyer pledges something of value that commits him to action and shows his earnestness in the matter.

Even though the intent and substance of the preliminary agreement is the same throughout the country, the form and wording in various jurisdictions can vary widely. Some versions of the document are also protected by copyright. Therefore, we have designed our own version for use throughout this book. Our model may not be a paragon of documentary perfection, but it is at least straightforward and comprehensive enough to serve as an adequate instructional tool for examining the principles of making risk-free offers. Here is the masterpiece we came up with after examining counterparts from all areas of the country and conferring with competent legal counsel:

UNIVERSAL EARNEST MONEY RECEIPT
AND OFFER TO PURCHASE

"This is a legally binding contract: if not understood, seek competent advice."

1. Date and Place of Offer: _____ 19 _____ ; _____

(city)   (state)

2. Principals: The undersigned Buyer _____
agrees to buy and Seller agrees to sell, according to the indicated terms and conditions, the property described as follows:

3. Property: located at _____

(street address)   (city)   (state)

with the following legal description: _____

including any of the following items if at present attached to the premises: plumbing, heating, and cooling equipment, including stoker and oil tanks, burners, water heaters, electric light fixtures, bathroom fixtures, roller shades, curtain rods and fixtures, draperies, venetian blinds, window and door screens, towel racks, linoleum and other attached floor coverings,

including carpeting, attached television antennas, mailboxes, all trees and shrubs, and any other fixtures EXCEPT _____

The following personal property shall also be included as part of the purchase: _____
At the closing of the transaction, the Seller, at his expense, shall provide the Buyer with a Bill Of Sale containing a detailed inventory of the personal property included.

4. Earnest Money Deposit: Agent (or Seller) acknowledges receipt from Buyer of _____ dollars $ _____

in the form of ( ) cash; ( ) personal check; ( ) cashier's check; ( ) promissory note at _____ % interest per annum due _____ 19 _____ ; or

other _____
as earnest money deposit to secure and apply on this purchase. Upon acceptance of this agreement in writing and delivery of same to Buyer, the earnest money deposit shall be assigned

to and deposited in the listing Realtor's trust account or _____, to apply on the
purchase price at the time of closing.

5. Purchase Price: The total purchase price of the property shall be _____ dollars $ _____

6. Payment: Purchase price is to be paid by Buyer as follows:

    Aforedescribed earnest money deposit . . . . $ _____

    Additional payment due upon acceptance of this offer . . . . $ _____

    Additional payment due at closing . . . . $ _____

Balance to be paid as follows:

_____
_____

7. Title: Seller agrees to furnish good and marketable title free of all encumbrances and defects, except mortgage liens and encumbrances as set forth in this agreement, and to make

conveyance by Warranty Deed or _____. Seller shall furnish in due course
to the Buyer a title insurance policy insuring the Buyer of a good and marketable title in keeping with the terms and conditions of this agreement. Prior to the closing of this transaction, the Seller, upon request, will furnish to the Buyer a preliminary title report made by a title insurance company showing the condition of the title to said property. If the Seller cannot furnish marketable title within thirty days after receipt of the notice to the Buyer containing a written statement of the defects, the earnest money deposit herein receipted shall be refunded to the Buyer and this agreement shall be null and void. The following shall not be deemed encumbrances or defects: building and use restrictions general to the area; utility easements; other easements not inconsistent with Buyer's intended use; zoning or subdivision laws, covenants, conditions, restrictions, or reservations of record; tenancies of record. In the event of sale of other than real property relating to this transaction, Seller will provide evidence of title or right to sell or lease such personal property.

8. Special Representations: Seller warrants and represents to Buyer (1) that the subject property is connected to ( ) public sewer system, ( ) cesspool or septic tank, ( ) sewer system available but not connected, ( ) city water system, ( ) private water system, and that the following special improvements are included in the sale: ( ) sidewalk, ( ) curb and gutter, ( ) special street paving, ( ) special street lighting; (2) that the Seller knows of no material structural defects; (3) that all electrical wiring, heating, cooling, and plumbing systems are free of material defects and will be in good working order at the time the Buyer is entitled to possession; (4) that the Seller has no notice from any government agency of any violation or knowledge of probable violations of the law relating to the subject property; (5) that the Seller has no notice or knowledge of planned or commenced public improvements which may result in special assessments or otherwise directly and materially affect the property; and (6) that the Seller has no notice or knowledge of any liens to be assessed against the property,

EXCEPT _____.

9. Escrow Instructions: This sale shall be closed on or before _____ 19 _____ by _____
or such other closing agent as mutually agreed upon by Buyer and Seller. Buyer and Seller will, immediately on demand, deposit with closing agent all instruments and monies required

to complete the purchase in accordance with the provisions of this agreement. Contract of Sale or Instrument of Conveyance to be made in the name of _____

_____

10. Closing Costs and Pro-Ration: Seller agrees to pay for title insurance policy, preliminary title report (if requested), termite inspection as set forth below, real estate commission, cost of preparing and recording any corrective instruments, and one-half of the escrow fees. Buyer agrees to pay for recording fees for mortgages and deeds of conveyance, all costs or expenses in securing new financing or assuming existing financing, and one-half of the escrow fees. Taxes for the current year, insurance acceptable to the Buyer, rents, interest, mortgage reserves, maintenance fees, and water and other utilities constituting liens, shall be pro-rated as of closing. Renters' security deposits shall accrue to Buyer at closing. Seller to provide Buyer with all current rental or lease agreements prior to closing.

11. Termite Inspection: Seller agrees, at his expense, to provide written certification by a reputable licensed pest control firm that the property is free of termite infestation. In the event termites are found, the Seller shall have the property treated at his expense and provide acceptable certification that treatment has been rendered. If any structural repairs are required by reason of termite damage as established by acceptable certification, Seller agrees to make necessary repairs not to exceed $500. If repairs exceed $500, Buyer shall first have the right to accept the property "as is" with a credit to the Buyer at closing of $500, or the Buyer may terminate this agreement with the earnest money deposit being promptly returned to the Buyer if the Seller does not agree to pay all costs of treatment and repair.

12. Conditions of Sale: The following conditions shall also apply, and shall, if conflicting with the printed portions of this agreement, prevail and control:

_____
_____

13. Liability and Maintenance: Seller shall maintain subject property, including landscaping, in good condition until the date of transfer of title or possession by Buyer, whichever occurs first. All risk of loss and destruction of property, and all expenses of insurance, shall be borne by the seller until the date of possession. If the improvements on the property are destroyed or materially damaged prior to closing, then the Buyer shall have the right to declare this agreement null and void, and the earnest money deposit and all other sums paid by Buyer toward the purchase price shall be returned to the Buyer forthwith.

14. Possession: The Buyer shall be entitled to possession of property upon closing or _____, 19 _____.

15. Default: In the event the Buyer fails to complete the purchase as herein provided, the earnest money deposit shall be retained by the Seller as the total and entire liquidated damages. In the event the Seller fails to perform any condition of the sale as herein provided, then the Buyer may, at his option, treat the contract as terminated, and all payments made by the Buyer hereunder shall be returned to the Buyer forthwith, provided the Buyer may, at his option, treat this agreement as being in full force and effect with the right to action for specific performance and damages. In the event that either Buyer, Seller, or Agent shall institute suit to enforce any rights hereunder, the prevailing party shall be entitled to court costs and a reasonable attorney's fee.

16. Time Limit of Offer: The Seller shall have until

_____, 19 _____ to accept this
     (hour)   (date)
offer by delivering a signed copy hereof to the Buyer. If this offer is not so accepted, it shall lapse and the agent (or Seller) shall refund the earnest money deposit to the Buyer forthwith.

17. General Agreements: (1) Both parties to this purchase reserve their rights to assign and hereby otherwise agree to cooperate in effecting an Internal Revenue Code 1031 exchange or similar tax-related arrangement prior to close of escrow, upon either party's written notice of intention to do so. (2) Upon approval of this offer by the Seller, this agreement shall become a contract between Buyer and Seller and shall inure to the benefit of the heirs, administrators, executors, successors, personal representatives, and assigns of said parties. (3) Time is of the essence and an essential part of this agreement. (4) This contract constitutes the sole and entire agreement between the parties hereto and no modification of this contract shall be binding unless attached hereto and signed by all parties to the contract. No representations, promises, or inducements not included in this contract shall be binding upon any party hereto.

18. Buyer's Statement and Receipt: "I/we hereby agree to purchase the above property in accordance with the terms and conditions above stated and acknowledge receipt of a

completed copy of this agreement, which I/we have fully read and understand." Dated _____ 19 _____, _____
                                                                                                                        (hour)

Address _____   _____ Buyer

        _____   _____ Buyer

Phone No: Home _____ Business _____

19. Seller's Statement and Response: "I/we approve and accept the above offer, which I/we have fully read and understand, and agree to the above terms and conditions this day

of _____, 19 _____, _____
                                                        (hour)

Address _____   _____ Seller

Phone No: Home _____ Business _____ _____ Seller

20. Commission Agreement: Seller agrees to pay a commission of _____% of the gross sales price to _____
for services in this transaction, and agrees that, in the event of forfeiture of the earnest money deposit by the Buyer, said deposit shall be divided between the Seller's broker and the Seller
(one half to each party), the Broker's part not to exceed the amount of the commission.

21. Buyer's Receipt for Signed Offer: The Buyer hereby acknowledges receipt of a copy of the above agreement bearing the Seller's signature in acceptance of this offer.

Dated _____, 19 _____ _____ Buyer

_____ Buyer

Commentary on the Universal Earnest Money Receipt and Offer to Purchase

The 21 divisions of the document address the following questions, all of which are centrally important to the transaction:

1. When and where is the offer made?
2. Who is involved in the transaction?
3. Which property is involved and exactly what is included in the sale?
4. What is the amount of the deposit and in what form is it given?
5. What is the purchase price?
6. How is the price to be paid?
7. Can the seller deliver clear title to the property?
8. Can the seller attest to the quality of the property?
9. When and how is the closing to take place?
10. Who pays for what at the closing?
11. Is the structure free of termite problems, and if not, how to proceed?
12. What special conditions of the sale are there?
13. Who is liable for the property from the time of acceptance until the closing?
14. When can the buyer have possession of the property?
15. What happens in case the buyer or the seller fail to comply with the terms of the agreement as promised?
16. How long does the seller have to accept or reject the offer?
17. What general agreements are binding on the parties to the agreement?
18. Is the buyer willing to accept the agreement as stated?
19. Does the seller accept the offer?
20. What commission is involved, and how and to whom is it to be paid?
21. Does the buyer acknowledge receipt of the final signed offer?

If the verbiage to answer all those question had to be written out and negotiated from scratch every time an offer were made, buyers and sellers would be smothered in the paralysis of analysis and never get much done. Fortunately, a preprinted form such as the one reproduced above takes care of most of the boilerplate basics — all of which are important — leaving spaces for the optional items constituting the heart of the offer. Let's examine the earnest money form step by step and see how it can be filled out using risk-free entries.

1. **Date and Place of Offer.** Everyone can get this far on their own without the slightest tinge of fear and concern.

2. **Principals.** Here the name of the buyer is filled out but with the addition of the vital words "or Assigns." If "John Doe" appears on this line, then John Doe must follow through with the purchase. But if "John Doe or Assigns" appears there, then John Doe may, at his option, assign the agreement to someone else prior to closing and let that someone take over the purchase. What if you strike a spectacular bargain on a piece of property and then an associate, to whom you mention it, wants to step in and take over your interest? With the words "or Assigns" to back you up, you could effectively "sell" him your interest in the property and perhaps realize a handsome profit. Your "interest" in the property is effectively the earnest money you put down and the right it gives you to control the property according to the terms of the agreement. An earnest money agreement is, in fact, a short-term option to purchase: Technique No. 49 in the Nothing Down System of creative finance described below. In most cases John Doe has every intention of following through with the purchase himself, but those two extra little words "or Assigns" enlarge his options and add an element of insurance to the undertaking. It is possible, after all, that circumstances may on occasion prevent John from following through on his plan to purchase the property. He may be forced to assign his interest and needs the legal right to do so.

3. **Property.** If the legal description is not available to you at the time, you may enter the street address and add the words "to be supplied prior to closing" or "Escrow Agent authorized to add legal description to the agreement." An example of a legal description as recorded in the official records might be: "Lot 23 in Block 16 of Joseph Strator's 1st Addition to the City of Midvale, as per plat recorded in Volume 7 of Plats, Page 78, records of Everett County." As you can see, that is not something you might have access to as you are sitting there writing out an offer on a property that is in high demand.

The rest of Item No. 3 is boilerplate identifying as part of the offer anything that might be attached to the property. It is important to list separately any unattached items you hope to acquire as part of the property, e.g., refrigerators, ranges, furniture, wall-hangings, and so on. Such personal property might be depreciable for tax purposes at a faster rate than the improvements; therefore, Item No. 3 requires the seller to provide a bill of sale inventorying such items.

4. **Earnest Money Deposit.** The buyer can use as earnest "money" any consideration acceptable to the seller. The payment is usually in the form of cash (checks). However, many buyers prefer to use non-interest-bearing promissory notes made out in favor of the seller. If the buyer backs out of his commitments, then the seller has recourse through the note, which must be paid according to the terms agreed on. If the deal goes through as planned, the note is retired in favor of the payment schedule agreed to in Item No. 6. Paying the earnest money via a note has two advantages: no cash is tied up during the process of purchasing the property, and the buyer can offer a larger sum. One of the Nothing Down graduates in Los Angeles who specializes in multi-unit apartment buildings, makes it a practice of using $5,000 earnest money notes when submitting offers. The generous amount of the notes impresses the sellers.

If cash is used (currency, checks, etc.), the buyer should put down as little as possible and still stay within the "trust comfort zone" of the seller. Sometimes $100 will suffice; sometimes it will take $500 or more to demonstrate to the seller that there is a sincere desire to follow through with the purchase. The deposit should be held by a third party — in the real estate broker's trust account or in the trust account of an attorney or escrow officer. If the amount of deposit is small and no agent is involved, letting the seller hold it might be a gesture of trust that could elicit similar flexibilities on the part of the seller.

It is also possible to make an earnest "money" payment in the form of personal property: a car, a boat, a stereo, a piece of equipment — anything perceived by the seller as having value. Naturally the buyer will need to measure the value of personal property against the risks involved.

5. **Purchase Price.** This figure will represent either the outcome of a process of negotiation already completed, or it will represent the buyer's opening figure. Beginning investors will often attach their risk-sensitivity to this figure. They prepare to do battle down to the penny in order to feel secure about the transaction. Actually, the price is in general not as important as the terms of repayment. One of the techniques, in fact, is called "Raise the Price, Lower the Terms" (No. 5). There is less risk involved if the terms are "soft," i.e., flexible in the interest rate, size, and frequency of the installments, and length of note, than if the price is a bit too high. Of course, in a "wholesale" transaction (one involving a heavily discounted property), the price may be very important if the buyer is cashing the seller out. The buyer has to offset his risk in providing a great deal of cash by insisting on a lower price (as much as 15 to 50% below market). It all depends on the situation at hand.

6. **Payment.** This item represents the most important aspect of the negotiation process. Once again, the parties may have agreed orally on the terms and are now providing formal language to prepare for closing. On the other hand, the buyer may be using the earnest money agreement as a tool for negotiation. The terms he is suggesting may be his opening salvo; in this case, he will want them to minimize risk to himself while avoiding insult to the seller with too high a degree of one-sidedness. This is the realm where only two rules prevail: "You never know until you ask" and "A lasting and satisfying deal is a win/win deal."

Sometimes the seller will insist on additional earnest money upon acceptance of the offer. If so, the form provides a place for the figure. The balance of the down payment, if there is to be any, is entered on the line "Additional payment due at closing." The balance of the sales price (after the down payment) is then expressed in terms of the combination of existing encumbrances and new arrangements for paying out the seller's equity.

What are the possibilities? Most transactions are completed using one or more of the following approaches:

(1) **All cash** (as in a wholesale deal) — this is easy to express.

(2) **Assumption of an existing encumbrance:** For example, "This purchase is subject to Buyer assuming and paying Seller's current first mortgage and note (first trust deed and note) held by ABC Mortgage Company with monthly payments on the approximate balance of $_____ to be amortized over _____ years and to include interest not in excess of _____ percent per annum, together with monthly allowances for estimated annual property tax and insurance escrows."

Commentary: In an assumption process, the buyer may have to deal with the original lender, who may want to increase the interest rate prevailing on the existing loan. By using the terms "subject to" and specifying a maximum interest rate ("not in excess of"), the buyer is adding a contingency clause to protect himself in the event the assumption terms of the lender are unacceptable. In the case of an FHA or VA mortgage, the loan will be assumable as is, and the terms of the loan can be stated in the earnest money without a contingency. The assumption process can also apply to a second mortgage (or second trust deed), an all-inclusive trust deed, a contract, or other existing encumbrance.

(3) **Purchasing the property subject to an existing encumbrance:** For example, "Buyer to purchase property subject to an existing first mortgage and note (first trust deed and note) of record in the

approximate amount of $_____, payable approximately $_____ per month, including interest at _____ percent per annum and allowances for estimated annual property tax and insurance escrows (PITI)."

Commentary: Purchasing a property "subject to" existing encumbrances means that no formal assumption takes place. The buyer does not go to the lender and pass muster according to the institional policies for qualifying. What risk is involved in buying "subject to"? In the case of an underlying FHA or VA loan, none at all, since such loans are fully assumable. In the case of a commercial loan in which the trust document contains a "due-on-sale" clause (acceleration clause), the seller may be in violation of his agreement with the bank unless he requires the buyer to go through a formal assumption process. This is a hot issue today — one that will likely be resolved by the Supreme Court in the near future. There are outspoken advocates on both sides. Friends of the banking industry claim that the banks have every right to force new buyers to qualify and pay higher rates of interest (plus assumption fees up front). Friends of the buying public claim that sellers have the right of "alienation" — the right to sell their property without restraint as long as the loans are not rendered less secure as a result. In this period of tight money, the banks and savings and loan associations are frequently very aggressive about accelerating their loans when sellers sell "subject to" and not through the "assumption" process.

What is the down-side risk for the buyer who structures his offers on a "subject to" basis? At the very least, he should be prepared (in the case of due-on-sale loans) to respond to a call from the lender to come in and qualify for the loan, pay additional points up front, and pay higher monthly payments due to a hike in the interest rates. In many cases, this penalty may be far more acceptable than to go after new financing at prevailing high rates of interest. In the case of assumptions and new loans, the lender may very well replace the long-term note with one based on a variable rate of interest. Buyers who are concerned about the legalities of the due-on-sale issue should consult competent legal advice before acting.

The example above had to do with a first mortgage. A "subject to" purchase can also apply to second mortgages (second trust deeds), all-inclusive trust deeds, contracts, or other existing encumbrances.

(4) **New loan:**
For example:
"This purchase is subject to the Buyer obtaining a new loan on the subject property from (name of lender) _____ in the amount of $_____ payable in monthly installments of $_____, including interest of

not more than _____ percent per annum, amortized over a period of not less than _____ years, plus monthly allowances for estimated annual property tax and insurance escrows."

Commentary: The words "subject to" constitute an important element of protection for the buyer. If the new loan is not obtainable according to the terms indicated, then the buyer is not committed to proceed with the purchase. If the seller or the seller's agent is on the ball, he may want to eliminate the specifics from the statement and try to get the buyer to generalize the conditions by saying "at prevailing interest rates." The seller may also insist on a time limit for obtaining the new loan, using wording such as this: "Buyer agrees to make application for the new loan within five (5) business days after acceptance of this offer, and to advise the seller in writing within fifteen (15) business days after acceptance of this offer of his ability or inability to obtain said loan in accordance with the indicated terms and conditions."

The new loan may also be in the form of a second mortgage and note (second trust deed and note).

(5) **Promissory note taken back by seller:**
For example:
"Buyer to execute promissory note in favor of Seller secured by first mortgage in the amount of $_____, payable $_____ per month, including _____ percent interest per annum, amortized over a period of _____ years, balance all due and payable _____ years from the date of execution."

Commentary: This is the now popular owner carry-back arrangement so common during tight-money times. Security for the note, depending on the circumstances and local practice, could be in the form of a second mortgage (second trust deed), third mortgage (third trust deed), all-inclusive trust deed (wrap-around mortgage), etc. Some states use mortgages, some use trust deeds. An all-inclusive trust deed or wrap-around mortgage pertains to the situation where the agreement encloses or wraps around an existing encumbrance.

The example used above includes a balloon payment. Not all do. Several of the case studies in this book involve owner carry-back arrangements with fully amortized notes. In today's strained real estate market, balloons of less than 5 years' duration are risky. Seven years or more would be advisable.

(6) **Contract:**
For example:
"Buyer to execute a real estate contract (land sales contract, installment land contract, contract for deed, etc.) in favor of seller in the amount of $_____, payable $_____ per

month, including _____ percent interest per annum, amortized over a period of _____ years, principal and interest all due and payable _____ years from the date of execution."

Commentary: The word contract (and its variations) implies that the buyer must satisfy the conditions of the agreement before title actually passes. In practice, the buyer should see to it that the escrow agent prepares the deed in favor of the buyer and holds it in escrow. Escrow instructions signed by buyer and seller should provide for release of the deed to the buyer when the contract terms have been satisfied. If the seller is on the ball, he will insist that a quitclaim deed from buyer to seller be prepared and placed in escrow in case of a default.

The example above contains provisions for a balloon payment. Not all do. Some buyers are fortunate enough to negotiate a contract covering a fully amortized note.

By way of summary concerning Item No. 6 of the earnest money agreement, payment of the balance of the sales price (after the down payment) occurs through one or more of the following approaches:

(1) Cash
(2) Assumption of existing encumbrances
(3) Purchase subject to existing encumbrances
(4) New loan
(5) Promissory note taken back by seller
(6) Contract

There are several important security contingencies that the buyer can add to the financial terms where applicable in order to reduce the risk or enhance future options:

(1) **Substitution of Collateral.** A mortgage consists of two basic documents: a note covering the amount owing and the terms of repayment, plus a security document offering real property collateral to back up the note in case of default. Usually a note is secured by the subject property being purchased; however, it is always wise to negotiate the right to substitute other property acceptable to the seller at any time in the future. Here is a sample of a statement that could be added to the earnest money agreement giving the buyer that right:

"Buyer has the right to substitute collateral of equal or greater value on the second mortgage at any time, with the Seller having the right of approval."

The title company handling the documentation can provide the technical language to secure the right of collateral substitution (as in Case No. 27 printed later on in this volume). The right to "move the mortgage" from the subject property to another property acceptable to the seller permits the buyer later on (as we shall see) to pull money out of acquired properties or fully leverage others.

In many cases the substitution of collateral is explicit in the earnest money itself, as in this example:

"Buyer agrees to execute note in favor of the Seller for the principal amount of $_____, secured by a first (second, third, etc.) mortgage (first trust deed, second trust deed, etc.) on a property located at _____, amortized for a period of _____ years, payable $_____ per month, including interest of _____ percent per annum, balance of principal and interest all due and payable _____ years from the date of execution."

(2) **Subordination.** The buyer may have given a note to the seller secured by a mortgage (trust deed) in second position above an existing first mortgage (trust deed). And the buyer may wish for this note to remain in second position, even though he may wish one day to refinance this first. What is called for is a subordination clause similar to this one:

"Seller agrees to subordinate the second note and deed of trust to the first note and deed of trust or any replacement thereof."

(3) **Rollover Provision on a Balloon.** An important risk-reduction clause provides the buyer with the right to extend a balloon payment in case he is unable to comply at the time:

"Buyer shall have the right to extend the balloon payment, at his option, for an additional twelve months, provided a principal payment of $_____ is made to the Seller on the original due date of the balloon."

An alternate way of inducing the seller to accept the rollover provision might be to offer a higher rate of interest on the balance during the extra year. Whatever sweetener is used, the buyer must attempt to secure this extension privilege because of the unpredictability of the economy over the next few years.

(4) **Prepayment Provision.** It is important for the buyer to negotiate the right to pay off his obligations to the seller at any time without penalty in the event he should wish to sell. The following kind of stipulation should do the trick:

"Buyer may at any time and without penalty pay in full all amounts owing to the Seller under conditions and terms of this agreement."

(5) **Assumption Provision.** The buyer's note to the seller should contain a stipulation that the note and mortgage (trust deed) are fully assumable. This would allow the buyer to sell the property subject to his obligations to the original seller. The wording need not be complicated:

". . . said note and trust deed to be fully assumable, with no due-on-sale clause."

(6) **First Right of Refusal on Note.** It is in the best interests of the buyer to negotiate the option of having the first right of refusal should the seller ever want to sell a note the buyer had given him. In this way the buyer might benefit from a discount purchase and also

protect himself from undesirable holders of the note. Here is an example:

"This arrangement is contingent upon Buyer having first right of refusal on the third note and deed of trust if Seller should decide to sell the note."

In all of these terms pertaining to Item No. 6 of the earnest money agreement, it is important to seek competent professional advice concerning the wording and the implications of what is being agreed to. The above examples are only illustrations. There are many variations — interest-free notes, interest-only notes, notes calling for annual payments only, amortized notes with several intermittent balloons, etc. The best risk-reduction strategy is to consult expert advice as you go. Once the agreement is signed, it becomes a binding legal contract.

7. **Title.** In some areas of the country, it may be customary for the buyer to share in the costs of title insurance. However, this version of the earnest money agreement presumes that the seller will bear the full burden. That is where the negotiation should always begin. This section is an important contingency for the buyer. On occasion a title search will disclose problems with the title — liens or judgments that effect the marketability of the property adversely. The boilerplate of Item No. 7 protects the buyer against such cases and provides an escape from the earnest money agreement if the title defects cannot be resolved.

8. **Special Representations.** Once more, this section contains important protections for the buyer and reduces the risk of the offer. After the section on utilities, there are assurances concerning the structural integrity of the building and its major systems, also a "clean bill of health" in regard to compliance with government agency regulations, freedom from future liens and assessments, etc.

9. **Escrow Instructions.** This item specifies when the closing will take place and which agency will provide third-party (neutral) escrow services. In some states, it is customary for the earnest money offer to specify that complete escrow instructions will be provided by the buyer and seller within a specified number of days following acceptance of the offer.

The matter of how conveyance will be made (in whose name and precisely how it is to be stated) is a legal question for the buyer to review with competent legal help. For purposes of the earnest money agreement, one might state "To be provided prior to closing."

10. **Closing Costs.** In this section, the responsibility of who pays for what at closing is spelled out. The escrow fees are divided equally between the buyer and seller in this version; however, everything is negotiable. The boilerplate can be changed to fit the circumstances by simply striking out what does not apply or adding different wording. In the case of changes to the printed text, both buyer and seller must initial the change to show their agreement.

11. **Termite Inspection.** Once again, an important contingency for the buyer. No one wants to wind up with a property that is going to collapse because of the work of termites.

12. **Conditions of Sale.** Apart from Section No. 6 on financing, this may well be the most important risk-reduction section of all. Here is the place to state whatever contingencies the buyer wants to use for his own protection. Some examples follow:

(1) Inspection and approval of buyer or buyer's partner:

"This offer is subject to inspection and approval of the property by buyer (buyer's partner) within 72 hours of seller's acceptance."

Commentary: Offers are frequently made prior to a thorough inspection. This contingency is an important escape clause for the buyer who finds that he does not want the property after all.

(2) Building Inspection:

"This sale is subject to a building inspection at the buyer's expense and with the buyer's approval within seven days of the acceptance of this offer."

(3) Repairs. The buyer may already be aware of needed repairs, in which case the following wording may be used:

"This offer is contingent on the seller completing repairs to the roof at seller's expense. Roof to be in good condition and watertight at time of closing." Etc.

(4) Exculpatory Clause. The buyer is well advised to insist on wording that limits his liability to the value of the property offered as collateral for the notes taken back by the seller. The point is to protect the buyer from personal liability, i.e., liability that could extend beyond the real estate collateral to his personal assets. The following is an example of an exculpatory clause of this type:

"The liability on the part of the buyer to satisfy the terms and conditions of the note(s) executed in favor of the seller shall be limited to the property securing such note(s) and shall not extend beyond this."

(5) Warranty Policy. In some cases the buyer is able to negotiate for himself the added protection of a warranty policy paid for by the seller. The following wording covers this for a single family home:

"The seller shall place on the property a one-year home warranty policy available through _____(name of company)."

(6) Cleanliness:

"Seller agrees to delivery the premises in a clean and orderly condition at the time of closing."

Note: There are many contingencies that might be warranted in the case of a particular property. The buyer needs to decide what is needed for his own protection. A fairly obvious limitation on the number of contingencies used in the offer is the need to avoid frightening the seller unduly. As Bob Allen says, "A confused mind always says 'No.'"

13. **Liability and Maintenance.** An earnest money offer in force (signed by all parties) is a legally binding contract. Without Item No. 13, the buyer may be responsible to cover all or part of the damages that might occur to a property between the time of acceptance and the time of closing.

14. **Possession.** Not all sellers automatically vacate a property upon closing. This item protects the buyer by stating exactly when he is to have possession. In some cases the buyer may work out a deal with the seller to let him continue occupying the premises for a period of time. The following wording added to the agreement would cover this point:

> "Buyer agrees to permit seller to continue residence on the property following close of escrow for a period of time not to exceed _____ months and at a monthly rental rate of $_____. Rental agreement to be executed and signed at the time of closing."

15. **Default.** What happens if the buyer or the seller fails to perform according to the terms and conditions of the earnest money agreement? It is important for the protection of the buyer that his liability in case of default be limited to the earnest money deposit and no more. That is why this particular version of the earnest money receipt and offer to purchase contains the vital phrase:

> "In the event the Buyer fails to complete the purchase as herein provided, the earnest money deposit shall be retained by the Seller as the total and entire liquidated damages."

In most preprinted earnest money forms this phrase is not present. Frequently the buyer's liability is expressed as being the amount of the earnest money deposit or a certain percentage of the gross sales price (for example, not more than 3%). It might be that the seller will want to retain the right to demand specific performance on the contract, i.e., have recourse to legal means (in addition to retaining the deposit) to force the buyer to comply. According to the principles of making risk-free offers, the buyer should insist on using the "total liquidated damages approach" stated in our model earnest money. Of course, the buyer should make the offer in good faith. Only a win/win deal will prove to be satisfying in the long run. However, if the seller is adamant about having the right of specific performance, it may be that this particular seller will be inflexible in every aspect of the transaction. If so, the buyer may want to take the hint and not follow through with the earnest money offer. There are plenty of don't wanter sellers out there to deal with.

16. **Time Limit of Offer.** This is another important risk-reduction provision to protect the buyer. It is also a wise negotiating tool. The seller cannot have forever to make up his mind. Sometimes an earnest money agreement will state that the seller has to give his approval "upon presentation of the offer." That is really putting the pressure on!

17. **General Agreements.** This is a collection of legal provisions placed in virtually every version of the earnest money form. Each provision has its specific purpose in helping to make the contract accomplish the purpose intended by the buyer and seller. Of special interest is the provision of mutual assent and cooperation in effecting an IRS 1031 tax-deferred exchange. If the buyer should find a property meanwhile that he could acquire using the subject property of the offer as an exchange, this provision would facilitate the process. Once more, the presence of the provision is designed to expand the options of the buyer and limit his risks.

Items 18-21 constitute formal approval of the offer on the part of both buyer and seller. Item No. 20 covers the real estate commission, which, according to the current conventions of practice, is paid by the seller. Naturally, this item is also negotiable, and many of the cases included in this book involve situations where the buyer assumes the responsibilities to pay the commission over time, usually in exchange for a reduction in the down payment. If this is the case, details should be spelled out under Item No. 6 of the earnest money agreement.

Documentation Used In The Case Studies

Each of the case studies used in this book is authentic. We have transferred to our own "universal earnest money receipt and offer to purchase" the precise data provided by the investors through copies of their own offers. Nothing is embellished. Only the names and addresses have been replaced with fictitious ones. Where we feel the original offer is exemplary in this or that point, or perhaps capable of improvement, our comments and opinions will be added in a special section of the case study.

Please note that the purchase offers included with the case studies are often the **initial** offers. Some variance from the details of the **ultimate** financial arrangement may be expected.

The readers should take careful note of this warning: these case studies and documents are provided as illustrations of the author's opinion concerning the subject matter covered. It is expressly not the intention of the author or the publishers that this material constitute legal or professional advice to readers engaged in pursuits similar to those reflected in the case studies. It is imperative that the reader consult competent professionals if legal advice or other expert service is required.

The R.A.N.D. Program in Action: Case Studies and Techniques

"The real disgrace of poverty lies not in owning to the fact but in declining the struggle against it."

—Thucydides

"Man's mind, stretched to a new idea, never goes back to its original dimension."

—Oliver Wendell Holmes

"Wealth depends on diligence."

—Hegel

The main body of this volume consists of authentic case studies organized as a manual of action for real estate investors. The amount of property involved exceeds ten million dollars in value. The setting is today's real estate world. The approach is creative finance. The participants are everyday people—your neighbors, colleagues, and friends. With the exception of names and addresses, all the facts are true.

We have stayed clear of the hypothetical for two essential reasons. First, the use of actual transactions is a more compelling way to share important concepts; it puts flesh and blood to what would otherwise be lifeless ideas and theories. Second, the use of actual purchases carried out successfully by a wide variety of real people from all walks of life and in all areas of the country is intended strategically to suggest to the reader: "Whoever you are—if **these** people can make it

work, so can you!"

We have attempted to present this material from multiple points of view. The three main questions are these:

1. What areas of flexibility can the knowledgeable creative buyer turn to in working out a nothing down deal?
2. What creative finance techniques work best in a given situation?
3. What are the actual steps the buyer must go through in acquiring a property, including the preparation of a written offer that is as risk-free as possible?

In working with my brother, Robert Allen, several years ago to improve the organization and structure of the Nothing Down Seminar materials, I suggested that the fifty basic creative finance techniques of the system be arranged and sequenced according to the areas of flexibility available to the buyer. The areas of flexibility relate to the principals involved in the standard transaction, i.e., the seller, the buyer, the Realtor, the renters, the hard-money lenders, the holders of underlying mortgages, investors, and partners. Most buyers quite naturally set up their inventory of nothing down resources according to these eight categories of people, all of whom play a role in the development of an investment portfolio. In addition, there is a ninth source of nothing down capital: the property itself, which is a valuable resource that many buyers overlook. To these nine areas of flexibility we add a tenth, the realm of the "option," which provides additional strategies for avoiding or delaying down payment outlays. These ten areas of capital flexibility define the organizational structure for the remainder of the book. There is one division assigned to each.

The second major dimension to look for in what follows is the system of fifty basic creative finance techniques that form the core of the Robert Allen Nothing Down Program. Each of the ten parts to Section Two of the book opens with a brief descriptive explanation of the techniques that pertain to that part of the case study material. The reader is urged to read through all ten sets of these descriptive vignettes prior to plunging into the case study material in earnest. Each case study has a dominant technique for which it provides the illustration; in addition, any other techniques used in that particular transaction are identified in the "Nutshell" section at the head of the case study. By keeping the techniques in focus throughout, the reader will be able to learn which combinations and groupings were most useful in a given situation. The case study/techniques matrix in the appendix permits a reader to trace each technique longitudinally across all fifty case studies.

Finally, the third dimension to look for in the remainder of the book is the five-stage process used in the actual purchase:

1. Locating the property,
2. Defining the situation at hand,
3. Negotiating the agreement,
4. The closing process, including the preparation of documents, and
5. Outcomes and future plans.

A commentary to the acquisitions process and to the documentation guides the reader to a more critical look at what actually transpired in each case study. Opinions—pro and con—are given for the reader's consideration.

Each case study includes one or more illustrative stick houses summarizing how the financial aspects of the transaction went together. According to the conventions adopted for this book, shaded portions of the stick houses show liens against the property; unshaded portions show the buyer's post-transaction equities as defined by down payments, unsecured obli-

gations, or mortgages moved to other properties. Dotted portions show the buyer's additional equity above the selling price in the case of discounted properties. The following model shows the pattern:

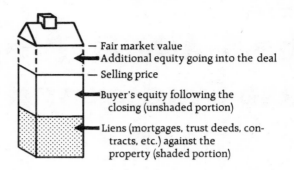

— Fair market value
Additional equity going into the deal
— Selling price
Buyer's equity following the closing (unshaded portion)
Liens (mortgages, trust deeds, contracts, etc.) against the property (shaded portion)

The case studies can be read individually as complete units or, because of the uniform structure of the cases, readers might choose to read "across" groups of them to satisfy a particular interest, e.g., negotiation, cash flow outcomes, documentation, commentary, etc.

The theme of this book is fairly obviously "How to Write a Nothing Down Offer so That Everyone Wins." But the scope is just as obviously much broader. We want the reader to come away from the book with a comprehensive grasp of what it means to invest in real estate using the kinds of alternative methods that must be mastered if success is to be assured in the eighties. In planning his or her strategies, the reader should keep in mind the fact that every nothing down offer, if it is to have meaning, must have a context. For the purpose of this book, the context has been defined three dimensionally as the following diagram:

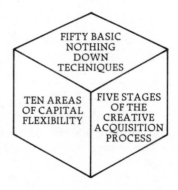

FIFTY BASIC NOTHING DOWN TECHNIQUES

TEN AREAS OF CAPITAL FLEXIBILITY

FIVE STAGES OF THE CREATIVE ACQUISITION PROCESS

The fifty case studies reflect these dimensions throughout. Included are 61 transactions in 35 different cities—in all, 543 rental units in 256 different properties ranging from $3,000 to $3,000,000 in value per transaction. By setting realistic goals and following carefully the principles outlined in the Robert Allen Nothing Down System, any person with conviction and a willingness to work for financial independence can succeed in real estate investments. It is hoped that this book may contribute to that success by showing the system in action.

Part I

The Seller

Among the nine major sources of down payment funds for property acquisition, the seller is no doubt the most important. If the buyer has done his selection job well, he will be dealing with a person who is anxious to sell and therefore flexible with financing arrangements. The seller will need to take on a role that might be new for him — that of lender. But if the buyer is sensitive to the needs of the seller, he will foster trust and see to it that both parties win. (Lending can, after all, be a lucrative business with its own slate of benefits, even for property sellers.)

This section reviews eight nothing down techniques involving seller financing, with nine case studies as illustrations. The outline follows:

Technique No. 1 — The Ultimate Paper Out
    Case No. 1:   How To Soften Up A Hard-Money Lender
    Case No. 2:   Can You Have 100% Financing And Cash Flow At The Same Time?
    Case No. 3:   Picking Up A Rental Home—Interest Free
    Case No. 4:   Four Houses For The Price Of Two

Technique No. 2 — The Blanket Mortgage

Technique No. 3 — Life Insurance Policy

Technique No. 4 — Contract or Wrap-Around Mortgage
    Case No. 5:   Using Your Reputation (Instead of Cash) As Down Payment
    Case No. 6:   Buyer Teaches Seller New Trick—And They Both Win

Technique No. 5 — Raise the Price, Lower The Terms
    Case No. 7:   How To Buy A Mansion For Nothing Down

Technique No. 6 — The Balloon Down Payment
    Case No. 8:   Ever Hear Of An $18,000 5-Year Loan—No Interest, No Payments?
    Case No. 9:   Seven-Plex Buyer Wouldn't Take ''No'' For An Answer

Technique No. 7 — High Monthly Down Payments

Technique No. 8 — Defer the Down Payment with No Mortgage Payments

---

Technique No. 1   The Ultimate Paper Out

When we are talking about buying or selling a piece of real estate, we are really talking about the problem of defining and dealing with the seller's equity. Equity as a concept is straightforward enough. Everyone knows that it represents that portion of the value of a property that is not encumbered, that belongs lock, stock, and barrell to the owner. But equity is a fluid concept. It can be specified only in relation to that mysterious and shifting quantity called the "fair market value." The owner has dreams about an equity of such and such — usually an optimistically high number. But the truth of the matter is that market forces determine his equity by determining how much his property is really worth at any moment in time. The members of the market club — you and I — gang up on the poor old seller and say, collectively, "You have a nice little place, but we've taken a vote around town, and the best we could come up with is a price of such and such." At that moment in time, the seller's equity is defined, and the problem becomes how to transfer to him value equal to the equity involved.

The majority of sellers, of course, will want to hold out for a selling price at the high end of the scale. They want their equity to be overweight. No one can blame them for that. But among the army of sellers in the marketplace at any given time, there are always a few — perhaps five percent or less — who say to themselves, "We like our equity and want to preserve it and derive benefit from it, but we are very anxious to sell. So anxious in fact, that we might give up some of that equity in order to get rid of the property quickly." Alternately, these don't wanter sellers might be thinking, "I don't really feel like discounting my equity for a quick sale, but I would be willing to wait until later for a part or all of my equity to be converted to cash."

And that is the issue when it comes to "papering out" a deal. After the seller and the buyer have determined what equity is involved, the next step is to decide how soon the equity is to be converted. It all boils down to a matter of patience. The seller with infinite patience (and infinite desperation) will say, "Here's my equity; take it all and just get me out of this place." In a case like that the selling price is equal to the liens. But such cases are rare.

The next best situation is the case in which the seller says, "Here's my equity; pay me for it when you can. Let's work out the schedule." That is the technique referred to as "The Ultimate Paper Out." All of the seller's equity is converted to paper before it is converted to cash. When the buyer takes over the property, he gives the seller paper for his equity and obligates himself to redeem the paper according to mutually agreeable terms.

There are four case studies included in this section to illustrate "The Ultimate Paper Out." In Case No. 1, a bank president disposing of a triplex is willing to wait three years (interest free) for part of his equity and receive the rest in monthly payments over the same span of time. In Case No. 2, an absentee seller of a duplex is willing to receive all of his equity in monthly payments over seven years (after the buyer helped out a little on arrears taxes and other obligations). Case No. 3 describes how the seller of a single family home papered

out all of his equity — $36,500 — for five years — no payments and no interest! And finally, Case No. 4 tells the unusual story of a seller who was willing to receive all of her equity on a free and clear home by means of monthly payments on a personal note — interest free.

Not all sellers will agree to an "Ultimate Paper Out." But creative buyers should always ask. You never know exactly what the seller is thinking or how anxious he really is to sell. Perhaps only one seller in twenty will be willing to enter into a nothing down deal; and of these, perhaps only one in ten will agree to an "Ultimate Paper Out." That means that Technique No. 1 will show up in only one out of every 200 creative deals. But it does happen from time to time — much to the surprise and delight of the creative buyer.

Technique No. 2   The Blanket Mortgage

The key to using the seller as lender in a real estate transaction is trust. The seller has got to trust us to pay him his equity according to the terms of the agreement we work out with him. The conventional way to "buy" trust is to give the seller a large cash down payment. That way he knows that we will not likely walk away from the property. We are going to stay around and take care of our obligations; otherwise the seller will be able to take back the property, and we will lose not only that big cash down payment but also any appreciated value above the seller's equity.

But how do we develop trust when there is little or no cash put down on the property? How does the buyer make the seller feel secure in such cases? Often the buyer can develop personal trust with the seller simply on the basis of personal qualities and win/win attitudes. In such cases, the security of the subject property itself is sufficient to close the deal.

In some instances, however, a little extra is needed to remove lingering suspicions on the part of the seller. That is where the blanket mortgage comes into play. In any mortgage or trust deed arrangement, there are two basic documents that are prepared: one is a note given by the buyer to the seller setting forth the terms for converting the equity to cash; the other is a security agreement in which the buyer says to the seller, in effect, "If I don't perform according to the terms of the note, then you can take back the property." In a cashless or near cashless transaction, the security of the subject property may not be enough to satisfy the seller. Therefore, the buyer may choose to secure the note with additional collateral — not only the subject property but also additional property (equity) he may have in his portfolio. The note itself stays the same, but the security agreement is changed to increase the collateral and build trust with the seller. Naturally, the buyer will want to arrange to have the seller release the additional collateral as soon as the subject property appreciates to a predetermined value or as soon as the buyer has proven himself to be dependable and prompt in making his payments.

The blanket mortgage technique is not among the most frequently used in creative finance. The buyer hopes to build trust without having to tie up his other equities. Still, when a seller needs that extra bit of persuasion, the blanket mortgage technique can come in handy. None of the fifty featured case studies in this book features the blanket mortgage; however, readers can turn to the addendum of Case No. 29 to see how a California investor used the technique to cement a deal in which no cash came out of his own pocket.

Technique No. 3   Life Insurance Policy

There is another strategy the buyer can use to persuade the seller to play lender in a transaction. As in the case of the blanket mortgage, the key is building trust. What if you say to the still somewhat incredulous seller, "Since you are permitting me to pay off your equity in cash over a period of time, how would it be if I took out an insurance policy in the amount of the note and made you the beneficiary? That way you will feel secure that the note will be paid off no matter what."

This technique is not usually necessary; still, it is an inexpensive way to build trust if the seller cannot quite see it your way and needs just a bit more persuasion. None of the fifty case studies featured in this book illustrate the need to build trust in this way; however, Case No. 3, described below, has an interesting reverse twist on the life insurance technique. The banker had tacked on the cost of credit life insurance to the buyer's mortgage loan as additional security (banks frequently like to do this). But the buyer simply refused the service, so the banker cut him a check for the $1,400 premium and left the larger mortgage note intact! The buyer put an extra $1,400 in his pocket at closing. Such is life!

Technique No. 4   Contract or Wrap-Around Mortgage

This technique is one of the most frequently used creative finance tools. It is the foundation of seller financing. Rather than refinancing the property or formally assuming the existing mortgage, the buyer uses a contract as the purchase instrument. Technically he does not get title to the property until he has performed according to the provisions of the agreement. In effect, he says to the seller, "I'll pay your equity off in installments over time. And as soon as I have paid everything off, you will give me the deed for the property, and it will be mine. In the meantime, I will act as the owner by taking over the management and getting all the tax benefits and the appreciated equity above what the property is worth at the time of purchase. Of course, all the expenses in the meantime are mine as well."

If the property is free and clear at the time of purchase, the seller pockets all the installment payments on the contract. If there are existing encumbrances on the property, then the contract is referred to as a wrap-around contract or wrap-around mortgage. It "wraps around" the existing first and subsequent mortgages or trust deeds. When the seller receives the installment payments, he has to first make payments on the existing notes before he can pocket the rest. The advantage to him is that the interest rate on the total wrap-around contract will be higher than on the underlying loans. Therefore, he will be making an interest spread on the underlying part of the note — not a bad deal for a seller turned lender. In addition, he will be able to spread his capital gains profit out over time rather than receiving all of it during one year. The tax advantages are considerable. With the recent liberalization of installment sale provisions by the IRS, sellers have great leeway in how contracts are set up for maximum tax benefits. A competent tax accountant can spell out the details.

The advantage to the buyer is that he does not need to come up with a large cash down payment. Frequently a moderate amount down will close the deal. In addition, the interest rates acceptable to sellers are usually far below conventional market rates for new financing.

In practice, a contract sale is handled by an escrow company, which holds the pre-executed deed from the seller in favor of the buyer until the latter satisfies the terms of the contract. Generally the escrow or title company will also hold a quitclaim deed made out by the buyer in favor of the seller, which is to be released to the seller in case of default. It is in the best interests of the buyer if the escrow company is also empowered to receive his installment payments and take care of making the payments on the underlying loans before disbursing the balance to the seller. That way the buyer can be assured that his money winds up in the right places.

In the present volume, there are two case studies that feature Technique No. 4, "Contract or Wrap-Around Mortgage." In the first (Case No. 5), the buyer acquires a tri-plex with minimal down and a wrap-around contract for the balance of $68,000 at only 10.75%. In Case No. 6, the contract on a free and clear single family home (therefore not a "wrap" in this instance) provides for a carry back of $76,000 for 25 years at 12% interest.

An alternative form of the "contract/wrap" technique is the situation where a buyer takes title subject to the existing financing (agrees to take over the seller's obligations) or goes through the formal procedure of assuming the existing financing (qualification, credit checks, transfer of title). The buyer then signs a contract with the seller for the equity above the existing loans and makes payments according to a mutually agreeable schedule. The seller's equity is covered by a note secured by the property itself. The usual term for this arrangement is "owner carry back." There are dozens of such instances included in the case studies featured in this volume. Refer to the cross-reference chart in the appendix for guidance. Purchase money mortgages are also assigned to this category.

Technique No. 5   Raise the Price, Lower the Terms

Seller financing has already become a convention for real estate transactions in the decade of the 1980s. Currently nearly two-thirds of all home sales involve contract sales or assumptions with owner carry-back second-mortgages. Tight money conditions always foster seller financing of this type. Yet even though the concept of "seller as lender" is no longer foreign to the American way of real property transfer, there are variations to the game that give creative buyers the advantage over the competition.

One such variation is the important technique called "Raise the Price, Lower the Terms." Simply put, this technique calls for the buyer to offer the seller more than he is asking for the property in exchange for flexibility with the terms. In Case No. 7, discussed below, the buyer of a mansion with adjoining tri-plex offered to raise the sales price by $5,000 if the seller would lower the down payment requirement and accept payments over 15 years. By using this technique, he outpaced the competition and won over the seller despite the hue and cry of all the relatives in the background.

Technique No. 6   The Balloon Down Payment

It is not uncommon for seller-financing arrangements to include provisions for a balloon payment in the future. In fact, balloons are an important inducement to get the seller to play the part of the lender in the first place. Knowing that the major part of his equity is coming in the near future, the seller is willing to carry the financing at rates below the conventional market. Occasionally a seller is willing to amortize the entire amount of the carry back over a long period of time — fifteen or twenty years or longer. Most of the time, however, the seller wants to be paid off sooner, in fact, as soon as possible.

And that is the danger the buyer must beware of. Short fuse balloon notes can rob the buyer of health, sleep, and sometimes the property itself. In theory, the time of the balloon payment should be far enough away to take advantage of interim appreciation. Property values and rents must grow enough to permit a refinance solution to the balloon payment.

But what if local property values — particularly during a period of sustained high interest rates and sluggish real estate sales — do not grow as anticipated? The buyer may be forced to sell the property, or another piece of real estate in his control, to pay off the balloon. Alternately, he may have to bring in an equity-participation cash-partner to bail him out, thus giving away important benefits. In the worst case, he might have to give the property back to the seller and lose all his investment.

Despite its liabilities, the balloon payment technique can be a valuable way to get into a property for little or nothing down up front. Buyers should resist pressures to accept anything less than five years for pay out. Seven years or more would be preferable.

There are two case studies appearing in this section to illustrate how the balloon arrangement works. Case No. 8 features a small single family home for which the seller carried back $17,000 with no payments — and no interest — for five years. Case No. 9 describes the sale of a seven-plex involving a carry back of $84,000 at 12% for 30 years, with payments to start after nine months and a balloon after ten years.

In addition to these featured case studies, some two-dozen of the other fifty cases involve balloon payments — a rich variety of transactions through which much insight can be gained on how the balloon technique works. Happy reading!

Technique No. 7   High Monthly Down Payments

This technique is a variation of Technique No. 4, "Contract or Wrap-Around Mortgage." Usually a contract sale requires at least a token down payment to substantiate the good faith of the buyer and put a little cash into the pocket of the seller. Sometimes a hefty down is required, in which case funds have to be "cranked" out of the property (Techniques 32 and 33) or a cash partner must be brought in (Techniques 43, 44, and 45).

But what if the buyer has nothing at all to put down except an income that gives him the ability to make monthly payments of several hundred dollars toward the purchase of a piece of property? Perhaps the seller would permit him to purchase the property now and make high monthly payments over a couple of years until a mutually acceptable down payment had been constituted. There is no case quite like this among the fifty reviewed in this book, but there is always the possibility of finding a seller who would be sufficiently tempted by an extra income of several hundred dollars a month to approve a sale with nothing down at all.

There are certain similarities between this approach and Technique No. 50, "Lease With An Option To Purchase." Readers might want to review Cases No. 49 and 50 as illustrations of this approach.

Technique No. 8   Defer the Down Payment with No Mortgage Payment

There are endless variations of how seller financing might be set up. Here is one more — not illustrated in this book — which could prove useful under certain circumstances. A seller of a free and clear property who needed cash down only to build trust in his buyer might be induced to forego rental income for a few months while the buyer accumulated enough to put together the required down. It is not a common opportunity, but it has happened in the past and will happen again in the future — perhaps to you.

This technique, together with the other seven described and illustrated in this section, should stimulate creative buyers to take advantage of seller flexibilities in financing. Seller financing, after all, is one of the major sources for down payment capital.

"... which brings me to my 431st Nothing Down technique . . ."

Reprinted by permission from the *Nothing Down Advisor.*

1

How To Soften Up A Hard-Money Lender

**Featuring Technique No. 1
"The Ultimate Paper Out"**

In A Nutshell . . .

Type: Tri-plex
Price: $48,000
Source: Realtor
Means: Refinance, carry back
Techniques: No. 1 — Ultimate Paper Out
No. 4 — Contract/Wrap
No. 6 — Balloon
No. 37 — Creative Refinance
Strategies: Stepped interest on 2d

Dr. Richard Austin is a successful health-care professional in Milwaukee. His goal in becoming a practitioner of the Nothing Down System is to use his real estate investments as a vehicle for achieving financial independence within seven years. He explains his motivation in this excerpt from a recent letter: "After making more money each year but never seeming to have any more money at the end of the year — other than an increase in my net worth because of the three properties I owned — I figured I had to do something different to protect my income. I took the Nothing Down Seminar and became totally convinced that real estate is the best investment to have. I can control it and not let the whim of a Joe Granville or wrong sneeze of the President drop my stocks down by thousands of dollars."

To launch his program, Richard looked at approximately 200 properties in his county to see what was available and get a good idea of property values. He interviewed many real estate agents before finding one who would listen to what he wanted to accomplish. With the help of this one agent alone he acquired eight excellent properties in the course of a year's time. With three additional purchases during the same period, his portfolio at last count consisted of eight single family houses (all in the price range of $35,000 to $45,000), four duplexes, and one triplex — with an aggregate value of over $700,000. The following case study concerns the triplex.

LOCATING

The triplex was located in Lake Geneva, a community with a resort flavor some 30 miles southwest of Milwaukee. Rents in the area were somewhat higher than closer in, and the property values seemed more reasonable. All in all the location of the triplex was ideal.

SITUATION

At first, Richard did not like the property. Its appearance left something to be desired; clearly a bit of fix-up would be called for. But the Realtor pointed out to him that a little strategic renovation would do wonders and assure a positive cash flow.

The owner was the president of a bank in the community. He had an unusual problem that was prompting him to get rid of the property. The tenant in the efficiency apartment of the triplex was the banker's brother-in-law, a person who was evidently proving to be less than desirable. Rent on the efficiency was only $50. Since the brother-in-law could hardly be "liquidated," the banker apparently felt the next best course of action would be to liquidate the property. That all added up to a severe case of don't wanteritis.

NEGOTIATION

The Realtor convinced the banker that Richard would be a good risk. As a result, the negotiations went smoothly. The banker agreed to arrange for a new first mortgage of $34,000 at 13½% for 25 years with payments of approximately $400 per month. He then agreed to carry back a second of $11,000 with stepped interest payments (8% on the first year, 10% the next, and 12% the third), the principal sum being all due and payable after three years. Since the agreed upon selling price for the triplex was $48,000, the balance of the equity yet to be paid was $3,000. Where did Richard get that amount? Once more, from the banker, who agreed to accept a personal unsecured note for the required amount, no interest, no payments, all due and payable in three years. (He really **did** want to get rid of his brother-in-law.)

CLOSING

The banker paid the Realtor's commission out of the proceeds of the new first mortgage. Thus all the bases were covered. The sketch shows a summary of the financing on the triplex:

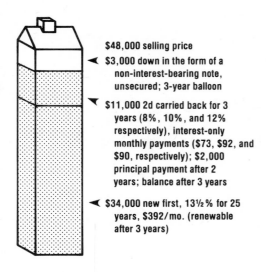

$48,000 selling price

◄ $3,000 down in the form of a non-interest-bearing note, unsecured; 3-year balloon

◄ $11,000 2d carried back for 3 years (8%, 10%, and 12% respectively), interest-only monthly payments ($73, $92, and $90, respectively); $2,000 principal payment after 2 years; balance after 3 years

◄ $34,000 new first, 13½% for 25 years, $392/mo. (renewable after 3 years)

COMMENTARY

1. The Realtor's lesson for Richard was to develop the ability to visualize properties as they might be, rather than as they are. That is good advice for all investors, whether change will come in the form of improvements or a total conversion to other uses. The essence of creativity is a shift to a higher perspective, one where new combinations and solutions come into view, but only to those willing to leave the comfortable old patterns of looking. Was the triplex an ugly duckling waiting to become a swan? Hardly! The real beauty comes in strategies for solving negative cash flow and increasing the value of properties through improvements and skillful management.

2. The irony of this case study is the fact that the seller who gladly went along with the nothing down deal was a banker. Even bankers, despite their stereotype as persons who constantly "go by the book," can be flexible, especially where a brother-in-law problem exists. But also institutionally when it comes to "REO's" — Real Estate Owned. During the next period of higher interest rates and increased numbers of foreclosures, investors would do well to stay in touch with their banker associates who might steer them to excellent nothing down or low down deals. It is instructive, also, that the banker came up with a creative (lower interest) refinance arrangement in order to close the deal.

3. Richard went through some dozen-odd agents before finding the Realtor who brought him this deal and six others. The creative Realtor who can see further than beyond the next cash commission is worth his (or her) weight in gold. Once the agent understands the parameters — in this case bread-and-butter properties with no or low mortgages and the possibility of attractive discounts — things begin to click. One of the most important competencies of creative real estate investing is the effective use of professionals — Realtors, attorneys, title company officers, bankers, appraisers, and partners! Creative real estate investing is almost always teamwork.

OUTCOMES AND FUTURE PLANS

Richard immediately raised the rent on the brother-in-law from $50 to $175 per month. The man couldn't take such a strong dose of logic and took off. The other two units were likewise adjusted, with the result that the property showed a positive cash flow of $50 per month, helped in part by the stepped interest rate on the second. To justify the increase, Richard borrowed home-improvement funds to pay for new siding, a new roof, and interior touch-up. The $4,500 investment had the effect of raising the property value to around $70,000.

The new owner has an admirable philosophy of how to hold real estate — he insists on improving it and keeping it in top notch condition. His experience has been that his attempts to improve his properties have had a positive effect on others living close by or operating other rental units in the neighborhood. They have in many cases followed suit by renovating their own buildings, the result being a general improvement in the appearance of the neighborhood. Looking at things this way, investors can regard their program for financial independence as a form of "community service." Why not!

DOCUMENTATION

UNIVERSAL EARNEST MONEY RECEIPT AND OFFER TO PURCHASE

"This is a legally binding contract: if not understood, seek competent advice."

1. Date and Place of Offer: __March 31__ 19 __81__ ; __Lake Geneva__ __Wisconsin__
   (city)   (state)

2. Principals: The undersigned Buyer __Richard Austin__
   agrees to buy and Seller agrees to sell, according to the indicated terms and conditions, the property described as follows:

3. Property: located at __1675 Walnut Street__ __Lake Geneva__ __Wisconsin__
   (street address)   (city)   (state)

   with the following legal description: __Lot 17, Block 12 Original Plat. City of Lake Geneva.__

   __County of Walworth.__

including any of the following items if at present attached to the premises: plumbing, heating, and cooling equipment, including stoker and oil tanks, burners, water heaters, electric light fixtures, bathroom fixtures, roller shades, curtain rods and fixtures, draperies, venetian blinds, window and door screens, towel racks, linoleum and other attached floor coverings,

including carpeting, attached television antennas, mailboxes, all trees and shrubs, and any other fixtures EXCEPT _____None_____

The following personal property shall also be included as part of the purchase: _____
At the closing of the transaction, the Seller, at his expense, shall provide the Buyer with a Bill Of Sale containing a detailed inventory of the personal property included.

4. Earnest Money Deposit: Agent (or Seller) acknowledges receipt from Buyer of __Three Thousand and 00/100__ dollars $ __3,000.00__

in the form of ( ) cash; ( ) personal check; ( ) cashier's check; (X) promissory note at _____% interest per annum due __April 1,__ 19 __84__ ; or

other ____non-interest bearing note, unsecured____

as earnest money deposit to secure and apply on this purchase. Upon acceptance of this agreement in writing and delivery of same to Buyer, the earnest money deposit shall be assigned

to and deposited in the listing Realtor's trust account or _____, to apply on the purchase price at the time of closing.

5. Purchase Price: The total purchase price of the property shall be __Forty-eight Thousand and 00/100__ dollars $ __48,000.00__

6. Payment: Purchase price is to be paid by Buyer as follows:

Aforedescribed earnest money deposit .... $ __3,000.00__

Additional payment due upon acceptance of this offer .... $ __0__

Additional payment due at closing .... $ __0__

Balance to be paid as follows:

1. This purchase is subject to the Buyer obtaining a new loan on the subject property from Wisconsin National Bank in the amount of $34,000 payable in monthly installments of $392, including interest of not more than 13.5% per annum, amortized over a period of not less than 25 years, plus monthly allowances for estimated annual property tax and insurance escrows. (Note to be drawn for three years renewable at current market rate.) Proceeds to Seller.
2. Buyer to execute promissory note for balance in favor of Seller secured by second mortgage in the amount of $11,000 payable in interest-only monthly payments as follows: 8% ($73 per month) from April 2, 1981 to January 31, 1982; 10% ($92 per month) from January 31, 1982 to January 31, 1983; and 12% ($90 per month) from January 31, 1983 to March 31, 1984, when balance is due and payable. A principal payment of $2,000 shall be due January 29, 1983.

7. Title: Seller agrees to furnish good and marketable title free of all encumbrances and defects, except mortgage liens and encumbrances as set forth in this agreement, and to make

conveyance by Warranty Deed or _____. Seller shall furnish in due course to the Buyer a title insurance policy insuring the Buyer of a good and marketable title in keeping with the terms and conditions of this agreement. Prior to the closing of this transaction, the Seller, upon request, will furnish to the Buyer a preliminary title report made by a title insurance company showing the condition of the title to said property. If the Seller cannot furnish marketable title within thirty days after receipt of the notice to the Buyer containing a written statement of the defects, the earnest money deposit herein receipted shall be refunded to the Buyer and this agreement shall be null and void. The following shall not be deemed encumbrances or defects: building and use restrictions general to the area; utility easements; other easements not inconsistent with Buyer's intended use; zoning or subdivision laws, covenants, conditions, restrictions, or reservations of record; tenancies of record. In the event of sale of other than real property relating to this transaction, Seller will provide evidence of title or right to sell or lease such personal property.

8. Special Representations: Seller warrants and represents to Buyer (1) that the subject property is connected to ( ) public sewer system, ( ) cesspool or septic tank, ( ) sewer system available but not connected, ( ) city water system, ( ) private water system, and that the following special improvements are included in the sale: ( ) sidewalk, ( ) curb and gutter, ( ) special street paving, ( ) special street lighting; (2) that the Seller knows of no material structural defects; (3) that all electrical wiring, heating, cooling, and plumbing systems are free of material defects and will be in good working order at the time the Buyer is entitled to possession; (4) that the Seller has no notice from any government agency of any violation or knowledge of probable violations of the law relating to the subject property; (5) that the Seller has no notice or knowledge of planned or commenced public improvements which may result in special assessments or otherwise directly and materially affect the property; and (6) that the Seller has no notice or knowledge of any liens to be assessed against the property,

EXCEPT ____None____

9. Escrow Instructions: This sale shall be closed on or before __April 7,__ 19 81 by __Wisconsin National Bank,__
__711 Weber Square__

or such other closing agent as mutually agreed upon by Buyer and Seller. Buyer and Seller will, immediately on demand, deposit with closing agent all instruments and monies required

to complete the purchase in accordance with the provisions of this agreement. Contract of Sale or Instrument of Conveyance to be made in the name of _____

10. Closing Costs and Pro-Ration: Seller agrees to pay for title insurance policy, preliminary title report (if requested), termite inspection as set forth below, real estate commission, cost of preparing and recording any corrective instruments, and one-half of the escrow fees. Buyer agrees to pay for recording fees for mortgages and deeds of conveyance, all costs or expenses in securing new financing or assuming existing financing, and one-half of the escrow fees. Buyer agrees to pay for recording fees for mortgages and deeds of conveyance, all costs or expenses in securing new financing or assuming existing financing, and one-half of the escrow fees. Taxes for the current year, insurance acceptable to the Buyer, rents, interest, mortgage reserves, maintenance fees, and water and other utilities constituting liens, shall be pro-rated as of closing. Renters' security deposits shall accrue to Buyer at closing. Seller to provide Buyer with all current rental or lease agreements prior to closing.

Note: The three units are rented month-to-month oral at rates of $50 per month (down rear), $200 per month (up front), $180 per month (down front).

11. Termite Inspection: Seller agrees, at his expense, to provide written certification by a reputable licensed pest control firm that the property is free of termite infestation. In the event termites are found, the Seller shall have the property treated at his expense and provide acceptable certification that treatment has been rendered. If any structural repairs are required by reason of termite damage as established by acceptable certification, Seller agrees to make necessary repairs not to exceed $500. If repairs exceed $500, Buyer shall first have the right to accept the property "as is" with a credit to the Buyer at closing of $500, or the Buyer may terminate this agreement with the earnest money deposit being promptly returned to the Buyer if the Seller does not agree to pay all costs of treatment and repair.

12. Conditions of Sale: The following conditions shall also apply, and shall, if conflicting with the printed portions of this agreement, prevail and control:

This offer is not subject to the sale of other property.

13. Liability and Maintenance: Seller shall maintain subject property, including landscaping, in good condition until the date of transfer of title or possession by Buyer, whichever occurs first. All risk of loss and destruction of property, and all expenses of insurance, shall be borne by the seller until the date of possession. If the improvements on the property are destroyed or materially damaged prior to closing, then the Buyer shall have the right to declare this agreement null and void, and the earnest money deposit and all other sums paid by Buyer toward the purchase price shall be returned to the Buyer forthwith.

14. Possession: The Buyer shall be entitled to possession of property upon closing or _____ NA _____, 19 _____.

15. Default: In the event the Buyer fails to complete the purchase as herein provided, the earnest money deposit shall be retained by the Seller as the total and entire liquidated damages. In the event the Seller fails to perform any condition of the sale as herein provided, then the Buyer may, at his option, treat the contract as terminated, and all payments made by the Buyer hereunder shall be returned to the Buyer forthwith, provided the Buyer may, at his option, treat this agreement as being in full force and effect with the right to action for specific performance and damages. In the event that either Buyer, Seller, or Agent shall institute suit to enforce any rights hereunder, the prevailing party shall be entitled to court costs and a reasonable attorney's fee.

16. Time Limit of Offer: The Seller shall have until

_____ (hour) _____ April 1, _____ (date) _____, 19 81 to accept this offer by delivering a signed copy hereof to the Buyer. If this offer is not so accepted, it shall lapse and the agent (or Seller) shall refund the earnest money deposit to the Buyer forthwith.

17. General Agreements: (1) Both parties to this purchase reserve their rights to assign and hereby otherwise agree to cooperate in effecting an Internal Revenue Code 1031 exchange or similar tax-related arrangement prior to close of escrow, upon either party's written notice of intention to do so. (2) Upon approval of this offer by the Seller, this agreement shall become a contract between Buyer and Seller and shall inure to the benefit of the heirs, administrators, executors, successors, personal representatives, and assigns of said parties. (3) Time is of the essence and an essential part of this agreement. (4) This contract constitutes the sole and entire agreement between the parties hereto and no modification of this contract shall be binding unless attached hereto and signed by all parties to the contract. No representations, promises, or inducements not included in this contract shall be binding upon any party hereto.

18. Buyer's Statement and Receipt: "I/we hereby agree to purchase the above property in accordance with the terms and conditions above stated and acknowledge receipt of a completed copy of this agreement, which I/we have fully read and understand." Dated _____ March 31 _____ 19 81 _____, _____ (hour) _____

Address _____ 17 Juniper Street _____ [signature] _____ Buyer

_____ East Troy, Wisconsin _____ _____ Buyer

Phone No: Home _____ 678-1400 _____ Business _____ 678-1400 _____

19. Seller's Statement and Response: "I/we approve and accept the above offer, which I/we have fully read and understand, and agree to the above terms and conditions this day

of _____, 19 _____, _____ (hour) _____

Address _____ _____ Seller

Phone No: Home _____ Business _____ _____ Seller

20. Commission Agreement: Seller agrees to pay a commission of _____ NA _____ % of the gross sales price to _____ for services in this transaction, and agrees that, in the event of forfeiture of the earnest money deposit by the Buyer, said deposit shall be divided between the Seller's broker and the Seller (one half to each party), the Broker's part not to exceed the amount of the commission.

21. Buyer's Receipt for Signed Offer: The Buyer hereby acknowledges receipt of a copy of the above agreement bearing the Seller's signature in acceptance of this offer.

Dated _____, 19 _____ _____ Buyer

COMMENTARY TO DOCUMENTATION

Item 3. For control and tax purposes, the buyer should have called for a separate bill of sale covering personal items included in the sale.

Item 2. The terms "or Assigns" should be added after the buyer's name.

Item 4. The use of a note as earnest money can be very effective; in this case, the amount of the note was a significant portion of the sales price and was left intact as part of the long-range financing of the property. The buyer should have attempted to secure a longer repayment term on the note.

Item 6. The new first mortgage was established on a "weighted" basis, hence below market interest rates. In the final mortgage note, the bank insisted on a provision that the note be drawn for three years renewable at current market rates. If the bank was inflexible on this issue, then the buyer should have insisted that the second mortgage be based on at least a five-year term. At a minimum, a rollover provision on the second should have been part of the offer. A substitution of collateral clause would also have been a useful goal in the negotiation process. As it turned out, the second mortgage note was drawn subject to prepayment without penalty — a decided advantage for the buyer.

Item 15. The original offer did not contain a provision that the earnest money (in this case a note) would constitute the total and entire liquidated damages in the case of a default by the buyer. Such a provision is always wise for the buyer.

2

Can You Have 100% Financing And Cash Flow At The Same Time?

Featuring Technique No. 1
"The Ultimate Paper Out"

In A Nutshell . . .

Type: Duplex
Price: $38,000
Source: Realtor
Means: Land contract
Techniques: No. 1 — Ultimate Paper Out
No. 4 — Contract/Wrap
No. 6 — Balloon
No. 11 — Assume Seller's Obligations
No. 19 — Borrowing Realtor's Commission
Strategies: Structuring payments for positive flow
Features: Discount, positive cash flow

LOCATING

In the previous example, Richard Austin of Milwaukee was able to acquire a triplex with 100% financing and positive cash flow. In case anyone considers that a fluke in this age of inflation and high interest rates, here is a second example of the same thing from his portfolio. As before, it was his Realtor who brought the property to his attention. The duplex was located ideally in a pleasant neighborhood in Lake Geneva, a resort area southwest of Milwaukee and northwest of Chicago.

SITUATION

Except for minor painting needs, the property was in fairly good condition. The owner had moved to New Mexico and was not anxious to attempt managing the duplex from so far away. For the past six months he had been advertising the place for $44,000 — all to no avail. The rental income totaled $425 per month.

NEGOTIATION

Richard's offer was straightforward. He would pay $38,000 for the duplex, $34,500 being carried on a land contract at 12% for seven years with payments set at $350. The balance after seven years would be paid in a lump sum. Richard agreed to cover the difference between the contract amount and the selling price ($3,500) by assuming the seller's obligations for arrears property taxes, commissions, and closing costs. The response of the seller was also straightforward — he said "Yes." Another "ultimate paper out" had been accomplished. Richard gives much of the credit for the agreement to the Realtor, who prepared a printout for the seller showing how much interest he would be making over the life of the contract.

CLOSING

One problem remained: how to pay the Realtor where there was no cash down payment. In this case,

the buyer agreed to pay the commission, which the Realtor took back in the form of a note, no interest, payable six months from the date of closing. The Realtor did all the paperwork for the transaction, and Richard had it reviewed, as always, by his attorney.

OUTCOMES AND FUTURE PLANS

The new owner had the trim painted at a cost of $329. A tenant volunteered to paint the interior free if the paint were provided. Richard gladly agreed but insisted on giving the man $100 for his services. His philosophy is to have the tenants participate in maintenance, where appropriate, and give them consideration for their efforts. "They seem to have more pride in the place if they do some of the work."

Except for the need to do some repairing of the building at a cost of $1,000, there were no major surprises. It was an excellent property in a desirable location. After improvements, the appraised value was around $49,000. Not bad for a pure nothing down deal. The sketch summarizes the facts in the case:

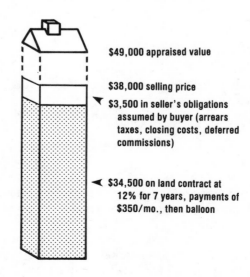

$49,000 appraised value

$38,000 selling price

$3,500 in seller's obligations assumed by buyer (arrears taxes, closing costs, deferred commissions)

$34,500 on land contract at 12% for 7 years, payments of $350/mo., then balloon

COMMENTARY

1. The seven-year balloon agreed to in this case study is tolerable. In the case study previous to this, Richard had set up financing with a three-year payout. In these times of uncertainty and unpredictable ups and downs in the rate of real estate growth, a three-year balloon is somewhat on the short side, as Richard himself is quick to confirm in retrospect. Five years is the shortest balloon period one should enter into for the foreseeable future, unless the investor plans a quick turn around. Even then, the presence of a very short term balloon can have a dampening effect at resale.

2. The willingness of the Realtor to take his commission in paper is less an indication of largesse than of a shrewd sense of survival. A sure sale with a paper commission that will soon be redeemed is far superior to a sale lost over the issue of cash at closing. As Richard put it in a recent telephone conversation, "Many Realtors are starving. They just sit on their duff and wait for business to come along." The aggressive and flexible agents, on the other hand, will not only survive but flourish.

3. The most important principle behind this case study has to be this: "You'll never know unless you ask." The "Ultimate Paper Out" does not work in every case, but it is always the place to begin.

DOCUMENTATION

UNIVERSAL EARNEST MONEY RECEIPT AND OFFER TO PURCHASE

"This is a legally binding contract: if not understood, seek competent advice."

1. Date and Place of Offer: __April 14__ 19 __81__ ; __Elkhorn__ __Wisconsin__
(city) (state)

2. Principals: The undersigned Buyer __Richard Austin__
agrees to buy and Seller agrees to sell, according to the indicated terms and conditions, the property described as follows:

3. Property: located at __926 Birch Street__ __Elkhorn__ __Wisconsin__
(street address) (city) (state)

with the following legal description: __Parcel S/W ¼ of Section 4. City of Elkhorn to Common.__

__204.1 feet South of S/E Corner, Lot 15, Block 24. Stanley addition,__

__Thence East to Wit 66 feet, Thence North 138.1, Thence West 66 feet,__

__Thence 138.1 feet to the Point of Beginning.__

including any of the following items if at present attached to the premises: plumbing, heating, and cooling equipment, including stoker and oil tanks, burners, water heaters, electric light fixtures, bathroom fixtures, roller shades, curtain rods and fixtures, draperies, venetian blinds, window and door screens, towel racks, linoleum and other attached floor coverings,

including carpeting, attached television antennas, mailboxes, all trees and shrubs, and any other fixtures EXCEPT __None__

The following personal property shall also be included as part of the purchase: _____
At the closing of the transaction, the Seller, at his expense, shall provide the Buyer with a Bill Of Sale containing a detailed inventory of the personal property included.

4. Earnest Money Deposit: Agent (or Seller) acknowledges receipt from Buyer of __None__ dollars $ __0__

in the form of ( ) cash; ( ) personal check; ( ) cashier's check; ( ) promissory note at _____% interest per annum due _____ 19 _____ ; or

other _____
as earnest money deposit to secure and apply on this purchase. Upon acceptance of this agreement in writing and delivery of same to Buyer, the earnest money deposit shall be assigned

to and deposited in the listing Realtor's trust account or _____, to apply on the purchase price at the time of closing.

5. Purchase Price: The total purchase price of the property shall be __Thirty-eight Thousand and 00/100__ dollars $ __38,000.00__

6. Payment: Purchase price is to be paid by Buyer as follows:

Aforedescribed earnest money deposit .... $ None

Additional payment due upon acceptance of this offer .... $ None

Additional payment due at closing .... $ None

Balance to be paid as follows:

1. This offer is not subject to the sale of other property.
2. This offer is subject to the Seller holding a Wisconsin Form II Land
Contract in the amount of $34,500 at an annual interest rate of 12%
per annum for a term of 84 months at a monthly payment of $350.00
per month. The first payment is to be made on June 1, 1981, 30 days

after closing.

3. Buyer is to pay all closing costs on Closing Statement attached and including all 1980 and 1981 real estate property taxes and assessments. Real estate taxes for 1980 were $729.32. Special assessment was $124.26. The total taxes were $853.58.

4. A current first mortgage is held by Rossiter Savings and Loan. Seller has received permission to convey property to Buyer from mortgage.

5. No cash at closing.

7. Title: Seller agrees to furnish good and marketable title free of all encumbrances and defects, except mortgage liens and encumbrances as set forth in this agreement, and to make conveyance by Warranty Deed or _____. Seller shall furnish in due course to the Buyer a title insurance policy insuring the Buyer of a good and marketable title in keeping with the terms and conditions of this agreement. Prior to the closing of this transaction, the Seller, upon request, will furnish to the Buyer a preliminary title report made by a title insurance company showing the condition of the title to said property. If the Seller cannot furnish marketable title within thirty days after receipt of the notice to the Buyer containing a written statement of the defects, the earnest money deposit herein receipted shall be refunded to the Buyer and this agreement shall be null and void. The following shall not be deemed encumbrances or defects; building and use restrictions general to the area; utility easements; other easements not inconsistent with Buyer's intended use; zoning or subdivision laws, covenants, conditions, restrictions, or reservations of record; tenancies of record. In the event of sale of other than real property relating to this transaction, Seller will provide evidence of title or right to sell or lease such personal property.

8. Special Representations: Seller warrants and represents to Buyer (1) that the subject property is connected to ( ) public sewer system, ( ) cesspool or septic tank, ( ) sewer system available but not connected, ( ) city water system, ( ) private water system, and that the following special improvements are included in the sale: ( ) sidewalk, ( ) curb and gutter, ( ) special street paving, ( ) special street lighting; (2) that the Seller knows of no material structural defects; (3) that all electrical wiring, heating, cooling, and plumbing systems are free of material defects and will be in good working order at the time the Buyer is entitled to possession; (4) that the Seller has no notice from any government agency of any violation or knowledge of probable violations of the law relating to the subject property; (5) that the Seller has no notice or knowledge of planned or commenced public improvements which may result in special assessments or otherwise directly and materially affect the property; and (6) that the Seller has no notice or knowledge of any liens to be assessed against the property,

EXCEPT _____ Special tax assessment of $124.26 yet to be billed. 1981 Tax Bill is to be the final assessment payment. _____

9. Escrow Instructions: This sale shall be closed on or before _April 25,_ 19_82_ by _Office of Richard Austin_ or such other closing agent as mutually agreed upon by Buyer and Seller. Buyer and Seller will, immediately on demand, deposit with closing agent all instruments and monies required to complete the purchase in accordance with the provisions of this agreement. Contract of Sale or Instrument of Conveyance to be made in the name of _____

10. Closing Costs and Pro-Ration: Seller agrees to pay for title insurance policy, preliminary title report (if requested), termite inspection as set forth below, real estate commission, cost of preparing and recording any corrective instruments, and one-half of the escrow fees. Buyer agrees to pay for recording fees for mortgages and deeds of conveyance, all costs or expenses in securing new financing or assuming existing financing, and one-half of the escrow fees. Buyer agrees to pay for recording fees for mortgages and deeds of conveyance, all costs or expenses in securing new financing or assuming existing financing, and one-half of the escrow fees. Taxes for the current year, insurance acceptable to the Buyer, rents, interest, mortgage reserves, maintenance fees, and water and other utilities constituting liens, shall be pro-rated as of closing. Renters' security deposits shall accrue to Buyer at closing. Seller to provide Buyer with all current rental or lease agreements prior to closing.

Oral lease to Jim Brady at $165.00 per month. Written one year lease to tenant on east upper and lower at $225.00 per month.

11. Termite Inspection: Seller agrees, at his expense, to provide written certification by a reputable licensed pest control firm that the property is free of termite infestation. In the event termites are found, the Seller shall have the property treated at his expense and provide acceptable certification that treatment has been rendered. If any structural repairs are required by reason of termite damage as established by acceptable certification, Seller agrees to make necessary repairs not to exceed $500. If repairs exceed $500, Buyer shall first have the right to accept the property "as is" with a credit to the Buyer at closing of $500, or the Buyer may terminate this agreement with the earnest money deposit being promptly returned to the Buyer if the Seller does not agree to pay all costs of treatment and repair.

12. Conditions of Sale: The following conditions shall also apply, and shall, if conflicting with the printed portions of this agreement, prevail and control:

Seller is to provide repairs to: garage door, replace gutter where missing, counter tops in kitchen.

13. Liability and Maintenance: Seller shall maintain subject property, including landscaping, in good condition until the date of transfer of title or possession by Buyer, whichever occurs first. All risk of loss and destruction of property, and all expenses of insurance, shall be borne by the seller until the date of possession. If the improvements on the property are destroyed or materially damaged prior to closing, then the Buyer shall have the right to declare this agreement null and void, and the earnest money deposit and all other sums paid by Buyer toward the purchase price shall be returned to the Buyer forthwith.

14. Possession: The Buyer shall be entitled to possession of property upon closing or _____, 19_____

15. Default: In the event the Buyer fails to complete the purchase as herein provided, the earnest money deposit shall be retained by the Seller as the total and entire liquidated damages. In the event the Seller fails to perform any condition of the sale as herein provided, then the Buyer may, at his option, treat the contract as terminated, and all payments made by the Buyer hereunder shall be returned to the Buyer forthwith, provided the Buyer may, at his option, treat this agreement as being in full force and effect with the right to action for specific performance and damages. In the event that either Buyer, Seller, or Agent shall institute suit to enforce any rights hereunder, the prevailing party shall be entitled to court costs and a reasonable attorney's fee.

16. Time Limit of Offer: The Seller shall have until

_____ _April 24,_ _____, 19 _81_ to accept this
(hour) (date)

offer by delivering a signed copy hereof to the Buyer. If this offer is not so accepted, it shall lapse and the agent (or Seller) shall refund the earnest money deposit to the Buyer forthwith.

17. General Agreements: (1) Both parties to this purchase reserve their rights to assign and hereby otherwise agree to cooperate in effecting an Internal Revenue Code 1031 exchange or similar tax-related arrangement prior to close of escrow, upon either party's written notice of intention to do so. (2) Upon approval of this offer by the Seller, this agreement shall become a contract between Buyer and Seller and shall inure to the benefit of the heirs, administrators, executors, successors, personal representatives, and assigns of said parties. (3) Time is of the

essence and an essential part of this agreement. (4) This contract constitutes the sole and entire agreement between the parties hereto and no modification of this contract shall be binding unless attached hereto and signed by all parties to the contract. No representations, promises, or inducements not included in this contract shall be binding upon any party hereto.

18. Buyer's Statement and Receipt: "I/we hereby agree to purchase the above property in accordance with the terms and conditions above stated and acknowledge receipt of a completed copy of this agreement, which I/we have fully read and understand." Dated ___ April 14, ___ 19 __81__ , ___
(hour)

Address ___ 17 Juniper Street ___ [signature] ___ Buyer

___ East Troy, Wisconsin ___ Buyer

Phone No: Home ___ 678-1400 ___ Business ___ 678-1400 ___

19. Seller's Statement and Response: "I/we approve and accept the above offer, which I/we have fully read and understand, and agree to the above terms and conditions this day of ___, 19 ___, ___ .
(hour)

Address ___ Seller

Phone No: Home ___ Business ___ Seller

20. Commission Agreement: Seller agrees to pay a commission of ___% of the gross sales price to __Buyer agrees to pay.__
for services in this transaction, and agrees that, in the event of forfeiture of the earnest money deposit by the Buyer, said deposit shall be divided between the Seller's broker and the Seller (one half to each party), the Broker's part not to exceed the amount of the commission.

21. Buyer's Receipt for Signed Offer: The Buyer hereby acknowledges receipt of a copy of the above agreement bearing the Seller's signature in acceptance of this offer.

Dated ___, 19 ___ Buyer

___ Buyer

COMMENTARY TO DOCUMENTATION

Item 2. The terms "or Assigns" should be added after the buyer's name.

Item 3. Personal property included, if any, should have been listed in the offer. For control and tax purposes, a bill of sale for such property should have been a requirement.

Item 6. A seven-year payout on the land contract is a fairly comfortable term; however, it would have been wise to seek a rollover provision for at least one additional year. As an added thought: since the bank seemed flexible on the underlying first, an alternative would have been for the buyer to assume the first and give the seller a promissory note for the balance of his equity secured by a second mortgage. The offer would then have required a substitution of collateral clause for the second, or the second could have been secured from the beginning with another property in the buyer's portfolio. This would have set the stage for later flexible dealings in resale, refinance, or "cranking" funds out of the property.

A safer way to state the provision on conveyance of the first would be this: "This agreement is contingent on the Buyer being able to purchase subject to the existing first mortgage without incurring additional expense." In other words, rather than stating in the offer that the seller had received permission to proceed with the sale, it seems more prudent to make permission a contingency of the offer.

Picking Up A Rental Home . . . Interest Free

**Featuring Technique No. 1
"The Ultimate Paper Out"**

In A Nutshell. . .

Type: SFH
Price: $66,500
Source: Classified ad
Means: Refinance, carry back
Techniques: No. 1 — Ultimate Paper Out
No. 4 — Contract/Wrap
No. 6 — Balloon
No. 20 — Rents
No. 21 — Deposits
No. 32 — Second Mortgage Crank
Strategies: No interest, no payment second

LOCATING

Twenty-five year old Troy Bigler of West Palm Beach, Florida, owns and operates a fashion store. Since attending the Nothing Down Seminar in his area, he has taken steps to plan for the future by investing in a number of single family rental units in the $40,000 to $60,000 range. His fifth property, described below, was located through the "Homes for Sale" section of the classified ads.

SITUATION

The well-maintained free and clear home was situated on a pleasant circle. The owner was an older man who had inherited the property and now needed to sell it in order to cover some hospital bills. The rent was set at $500, adequate for the area, with a built-in 5% cost of living increase every six months.

NEGOTIATION

Troy knew what he could afford and approached the seller with that in mind. He offered $66,500 for the property, with a down payment of $25,000 (which he intended to raise by obtaining a new mortgage). The owner countered with $30,000 down, whereupon Troy executed one of the classic negotiating maneuvers by acting as though his limit had been reached. In his own words: "I low-balled it. At that point he thought that was the most he could get out of me. I would have gone up to 40K."

Then Troy set the terms for the balance: the remaining equity of $36,500 would be repaid in five years and three months in one balloon payment, no interest. "I pointed out to him that mortgages are set up on thirty-year periods and that I would do him a favor and pay him in five years and three months." The owner agreed, evidently so pleased to be getting the rest of his equity in such a short time that he was willing to forego any interest. The seller was nearly three times the age of the buyer, and Troy permitted the paternal tendencies

of the gentleman to emerge: "I guess he took a liking to me."

CLOSING

The rest was easy. Troy's attorney drew up the papers, and the closing was arranged through a title company. The following sketch shows how the down payment was "cranked" out of the property (in this case a First Mortgage Crank), and the remainder was taken care of through an "Ultimate Paper Out":

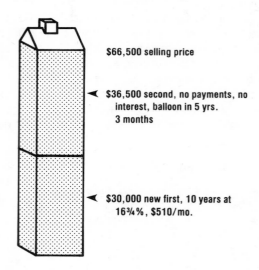

$66,500 selling price

$36,500 second, no payments, no interest, balloon in 5 yrs. 3 months

$30,000 new first, 10 years at 16¾%, $510/mo.

In a pleasant side-development, the mortgage company that granted Troy the loan added $1,400 to the principal amount as credit life insurance. Troy declined this service, so the lender cut him a check for $1,400. This amount, together with $500 for the first month's rent and a security deposit of $750, brought to $2,650 the amount of money Troy received at closing. His reaction: "If they continue to pay me these tidy sums of money every time I buy a house, I'm going to have to do something drastic like take a vacation — it will be the first one in four years."

OUTCOMES AND FUTURE PLANS

The property was essentially a "cream puff"; it needed very little attention. Six months after closing, the cash flow moved into the positive column. Troy is counting on steady appreciation of property values in his area for the next few years, at least sufficient for him to refinance the house in time for the no-interest balloon.

His main strategy in negotiating is to win the trust of the seller and to be explicit about what he can afford. "I find out in my negotiating that it is best to say that. They seem to sympathize with you." The most important advice he can give to others is: "Make those offers. It only takes one yes."

COMMENTARY

1. This is an unusual case study. Few people will carry back paper without interest. Absolutely no one will do this unless asked. In fact, Troy did not ask for these terms — he stated them. And the seller bought it. Granted, the seller had little emotional interest vested in the property, which he had inherited. Still, Troy is to be given credit as a courageous negotiator who dares to start at the point of greatest advantage to himself.

2. Another aspect of Troy's negotiating approach is worth reviewing. He went into the process knowing exactly how far he would go in yielding to the seller's demands. Then he started safely this side of that threshold and gave the seller the opportunity to give up too soon. This was fortunate, since any larger amount "cranked" out of the house would have generated a negative cash flow. Still, Troy was prepared to go further if necessary because he knew that an interest-free loan for the balance of the equity would have compensated handsomely. As it turned out, he had his cake and ate it, too. More power to him.

DOCUMENTATION

UNIVERSAL EARNEST MONEY RECEIPT
AND OFFER TO PURCHASE

"This is a legally binding contract: if not understood, seek competent advice."

1. Date and Place of Offer: __June 4,__ 19 __81__ ; __West Palm Beach__ __Florida__
                                                           (city)   (state)

2. Principals: The undersigned Buyer __Troy Bigler__
agrees to buy and Seller agrees to sell, according to the indicated terms and conditions, the property described as follows:

3. Property: located at __1406 Palmdale Street__ __West Palm Beach__ __Florida__
                     (street address)   (city)   (state)

with the following legal description: __Lot 81, Block 6, Plat #16. Jamaica Heights__

including any of the following items if at present attached to the premises: plumbing, heating, and cooling equipment, including stoker and oil tanks, burners, water heaters, electric light fixtures, bathroom fixtures, roller shades, curtain rods and fixtures, draperies, venetian blinds, window and door screens, towel racks, linoleum and other attached floor coverings,

including carpeting, attached television antennas, mailboxes, all trees and shrubs, and any other fixtures EXCEPT __None__

The following personal property shall also be included as part of the purchase: __Range, refrigerator, washer.__
At the closing of the transaction, the Seller, at his expense, shall provide the Buyer with a Bill Of Sale containing a detailed inventory of the personal property included.

4. Earnest Money Deposit: Agent (or Seller) acknowledges receipt from Buyer of __One-hundred and 00/100__ dollars $ __100.00__

in the form of (X) cash; ( ) personal check; ( ) cashier's check; ( ) promissory note at _____ % interest per annum due _____ 19 _____ ; or

other _____
as earnest money deposit to secure and apply on this purchase. Upon acceptance of this agreement in writing and delivery of same to Buyer, the earnest money deposit shall be assigned

to and deposited in the listing Realtor's trust account or __NA__ , to apply on the
purchase price at the time of closing.

5. Purchase Price: The total purchase price of the property shall be __Sixty-six Thousand Five Hundred and 00/100__

dollars $ __66,500__ .

6. Payment: Purchase price is to be paid by Buyer as follows:

    Aforedescribed earnest money deposit .... $ __100.00__

    Additional payment due upon acceptance of this offer .... $ __0__

    Additional payment due at closing .... $ __0__

Balance to be paid as follows:

1. $30,000 conventional mortgage, current rate and terms: proceeds to Seller.

2. $36,400 purchase money mortgage and note bearing interest at 0% on terms set forth below: purchase money mortgage to be a second mortgage in the amount of $36,400, payable in its entirety five (5) years from date of closing. Mortgage and note to be in a form acceptable to Seller's attorney. Mortgage to provide that in the event of a default, interest to activate at the rate of 18%. Additionally, mortgage to provide that in the event property is transferred, or any interest therein is conveyed, then in that event, mortgage to be paid in full. Buyer to pay all closing expenses attributable to mortgage, including attorney's fees in connection therewith. Buyer will pay all attorney's fees up to $100.00.

7. Title: Seller agrees to furnish good and marketable title free of all encumbrances and defects, except mortgage liens and encumbrances as set forth in this agreement, and to make conveyance by Warranty Deed or _____. Seller shall furnish in due course to the Buyer a title insurance policy insuring the Buyer of a good and marketable title in keeping with the terms and conditions of this agreement. Prior to the closing of this transaction, the Seller, upon request, will furnish to the Buyer a preliminary title report made by a title insurance company showing the condition of the title to said property. If the Seller cannot furnish marketable title within thirty days after receipt of the notice to the Buyer containing a written statement of the defects, the earnest money deposit herein receipted shall be refunded to the Buyer and this agreement shall be null and void. The following shall not be deemed encumbrances or defects; building and use restrictions general to the area; utility easements; other easements not inconsistent with Buyer's intended use; zoning or subdivision laws, covenants, conditions, restrictions, or reservations of record; tenancies of record. In the event of sale of other than real property relating to this transaction, Seller will provide evidence of title or right to sell or lease such personal property.

8. Special Representations: Seller warrants and represents to Buyer (1) that the subject property is connected to ( ) public sewer system, ( ) cesspool or septic tank, ( ) sewer system available but not connected, ( ) city water system, ( ) private water system, and that the following special improvements are included in the sale: ( ) sidewalk, ( ) curb and gutter, ( ) special street paving, ( ) special street lighting; (2) that the Seller knows of no material structural defects; (3) that all electrical wiring, heating, cooling, and plumbing systems are free of material defects and will be in good working order at the time the Buyer is entitled to possession; (4) that the Seller has no notice from any government agency of any violation or knowledge of probable violations of the law relating to the subject property; (5) that the Seller has no notice or knowledge of planned or commenced public improvements which may result in special assessments or otherwise directly and materially affect the property; and (6) that the Seller has no notice or knowledge of any liens to be assessed against the property,

EXCEPT _____ None _____

9. Escrow Instructions: This sale shall be closed on or before ___ July 15, ___ 19 81 ,by _____ or such other closing agent as mutually agreed upon by Buyer and Seller. Buyer and Seller will, immediately on demand, deposit with closing agent all instruments and monies required to complete the purchase in accordance with the provisions of this agreement. Contract of Sale or Instrument of Conveyance to be made in the name of _____

10. Closing Costs and Pro-Ration: Seller agrees to pay for title insurance policy, preliminary title report (if requested), termite inspection as set forth below, real estate commission, cost of preparing and recording any corrective instruments, and one-half of the escrow fees. Buyer agrees to pay for recording fees for mortgages and deeds of conveyance, all costs or expenses in securing new financing or assuming existing financing, and one-half of the escrow fees. Buyer agrees to pay for recording fees for mortgages and deeds of conveyance, all costs or expenses in securing new financing or assuming existing financing, and one-half of the escrow fees. Taxes for the current year, insurance acceptable to the Buyer, rents, interest, mortgage reserves, maintenance fees, and water and other utilities constituting liens, shall be pro-rated as of closing. Renters' security deposits shall accrue to Buyer at closing. Seller to provide Buyer with all current rental or lease agreements prior to closing.

11. Termite Inspection: Seller agrees, at his expense, to provide written certification by a reputable licensed pest control firm that the property is free of termite infestation. In the event termites are found, the Seller shall have the property treated at his expense and provide acceptable certification that treatment has been rendered. If any structural repairs are required by reason of termite damage as established by acceptable certification, Seller agrees to make necessary repairs not to exceed $500. If repairs exceed $500, Buyer shall first have the right to accept the property "as is" with a credit to the Buyer at closing of $500, or the Buyer may terminate this agreement with the earnest money deposit being promptly returned to the Buyer if the Seller does not agree to pay all costs of treatment and repair.

12. Conditions of Sale: The following conditions shall also apply, and shall, if conflicting with the printed portions of this agreement, prevail and control:

1. Buyer may not assign contract.

2. Subject to Buyer's approval of termite report and loan approval.

13. Liability and Maintenance: Seller shall maintain subject property, including landscaping, in good condition until the date of transfer of title or possession by Buyer, whichever occurs first. All risk of loss and destruction of property, and all expenses of insurance, shall be borne by the seller until the date of possession. If the improvements on the property are destroyed or materially damaged prior to closing, then the Buyer shall have the right to declare this agreement null and void, and the earnest money deposit and all other sums paid by Buyer toward the purchase price shall be returned to the Buyer forthwith.

14. Possession: The Buyer shall be entitled to possession of property upon closing or _____, 19 _____.

15. Default: In the event the Buyer fails to complete the purchase as herein provided, the earnest money deposit shall be retained by the Seller as the total and entire liquidated damages. In the event the Seller fails to perform any condition of the sale as herein provided, then the Buyer may, at his option, treat the contract as terminated, and all payments made by the Buyer hereunder shall be returned to the Buyer forthwith, provided the Buyer may, at his option, treat this agreement as being in full force and effect with the right to action for specific performance and damages. In the event that either Buyer, Seller, or Agent shall institute suit to enforce any rights hereunder, the prevailing party shall be entitled to court costs and a reasonable attorney's fee.

16. Time Limit of Offer: The Seller shall have until

_____ June 9, _____, 19 81 to accept this
(hour)   (date)

offer by delivering a signed copy hereof to the Buyer. If this offer is not so accepted, it shall lapse and the agent (or Seller) shall refund the earnest money deposit to the Buyer forthwith.

17. General Agreements: (1) Both parties to this purchase reserve their rights to assign and hereby otherwise agree to cooperate in effecting an Internal Revenue Code 1031 exchange or similar tax-related arrangement prior to close of escrow, upon either party's written notice of intention to do so. (2) Upon approval of this offer by the Seller, this agreement shall become a contract between Buyer and Seller and shall inure to the benefit of the heirs, administrators, executors, successors, personal representatives, and assigns of said parties. (3) Time is of the essence and an essential part of this agreement. (4) This contract constitutes the sole and entire agreement between the parties hereto and no modification of this contract shall be binding unless attached hereto and signed by all parties to the contract. No representations, promises, or inducements not included in this contract shall be binding upon any party hereto.

18. Buyer's Statement and Receipt: "I/we hereby agree to purchase the above property in accordance with the terms and conditions above stated and acknowledge receipt of a completed copy of this agreement, which I/we have fully read and understand." Dated ___June 4,___ 19 __81__ , _____ (hour)

Address ___16 Devonshire Place___   ___[signature]___ Buyer

___West Palm Beach, Florida___   _____ Buyer

Phone No: Home ___225-1593___ Business ___682-1436___

19. Seller's Statement and Response: "I/we approve and accept the above offer, which I/we have fully read and understand, and agree to the above terms and conditions this day of _____ , 19 _____ , _____ (hour)

Address _____   _____ Seller

Phone No: Home _____ Business _____   _____ Seller

20. Commission Agreement: Seller agrees to pay a commission of ___5___ % of the gross sales price to ___Jules Madsen Realty___ for services in this transaction, and agrees that, in the event of forfeiture of the earnest money deposit by the Buyer, said deposit shall be divided between the Seller's broker and the Seller (one half to each party), the Broker's part not to exceed the amount of the commission.

21. Buyer's Receipt for Signed Offer: The Buyer hereby acknowledges receipt of a copy of the above agreement bearing the Seller's signature in acceptance of this offer.

Dated _____ , 19 _____   _____ Buyer

_____ Buyer

COMMENTARY TO DOCUMENTATION

Item 2. The words "or Assigns" should be written after the buyer's name in every offer. However, in this case, there is a special contingency imposed by the seller under Item No. 12 to the effect that the contract is not assignable. With terms as soft as those built into this transaction, the buyer is not likely to want to assign this contract anyway.

Item 3. The buyer is wise to list personal property items separately.

Item 6. The buyer would have been well advised to try for a rollover provision on the five-year balloon. Clearly the seller was opposed to a non-acceleration clause — not much progress to be made there. However, a substitution of collateral clause would have been useful, as well as a first right of refusal on the mortgage note.

In regard to the terms on the new first mortgage: stating them precisely (interest rate and length of term) is an added contingency for the buyer. The way it is stated now constitutes a blank check.

Item 9. No title company is mentioned. However, in a separate letter to the author, the buyer in this transaction passed on this interesting bit of advice: "By the way, Rich, you might want to put this clause in the book (it works very well for me): 'Buyer to choose title company.' Being that the seller is paying for the title policy, I worked a deal out with my lawyer that I would give him all the title work if in return he represents me at no charge. Win/win."

Item 15. The "entire liquidated damages" provision was not in the buyer's original offer. It is always a good idea to put it in (as in this version of the preprinted earnest money agreement).

Four Houses For The Price Of Two

**Featuring Technique No. 1
"The Ultimate Paper Out"**

In A Nutshell. . .

Type: SFH, with extra building
Price: $35,000
Source: Friend
Means: Personal Note
Techniques: No. 1 — Ultimate Paper Out
No. 4 — Contract/Wrap
Features: Conversion, positive cash flow

James Judd of Albuquerque was no stranger to nothing down purchases. In 1960 he bought his first home for nothing down using "sweat equity." His second home came in 1965 for $250 down during a small recession in the mining community. Two years later he took advantage of a slow real estate market to buy another home, this time for $200 down. He knew that real estate could be acquired for nothing down, but until he took the Nothing Down Seminar, he was not aware of the principles that would enable him to hold property creatively and profitably. Besides having to overcome the "knowledge barrier," he had to adjust the attitudes about landholding that his parents had passed on to him. For them — they had never owned their own home — the landlord was a "rich man" in a different and inaccessible world. Following the Nothing Down Seminar, James decided that he was going to become part of that new world.

LOCATING

After trying his hand unsuccessfully at two condos in a less than desirable location, he set out to find a solid family home. A friend of a friend told him of a nice unlisted two-bedroom house up for sale in a much better area of town. Immediately he went to investigate.

SITUATION

The free-and-clear property was immaculate on the outside; the landscaping was plush. This somewhat compensated for the inside, which needed considerable fix-up attention. The owner-occupant was an elderly lady who needed retirement income. In addition to the small two-bedroom house, there was a one-bedroom house in the rear of the property included in the deal. At the time, it was being rented for $175/mo. James figured this extra building must be adequate if it brought in that much rent, so he did not even inspect it.

NEGOTIATION

This was the simplest part of the transaction, especially since it turned out that the lady knew James' wife and thus brought considerable trust to the negotiation process. James simply asked the lady what price and terms she wanted for her property. Much to his surprise, she said she would be satisfied with $35,000 for the package, with zero down and payments of $250 per month, no interest. James thought long and hard about it — perhaps three seconds. Based on real estate patterns in the area, he figured the property to be 50% underpriced. Payout would take only 11 years and 8 months using her terms. Was she sure that her needs would be satisfied in that way? She confirmed it, so he agreed.

CLOSING

James' obligations were drawn up in the form of a personal note for $35,000, signed by his wife Emily. The lady, who was 83 years old, deeded the property over to Emily using a quitclaim deed. She insisted on a provision that would forgive the balance of the note in the event of her death. The sketch shows what he had gained:

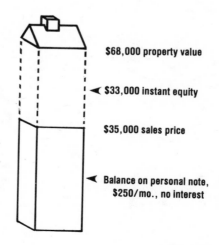

$68,000 property value

◄ $33,000 instant equity

$35,000 sales price

◄ Balance on personal note,
$250/mo., no interest

OUTCOMES AND FUTURE PLANS

James invested $1,500 to renovate the interior of the two-bedroom house and rented it out for $275/mo. Soon thereafter, the tenant in the rear building left, so James invested another $2,500 to convert this unit into a duplex with two efficiency apartments. These he has rented for $165/mo. each. After taxes of $139 and insurance of $127 (annual payments), James has a positive cash flow on the property of $355 per month. With the improvements, the property value is actually around $72,000.

Incidentally, the seller has asked James to consider buying another house from her with similar terms. Talk about trust!

ADDENDUM

Soon after the closing of this deal, James noticed that the duplex across the street was also being offered for sale. The listed price was $50,000. James offered $2,000 down with a 10% wrap-around mortgage on the balance. The seller accepted, and this transaction also went to closing. Then the unimaginable happened. As James tells it: "At closing I was asked to sign two warranty deeds for escrow. TWO? It seems that a small one-bedroom house next door was included in the original mortgage and went with the deal even though the real estate salesman was unaware of it. (A genuine FREEBEE!)" Once again James had done it — two for the price of one. The upshot of these two deals: four houses for the price of two.

As to the outcomes on the duplex: payments are $423 per month, with income of only $420. As James puts it: "I figured I could handle this large negative for a few months." The extra one-bedroom unit is rented out for $120/mo. to a tenant who won't let James renovate ("He's afraid I'll raise the rent."). So this unit just sits there cranking out a monthly cash flow.

COMMENTARY

1. Is James taking advantage of the elderly lady? Certainly not. She herself suggested the price and terms. The secret for success is the fact that James was able to generate trust. As always, it is important to be thorough about the preparation of the documents. This is especially true of discounted properties of the type involved in this case study. Investors should use the services of competent professionals (title company officers, real estate attorneys, etc.).

2. James cannot be faulted for jumping at a good opportunity like the two-bedroom house with the extra building in the rear; however, a thorough inspection before closing is always the universal rule.

DOCUMENTATION

The only paperwork originating with the buyers in this transaction was the following promissory note to the seller. No earnest money agreement was used. All the preliminary understandings were oral in nature.

PROMISSORY NOTE

$ 35,000.00

Albuquerque, Bernalillo County, New Mexico

Emily Judd after date, for value received, I or either of us, promise to pay to the order of Mary Bradford the sum of Thirty-five thousand dollars and 00/100----------Dollars ($35,000.00) with interest from 2-16-81 until paid, at the rate of none percent (-0-%). Payable at the rate of $250.00 per month, on the first day of the month, until paid in full. In the event of death of holder, this note becomes null and void and shall be considered paid in full.

COMMENTARY TO DOCUMENTATION

The Internal Revenue Service is always concerned about notes at zero percent interest. The issue is whether sellers should be allowed to assign the entire amount of a payment as principal (with long-term capital gains tax advantages) or whether a portion of the payment must be considered interest income (taxed as ordinary income). According to current regulations, the latter is the case. The IRS will likely impute interest at 10% in a situation like the one discussed here. The seller will probably have to allocate a percentage of the $250 monthly payment as interest income. Similarly, the buyer will allocate the same percentage as an interest payment (rather than all principal). It is imperative that competent tax advice be obtained in such cases. The formulas used in imputing interest are not without their complexities.

5

Using Your Reputation (Instead Of Cash) As Down Payment

**Featuring Technique No. 4
"Contract Or Wrap-Around Mortgage"**

In A Nutshell . . .

Type: Tri-plex
Price: $69,300
Source: Classified Ad
Means: Wrap
Techniques: No. 4 — Contract/Wrap
No. 19 — Borrowing Realtor's Commission
No. 21 — Deposits

LOCATING

In the previous case study, James Judd of Albuquerque demonstrated his expertise in using the "Ultimate Paper Out" technique. In the present example, also located through the classified ads, he shows his colors with the wrap-around mortgage technique as applied to a tri-plex.

SITUATION

The tri-plex was located in a low-cost area of the city currently being upgraded and developed. The block and stucco building was structurally sound, although cosmetic improvements were called for. The listing was explicit about the price and terms: $74,000, with $15,000 down and the balance on contract at 12%. There was a fairly small conventional underlying mortgage at 7¾%.

NEGOTIATION

James' goal was to buy the property with nothing down. From $15,000 to zero was a considerable distance, and it took nine offers and counteroffers to bring the seller nearly all the way. The final agreement called for a sales price of $69,300, with a down payment of $1,300, the balance on a wrap-around contract at 10.75% for 35 years with a 12-year payout.

How did James get the seller to agree to a near nothing down deal? The major factor was James' reputation as an efficient property manager. Being a building designer, James knew how to get action on property renovation. Being an experienced landlord, he knew how to keep occupancy to a maximum.

James did not need to toot his own horn — that's where the skillful real estate agent came in. The agent sold James to the seller, who knew all too much about management headaches, especially in that part of town. He wanted to turn the property over to someone who could make it click. In effect, James invested his reputation as a down payment and got off with a minimum down of $1,000. The additional $300 came

from renters' deposits being held by the seller.

The agent's service did not stop with that. He also agreed to take his commission in the form of a note from the seller, thus contributing his part to the relaxation of the down payment requirement.

CLOSING

The necessary papers were drawn up by a title company. James was careful to stipulate that the payout (in this case after 12 years) would cover only the seller's equity. The long-term first-mortgage at 7¾% would thus be left intact. The sketch summarizes the facts:

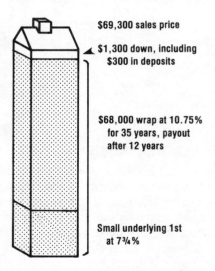

$69,300 sales price

$1,300 down, including $300 in deposits

$68,000 wrap at 10.75% for 35 years, payout after 12 years

Small underlying 1st at 7¾%

OUTCOMES AND FUTURE PLANS

The property is worth approximately $74,000. James' instant equity is therefore $4,700. Rents are locked in by leases for another 6 months; the income of $525/mo. is short by nearly $100 of matching the debt service. James plans to complete some cosmetic improvements and raise the rents as soon as possible in order to convert the flow to the positive side of the ledger. The negative doesn't bother him in the meantime, as he is in the 40% tax bracket and has offsetting cash flows from his other units.

COMMENTARY

1. Those who lose the faith after one "no" should take heart in James' persistence. With nine offers and counteroffers under his belt on this one deal, he has a right to celebrate. Nothing down investors average five offers to achieve one deal and ten offers for a true nothing down deal. Generally that means offers on different properties. In this case, the nearly ten offers applied to the **same** property. There is a lesson for us all.

2. Here is yet another example of down payment being equivalent to "trust payment." The seller did not need the money, only the peace of mind. The case study underscores the importance of a competent and insightful real estate agent; in any real estate transaction, not only **properties** are sold but — even chiefly — **people** are sold. The agent earned his money in this one or rather his note. And that is another point in his favor: when it comes to commissions, a note in the hand is worth more than imaginary cash in the bank. Every creative Realtor knows that, especially in times of tight money. The seller won, the buyer won, the agent won — everyone won.

DOCUMENTATION

UNIVERSAL EARNEST MONEY RECEIPT AND OFFER TO PURCHASE

"This is a legally binding contract: if not understood, seek competent advice."

1. Date and Place of Offer: __November 6,__ 19 __81__ ; __Albuquerque__ (city) __New Mexico__ (state)

2. Principals: The undersigned Buyer __James Judd__
agrees to buy and Seller agrees to sell, according to the indicated terms and conditions, the property described as follows:

3. Property: located at __986 Pleasant View Drive__ (street address) __Albuquerque__ (city) __New Mexico__ (state)

with the following legal description: __To be supplied prior to closing.__

including any of the following items if at present attached to the premises: plumbing, heating, and cooling equipment, including stoker and oil tanks, burners, water heaters, electric light fixtures, bathroom fixtures, roller shades, curtain rods and fixtures, draperies, venetian blinds, window and door screens, towel racks, linoleum and other attached floor coverings,

including carpeting, attached television antennas, mailboxes, all trees and shrubs, and any other fixtures EXCEPT __None__

The following personal property shall also be included as part of the purchase: ____
At the closing of the transaction, the Seller, at his expense, shall provide the Buyer with a Bill Of Sale containing a detailed inventory of the personal property included.

4. Earnest Money Deposit: Agent (or Seller) acknowledges receipt from Buyer of __One Thousand and 00/100__ dollars $ __1,000.00__

in the form of ( ) cash; (X) personal check; ( ) cashier's check; ( ) promissory note at ____% interest per annum due ____ 19 ____ ; or

other ____
as earnest money deposit to secure and apply on this purchase. Upon acceptance of this agreement in writing and delivery of same to Buyer, the earnest money deposit shall be assigned

to and deposited in the listing Realtor's trust account or __NA__ , to apply on the
purchase price at the time of closing.

5. Purchase Price: The total purchase price of the property shall be __Sixty-nine Thousand Three Hundred and 00/100__

dollars $ __69,300.00__

6. Payment: Purchase price is to be paid by Buyer as follows:

Aforedescribed earnest money deposit .... $ __1,000.00__

Additional payment due upon acceptance of this offer .... $ ____

Additional payment due at closing .... $ __300.00__

Balance to be paid as follows:
__The balance of $68,000 payable together with interest on the unpaid balance at the rate of 10 3/4 percent per annum, in monthly installments of not less than $623.90 each, or more per month including interest; 1st payment is payable on the 25th day of November, 1981, and subsequent payments shall be due on the 25th day of each month thereafter until twelve (12) years from the date of closing, at which time the entire balance of principal and interest shall be due and payable. In addition to the__

payments for principal and interest, Buyer shall pay with each installment
a pro rata portion of the estimated annual taxes and of the insurance premium for hazard insurance on said property.

7. Title: Seller agrees to furnish good and marketable title free of all encumbrances and defects, except mortgage liens and encumbrances as set forth in this agreement, and to make

conveyance by Warranty Deed or _____. Seller shall furnish in due course
to the Buyer a title insurance policy insuring the Buyer of a good and marketable title in keeping with the terms and conditions of this agreement. Prior to the closing of this transaction, the Seller, upon request, will furnish to the Buyer a preliminary title report made by a title insurance company showing the condition of the title to said property. If the Seller cannot furnish marketable title within thirty days after receipt of the notice to the Buyer containing a written statement of the defects, the earnest money deposit herein receipted shall be refunded to the Buyer and this agreement shall be null and void. The following shall not be deemed encumbrances or defects; building and use restrictions general to the area; utility easements; other easements not inconsistent with Buyer's intended use; zoning or subdivision laws, covenants, conditions, restrictions, or reservations of record; tenancies of record. In the event of sale of other than real property relating to this transaction, Seller will provide evidence of title or right to sell or lease such personal property.

8. Special Representations: Seller warrants and represents to Buyer (1) that the subject property is connected to ( ) public sewer system, ( ) cesspool or septic tank, ( ) sewer system available but not connected, ( ) city water system, ( ) private water system, and that the following special improvements are included in the sale: ( ) sidewalk, ( ) curb and gutter, ( ) special street paving, ( ) special street lighting; (2) that the Seller knows of no material structural defects; (3) that all electrical wiring, heating, cooling, and plumbing systems are free of material defects and will be in good working order at the time the Buyer is entitled to possession; (4) that the Seller has no notice from any government agency of any violation or knowledge of probable violations of the law relating to the subject property; (5) that the Seller has no notice or knowledge of planned or commenced public improvements which may result in special assessments or otherwise directly and materially affect the property; and (6) that the Seller has no notice or knowledge of any liens to be assessed against the property,

EXCEPT _____ None _____

9. Escrow Instructions: This sale shall be closed on or before November 11, 19 81 by _____
or such other closing agent as mutually agreed upon by Buyer and Seller. Buyer and Seller will, immediately on demand, deposit with closing agent all instruments and monies required

to complete the purchase in accordance with the provisions of this agreement. Contract of Sale or Instrument of Conveyance to be made in the name of _____

10. Closing Costs and Pro-Ration: Seller agrees to pay for title insurance policy, preliminary title report (if requested), termite inspection as set forth below, real estate commission, cost of preparing and recording any corrective instruments, and one-half of the escrow fees. Buyer agrees to pay for recording fees for mortgages and deeds of conveyance, all costs or expenses in securing new financing or assuming existing financing, and one-half of the escrow fees. Buyer agrees to pay for recording fees for mortgages and deeds of conveyance, all costs or expenses in securing new financing or assuming existing financing, and one-half of the escrow fees. Taxes for the current year, insurance acceptable to the Buyer, rents, interest, mortgage reserves, maintenance fees, and water and other utilities constituting liens, shall be pro-rated as of closing. Renters' security deposits shall accrue to Buyer at closing. Seller to provide Buyer with all current rental or lease agreements prior to closing.

11. Termite Inspection: Seller agrees, at his expense, to provide written certification by a reputable licensed pest control firm that the property is free of termite infestation. In the event termites are found, the Seller shall have the property treated at his expense and provide acceptable certification that treatment has been rendered. If any structural repairs are required by reason of termite damage as established by acceptable certification, Seller agrees to make necessary repairs not to exceed $500. If repairs exceed $500, Buyer shall first have the right to accept the property "as is" with a credit to the Buyer at closing of $500, or the Buyer may terminate this agreement with the earnest money deposit being promptly returned to the Buyer if the Seller does not agree to pay all costs of treatment and repair.

12. Conditions of Sale: The following conditions shall also apply, and shall, if conflicting with the printed portions of this agreement, prevail and control:

Subject to inspection and approval of interiors by Buyer within 72
hours of the acceptance by Seller.

13. Liability and Maintenance: Seller shall maintain subject property, including landscaping, in good condition until the date of transfer of title or possession by Buyer, whichever occurs first. All risk of loss and destruction of property, and all expenses of insurance, shall be borne by the seller until the date of possession. If the improvements on the property are destroyed or materially damaged prior to closing, then the Buyer shall have the right to declare this agreement null and void, and the earnest money deposit and all other sums paid by Buyer toward the purchase price shall be returned to the Buyer forthwith.

14. Possession: The Buyer shall be entitled to possession of property upon closing or _____ NA _____, 19 _____.

15. Default: In the event the Buyer fails to complete the purchase as herein provided, the earnest money deposit shall be retained by the Seller as the total and entire liquidated damages. In the event the Seller fails to perform any condition of the sale as herein provided, then the Buyer may, at his option, treat the contract as terminated, and all payments made by the Buyer hereunder shall be returned to the Buyer forthwith, provided the Buyer may, at his option, treat this agreement as being in full force and effect with the right to action for specific performance and damages. In the event that either Buyer, Seller, or Agent shall institute suit to enforce any rights hereunder, the prevailing party shall be entitled to court costs and a reasonable attorney's fee.

16. Time Limit of Offer: The Seller shall have until

_____   _____, 19 _____ to accept this
         (hour)   (date)
offer by delivering a signed copy hereof to the Buyer. If this offer is not so accepted, it shall lapse and the agent (or Seller) shall refund the earnest money deposit to the Buyer forthwith.

17. General Agreements: (1) Both parties to this purchase reserve their rights to assign and hereby otherwise agree to cooperate in effecting an Internal Revenue Code 1031 exchange or similar tax-related arrangement prior to close of escrow, upon either party's written notice of intention to do so. (2) Upon approval of this offer by the Seller, this agreement shall become a contract between Buyer and Seller and shall inure to the benefit of the heirs, administrators, executors, successors, personal representatives, and assigns of said parties. (3) Time is of the essence and an essential part of this agreement. (4) This contract constitutes the sole and entire agreement between the parties hereto and no modification of this contract shall be binding unless attached hereto and signed by all parties to the contract. No representations, promises, or inducements not included in this contract shall be binding upon any party hereto.

18. Buyer's Statement and Receipt: "I/we hereby agree to purchase the above property in accordance with the terms and conditions above stated and acknowledge receipt of a

completed copy of this agreement, which I/we have fully read and understand." Dated _____ November 6 _____ 19 81 , _____
                                                                                                                    (hour)

Address _____ 1643 Falcrest Court _____   _____ [signature] _____ Buyer

_____ Albuquerque, New Mexico _____   _____ Buyer

Phone No: Home ___ 631-6119 ___ Business ___ 629-1407 ___

19. Seller's Statement and Response: "I/we approve and accept the above offer, which I/we have fully read and understand, and agree to the above terms and conditions this day

of _____ , 19 _____ , _____ .
(hour)

Address _____   _____ Seller

Phone No: Home _____ Business _____   _____ Seller

20. Commission Agreement: Seller agrees to pay a commission of _____% of the gross sales price to _____
for services in this transaction, and agrees that, in the event of forfeiture of the earnest money deposit by the Buyer, said deposit shall be divided between the Seller's broker and the Seller (one half to each party), the Broker's part not to exceed the amount of the commission.

21. Buyer's Receipt for Signed Offer: The Buyer hereby acknowledges receipt of a copy of the above agreement bearing the Seller's signature in acceptance of this offer.

Dated _____ , 19 _____   _____ Buyer

_____ Buyer

COMMENTARY TO DOCUMENTATION

Item 2. The words "or Assigns" should always be written after the buyer's name.

Item 6. In the closing papers, the buyer was careful to stipulate that the 12-year payout applied only to the seller's equity, not the underlying first mortgage of 7¾%. This stipulation should also have been part of the earnest money agreement to avoid any subsequent misunderstandings.

The security for the balance of $68,000 was, in this case, a real estate contract that wrapped around the underlying first (hence a wrap-around contract, with the purchase made "subject to" the existing financing). An alternate approach might have been to assume the underlying first and execute a second trust deed (mortgage) on the balance. This might have brought to the buyer some added flexibilities in future resale, refinance, exchanging, etc., especially if a substitution of collateral provision applied to the second.

The arrangement should have included provisions for rolling the balloon over for an additional period of time if necessary, as well as prepaying the balance without penalty.

Item 12. The inspection and approval provision is an excellent contingency for the buyer, who in this case had not seen the interiors of the building.

Item 16. No time limit was imposed on the seller — a risky omission in any case. Usually 2 to 3 days would be a sufficient time to allow for the response. Some buyers insist on approval or disapproval on receipt of the offer.

Item 20. The original earnest money form did not stipulate the responsibility for the commission.

Buyer Teaches Seller
New Trick —
And They Both Win

Featuring Technique No. 4
"Contract or Wrap-Around Mortgage"

In A Nutshell . . .

Type: SFH
Price: $80,000
Source: Realtor
Means: New first (Purchase money mortgage)
Techniques: No. 4: — Contract/Wrap
Features: $200/mo. positive cash flow

LOCATING

Kent Bradford is an investor in Longmeadow, Massachusetts, a small city south of Springfield. His goal recently was to acquire a single family home in the $80,000 to $90,000 range as a long-term investment. With the help of a Realtor, he located a promising property.

SITUATION

The owner was a woman who was about to retire. She was offering her free and clear rental home for $85,000. Her terms: all cash, with conventional financing. In this era of high-interest financing, the ordinary cash-poor buyer might have passed this deal up as too prone to generate a painful negative cash flow. But Kent did not yet know enough about the seller to make a judgment.

NEGOTIATION

The next phase of the process went something this:

Kent: "What will you do with the proceeds of the sale?"
Seller: "I plan to invest the cash in Certificates of Deposit."
Kent: "What interest will your money be earning in C.D.'s?"
Seller: "Currently around 11.5% — much better than passbook savings."
Kent: "If I could show you a way to earn an even higher rate of interest, would you be interested?"
Seller: "Certainly I would. What do you have in mind?"
Kent: "Will you take a mortgage for your property?"
Seller: "I didn't know I could."
Kent: "Absolutely. It's done frequently these days. I could give you a note for your equity, secured by the property, and make monthly payments to you just as if you were the bank. How does 12% interest sound to

you, with regular payments each month. You don't have to wait for a long period of time as with a Certificate of Deposit. The payments will start right away."

The outcome of the negotiation was this — the woman was delighted with the prospect of getting a higher rate of interest. She accepted Kent's offer of $80,000, with $4,000 down, and the balance at 12% for 25 years.

CLOSING

As part of the arrangement, the seller agreed to reshingle the roof and repair the porch at her own expense. The Realtor's commission was paid in cash by the seller out of the proceeds of the escrow. As it turned out, the Realtor was a friend of the seller and agreed to accept a 3% fee — it pays to negotiate! The financing, shown in the following sketch, was very simple:

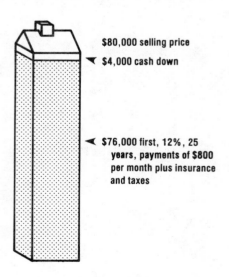

$80,000 selling price
$4,000 cash down
$76,000 first, 12%, 25 years, payments of $800 per month plus insurance and taxes

OUTCOMES AND FUTURE PLANS

Debt service and expenses amount to around $900 per month. The rental income is $1,100 per month, leaving a positive cash flow of $200. Just two months after the closing, the house appraised for $110,000, $30,000 more than Kent paid for it. He plans to hold the property for the long term, refinancing it in perhaps 5 to 7 years — after it has doubled in value.

His secret for creative investing is, in his own words, "solving the seller's problem." If he had it to do over again, he would have changed the commission arrangement: "I might have been able to negotiate a 100% nothing down deal if I had asked the Realtor to take her commission in monthly payments."

COMMENTARY

1. One advantage to the arrangement probably did not escape the seller in this case — her tax liability in not accepting the full equity in cash up front (as she at first planned) was considerably reduced. This is perhaps the most important aspect of a contract sale (also called a land sales contract, contract for deed, purchase money mortgage, etc.) to be explained to the seller.

2. What is conspicuously missing in this deal — much to the buyer's delight, no doubt? There is no balloon payment involved. The woman was willing to accept her payments for 25 years. The indebtedness will be fully amortized. So often these days buyers accede to financing involving short-term balloon notes. Such buyers don't sleep well unless they have planned from the beginning to cure the balloons in acceptable ways. But balloons are not always necessary, as this case demonstrates.

3. Kent is fortunate that the rent levels in this area are high enough to cover the debt service on this property. In many areas of the country, this deal would have generated a considerable negative cash flow and forced the buyer to bring in a partner, adjust the financing, or set up a lease-option with the tenant in order to solve the negative problem.

4. There might have been an advantage to setting up the financing using two separate notes rather than just one. In that case, Kent would have had more flexibility in the event he might have wanted to move the mortgage to another property — if the seller agreed at the outset to a substitution of collateral — or manipulate the financing in other ways.

DOCUMENTATION

[The following illustrative document was completed using data supplied by the buyer.]

UNIVERSAL EARNEST MONEY RECEIPT AND OFFER TO PURCHASE

"This is a legally binding contract: if not understood, seek competent advice."

1. Date and Place of Offer: __May 1,__ 19 __81__ ; __Longmeadow__ (city) __Massachusetts__ (state)

2. Principals: The undersigned Buyer __Kent Bradford or Assigns__
agrees to buy and Seller agrees to sell, according to the indicated terms and conditions, the property described as follows:

3. Property: located at __1214 Hippard Lane__ (street address) __Longmeadow__ (city) __Massachusetts__ (state)

with the following legal description: __To be supplied prior to closing.__
including any of the following items if at present attached to the premises: plumbing, heating, and cooling equipment, including stoker and oil tanks, burners, water heaters, electric light fixtures, bathroom fixtures, roller shades, curtain rods and fixtures, draperies, venetian blinds, window and door screens, towel racks, linoleum and other attached floor coverings,

including carpeting, attached television antennas, mailboxes, all trees and shrubs, and any other fixtures EXCEPT __None__

The following personal property shall also be included as part of the purchase: __Range__
At the closing of the transaction, the Seller, at his expense, shall provide the Buyer with a Bill Of Sale containing a detailed inventory of the personal property included.

4. Earnest Money Deposit: Agent (or Seller) acknowledges receipt from Buyer of __One Hundred and 00/100__ dollars $ __100.00__

in the form of ( ) cash; (X) personal check; ( ) cashier's check; ( ) promissory note at _____% interest per annum due _____ 19 _____ ; or

other _____
as earnest money deposit to secure and apply on this purchase. Upon acceptance of this agreement in writing and delivery of same to Buyer, the earnest money deposit shall be assigned

to and deposited in the listing Realtor's trust account or __NA__ , to apply on the
purchase price at the time of closing.

5. Purchase Price: The total purchase price of the property shall be __Eighty Thousand and 00/100__ dollars $ __80,000.00__

6. Payment: Purchase price is to be paid by Buyer as follows:

Aforedescribed earnest money deposit .... $ __100.00__

Additional payment due upon acceptance of this offer .... $ _____

Additional payment due at closing .... $ __3,900.00__

Balance to be paid as follows:

Buyer to execute promissory note in favor of Seller secured by a
purchase money mortgage in the amount of $76,000, payable $800.45
per month, including 12% interest per annum, amortized over a period
of 25 years.

7. Title: Seller agrees to furnish good and marketable title free of all encumbrances and defects, except mortgage liens and encumbrances as set forth in this agreement, and to make

conveyance by Warranty Deed or _____ Seller shall furnish in due course to the Buyer a title insurance policy insuring the Buyer of a good and marketable title in keeping with the terms and conditions of this agreement. Prior to the closing of this transaction, the Seller, upon request, will furnish to the Buyer a preliminary title report made by a title insurance company showing the condition of the title to said property. If the Seller cannot furnish marketable title within thirty days after receipt of the notice to the Buyer containing a written statement of the defects, the earnest money deposit herein receipted shall be refunded to the Buyer and this agreement shall be null and void. The following shall not be deemed encumbrances or defects: building and use restrictions general to the area; utility easements; other easements not inconsistent with Buyer's intended use; zoning or subdivision laws, covenants, conditions, restrictions, or reservations of record; tenancies of record. In the event of sale of other than real property relating to this transaction, Seller will provide evidence of title or right to sell or lease such personal property.

8. Special Representations: Seller warrants and represents to Buyer (1) that the subject property is connected to ( ) public sewer system, ( ) cesspool or septic tank, ( ) sewer system available but not connected, ( ) city water system, ( ) private water system, and that the following special improvements are included in the sale: ( ) sidewalk, ( ) curb and gutter, ( ) special street paving, ( ) special street lighting; (2) that the Seller knows of no material structural defects; (3) that all electrical wiring, heating, cooling, and plumbing systems are free of material defects and will be in good working order at the time the Buyer is entitled to possession; (4) that the Seller has no notice from any government agency of any violation or knowledge of probable violations of the law relating to the subject property; (5) that the Seller has no notice or knowledge of planned or commenced public improvements which may result in special assessments or otherwise directly and materially affect the property; and (6) that the Seller has no notice or knowledge of any liens to be assessed against the property,

EXCEPT _____None_____

9. Escrow Instructions: This sale shall be closed on or before __May 15,__ 19__81__ by __Stirling Escrow Company__ or such other closing agent as mutually agreed upon by Buyer and Seller. Buyer and Seller will, immediately on demand, deposit with closing agent all instruments and monies required

to complete the purchase in accordance with the provisions of this agreement. Contract of Sale or Instrument of Conveyance to be made in the name of _____

__To be determined prior to closing.__

10. Closing Costs and Pro-Ration: Seller agrees to pay for title insurance policy, preliminary title report (if requested), termite inspection as set forth below, real estate commission, cost of preparing and recording any corrective instruments, and one-half of the escrow fees. Buyer agrees to pay for recording fees for mortgages and deeds of conveyance, all costs or expenses in securing new financing or assuming existing financing, and one-half of the escrow fees. Buyer agrees to pay for recording fees for mortgages and deeds of conveyance, all costs or expenses in securing new financing or assuming existing financing, and one-half of the escrow fees. Taxes for the current year, insurance acceptable to the Buyer, rents, interest, mortgage reserves, maintenance fees, and water and other utilities constituting liens, shall be pro-rated as of closing. Renters' security deposits shall accrue to Buyer at closing. Seller to provide Buyer with all current rental or lease agreements prior to closing.

11. Termite Inspection: Seller agrees, at his expense, to provide written certification by a reputable licensed pest control firm that the property is free of termite infestation. In the event termites are found, the Seller shall have the property treated at his expense and provide acceptable certification that treatment has been rendered. If any structural repairs are required by reason of termite damage as established by acceptable certification, Seller agrees to make necessary repairs not to exceed $500. If repairs exceed $500, Buyer shall first have the right to accept the property "as is" with a credit to the Buyer at closing of $500, or the Buyer may terminate this agreement with the earnest money deposit being promptly returned to the Buyer if the Seller does not agree to pay all costs of treatment and repair.

12. Conditions of Sale: The following conditions shall also apply, and shall, if conflicting with the printed portions of this agreement, prevail and control:

__Seller agrees to reshingle the roof and repair the porch at her own
expense prior to closing.__

13. Liability and Maintenance: Seller shall maintain subject property, including landscaping, in good condition until the date of transfer of title or possession by Buyer, whichever occurs first. All risk of loss and destruction of property, and all expenses of insurance, shall be borne by the seller until the date of possession. If the improvements on the property are destroyed or materially damaged prior to closing, then the Buyer shall have the right to declare this agreement null and void, and the earnest money deposit and all other sums paid by Buyer toward the purchase price shall be returned to the Buyer forthwith.

14. Possession: The Buyer shall be entitled to possession of property upon closing or __NA_____, 19_____

15. Default: In the event the Buyer fails to complete the purchase as herein provided, the earnest money deposit shall be retained by the Seller as the total and entire liquidated damages. In the event the Seller fails to perform any condition of the sale as herein provided, then the Buyer may, at his option, treat the contract as terminated, and all payments made by the Buyer hereunder shall be returned to the Buyer forthwith, provided the Buyer may, at his option, treat this agreement as being in full force and effect with the right to action for specific performance and damages. In the event that either Buyer, Seller, or Agent shall institute suit to enforce any rights hereunder, the prevailing party shall be entitled to court costs and a reasonable attorney's fee.

16. Time Limit of Offer: The Seller shall have until

_____ __May 4,__ _____, 19 __81__ to accept this
(hour)   (date)

offer by delivering a signed copy hereof to the Buyer. If this offer is not so accepted, it shall lapse and the agent (or Seller) shall refund the earnest money deposit to the Buyer forthwith.

17. General Agreements: (1) Both parties to this purchase reserve their rights to assign and hereby otherwise agree to cooperate in effecting an Internal Revenue Code 1031 exchange or similar tax-related arrangement prior to close of escrow, upon either party's written notice of intention to do so. (2) Upon approval of this offer by the Seller, this agreement shall become a contract between Buyer and Seller and shall inure to the benefit of the heirs, administrators, executors, successors, personal representatives, and assigns of said parties. (3) Time is of the essence and an essential part of this agreement. (4) This contract constitutes the sole and entire agreement between the parties hereto and no modification of this contract shall be binding unless attached hereto and signed by all parties to the contract. No representations, promises, or inducements not included in this contract shall be binding upon any party hereto.

18. Buyer's Statement and Receipt: "I/we hereby agree to purchase the above property in accordance with the terms and conditions above stated and acknowledge receipt of a

completed copy of this agreement, which I/we have fully read and understand." Dated __May 1,__ 19 __81__ , _____
                                                                                                              (hour)

Address ____1412 Lancaster Blvd.____   ____[signature] or Assigns_____
                                                                                      Buyer
_____Longmeadow, Massachusetts_____   _____
                                                                                      Buyer

Phone No: Home ___425-1916___ Business ___721-1209___

19. Seller's Statement and Response: "I/we approve and accept the above offer, which I/we have fully read and understand, and agree to the above terms and conditions this day

of _____, 19 _____, _____

(hour)

Address _____ _____ Seller

Phone No: Home _____ Business _____ _____ Seller

20. Commission Agreement: Seller agrees to pay a commission of _____3_____% of the gross sales price to ___McMann Realty_____

for services in this transaction, and agrees that, in the event of forfeiture of the earnest money deposit by the Buyer, said deposit shall be divided between the Seller's broker and the Seller (one half to each party), the Broker's part not to exceed the amount of the commission.

21. Buyer's Receipt for Signed Offer: The Buyer hereby acknowledges receipt of a copy of the above agreement bearing the Seller's signature in acceptance of this offer.

Dated _____, 19 _____ _____ Buyer

_____ Buyer

COMMENTARY TO DOCUMENTATION

Item 6. The buyer should have stipulated that the mortgage would not be subject to a non-acceleration provision or any prepayment penalties. A late note: just prior to press time for this volume, the buyer communicated by phone that the seller had negotiated with him after the fact a provision for paying off the balance of the note after five years. Even though the new terms are not as glorious as a 25-year amortization, a five-year balloon is tolerable, especially if a rollover provision is included.

7

How To Buy A Mansion For Nothing Down

Featuring Technique No. 5
"Raise The Price, Lower The Terms"

In A Nutshell. . .

Type: Mansion, with adjoining tri-plex
Price: $80,000
Source: Realtor
Means: Purchase money mortgage
Techniques: No. 4 — Contract/Wrap
No. 5 — Raise Price, Lower Terms
No. 10 — Supply Seller's Needs
No. 14 — Anything Goes
No. 45 — Partner's Cash/Your Expertise
Features: Positive cash flow

LOCATING

Malcolm Rutledge is a Realtor Associate in Jacksonville, Florida. In the late Spring of 1981 he was participating in a real estate agents' "caravan" for the purpose of getting acquainted with the latest listings. It was a fairly routine tour until the group came to an impressive mansion in the historic district. When the listing agent pointed out that the property had a gross monthly income of $1,400, Malcolm's ears perked up. He had been looking for some investment property for his own portfolio, and this property had promise.

SITUATION

The two-and-a-half story manor house was in exceptionally good condition. It featured marble steps, beamed ceilings, inlaid floors, and hanging fixtures throughout. It had space for 9 roomers. In addition, there was a two story tri-plex in the rear and off to the side of the mansion.

The owner was an elderly lady of moderate means who was about to move to California. She was asking $75,000, with $25,000 down. The property was free of any encumbrances.

NEGOTIATION

Malcolm's first question to the seller was, "Why are you selling?" She told him that her first grandchild had just been born in California, that the child had red hair and bore a resemblance to her late departed husband, and that she now wanted to move to the West in order to help raise the new addition to the family. She, therefore, needed to sell her home and her business and clear up her affairs in preparation for the move.

Since Malcolm's motto for negotiation is "Ask questions and listen to the answers," he took her needs to heart and structured the following offer:

Because the property was considerably underpriced, he offered a sales price of $80,000, rather than the $75,000 she originally wanted. His down payment was

to be $16,000 — less than she asked for — with 10% interest on the carry back for 15 years. This is the useful technique known as "Raise the Price, Lower the Terms." The monthly payments on the carry back were designed to provide her with a regular cash flow in California. In addition, Malcolm suggested that she feel free to remain a resident in the mansion for up to six months — rent free — while she sold her business.

All five of her relatives ("family counselors") in the area urged her to reject Malcolm's offer. But she was impressed that he had raised the sales price when all of the other offers she had received were "low ball" in nature. Moreover, she was appreciative of the fact that he would be willing to let her stay in her home until she had taken care of her affairs. Peace of mind and a minimum of dislocation were the "hot buttons" that were important to her, and Malcolm was smart enough — thoughtful enough — to understand these needs. Her only request was that the carry back — in this case it took the form of a purchase money mortgage — yield 12% interest rather than the 10% of the offer. Malcolm assented readily.

CLOSING

There was only one problem that Malcolm could foresee: he didn't have any money for the down payment he had agreed to! Because of the excellent property he now had an interest in, it took him exactly six hours to find a partner willing to put up the down payment in exchange for half interest. Unfortunately, this first partner had to pull out of the deal because he unexpectedly had to divert his assets to pay for medical bills. However, he knew another fellow who gladly took over his position in the arrangement in exchange for five truck loads of topsoil for the first investor's other rental property — the "Anything Goes" technique applied to partnerships. The closing then proceeded without a hitch. The sketch summarizes the facts:

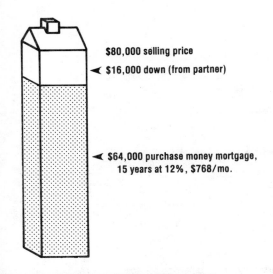

$80,000 selling price
◄ $16,000 down (from partner)

◄ $64,000 purchase money mortgage,
15 years at 12%, $768/mo.

the monthly positive cash flow is $272. This is an annual return of $3,264 or 20.4% on the $16,000 down payment the first year.

Future plans include converting the buildings to law offices in order to increase the income substantially.

OUTCOMES AND FUTURE PLANS

Malcolm immediately raised the rents by $200 so that the gross monthly income now totaled $1,600. Payments on the mortgage are $768/mo. After expenses,

COMMENTARY

1. This case study is an unusually good illustration of how to listen to the seller and maintain an awareness of the seller's needs.
2. Malcolm should have negotiated a "substitution of collateral" clause for the mortgage. This would have enabled him to definance (disencumber) the property at a future date in order to pull money out of it for coming needs such as the conversion. Moving the mortgage off the property in the future would also have opened up the way for exchanging or the creation of paper against the property. Still, he does have $16,000 in equity — probably much more if the property was in effect underpriced — to be used in creative ways.

DOCUMENTATION

UNIVERSAL EARNEST MONEY RECEIPT
AND OFFER TO PURCHASE

"This is a legally binding contract: if not understood, seek competent advice."

1. Date and Place of Offer: __July 29,__ 19 __81__ ; __Jacksonville__ (city) __Florida__ (state)

2. Principals: The undersigned Buyer __George Gross and Malcolm Rutledge, a registered real estate salesman__

agrees to buy and Seller agrees to sell, according to the indicated terms and conditions, the property described as follows:

3. Property: located at __5829 Falcon Way__ (street address) __Jacksonville__ (city) __Florida__ (state)

with the following legal description: __Lot 17, Block 12--Watercrest--Plat. Book 6, Page 12__

including any of the following items if at present attached to the premises: plumbing, heating, and cooling equipment, including stoker and oil tanks, burners, water heaters, electric light fixtures, bathroom fixtures, roller shades, curtain rods and fixtures, draperies, venetian blinds, window and door screens, towel racks, linoleum and other attached floor coverings,

including carpeting, attached television antennas, mailboxes, all trees and shrubs, and any other fixtures EXCEPT __None__

The following personal property shall also be included as part of the purchase: __All kitchen stoves and refrigerators and also all installed window A/C units.__

At the closing of the transaction, the Seller, at his expense, shall provide the Buyer with a Bill Of Sale containing a detailed inventory of the personal property included.

4. Earnest Money Deposit: Agent (or Seller) acknowledges receipt from Buyer of __One Hundred and 00/100__ dollars $ __100.00__

in the form of ( ) cash; (X) personal check; ( ) cashier's check; ( ) promissory note at _____% interest per annum due _____ 19 _____; or

other _____

as earnest money deposit to secure and apply on this purchase. Upon acceptance of this agreement in writing and delivery of same to Buyer, the earnest money deposit shall be assigned

to and deposited in the listing Realtor's trust account or _____, to apply on the purchase price at the time of closing.

5. Purchase Price: The total purchase price of the property shall be __Eighty Thousand and 00/100__ dollars $ __80,000.00__

6. Payment: Purchase price is to be paid by Buyer as follows:

Aforedescribed earnest money deposit .... $ __100.00__

Additional payment due upon acceptance of this offer .... $ _____

Additional payment due at closing .... $ __15,900.00__

Balance to be paid as follows:

Balance due to the Seller to be evidenced by a negotiable promissory
note of the Buyer, secured by a valid purchase money mortgage, in a form
acceptable to Seller, containing standard provisions unless noted in item
12 below, on said property executed and delivered by the Buyer to the
Seller, dated the date of closing, bearing interest at the rate of 12%
per annum and payable $768.11 per month. Mortgage amounts 180.

7. **Title:** Seller agrees to furnish good and marketable title free of all encumbrances and defects, except mortgage liens and encumbrances as set forth in this agreement, and to make

conveyance by Warranty Deed or _____ . Seller shall furnish in due course
to the Buyer a title insurance policy insuring the Buyer of a good and marketable title in keeping with the terms and conditions of this agreement. Prior to the closing of this transaction, the Seller, upon request, will furnish to the Buyer a preliminary title report made by a title insurance company showing the condition of the title to said property. If the Seller cannot furnish marketable title within thirty days after receipt of the notice to the Buyer containing a written statement of the defects, the earnest money deposit herein receipted shall be refunded to the Buyer and this agreement shall be null and void. The following shall not be deemed encumbrances or defects; building and use restrictions general to the area; utility easements; other easements not inconsistent with Buyer's intended use; zoning or subdivision laws, covenants, conditions, restrictions, or reservations of record; tenancies of record. In the event of sale of other than real property relating to this transaction, Seller will provide evidence of title or right to sell or lease such personal property.

Within five (5) days after date of acceptance, the Seller will furnish
and deliver to the Buyer, Agent, or Closing Attorney: Title insurance
binder for a fee policy in the amount of the purchase price, plus survey.

8. **Special Representations:** Seller warrants and represents to Buyer (1) that the subject property is connected to ( ) public sewer system, ( ) cesspool or septic tank, ( ) sewer system available but not connected, ( ) city water system, ( ) private water system, and that the following special improvements are included in the sale: ( ) sidewalk, ( ) curb and gutter, ( ) special street paving, ( ) special street lighting; (2) that the Seller knows of no material structural defects; (3) that all electrical wiring, heating, cooling, and plumbing systems are free of material defects and will be in good working order at the time the Buyer is entitled to possession; (4) that the Seller has no notice from any government agency of any violation or knowledge of probable violations of the law relating to the subject property; (5) that the Seller has no notice or knowledge of planned or commenced public improvements which may result in special assessments or otherwise directly and materially affect the property; and (6) that the Seller has no notice or knowledge of any liens to be assessed against the property,

EXCEPT ___ Seller is aware of malfunction in basement water-clearance pump.

9. **Escrow Instructions:** This sale shall be closed on or before August 7, 19 81 by _____
or such other closing agent as mutually agreed upon by Buyer and Seller. Buyer and Seller will, immediately on demand, deposit with closing agent all instruments and monies required

to complete the purchase in accordance with the provisions of this agreement. Contract of Sale or Instrument of Conveyance to be made in the name of _____

10. **Closing Costs and Pro-Ration:** Seller agrees to pay for title insurance policy, preliminary title report (if requested), termite inspection as set forth below, real estate commission, cost of preparing and recording any corrective instruments, and one-half of the escrow fees. Buyer agrees to pay for recording fees for mortgages and deeds of conveyance, all costs or expenses in securing new financing or assuming existing financing, and one-half of the escrow fees. Buyer agrees to pay for recording fees for mortgages and deeds of conveyance, all costs or expenses in securing new financing or assuming existing financing, and one-half of the escrow fees. Taxes for the current year, insurance acceptable to the Buyer, rents, interest, mortgage reserves, maintenance fees, and water and other utilities constituting liens, shall be pro-rated as of closing. Renters' security deposits shall accrue to Buyer at closing. Seller to provide Buyer with all current rental or lease agreements prior to closing.

11. **Termite Inspection:** Seller agrees, at his expense, to provide written certification by a reputable licensed pest control firm that the property is free of termite infestation. In the event termites are found, the Seller shall have the property treated at his expense and provide acceptable certification that treatment has been rendered. If any structural repairs are required by reason of termite damage as established by acceptable certification, Seller agrees to make necessary repairs not to exceed $500. If repairs exceed $500, Buyer shall first have the right to accept the property "as is" with a credit to the Buyer at closing of $500, or the Buyer may terminate this agreement with the earnest money deposit being promptly returned to the Buyer if the Seller does not agree to pay all costs of treatment and repair.

12. **Conditions of Sale:** The following conditions shall also apply, and shall, if conflicting with the printed portions of this agreement, prevail and control:

A. The $100.00 binder deposit shall be retained by the Seller as total
   liquidated damages in the event of default by Buyer.

B. Buyer assumes all risk of loss to property from date of closing, shall
   be responsible and liable for maintenance thereof from said date, and
   shall be deemed to have accepted the property, real and personal, in
   its existing condition as of date of closing.

C. Buyer does hereby allow the Seller to continue residence on the property for a time period sufficient to finalize personal affairs, said
   time period not to exceed six months. Buyer does allow the Seller to
   stay past closing date at no charge for space and use if the Seller
   will give the Buyer fifteen days notice prior to quitting the subject
   property.

D. Seller to retain complete use of first floor through September 15,
   1981, as she is presently occupying, including her furniture and air
   conditioner units (2), in order to sell her personal furniture in
   comfort.

13. **Liability and Maintenance:** Seller shall maintain subject property, including landscaping, in good condition until the date of transfer of title or possession by Buyer, whichever occurs

first. All risk of loss and destruction of property, and all expenses of insurance, shall be borne by the seller until the date of possession. If the improvements on the property are destroyed or materially damaged prior to closing, then the Buyer shall have the right to declare this agreement null and void, and the earnest money deposit and all other sums paid by Buyer toward the purchase price shall be returned to the Buyer forthwith.

14. Possession: The Buyer shall be entitled to possession of property upon closing or _____, 19 _____.

     See item 12-C above.

15. Default: In the event the Buyer fails to complete the purchase as herein provided, the earnest money deposit shall be retained by the Seller as the total and entire liquidated damages. In the event the Seller fails to perform any condition of the sale as herein provided, then the Buyer may, at his option, treat the contract as terminated, and all payments made by the Buyer hereunder shall be returned to the Buyer forthwith, provided the Buyer may, at his option, treat this agreement as being in full force and effect with the right to action for specific performance and damages. In the event that either Buyer, Seller, or Agent shall institute suit to enforce any rights hereunder, the prevailing party shall be entitled to court costs and a reasonable attorney's fee.

16. Time Limit of Offer: The Seller shall have until

_____   July 31,   , 19 __81__ to accept this
    (hour)   (date)

offer by delivering a signed copy hereof to the Buyer. If this offer is not so accepted, it shall lapse and the agent (or Seller) shall refund the earnest money deposit to the Buyer forthwith.

17. General Agreements: (1) Both parties to this purchase reserve their rights to assign and hereby otherwise agree to cooperate in effecting an Internal Revenue Code 1031 exchange or similar tax-related arrangement prior to close of escrow, upon either party's written notice of intention to do so. (2) Upon approval of this offer by the Seller, this agreement shall become a contract between Buyer and Seller and shall inure to the benefit of the heirs, administrators, executors, successors, personal representatives, and assigns of said parties. (3) Time is of the essence and an essential part of this agreement. (4) This contract constitutes the sole and entire agreement between the parties hereto and no modification of this contract shall be binding unless attached hereto and signed by all parties to the contract. No representations, promises, or inducements not included in this contract shall be binding upon any party hereto.

18. Buyer's Statement and Receipt: "I/we hereby agree to purchase the above property in accordance with the terms and conditions above stated and acknowledge receipt of a completed copy of this agreement, which I/we have fully read and understand." Dated __July 29,__ 19 __81__ , _____
                  (hour)

Address __14 Overbrook Street__   __[signature]__ _____ Buyer

__Jacksonville, Florida__   _____ Buyer

Phone No: Home __225-1213__ Business __659-1819__

19. Seller's Statement and Response: "I/we approve and accept the above offer, which I/we have fully read and understand, and agree to the above terms and conditions this day

of _____ , 19 _____ , _____.
                      (hour)

Address _____ _____ Seller

Phone No: Home _____ Business _____ _____ Seller

20. Commission Agreement: Seller agrees to pay a commission of __6.5__ % of the gross sales price to __Jackobson Realty, Co.__

for services in this transaction, and agrees that, in the event of forfeiture of the earnest money deposit by the Buyer, said deposit shall be divided between the Seller's broker and the Seller (one half to each party), the Broker's part not to exceed the amount of the commission.

21. Buyer's Receipt for Signed Offer: The Buyer hereby acknowledges receipt of a copy of the above agreement bearing the Seller's signature in acceptance of this offer.

Dated _____ , 19 _____   _____ Buyer

COMMENTARY TO DOCUMENTATION

Item 2. The wording "or Assigns" should always appear after the name of the buyer. In this case, the partner (we have called him George Gross) had to back out prior to closing; the buyer had to arrange for an assignment of their mutual interest in the "Deposit Receipt and Purchase and Sale Agreement" to the next partner, who was recruited at the last minute to step in. Had the words "or Assigns" appeared, the substitution would have been less involved.

Notice that the buyer identified himself as a "registered real estate salesman." Agents are required by law in most jurisdictions to so identify themselves. If they do not, they expose themselves (and their profession) to the dangers of legal recourse by sellers who may come back and claim they were taken advantage of.

Item 6. The buyer should have negotiated the privilege of prepayment on the mortgage note without penalty. A clause rendering the note assumable would also have been wise.

Item 8. Buyer should have specified that the Seller was required to repair the water pump prior to closing.

Item 15. The "Universal Earnest Money Receipt" used in the documentary illustration above contains a "total liquidated damages" clause. However, the original form used by the buyer in this transaction was worded this way: "If the said Buyer fails to perform the covenants herein contained within the time specified, Seller shall have all remedies available under the law to include, but not limited to (a) require specific performance on the part of the Buyer, (b) bring suit against Buyer for damages resulting from the breach, (c) after deducting any funds expended for Buyer to Seller's processing costs, the Owner shall retain as liquidated damages one-half of the remainder of the binder deposit. The remaining one-half of net deposit shall be paid to the Agent as compensation not to exceed the total amount of his commission." It should be clear from points (a) and (b) why the buyer wisely insisted on the special condition entered under Item 12(a) in our illustrative document.

Ever Hear Of A $17,000 5-Year Loan — No Interest, No Payments?

**Featuring Technique No. 6
''The Balloon Down Payment''**

In A Nutshell . . .

Type: SFH
Price: $35,000
Source: Realtor
Means: New first, with carry back
Techniques: No. 6 — Balloon
No. 10 — Supply Seller's Needs
No. 34 — Buy Low, Refinance High
Strategies: No-interest balloon
Features: Positive cash flow

We have already seen how Richard Austin of Milwaukee makes the ''Ultimate Paper Out'' and ''Contract Sale/Wrap Around Mortgage'' techniques work to his advantage. In the following case study, he demonstrates his skill at structuring balloon notes of a very unusual kind.

LOCATING

With the help of his trusty Realtor friend, Richard located a single family home in the Lake Geneva area (southwest of Milwaukee) that fit his buying parameters — low or no mortgage bread-and-butter properties that might be discounted by the owner. In this case, the asking price was $41,000. The property was free of any liens or encumbrances but was subject to some potential judgments, as explained below.

SITUATION

The owner had received the property through inheritance two years earlier when his uncle passed away. But he had also inherited something he did not especially want — $18,000 in expenses, including the costs of the funeral, the attorney's fees, and water bills. The creditors had been after him for two years to pay up, but now they were out looking for blood — his blood. Since he had no money, he needed to dispose of the house as quickly as possible to get relief from all the pressure of the bill collectors. In this case, relief was spelled A-U-S-T-I-N, and the medicine was creative finance.

NEGOTIATION

Richard offered the gentleman $35,000 for the property, with a cash down payment of $3,000, the proceeds of a new $15,000 first, and a carry back second of $17,000 for five years — no interest and no payments. The thought of the $18,000 in down payment and loan proceeds was music to the ears of the seller, so much so that he did not care about the no-interest discord on the balance!

Why would he accept such an offer? Because it solved his problem. He was thrilled to get the bill collectors off his back and have a little peace and quiet. He was happy to wait five years for the rest of his equity — which was inherited anyway.

CLOSING

The Realtor helped Richard obtain a new $15,000 first mortgage at the bank, 16% interest with an eight-year amortization, payments of $278 per month. The sketch summarizes the arrangement:

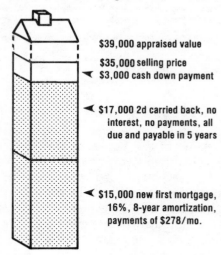

$39,000 appraised value

$35,000 selling price
$3,000 cash down payment

$17,000 2d carried back, no interest, no payments, all due and payable in 5 years

$15,000 new first mortgage, 16%, 8-year amortization, payments of $278/mo.

OUTCOMES AND FUTURE PLANS

Following the closing, Richard raised the rent from $300 to $325. The cash flow on the property is therefore slightly positive after expenses. Since the property is appraised at $39,000, the new buyer picked up $4,000 in instant equity going into the deal. He plans to hold the property for long-term growth and tax shelter.

COMMENTARY

1. Richard's formula is wise: looking for free and clear

or low mortgage properties in the bread-and-butter range. Such situations lend themselves very well to creative finance and provide the best insurance for future low vacancy. As long as interest rates remain high and inflation continues to eat away at the wage earner's buying power, the bread-and-butter units will continue to be in especially high demand.

2. Once more, this case study illustrates the benefits of locating a dependable Realtor who understands creative finance and listens to the buyer's needs and restrictions.

3. $3,000 cash down on this property amounts to around 8% of the selling price, somewhat beyond the 5% or less guidelines of the Nothing Down System. However, the $17,000 second costs Richard nothing for five years. If the seller had charged him, say, 12% interest compounded annually during the same period, Richard would have had to pay $12,500 in interest charges by the time the balloon came due. Did he make a good choice in paying a little more up front? Would you do the same?

DOCUMENTATION

UNIVERSAL EARNEST MONEY RECEIPT
AND OFFER TO PURCHASE

"This is a legally binding contract: if not understood, seek competent advice."

1. Date and Place of Offer: __December 8,__ 19 __80__ ; __Lake Geneva__ __Wisconsin__
                (city)   (state)

2. Principals: The undersigned Buyer __Richard Austin__
agrees to buy and Seller agrees to sell, according to the indicated terms and conditions, the property described as follows:

3. Property: located at __451 Crestview Way__ __Lake Geneva__ __Wisconsin__
            (street address)   (city)   (state)

with the following legal description: __North 1/2 of lot 42, Glenn's Addition, City of Lake__ __Geneva, County of Walworth.__

including any of the following items if at present attached to the premises: plumbing, heating, and cooling equipment, including stoker and oil tanks, burners, water heaters, electric light fixtures, bathroom fixtures, roller shades, curtain rods and fixtures, draperies, venetian blinds, window and door screens, towel racks, linoleum and other attached floor coverings,

including carpeting, attached television antennas, mailboxes, all trees and shrubs, and any other fixtures EXCEPT __None__

The following personal property shall also be included as part of the purchase: __Buyer does not want any of the personal property.__

At the closing of the transaction, the Seller, at his expense, shall provide the Buyer with a Bill Of Sale containing a detailed inventory of the personal property included.

4. Earnest Money Deposit: Agent (or Seller) acknowledges receipt from Buyer of __One Hundred and 00/100__ dollars $ __100.00__

in the form of ( ) cash; (X) personal check; ( ) cashier's check; ( ) promissory note at _____ % interest per annum due _____ 19 _____ ; or

other _____
as earnest money deposit to secure and apply on this purchase. Upon acceptance of this agreement in writing and delivery of same to Buyer, the earnest money deposit shall be assigned

to and deposited in the listing Realtor's trust account or _____, to apply on the
purchase price at the time of closing.

5. Purchase Price: The total purchase price of the property shall be __Thirty-five Thousand and 00/100__ dollars $ __35,000.00__

6. Payment: Purchase price is to be paid by Buyer as follows:

Aforedescribed earnest money deposit .... $ __100.00__

Additional payment due upon acceptance of this offer __Within 3 days of acceptance of offer.__ $ __900.00__

Additional payment due at closing __See below.__ .... $ _____

Balance to be paid as follows:
__This offer not subject to the sale of other property.__

__1. This offer is subject to the Buyer obtaining a Purchase Money Mortgage__
     __in the amount of $15,000.00 at an annual rate of 16% per annum for a__
     __term of eight years (8). The Buyer and Lender shall set and agree to__
     __closing costs including the loan origination fee. This application__
     __shall be completed by December 24, 1980, or the offer shall become null__

and void.

2. Buyer shall issue a second mortgage to the Seller in a no-interest, no principal bearing note to secure Seller with the balance being due in the amount of $17,000.00. The term of this second mortgage shall be five years (5) and due in full at that date.

3. And the balance in cash at closing ($18,000) less closing expenses/pro-ration.

7. Title: Seller agrees to furnish good and marketable title free of all encumbrances and defects, except mortgage liens and encumbrances as set forth in this agreement, and to make conveyance by Warranty Deed or _____ Seller shall furnish in due course to the Buyer a title insurance policy insuring the Buyer of a good and marketable title in keeping with the terms and conditions of this agreement. Prior to the closing of this transaction, the Seller, upon request, will furnish to the Buyer a preliminary title report made by a title insurance company showing the condition of the title to said property. If the Seller cannot furnish marketable title within thirty days after receipt of the notice to the Buyer containing a written statement of the defects, the earnest money deposit herein receipted shall be refunded to the Buyer and this agreement shall be null and void. The following shall not be deemed encumbrances or defects; building and use restrictions general to the area; utility easements; other easements not inconsistent with Buyer's intended use; zoning or subdivision laws, covenants, conditions, restrictions, or reservations of record; tenancies of record. In the event of sale of other than real property relating to this transaction, Seller will provide evidence of title or right to sell or lease such personal property.

8. Special Representations: Seller warrants and represents to Buyer (1) that the subject property is connected to ( ) public sewer system, ( ) cesspool or septic tank, ( ) sewer system available but not connected, ( ) city water system, ( ) private water system, and that the following special improvements are included in the sale: ( ) sidewalk, ( ) curb and gutter, ( ) special street paving, ( ) special street lighting; (2) that the Seller knows of no material structural defects; (3) that all electrical wiring, heating, cooling, and plumbing systems are free of material defects and will be in good working order at the time the Buyer is entitled to possession; (4) that the Seller has no notice from any government agency of any violation or knowledge of probable violations of the law relating to the subject property; (5) that the Seller has no notice or knowledge of planned or commenced public improvements which may result in special assessments or otherwise directly and materially affect the property; and (6) that the Seller has no notice or knowledge of any liens to be assessed against the property,

EXCEPT _____ None _____

9. Escrow Instructions: This sale shall be closed on or before December 30, 19 80 by Stewart Bromberg Agency or such other closing agent as mutually agreed upon by Buyer and Seller. Buyer and Seller will, immediately on demand, deposit with closing agent all instruments and monies required to complete the purchase in accordance with the provisions of this agreement. Contract of Sale or Instrument of Conveyance to be made in the name of ___ to be provided prior to closing.

10. Closing Costs and Pro-Ration: Seller agrees to pay for title insurance policy, preliminary title report (if requested), termite inspection as set forth below, real estate commission, cost of preparing and recording any corrective instruments, and one-half of the escrow fees. Buyer agrees to pay for recording fees for mortgages and deeds of conveyance, all costs or expenses in securing new financing or assuming existing financing, and one-half of the escrow fees. Buyer agrees to pay for recording fees for mortgages and deeds of conveyance, all costs or expenses in securing new financing or assuming existing financing, and one-half of the escrow fees. Taxes for the current year, insurance acceptable to the Buyer, rents, interest, mortgage reserves, maintenance fees, and water and other utilities constituting liens, shall be pro-rated as of closing. Renters' security deposits shall accrue to Buyer at closing. Seller to provide Buyer with all current rental or lease agreements prior to closing.

Month to month tenancy at a rate of $300.000 per month. Ben and Ruth Hansen, tenants. Taxes for 1979 were $524.04.

11. Termite Inspection: Seller agrees, at his expense, to provide written certification by a reputable licensed pest control firm that the property is free of termite infestation. In the event termites are found, the Seller shall have the property treated at his expense and provide acceptable certification that treatment has been rendered. If any structural repairs are required by reason of termite damage as established by acceptable certification, Seller agrees to make necessary repairs not to exceed $500. If repairs exceed $500, Buyer shall first have the right to accept the property "as is" with a credit to the Buyer at closing of $500, or the Buyer may terminate this agreement with the earnest money deposit being promptly returned to the Buyer if the Seller does not agree to pay all costs of treatment and repair.

12. Conditions of Sale: The following conditions shall also apply, and shall, if conflicting with the printed portions of this agreement, prevail and control:

None

13. Liability and Maintenance: Seller shall maintain subject property, including landscaping, in good condition until the date of transfer of title or possession by Buyer, whichever occurs first. All risk of loss and destruction of property, and all expenses of insurance, shall be borne by the seller until the date of possession. If the improvements on the property are destroyed or materially damaged prior to closing, then the Buyer shall have the right to declare this agreement null and void, and the earnest money deposit and all other sums paid by Buyer toward the purchase price shall be returned to the Buyer forthwith.

14. Possession: The Buyer shall be entitled to possession of property upon closing or _____ NA _____, 19 ____.

15. Default: In the event the Buyer fails to complete the purchase as herein provided, the earnest money deposit shall be retained by the Seller as the total and entire liquidated damages. In the event the Seller fails to perform any condition of the sale as herein provided, then the Buyer may, at his option, treat the contract as terminated, and all payments made by the Buyer hereunder shall be returned to the Buyer forthwith, provided the Buyer may, at his option, treat this agreement as being in full force and effect with the right to action for specific performance and damages. In the event that either Buyer, Seller, or Agent shall institute suit to enforce any rights hereunder, the prevailing party shall be entitled to court costs and a reasonable attorney's fee.

16. Time Limit of Offer: The Seller shall have until

_____ December 11, _____, 19 80 to accept this
(hour)   (date)

offer by delivering a signed copy hereof to the Buyer. If this offer is not so accepted, it shall lapse and the agent (or Seller) shall refund the earnest money deposit to the Buyer forthwith.

17. General Agreements: (1) Both parties to this purchase reserve their rights to assign and hereby otherwise agree to cooperate in effecting an Internal Revenue Code 1031 exchange or similar tax-related arrangement prior to close of escrow, upon either party's written notice of intention to do so. (2) Upon approval of this offer by the Seller, this agreement shall become a contract between Buyer and Seller and shall inure to the benefit of the heirs, administrators, executors, successors, personal representatives, and assigns of said parties. (3) Time is of the essence and an essential part of this agreement. (4) This contract constitutes the sole and entire agreement between the parties hereto and no modification of this contract shall be binding unless attached hereto and signed by all parties to the contract. No representations, promises, or inducements not included in this contract shall be binding upon any party hereto.

18. Buyer's Statement and Receipt: "I/we hereby agree to purchase the above property in accordance with the terms and conditions above stated and acknowledge receipt of a

completed copy of this agreement, which I/we have fully read and understand." Dated _____ 19 _____ , _____

(hour)

Address ___ 17 Juniper Street _____   [signature] _____ Buyer

___ East Troy, Wisconsin _____   _____ Buyer

Phone No: Home ___ 678-1400 ___ Business ___ 678-1400 ___

19. Seller's Statement and Response: "I/we approve and accept the above offer, which I/we have fully read and understand, and agree to the above terms and conditions this day

of _____ , 19 _____ , _____

(hour)

Address _____   _____ Seller

Phone No: Home _____ Business _____   _____ Seller

20. Commission Agreement: Seller agrees to pay a commission of ___ 6 ___% of the gross sales price to ___ Henry Accord Realty _____

for services in this transaction, and agrees that, in the event of forfeiture of the earnest money deposit by the Buyer, said deposit shall be divided between the Seller's broker and the Seller (one half to each party), the Broker's part not to exceed the amount of the commission.

21. Buyer's Receipt for Signed Offer: The Buyer hereby acknowledges receipt of a copy of the above agreement bearing the Seller's signature in acceptance of this offer.

Dated _____ , 19 _____   _____ Buyer

_____ Buyer

COMMENTARY TO DOCUMENTATION

Item 2. The words "or Assigns" should appear after the buyer's name.

Item 6. A Purchase Money Mortgage is the general designation for a loan extended by the seller to the buyer, without an intermediary lending institution, but with the security of a mortgage. What was evidently intended in the earnest money form at this point in the entry was the term "new loan" or "new first mortgage."

The conditions governing the second mortgage should have included a provision for substitution of collateral plus rollover of the balloon. It would have been wise for the buyer to have negotiated an assumption clause for the note, as well as a prepayment privilege without penalty. A further refinement would have been to secure first right of refusal in the event the seller were to sell the note.

Note that the IRS will likely impute 10% interest on the no-interest note secured by the second mortgage. See the "Commentary To Documentation" on Case No. 4.

The wording on the cash balance is a bit vague the way it stands. It would have been clearer to add "Proceeds to Seller" after the reference to the new loan, then state "Balance of $2,000.00 in cash at closing, less closing expenses/pro-ration." However, all parties to the transaction evidently understood what was intended, as everything worked out well in the closing.

Seven-Plex Buyer Wouldn't Take ''No'' For An Answer

Featuring Technique No. 6
''The Balloon Down Payment''

In A Nutshell . . .

Type: 7-Plex Plus Lot
Price: $245,000
Source: Classified Ad
Means: Assumption, Owner Carry Back
Techniques: No. 6 — Balloon
No. 8 — Defer Down/No Payments
No. 20 — Rents
No. 21 — Deposits
No. 45 — Partner's Cash/Your Expertise
Strategies: Delayed payment on 2d
Features: $1,200 positive cash flow

LOCATING

Real estate investor Bruce Clark of Lake Worth, Florida, spotted an interesting classified ad featuring a seven-unit apartment building with extra tri-plex lot. Bruce thought the seller must be a don't wanter when he read ''reduced $100,000'' in the ad. A call to the listing office confirmed the fact that the price was indeed reduced from $349,000 to $249,000 for a quick sale.

SITUATION

The 7-plex belonged to an older woman who was living in one of the units and who had developed an incurable case of manager's blues. She felt the property was just too much for a single woman to handle. The package included an adjacent lot laid out for a tri-plex. The 7-plex itself was a solid building that was 100% rented and showed a positive cash flow.

The problem was that the listing had gone eight months without any action. Now the woman wanted out — quickly. There was a first mortgage against the property of around $111,000. The seller and the agents indicated that the mortgage was non-assumable.

NEGOTIATION

Acting on the assumption that he could not take over the existing financing, Bruce submitted an offer of $200,000, with enough cash down to pay off the mortgage, the rest being carried back by the seller. This first offer was rejected without a counteroffer. Next, Bruce offered $225,000 with $50,000 down, buyer to assume the first mortgage — there is no harm in trying — and the rest ($64,000) carried back as a first against a free and clear 4-plex in Bruce's portfolio. Again, a rejection with no counteroffer.

''The feeling at this time,'' as Bruce put it, ''was that the Realtor was very negative due to his lack of experience with anything but conventional finance. Three days later at our regular RAND meeting the deal was discussed; the feeling was that it was a good deal if we could put something together.'' The following day Bruce's wife went to research the mortgage and the zoning on the lot. She found out that the seller and her broker were mistaken concerning the underlying financing — the mortgage was indeed assumable, with an interest rate of 8¾% and 26 years to go!

At that point in time a fellow graduate in the RAND group offered his help as a Realtor. He told the Clarks: ''This is an excellent opportunity. If you don't buy the property, I'll see that someone else does!'' So Bruce submitted his third offer: $240,000 with $50,000 down, assumption of the first, and the balance of $84,000 at 12% for 30 years ballooned out after 10 years, no payments for one year. This time the RAND Realtor insisted on a counteroffer. (''Don't tell me what you won't do; tell me what you will do!'' — Bob Allen.)

The seller countered with $245,000, no payments on the second for nine months. The Clarks accepted.

CLOSING

Coming up with the down payment was no problem. Bruce's brother-in-law was in a position to serve as cash partner in exchange for all the tax benefits for two years and half ownership in the property. The arrangements were handled by a local title company. The Clarks received $2,600 back at closing, together with $2,500 in rents. The sketch summarizes the financing:

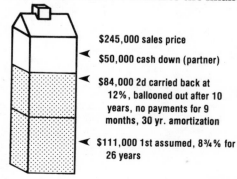

$245,000 sales price

$50,000 cash down (partner)

$84,000 2d carried back at 12%, ballooned out after 10 years, no payments for 9 months, 30 yr. amortization

$111,000 1st assumed, 8¾% for 26 years

OUTCOMES AND FUTURE PLANS

For the first nine months of ownership, the positive cash flow will be $1,200 per month ($2,182 less $982 on the first mortgage). By the time the payments start on the second mortgage ($864/mo.), the Clarks will have completed a new tri-plex on the adjacent lot using capital provided by the partner. The gross monthly income is then projected to be $5,300, leaving a positive cash flow of $1,600 per month.

The value of the complex will then be $425,000, with an equity of around $110,000 (after all improvements are financed). Not bad progress for a short period of time.

Looking back at the transaction, Bruce believes that his persistence was the key to the negotiations. The major breakthrough came when he found out that the underlying loan was assumable. As he says: "It pays to do your own research." His advice for other investors: "Don't get discouraged. Keep a positive attitude."

A final possibility to consider: since the underlying mortgage is held by a private individual, Bruce intends at some future time to explore with this person some creative techniques that apply to such situations.

COMMENTARY

1. This case study is a good illustration of the fact that a nothing down offer is not necessarily a no-cash offer. The $50,000 down payment made the seller happy and cemented the deal; but none of the money came out of Bruce's pocket. He got in for absolutely nothing down because of his skill at generating win/win opportunities for his partner.

2. In his second offer, Bruce tried to persuade the seller to move the second mortgage to another property. This wise approach would have freed up a great deal of equity in the 7-plex to use in the creation of paper or in subsequent cash-generating techniques. Even though the seller would not agree to a substitution of collateral in the final offer, it is a smart investor who will try to achieve such an agreement in as many deals as possible.

3. The ten-year balloon was possible, no doubt, because Bruce was able to provide a large down payment. Such a long-term balloon will hardly affect the Clarks' sleep at night (at least for nine years) — they will have plenty of leeway to plan for the payment while the property appreciates in value.

4. Horror stories abound concerning the recalcitrant Realtor who refuses to cooperate in facilitating creative deals, either out of ignorance or conventional habit. In this case, the buyer lost confidence in the listing agent. Things were going nowhere. The listing information was erroneous. No counteroffers were forthcoming. So Bruce did what he thought was necessary — he changed agents, and things began to fall in place. As Bruce recounts things, the original agent did not even recognize him at the closing (although the seller did). A Realtor who understands creative finance and is able to come up with alternative solutions to problems is worth his or her weight in gold. Therefore, one solution to the Realtor impasse — get another Realtor!

DOCUMENTATION

UNIVERSAL EARNEST MONEY RECEIPT AND OFFER TO PURCHASE

"This is a legally binding contract: if not understood, seek competent advice."

1. Date and Place of Offer: ___July 25,___ 19_81_ ; ___Lake Worth___ (city) ___Florida___ (state)

2. Principals: The undersigned Buyer ___Jeffrey Maddock and Lillian Maddock or Assigns___
agrees to buy and Seller agrees to sell, according to the indicated terms and conditions, the property described as follows:

3. Property: located at ___175 West Oldridge Street___ (street address) ___Lake Worth___ (city) ___Florida___ (state)

with the following legal description: ___(to be supplied prior to closing) Includes residence, 4-unit, with pool, vacant lot, parcels 1, 2 and 3.___

including any of the following items if at present attached to the premises: plumbing, heating, and cooling equipment, including stoker and oil tanks, burners, water heaters, electric light fixtures, bathroom fixtures, roller shades, curtain rods and fixtures, draperies, venetian blinds, window and door screens, towel racks, linoleum and other attached floor coverings,

including carpeting, attached television antennas, mailboxes, all trees and shrubs, and any other fixtures EXCEPT ___None___

The following personal property shall also be included as part of the purchase: ___List of furniture and other chattel to be supplied by Seller.___

At the closing of the transaction, the Seller, at his expense, shall provide the Buyer with a Bill Of Sale containing a detailed inventory of the personal property included.

4. Earnest Money Deposit: Agent (or Seller) acknowledges receipt from Buyer of __Five Hundred and 00/100__ dollars $ __500.00__

in the form of (X cash; ( ) personal check; ( ) cashier's check; ( ) promissory note at _____% interest per annum due _____ 19 _____; or

other _____
as earnest money deposit to secure and apply on this purchase. Upon acceptance of this agreement in writing and delivery of same to Buyer, the earnest money deposit shall be assigned

to and deposited in the listing Realtor's trust account or _____, to apply on the
purchase price at the time of closing.

5. Purchase Price: The total purchase price of the property shall be __Two Hundred Forty-five Thousand and 00/100__ dollars
$ __245,000.00__

6. Payment: Purchase price is to be paid by Buyer as follows:

Aforedescribed earnest money deposit .... $ __500.00__

Additional payment due upon acceptance of this offer .... $ _____

Additional payment due at closing .... $ __49,500.00__

Balance to be paid as follows:

__Approximate principal balance of first mortgage to which conveyance shall__
__be subject: $111,000 at 8 3/4% interest per annum. Method of payment__
__$982.47. Seller to take 2nd mortgage for 30 years at 12% interest, 10 year__
__balloon, in the amount of $84,000. First payment and interest to start__
__May 1, 1982, payments of $864.03 per month.__

7. Title: Seller agrees to furnish good and marketable title free of all encumbrances and defects, except mortgage liens and encumbrances as set forth in this agreement, and to make

conveyance by Warranty Deed or _____. Seller shall furnish in due course
to the Buyer a title insurance policy insuring the Buyer of a good and marketable title in keeping with the terms and conditions of this agreement. Prior to the closing of this transaction, the Seller, upon request, will furnish to the Buyer a preliminary title report made by a title insurance company showing the condition of the title to said property. If the Seller cannot furnish marketable title within thirty days after receipt of the notice to the Buyer containing a written statement of the defects, the earnest money deposit herein receipted shall be refunded to the Buyer and this agreement shall be null and void. The following shall not be deemed encumbrances or defects; building and use restrictions general to the area; utility easements; other easements not inconsistent with Buyer's intended use; zoning or subdivision laws, covenants, conditions, restrictions, or reservations of record; tenancies of record. In the event of sale of other than real property relating to this transaction, Seller will provide evidence of title or right to sell or lease such personal property.

8. Special Representations: Seller warrants and represents to Buyer (1) that the subject property is connected to ( ) public sewer system, ( ) cesspool or septic tank, ( ) sewer system available but not connected, ( ) city water system, ( ) private water system, and that the following special improvements are included in the sale: ( ) sidewalk, ( ) curb and gutter, ( ) special street paving, ( ) special street lighting; (2) that the Seller knows of no material structural defects; (3) that all electrical wiring, heating, cooling, and plumbing systems are free of material defects and will be in good working order at the time the Buyer is entitled to possession; (4) that the Seller has no notice from any government agency of any violation or knowledge of probable violations of the law relating to the subject property; (5) that the Seller has no notice or knowledge of planned or commenced public improvements which may result in special assessments or otherwise directly and materially affect the property; and (6) that the Seller has no notice or knowledge of any liens to be assessed against the property,

EXCEPT __None__.

9. Escrow Instructions: This sale shall be closed on or before __September 1,__ 19 __81__ by _____
or such other closing agent as mutually agreed upon by Buyer and Seller. Buyer and Seller will, immediately on demand, deposit with closing agent all instruments and monies required

to complete the purchase in accordance with the provisions of this agreement. Contract of Sale or Instrument of Conveyance to be made in the name of _____
_____

10. Closing Costs and Pro-Ration: Seller agrees to pay for title insurance policy, preliminary title report (if requested), termite inspection as set forth below, real estate commission, cost of preparing and recording any corrective instruments, and one-half of the escrow fees. Buyer agrees to pay for recording fees for mortgages and deeds of conveyance, all costs or expenses in securing new financing or assuming existing financing, and one-half of the escrow fees. Buyer agrees to pay for recording fees for mortgages and deeds of conveyance, all costs or expenses in securing new financing or assuming existing financing, and one-half of the escrow fees. Taxes for the current year, insurance acceptable to the Buyer, rents, interest, mortgage reserves, maintenance fees, and water and other utilities constituting liens, shall be pro-rated as of closing. Renters' security deposits shall accrue to Buyer at closing. Seller to provide Buyer with all current rental or lease agreements prior to closing.

11. Termite Inspection: Seller agrees, at his expense, to provide written certification by a reputable licensed pest control firm that the property is free of termite infestation. In the event termites are found, the Seller shall have the property treated at his expense and provide acceptable certification that treatment has been rendered. If any structural repairs are required by reason of termite damage as established by acceptable certification, Seller agrees to make necessary repairs not to exceed $500. If repairs exceed $500, Buyer shall first have the right to accept the property "as is" with a credit to the Buyer at closing of $500, or the Buyer may terminate this agreement with the earnest money deposit being promptly returned to the Buyer if the Seller does not agree to pay all costs of treatment and repair.

12. Conditions of Sale: The following conditions shall also apply, and shall, if conflicting with the printed portions of this agreement, prevail and control:

__Subject to Buyer seeing all units by August 1, 1981.__

__Subject to Buyer getting proper license for use of duplex by August 31,__
__1981.__

__Seller to pay rent for 30 days of $500.00 per month after the closing,__
__plus utilities.__

13. Liability and Maintenance: Seller shall maintain subject property, including landscaping, in good condition until the date of transfer of title or possession by Buyer, whichever occurs first. All risk of loss and destruction of property, and all expenses of insurance, shall be borne by the seller until the date of possession. If the improvements on the property are destroyed or materially damaged prior to closing, then the Buyer shall have the right to declare this agreement null and void, and the earnest money deposit and all other sums paid by Buyer toward the purchase price shall be returned to the Buyer forthwith.

14. Possession: The Buyer shall be entitled to possession of property upon closing or _____ September 1, _____ 19 81

15. Default: In the event the Buyer fails to complete the purchase as herein provided, the earnest money deposit shall be retained by the Seller as the total and entire liquidated damages. In the event the Seller fails to perform any condition of the sale as herein provided, then the Buyer may, at his option, treat the contract as terminated, and all payments made by the Buyer hereunder shall be returned to the Buyer forthwith, provided the Buyer may, at his option, treat this agreement as being in full force and effect with the right to action for specific performance and damages. In the event that either Buyer, Seller, or Agent shall institute suit to enforce any rights hereunder, the prevailing party shall be entitled to court costs and a reasonable attorney's fee.

16. Time Limit of Offer: The Seller shall have until

_____ July 25, _____ 19 81 to accept this
(hour)   (date)

offer by delivering a signed copy hereof to the Buyer. If this offer is not so accepted, it shall lapse and the agent (or Seller) shall refund the earnest money deposit to the Buyer forthwith.

17. General Agreements: (1) Both parties to this purchase reserve their rights to assign and hereby otherwise agree to cooperate in effecting an Internal Revenue Code 1031 exchange or similar tax-related arrangement prior to close of escrow, upon either party's written notice of intention to do so. (2) Upon approval of this offer by the Seller, this agreement shall become a contract between Buyer and Seller and shall inure to the benefit of the heirs, administrators, executors, successors, personal representatives, and assigns of said parties. (3) Time is of the essence and an essential part of this agreement. (4) This contract constitutes the sole and entire agreement between the parties hereto and no modification of this contract shall be binding unless attached hereto and signed by all parties to the contract. No representations, promises, or inducements not included in this contract shall be binding upon any party hereto.

18. Buyer's Statement and Receipt: "I/we hereby agree to purchase the above property in accordance with the terms and conditions above stated and acknowledge receipt of a completed copy of this agreement, which I/we have fully read and understand." Dated _____ July 25, _____ 19 81 _____, _____
(hour)

Address _____ 25 Wexler Avenue _____   [signature] or Assigns _____ Buyer

_____ Miami, Florida _____   [signature] _____ Buyer

Phone No: Home _____ 251-1347 _____ Business _____ 625-1701

19. Seller's Statement and Response: "I/we approve and accept the above offer, which I/we have fully read and understand, and agree to the above terms and conditions this day of _____ 19 _____, _____
(hour)

Address _____ _____ Seller

Phone No: Home _____ Business _____ _____ Seller

20. Commission Agreement: Seller agrees to pay a commission of _____ 6 _____ % of the gross sales price to _____ Harvey Flax, Realtor _____ for services in this transaction, and agrees that, in the event of forfeiture of the earnest money deposit by the Buyer, said deposit shall be divided between the Seller's broker and the Seller (one half to each party), the Broker's part not to exceed the amount of the commission.

21. Buyer's Receipt for Signed Offer: The Buyer hereby acknowledges receipt of a copy of the above agreement bearing the Seller's signature in acceptance of this offer.

Dated _____ , 19 _____   _____ Buyer

_____ Buyer

COMMENTARY TO DOCUMENTATION

Item 2. The offer was made by relatives with the addition of the words "or Assigns" to facilitate assignment of interest in the agreement to the final buyers at closing.

Item 6. The second mortgage should have included provisions for rollover, prepayment without penalty, assumption, and first right of refusal should note be sold by seller. The substitution of collateral had already been turned back by the seller in a previous offer.

Item 12. The buyer was wise to make the purchase subject to his obtaining proper permits for the intended use. The contingency for "seeing" all the units by a given date should also have contained the provision that the units be "approved by the buyer." Technically, the contingency as stated is satisfied if the buyer just looks at the units, whereas the intention is to look AND approve.

Item 15. The original earnest money form contained this strong buyer-oriented default statement: "If Buyer fails to perform any of the covenants of this contract, all money paid pursuant to this contract by Buyer as aforesaid shall be retained by or for the account of the Seller as consideration for the execution of this contract and as agreed liquidated damages and in full settlement of any claims for damages."

The Buyer

The second area of flexibility in solving the problem of down payments has to do with the buyer's own resources. "But," you say, "if we are trying to spare the downtrodden, cash-poor buyer from coming up with down payments in the first place, why bother to look to his personal resources?" The reason is that buyers often overlook valuable resources right under their own noses. They frequently have personal property, talents, expertise, or equity resources that could be used to acquire desirable income-producing property without the need for cash. And sometimes they even have cash or inheritances that could be applied—there's no shame to that, if you have the money at hand!

This section reviews ten techniques and nine case studies in the area of buyer flexibility. The following outline summarizes the material:

Technique No. 9   Your Own Savings and Inheritances

Practitioners of the Nothing Down System sometimes get the notion that putting their own money into a deal is somehow tantamount to failure. Nonsense! If you have it, use it; but use it with skill and creativity. The conventional buyer with $25,000 to spare will go out into the marketplace and plunk the full amount down on a single property. He might find a nice rental home worth $60,000 with a $35,000 mortgage. His first instinct is to take his $25,000 and cash out the seller. There will be no contract payments or balloon mortgages to worry about. Very likely there will be a modest positive cash flow after expenses and debt service are taken care of. He is happy watching his rental unit appreciate in value.

By way of contrast, the creative buyer takes his $25,000 and distributes it over, let's say, five rental homes worth a total of $300,000. By using a combination of creative acquisition techniques and strategies for avoiding negative cash flows, this buyer puts down only $5,000 on each of the homes. He must be careful to structure his deals advantageously, but the outcome is that he controls the growth of five times the real estate for the same amount of investment. His yield will, therefore, be much greater.

In either case, the best approach might be to use the cash resources as collateral to borrow down payment funds. That way, the cash assets can remain in the hands of the buyer and earn a substantial amount of interest. The same might be true of coming inheritances that would be acceptable as collateral on loans.

This technique is not central to any of the fifty case studies outlined in this book; however, the use of personal cash assets was important as a contributing element in four of the case studies. Consult the cross-reference matrix in the appendix for details.

Technique No. 10   Supply the Seller What He Needs

The question of seller needs is a complex one. Often buyers resort to sophisticated psychological observation and strategic interrogation in order to penetrate the seller's wall of secrecy. That is fine as far as it goes. But the best approach is nearly always the direct one in the form of one simple question: "What do you need the money for?" There are more subtle variations, such as "What do you plan to do with the proceeds of the transaction?" But it all boils down to the same thing — letting the seller know that you can solve his problem best if you know what he plans to do with the cash coming to him as a result of the sale.

Often the seller has consumer needs that the buyer could satisfy by carrying the necessary amounts on charge accounts or credit cards. In this way, the immediate up-front cash needs are spread out over time. Frequently the seller will be anticipating financial obligations that will require a set amount of cash each month beginning at some time in the future. If the buyer is on his toes, he can help the seller translate the down payment into installment payments that can be taken over by the buyer in lieu of a heavy cash down payment.

In Case No. 10, featured below, the buyer gained insight into the seller's need for future day-care funds and persuaded her to reduce the down payment by $13,500 in exchange for his providing monthly payments toward her day care for the next thirty years at very low interest. He was able to supply the seller what was needed and spare himself a heavy down payment obligation. Other examples of this technique can be identified through the cross-reference matrix in the appendix.

Technique No. 11   Assume Seller's Obligations

Often a seller is planning to apply down payment funds to debts he may have or payments that may be overdue. If the buyer can arrange to assume these debts and then pay for them over time, he can avoid having to come up with the down payment funds all at once.

In Case No. 11, the buyer was able to take care of the seller's arrears mortgage payments and utility bills and then cover some consumer debt obligations through installment payments. The result was the relaxation of the up-front cash requirements for the transaction.

Technique No. 12   Using Talents, Not Money

A buyer will often have professional expertise that can be "traded" in lieu of down payment funds. Contractors, painters, landscapers, health-care professionals, lawyers, Realtors, insurance agents, car dealers, merchants — all of these can provide valuable services or discounts that could be used in place of down payments. The potential list is not restricted to professional consideration either; sometimes a supply of plain elbow grease can help swing a deal in the absence of funds.

That is true of the arrangement described in Case No. 25 (printed elsewhere in this volume in the section on Hard Money Lenders) where the buyer was able to assume a seller's obligations and work off part of the debt by providing maintenance and management services for the creditor.

Technique No. 13   Borrow Against Life Insurance Policy

In an age of oppressively high interest rates, it is inconceivable why people will leave assets lying around unused in the cash-value accounts of their life insurance policies. But many do it, not realizing that for a pittance (perhaps as low as 5 or 6 percent interest) they can pull those funds out of their policies and apply them to other investments.

In two Case Studies included in this section, Technique No. 13 proved to be centrally important. In Case No. 12, the buyer found out he could qualify for essential secondary financing only if he was able to put 10% ($5,000) down on the property. He turned to his insurance assets and borrowed the money out at 5% interest. In Case No. 13, the buyer took care of the entire down payment by borrowing $8,000 out of his insurance assets at the same low rate of 5%. The beauty of insurance loans of this type is that the principal need not ever be paid back (except out of the death or annuity benefits of the policy).

Technique No. 14   Anything Goes

Down payments need not be in the form of cash. We have already seen how professional services can be used in lieu of cash. The same is true of personal property that the buyer might offer the seller to satisfy down payment needs. Cars, boats, furniture, art, clothing, musical instruments — anything acceptable to the seller might be used. We have even heard of pets such as rare monkeys or valuable cats being used as down payments.

In Case No. 14, described below, the buyer acquired a luxurious new home by using gems — diamonds, rubies, and emeralds — as the down payment. In an earlier case study (No. 7), five truck loads of topsoil did the trick. Anything goes if it satisfies the seller's needs.

Technique No. 15   Creation of Paper

Frequently a cashless buyer can solve down payment hurdles by applying the value of his other equities to the deal at hand. If the seller is amenable, it is a simple matter to prepare a note secured by the buyer's equity in other properties and hand it to the seller as all or part of the down payment on the subject property. In effect, the buyer says, "I don't have the cash to give you as a down payment, but I can give you this note in exchange for your equity. The note will generate payments to you on mutually acceptable terms. I will maintain the collateral property in excellent condition as security for the note." Then the buyer has a trust deed prepared in favor of the seller to back up the trust deed note.

What the buyer has done is magic — he has created paper out of thin air. But his paper has value. It is solid consideration for the seller's equity and is used in good faith in lieu of all or part of the cash down payment required. If the seller is dependent on such an exchange to consummate the deal but hungry for the cash just the same, he can always sell the note at a discount for cash (Technique No. 40, explained later in the book).

Two case studies in this section illustrate the creation of paper technique. The first (Case No. 15) shows how a buyer was able to acquire a single family home by giving the seller a trust deed note for $11,600 against another property, with terms of 14%, no payments for one year, thereafter interest-only payments each month for four years until a balloon came due for the balance. In Case No. 16, a note for $22,500 (10%, seven-year balloon) secured against another property in the buyer's portfolio was used to get into a single family home. Three other case studies printed elsewhere in this volume provide further illustrations of how paper can be created. (See the cross-reference matrix in the appendix.)

Not only is the Creation of Paper technique valuable in property acquisition, it permits the complete leveraging of a buyer's other holdings. Usually commercial lenders will lend only up to 80% of the value of a collateral property. If an owner wants to borrow against his assets at levels higher than 80%, he can readily create paper against the top 20% of value and use it for exchange purposes. Rarely will a seller ask for credit checks or complicated paperwork to back up such a technique.

Technique No. 16   The Two-Way Exchange

In the Creation of Paper Technique, the buyer retains ownership of the property used to secure the note given to the seller as down payment on the subject property. In an exchange, the seller actually receives the buyer's property in exchange for his own. Title transfers.

Buying property by means of an exchange, if correctly done, provides great benefits in the form of tax deferrals. Section 1031 of the Internal Revenue Service Code permits trading of properties without triggering taxation on the gains. This is one of the single most important strategies in building up a real estate portfolio.

Case No. 17 shows how a creative buyer used this approach to trade his 7-plex into a more desirable 12-plex. Case No. 18 is an illustration of the pyramiding potential in exchanges. In this situation, a buyer traded a single family home with a large equity for three other properties worth nearly twice as much.

Technique No. 17   The Three-Way Exchange

The principles are the same as in the two-way exchange except that the seller, while anxious to get rid of his own property, is not willing to accept the buyer's property in exchange. However, if someone with a property acceptable to the seller is willing to take over the buyer's property, then everything will fall into place. The end result is the same as a simple exchange except that an extra link is added to the chain. Theoretically any number of links might be added. As a result, the business can get complicated. Unfortunately none of the fifty case studies in this volume involves a multiple exchange. You will have to use your imagination!

Technique No. 18   Lemonading

In exchanging parlance, lemonading refers to the technique of adding cash to a property that, for one reason or another, has not sold as readily as the seller had hoped (a "lemon"). The new package of property-plus-cash is then offered in exchange for any acceptable package on the market. With the cash sweetener added, the lemon is supposed to become more palatable to the marketplace — "lemonade."

The Buyer

This technique is not central to any of the case studies reviewed in this volume. However, Case No. 17, printed below, gives a taste of how the technique works. The seller of a 12-plex had to add $11,000 cash to his package in order for his equity to match the equity of a 7-plex being offered by the buyer in exchange. The need to add cash ("boot") to an exchange for the purpose of balancing equities is a common practice. If the seller had actually gone into the marketplace with his 12-plex and offered $11,000 cash as an inducement for an exchange, he would have been "lemonading." If a buyer has the fortune of finding a property he actually wants with a lemonade sweetener attached, he can not only get in for nothing down, he can walk away with cash in his pocket.

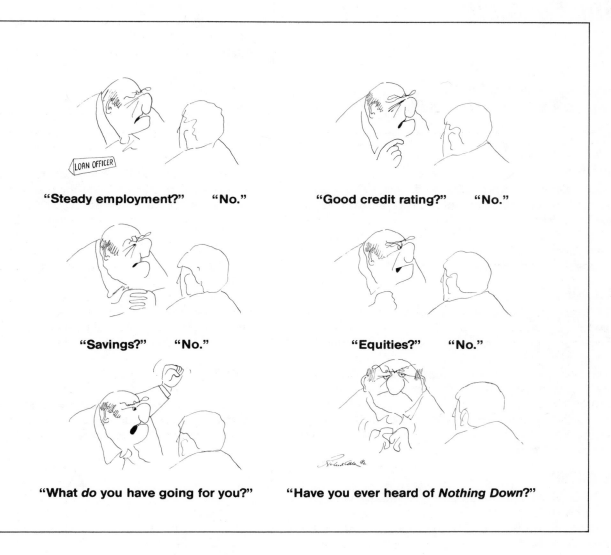

10

6½% Mortgages Are Still Possible

Featuring Technique No. 10
''Supply The Seller What He Needs''

In A Nutshell. . .

Type: SFH
Price: $155,000
Source: Classified ad
Means: AITD
Techniques: No. 4 — Contract/Wrap
No. 6 — Balloon
No. 10 — Supply Seller's Needs
Strategies: Stepped interest
Features: Positive cash flow

LOCATING

Jules Peffer of Stanford, California, was in the market for a single family home at around the $150,000 level. He noticed a classified ad for a property in Conoga Park, an area he was interested in. The listing agent quickly responded to his call and arranged for an inspection and a meeting with the owner.

SITUATION

The home was being occupied by an elderly widow who was about to move into a day-care center. She had worked out two options for prospective buyers: a purchase plan with $20,000 down and the balance carried back, or a five-year lease-option plan with $10,000 up front and $800 per month rent. Jules was concerned when he learned that the agent involved was a sister to the owner who was especially cautious about finding just the right buyer. The home had a $28,000 assumable first mortgage against it.

NEGOTIATION

As Jules perceived the situation in talking with the seller, she was mainly interested in receiving a dependable monthly cash flow to support herself in the day-care center. Beyond that, her cash needs were limited to the commission, around $10,000. Jules also knew that since she was over 55 years of age, she could exercise the one time exclusion (then $100,000) in escaping tax liability on most of her long-term capital gain.

His strategy was, therefore, to persuade her to sell the property to him immediately but with a much lower down payment and with modest monthly payments for the first few years. He offered her $6,500 down, with an additional principal payment of $3,500 in 6 months. These amounts would take care of the commission. For the first five years she would receive $800 per month in interest payments on the balance, precisely the amount she would need for the purpose of

paying for her day-care expenses. The interest rate that would yield this amount during the first 6 months was calculated to be 6.46% annually; after the 6-month balloon, the interest rate would change to 6.62% annually to generate the $800/mo. payment. After a period of five years, Jules would pay down the balance by an additional $20,000, and the amount due would be amortized over 30 years at 12½%.

After conferring with her sister, the lady agreed with the terms, and the offer was accepted. For the first five years of the financing, Jules had, in effect, negotiated what amounted to a 6½% mortgage!

CLOSING

The transaction was completed using an all-inclusive purchase money promissory note secured by an all-inclusive purchase money deed of trust. The sketches will summarize the steps in the financing process:

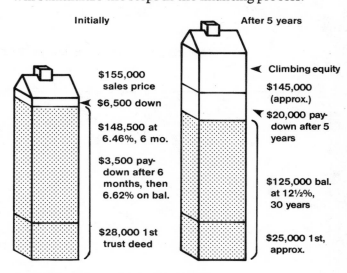

Initially

$155,000 sales price
$6,500 down
$148,500 at 6.46%, 6 mo.
$3,500 pay-down after 6 months, then 6.62% on bal.
$28,000 1st trust deed

After 5 years

◄ Climbing equity
$145,000 (approx.)
$20,000 pay-down after 5 years
$125,000 bal. at 12½%, 30 years
$25,000 1st, approx.

OUTCOMES AND FUTURE PLANS

Under the above arrangement, the property can be rented out with a positive cash flow. How will Jules raise the $20,000 for the five-year balloon payment? He plans to put a second on the property at that time, then hold it for a few years longer before selling.

His advice for other investors: "Understand the tax laws and everything involved, then exercise your knowledge."

COMMENTARY

1. How could Jules have avoided the $6,500 up front? Perhaps the agent involved would have taken back paper for the commission secured by a trust deed on the property. If the agent balked, perhaps a higher commission could have been negotiated.

2. This case study is a splendid example of keying in to the needs of the seller and providing exactly that which was needed — no more, no less — so that everyone involved won. The 6½% interest on the first five years is unusual — you never know until you ask!

DOCUMENTATION

[The following illustrative document was completed using data supplied by the buyer.]

UNIVERSAL EARNEST MONEY RECEIPT
AND OFFER TO PURCHASE

"This is a legally binding contract: if not understood, seek competent advice."

1. Date and Place of Offer: __June 30,__ 19 __81__ ; __Stanford__ (city) __California__ (state)

2. Principals: The undersigned Buyer __Jules Peffer__
agrees to buy and Seller agrees to sell, according to the indicated terms and conditions, the property described as follows:

3. Property: located at __1514 Bellvedere Avenue__ (street address) __Canoga Park__ (city) __California__ (state)

with the following legal description: __(To be supplied prior to closing)__

including any of the following items if at present attached to the premises: plumbing, heating, and cooling equipment, including stoker and oil tanks, burners, water heaters, electric light fixtures, bathroom fixtures, roller shades, curtain rods and fixtures, draperies, venetian blinds, window and door screens, towel racks, linoleum and other attached floor coverings,

including carpeting, attached television antennas, mailboxes, all trees and shrubs, and any other fixtures EXCEPT __None__

The following personal property shall also be included as part of the purchase: _____
At the closing of the transaction, the Seller, at his expense, shall provide the Buyer with a Bill Of Sale containing a detailed inventory of the personal property included.

4. Earnest Money Deposit: Agent (or Seller) acknowledges receipt from Buyer of __Five Hundred and 00/100__ dollars $ __500.00__

in the form of ( ) cash; (X) personal check; ( ) cashier's check; ( ) promissory note at _____ % interest per annum due _____ 19 _____ ; or

other _____
as earnest money deposit to secure and apply on this purchase. Upon acceptance of this agreement in writing and delivery of same to Buyer, the earnest money deposit shall be assigned

to and deposited in the listing Realtor's trust account or _____, to apply on the purchase price at the time of closing.

5. Purchase Price: The total purchase price of the property shall be __One Hundred Fifty-five Thousand and 00/100__ dollars
$ __155,000.00__

6. Payment: Purchase price is to be paid by Buyer as follows:

Aforedescribed earnest money deposit .... $ __500.00__

Additional payment due upon acceptance of this offer .... $ __0__

Additional payment due at closing .... $ __6,000.00__

Balance to be paid as follows:
__Buyer to execute all-inclusive purchase money promissory note in favor of__
__Seller secured by all-inclusive purchase money deed of trust in the amount__
__of $148,500.00, payable as follows: interest shall accrue at 6.46% per__
__annum payable monthly beginning September 1981 until February 1982 at__
__which time the interest rate shall be increased to 6.62% per annum payable__
__monthly until September 1986 at which time the interest rate shall be__

increased to 12.50% per annum calling for principal and interest payments of $1,334.08 per month. On January 10, 1982, there shall be due a principal payment of $3,500.00. On August 1, 1986, there shall be due a principal payment of $20,000.

Buyer shall have the right to pre-pay the note in part or in full prior to maturity without penalty.

7. Title: Seller agrees to furnish good and marketable title free of all encumbrances and defects, except mortgage liens and encumbrances as set forth in this agreement, and to make conveyance by Warranty Deed or _____. Seller shall furnish in due course to the Buyer a title insurance policy insuring the Buyer of a good and marketable title in keeping with the terms and conditions of this agreement. Prior to the closing of this transaction, the Seller, upon request, will furnish to the Buyer a preliminary title report made by a title insurance company showing the condition of the title to said property. If the Seller cannot furnish marketable title within thirty days after receipt of the notice to the Buyer containing a written statement of the defects, the earnest money deposit herein receipted shall be refunded to the Buyer and this agreement shall be null and void. The following shall not be deemed encumbrances or defects; building and use restrictions general to the area; utility easements; other easements not inconsistent with Buyer's intended use; zoning or subdivision laws, covenants, conditions, restrictions, or reservations of record; tenancies of record. In the event of sale of other than real property relating to this transaction, Seller will provide evidence of title or right to sell or lease such personal property.

8. Special Representations: Seller warrants and represents to Buyer (1) that the subject property is connected to ( ) public sewer system, ( ) cesspool or septic tank, ( ) sewer system available but not connected, ( ) city water system, ( ) private water system, and that the following special improvements are included in the sale: ( ) sidewalk, ( ) curb and gutter, ( ) special street paving, ( ) special street lighting; (2) that the Seller knows of no material structural defects; (3) that all electrical wiring, heating, cooling, and plumbing systems are free of material defects and will be in good working order at the time the Buyer is entitled to possession; (4) that the Seller has no notice from any government agency of any violation or knowledge of probable violations of the law relating to the subject property; (5) that the Seller has no notice or knowledge of planned or commenced public improvements which may result in special assessments or otherwise directly and materially affect the property; and (6) that the Seller has no notice or knowledge of any liens to be assessed against the property,

EXCEPT   None

9. Escrow Instructions: This sale shall be closed on or before ___July 15,___ 19 81 by _____ or such other closing agent as mutually agreed upon by Buyer and Seller. Buyer and Seller will, immediately on demand, deposit with closing agent all instruments and monies required to complete the purchase in accordance with the provisions of this agreement. Contract of Sale or Instrument of Conveyance to be made in the name of ___(To be provided prior to closing)

10. Closing Costs and Pro-Ration: Seller agrees to pay for title insurance policy, preliminary title report (if requested), termite inspection as set forth below, real estate commission, cost of preparing and recording any corrective instruments, and one-half of the escrow fees. Buyer agrees to pay for recording fees for mortgages and deeds of conveyance, all costs or expenses in securing new financing or assuming existing financing, and one-half of the escrow fees. Buyer agrees to pay for recording fees for mortgages and deeds of conveyance, all costs or expenses in securing new financing or assuming existing financing, and one-half of the escrow fees. Taxes for the current year, insurance acceptable to the Buyer, rents, interest, mortgage reserves, maintenance fees, and water and other utilities constituting liens, shall be pro-rated as of closing. Renters' security deposits shall accrue to Buyer at closing. Seller to provide Buyer with all current rental or lease agreements prior to closing.

11. Termite Inspection: Seller agrees, at his expense, to provide written certification by a reputable licensed pest control firm that the property is free of termite infestation. In the event termites are found, the Seller shall have the property treated at his expense and provide acceptable certification that treatment has been rendered. If any structural repairs are required by reason of termite damage as established by acceptable certification, Seller agrees to make necessary repairs not to exceed $500. If repairs exceed $500, Buyer shall first have the right to accept the property "as is" with a credit to the Buyer at closing of $500, or the Buyer may terminate this agreement with the earnest money deposit being promptly returned to the Buyer if the Seller does not agree to pay all costs of treatment and repair.

(Seller and Buyer acknowledge that property is being purchased without benefit of a termite report with no demands to be placed on the Seller for corrective work now or in the future.)

12. Conditions of Sale: The following conditions shall also apply, and shall, if conflicting with the printed portions of this agreement, prevail and control:
None

13. Liability and Maintenance: Seller shall maintain subject property, including landscaping, in good condition until the date of transfer of title or possession by Buyer, whichever occurs first. All risk of loss and destruction of property, and all expenses of insurance, shall be borne by the seller until the date of possession. If the improvements on the property are destroyed or materially damaged prior to closing, then the Buyer shall have the right to declare this agreement null and void, and the earnest money deposit and all other sums paid by Buyer toward the purchase price shall be returned to the Buyer forthwith.

14. Possession: The Buyer shall be entitled to possession of property upon closing or _____NA_____, 19_____.

15. Default: In the event the Buyer fails to complete the purchase as herein provided, the earnest money deposit shall be retained by the Seller as the total and entire liquidated damages. In the event the Seller fails to perform any condition of the sale as herein provided, then the Buyer may, at his option, treat the contract as terminated, and all payments made by the Buyer hereunder shall be returned to the Buyer forthwith, provided the Buyer may, at his option, treat this agreement as being in full force and effect with the right to action for specific performance and damages. In the event that either Buyer, Seller, or Agent shall institute suit to enforce any rights hereunder, the prevailing party shall be entitled to court costs and a reasonable attorney's fee.

16. Time Limit of Offer: The Seller shall have until

_____ ___July 3,___ , 19 81 _____ to accept this
(hour)   (date)

offer by delivering a signed copy hereof to the Buyer. If this offer is not so accepted, it shall lapse and the agent (or Seller) shall refund the earnest money deposit to the Buyer forthwith.

17. General Agreements: (1) Both parties to this purchase reserve their rights to assign and hereby otherwise agree to cooperate in effecting an Internal Revenue Code 1031 exchange or similar tax-related arrangement prior to close of escrow, upon either party's written notice of intention to do so. (2) Upon approval of this offer by the Seller, this agreement shall become a contract between Buyer and Seller and shall inure to the benefit of the heirs, administrators, executors, successors, personal representatives, and assigns of said parties. (3) Time is of the essence and an essential part of this agreement. (4) This contract constitutes the sole and entire agreement between the parties hereto and no modification of this contract shall be binding unless attached hereto and signed by all parties to the contract. No representations, promises, or inducements not included in this contract shall be binding upon any party hereto.

18. Buyer's Statement and Receipt: "I/we hereby agree to purchase the above property in accordance with the terms and conditions above stated and acknowledge receipt of a

completed copy of this agreement, which I/we have fully read and understand." Dated _____ June 30, _____ 19 81 _____

(hour)

Address _____ 1521 North Broad Street _____   [signature] _____ Buyer

_____ Stanford, California _____   _____ Buyer

Phone No: Home _____ 659-1413 _____ Business _____ 279-8112 _____

19. Seller's Statement and Response: "I/we approve and accept the above offer, which I/we have fully read and understand, and agree to the above terms and conditions this day

of _____ . _____ , 19 _____ , _____ .

(hour)

Address _____ Seller

Phone No: Home _____ Business _____ Seller

20. Commission Agreement: Seller agrees to pay a commission of _____ 6 _____ % of the gross sales price to _____ Mark Evans Realty, Co. _____ for services in this transaction, and agrees that, in the event of forfeiture of the earnest money deposit by the Buyer, said deposit shall be divided between the Seller's broker and the Seller (one half to each party), the Broker's part not to exceed the amount of the commission.

21. Buyer's Receipt for Signed Offer: The Buyer hereby acknowledges receipt of a copy of the above agreement bearing the Seller's signature in acceptance of this offer.

Dated _____ , 19 _____   _____ Buyer

_____ Buyer

COMMENTARY TO DOCUMENTATION

Item 2. The words "or Assigns" should be added after the buyer's name.

Item 6. The acceleration issue was evidently important to the seller, as the final note contained this condition: "In the event Trustor sells, agrees to sell, transfers or conveys its interest in the real property or any part thereof or any interest therein beneficiary has the option to renegotiate the above stated interest rate should she/they so desire."

The financing instrument used is referred to as an all-inclusive purchase money note secured by an all-inclusive purchase money deed of trust. The reference to "purchase money" indicates that the seller is the lender. The reference to "all inclusive" indicates that the note "wraps" around an existing encumbrance (in this case a first trust deed of $28,000). The reference to the words "trust deed" (rather than contract, land contract, contract for deed, etc.) indicates that the seller's recourse is through the same channels as would apply to a trust deed in that jurisdiction. Just how the buyer can offer an all-encompassing trust deed to the seller as security when there is an existing first trust encumbrance against the property which he has not assumed is a fine point of the law that escapes this author — and evidently causes some discomfort among the attorneys in jurisdictions where the all-inclusive trust deeds are used. All the more reason to fall back on professional expertise when these documents are drawn up!

Distress Situation Can Be Win/Win, Too

Featuring Technique No. 11
"Assume Seller's Obligations"

In A Nutshell. . .

Type: SFH
Price: $43,221
Source: Classified ad
Means: VA assumption
Techniques: No. 11 — Assume Seller's Obligations
No. 24 — Small Amounts From Banks
No. 42 — Partner's Money For Down
Features: Positive cash flow

LOCATING

Attorney Fred Jenkins of Cleveland was looking around for a single-family rental house in the $50,000 range. He spotted a promising FSBO ad in the classified section of the local newspaper and called to get more information. His call confirmed the possibility of a deal.

SITUATION

The owner was a woman who had just gone through a divorce settlement. According to the divorce decree, she was to sell the home and split the proceeds with her former husband. Her asking price was $49,900 with 20% down and a conventional refinance of the existing $39,000 VA loan. She seemed to be under considerable pressure.

The house was located on an attractive suburban street near shopping, schools, and transportation. Though solidly built, it was in fact the "worst house in the best neighborhood," and it needed considerable cosmetic attention.

NEGOTIATION

Fred got right to the heart of the matter by asking the following questions: 1. What do you really need in the way of cash? 2. When would you prefer to move? and 3. Can you make the next mortgage payment?

Her response was that she needed around $1,500 to take care of arrears mortgage payments and utility bills, that she could not move for around three months, and she could unfortunately not make the next mortgage payment. Clearly this was a distress situation — a painful divorce and no money for living expenses.

Fred offered her $42,700 for the house in exchange for his assuming her obligations and arrears payments and allowing her to lease the property back for three months. She agreed in principle but asked for time to check with her attorney and finalize plans for moving. They executed a preliminary 60-day option secured by a note.

As it turned out, her attorney was a law professor who wanted the contract to be a work of art — "even though the house was not" — as Fred put it. Altogether the process of finalizing the papers in preparation for closing took eight separate drafts and three months! The final product is reproduced below in somewhat shortened form.

Essentially, Fred agreed to assume the VA loan of $39,220, pay the arrears mortgage payment of $434, pay an additional mortgage payment of $434 (for the due date just prior to closing), and provide an additional $3,133 in cash and other consideration as follows:

$1,800	in prepaid rents and deposit credited to seller under a lease agreement (for the 3 months after closing)
$ 300	in cash to cover arrears utility bills
$ 500	in cash 30 days after closing (for other needs of seller)
$ 533	in cash 60 days after closing
$3,133	total

To protect himself, Fred had the seller give him a 90-day option plus a repayment note just in case the deal was never finalized.

CLOSING

In fact, everything went as planned. In all, Fred paid $868 for mortgage payments that applied to the two months prior to closing (borrowed from a friend), plus the additional $3,133 that applied to obligations following closing, for a total outlay of $4,001 as down payment or deferred down payment. By extending the obligation over a period of three months following closing, Fred was able to absorb the outlays without undue difficulty. In fact, all subsequent down money was borrowed on a line of credit. Fred was even able to negotiate a discount from the escrow agent.

The sketch summarizes the financing:

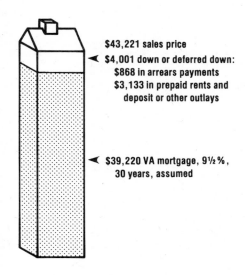

$43,221 sales price
$4,001 down or deferred down:
$868 in arrears payments
$3,133 in prepaid rents and
deposit or other outlays

$39,220 VA mortgage, 9½%,
30 years, assumed

COMMENTARY

1. Having gone through eight revisions of the negotiated contract on this one small home, Fred knows
the value of persistence. The work of the law professor in this case is a splendid example of conservative documentation.
2. Of interest is the set of questions used by Fred — in
effect: How much cash do you need? When can you
leave? and Where does it hurt? In creative finance
transactions, there is no time to beat around the
bush. If the investor cannot solve the seller's
problems to the mutual benefit of both parties, he
needs to move on to the next deal.
3. What is fair in a distress situation? In this case, Fred
put his neck on the line to the extent of $4,001 in
cash outlays (borrowed, out of pocket, or deferred).
If the appraisal of $50,000 was accurate, the seller's
equity above the VA loan of $39,220 amounted to
$10,780. Fred came up with nearly 39% of that
figure, certainly a generous share. The important
thing is that the buyer and seller come to a mutually
agreeable solution. Occasionally you hear of stories
where an investor will come into a distress situation
and simply arrange to take the property off the
hands of the unfortunate seller, who often gives up
a large amount of equity in exchange for the relief.
Does that kind of arrangement lead to satisfying
outcomes? Perhaps. Perhaps not. Sometimes one has
to go by the heart in addition to the HP-138c. In this
case, both Fred and the seller have got to be feeling
rather good about how things turned out. Even a
distress sale can be a win/win situation.

OUTCOMES AND FUTURE PLANS

With rental income of $500/mo. and a mortgage
payment of $434 PITI, the property shows a modest
positive cash flow. An appraisal of the property came in
at $50,000, giving Fred an instant equity of $6,779 for use
in future deals calling for the creation of paper.

In retrospect, Fred believes that the key to negotiation success is this: "Make overt efforts to find the
seller's 'hot buttons' and needs. I walked away twice,
finally offered the lease-back as part of the price."

His advice to others: "Be fair to the seller and make
clear how far you will go on the price and terms. Keep
all promises."

DOCUMENTATION

[The following is a transcription of the purchase agreement in somewhat shortened form.]

PURCHASE AGREEMENT

THIS AGREEMENT for the purchase and sale of REAL ESTATE, made in quadruplicate, at Cleveland Hts., Ohio, as of the 6th day of September, 1981.

WITNESSETH:

The Undersigned (Purchaser), hereby offers and agrees to buy the following described property, situated in the City of Cleveland Heights, County of Cuyahoga and State of Ohio:

[legal description]

And further commonly known as 1215 Stewart Avenue, single family frame house (3 bedroom) and two car detached garage together with all buildings and appurtenances now thereon and appurtenant thereto or thereon, in their present condition.

For which PURCHASER agrees to pay the sum of FORTY-THREE THOUSAND TWO HUNDRED TWENTY-ONE and 11/100 Dollars ($43,221.11), as hereinafter set forth, upon the following terms and conditions.

The purchase price is to be paid as follows by the Purchaser.

(1) Delivering to Owner Purchaser's promissory note of even date in the form of the form of Promissory Note annexed hereto as "Exhibit A" and hereby made a part hereof, receipt of which note is hereby acknowledged, — $ 3,133.00

(2) Cash paid by Purchaser to cover mortgage payment due 8/1/81, receipt of which is hereby acknowledged (the Purchaser agrees to cancel the note given by the Owner in consideration of this payment at the time of the transfer of title). — $ 434.00

(3) Cash to be paid by Purchaser to the holder of the mortgage on the premises in payment of the mortgage payment due 9/1/81, which payment the Purchaser promises shall be made before the mortgage becomes in default — $ 434.00

(4) Assumption by Purchaser, as set forth in paragraph (3), below fully hereinafter described, of the First Mortgage now on said premises, the unpaid balance of which is agreed by the parties for the purposes of calculating the amount to be credited to the Purchaser for such assumption, to be — $39,220.11

$43,221.11

And it is further agreed between the parties that the following terms and conditions are part of this agreement.

(1) The Purchaser shall pay all of the closing costs (except for Owner's attorney's fees) including the escrow fee and the cost of the title guarantee to be supplied by the Owner as provided below.

(2) The Purchaser shall assume and take the property subject to all building code violations noted on certificate, dated 7/23/81 only, except for two items of hauling rubbish, which Owner will haul to street before transfer of title.

(3) The Purchaser shall assume the Owner's obligations with respect to, and pay in accordance with its terms, the note or other obligation secured by that certain mortgage, dated September 26, 1978, made by George Simpson and Bonnie Simpson to the ABC Savings and Loan Company to secure the original principal indebtedness of $40,000, with interest at 9½% per annum and with payments for principal, interest, tax, and insurance to the holder currently being $434 per month; which mortgage constitutes a first mortgage lien upon the above-described premises. The Purchaser's obligation under this agreement is expressly subject to the Purchaser's being able, at the time scheduled for the transfer of title, to assume said mortgage at 9½% interest on exactly the terms stated therein.

(4) All window shades, window and door screens, storm doors, storm windows, electric fixtures, curtain rods, bath room fixtures, heat regulator, landscaping and gas Kenmore stove, Admiral Duplex Refrigerator, Window Sash for Sunroom, Fireplace Grate & Screen, and Dining Room Chandelier, now in said property and belonging to the Owner shall pass with the title to the above mentioned property.

(5) Owner shall deliver or cause to be delivered to Purchaser a warranty deed in the form of the form of deed annexed hereto as "Exhibit B," and hereby made a part hereof, conveying a good title to the said premises free and clear of all liens and encumbrances whatsoever, except

    (i)   The mortgage described in Paragraph (3), above;

    (ii)   The violations referred to in Paragraph (2), above;

    (iii)   Other matters noted herein;

    (iv)   Restrictions of record, easements, zoning ordinances, if any, and taxes and assessments, both general and special, after December 31, 1980. Interest due with respect to mortgages assumed and taxes and assessments shall not be prorated and any unpaid at the time of transfer of title or any time thereafter shall be the obligation of the Purchaser. All escrowed taxes to be credited to Purchaser in escrow.

(6) Subject to the provisions of Paragraph (1), above, Owner shall deliver or cause to be delivered to Purchaser a Title Guarantee showing title good in Purchaser at the time of the delivery of the deed. Said Title Guarantee to be in the amount of the purchase price.

(7) Prepaid interest on assumed mortgages, and prepaid insurance premiums are assigned to Purchaser as of the date of transfer. Assumption of present existing insurance is hereby agreed. Owner hereby assigns, transfers and sets over all right, title and interest in fire and liability policy #66159 issued by Gem Insurance Co., effective to 9/25/82, and proceeds thereof to Purchaser as of the date of transfer of title to the premises. Purchaser hereby accepts such assignment.

(8) Subject to the provisions of the lease described in paragraph (16), below, possession of the herein described premises shall be given by the Owner to the Purchaser with keys (to fit all 3 outside doors), except one set, on date of title transfer.

(9) If this offer is NOT ACCEPTED, all sums paid by the Purchaser on account of the purchase price shall be repaid and the note of the Purchaser delivered as part of the purchase price shall be returned without liability upon the part of any party connected with this transaction. When this offer is accepted by the Owner, it shall constitute a contract for the purchase and sale of said property. This contract shall be performed within 14 days from the date of acceptance, and if within said time Purchaser defaults in the performance of any of the obligations imposed by the terms hereof, the Owner may at her option treat this contract as null and void. If the Owner does not perform her obligation under this contract within said time Purchaser may at his option treat this contract as null and void and receive the repayment of all sums paid by the Purchaser on account of the purchase price and the return of the note described above in this paragraph (9).

(10) All documents and funds pertaining to this conveyance are to be placed in escrow with American Title Insurance Co., within 14 days from date of acceptance hereof.

(11) Purchaser is buying this property for investment and 90% of the price is allocated to the improvements on the property.

(12) This contract is made for the benefit of each party, their heirs, beneficiaries, personal representatives, successors or assigns, but assignment by Purchaser is subject to the approval by Owner of the assignee which approval shall not be unreasonably withheld.

(13) The parties hereby acknowledge receipt of a full and complete copy of this agreement.

(14) The parties agree and represent, each to the other, that no broker was instrumental in bringing about this sale.

(15) This offer remains open to September 6, 1981.

(16) Lease: immediately after closing, the parties will execute a lease in the form of lease annexed hereto as "Exhibit C," by which Purchaser will lease back the property in its present condition to Owner.

(17) Upon acceptance of offer, Owner will loan Purchaser:

    (a)   existing deed;

    (b)   window sash for sunroom;

    (c)   a copy of the existing mortgage;

    (d)   a copy of the limited warranty deed from Bonnie Simpson to Owner; and

    (e)   a copy of the separation agreement between Bonnie Simpson and Owner.

Transaction is subject to Purchaser's approval of the above documents, which approval shall not be unreasonably withheld.

(18) Owner warrants and represents: (a) that as of the date of this agreement and as of the date of closing, all plumbing, sewers, drains, furnace, wiring, water heater, electric fixtures, fireplace, appliances and upstairs toilet (but not downstairs toilet) are in good operating condition and basement is dry (except for leaking toilet); and (b) that she is divorced and unremarried and that there are no terms in her divorce decree or separation agreement or later proceedings in her dissolution action which will affect the property after closing. These warranties and representations shall survive closing but shall be of no further force and effect after the expiration of 30 days after Owner vacates the property.

(19) If the above-described premises are destroyed or substantially damaged by fire or other casualty before the time of the transfer of title to the Purchaser the Purchaser may, at his option, terminate this contract and, upon such termination, all sums paid by the Purchaser on account of the purchase price shall be repaid and the note of the Purchaser delivered as part of the purchase price shall be returned without liability upon the part of any party connected with this transaction, and neither party shall thereafter have any rights against the other in respect of this agreement.

(20) Purchaser is to assume water and sewer arrearage, current bill and deposit and pay separately, directly to City of Cleveland Heights.

(21) All promissory notes and offers to purchase given by Purchaser to Owner, prior to and other than the promissory note of even date which is annexed hereto and made a part hereof, are null and void.

[signature]

DEPOSIT RECEIPT

Acknowledgment is hereby made of receipt of the promissory note of even date in the amount of THREE THOUSAND ONE HUNDRED THIRTY-THREE DOLLARS ($3,133.00).

[signature]

COMMENTARY TO DOCUMENTATION

Even though the buyer looked askance at the many drafts this agreement went through before being finalized, the finished product is not infected with legal boilerplate too far beyond what the ordinary earnest money form contains. The language is a bit florid, but the buyer comes out with some rather good protections. For example:

1. Seller to haul away rubbish (Item 2); 2. Subject to buyer being able to assume the first according to precisely identified terms (Item 3); Strictly limited recourse for Seller in the event of a default by the Buyer (Item 9); Absence of any divorce judgment impairing the sale (Item 18).

Reprinted by permission from the *Nothing Down Advisor*.

"I don't care who you are . . . we require 20% down!"

12

Eleventh-Hour Loan On Insurance Policy Saves Deal

Featuring Technique No. 13
"Borrow Against Life Insurance Policy"

In A Nutshell . . .

Type: SFH
Price: $57,500
Source: MLS Book
Means: Assumption, Hard-Money 2d, Owner Carry-Back
Techniques: No. 6 — Balloon
No. 13 — Borrow Against Insurance
No. 32 — Second Mortgage Crank
Strategies: Lease option

LOCATING

Dale Fields of San Jose, California, was looking for properties in Arizona. His target was a single family home in the range of $40,000 to $60,000. In perusing a Multiple Listing Service Book he spotted an interesting entry for Cottonwood, Arizona, a small city south of Flagstaff. The house was listed as vacant.

SITUATION

The owner was living in Ohio. The house, listed at $57,500 with a first mortgage of $25,400, had been vacant for three months. The vacancy and out-of-state factors were good clues to don't wanteritis, especially in combination. Since Dale's philosophy was to determine the owner's needs and structure the transaction accordingly, he asked the listing agent why the seller was requesting "cash to mortgage" in the deal.

Through the agent, Dale learned that the owner had incurred some heavy moving expenses and for this and other reasons would need at least $20,000 cash. Would the seller be willing to carry back some paper on the deal? Yes.

NEGOTIATION

With that word of encouragement, Dale structured his offer. He would assume the first mortgage of $25,400 at 10% ($266 per month), put a hard-money second on the property in the amount of $20,000 (proceeds to the seller), and ask the seller to carry back the balance of $12,100 at 10% for 30 years (ballooned after 7 years). The property would then be 100% papered out.

The owner, who was a single parent, liked the terms offered: the monthly payments would provide a steady supplement to his income, and the balloon in seven years would coincide with a need for college money in the family. Dale's strategy had worked out. His negotiation "secret" was, in his own words, "determining and meeting the seller's needs using the win/win philosophy and understanding ways to structure 'nothing down'

transactions."

CLOSING

Now he needed only to come up with the $20,000 hard-money second to complete the deal. At first he tried to locate some money through private sources. Twice he thought he had partnership funds nailed down, only to see the money evaporate because of extenuating circumstances in the lives of the partners.

Attempts to arrange for hard money also proved difficult because he was an out-of-state buyer. Finally, on the suggestion of the chairman of the Phoenix R.A.N.D. Group (the local organization of the "Robert Allen Nothing Down" graduates), Dale went to the Citicorp Person-to-Person Financial Center and made arrangements for a loan.

The only problem was that Person-to-Person required new buyers to put 10% down on properties for which they were providing secondary financing. In Dale's case, this would amount to $5,750, just about $5,750 more than he had. Solution? Dale borrowed $5,800 against the cash value of his life insurance policy at 5% interest. Even though Person-to-Person raised the interest rate on their second ½ point because Dale was an out-of-state borrower, everything after that fell in place, and the deal was closed. The sketch summarizes the financing on the property, including the second mortgage crank.

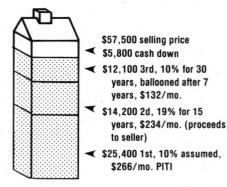

$57,500 selling price
◄ $5,800 cash down

◄ $12,100 3rd, 10% for 30 years, ballooned after 7 years, $132/mo.

◄ $14,200 2d, 19% for 15 years, $234/mo. (proceeds to seller)

◄ $25,400 1st, 10% assumed, $266/mo. PITI

OUTCOMES AND FUTURE PLANS

Total debt service on the financing for Dale's new SFH amounts to $632 per month, about $200 more than it could rent for. His strategy for dealing with this unacceptable level of negative cash flow was to find a tenant who was willing to sign a lease-option agreement based on rent of $450 per month with an additional $200 per month going toward the future purchase (two-year option).

Dale figures the price he paid for the house is around $3,000 below market, giving him some instant equity above the financing — not bad for a nothing down deal. As a matter of fact, he was approached just two hours after the closing by a buyer who wanted to pay $62,500 for the house — $5,000 more than Dale had just paid for it! He passed up the deal on the theory that a longer holding period would yield even better results.

COMMENTARY

1. Dale was correct in turning first to the seller for financing. He was also correct in attempting to find partnership funds before going to the hard-money lenders for help. However, it was only under pressures of the moment that he thought of borrowing against the cash value of his life insurance policy. So few take advantage of this cheap source of money. In this day and age of high interest rates, money should never be left in cash value insurance accounts. Borrowing this money out gives the policy-holder the added advantage of not being under any restraints to pay it back (except annual interest payments). The only question one might have is why Dale did not borrow more in this way and less from the finance company?

2. A further question for the buyer is this: if the finance company required 10% down, could this not have come in the form of a note secured by Dale against other equity he might have had? The note could have been offered to the seller, who could have indicated to potential lenders that the requirement for down was satisfied.

3. The lease-option arrangement was a stroke of genius in this case. Not only did Dale avoid the negative cash flow generated by a 100% financed property, he also solved the management problem of having to care for a property many hundreds of miles away from his home. Does it not stand to reason that the lessee will take extra good care of the house, knowing that in two years he has the right to apply his $4,800 in accumulated option funds toward the purchase of the property? Of course, the long-term lease-option works best in areas where property values are still reasonable and the option increment therefore tolerable to the tenant.

4. Dale was wise to require the seller to subordinate the third note and deed of trust to the second (or its replacement). He was also wise to retain first right of refusal on the third in order to preserve his options for fuller ownership in the future.

DOCUMENTATION (INITIAL OFFER)

UNIVERSAL EARNEST MONEY RECEIPT AND OFFER TO PURCHASE

"This is a legally binding contract: if not understood, seek competent advice."

1. Date and Place of Offer: __July 4,__ 19 __81__ ; __Cottonwood__ __Arizona__
   (city) (state)

2. Principals: The undersigned Buyer __Dale Fields and Sarah Fields, H and W as community property__
   agrees to buy and Seller agrees to sell, according to the indicated terms and conditions, the property described as follows:

3. Property: located at __1643 Gem Avenue__ __Cottonwood__ __Arizona__
   (street address) (city) (state)

   with the following legal description: __Lot 14, Wildrower Terrace, #12__

including any of the following items if at present attached to the premises: plumbing, heating, and cooling equipment, including stoker and oil tanks, burners, water heaters, electric light fixtures, bathroom fixtures, roller shades, curtain rods and fixtures, draperies, venetian blinds, window and door screens, towel racks, linoleum and other attached floor coverings,

including carpeting, attached television antennas, mailboxes, all trees and shrubs, and any other fixtures EXCEPT __None__

The following personal property shall also be included as part of the purchase: _____
At the closing of the transaction, the Seller, at his expense, shall provide the Buyer with a Bill Of Sale containing a detailed inventory of the personal property included.

4. Earnest Money Deposit: Agent (or Seller) acknowledges receipt from Buyer of __One Hundred and 00/100__ dollars $ __100.00__

in the form of ( ) cash; (X) personal check; ( ) cashier's check; ( ) promissory note at _____% interest per annum due _____ 19 _____ ; or

other _____

as earnest money deposit to secure and apply on this purchase. Upon acceptance of this agreement in writing and delivery of same to Buyer, the earnest money deposit shall be assigned

to and deposited in the listing Realtor's trust account or _____, to apply on the purchase price at the time of closing.

5. Purchase Price: The total purchase price of the property shall be <u>Fifty-seven Thousand Five Hundred and 00/100</u> dollars
$ <u>57,500.00</u>

6. Payment: Purchase price is to be paid by Buyer as follows:

Aforedescribed earnest money deposit **To be applied to Buyer's Closing Costs.** $ _____ --

Additional payment due upon acceptance of this offer .... $ _____ --

Additional payment due at closing .... $ _____ --

Balance to be paid as follows:

<u>$25,400 Buyer assumes and agrees to pay at $266.00 per month including</u>
<u>interest at 10% per annum through First State Bank #776-987-5678.</u>
<u>Seller shall remain liable for the First Mortgage.</u>

<u>$20,000 Cash to Seller, subject to Buyer obtaining Second Note and Deed</u>
<u>of Trust within 30 days of acceptance of this offer.</u>

<u>$12,100 By Note and Third Deed of Trust payable at $132.00 or more per</u>
<u>month including interest at the rate of 10% per annum, entire balance</u>
<u>due seven (7) years from the close of escrow. Any difference in the</u>
<u>first mortgage balance shall be reflected in the Third Note and Deed of</u>
<u>Trust.</u>

<u>Contingent upon: Buyer to have the first right of refusal on the Third</u>
<u>Note and Deed of Trust if Seller should decide to sell the note.</u>
<u>Seller agrees to subordinate the Third Note and Deed of Trust to the Second</u>
<u>Note and Deed of Trust or any replacement thereof.</u>
<u>Buyer shall approve the Preliminary Title Report within 10 days of receipt</u>
<u>of same.</u>

7. Title: Seller agrees to furnish good and marketable title free of all encumbrances and defects, except mortgage liens and encumbrances as set forth in this agreement, and to make

conveyance by Warranty Deed or _____. Seller shall furnish in due course to the Buyer a title insurance policy insuring the Buyer of a good and marketable title in keeping with the terms and conditions of this agreement. Prior to the closing of this transaction, the Seller, upon request, will furnish to the Buyer a preliminary title report made by a title insurance company showing the condition of the title to said property. If the Seller cannot furnish marketable title within thirty days after receipt of the notice to the Buyer containing a written statement of the defects, the earnest money deposit herein receipted shall be refunded to the Buyer and this agreement shall be null and void. The following shall not be deemed encumbrances or defects; building and use restrictions general to the area; utility easements; other easements not inconsistent with Buyer's intended use; zoning or subdivision laws, covenants, conditions, restrictions, or reservations of record; tenancies of record. In the event of sale of other than real property relating to this transaction, Seller will provide evidence of title or right to sell or lease such personal property.

8. Special Representations: Seller warrants and represents to Buyer (1) that the subject property is connected to ( ) public sewer system, ( ) cesspool or septic tank, ( ) sewer system available but not connected, ( ) city water system, ( ) private water system, and that the following special improvements are included in the sale: ( ) sidewalk, ( ) curb and gutter, ( ) special street paving, ( ) special street lighting; (2) that the Seller knows of no material structural defects; (3) that all electrical wiring, heating, cooling, and plumbing systems are free of material defects and will be in good working order at the time the Buyer is entitled to possession; (4) that the Seller has no notice from any government agency of any violation or knowledge of probable violations of the law relating to the subject property; (5) that the Seller has no notice or knowledge of planned or commenced public improvements which may result in special assessments or otherwise directly and materially affect the property; and (6) that the Seller has no notice or knowledge of any liens to be assessed against the property,

EXCEPT _____ **None**

9. Escrow Instructions: This sale shall be closed on or before <u>August 14,</u> 19<u>81</u> by <u>Arizona Title Company</u> or such other closing agent as mutually agreed upon by Buyer and Seller. Buyer and Seller will, immediately on demand, deposit with closing agent all instruments and monies required

to complete the purchase in accordance with the provisions of this agreement. Contract of Sale or Instrument of Conveyance to be made in the name of <u>(To be</u>
<u>provided prior to closing.)</u>

10. Closing Costs and Pro-Ration: Seller agrees to pay for title insurance policy, preliminary title report (if requested), termite inspection as set forth below, real estate commission, cost of preparing and recording any corrective instruments, and one-half of the escrow fees. Buyer agrees to pay for recording fees for mortgages and deeds of conveyance, all costs or expenses in securing new financing or assuming existing financing, and one-half of the escrow fees. Buyer agrees to pay for recording fees for mortgages and deeds of conveyance, all costs or expenses in securing new financing or assuming existing financing, and one-half of the escrow fees. Taxes for the current year, insurance acceptable to the Buyer, rents, interest, mortgage reserves, maintenance fees, and water and other utilities constituting liens, shall be pro-rated as of closing. Renters' security deposits shall accrue to Buyer at closing. Seller to provide Buyer with all current rental or lease agreements prior to closing.

11. Termite Inspection: Seller agrees, at his expense, to provide written certification by a reputable licensed pest control firm that the property is free of termite infestation. In the event termites are found, the Seller shall have the property treated at his expense and provide acceptable certification that treatment has been rendered. If any structural repairs are required by reason of termite damage as established by acceptable certification, Seller agrees to make necessary repairs not to exceed $500. If repairs exceed $500, Buyer shall first have the right to accept the property "as is" with a credit to the Buyer at closing of $500, or the Buyer may terminate this agreement with the earnest money deposit being promptly returned to the Buyer if the Seller does not agree to pay all costs of treatment and repair.

12. Conditions of Sale: The following conditions shall also apply, and shall, if conflicting with the printed portions of this agreement, prevail and control:

None

13. Liability and Maintenance: Seller shall maintain subject property, including landscaping, in good condition until the date of transfer of title or possession by Buyer, whichever occurs first. All risk of loss and destruction of property, and all expenses of insurance, shall be borne by the seller until the date of possession. If the improvements on the property are destroyed or materially damaged prior to closing, then the Buyer shall have the right to declare this agreement null and void, and the earnest money deposit and all other sums paid by Buyer toward the purchase price shall be returned to the Buyer forthwith.

14. Possession: The Buyer shall be entitled to possession of property upon closing or _____ NA _____, 19 _____.

15. Default: In the event the Buyer fails to complete the purchase as herein provided, the earnest money deposit shall be retained by the Seller as the total and entire liquidated damages. In the event the Seller fails to perform any condition of the sale as herein provided, then the Buyer may, at his option, treat the contract as terminated, and all payments made by the Buyer hereunder shall be returned to the Buyer forthwith, provided the Buyer may, at his option, treat this agreement as being in full force and effect with the right to action for specific performance and damages. In the event that either Buyer, Seller, or Agent shall institute suit to enforce any rights hereunder, the prevailing party shall be entitled to court costs and a reasonable attorney's fee.

16. Time Limit of Offer: The Seller shall have until

_____ July 13, _____, 19 __81__ to accept this
(hour)   (date)

offer by delivering a signed copy hereof to the Buyer. If this offer is not so accepted, it shall lapse and the agent (or Seller) shall refund the earnest money deposit to the Buyer forthwith.

17. General Agreements: (1) Both parties to this purchase reserve their rights to assign and hereby otherwise agree to cooperate in effecting an Internal Revenue Code 1031 exchange or similar tax-related arrangement prior to close of escrow, upon either party's written notice of intention to do so. (2) Upon approval of this offer by the Seller, this agreement shall become a contract between Buyer and Seller and shall inure to the benefit of the heirs, administrators, executors, successors, personal representatives, and assigns of said parties. (3) Time is of the essence and an essential part of this agreement. (4) This contract constitutes the sole and entire agreement between the parties hereto and no modification of this contract shall be binding unless attached hereto and signed by all parties to the contract. No representations, promises, or inducements not included in this contract shall be binding upon any party hereto.

18. Buyer's Statement and Receipt: "I/we hereby agree to purchase the above property in accordance with the terms and conditions above stated and acknowledge receipt of a completed copy of this agreement, which I/we have fully read and understand." Dated _____ July 4, _____ 19 __81__, _____
(hour)

Address _____ 48 Victor Street _____   [signature] _____ Buyer

_____ San Jose, California _____   [signature] _____ Buyer

Phone No: Home __492-3516__   Business __615-4122__

19. Seller's Statement and Response: "I/we approve and accept the above offer, which I/we have fully read and understand, and agree to the above terms and conditions this day

of _____, 19 _____, _____
(hour)

Address _____ Seller

Phone No: Home _____ Business _____ Seller

20. Commission Agreement: Seller agrees to pay a commission of __6__ % of the gross sales price to __M.R. Duke Associates__ for services in this transaction, and agrees that, in the event of forfeiture of the earnest money deposit by the Buyer, said deposit shall be divided between the Seller's broker and the Seller (one half to each party), the Broker's part not to exceed the amount of the commission.

21. Buyer's Receipt for Signed Offer: The Buyer hereby acknowledges receipt of a copy of the above agreement bearing the Seller's signature in acceptance of this offer.

Dated _____, 19 _____ _____ Buyer

_____ Buyer

COMMENTARY TO DOCUMENTATION

Item 2. The words "or Assigns" should be written after the names of the buyers to assure future flexibility in the event of a change prior to closing (need of partner, opportunity to sell interest in purchase contract at a profit, etc.).

Item 6. As it turned out, the secondary lender required the buyers to come up with 10% cash down in order to complete the loan. Thus, the amount of the loan was only $14,200. The rest was obtained through an insurance loan.

The buyer was wise to insert a contingency about the second trust deed. If he had not been successful in obtaining it, then the offer would become null and void. As it turned out, the insurance loan saved the day anyway.

The contingency about subordination and first right of refusal on the third was a smart move on the part of the buyer. But he should also have added four other conditions: substitution of collateral, rollover on the balloon, prepayment without penalty, and assumability. Sellers will not always go for all of these, but it never hurts to try.

Item 15. The original offer was less favorable to the buyer in regard to buyer default than our "Universal Earnest Money Receipt." The original stated: "In the event the said purchaser shall fail to pay the balance of the cash payment, or complete said purchase, as herein provided, Seller may demand specific performance of this contract, or may retain the amount paid herein as liquidated and agreed damages, or pursue any other remedy at law or equity as he may elect."

Alert Duplex Buyer Gets Second One — Just For The Asking

Featuring Technique No. 13
''Borrow Against Life Insurance Policy''

In A Nutshell. . .

Type: Duplexes
Price: $64,000 and $60,000
Source: MLS book; ads; friend
Means: Contract
Techniques: No. 1 — Ultimate Paper Out
No. 4 — Contract/Wrap
No. 13 — Borrow Against Life Insurance Policy
Features: Alert follow through

By nature, Eldon Barnes is an energetic and alert individual who does things in a thorough way. By the time he took the Nothing Down Seminar in June, 1981, in Eugene, Oregon, he had already done fairly well with real estate — a duplex, a single family rental home, and a piece of recreational property. But in 1980 he took a rather severe beating with his income taxes and was prepared for the impetus the seminar gave to him.

LOCATING

He began looking for a duplex in the $60,000 to $70,000 range in his home city of Albany (near Corvallis). By reviewing the MLS book and scanning the classified ads, he identified twelve of the most promising properties on the market. He checked the values on these properties at the county court house and then drove by to inspect the cream of the crop. Two particularly appealed to him because of appearance and location.

The owner of the first was staring a large balloon in the face. Since a refinance would be too expensive, Eldon passed this one by and went on to the second. He struck pay dirt.

SITUATION

The second duplex was being offered as part of an estate sale. It had been listed at $66,000 two years prior to that without a sale, and the asking price for the past several months had been $69,900. It was one of four identical duplexes on a cul-de-sac in an excellent area of town. The building was fairly new — only four years old. The heirs were living in Germany and were anxious to sell.

It was at that moment in time that Eldon did something that proved to be very profitable. He asked an investor friend for advice concerning the duplex. Since the friend was knowledgeable about properties in the area, he was able to do a comparative study and came up with $64,000 as a fair price for the duplex.

It was through contact with his friend that Eldon stumbled upon the best news of all — the friend just happened to own one of the other identical duplexes in the group. Would he be interested in selling his duplex? (This is the question every astute creative real estate investor learns to ask.) The answer: "Yes, I would consider selling." That set the stage for the first round of negotiations.

NEGOTIATION

Eldon set aside the question of the first duplex for the time being and concentrated on his friend's property. The opening question was: "How much do you need in the way of cash?" When the friend replied that he would need around $10,000, Eldon asked the next logical question: "What do you need the money for?" He got a straight answer. The friend needed the money to make a down payment on some properties (a piece of recreational land and a lot next to his home), complete some repairs to his home, and set up a monthly income for his daughters in college. In addition, he would need a five-year balloon on the balance of his equity because of a European trip he was planning to take.

The two decided on a price of $64,000, with $8,000 down, and a carry back of $18,500 at 12% for 30 years ballooned out after five, the property being taken subject to the existing $37,500 mortgage at 9¼%.

In addition, they agreed to the following terms: interest on the second would drop from 12% to 10% if the prime rate ever dropped as low as 15%. The interest rate would revert to 12% if the prime went above 15%. The buyer also had the option of prepaying the note to a ceiling of $6,000 per year or reducing the payments on the note to interest only. Eldon also negotiated the right to reduce the size of the balloon when due and pay the balance on a new note.

Since the first mortgage contained a due-on-sale clause, Eldon and his friend agreed that the buyer would assume the liability in case the note were accelerated by the lender, except that interest on the second would drop to 11%. Finally, if the note were actually called, the obligation would be split by both parties, and the buyer would then have the option of drawing up a contract with the seller to retire the seller's outlay.

CLOSING

Eldon's only problem was how to come up with the $8,000 down payment he had agreed to. At first he considered setting up a joint venture partnership but then decided instead to borrow the money out of the cash value reserves of his insurance policy at 5%.

The instrument of sale was a Land Sale Contract drawn up by an attorney. All the arrangements were handled through a title company. In an interesting sidelight, the escrow was set up so that every other payment on the second went straight to the seller's daughters at college.

The important facts are summarized in the following sketch:

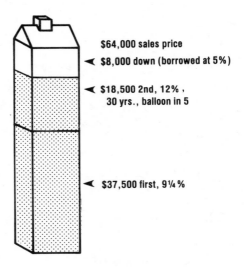

$64,000 sales price

$8,000 down (borrowed at 5%)

$18,500 2nd, 12%, 30 yrs., balloon in 5

$37,500 first, 9¼%

OUTCOMES AND FUTURE PLANS

The duplex has a negative cash flow of some $41 per month — not a problem for Eldon, who needs the tax write off anyway. Currently the payments on the first are $341/mo. and on the second $200/mo. He plans to raise the rents gradually and hold the property for a later sale or exchange.

His advice in retrospect: try to avoid balloon payments altogether or push them off as far into the future as possible. "Look carefully and talk with others you can trust. Luck helps."

ADDENDUM

After completing the transaction on the duplex owned by his friend, Eldon returned to the duplex he had originally targeted. The heirs settled on a price of $60,000 with the property taken subject to the existing 9¼% mortgage and their balance paid out at 10% for 25 years — nothing down. Who said the "Ultimate Paper Out" doesn't work?

COMMENTARY

1. The first lesson to be gained from Eldon's experiences is that it pays to be thorough and cautious at every step of the way: finding the property, analyzing it, negotiating the deal, and preparing the documentation. If he had not sought the opinion of his friend and been alert to additional opportunities, he would not have picked up the extra duplex. A crucial question for an investor to wear on his lips wherever he or she goes is: "Do you know of someone who might consider selling his real estate?"

2. The second lesson is that it pays to plan ahead — right from the word go. Eldon wrote into the contract a contingency about dealing with the balloon payment in the eventuality that he could not (or would not want to) pay it all off in five years. Furthermore, he tied the interest rate on the second to the prime rate itself. In addition, he set up the ground rules for dealing with the potential acceleration problem and lessening its impact on the investment.

3. The idea of $8,000 sitting in the cash value reserves of an insurance policy when it could be borrowed out at 5% and put to work is incomprehensible given today's economic climate. Eldon did the right thing. Naturally the borrower can choose to wait until death to pay back the principal (automatically deducted from the death benefit).

4. The question of due-on-sale clauses is at the forefront of discussion in many real estate circles these days. Many states have passed legislation restricting the recourse of lenders in situations where borrowers sell or transfer properties that have mortgages or trust deeds with non-assumption (acceleration, due-on-sale) clauses. Still, lenders in many areas have been fairly aggressive in the enforcement of such clauses by requiring the new buyers to qualify for the loans and go through a formal assumption process. In such cases, the interest rate on the note is raised, and up front "points" are charged. Buyers should consult with competent legal experts in any such cases. Where due-on-sale problems could present concerns, buyers should look for properties with readily assumable FHA or VA mortgages or mortgages sold by lenders to Fannie Mae (and hence subject to refinance at interest levels that could be well below the market.) Naturally the most flexible of all situations is the one involving free-and-clear properties where the seller himself is willing to serve as the lender. The whole issue of due-on-sale provisions may well have to be resolved eventually by the U. S. Supreme Court.

DOCUMENTATION

[The following illustrative document was completed on the basis of data supplied by the buyer.]

UNIVERSAL EARNEST MONEY RECEIPT
AND OFFER TO PURCHASE

"This is a legally binding contract: if not understood, seek competent advice."

1. Date and Place of Offer: __July 15,__ 19 __81__ ; __Albany__ __Oregon__
   (city) (state)

2. Principals: The undersigned Buyer __Eldon Barnes and Julia Barnes or Assigns__
   agrees to buy and Seller agrees to sell, according to the indicated terms and conditions, the property described as follows:

3. Property: located at __1582-1584 Forest Avenue__ __Albany__ __Oregon__
   (street address) (city) (state)

   with the following legal description: __Lot 18, Davidson's Subdivision, in the City of Albany, Linn__

   __County, Oregon__

   including any of the following items if at present attached to the premises: plumbing, heating, and cooling equipment, including stoker and oil tanks, burners, water heaters, electric light fixtures, bathroom fixtures, roller shades, curtain rods and fixtures, draperies, venetian blinds, window and door screens, towel racks, linoleum and other attached floor coverings,

   including carpeting, attached television antennas, mailboxes, all trees and shrubs, and any other fixtures EXCEPT __None__

   The following personal property shall also be included as part of the purchase: _____
   At the closing of the transaction, the Seller, at his expense, shall provide the Buyer with a Bill Of Sale containing a detailed inventory of the personal property included.

4. Earnest Money Deposit: Agent (or Seller) acknowledges receipt from Buyer of __Two Hundred and 00/100__ dollars $ __200.00__

   in the form of ( ) cash; (X) personal check; ( ) cashier's check; ( ) promissory note at _____% interest per annum due _____ 19 _____; or

   other _____
   as earnest money deposit to secure and apply on this purchase. Upon acceptance of this agreement in writing and delivery of same to Buyer, the earnest money deposit shall be assigned

   to and deposited in the listing Realtor's trust account or _____, to apply on the
   purchase price at the time of closing.

5. Purchase Price: The total purchase price of the property shall be __Sixty-four Thousand and 00/100__ dollars $ __64,000.00__

6. Payment: Purchase price is to be paid by Buyer as follows:

   Aforedescribed earnest money deposit .... $ __$200.00__

   Additional payment due upon acceptance of this offer .... $ __0__

   Additional payment due at closing .... $ __7,800.00__

   Balance to be paid as follows:

   Buyer to execute land sale contract in favor of Seller encompassing the
   following obligations:

   1. Buyer to purchase property subject to an existing first trust deed and
      note in the approximate amount of $37,500, payable approximately $341
      per month, including interest at 9 1/4% per annum and allowances for
      estimated annual insurance escrows.

   2. Buyer to execute promissory note in favor of Seller secured by the land
      sale contract in the amount of $18,500, payable not less than $185 per
      month, including 12% interest per annum, amortized over a period of 30
      years, balance all due and payable 5 years from the date of execution.
      Buyer to retain right to pay this note in part or in full at any time
      without penalty.

   In the event an existing underlying lien holder on the subject property
   should, by reason of this contract, increase the annual rate of interest on
   a remaining underlying balance or charge against Sellers or Purchasers an
   assumption fee or a fee of some other nature, Purchasers agree to assume
   and pay any such interest increase or fee and to hold Sellers harmless
   therefrom. In addition, the interest rate payable on the promissory note

provided for in paragraph 2 above shall be adjusted to eleven percent (11%) per annum, effective on the date of the aforementioned fee or interest increase.

Further, in the event an underlying lien holder should, by reason of this Contract, exercise its rights under a due-on-sale cr acceleration provision contained in an underlying security agreement, Purchasers and Sellers shall each pay one-half (1/2) of any obligation of Sellers arising out of such exercise of said clause. Purchasers shall then have the option of financing through a contract with Sellers the amount so paid by Sellers, with terms to be mutually agreed upon at that time.

The provisions of this paragraph shall be contingent upon Seller's prompt notification to Purchasers that an underlying lien holder has elected to assess a fee or exercise an acceleration provision, and Sellers permitting Purchasers to negotiate with said lien holder on the amounts and terms of such actions. Purchasers may, at any time, assume any underlying obligation owed by Sellers on the subject property.

7. Title: Seller agrees to furnish good and marketable title free of all encumbrances and defects, except mortgage liens and encumbrances as set forth in this agreement, and to make conveyance by Warranty Deed or _____. Seller shall furnish in due course to the Buyer a title insurance policy insuring the Buyer of a good and marketable title in keeping with the terms and conditions of this agreement. Prior to the closing of this transaction, the Seller, upon request, will furnish to the Buyer a preliminary title report made by a title insurance company showing the condition of the title to said property. If the Seller cannot furnish marketable title within thirty days after receipt of the notice to the Buyer containing a written statement of the defects, the earnest money deposit herein receipted shall be refunded to the Buyer and this agreement shall be null and void. The following shall not be deemed encumbrances or defects; building and use restrictions general to the area; utility easements; other easements not inconsistent with Buyer's intended use; zoning or subdivision laws, covenants, conditions, restrictions, or reservations of record; tenancies of record. In the event of sale of other than real property relating to this transaction, Seller will provide evidence of title or right to sell or lease such personal property.

8. Special Representations: Seller warrants and represents to Buyer (1) that the subject property is connected to ( ) public sewer system, ( ) cesspool or septic tank, ( ) sewer system available but not connected, ( ) city water system, ( ) private water system, and that the following special improvements are included in the sale: ( ) sidewalk, ( ) curb and gutter, ( ) special street paving, ( ) special street lighting; (2) that the Seller knows of no material structural defects; (3) that all electrical wiring, heating, cooling, and plumbing systems are free of material defects and will be in good working order at the time the Buyer is entitled to possession; (4) that the Seller has no notice from any government agency of any violation or knowledge of probable violations of the law relating to the subject property; (5) that the Seller has no notice or knowledge of planned or commenced public improvements which may result in special assessments or otherwise directly and materially affect the property; and (6) that the Seller has no notice or knowledge of any liens to be assessed against the property,

EXCEPT _____ None _____.

9. Escrow Instructions: This sale shall be closed on or before August 1, 19 81 by Johnson Title and Escrow or such other closing agent as mutually agreed upon by Buyer and Seller. Buyer and Seller will, immediately on demand, deposit with closing agent all instruments and monies required

to complete the purchase in accordance with the provisions of this agreement. Contract of Sale or Instrument of Conveyance to be made in the name of _____

(to be supplied prior to closing.)

10. Closing Costs and Pro-Ration: Seller agrees to pay for title insurance policy, preliminary title report (if requested), termite inspection as set forth below, real estate commission, cost of preparing and recording any corrective instruments, and one-half of the escrow fees. Buyer agrees to pay for recording fees for mortgages and deeds of conveyance, all costs or expenses in securing new financing or assuming existing financing, and one-half of the escrow fees. Buyer agrees to pay for recording fees for mortgages and deeds of conveyance, all costs or expenses in securing new financing or assuming existing financing, and one-half of the escrow fees. Taxes for the current year, insurance acceptable to the Buyer, rents, interest, mortgage reserves, maintenance fees, and water and other utilities constituting liens, shall be pro-rated as of closing. Renters' security deposits shall accrue to Buyer at closing. Seller to provide Buyer with all current rental or lease agreements prior to closing.

11. Termite Inspection: Seller agrees, at his expense, to provide written certification by a reputable licensed pest control firm that the property is free of termite infestation. In the event termites are found, the Seller shall have the property treated at his expense and provide acceptable certification that treatment has been rendered. If any structural repairs are required by reason of termite damage as established by acceptable certification, Seller agrees to make necessary repairs not to exceed $500. If repairs exceed $500, Buyer shall first have the right to accept the property "as is" with a credit to the Buyer at closing of $500, or the Buyer may terminate this agreement with the earnest money deposit being promptly returned to the Buyer if the Seller does not agree to pay all costs of treatment and repair.

12. Conditions of Sale: The following conditions shall also apply, and shall, if conflicting with the printed portions of this agreement, prevail and control:

None

13. Liability and Maintenance: Seller shall maintain subject property, including landscaping, in good condition until the date of transfer of title or possession by Buyer, whichever occurs first. All risk of loss and destruction of property, and all expenses of insurance, shall be borne by the seller until the date of possession. If the improvements on the property are destroyed or materially damaged prior to closing, then the Buyer shall have the right to declare this agreement null and void, and the earnest money deposit and all other sums paid by Buyer toward the purchase price shall be returned to the Buyer forthwith.

14. Possession: The Buyer shall be entitled to possession of property upon closing or ___ NA _____, 19 _____.

15. Default: In the event the Buyer fails to complete the purchase as herein provided, the earnest money deposit shall be retained by the Seller as the total and entire liquidated damages. In the event the Seller fails to perform any condition of the sale as herein provided, then the Buyer may, at his option, treat the contract as terminated, and all payments made by the Buyer hereunder shall be returned to the Buyer forthwith, provided the Buyer may, at his option, treat this agreement as being in full force and effect with the right to action for specific performance and damages. In the event that either Buyer, Seller, or Agent shall institute suit to enforce any rights hereunder, the prevailing party shall be entitled to court costs and a reasonable attorney's fee.

16. Time Limit of Offer: The Seller shall have until

_____ July 18, _____ 19 __81__ to accept this
             (hour)   (date)

offer by delivering a signed copy hereof to the Buyer. If this offer is not so accepted, it shall lapse and the agent (or Seller) shall refund the earnest money deposit to the Buyer forthwith.

17. General Agreements: (1) Both parties to this purchase reserve their rights to assign and hereby otherwise agree to cooperate in effecting an Internal Revenue Code 1031 exchange or similar tax-related arrangement prior to close of escrow, upon either party's written notice of intention to do so. (2) Upon approval of this offer by the Seller, this agreement shall become a contract between Buyer and Seller and shall inure to the benefit of the heirs, administrators, executors, successors, personal representatives, and assigns of said parties. (3) Time is of the essence and an essential part of this agreement. (4) This contract constitutes the sole and entire agreement between the parties hereto and no modification of this contract shall be binding unless attached hereto and signed by all parties to the contract. No representations, promises, or inducements not included in this contract shall be binding upon any party hereto.

18. Buyer's Statement and Receipt: "I/we hereby agree to purchase the above property in accordance with the terms and conditions above stated and acknowledge receipt of a completed copy of this agreement, which I/we have fully read and understand." Dated __July 15,__ _____ 19 __81__, _____
                                                                                     (hour)

Address ____112 Elmcrest_____ [signature] or Assigns _____ Buyer

_____Albany, Oregon_____ [signature] _____ Buyer

Phone No: Home ___277-1399___ Business ___421-5617___

19. Seller's Statement and Response: "I/we approve and accept the above offer, which I/we have fully read and understand, and agree to the above terms and conditions this day

of _____, 19 _____, _____.
                                                                  (hour)

Address _____ Seller

Phone No: Home _____ Business _____ _____ Seller

20. Commission Agreement: Seller agrees to pay a commission of _____% of the gross sales price to _____ for services in this transaction, and agrees that, in the event of forfeiture of the earnest money deposit by the Buyer, said deposit shall be divided between the Seller's broker and the Seller (one half to each party), the Broker's part not to exceed the amount of the commission.

21. Buyer's Receipt for Signed Offer: The Buyer hereby acknowledges receipt of a copy of the above agreement bearing the Seller's signature in acceptance of this offer.

Dated _____, 19 _____ _____ Buyer

_____ Buyer

COMMENTARY TO DOCUMENTATION

Item 6. In effect, the payments on the carry-back note amounted to "interest only" payments. In addition to the prepayment provision, the buyer should have attempted to secure the right to roll the balloon over for an additional year.

As it turned out, the final contract of sale provided a ceiling of $6,000 per year on prepayment of principal, evidently to protect the seller from adverse tax consequences.

The "due on sale" provisions in the earnest money agreement provide an interesting exercise in one approach to this recurring and challenging problem. The parties to the contract had thought through all of the exigencies and had prepared an action plan for any eventuality. It is interesting that they agreed to a reduction of interest on the carry-back note in the event the mortgagee on the first were to increase his interest rate or impose assumption fees. The final contract of sale contained involved provisions for insuring the property, with policies maintained in the name of the seller but paid by the buyer.

In addition, the final contract contained provisions indemnifying the seller against any liability arising out of the buyer's use of the subject property. The buyer agreed to keep the subject property "free and clear of all other assessments, liens, or encumbrances of every type and nature," a rather broad accommodation that the buyer may live to regret in the event he should wish to make creative use of the equity under his control. The seller also retained first right of refusal should the buyer wish in the future to sell the property.

Reprinted by permission from the *Nothing Down Advisor.*

14

Gems Used To Buy Beautiful New Home In Cashless Deal

Featuring Technique No. 14
''Anything Goes''

In A Nutshell . . .

Type: SFH
Price: $195,000
Source: MLS Book
Means: Refinance
Techniques: No. 14 — Anything Goes
Strategies: Rebate

LOCATING

Perry Brandt of San Diego is a Realtor who specializes in creative sales for builders and developers. A local gemologist approached him to see if he might have a residence for sale in the $175,000 range. Through the MLS book, Perry found a home of the type desired.

SITUATION

The property was part of a group of spacious homes in a planned residential development being offered by the same builder. He was a multi-millionaire who understood the techniques of creative finance and was willing to strike a bargain in order to move his inventory.

NEGOTIATION

Perry asked the developer if he needed a large cash down payment and learned that only the closing costs and commissions needed to be covered. The seller suggested a price of $175,500, with $8,000 down and the balance of the equity on a $69,000 second at 10% for five years (interest only payments). The buyer would assume a $98,500 first put on the property to pay off the construction loan.

With that one option open, Perry asked whether the builder would accept precious gems in lieu of the down payment and carry back. He also asked whether a rebate of $20,000 could be built into the transaction by raising the price correspondingly. The seller assented to both requests.

Since the buyer was a professional gemologist with a collection of gems worth in the neighborhood of 4 or 5 million dollars, there was a wide range to choose from. The offer was therefore structured as follows: Selling price of $195,000, with $59,000 in precious gems as down payment, and the balance in the form of proceeds from a new first of $136,000 at prevailing interest rates.

It was the buyer's intentions to provide gems at their appraised value of $59,000. However, Perry and his client (the seller) were aware of the difference between appraised value and cash value in precious stones. They insisted on a selection of gems with a cash value of $59,000 as certified by an independent gemological appraisal, with a second appraisal at the seller's option and cost. To this the buyer readily agreed — no doubt his expertise in acquiring the gems in the first place would have assured him of at least some leverage going in.

CLOSING

As things turned out, the buyer provided gems with a gemologically certified appraised value of $125,000 to yield a cash value of $59,000 as required by the agreement: $100,000 worth of rubies and emeralds and $25,000 in diamonds. The commissions also came back creatively: 35% of the fees in cash and 65% in gems. Perry received a beautiful 0.81 carat diamond for his troubles.

The buyer executed a new first mortgage against the property in the amount of $136,000 at 18¼% for 15 years, with payments of around $2,200 per month. The sketch summarizes the financing:

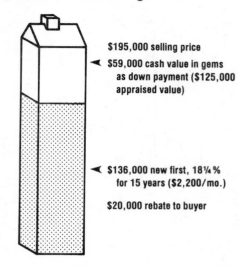

$195,000 selling price

$59,000 cash value in gems as down payment ($125,000 appraised value)

$136,000 new first, 18¼% for 15 years ($2,200/mo.)

$20,000 rebate to buyer

OUTCOMES AND FUTURE PLANS

When the planned residential development sells out — at this writing only one home remains on the market — the value of each of the some two dozen homes will rise to around $225,000 under the influence of new construction in the area. The buyer's paper profit at that point will be $30,000. The payments on his new residence are, of course, rather steep. However, he has a servicing fund of $20,000 from the escrow to use as an offset to the high payments. The bank was accorded full disclosure concerning the rebate and assented in view of the imminent rise in property values in the area.

For his creative sales approach, Perry was not only rewarded with a commission but also the opportunity to handle a group of additional properties for the same developer: 17 condos at present with 60 more coming on line.

Everyone came away from the cashless deal with a smile on his face. The builder sold another home and has a bundle of cash in his pocket (from the proceeds of the refinance) plus a collection of valuable gems — which he intends to keep as an investment. The buyer has a beautiful new home completely furnished with the latest and most popular style of rebate (cash!). The bank has a new qualified first on its books. The Realtor has a commission and a rosy future. And the readers of this book — we hope — are pleased to add another insight to their store of creative techniques.

COMMENTARY

1. In this era of sluggish sales and high interest rates, only the creative Realtors and brokers can survive and flourish. Perry Brandt is one example of an agent who refuses to be discouraged by the state of affairs. If anything, his business is better than ever. Word has got around to builders and developers in his area that he knows how to do things. They like his creativity and mobility (he sometimes distributes 2,000 flyers to local sales offices concerning a single sale). As a result, his level of income is rather satisfying. Even when he has to take commissions in the form of paper, he is not concerned. He knows the future income will be steady and dependable because of it.

2. Is the rebate technique used in this deal inflationary? Some critics of creative finance argue that alternative financing methods are artificially hiking the price of homes in many areas, especially in California. It may be that in some cases uninformed or desperate sellers have agreed to raise their prices considerably beyond the market in order to arrange creative deals for anxious buyers. If that is so, the larger context of supply and demand in the real estate market will bring about an adjustment sooner or later. Something like a cresting of values seems to have taken place in certain markets already. However, with the enormous pent up demand for housing in the United States, such adjustments will no doubt soon be swallowed up in the long-range growth of real estate values generally. Real estate remains the best long-term investment still available to the general public. Creative finance, with its leveraging opportunities, remains the only avenue of access for most buyers.

   In the case study just reviewed, there was no inflationary factor to the rebate because the value of the home was about to rise well beyond the rebate amount anyway. Everyone knew it, including the bank. What would the alternative have been? The buyer could have waited for a short while, got a new appraisal on his home at $225,000, and put on a new second for the rebate amount needed. He was just being creative in anticipating the inevitable and taking advantage of it under professional scrutiny and approval.

3. Why did the buyer not take the seller's first suggestion of $8,000 down, assumption of a $98,500 new first, and the balance of the $175,500 in the form of a second for $69,000 at 10% for five years (interest only)? The payments on the smaller first plus interest on the second would have approximated the payments on the larger first. The cash outflow would have been about the same, and he would have been hampered in resale by the presence of the second. Evidently it seemed cleaner to him to endure the larger payments (sweetened by the rebate) and hope to sell in a year or so with less difficulty. Who knows, he may also not have had the $8,000 down!

UNIVERSAL EARNEST MONEY RECEIPT
AND OFFER TO PURCHASE

"This is a legally binding contract: if not understood, seek competent advice."

1. Date and Place of Offer: _____ June 19, _____ 19 81 ; _____ San Diego _____ California
                                                                        (city)   (state)

2. Principals: The undersigned Buyer _____ R. Stanley Mitchell or Assignee
agrees to buy and Seller agrees to sell, according to the indicated terms and conditions, the property described as follows:

3. Property: located at _____ 48 Cliff Avenue _____ San Diego _____ California
                                        (street address)   (city)   (state)

with the following legal description: _____ to be provided prior to closing.

including any of the following items if at present attached to the premises: plumbing, heating, and cooling equipment, including stoker and oil tanks, burners, water heaters, electric light fixtures, bathroom fixtures, roller shades, curtain rods and fixtures, draperies, venetian blinds, window and door screens, towel racks, linoleum and other attached floor coverings,

including carpeting, attached television antennas, mailboxes, all trees and shrubs, and any other fixtures EXCEPT _____ None

The following personal property shall also be included as part of the purchase: _____
At the closing of the transaction, the Seller, at his expense, shall provide the Buyer with a Bill Of Sale containing a detailed inventory of the personal property included.

4. Earnest Money Deposit: Agent (or Seller) acknowledges receipt from Buyer of _____ One Thousand and 00/100 _____ dollars $ _____ 1,000.00

in the form of ( ) cash; (X) personal check; ( ) cashier's check; ( ) promissory note at _____ % interest per annum due _____ 19 _____ ; or

other _____
as earnest money deposit to secure and apply on this purchase. Upon acceptance of this agreement in writing and delivery of same to Buyer, the earnest money deposit shall be assigned

to and deposited in the listing Realtor's trust account or _____ Deposit to be returned to Buyer at close of escrow.
., to apply on the purchase price at the time of closing.

5. Purchase Price: The total purchase price of the property shall be _____ One Hundred Ninety-five Thousand and 00/100

dollars $ _____ 195,000.00

6. Payment: Purchase price is to be paid by Buyer as follows:

    Aforedescribed earnest money deposit .... $ _____ --

    Additional payment due upon acceptance of this offer .... $ _____ --

    Additional payment due at closing .... $ _____ --

    Balance to be paid as follows:

    1. Buyer to obtain and qualify for a new 30-year conventional loan in
        the amount of $136,000 including 16% interest per annum. Buyer to
        make loan application within 5 days of opening of escrow. Buyer's
        signature on loan documents will indicate his approval of all terms
        of said loan. Down payment of $59,000 will be in the form of $118,000
        worth of precious gems.
    2. From proceeds of loan, Buyer to receive $20,000 cash credit rebate for
        improvements.

7. Title: Seller agrees to furnish good and marketable title free of all encumbrances and defects, except mortgage liens and encumbrances as set forth in this agreement, and to make

conveyance by Warranty Deed or _____ . Seller shall furnish in due course
to the Buyer a title insurance policy insuring the Buyer of a good and marketable title in keeping with the terms and conditions of this agreement. Prior to the closing of this transaction, the Seller, upon request, will furnish to the Buyer a preliminary title report made by a title insurance company showing the condition of the title to said property. If the Seller cannot furnish marketable title within thirty days after receipt of the notice to the Buyer containing a written statement of the defects, the earnest money deposit herein receipted shall be refunded to the Buyer and this agreement shall be null and void. The following shall not be deemed encumbrances or defects; building and use restrictions general to the area; utility easements; other easements not inconsistent with Buyer's intended use; zoning or subdivision laws, covenants, conditions, restrictions, or reservations of record; tenancies of record. In the event of sale of other than real property relating to this transaction, Seller will provide evidence of title or right to sell or lease such personal property.

    Seller to provide Buyer with preliminary title report. Sale subject to
    Buyer's approval of PTR with 5 days of receipt of same.

8. Special Representations: Seller warrants and represents to Buyer (1) that the subject property is connected to ( ) public sewer system, ( ) cesspool or septic tank, ( ) sewer system available but not connected, ( ) city water system, ( ) private water system, and that the following special improvements are included in the sale: ( ) sidewalk, ( ) curb and gutter, ( ) special street paving, ( ) special street lighting; (2) that the Seller knows of no material structural defects; (3) that all electrical wiring, heating, cooling, and plumbing systems are free of material defects and will be in good working order at the time the Buyer is entitled to possession; (4) that the Seller has no notice from any government agency of any violation or knowledge of probable violations of the law relating to the subject property; (5) that the Seller has no notice or knowledge of planned or commenced public improvements which may result in special assessments or otherwise directly and materially affect the property; and (6) that the Seller has no notice or knowledge of any liens to be assessed against the property,

EXCEPT _____ None _____

9. Escrow Instructions: This sale shall be closed on or before __within 30 days of Seller's acceptance__

by __any reliable title company__

or such other closing agent as mutually agreed upon by Buyer and Seller. Buyer and Seller will, immediately on demand, deposit with closing agent all instruments and monies required

to complete the purchase in accordance with the provisions of this agreement. Contract of Sale or Instrument of Conveyance to be made in the name of _____

__to be provided prior to closing.__

10. Closing Costs and Pro-Ration: Seller agrees to pay for title insurance policy, preliminary title report (if requested), termite inspection as set forth below, real estate commission, cost of preparing and recording any corrective instruments, and one-half of the escrow fees. Buyer agrees to pay for recording fees for mortgages and deeds of conveyance, all costs or expenses in securing new financing or assuming existing financing, and one-half of the escrow fees. Buyer agrees to pay for recording fees for mortgages and deeds of conveyance, all costs or expenses in securing new financing or assuming existing financing, and one-half of the escrow fees. Taxes for the current year, insurance acceptable to the Buyer, rents, interest, mortgage reserves, maintenance fees, and water and other utilities constituting liens, shall be pro-rated as of closing. Renters' security deposits shall accrue to Buyer at closing. Seller to provide Buyer with all current rental or lease agreements prior to closing.

11. Termite Inspection: Seller agrees, at his expense, to provide written certification by a reputable licensed pest control firm that the property is free of termite infestation. In the event termites are found, the Seller shall have the property treated at his expense and provide acceptable certification that treatment has been rendered. If any structural repairs are required by reason of termite damage as established by acceptable certification, Seller agrees to make necessary repairs not to exceed $500. If repairs exceed $500, Buyer shall first have the right to accept the property "as is" with a credit to the Buyer at closing of $500, or the Buyer may terminate this agreement with the earnest money deposit being promptly returned to the Buyer if the Seller does not agree to pay all costs of treatment and repair.

12. Conditions of Sale: The following conditions shall also apply, and shall, if conflicting with the printed portions of this agreement, prevail and control:

   1. Seller to warrant the structure sound, all construction completed in a satisfactory manner to Buyer, and plumbing, electrical, heating, and appliances to be in good working order at close of escrow. Buyer to have a walk thru before close of escrow to inspect same.

   2. Seller to repair water damage and replace wet carpeting with new carpeting in downstairs closets and hallway.

   3. Buyer to receive solar tax credit.

   4. Buyer is a California licensed real estate agent.

13. Liability and Maintenance: Seller shall maintain subject property, including landscaping, in good condition until the date of transfer of title or possession by Buyer, whichever occurs first. All risk of loss and destruction of property, and all expenses of insurance, shall be borne by the seller until the date of possession. If the improvements on the property are destroyed or materially damaged prior to closing, then the Buyer shall have the right to declare this agreement null and void, and the earnest money deposit and all other sums paid by Buyer toward the purchase price shall be returned to the Buyer forthwith.

14. Possession: The Buyer shall be entitled to possession of property upon closing or _____ NA _____, 19 _____.

15. Default: In the event the Buyer fails to complete the purchase as herein provided, the earnest money deposit shall be retained by the Seller as the total and entire liquidated damages. In the event the Seller fails to perform any condition of the sale as herein provided, then the Buyer may, at his option, treat the contract as terminated, and all payments made by the Buyer hereunder shall be returned to the Buyer forthwith, provided the Buyer may, at his option, treat this agreement as being in full force and effect with the right to action for specific performance and damages. In the event that either Buyer, Seller, or Agent shall institute suit to enforce any rights hereunder, the prevailing party shall be entitled to court costs and a reasonable attorney's fee.

16. Time Limit of Offer: The Seller shall have until

_____ On presentation _____, 19 _____ to accept this
      (hour)   (date)

offer by delivering a signed copy hereof to the Buyer. If this offer is not so accepted, it shall lapse and the agent (or Seller) shall refund the earnest money deposit to the Buyer forthwith.

17. General Agreements: (1) Both parties to this purchase reserve their rights to assign and hereby otherwise agree to cooperate in effecting an Internal Revenue Code 1031 exchange or similar tax-related arrangement prior to close of escrow, upon either party's written notice of intention to do so. (2) Upon approval of this offer by the Seller, this agreement shall become a contract between Buyer and Seller and shall inure to the benefit of the heirs, administrators, executors, successors, personal representatives, and assigns of said parties. (3) Time is of the essence and an essential part of this agreement. (4) This contract constitutes the sole and entire agreement between the parties hereto and no modification of this contract shall be binding unless attached hereto and signed by all parties to the contract. No representations, promises, or inducements not included in this contract shall be binding upon any party hereto.

18. Buyer's Statement and Receipt: "I/we hereby agree to purchase the above property in accordance with the terms and conditions above stated and acknowledge receipt of a completed copy of this agreement, which I/we have fully read and understand." Dated __June 29,__ 19 __81__, _____
                                               (hour)

Address __76 Pomroy Lane__   __[signature] or Assigns__ _____ Buyer

__San Diego, California__   _____ Buyer

Phone No: Home __365-1212__ Business __461-7892__

19. Seller's Statement and Response: "I/we approve and accept the above offer, which I/we have fully read and understand, and agree to the above terms and conditions this day

of _____, 19 _____, _____.

(hour)

Address _____ _____ Seller

Phone No: Home _____ Business _____ _____ Seller

20. Commission Agreement: Seller agrees to pay a commission of _____% of the gross sales price to ___see below___

for services in this transaction, and agrees that, in the event of forfeiture of the earnest money deposit by the Buyer, said deposit shall be divided between the Seller's broker and the Seller (one half to each party), the Broker's part not to exceed the amount of the commission.

21. Buyer's Receipt for Signed Offer: The Buyer hereby acknowledges receipt of a copy of the above agreement bearing the Seller's signature in acceptance of this offer.

Dated _____, 19 _____ _____ Buyer

_____ Buyer

COMMENTARY TO DOCUMENTATION

The following provisions were conveyed in a counteroffer dated June 30, 1981: (1) Seller to pick independent certified gemologist. Buyer and Seller to agree on selection. Buyer and Seller to split appraisal of such. Appraisal of precious stones to be valued retail at $125,000. $100,000 of retail appraised gems to be in the form of rubies and emeralds. $25,000 worth of retail appraised gems to be in the form of diamonds. Seller to approve of size and quality of gems. (2) Seller to keep solar tax credit. (3) Buyer to be prequalified by lender of choice within 5 working days. Buyer to submit loan application prior to this time. Buyer to obtain new loan at current interest rates. Title escrow with San Diego Title and Escrow Co. Buyer aware of $22 maintenance fee. 2½% to Lane Realty, 35% of 2½% to be in the form of cash, the difference to be in the form of diamonds. 2½% to Morgan Real Estate Company, 35% of 2½% to be in the form of cash. The difference to be in the form of precious gems at retail price. Same ratio as gems down payment.

The following provisions were conveyed in a counter to the counteroffer: Buyer to provide independent impartial gemological certificated gemstones. Seller reserves right for 2nd certificated opinion at his cost.

Seller to have a choice of type of gemstones between ruby, sapphire, emerald, and diamond. Seller to be assured satisfaction and/or compensation in event values on gemstones are different than values placed by 2nd appraisal. All other terms and conditions accepted by Buyer.

Item 2. "Or Assignee" is an alternate version of "or Assigns."

Item 6. The Buyer specified 16% as the interest rate on the new financing, but the seller (a wise bird, no doubt) countered with the phrase "at current interest rates." The buyer lost a contingency but gained a house, even though he had to pay 18¼% when all was said and done.

The cash rebate at closing is a common practice, especially where a need exists to renovate a property or complete the furnishings. In this case, the escrow instructions justified the rebate "to offset lender's high interest rate." Cash-to-buyer transactions are getting more and more frequent, but the real estate and banking industry scrutinize them closely because of occasional abuses on the part of con artists who walk away with cash at closing and leave the unsuspecting seller holding a bag full of mortgages.

Reprinted by permission from the *Nothing Down Advisor.*

"Henry, I hope you didn't accept anything but cash
from that flakey Nothing Down buyer."

15

Creative Finance: Putting The Pieces Together In Better Ways

**Featuring Technique No. 15
"The Creation of Paper"**

In A Nutshell . . .

Type: SFH
Price: $56,000
Source: Realtor
Means: Subject to, carry back
Techniques: No. 6 — Balloon
No. 15 — Creation of Paper
No. 19 — Borrowing Realtor's Commission
No. 24 — Small Amounts from Banks
No. 32 — Second Mortgage Crank
No. 36 — Moving the Mortgage
Strategies: Create fund to service negatives

Ted Welch of Sacramento dabbles in creative real estate investing when he is not busy with his full-time job in government service. As the following case study shows, he has a penchant for seeing how to regroup the various elements of a transaction in order to solve problems creatively.

LOCATING

With the help of a Realtor, Ted located a 3-bedroom, 2-bath single family home in a pleasant tract development that seemed to reflect acceptable pride of ownership. Schools and shopping were nearby, and the area seemed promising from the standpoint of long-term growth and appreciation.

SITUATION

The owner had rented the SFH with an option to purchase. However, the tenant failed to exercise the option when the time came, so the owner generously allowed him to stay and use up the option fund as rent. That was clearly a mistake, as the tenant permitted the home to fall into disrepair. The neighbors then petitioned the owner to take action aimed at evicting the tenant and restoring the property to its former state.

Encumbrances included a long-term first of $28,200 and a $7,700 second due in seven months.

NEGOTIATION

Ted knew from the Realtor why the seller was anxious to dispose of the property. Still, when he asked the question of the seller directly, the verbal response was evasive, although the facial expression confirmed the truth.

Since he saw that he could not induce the seller to open up fully, Ted proceeded on the basis of what he knew with certainty, i.e., his own need to get in with nothing down and not be strapped with a severe negative cash flow problem. He, therefore, offered to give the seller his asking price of $56,000, taking title

subject to the existing first and second, if the seller would be willing to carry back a portion of his equity on a note secured by another property in Ted's portfolio. Since the Realtor was willing to take paper for $2,500 of the commissions, Ted structured the transaction so that he needed to come up with only $6,000 cash down. In so doing, he was violating his own nothing down principles — at least until he could play the ace up his sleeve.

The carry back amount was $11,600, precisely how much equity Ted had in a duplex he owned elsewhere in town. By creating paper against this duplex and applying it to the purchase of the single family home, Ted was able to leverage the duplex fully and prepare the way to crank his way out of cash obligations he was picking up with the latest property.

Looking at it another way, Ted was covering $11,600 of the seller's equity by creating a note for this amount in favor of the seller, then moving the mortgage from the subject property (where it would have been in third position) to another property acceptable to the seller (where it was in second position). That left the Realtor in third position on the single family home holding a note for $2,500 for eight months, with interest of 10%. The second on Ted's duplex yielded 14% interest, no payments for 12 months, thereafter interest only with a balloon after four more years.

CLOSING

Ted came up with the $6,000 cash down payment through a credit union loan. The closing, which was handled by a title company, went without a hitch. The sketch shows the financing to that point, including the results of an appraisal that Ted ordered:

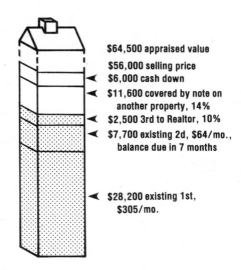

$64,500 appraised value

$56,000 selling price

$6,000 cash down

$11,600 covered by note on another property, 14%

$2,500 3rd to Realtor, 10%

$7,700 existing 2d, $64/mo., balance due in 7 months

$28,200 existing 1st, $305/mo.

OUTCOMES AND FUTURE PLANS

After closing, Ted surveyed his situation. He had just put down $6,000 in cash and was now staring two short-term balloons in the face — one for $7,700 due in seven months and another for $2,500 due one month after that. $16,200 in cash outlays don't add up to nothing down.

He therefore played his ace by going into the second-mortgage market and putting a new hard money second on the property in the amount of $23,000. With this amount, he paid off the $6,000 loan at the credit union and retired the two short-term balloons, leaving a fund of $6,800 to handle the negative cash flow of $255 per month. Meanwhile, the second he had put on his duplex required no payments for the first 12 months and only interest payments thereafter. The alligator had been caged, at least for the time being.

Looking back on this second mortgage crank transaction, Ted feels that he should have allowed only 12% interest on the $11,600 carry back, rather than 14%. Other than that, he is happy with the way things turned out. A little paint put the house in order and made the neighbors accepting once again.

COMMENTARY

1. Investors soon develop their own inventory of useful contract clauses. In Ted's case, two clauses of particular importance are those dealing with delayed payments and substitution of collateral. The 12-month breather before the beginning of debt service on the duplex second was a significant strategy in dealing with the negative cash flow. Moreover, not only did Ted induce the seller to substitute collateral on the single family home, he also insisted on having the same flexibility with the duplex second itself. If Ted should need to definance the duplex in the future (relieve it of part or all of its liens) — for whatever reason — he has the seller's written agreement to proceed, at least as far as the second is concerned, and as long as the new collateral is acceptable.

2. This case study was a little complicated with regard to the financing; however, the buyer at any moment knew exactly what he wanted and proceeded accordingly. This singleness of purpose is one of the principle characteristics that distinguish the creative investor from the ordinary man on the street. Ted knew that he was going to achieve a nothing down deal without succumbing to the ravages of negative cash flows and short-term balloons — and that is what he accomplished.

3. What makes the creative mind tick the way it does? The ordinary person would look at this transaction somewhat in this way: here is a 3/2 tract home with encumbrances of $35,900 and equity of $21,100. "If I want to buy this house," Mr. Ordinary says, "I'll have to put down $21,100 in cash now and then pay off the second in seven months by handing over another $7,700. That's a total outlay of $28,800, and all I've got is a modest little house that needs a paint job. Doesn't interest me all that much."

By contrast, the creative buyer begins to put the pieces of the puzzle together in different ways — ways the ordinary person somehow cannot even conceive of. The creative buyer says, "All right, I can create paper against my duplex in the amount of $11,600 — the minimum I will want the seller to carry back. That leaves $9,500 in equity to take care of. If the Realtor will carry back paper for $2,500 of the commission, I can get by for the time being with only $6,000 cash down. But wait, there is a $7,700 balloon coming up in seven months. This, together with the $2,500 balloon due the Realtor the month after that and the $6,000 note to the credit union, comes to $16,200 in immediate or imminent cash outlays. I don't like that, so I am going to relieve the pressure with a new longer-term hard money second.

"Ordinarily the carry back would have been secured against the subject property, meaning that the lender would be frightened off with all the encumbrances above the first. However, in this case I have been shrewd — the carry back is secured against my duplex, and I will have no trouble cranking out at least enough to pay off the credit union and the two short-fuse balloons ($16,200). But wait, why not crank out as much as the lender will allow? If the property appraised for $64,500, there is probably an upper limit of 80%, or $51,600, for secondary financing. That still leaves $23,400 leeway above the first of $28,200. Let's see if the lender will give me $23,000, enough to pay my obligations and still have sufficient to cover the negatives for a period of 26 months."

Somehow the creative mind is able to dissect and reassemble all the pieces in combinations that add up to maximum benefits. Is the secret tied into a certain innate ability with which a select few are endowed? Not really. The key is attitude — a willingness to look at old problems in new and productive ways.

4. What made this transaction especially attractive was its wholesale character. The selling price was discounted $8,500 (over 13% off the actual value). Since the first of $28,200 represented around a 50%

encumbrance (a little higher perhaps than in the typical second mortgage crank), the discount was an essential feature in assuring the success of the crank in this case. Ted had to steer a tight course, but it all came together.

DOCUMENTATION

UNIVERSAL EARNEST MONEY RECEIPT AND OFFER TO PURCHASE

"This is a legally binding contract: if not understood, seek competent advice."

1. Date and Place of Offer: ___May 27,___ 19_81_ ; ___Sacramento___ ___California___
                                                             (city)   (state)

2. Principals: The undersigned Buyer ___Ted Welch___
agrees to buy and Seller agrees to sell, according to the indicated terms and conditions, the property described as follows:

3. Property: located at ___529 Benton Avenue___ ___Sacramento___ ___California___
                  (street address)   (city)   (state)

with the following legal description: ___to be supplied prior to closing.___

including any of the following items if at present attached to the premises: plumbing, heating, and cooling equipment, including stoker and oil tanks, burners, water heaters, electric light fixtures, bathroom fixtures, roller shades, curtain rods and fixtures, draperies, venetian blinds, window and door screens, towel racks, linoleum and other attached floor coverings,

including carpeting, attached television antennas, mailboxes, all trees and shrubs, and any other fixtures EXCEPT ___None___

The following personal property shall also be included as part of the purchase: ___kitchen range___

At the closing of the transaction, the Seller, at his expense, shall provide the Buyer with a Bill Of Sale containing a detailed inventory of the personal property included.

4. Earnest Money Deposit: Agent (or Seller) acknowledges receipt from Buyer of ___One Hundred and 00/100___ dollars $ ___100.00___

in the form of ( ) cash; (X) personal check; ( ) cashier's check; ( ) promissory note at ___% interest per annum due ___ 19___ ; or

other ___

as earnest money deposit to secure and apply on this purchase. Upon acceptance of this agreement in writing and delivery of same to Buyer, the earnest money deposit shall be assigned

to and deposited in the listing Realtor's trust account or ___, to apply on the purchase price at the time of closing.

5. Purchase Price: The total purchase price of the property shall be ___Fifty-six Thousand and 00/100___ dollars $ ___56,000.00___

6. Payment: Purchase price is to be paid by Buyer as follows:

Aforedescribed earnest money deposit .... $ ___100.00___

Additional payment due upon acceptance of this offer .... $ ___--___

Additional payment due at closing .... $ ___5,900.00___

Balance to be paid as follows:

1. Buyer to take title subject to existing first note and deed of trust in approximate amount of $28,200 payable at $305 per month.

2. Buyer to take title subject to 2nd note in amount of $7,700 payable at $64 per month due October, 1981.

3. Buyer to create a 2nd note secured by deed of trust on Buyer's property located at 980 Hillcrest Lane, Rancho Cordova, in amount of $11,600 payable at 14% compounded annually, payments to begin 12 months after close of escrow and to be interest only monthly, all due in 48 months. Note to contain an assumption clause and not due-on-sale clause.

4. Buyer to create a third note in favor of Elexis Stewart in the amount of $2,500 payable November 15, 1981, bearing interest at 10% annually simple, payment secured by 529 Benton Avenue, Sacramento.

5. Buyer's created note on duplex at 980 Hillcrest Lane to contain substitution of collateral clause with Seller's approval of collateral.

6. Buyer to obtain fire insurance on duplex sufficient to cover additional

loan and name Seller as 2nd loss payee.

7.   Duplex property subject to Seller's approval.

8.   Seller's impound account to be current and transferred free to Buyer.

7. Title: Seller agrees to furnish good and marketable title free of all encumbrances and defects, except mortgage liens and encumbrances as set forth in this agreement, and to make

conveyance by Warranty Deed or _____. Seller shall furnish in due course to the Buyer a title insurance policy insuring the Buyer of a good and marketable title in keeping with the terms and conditions of this agreement. Prior to the closing of this transaction, the Seller, upon request, will furnish to the Buyer a preliminary title report made by a title insurance company showing the condition of the title to said property. If the Seller cannot furnish marketable title within thirty days after receipt of the notice to the Buyer containing a written statement of the defects, the earnest money deposit herein receipted shall be refunded to the Buyer and this agreement shall be null and void. The following shall not be deemed encumbrances or defects; building and use restrictions general to the area; utility easements; other easements not inconsistent with Buyer's intended use; zoning or subdivision laws, covenants, conditions, restrictions, or reservations of record; tenancies of record. In the event of sale of other than real property relating to this transaction, Seller will provide evidence of title or right to sell or lease such personal property.

8. Special Representations: Seller warrants and represents to Buyer (1) that the subject property is connected to ( ) public sewer system, ( ) cesspool or septic tank, ( ) sewer system available but not connected, ( ) city water system, ( ) private water system, and that the following special improvements are included in the sale: ( ) sidewalk, ( ) curb and gutter, ( ) special street paving, ( ) special street lighting; (2) that the Seller knows of no material structural defects; (3) that all electrical wiring, heating, cooling, and plumbing systems are free of material defects and will be in good working order at the time the Buyer is entitled to possession; (4) that the Seller has no notice from any government agency of any violation or knowledge of probable violations of the law relating to the subject property; (5) that the Seller has no notice or knowledge of planned or commenced public improvements which may result in special assessments or otherwise directly and materially affect the property; and (6) that the Seller has no notice or knowledge of any liens to be assessed against the property,

EXCEPT _____ None

9. Escrow Instructions: This sale shall be closed on or before _____ June 15, _19_ 81 _by_ _____ or such other closing agent as mutually agreed upon by Buyer and Seller. Buyer and Seller will, immediately on demand, deposit with closing agent all instruments and monies required

to complete the purchase in accordance with the provisions of this agreement. Contract of Sale or Instrument of Conveyance to be made in the name of _____

10. Closing Costs and Pro-Ration: Seller agrees to pay for title insurance policy, preliminary title report (if requested), termite inspection as set forth below, real estate commission, cost of preparing and recording any corrective instruments, and one-half of the escrow fees. Buyer agrees to pay for recording fees for mortgages and deeds of conveyance, all costs or expenses in securing new financing or assuming existing financing, and one-half of the escrow fees. Buyer agrees to pay for recording fees for mortgages and deeds of conveyance, all costs or expenses in securing new financing or assuming existing financing, and one-half of the escrow fees. Taxes for the current year, insurance acceptable to the Buyer, rents, interest, mortgage reserves, maintenance fees, and water and other utilities constituting liens, shall be pro-rated as of closing. Renters' security deposits shall accrue to Buyer at closing. Seller to provide Buyer with all current rental or lease agreements prior to closing.

11. Termite Inspection: Seller agrees, at his expense, to provide written certification by a reputable licensed pest control firm that the property is free of termite infestation. In the event termites are found, the Seller shall have the property treated at his expense and provide acceptable certification that treatment has been rendered. If any structural repairs are required by reason of termite damage as established by acceptable certification, Seller agrees to make necessary repairs not to exceed $500. If repairs exceed $500, Buyer shall first have the right to accept the property "as is" with a credit to the Buyer at closing of $500, or the Buyer may terminate this agreement with the earnest money deposit being promptly returned to the Buyer if the Seller does not agree to pay all costs of treatment and repair.

Property purchased "as is" but with Buyer's approval on inspection report.

12. Conditions of Sale: The following conditions shall also apply, and shall, if conflicting with the printed portions of this agreement, prevail and control:

None

13. Liability and Maintenance: Seller shall maintain subject property, including landscaping, in good condition until the date of transfer of title or possession by Buyer, whichever occurs first. All risk of loss and destruction of property, and all expenses of insurance, shall be borne by the seller until the date of possession. If the improvements on the property are destroyed or materially damaged prior to closing, then the Buyer shall have the right to declare this agreement null and void, and the earnest money deposit and all other sums paid by Buyer toward the purchase price shall be returned to the Buyer forthwith.

14. Possession: The Buyer shall be entitled to possession of property upon closing or _____ Upon recordation of deed _____, 19 ____.

15. Default: In the event the Buyer fails to complete the purchase as herein provided, the earnest money deposit shall be retained by the Seller as the total and entire liquidated damages. In the event the Seller fails to perform any condition of the sale as herein provided, then the Buyer may, at his option, treat the contract as terminated, and all payments made by the Buyer hereunder shall be returned to the Buyer forthwith, provided the Buyer may, at his option, treat this agreement as being in full force and effect with the right to action for specific performance and damages. In the event that either Buyer, Seller, or Agent shall institute suit to enforce any rights hereunder, the prevailing party shall be entitled to court costs and a reasonable attorney's fee.

16. Time Limit of Offer: The Seller shall have until

_____, 19 _____ to accept this
      (hour)   (date)

offer by delivering a signed copy hereof to the Buyer. If this offer is not so accepted, it shall lapse and the agent (or Seller) shall refund the earnest money deposit to the Buyer forthwith.

17. General Agreements: (1) Both parties to this purchase reserve their rights to assign and hereby otherwise agree to cooperate in effecting an Internal Revenue Code 1031 exchange or similar tax-related arrangement prior to close of escrow, upon either party's written notice of intention to do so. (2) Upon approval of this offer by the Seller, this agreement shall become a contract between Buyer and Seller and shall inure to the benefit of the heirs, administrators, executors, successors, personal representatives, and assigns of said parties. (3) Time is of the essence and an essential part of this agreement. (4) This contract constitutes the sole and entire agreement between the parties hereto and no modification of this contract shall be binding unless attached hereto and signed by all parties to the contract. No representations, promises, or inducements not included in this contract shall be binding upon any party hereto.

18. Buyer's Statement and Receipt: "I/we hereby agree to purchase the above property in accordance with the terms and conditions above stated and acknowledge receipt of a

completed copy of this agreement, which I/we have fully read and understand." Dated _____ June 2, _____ 19_ 81 _____, _____
                                                                               (hour)

Address _____ 1529 Wenstaff Avenue _____   [signature] _____ Buyer

                Sacramento, California _____   _____ Buyer

Phone No: Home _____ 266-2193 _____ Business _____ 255-1207

19. Seller's Statement and Response: "I/we approve and accept the above offer, which I/we have fully read and understand, and agree to the above terms and conditions this day

of _____ , 19 _____ , _____ .

(hour)

Address _____ _____ Seller

Phone No: Home _____ Business _____ _____ Seller

20. Commission Agreement: Seller agrees to pay a commission of _____% of the gross sales price to _____

for services in this transaction, and agrees that, in the event of forfeiture of the earnest money deposit by the Buyer, said deposit shall be divided between the Seller's broker and the Seller (one half to each party), the Broker's part not to exceed the amount of the commission.

21. Buyer's Receipt for Signed Offer: The Buyer hereby acknowledges receipt of a copy of the above agreement bearing the Seller's signature in acceptance of this offer.

Dated _____ , 19 _____ _____ Buyer

_____ Buyer

COMMENTARY TO DOCUMENTATION

Item 2. The words "or Assigns" should appear after the buyer's name.

Item 6. The amounts given for each ingredient of the financing varied somewhat in the final analysis, but the recipe yielded a cake that everyone could have and eat as well.

The balloon on the moved mortgage should have had a rollover provision, particularly since the fuse was a bit on the short side (4 years). It would have been useful, also, to obtain a prepayment provision for this note, as well as first right of refusal.

Item 15. The original offer contained this option: "By initialing this provision Purchaser_____ and Seller_____: agree that in the event Purchaser defaults in the performance of this agreement, Seller shall retain said deposit, or three percent (3%) of the purchase price, whichever is the lesser, as liquidated damages for such default. The remainder of the deposit, if any, shall be refunded to Purchaser." Since this option was not exercised by the buyer, the seller was left with a much broader recourse in the event of default. It would have been wise for the buyer to go after the liquidated damages clause (such as in our Universal Earnest Money Receipt) and strike the provision for the 3% alternative.

Item 16. Buyer did not indicate any time limit for seller's approval, a rather risky practice.

Item 20. No commission entry is called for because the buyer has agreed to cover the commission via a note.

Reprinted by permission from the *Nothing Down Advisor*.

". . . Well, the interest rate is acceptable, but this unsecured balloon note
for my equity, all due and payable in the year 2029,
does give me a slight bit of concern . . . "

Creative Mortgaging: A Very ''Moving'' Experience

Featuring Technique No. 15
''The Creation of Paper''

In A Nutshell. . .

Type: SFH
Price: $42,500
Source: MLS Book
Means: Purchase Money Second Mortgage
Techniques: No. 6 — Balloon
No. 15 — Creation of Paper
No. 36 — Moving the Mortgage
No. 44 — Cash/Equity Combo
Strategies: No payments on second
Features: Leads into Second Mortgage Crank, Positive Cash Flow

LOCATING

An earlier case study featured Troy Bigler's success in achieving an ''Ultimate Paper Out'' on a ''cream puff'' single family home in West Palm Beach, Florida. The following case study shows Troy back at work again, this time putting together a deal involving the moving of a mortgage. The source of this additional SFH was the MLS Book.

SITUATION

The brand new free and clear home had been listed for a full year at $46,000 without any takers. The seller had not been willing to face the truth that his price was just too high. It was Troy's job to open the man's eyes.

NEGOTIATION

His strategy was simple — just make the offer. Selling price was to be $42,500, with $20,000 down (proceeds from a new first on the property) and the balance of $22,500 in the form of a second created against another home (10% interest, one lump sum payment in seven years). During the course of the negotiations, the arrangement was shifted so that the $20,000 cash down payment was to originate in a second mortgage against a partner's home, leaving the subject property free and clear as at first. The whole negotiation process was facilitated by the Realtor, a creative person who happened to be a member of the R.A.N.D. Group in Troy's area.

CLOSING

Papers were drawn up by Troy's attorney. The closing, handled by a title company, was without complication. The following sketch shows the financing arrangement, involving three properties:

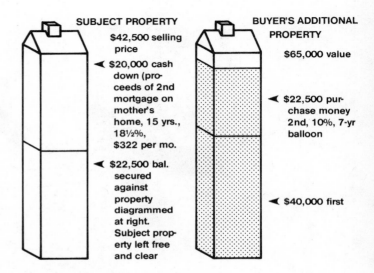

SUBJECT PROPERTY
$42,500 selling price
◄ $20,000 cash down (proceeds of 2nd mortgage on mother's home, 15 yrs., 18½%, $322 per mo.
◄ $22,500 bal. secured against property diagrammed at right. Subject property left free and clear

BUYER'S ADDITIONAL PROPERTY
$65,000 value
◄ $22,500 purchase money 2nd, 10%, 7-yr balloon
◄ $40,000 first

OUTCOMES AND FUTURE PLANS

Rental income on the new property is $465 per month, leaving a modest positive cash flow after the usual expenses plus debt service on the $20,000 second. The cash flow situation was possible only because of the willingness of the seller to accept a no-payment second for seven years for the balance of his equity. Troy wisely insisted on a rollover provision allowing him to extend the balloon for an additional year with the payment of an extra fee of $500.

By setting things up to leave the subject property free and clear, Troy has set the stage to ''crank'' funds out of his new rental home through future mortgage arrangements. Alternately, he can create paper against the property or trade it when that ''big one'' comes along.

COMMENTARY

1. Though young, this investor has already mastered the art of moving mortgages to achieve maximum benefits from creative finance. Even if the immediate transaction does not require moving the mortgage,

the buyer should always try to persuade the seller to accept a substitution of collateral clause as part of the agreement. That way, future needs can be fulfilled without the usually troublesome task of renegotiating the terms.

2. Why did Troy not follow through with his original plan of raising the down payment through the proceeds of a new first mortgage against the property? By policy, hard-money lenders will not loan beyond 80% of the value of the property, including any secondary financing. Troy could have presented his case on the basis of not having any secondary

financing against the property (the down payment was, in effect, a note secured against another property altogether). However, it seemed simpler to raise the needed cash by looking to partnership funding. It would now be an easy matter, depending on Troy's needs, to put on a new first and pay off the partner's second.

3. The arrangements required the seller to pay the first $395 of the buyer's closing costs. Sellers will not customarily accept such a provision, but it never hurts to try. This seller did accept it — without even flinching.

DOCUMENTATION (INITIAL OFFER)

UNIVERSAL EARNEST MONEY RECEIPT
AND OFFER TO PURCHASE

"This is a legally binding contract: if not understood, seek competent advice."

1. Date and Place of Offer: September 21, 19 81 ; West Palm Beach Florida
(city) (state)

2. Principals: The undersigned Buyer Troy Bigler and Assigns
agrees to buy and Seller agrees to sell, according to the indicated terms and conditions, the property described as follows:

3. Property: located at 253 Loreley Street West Palm Beach Florida
(street address) (city) (state)

with the following legal description: South Hills Estates, Lots 21 and 22, Block 6

including any of the following items if at present attached to the premises: plumbing, heating, and cooling equipment, including stoker and oil tanks, burners, water heaters, electric light fixtures, bathroom fixtures, roller shades, curtain rods and fixtures, draperies, venetian blinds, window and door screens, towel racks, linoleum and other attached floor coverings,

including carpeting, attached television antennas, mailboxes, all trees and shrubs, and any other fixtures EXCEPT None

The following personal property shall also be included as part of the purchase: range and refrigerator

At the closing of the transaction, the Seller, at his expense, shall provide the Buyer with a Bill Of Sale containing a detailed inventory of the personal property included.

4. Earnest Money Deposit: Agent (or Seller) acknowledges receipt from Buyer of One Hundred and 00/100 dollars $ 100.00

in the form of ( ) cash; (X) personal check; ( ) cashier's check; ( ) promissory note at _____% interest per annum due _____ 19 _____ ; or

other _____
as earnest money deposit to secure and apply on this purchase. Upon acceptance of this agreement in writing and delivery of same to Buyer, the earnest money deposit shall be assigned

to and deposited in the listing Realtor's trust account or _____, to apply on the purchase price at the time of closing.

5. Purchase Price: The total purchase price of the property shall be Forty-two Thousand Five Hundred and 00/100 dollars
$ 42,500.00

6. Payment: Purchase price is to be paid by Buyer as follows:

Aforedescribed earnest money deposit .... $ 100.00

Additional payment due upon acceptance of this offer .... $ --

Additional payment due at closing .... $ 19,900.00

Balance to be paid as follows:

$22,500.00, seller purchase money mortgage 2nd. (See contingent addendum below).

1. Buyer to place new 1st mortgage on property, from which $20,000.00 down payment will originate. Financing subject to Buyer approval.

2. Seller to take PMM 2nd of approximately $22,500.00 plus 10% amortized accumulating, payable in one lump sum in 7 years and 0 months. Should

financing be difficult then, buyer will pay extra $500 plus 10% amortized, to extend an additional 12 months. The requested PMM is to be secured by a $65,000 townhouse in Cherry Lane at 8775 Vista Circle. The townhouse currently has a $25,000 equity with a $40,000 first mortgage, with monthly PITI of $510. Sellers to approve any transfer of 2nd mortgage.

7. Title: Seller agrees to furnish good and marketable title free of all encumbrances and defects, except mortgage liens and encumbrances as set forth in this agreement, and to make conveyance by Warranty Deed or _____. Seller shall furnish in due course to the Buyer a title insurance policy insuring the Buyer of a good and marketable title in keeping with the terms and conditions of this agreement. Prior to the closing of this transaction, the Seller, upon request, will furnish to the Buyer a preliminary title report made by a title insurance company showing the condition of the title to said property. If the Seller cannot furnish marketable title within thirty days after receipt of the notice to the Buyer containing a written statement of the defects, the earnest money deposit herein receipted shall be refunded to the Buyer and this agreement shall be null and void. The following shall not be deemed encumbrances or defects: building and use restrictions general to the area; utility easements; other easements not inconsistent with Buyer's intended use; zoning or subdivision laws, covenants, conditions, restrictions, or reservations of record; tenancies of record. In the event of sale of other than real property relating to this transaction, Seller will provide evidence of title or right to sell or lease such personal property.

Within 30 days from the date of this contract, the Seller shall, at his expense, deliver to the Buyer or his attorney a Title Guarantee.

8. Special Representations: Seller warrants and represents to Buyer (1) that the subject property is connected to ( ) public sewer system, ( ) cesspool or septic tank, ( ) sewer system available but not connected, ( ) city water system, ( ) private water system, and that the following special improvements are included in the sale: ( ) sidewalk, ( ) curb and gutter, ( ) special street paving, ( ) special street lighting; (2) that the Seller knows of no material structural defects; (3) that all electrical wiring, heating, cooling, and plumbing systems are free of material defects and will be in good working order at the time the Buyer is entitled to possession; (4) that the Seller has no notice from any government agency of any violation or knowledge of probable violations of the law relating to the subject property; (5) that the Seller has no notice or knowledge of planned or commenced public improvements which may result in special assessments or otherwise directly and materially affect the property; and (6) that the Seller has no notice or knowledge of any liens to be assessed against the property,

EXCEPT _____ None _____

9. Escrow Instructions: This sale shall be closed on or before October 23, 19 81 by _____ or such other closing agent as mutually agreed upon by Buyer and Seller. Buyer and Seller will, immediately on demand, deposit with closing agent all instruments and monies required to complete the purchase in accordance with the provisions of this agreement. Contract of Sale or Instrument of Conveyance to be made in the name of _____

to be provided prior to closing.

10. Closing Costs and Pro-Ration: Seller agrees to pay for title insurance policy, preliminary title report (if requested), termite inspection as set forth below, real estate commission, cost of preparing and recording any corrective instruments, and one-half of the escrow fees. Buyer agrees to pay for recording fees for mortgages and deeds of conveyance, all costs or expenses in securing new financing or assuming existing financing, and one-half of the escrow fees. Buyer agrees to pay for recording fees for mortgages and deeds of conveyance, all costs or expenses in securing new financing or assuming existing financing, and one-half of the escrow fees. Taxes for the current year, insurance acceptable to the Buyer, rents, interest, mortgage reserves, maintenance fees, and water and other utilities constituting liens, shall be pro-rated as of closing. Renters' security deposits shall accrue to Buyer at closing. Seller to provide Buyer with all current rental or lease agreements prior to closing.

11. Termite Inspection: Seller agrees, at his expense, to provide written certification by a reputable licensed pest control firm that the property is free of termite infestation. In the event termites are found, the Seller shall have the property treated at his expense and provide acceptable certification that treatment has been rendered. If any structural repairs are required by reason of termite damage as established by acceptable certification, Seller agrees to make necessary repairs not to exceed $500. If repairs exceed $500, Buyer shall first have the right to accept the property "as is" with a credit to the Buyer at closing of $500, or the Buyer may terminate this agreement with the earnest money deposit being promptly returned to the Buyer if the Seller does not agree to pay all costs of treatment and repair.

12. Conditions of Sale: The following conditions shall also apply, and shall, if conflicting with the printed portions of this agreement, prevail and control:

1. Seller to pay for title insurance, brokerage fees, and first $395 of buyer's costs.

2. Buyer to choose title agency for title work paid for by Seller.

3. Seller to provide Buyer with copies of any current title and/or insurance policies on property.

4. Buyer allowed to inspect property or show property to persons of Buyer's choice during interim between Seller acceptance and closing.

5. Seller warrants there are no hidden or undisclosed defects to property. Should the listing agent not yet already have done so, the Seller shall place on the property a one-year home warranty policy available through the selling agent.

13. Liability and Maintenance: Seller shall maintain subject property, including landscaping, in good condition until the date of transfer of title or possession by Buyer, whichever occurs first. All risk of loss and destruction of property, and all expenses of insurance, shall be borne by the seller until the date of possession. If the improvements on the property are destroyed or materially damaged prior to closing, then the Buyer shall have the right to declare this agreement null and void, and the earnest money deposit and all other sums paid by Buyer toward the purchase price shall be returned to the Buyer forthwith.

14. Possession: The Buyer shall be entitled to possession of property upon closing or _____ NA _____, 19 _____.

15. Default: In the event the Buyer fails to complete the purchase as herein provided, the earnest money deposit shall be retained by the Seller as the total and entire liquidated damages. In the event the Seller fails to perform any condition of the sale as herein provided, then the Buyer may, at his option, treat the contract as terminated, and all payments made by the Buyer hereunder shall be returned to the Buyer forthwith, provided the Buyer may, at his option, treat this agreement as being in full force and effect with the right to action for specific performance

and damages. In the event that either Buyer, Seller, or Agent shall institute suit to enforce any rights hereunder, the prevailing party shall be entitled to court costs and a reasonable attorney's fee.

16. Time Limit of Offer: The Seller shall have until

_____ October 22, _____, 19 81 _____ to accept this
(hour)   (date)

offer by delivering a signed copy hereof to the Buyer. If this offer is not so accepted, it shall lapse and the agent (or Seller) shall refund the earnest money deposit to the Buyer forthwith.

17. General Agreements: (1) Both parties to this purchase reserve their rights to assign and hereby otherwise agree to cooperate in effecting an Internal Revenue Code 1031 exchange or similar tax-related arrangement prior to close of escrow, upon either party's written notice of intention to do so. (2) Upon approval of this offer by the Seller, this agreement shall become a contract between Buyer and Seller and shall inure to the benefit of the heirs, administrators, executors, successors, personal representatives, and assigns of said parties. (3) Time is of the essence and an essential part of this agreement. (4) This contract constitutes the sole and entire agreement between the parties hereto and no modification of this contract shall be binding unless attached hereto and signed by all parties to the contract. No representations, promises, or inducements not included in this contract shall be binding upon any party hereto.

18. Buyer's Statement and Receipt: "I/we hereby agree to purchase the above property in accordance with the terms and conditions above stated and acknowledge receipt of a completed copy of this agreement, which I/we have fully read and understand." Dated _____ September 21, _____ 19 81 _____, _____
                                                                                                                                                                          (hour)

Address _____ 4321 Brentwood Circle _____   _____ [signature] and Assigns _____ Buyer
_____ West Palm Beach, Florida _____   _____ Buyer

Phone No: Home _____ 631-1812 _____ Business _____ 661-200 X 35

19. Seller's Statement and Response: "I/we approve and accept the above offer, which I/we have fully read and understand, and agree to the above terms and conditions this day

of _____, 19 _____, _____.
                                                                                        (hour)

Address _____ Seller

Phone No: Home _____ Business _____   _____ Seller

20. Commission Agreement: Seller agrees to pay a commission of _____ 7 _____ % of the gross sales price to _____ Joseph Aldredge Realty _____ for services in this transaction, and agrees that, in the event of forfeiture of the earnest money deposit by the Buyer, said deposit shall be divided between the Seller's broker and the Seller (one half to each party), the Broker's part not to exceed the amount of the commission.

21. Buyer's Receipt for Signed Offer: The Buyer hereby acknowledges receipt of a copy of the above agreement bearing the Seller's signature in acceptance of this offer.

Dated _____, 19 _____   _____ Buyer
                                                                         _____ Buyer

COMMENTARY TO DOCUMENTATION

Note that the ultimate arrangement differed somewhat from that of the initial offer shown above.

Item 2. The wording "and Assigns" permits the buyer to enter into a partnership of his choice. The more flexible wording would be "or Assigns," which permits the buyer to escape the agreement altogether if it were to his advantage to bring someone else in to fulfill the terms of the contract.

Item 6. The rollover provision on the balloon is a smart move. The buyer offered a $500 extra sweetener to gain this clause. It would have been better to offer to pay down the principal by a certain amount — say $1,000 — for the same privilege. At least it is worth a try before adding a bonus on top of the principal amount.

It is interesting that the buyer secured the right to determine which title agency would be making the arrangements. Why would he want to do this? In a recent letter to the author, he explained that he took all his titling work to a specific attorney, who in return provided legal services to the buyer without charge.

The seller, of course, paid for the titling work. Win/win!

As indicated in the case study, a second against a partner's property, rather than the new first against the subject property, was the avenue for raising the down payment.

The addition of the home warranty provision is a good risk-reduction clause. Others that might have been considered for the moved second: a prepayment provision, an assumption provision, and first right of refusal on the note.

Item 15. The wording in the actual offer is akin to the "entire liquidated damages" clause in our "Universal Earnest Money Receipt" form. It stated: "If Buyer fails to perform any of the covenants of this contract, the aforesaid money paid pursuant to this contract by Buyer as aforesaid shall be retained by or for the account of the Seller as consideration for the execution of this contract and as agreed liquidated damages and in full settlement of any claims for damages." This is a strong clause of the type we like to see!

17

How To Exchange Multi-Units — On Your Terms

Featuring Technique No. 16
"The Two-Way Exchange"

In A Nutshell. . .

Type: 12-plex
Price: $280,000
Source: Buyer's ad
Means: Exchange agreement, assumption
Techniques: No. 16 — Two-Way Exchange
No. 19 — Borrowing Realtor's Commission
No. 20 — Rents
No. 21 — Deposits
Features: Even cash flow

LOCATING

George Barker of Milwaukee was in the market for a multi-unit apartment building in the size range 8 to 24 units and price range $200,000 to $375,000. To attract potential sellers, he listed his $175,000 7-plex for trade. He had purchased the 7-plex in 1971 for $73,500. The balance on the 7½% mortgage being $47,000, George's equity was $128,000 as he entered the market.

SITUATION

A local real estate broker took the bait. His client was the out-of-state owner of a brick 12-plex of 2-bedroom units listed at $295,000. The buyer was to assume the underlying first mortgage of $168,000 at 10¾%. At the asking price, the seller's equity was therefore $127,000, very close to George's own equity position in the 7-plex. Rents on the 12-plex were slightly under market.

NEGOTIATION

Knowing that he had plenty of time to look and that the seller of the 12-plex was out-of-state, George entered the negotiation with the attitude: "Hold out when you're in an advantageous position."

His first offer was to trade buildings outright, subject to inspection. However, when his inspection revealed the need for some repairs, he withdrew the offer and replaced it with a second offer of $280,000 (rather than $295,000), his 7-plex remaining at the $175,000 price.

The seller countered with exchange prices at $280,000 and $170,000. Again, George was in no hurry. He was at that time also working on a four-building exchange involving a 36-plex. His response to the counter-offer was therefore to balk. Moreover, the mortgage company had meanwhile specified its assumption terms at 15%, three percentage points higher than the 12% rate George had written into his offer as a contingency. It was clearly a time for waiting.

The broker, who was hungry, quickly came around. He persuaded the seller to commit to specified repairs

to the sewage system and the windows of the 12-plex. In addition, the broker agreed to subsidize the transaction by paying from his commission of $16,800 an amount equal to two interest points on the assumption for the first 36 payments or $10,095! George's condition of a lower interest rate on assumption was therefore met, and since he had negotiated the seller's price on the 12-plex from $295,000 to $280,000, while yielding only $5,000 on his own 7-plex, he was to receive $11,000 cash to equalize the exchange. The sketch shows the details:

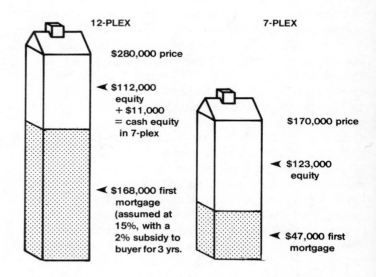

12-PLEX — $280,000 price

$112,000 equity + $11,000 = cash equity in 7-plex

$168,000 first mortgage (assumed at 15%, with a 2% subsidy to buyer for 3 yrs.

7-PLEX — $170,000 price

$123,000 equity

$47,000 first mortgage

CLOSING

The arrangements were made by an attorney, and the processing was accomplished through a title company. The broker's subsidy of $10,095 was listed as "repair credit." George received credits of $3,800 for deposits and $2,000 for rents. After all closing costs, including a 6% commission on the 7-plex, George came away from the closing with $12,756 in cash.

OUTCOMES AND FUTURE PLANS

George immediately raised the rents from $280 to $300 per month on all twelve units. The monthly rental income will cover expenses and debt service (thanks to the broker's subsidy), perhaps even with a small positive cash flow. Gross annual income, including $600 from the laundry facilities, amounts to $43,800. With expenses of $16,004, the net operating income is $27,796. The capitalization rate — for cap enthusiasts — is NOI over Value ($27,796 over $280,000) × 100 or 9.9% in this case.

George plans to invest $5,000 in fix-up, with an anticipated return of $15,000 to $25,000. He will hold the 12-plex for three years and then trade up. Meanwhile, the seller has refinanced the 7-plex for $100,000 at 12½% for 30 years on a shared appreciation mortgage.

In retrospect, George wishes that he had held out for even more benefits on the exchange. His advice to other investors: "It's a buyer's market — hold out for big reductions or move on to another deal."

COMMENTARY

1. George accomplished a shrewd tax-deferred exchange. His gain on the 7-plex would have been $170,000 − $73,500 = $96,500 (less improvements), otherwise a considerable tax liability. Of course, he will have to pay taxes on the $11,000 cash added to the exchange ("boot").

2. The negotiation strategy used — hold out for better terms — worked to George's advantage. Such a strategy has to be balanced with the traditional dictum known to all investors, "You don't steal in slow motion," i.e., good deals won't stay on the market for very long so act fast!

DOCUMENTATION

The offer made by the buyer was not executed on a standard Earnest Money Receipt and Offer To Purchase, but rather on a standard "Offer to Exchange" form. The Offer to Exchange form embodies essentially the same legal representations and provisions contained in the earnest money form, except that the financial aspect involves payment of equities for equities rather than the buyer's cash (or notes) for the seller's equity.

Here are the important excerpts from the actual documentation to show the kind of language used to effect the transaction. Notice how thoroughly and carefully the contingencies are laid out.

FIRST PARTY EXCHANGES THE FOLLOWING PROPERTY.

Subject to approval of the first party's counsel within five days hereof; 210 Acorn Ave., Milwaukee, WI 53209; Assessor's Tax Key #1234; (Legal description to follow as per Title Insurance commitment) being a seven-family apartment residence, with a market value of $170,000-; subject to an existing first mortgage in the amount of $47,000, more or less.

SECOND PARTY EXCHANGES THE FOLLOWING PROPERTY.

Subject to the second party's acquisition of the property at closing from its current owners — Hoyt and Jerrie Mason: 912 Bell St., Milwaukee, WI 53225; Assessor's Tax Key #5678; (Legal description to follow as per Title Insurance commitment) being a twelve-family apartment building, with a market value of $280,000; subject to an existing first mortgage in the amount of $168,000, more or less.

To balance equities the second party or their nominee shall pay the first party $11,000 in cash at closing; said amount, to be increased or decreased in accordance with actual mortgage balances outstanding at time of closing.

THIS AGREEMENT IS SUBJECT TO AND/OR CONTINGENT UPON THE FOLLOWING TERMS AND CONDITIONS.

A) This offer is contingent upon the first party assuming the second party's current first mortgage with Charter Savings and Loan, with payments on the approximate balance of $168,000 to be amortized over 30 years and to include interest not in excess of 12% per annum, together with monthly allowances for estimated annual property tax and insurance escrows.

B) The second party's acceptance is contingent upon the second party securing first mortgage financing on the first party's property in a minimum amount of $100,000, retiring the first party's existing financing, with monthly payments to include interest not in excess of 12¼%, amortizing the principal over 30 years, and allowances for estimated annual property tax and insurance escrows.

C) The first party's offer acknowledges that the second party is a licensed Real Estate Broker in the State of Wisconsin, acting as a conduit to facilitate this and other tax-deferred exchanges in this transaction. The first parties agree that they have inspected 912 Bell St., acknowledge that this offer is a renegotiation of a prior withdrawn offer dated April 2, 1981, and agree that they have not relied on the second party or other agents for representations as to structural or cosmetic repairs that could be required in the future. The first parties offer their property with the covenant to hold harmless the second party or other agents for any such representations.

D) The first party's conveyance of 210 Acorn Ave. and the second party's acquisition of 912 Bell St. shall be by Warranty Deeds. The first party's acquisition of 912 Bell St. shall be via a State of Wisconsin approved form five Warranty Deed.

E) Personal property offered with each building shall be inventoried within seven days of acceptance, and conveyed in good working order as fixtures to the improvements or appurtenances to the land at closing. It is understood that the first party's offering of 210 Acorn Ave. includes seven stoves, seven refrigerators, seven garbage disposals, waste cans and keys provided to the tenants. Each property offering, excludes the property of tenants in possession. The second party's offering of 912 Bell St. is understood to include 11 stoves, 10 working and one damaged refrigerator, 12 existing air conditioners (four of which are reported to be in need of repair), three functional and one malfunctional garbage disposal, the building's present garbage hamper, and miscellaneous interior-common area and exterior-maintenance-equipment supplies.

F) As regards [the earlier representation that no government notices of violations or probable planned improvements had been received]: While no "Notices" have been received, neither party or their agent makes representations or warranty as to "planned public improvements" which may be inacted by the Milwaukee Metropolitan Sewerage District.

This offer does not entail business opportunities and reference to these in the standard printed contract do not apply.

Time is of the essence of this agreement.

The undersigned, first party, has read and fully understands and hereby makes the foregoing offer at Milwaukee, Wisconsin on this 20th day of April, 1981, and acknowledges receipt of a copy of said offer.

[Signatures]

The undersigned, second party, has read and fully understands and hereby accepts the foregoing offer at Milwaukee, Wisconsin on this _____ day of 4/20, 1981, upon the terms and conditions stated and acknowledges receipt of a copy of this agreement.

[Signature]

* [The following amendment to the offer finalized the arrangement:]

AMENDMENT TO OFFER TO EXCHANGE

It is hereby mutually agreed that the contract dated April 20, 1981, between the undersigned for the exchange of real estate at 210 Acorn Ave. and 912 Bell St. be amended to include the below recital and agreements between principals and agents.

Whereas, Charter Savings and Loan has agreed to permit assumption of its outstanding first mortgage balance of approximately $166,528 being secured by the second party's property and having a remaining amortization of about 304 monthly payments, but only at 15% interest per annum, thereafter to be payable at approximately $2,130 per month, together with allowances for 1/12th the estimated annual taxes and insurance premium escrows, NOW THEREFORE, the parties hereby agree to the following:

1)   The Barkers hereby agree to accept said financing provided the agents and/or their nominees (if any) as principals agree to subsidize said interest 2% per annum for the first thirty-six payments, so as to reduce the costs of said interest to an effective rate of 13% per annum during said period.

Said interest subsidy, to be exclusive of principal retirements, shall be conveyed as a capital or cosmetic "repair credit," based on the following schedule:

	At 15%	At 13%	Subsidy Difference
First year's interest:	$24,937	$21,596	$ 3,341
Second year's interest:	$24,836	$21,471	$ 3,365
Third year's interest:	$24,719	$21,330	$ 3,389
Total Subsidy:			$10,095

(The apparent escalation in subsidy difference, being a manifestation of decreased principal retirement.)

Said interest subsidy of $10,095 shall be credited the Barkers in cash at closing, subject to agreement between the agents, other principals or their nominees.

2)   It is understood that there shall be no loan fee due from the Barkers, but that these same shall pay a $205 assumption fee to Charter Savings and Loan. The Barkers, otherwise, accept the attached loan commitment: Exhibit A.

3)   Ben Stuart, as agent for other parties to this transaction and principal-nominee, hereby agrees to accept loan commitment on 210 Acorn Ave. at current market terms and conditions, thus satisfying said loan contingency described in paragraph B of the original contract, via State Savings and Loan Association.

4)   Due to extensive negotiations in this transaction, the close of escrow is hereby continued from the former stated contract date to June 10, 1981.

All other terms of the above mentioned contract shall remain unchanged and in full force and effect as though fully set forth at length herein.

[Signatures]

Reprinted by permission from the *Nothing Down Advisor.*

"One of the zippiest double-escrow settlements we have had in years."

Creative Exchange Involves Four Properties

**Featuring Technique No. 16
"The Two-Way Exchange"**

In A Nutshell. . .

Type: 1 SFH into 3 SFH's
Price: $150,000 into $102,104, $92,000, and $77,600
Source: Exchange broker
Means: Assumptions, 1031 exchange contracts
Techniques: No. 4 — Contract/Wrap
No. 17 — Two-way Exchange
Features: Positive cash flow

Investor Gerald Seibold of Palo Alto, California, had owned a 50-year old two-bedroom, one-bath rental home for several years. The property, now free and clear, had a value of $150,000. Four hours after he put the house on the market it sold to a strong cash buyer for the asking price of $150,000. The proceeds of a new first mortgage of $40,000 at 15% went to the seller, together with a cash down payment of $80,000 and a carry-back second for $30,000 at 12%, interest only for three years. With a cash fund of $120,000 and an agreement by the buyer to cooperate in an exchange arrangement, Gerald entered the market for other SFH's.

LOCATING

Gerald and his wife did extensive research and decided to look for properties in the Fremont/Union City area across the Bay from where they were living. The houses they finally decided upon are in good proximity to the new Dumbarton Bridge scheduled for completion in a year or two. The bridge will greatly improve access to the Stanford/Palo Alto/Silicon Valley area and make the Fremont/Union City location more desirable for employees on the east side of the Bay. The new exchange properties are only a 35 minute drive from the Seibolds' home as it is.

They contacted an exchange broker in Fremont and gave him the parameters for their search. "We were looking for houses at about the median and a little lower. Our experience suggests better returns in this range than those in higher price ranges . . . We decided to look in the Fremont/Union City area because our survey indicated better returns in that area . . . The broker is also an attorney, which was fortunate because on several occasions he had to help the escrow officer clear up some missteps that might have jeopardized our tax-deferred status. Also, we prefer to use a broker local to the area in which we are buying because of his familiarity with that market, proximity to lenders,

escrow people, etc."

With the proceeds of Property A in their pocket, the Seibolds managed to buy three other properties that matched their equity needs. All were located for them by their exchange broker. The details of the transactions follow.

Property B

SITUATION

The first of the exchange properties was an 18-year old three-bedroom, two-bath home listed for $106,000. The owners were about to move to Southern California to accept a new job offer and were therefore anxious to close quickly. The property had a 9¾% first mortgage with a balance of $56,342 and seven years to go.

NEGOTIATION

Seibolds offered $98,000 with a second of $15,000 at 15% after the cash down payment of $26,658, closing to take place in two months. This offer was rejected in favor of the following mutually-agreeable plan: Price of $102,104 with cash down of $45,762, no second carried back, and assumption of the existing first. Closing was set up for 6 weeks later.

CLOSING

The arrangements for this property and the other two homes purchased were handled by the same title company. Everything was accomplished in a simultaneous escrow through which the buyer of Property A (the Seibolds' free and clear house) purchased the three target homes and then traded them to the Seibolds as part of the agreement. The sketch shows the financing for Property B:

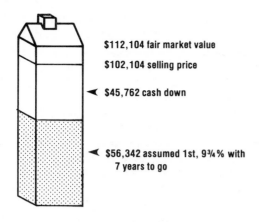

$112,104 fair market value

$102,104 selling price

◄ $45,762 cash down

◄ $56,342 assumed 1st, 9¾% with
7 years to go

OUTCOMES AND FUTURE PLANS

As part of the transaction, the Seibolds had inspections made to check the roof and appliances and test for termites. The upshot was a $3,500 credit for a new roof, a reworked shower area, and $150 towards a new dishwasher. After possession, Gerald cleaned up some "kooky wiring" that the seller had done and moved in a tenant for $625/mo. The after-tax cash flow for the unit is $499 per year positive.

Property C

SITUATION

The second rental property was a 9-year old three-bedroom, 1½ bath home in exceptionally fine condition. The existing first mortgage was at 9¾% assumable, with 20 years to run. It was listed for around $8,000 below market.

NEGOTIATION

"We didn't dicker on this one — it was a cream puff." Seibolds paid $92,000 for the property with $36,623 down and assumption of the first with a balance of $55,377.

CLOSING

Once again, everything was taken care of in a simultaneous escrow using the same title company. The sketch shows the details:

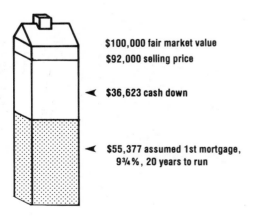

$100,000 fair market value
$92,000 selling price

◄ $36,623 cash down

◄ $55,377 assumed 1st mortgage,
9¾%, 20 years to run

OUTCOMES AND FUTURE PLANS

After shampooing the carpets, the new owners rented the property for $550 per month. The after-tax cash flow is $348 annually.

Property D

SITUATION

The third purchase involved a two-year old three-bedroom, one bath half-plex listed at $80,000. It had a $45,150 first mortgage at 9¾% with 21 years to run.

NEGOTIATION

Gerald first offered $75,000 for the property. The parties finally agreed on $77,600 with $17,450 cash down and a second of $15,000 carried back at 17%, interest only for three years.

CLOSING

Once again, Property D was part of the simultaneous closing involving Seibolds' free and clear house (Property A), plus Properties B and C described above. The financing for the final property is shown in this sketch:

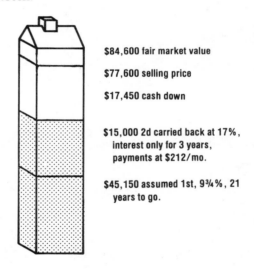

$84,600 fair market value

$77,600 selling price

$17,450 cash down

$15,000 2d carried back at 17%,
interest only for 3 years,
payments at $212/mo.

$45,150 assumed 1st, 9¾%, 21
years to go.

OUTCOMES AND FUTURE PLANS

Gerald summarizes what happened: "The seller agreed to repair some cosmetic fire damage in the kitchen, repaint the entire interior of the house, and deliver the property vacant. In addition, there was an agreement that was to survive closing requiring the seller to pay all of our carrying costs until he could deliver the house vacant and in the stipulated condition. This turned out to be a very important provision because of the timing of the 1031 exchange and the closing date stipulated by the Property B sellers, but also because the Property D seller ended up having to evict his tenants." Since it took several months for the seller to perform on his agreement, he covered the payments on the 1st and 2d and the buyers had no negative cash flow for the interim period.

One week after they took final possession, they rented the house for $499/mo. The after tax cash flow is $1,672 per year negative due to the payments on the second mortgage.

SUMMARY

What the Seibolds accomplished in this somewhat involved transaction was a two-way exchange involving their own property and a package of three other SFH's located by them and purchased as a package by their buyer for exchange in a simultaneous escrow.

The cash proceeds from the sale of Property A were $120,000. The down payments on the three purchases were as follows:

Property B. $45,762
Property C   36,623
Property D   17,450
Total $99,835

After paying commissions and other costs amounting to $7,865, the Seibolds had an excess of $12,300 considered "boot" in the exchange.

Their cash flow situation is shown in this chart:

Property A. . $3,600	(payments on their own carry back)
Property B . . 499	
Property C . . 348	
Property D . . (1,672)	(payments on the 2d mortgage carried back by the seller)
Net cash flow $2,742	(after taxes)

COMMENTARY

1. It is instructive that a set of three houses in the Bay area, one of the most expensive in the United States, can have a positive cash flow. The secret in this case was the fact that the Seibolds concentrated on what amounted to "bread and butter" homes for their area. Naturally, they were in a favorable position with so much equity to convert to cash down payments for the exchange purchases, the result of a judicious buy several years earlier.

2. Since their capital gain for Property A was $119,400 ($150,000 less their basis of $30,600), the 1031 exchange was the most effective way to defer the tax liability and still acquire three different SFH's with all the tax benefits available through the new accelerated depreciation schedules.

3. In each case, the buyers made purchases at below market levels. In fact, the instant equity in Properties B, C, and D amounted to $25,000 ($10,000 plus $8,000 plus $7,000). Not bad for one set of purchases.

4. Another admirable aspect of the exchange is the fact that all three properties involved assumable low-interest mortgages. This was no accident — the Seibolds were smart enough to make this a conscious goal in an era of the variable rate mortgage. When they go to sell, they will be in an excellent position to realize maximum benefits and terms.

5. One wonders why the Seibolds could not arrange for the second on Property D to be no payments (or smaller payments), all due and payable in three years (or preferably longer). That would have improved the positive cash flow situation measurably.

6. Especially significant is the Seibolds' practice of careful analysis of location, structure, and financing. They will be able to sleep well knowing that their three new "automatic pilots" are contributing to their financial security.

DOCUMENTATION—Property A (Sold by the buyers to obtain the 3 SFH's)

UNIVERSAL EARNEST MONEY RECEIPT
AND OFFER TO PURCHASE

"This is a legally binding contract: if not understood, seek competent advice."

1. Date and Place of Offer: __January 18,__ 19 __81__ ; __Palo Alto__ __California__
                                                    (city)   (state)

2. Principals: The undersigned Buyer __June Barlowe__
agrees to buy and Seller agrees to sell, according to the indicated terms and conditions, the property described as follows:

3. Property: located at __17 Benson Drive__ __Palo Alto__ __California__
                                  (street address)   (city)   (state)

with the following legal description: __to be supplied prior to closing.__

including any of the following items if at present attached to the premises: plumbing, heating, and cooling equipment, including stoker and oil tanks, burners, water heaters, electric light fixtures, bathroom fixtures, roller shades, curtain rods and fixtures, draperies, venetian blinds, window and door screens, towel racks, linoleum and other attached floor coverings,

including carpeting, attached television antennas, mailboxes, all trees and shrubs, and any other fixtures EXCEPT __None__

The following personal property shall also be included as part of the purchase: __stove and refrigerator__

At the closing of the transaction, the Seller, at his expense, shall provide the Buyer with a Bill Of Sale containing a detailed inventory of the personal property included.

4. Earnest Money Deposit: Agent (or Seller) acknowledges receipt from Buyer of __One Thousand Five Hundred__ dollars $ __1,500.00__

in the form of ( ) cash; (X) personal check; ( ) cashier's check; ( ) promissory note at _____% interest per annum due _____ 19 _____, or

other _____

as earnest money deposit to secure and apply on this purchase. Upon acceptance of this agreement in writing and delivery of same to Buyer, the earnest money deposit shall be assigned

to and deposited in the listing Realtor's trust account or _____, to apply on the purchase price at the time of closing.

5. Purchase Price: The total purchase price of the property shall be __One Hundred Fifty Thousand and 00/100__ dollars

$ __150,000.00__

6. Payment: Purchase price is to be paid by Buyer as follows:

Aforedescribed earnest money deposit .... $ __1,500.00__

Additional payment due upon acceptance of this offer .... $ __--__

Additional payment due at closing .... $ __78,500.00__

Balance to be paid as follows:

A. Conditioned on the buyer obtaining a conventional loan in the amount of $40,000 or less, secured by the property, with equal monthly payments to be amortized over a period of not less than 30 years, with an interest rate not to exceed 15% per annum. Buyer shall have 15 calendar days to obtain such a loan commitment or waive this condition. Loan fee not to exceed 2% plus $200.

B. Seller to carry back a second deed of trust in the amount of $30,000 at an interest rate not to exceed 12% per annum with interest only payments in the amount of $300 per month. Entire principal due and payable three years from close of escrow.

C. Buyer agrees to increase deposit to 3% of purchase price upon removal of loan contingency.

D. Close of escrow shall not be prior to March 3, 1981.

E. Buyer acknowledges that this is part of a 1031 exchange and agrees to cooperate fully in such exchange with no liability to buyer.

7. Title: Seller agrees to furnish good and marketable title free of all encumbrances and defects, except mortgage liens and encumbrances as set forth in this agreement, and to make

conveyance by Warranty Deed or _____. Seller shall furnish in due course to the Buyer a title insurance policy insuring the Buyer of a good and marketable title in keeping with the terms and conditions of this agreement. Prior to the closing of this transaction, the Seller, upon request, will furnish to the Buyer a preliminary title report made by a title insurance company showing the condition of the title to said property. If the Seller cannot furnish marketable title within thirty days after receipt of the notice to the Buyer containing a written statement of the defects, the earnest money deposit herein receipted shall be refunded to the Buyer and this agreement shall be null and void. The following shall not be deemed encumbrances or defects; building and use restrictions general to the area; utility easements; other easements not inconsistent with Buyer's intended use; zoning or subdivision laws, covenants, conditions, restrictions, or reservations of record; tenancies of record. In the event of sale of other than real property relating to this transaction, Seller will provide evidence of title or right to sell or lease such personal property.

8. Special Representations: Seller warrants and represents to Buyer (1) that the subject property is connected to ( ) public sewer system, ( ) cesspool or septic tank, ( ) sewer system available but not connected, ( ) city water system, ( ) private water system, and that the following special improvements are included in the sale: ( ) sidewalk, ( ) curb and gutter, ( ) special street paving, ( ) special street lighting; (2) that the Seller knows of no material structural defects; (3) that all electrical wiring, heating, cooling, and plumbing systems are free of material defects and will be in good working order at the time the Buyer is entitled to possession; (4) that the Seller has no notice from any government agency of any violation or knowledge of probable violations of the law relating to the subject property; (5) that the Seller has no notice or knowledge of planned or commenced public improvements which may result in special assessments or otherwise directly and materially affect the property; and (6) that the Seller has no notice or knowledge of any liens to be assessed against the property,

EXCEPT __None__

9. Escrow Instructions: This sale shall be closed on or before __45 calendar days from date of acceptance by Seller.__

or such other closing agent as mutually agreed upon by Buyer and Seller. Buyer and Seller will, immediately on demand, deposit with closing agent all instruments and monies required

to complete the purchase in accordance with the provisions of this agreement. Contract of Sale or Instrument of Conveyance to be made in the name of _____

10. Closing Costs and Pro-Ration: Seller agrees to pay for title insurance policy, preliminary title report (if requested), termite inspection as set forth below, real estate commission, cost of preparing and recording any corrective instruments, and one-half of the escrow fees. Buyer agrees to pay for recording fees for mortgages and deeds of conveyance, all costs or expenses in securing new financing or assuming existing financing, and one-half of the escrow fees. Buyer agrees to pay for recording fees for mortgages and deeds of conveyance, all costs or expenses in securing new financing or assuming existing financing, and one-half of the escrow fees. Taxes for the current year, insurance acceptable to the Buyer, rents, interest, mortgage reserves, maintenance fees, and water and other utilities constituting liens, shall be pro-rated as of closing. Renters' security deposits shall accrue to Buyer at closing. Seller to provide Buyer with all current rental or lease agreements prior to closing.

11. Termite Inspection: Seller agrees, at his expense, to provide written certification by a reputable licensed pest control firm that the property is free of termite infestation. In the event

termites are found, the Seller shall have the property treated at his expense and provide acceptable certification that treatment has been rendered. If any structural repairs are required by reason of termite damage as established by acceptable certification, Seller agrees to make necessary repairs not to exceed $500. If repairs exceed $500, Buyer shall first have the right to accept the property "as is" with a credit to the Buyer at closing of $500, or the Buyer may terminate this agreement with the earnest money deposit being promptly returned to the Buyer if the Seller does not agree to pay all costs of treatment and repair.

Buyer to pay for inspection; Seller to pay for any corrective work.

13. Liability and Maintenance: Seller shall maintain subject property, including landscaping, in good condition until the date of transfer of title or possession by Buyer, whichever occurs first. All risk of loss and destruction of property, and all expenses of insurance, shall be borne by the seller until the date of possession. If the improvements on the property are destroyed or materially damaged prior to closing, then the Buyer shall have the right to declare this agreement null and void, and the earnest money deposit and all other sums paid by Buyer toward the purchase price shall be returned to the Buyer forthwith.

14. Possession: The Buyer shall be entitled to possession of property upon closing or _____ NA _____, 19 _____.

15. Default: In the event the Buyer fails to complete the purchase as herein provided, the earnest money deposit shall be retained by the Seller as the total and entire liquidated damages. In the event the Seller fails to perform any condition of the sale as herein provided, then the Buyer may, at his option, treat the contract as terminated, and all payments made by the Buyer hereunder shall be returned to the Buyer forthwith, provided the Buyer may, at his option, treat this agreement as being in full force and effect with the right to action for specific performance and damages. In the event that either Buyer, Seller, or Agent shall institute suit to enforce any rights hereunder, the prevailing party shall be entitled to court costs and a reasonable attorney's fee.

16. Time Limit of Offer: The Seller shall have until

12 hours _____, 19 _____ to accept this
(hour)   (date)

offer by delivering a signed copy hereof to the Buyer. If this offer is not so accepted, it shall lapse and the agent (or Seller) shall refund the earnest money deposit to the Buyer forthwith.

17. General Agreements: (1) Both parties to this purchase reserve their rights to assign and hereby otherwise agree to cooperate in effecting an Internal Revenue Code 1031 exchange or similar tax-related arrangement prior to close of escrow, upon either party's written notice of intention to do so. (2) Upon approval of this offer by the Seller, this agreement shall become a contract between Buyer and Seller and shall inure to the benefit of the heirs, administrators, executors, successors, personal representatives, and assigns of said parties. (3) Time is of the essence and an essential part of this agreement. (4) This contract constitutes the sole and entire agreement between the parties hereto and no modification of this contract shall be binding unless attached hereto and signed by all parties to the contract. No representations, promises, or inducements not included in this contract shall be binding upon any party hereto.

18. Buyer's Statement and Receipt: "I/we hereby agree to purchase the above property in accordance with the terms and conditions above stated and acknowledge receipt of a completed copy of this agreement, which I/we have fully read and understand." Dated _____ January 18, _____ 19 _81_, _____
(hour)

Address _____ 14 Juniper Street _____   [signature] _____ Buyer

_____ Palo Alto, California _____   _____ Buyer

Phone No: Home _____ 719-9915 _____ Business _____ 651-3215 _____

19. Seller's Statement and Response: "I/we approve and accept the above offer, which I/we have fully read and understand, and agree to the above terms and conditions this day of _____, 19 _____, _____.
(hour)

Address _____   _____ Seller

Phone No: Home _____ Business _____   _____ Seller

20. Commission Agreement: Seller agrees to pay a commission of _6_ % of the gross sales price to _____ John Walker Realty _____ for services in this transaction, and agrees that, in the event of forfeiture of the earnest money deposit by the Buyer, said deposit shall be divided between the Seller's broker and the Seller (one half to each party), the Broker's part not to exceed the amount of the commission.

21. Buyer's Receipt for Signed Offer: The Buyer hereby acknowledges receipt of a copy of the above agreement bearing the Seller's signature in acceptance of this offer.

Dated _____, 19 _____   _____ Buyer

_____ Buyer

The following excerpt from the seller's counter offer of January 18, 1981, led to final acceptance:

Seller accepts all of the terms and conditions set forth in the above designated agreement with the following changes or amendments:

Clause A.   Interest will not exceed 15½ % instead of 15%.

Clause B.   Buyer agrees to standard due on sale acceleration clause and standard prepayment clause.

Buyer understands that drapes owned by tenants are not included. Close of escrow shall be within 65 days of date of this contract.

Seller liability under clause 11 Structural Pest Control Agreement is as follows: if estimated cost of repairs exceeds $1,500 then seller may elect to pay estimated cost or elect to give buyer 5 days notice to rescind this contract unless buyer agrees to pay excess over $1,500 within the 5 days' notice. If the contract is rescinded, all deposits will be refunded. Seller and Buyer agree to split the cost of ABC Home Warranty at $230.00.

Seller will use diligence in seeking exchange properties. If properties are not located within 45 days, Seller may rescind the contract unless Buyer extends this period to 75 days and extends escrow to 95 days.

SUPPLEMENT/ADDENDUM

The following excerpt from an addendum to the agreement outlines the exchange procedure:

In furtherance of Paragraph (1) E., wherein Buyer agreed to cooperate with Sellers in carrying out an IRS 1031 exchange, the parties agree as follows:

Seller has located the following three properties for Buyer to acquire and later convey to Sellers in exchange for Seller's Deed of 17 Benson Drive to Buyer:

1) 416 Bridge Avenue, Union City, California
2) 2421 Scott Street, Fremont, California
3) 2900 Bluebird Lane, Union City, California

Buyer hereby agrees to purchase the above properties on the terms shown on the Buyer's closing statements (estimated) in the following escrow accounts at American Title Insurance Co., Fremont, Ca., 21693, 21512, and 21651, respectively. In furtherance of Buyer's agreement, Sellers hereby assign to Buyer Seller's rights to acquire the above properties pursuant to relevant Deposit Receipts; and Buyer hereby accepts such assignment of rights.

Buyer agrees to convey title to the above three properties as called for in the relevant escrows, to Sellers simultaneously with Sellers' conveyance to Buyer of 17 Benson Drive, through an exchange, as shown by the estimated closing statements in American Title escrow 21563.

Except as specifically supplemented and amended hereby, the Real Estate Contract shall continue in full force and effect.

COMMENTARY TO DOCUMENTATION — Property A

Counteroffer: Seller was wise to limit his liability to $1,500 in regard to termite damage. His experience also shows up in his requirement that the carry back note contain a due-on-sale clause and a standard prepayment clause. Similarly, the added contingency for extending the time to locate the exchange properties reflects the hand of an experienced investor.

DOCUMENTATION—Property B (INITIAL OFFER)

UNIVERSAL EARNEST MONEY RECEIPT AND OFFER TO PURCHASE

"This is a legally binding contract: if not understood, seek competent advice."

1. Date and Place of Offer: __January 29,__ 19__81__ ; __Fremont__ (city) __California__ (state)

2. Principals: The undersigned Buyer __Gerald Seibold and Evelyn Seibold__
agrees to buy and Seller agrees to sell, according to the indicated terms and conditions, the property described as follows:

3. Property: located at __242 Scott Street__ (street address) __Fremont__ (city) __California__ (state)
with the following legal description: __to be supplied prior to closing.__

including any of the following items if at present attached to the premises: plumbing, heating, and cooling equipment, including stoker and oil tanks, burners, water heaters, electric light fixtures, bathroom fixtures, roller shades, curtain rods and fixtures, draperies, venetian blinds, window and door screens, towel racks, linoleum and other attached floor coverings,

including carpeting, attached television antennas, mailboxes, all trees and shrubs, and any other fixtures EXCEPT __None__

The following personal property shall also be included as part of the purchase: ____
At the closing of the transaction, the Seller, at his expense, shall provide the Buyer with a Bill Of Sale containing a detailed inventory of the personal property included.

4. Earnest Money Deposit: Agent (or Seller) acknowledges receipt from Buyer of __Five Hundred and 00/100__ dollars $ __500.00__

in the form of ( ) cash; (X) personal check; ( ) cashier's check; ( ) promissory note at ____% interest per annum due ____ 19____; or

other ____
as earnest money deposit to secure and apply on this purchase. Upon acceptance of this agreement in writing and delivery of same to Buyer, the earnest money deposit shall be assigned

to and deposited in the listing Realtor's trust account or ____, to apply on the
purchase price at the time of closing.

5. Purchase Price: The total purchase price of the property shall be __Ninety-eight Thousand and 00/100__ dollars $ __98,000.00__

6. Payment: Purchase price is to be paid by Buyer as follows:

Aforedescribed earnest money deposit .... $ __500.00__

Additional payment due upon acceptance of this offer .... $ __--__

Additional payment due at closing .... $ __26,158.00__

Balance to be paid as follows:
__Buyer to purchase subject to a First Trust Deed and Note of record in__
__the approximate amount of $56,342 payable approximately $490 per month,__
__including interest at 9.75% per annum. Loan documents subject to Buyer's__
__approval. Buyer to be assured that it can be taken over without change__
__in terms.__
__Seller's Purchase Money carryback: Balance of purchase price to be__
__evidenced by a note secured by a trust deed in the approximate amount of__
__$15,000 executed by the Buyer in favor of Seller. Said note to include__
__interest installments of $115 or more per month, beginning one month after__

the close of escrow to be all due and payable in three years from close of escrow.

7. Title: Seller agrees to furnish good and marketable title free of all encumbrances and defects, except mortgage liens and encumbrances as set forth in this agreement, and to make conveyance by Warranty Deed or _____. Seller shall furnish in due course to the Buyer a title insurance policy insuring the Buyer of a good and marketable title in keeping with the terms and conditions of this agreement. Prior to the closing of this transaction, the Seller, upon request, will furnish to the Buyer a preliminary title report made by a title insurance company showing the condition of the title to said property. If the Seller cannot furnish marketable title within thirty days after receipt of the notice to the Buyer containing a written statement of the defects, the earnest money deposit herein receipted shall be refunded to the Buyer and this agreement shall be null and void. The following shall not be deemed encumbrances or defects; building and use restrictions general to the area; utility easements; other easements not inconsistent with Buyer's intended use; zoning or subdivision laws, covenants, conditions, restrictions, or reservations of record; tenancies of record. In the event of sale of other than real property relating to this transaction, Seller will provide evidence of title or right to sell or lease such personal property.

8. Special Representations: Seller warrants and represents to Buyer (1) that the subject property is connected to ( ) public sewer system, ( ) cesspool or septic tank, ( ) sewer system available but not connected, ( ) city water system, ( ) private water system, and that the following special improvements are included in the sale: ( ) sidewalk, ( ) curb and gutter, ( ) special street paving, ( ) special street lighting; (2) that the Seller knows of no material structural defects; (3) that all electrical wiring, heating, cooling, and plumbing systems are free of material defects and will be in good working order at the time the Buyer is entitled to possession; (4) that the Seller has no notice from any government agency of any violation or knowledge of probable violations of the law relating to the subject property; (5) that the Seller has no notice or knowledge of planned or commenced public improvements which may result in special assessments or otherwise directly and materially affect the property; and (6) that the Seller has no notice or knowledge of any liens to be assessed against the property,

EXCEPT _____ None

9. Escrow Instructions: This sale shall be closed on or before _____ 19____ by American Escrow
or such other closing agent as mutually agreed upon by Buyer and Seller. Buyer and Seller will, immediately on demand, deposit with closing agent all instruments and monies required

to complete the purchase in accordance with the provisions of this agreement. Contract of Sale or Instrument of Conveyance to be made in the name of _____
_____ to be supplied later. See under 12 below.

10. Closing Costs and Pro-Ration: Seller agrees to pay for title insurance policy, preliminary title report (if requested), termite inspection as set forth below, real estate commission, cost of preparing and recording any corrective instruments, and one-half of the escrow fees. Buyer agrees to pay for recording fees for mortgages and deeds of conveyance, all costs or expenses in securing new financing or assuming existing financing, and one-half of the escrow fees. Buyer agrees to pay for recording fees for mortgages and deeds of conveyance, all costs or expenses in securing new financing or assuming existing financing, and one-half of the escrow fees. Taxes for the current year, insurance acceptable to the Buyer, rents, interest, mortgage reserves, maintenance fees, and water and other utilities constituting liens, shall be pro-rated as of closing. Renters' security deposits shall accrue to Buyer at closing. Seller to provide Buyer with all current rental or lease agreements prior to closing.

11. Termite Inspection: Seller agrees, at his expense, to provide written certification by a reputable licensed pest control firm that the property is free of termite infestation. In the event termites are found, the Seller shall have the property treated at his expense and provide acceptable certification that treatment has been rendered. If any structural repairs are required by reason of termite damage as established by acceptable certification, Seller agrees to make necessary repairs not to exceed $500. If repairs exceed $500, Buyer shall first have the right to accept the property "as is" with a credit to the Buyer at closing of $500, or the Buyer may terminate this agreement with the earnest money deposit being promptly returned to the Buyer if the Seller does not agree to pay all costs of treatment and repair.

12. Conditions of Sale: The following conditions shall also apply, and shall, if conflicting with the printed portions of this agreement, prevail and control:

Buyer is selling 17 Benson Drive, Palo Alto, and will acquire 242 Scott Street in exchange. If Benson title does not transfer on or before March 16, 1981 (through American Escrow), then this contract shall be rescinded and deposit refunded.

13. Liability and Maintenance: Seller shall maintain subject property, including landscaping, in good condition until the date of transfer of title or possession by Buyer, whichever occurs first. All risk of loss and destruction of property, and all expenses of insurance, shall be borne by the seller until the date of possession. If the improvements on the property are destroyed or materially damaged prior to closing, then the Buyer shall have the right to declare this agreement null and void, and the earnest money deposit and all other sums paid by Buyer toward the purchase price shall be returned to the Buyer forthwith.

14. Possession: The Buyer shall be entitled to possession of property upon closing or _____ NA _____, 19____.

15. Default: In the event the Buyer fails to complete the purchase as herein provided, the earnest money deposit shall be retained by the Seller as the total and entire liquidated damages. In the event the Seller fails to perform any condition of the sale as herein provided, then the Buyer may, at his option, treat the contract as terminated, and all payments made by the Buyer hereunder shall be returned to the Buyer forthwith, provided the Buyer may, at his option, treat this agreement as being in full force and effect with the right to action for specific performance and damages. In the event that either Buyer, Seller, or Agent shall institute suit to enforce any rights hereunder, the prevailing party shall be entitled to court costs and a reasonable attorney's fee.

16. Time Limit of Offer: The Seller shall have until
_____ Upon presentation. _____
_____ , 19 _____ to accept this
(hour)   (date)
offer by delivering a signed copy hereof to the Buyer. If this offer is not so accepted, it shall lapse and the agent (or Seller) shall refund the earnest money deposit to the Buyer forthwith.

17. General Agreements: (1) Both parties to this purchase reserve their rights to assign and hereby otherwise agree to cooperate in effecting an Internal Revenue Code 1031 exchange or similar tax-related arrangement prior to close of escrow, upon either party's written notice of intention to do so. (2) Upon approval of this offer by the Seller, this agreement shall become a contract between Buyer and Seller and shall inure to the benefit of the heirs, administrators, executors, successors, personal representatives, and assigns of said parties. (3) Time is of the essence and an essential part of this agreement. (4) This contract constitutes the sole and entire agreement between the parties hereto and no modification of this contract shall be binding unless attached hereto and signed by all parties to the contract. No representations, promises, or inducements not included in this contract shall be binding upon any party hereto.

18. Buyer's Statement and Receipt: "I/we hereby agree to purchase the above property in accordance with the terms and conditions above stated and acknowledge receipt of a completed copy of this agreement, which I/we have fully read and understand." Dated _____ January 29, __ 19 81 ____, _____
(hour)

Address ____ 2531 Allenbury Street _____   _____ [signature] _____ Buyer

_____ Palo Alto, California _____   _____ [signature] _____ Buyer

Phone No: Home ___ 261-1115 ___ Business ___ 359-2176 ___

19. Seller's Statement and Response: "I/we approve and accept the above offer, which I/we have fully read and understand, and agree to the above terms and conditions this day

of _____, 19 _____, _____

(hour)

Phone No: Home _____ Business _____   _____ Seller

20. Commission Agreement: Seller agrees to pay a commission of ___6___ % of the gross sales price to   Bergman Realty

for services in this transaction, and agrees that, in the event of forfeiture of the earnest money deposit by the Buyer, said deposit shall be divided between the Seller's broker and the Seller

Address _____   _____ Seller

(one half to each party), the Broker's part not to exceed the amount of the commission.

21. Buyer's Receipt for Signed Offer: The Buyer hereby acknowledges receipt of a copy of the above agreement bearing the Seller's signature in acceptance of this offer.

Dated _____, 19 _____   _____ Buyer

          _____ Buyer

COMMENTARY TO DOCUMENTATION — Property B

Item 2. The words "or Assigns" are always wise to add after the name(s) of the buyer(s). Alternate forms: "Assignees" or "Nominees."

Item 6. The buyer is cautious in covering his bases with the "subject to" provision. His contingency on approving the loan documents of the existing first will protect him from any change in the low interest terms of the note. In regard to the carry-back second, he

should have added a rollover provision to the balloon in case the buyer of the Benson Drive home is unable to pay his 3-year note to the Seibolds. Similarly, a prepayment without penalty clause and an assumption clause (non-accelerating) would have been desirable. (As it turned out, the carry-back was eliminated.)

Note how the buyer is careful to make the timeliness of the title transfer a contingency in the context of the exchange.

DOCUMENTATION — Property C

UNIVERSAL EARNEST MONEY RECEIPT AND OFFER TO PURCHASE

"This is a legally binding contract: if not understood, seek competent advice."

1. Date and Place of Offer: __January 19,__ 19 __81__ ; __Fremont__ __California__
(city) (state)

2. Principals: The undersigned Buyer __Gerald Seibold and Evelyn Seibold__
agrees to buy and Seller agrees to sell, according to the indicated terms and conditions, the property described as follows:

3. Property: located at __416 Bridge Avenue__ __Union City__ __California__
(street address) (city) (state)

with the following legal description: __to be supplied prior to closing.__

including any of the following items if at present attached to the premises: plumbing, heating, and cooling equipment, including stoker and oil tanks, burners, water heaters, electric light fixtures, bathroom fixtures, roller shades, curtain rods and fixtures, draperies, venetian blinds, window and door screens, towel racks, linoleum and other attached floor coverings,

including carpeting, attached television antennas, mailboxes, all trees and shrubs, and any other fixtures EXCEPT __None__

The following personal property shall also be included as part of the purchase: _____
At the closing of the transaction, the Seller, at his expense, shall provide the Buyer with a Bill Of Sale containing a detailed inventory of the personal property included.

__Stove to (a) be replaced with like kind approved by Buyer, or (b) stay or go, leaving a $250.00 credit in escrow.__

4. Earnest Money Deposit: Agent (or Seller) acknowledges receipt from Buyer of __Five-hundred and 00/100__ dollars $ __500.00__

in the form of ( ) cash; (X) personal check; ( ) cashier's check; ( ) promissory note at ____% interest per annum due _____ 19 ____; or

other _____
as earnest money deposit to secure and apply on this purchase. Upon acceptance of this agreement in writing and delivery of same to Buyer, the earnest money deposit shall be assigned

to and deposited in the listing Realtor's trust account or _____, to apply on the
purchase price at the time of closing.

5. Purchase Price: The total purchase price of the property shall be __Ninety-two Thousand and 00/100__ dollars $ __92,000.00__

6. Payment: Purchase price is to be paid by Buyer as follows:

Aforedescribed earnest money deposit .... $ __500.00__

Additional payment due upon acceptance of this offer .... $ __--__

Additional payment due at closing .... $ __36,122.67__

Balance to be paid as follows:

Buyer to purchase subject to a First Trust Deed and Note of record in the approximate amount of $55,377.33 payable approximately $580 per month, including interest at 9 3/4% per annum, including taxes and insurance. Loan documents to be approved by Buyer within 3 working days of receipt of copies.

7. **Title:** Seller agrees to furnish good and marketable title free of all encumbrances and defects, except mortgage liens and encumbrances as set forth in this agreement, and to make

conveyance by Warranty Deed or _____. Seller shall furnish in due course to the Buyer a title insurance policy insuring the Buyer of a good and marketable title in keeping with the terms and conditions of this agreement. Prior to the closing of this transaction, the Seller, upon request, will furnish to the Buyer a preliminary title report made by a title insurance company showing the condition of the title to said property. If the Seller cannot furnish marketable title within thirty days after receipt of the notice to the Buyer containing a written statement of the defects, the earnest money deposit herein receipted shall be refunded to the Buyer and this agreement shall be null and void. The following shall not be deemed encumbrances or defects; building and use restrictions general to the area; utility easements; other easements not inconsistent with Buyer's intended use; zoning or subdivision laws, covenants, conditions, restrictions, or reservations of record; tenancies of record. In the event of sale of other than real property relating to this transaction, Seller will provide evidence of title or right to sell or lease such personal property.

8. **Special Representations:** Seller warrants and represents to Buyer (1) that the subject property is connected to ( ) public sewer system, ( ) cesspool or septic tank, ( ) sewer system available but not connected, ( ) city water system, ( ) private water system, and that the following special improvements are included in the sale: ( ) sidewalk, ( ) curb and gutter, ( ) special street paving, ( ) special street lighting; (2) that the Seller knows of no material structural defects; (3) that all electrical wiring, heating, cooling, and plumbing systems are free of material defects and will be in good working order at the time the Buyer is entitled to possession; (4) that the Seller has no notice from any government agency of any violation or knowledge of probable violations of the law relating to the subject property; (5) that the Seller has no notice or knowledge of planned or commenced public improvements which may result in special assessments or otherwise directly and materially affect the property; and (6) that the Seller has no notice or knowledge of any liens to be assessed against the property,

EXCEPT ___None_____

9. **Escrow Instructions:** This sale shall be closed on or before _____ 19____ by __American Escrow__ or such other closing agent as mutually agreed upon by Buyer and Seller. Buyer and Seller will, immediately on demand, deposit with closing agent all instruments and monies required

to complete the purchase in accordance with the provisions of this agreement. Contract of Sale or Instrument of Conveyance to be made in the name of _____ to be supplied later. See under 12 below.

10. **Closing Costs and Pro-Ration:** Seller agrees to pay for title insurance policy, preliminary title report (if requested), termite inspection as set forth below, real estate commission, cost of preparing and recording any corrective instruments, and one-half of the escrow fees. Buyer agrees to pay for recording fees for mortgages and deeds of conveyance, all costs or expenses in securing new financing or assuming existing financing, and one-half of the escrow fees. Buyer agrees to pay for recording fees for mortgages and deeds of conveyance, all costs or expenses in securing new financing or assuming existing financing, and one-half of the escrow fees. Taxes for the current year, insurance acceptable to the Buyer, rents, interest, mortgage reserves, maintenance fees, and water and other utilities constituting liens, shall be pro-rated as of closing. Renters' security deposits shall accrue to Buyer at closing. Seller to provide Buyer with all current rental or lease agreements prior to closing.

11. **Termite Inspection:** Seller agrees, at his expense, to provide written certification by a reputable licensed pest control firm that the property is free of termite infestation. In the event termites are found, the Seller shall have the property treated at his expense and provide acceptable certification that treatment has been rendered. If any structural repairs are required by reason of termite damage as established by acceptable certification, Seller agrees to make necessary repairs not to exceed $500. If repairs exceed $500, Buyer shall first have the right to accept the property "as is" with a credit to the Buyer at closing of $500, or the Buyer may terminate this agreement with the earnest money deposit being promptly returned to the Buyer if the Seller does not agree to pay all costs of treatment and repair.

12. **Conditions of Sale:** The following conditions shall also apply, and shall, if conflicting with the printed portions of this agreement, prevail and control:

Close of escrow to be concurrent with close of escrow on property known as 12 Benson Drive at American Escrow. Buyer is selling 17 Benson Drive and is acquiring 416 Bridge Avenue in exchange. If Benson title does not transfer on or before March 16, 1981, then this contract shall be rescinded and deposit refunded.

13. **Liability and Maintenance:** Seller shall maintain subject property, including landscaping, in good condition until the date of transfer of title or possession by Buyer, whichever occurs first. All risk of loss and destruction of property, and all expenses of insurance, shall be borne by the seller until the date of possession. If the improvements on the property are destroyed or materially damaged prior to closing, then the Buyer shall have the right to declare this agreement null and void, and the earnest money deposit and all other sums paid by Buyer toward the purchase price shall be returned to the Buyer forthwith.

14. **Possession:** The Buyer shall be entitled to possession of property upon closing or ____NA_____, 19____.

15. **Default:** In the event the Buyer fails to complete the purchase as herein provided, the earnest money deposit shall be retained by the Seller as the total and entire liquidated damages. In the event the Seller fails to perform any condition of the sale as herein provided, then the Buyer may, at his option, treat the contract as terminated, and all payments made by the Buyer hereunder shall be returned to the Buyer forthwith, provided the Buyer may, at his option, treat this agreement as being in full force and effect with the right to action for specific performance and damages. In the event that either Buyer, Seller, or Agent shall institute suit to enforce any rights hereunder, the prevailing party shall be entitled to court costs and a reasonable attorney's fee.

16. **Time Limit of Offer:** The Seller shall have until

_____ Upon presentation. _____, 19____ to accept this
(hour) (date)

offer by delivering a signed copy hereof to the Buyer. If this offer is not so accepted, it shall lapse and the agent (or Seller) shall refund the earnest money deposit to the Buyer forthwith.

17. General Agreements: (1) Both parties to this purchase reserve their rights to assign and hereby otherwise agree to cooperate in effecting an Internal Revenue Code 1031 exchange or similar tax-related arrangement prior to close of escrow, upon either party's written notice of intention to do so. (2) Upon approval of this offer by the Seller, this agreement shall become a contract between Buyer and Seller and shall inure to the benefit of the heirs, administrators, executors, successors, personal representatives, and assigns of said parties. (3) Time is of the essence and an essential part of this agreement. (4) This contract constitutes the sole and entire agreement between the parties hereto and no modification of this contract shall be binding unless attached hereto and signed by all parties to the contract. No representations, promises, or inducements not included in this contract shall be binding upon any party hereto.

18. Buyer's Statement and Receipt: "I/we hereby agree to purchase the above property in accordance with the terms and conditions above stated and acknowledge receipt of a completed copy of this agreement, which I/we have fully read and understand." Dated __January 29,__ 19 __81__ , _____
(hour)

Address __2531 Allenbury Street__ ___[signature]___ Buyer

__Palo Alto, California__ ___[signature]___ Buyer

Phone No: Home __267-1115__ Business __359-2176__

19. Seller's Statement and Response: "I/we approve and accept the above offer, which I/we have fully read and understand, and agree to the above terms and conditions this day of _____, 19 _____, _____
(hour)

Address _____ Seller

Phone No: Home _____ Business _____ Seller

20. Commission Agreement: Seller agrees to pay a commission of _____% of the gross sales price to _____ for services in this transaction, and agrees that, in the event of forfeiture of the earnest money deposit by the Buyer, said deposit shall be divided between the Seller's broker and the Seller (one half to each party), the Broker's part not to exceed the amount of the commission.

21. Buyer's Receipt for Signed Offer: The Buyer hereby acknowledges receipt of a copy of the above agreement bearing the Seller's signature in acceptance of this offer.

Dated _____, 19 _____ _____ Buyer

_____ Buyer

COMMENTARY TO DOCUMENTATION — Property C

Item 2. Once again, the use of the words "or Assigns" (Assignee, Nominee) is recommended consistently.

Item 6. The condition stated relative to the first deed of trust is designed to protect the buyer from any hike in the interest rates on the part of the lender.

Item 12. The exchange is beginning to shape up. Everything hinges on the multiple escrow coming off — therefore, the necessary preoccupation with timing.

DOCUMENTATION — Property D

UNIVERSAL EARNEST MONEY RECEIPT
AND OFFER TO PURCHASE

"This is a legally binding contract: if not understood, seek competent advice."

1. Date and Place of Offer: __January 19,__ 19 __81__ ; __Fremont__ __California__
(city) (state)

2. Principals: The undersigned Buyer __Gerald Seibold and Evelyn Seibold__
agrees to buy and Seller agrees to sell, according to the indicated terms and conditions, the property described as follows:

3. Property: located at __2900 Bluebird Street__ __Union City__ __California__
(street address) (city) (state)

with the following legal description: __to be supplied__

_____

including any of the following items if at present attached to the premises: plumbing, heating, and cooling equipment, including stoker and oil tanks, burners, water heaters, electric light fixtures, bathroom fixtures, roller shades, curtain rods and fixtures, draperies, venetian blinds, window and door screens, towel racks, linoleum and other attached floor coverings,

including carpeting, attached television antennas, mailboxes, all trees and shrubs, and any other fixtures EXCEPT __None__

The following personal property shall also be included as part of the purchase: _____
At the closing of the transaction, the Seller, at his expense, shall provide the Buyer with a Bill Of Sale containing a detailed inventory of the personal property included.

4. Earnest Money Deposit: Agent (or Seller) acknowledges receipt from Buyer of __Five Hundred and 00/100__ dollars $ __500.00__

in the form of ( ) cash; (X) personal check; ( ) cashier's check; ( ) promissory note at _____% interest per annum due _____ 19 _____, or

other _____
as earnest money deposit to secure and apply on this purchase. Upon acceptance of this agreement in writing and delivery of same to Buyer, the earnest money deposit shall be assigned

to and deposited in the listing Realtor's trust account or _____, to apply on the
purchase price at the time of closing.

5. Purchase Price: The total purchase price of the property shall be __Seventy-seven Thousand Six Hundred and 00/100__

$ __77,600.00__

6. Payment: Purchase price is to be paid by Buyer as follows:

Aforedescribed earnest money deposit .... $ __500.00__

Additional payment due upon acceptance of this offer .... $ __--__

Additional payment due at closing .... $ __16,950.00__

Balance to be paid as follows:

> Buyer to purchase subject to a First Trust Deed and Note of record in the approximate amount of $45,100.00 payable approximately $493 per month, including interest at 9 3/4% per annum, including taxes and insurance. Loan documents to be approved by Buyer within 3 working days of receipt of copies. To be taken over without change of interest rate.
>
> Seller's Purchase Money Carryback: Balance of the purchase price to be evidenced by a note secured by a trust deed in the approximate amount of $15,000.00 executed by Buyer in favor of Seller. Said note to include interest at 17% per annum, to accrue from close of escrow, to be payable in principal and interest installments of $212.50 or more per month, beginning one month after the close of escrow to be all due and payable in three years from close of escrow.

7. Title: Seller agrees to furnish good and marketable title free of all encumbrances and defects, except mortgage liens and encumbrances as set forth in this agreement, and to make

conveyance by Warranty Deed or _____. Seller shall furnish in due course
to the Buyer a title insurance policy insuring the Buyer of a good and marketable title in keeping with the terms and conditions of this agreement. Prior to the closing of this transaction, the Seller, upon request, will furnish to the Buyer a preliminary title report made by a title insurance company showing the condition of the title to said property. If the Seller cannot furnish marketable title within thirty days after receipt of the notice to the Buyer containing a written statement of the defects, the earnest money deposit herein receipted shall be refunded to the Buyer and this agreement shall be null and void. The following shall not be deemed encumbrances or defects; building and use restrictions general to the area; utility easements; other easements not inconsistent with Buyer's intended use; zoning or subdivision laws, covenants, conditions, restrictions, or reservations of record; tenancies of record. In the event of sale of other than real property relating to this transaction, Seller will provide evidence of title or right to sell or lease such personal property.

8. Special Representations: Seller warrants and represents to Buyer (1) that the subject property is connected to ( ) public sewer system, ( ) cesspool or septic tank, ( ) sewer system available but not connected, ( ) city water system, ( ) private water system, and that the following special improvements are included in the sale: ( ) sidewalk, ( ) curb and gutter, ( ) special street paving, ( ) special street lighting; (2) that the Seller knows of no material structural defects; (3) that all electrical wiring, heating, cooling, and plumbing systems are free of material defects and will be in good working order at the time the Buyer is entitled to possession; (4) that the Seller has no notice from any government agency of any violation or knowledge of probable violations of the law relating to the subject property; (5) that the Seller has no notice or knowledge of planned or commenced public improvements which may result in special assessments or otherwise directly and materially affect the property; and (6) that the Seller has no notice or knowledge of any liens to be assessed against the property,

EXCEPT __None__.

9. Escrow Instructions: This sale shall be closed on or before _____ 19 _____ by __American Escrow__
or such other closing agent as mutually agreed upon by Buyer and Seller. Buyer and Seller will, immediately on demand, deposit with closing agent all instruments and monies required

to complete the purchase in accordance with the provisions of this agreement. Contract of Sale or Instrument of Conveyance to be made in the name of _____

> to be supplied later. See under 12 below.

10. Closing Costs and Pro-Ration: Seller agrees to pay for title insurance policy, preliminary title report (if requested), termite inspection as set forth below, real estate commission, cost of preparing and recording any corrective instruments, and one-half of the escrow fees. Buyer agrees to pay for recording fees for mortgages and deeds of conveyance, all costs or expenses in securing new financing or assuming existing financing, and one-half of the escrow fees. Buyer agrees to pay for recording fees for mortgages and deeds of conveyance, all costs or expenses in securing new financing or assuming existing financing, and one-half of the escrow fees. Taxes for the current year, insurance acceptable to the Buyer, rents, interest, mortgage reserves, maintenance fees, and water and other utilities constituting liens, shall be pro-rated as of closing. Renters' security deposits shall accrue to Buyer at closing. Seller to provide Buyer with all current rental or lease agreements prior to closing.

11. Termite Inspection: Seller agrees, at his expense, to provide written certification by a reputable licensed pest control firm that the property is free of termite infestation. In the event termites are found, the Seller shall have the property treated at his expense and provide acceptable certification that treatment has been rendered. If any structural repairs are required by reason of termite damage as established by acceptable certification, Seller agrees to make necessary repairs not to exceed $500. If repairs exceed $500, Buyer shall first have the right to accept the property "as is" with a credit to the Buyer at closing of $500, or the Buyer may terminate this agreement with the earnest money deposit being promptly returned to the Buyer if the Seller does not agree to pay all costs of treatment and repair.

12. Conditions of Sale: The following conditions shall also apply, and shall, if conflicting with the printed portions of this agreement, prevail and control:

> Buyer is selling 17 Benson Drive, Palo Alto, and will acquire 2900 Bluebird Lane in exchange. If Benson title does not transfer on or before

March 16, 1981 (through American Escrow), then this contract shall be rescinded and deposit refunded. The following added conditions shall be in force:

1. Close of escrow is to occur on March 3, 1981.

2. Repairs to be done by Seller before close of escrow: 1. Interior to be painted throughout. 2. Fire damage (floor, hood, wallpaper and smoke) to be repaired and cleaned to Buyer's reasonable satisfaction. 3. Garage door to be in good condition and properly operating. 4. Bath tub door to be repaired and water spout to be properly operating. 5. Black mold on window frames to be removed.

3. $1,000 of Seller's funds shall be held in escrow for payment of fire damage repairs, painting, cleaning, and other repairs per contract. As an agreement to survive close of escrow, Seller agrees to pay for all work required by the contract, even if the cost exceeds the monies held in escrow.

4. As a further agreement to survive close of escrow, Seller will take all reasonable steps to evict current tenants, and thereafter to do the painting, cleaning, and repairs required by the contract. Seller will reimburse Buyer for Buyer's carrying costs (1st loan PITI, 2nd loan interest) from the close of escrow to date possession is delivered to Buyers vacant and in the condition called for by this contract. Seller shall be entitled to retain any rents to date possession is delivered on condition specified.

13. Liability and Maintenance: Seller shall maintain subject property, including landscaping, in good condition until the date of transfer of title or possession by Buyer, whichever occurs first. All risk of loss and destruction of property, and all expenses of insurance, shall be borne by the seller until the date of possession. If the improvements on the property are destroyed or materially damaged prior to closing, then the Buyer shall have the right to declare this agreement null and void, and the earnest money deposit and all other sums paid by Buyer toward the purchase price shall be returned to the Buyer forthwith.

14. Possession: The Buyer shall be entitled to possession of property upon closing or _____NA_____, 19_____.

15. Default: In the event the Buyer fails to complete the purchase as herein provided, the earnest money deposit shall be retained by the Seller as the total and entire liquidated damages. In the event the Seller fails to perform any condition of the sale as herein provided, then the Buyer may, at his option, treat the contract as terminated, and all payments made by the Buyer hereunder shall be returned to the Buyer forthwith, provided the Buyer may, at his option, treat this agreement as being in full force and effect with the right to action for specific performance and damages. In the event that either Buyer, Seller, or Agent shall institute suit to enforce any rights hereunder, the prevailing party shall be entitled to court costs and a reasonable attorney's fee.

16. Time Limit of Offer: The Seller shall have until

Upon presentation.
_____(hour)_____ _____(date)_____, 19_____ to accept this

offer by delivering a signed copy hereof to the Buyer. If this offer is not so accepted, it shall lapse and the agent (or Seller) shall refund the earnest money deposit to the Buyer forthwith.

17. General Agreements: (1) Both parties to this purchase reserve their rights to assign and hereby otherwise agree to cooperate in effecting an Internal Revenue Code 1031 exchange or similar tax-related arrangement prior to close of escrow, upon either party's written notice of intention to do so. (2) Upon approval of this offer by the Seller, this agreement shall become a contract between Buyer and Seller and shall inure to the benefit of the heirs, administrators, executors, successors, personal representatives, and assigns of said parties. (3) Time is of the essence and an essential part of this agreement. (4) This contract constitutes the sole and entire agreement between the parties hereto and no modification of this contract shall be binding unless attached hereto and signed by all parties to the contract. No representations, promises, or inducements not included in this contract shall be binding upon any party hereto.

18. Buyer's Statement and Receipt: "I/we hereby agree to purchase the above property in accordance with the terms and conditions above stated and acknowledge receipt of a completed copy of this agreement, which I/we have fully read and understand." Dated ____January 19,____ 19 81 ____, _____ (hour)

Address ____2531 Allenburg Street____ [signature] ____ Buyer

____Palo Alto, California____ [signature] ____ Buyer

Phone No: Home ____267-1115____ Business ____359-2176____

19. Seller's Statement and Response: "I/we approve and accept the above offer, which I/we have fully read and understand, and agree to the above terms and conditions this day

of _____, 19_____, _____ (hour)

Address _____ Seller

Phone No: Home _____ Business _____ Seller

20. Commission Agreement: Seller agrees to pay a commission of _____% of the gross sales price to _____
for services in this transaction, and agrees that, in the event of forfeiture of the earnest money deposit by the Buyer, said deposit shall be divided between the Seller's broker and the Seller (one half to each party), the Broker's part not to exceed the amount of the commission.

21. Buyer's Receipt for Signed Offer: The Buyer hereby acknowledges receipt of a copy of the above agreement bearing the Seller's signature in acceptance of this offer.

Dated _____, 19 _____   _____ Buyer

_____ Buyer

COMMENTARY TO DOCUMENTATION — Property D

Item 2. "Or Assigns" should be written after the names of the buyers.

Item 6. Once again, the buyer is cautious in regard to the existing first. His contingencies protect him from adjustments by the lender to the terms of the note. The three-year balloon on the second is tolerable because the balloon note on the original property (first leg of the exchange) will fall due at the same time. However, just to be safe, the buyer should have negotiated a rollover provision for the note, as well as a prepayment clause and an assumption agreement.

Item 12. The buyer covers all his bases for repairs by insisting on an escrow fund as leverage — the sign of an expert.

As a final comment on this complicated exchange: through all of the detail and drudgery of the documentation, there emerges a feeling of bliss and satisfaction at having pulled the thing off! Exchanges are not simple — timing is crucial, every detail needs to be controlled with consummate skill. But when it is all done, the investor can look back and say, "Well done. You've disinherited the IRS once again!"

Part III

The Realtor

The third major source of down payment capital is the Realtor. By convention, most people assume that the real estate commission for listed properties is a fixed cash element of a transaction and that a seller is responsible for paying it. In fact, the commission is not fixed in any of its dimensions: rate, form, or source.

Like almost anything else, the percentage rate for calculating the commission is negotiable. Indeed, there would be legal problems if the real estate industry were to publish uniform fixed rates. Moreover, there is nothing written dictating that one must pay a commission in cash and cash only. Of course, almost all real estate professionals would prefer cash. It makes a deal clean and tidy and allows one to buy bread for the family table.

However, most informed agents know that some transactions may involve commissions in the form of paper — promissory notes that may provide for monthly payments or a single payment balloon note at the end of an acceptable period. Generally the time involved does not exceed a year or two. Occasionally the commission may be in the form of a share of ownership, with cash emerging upon sale of the property down the pike. Still other possibilities include commissions paid in personal property. In Case No. 14, printed earlier in this volume, the agent received a beautiful 0.81 carat diamond for his services. He was delighted, as are most agents who are shrewd enough to realize that a commission in an alternate form is better than no commission at all.

One of the important techniques available to the buyer who is interested in reducing the cash down payment for a deal is the technique of "Borrowing the Realtor's Commission" (No. 19). While it is true that according to current agency practice, the seller pays the commission, the buyer is at liberty to negotiate alternative arrangements with either the listing or selling agents (or both). If the buyer can induce the agents to defer the commission, the down payment can be reduced by the same amount because the seller's immediate obligation is relieved.

Who pays for the deferred commission in the final analysis? It is negotiable. If the buyer can strike a nothing down deal with the seller paying the commission over time, all the better. In many cases the buyer himself assumes the seller's obligation (Technique No. 11) and pays the deferred commission. Occasionally they share.

The whole point is that the flexibility of the Realtor may be an important factor in whether the deal comes together. Since the commission is usually the largest cash obligation of the seller in a transaction, the power of this technique cannot be overestimated.

There are three case studies in this section that illustrate how "Borrowing the Realtor's Commission" works in practice. In Case No. 19, the seller of an 8-plex arranged to pay $3,000 of the commission on a note, the balance being paid in the form of a real estate contract invested in the deal by the buyer's partner. The two notes not only constituted the entire commission, but the entire up front cash needs as well. Case No. 20 shows how a 35-unit motel and restaurant were acquired using, among other approaches, the technique of borrowing $30,000 in commissions ($15,000 in the form of a personal unsecured note signed by the buyer, and $15,000 in the form of a third mortgage on the buyer's home). Similarly, a note for the commissions was instrumental in closing a deal on two duplexes as described in Case No. 21. The cross-reference matrix in the appendix lists seven other case studies where this technique was used to good advantage.

Here is a summary of the case titles for this section:

Technique No. 19 — Borrowing The Realtor's Commission
    Case No. 19: Partner And Realtor Help With Cashless Deal On 8-Plex
    Case No. 20: Nine Techniques Net Buyer $700,000 Beach Motel
    Case No. 21: Buyer Wins Seller's Trust—Despite ''Funny Sounding'' Deal

---

Partner And Realtor Help With Cashless Deal On 8-Plex

**Featuring Technique No. 19
''Borrowing The Realtor's Commission''**

In A Nutshell . . .

Type: 8-Plex
Price: $165,000
Source: Classified Ad
Means: Wrap
Techniques: No. 4 — Contract/Wrap
No. 13 — Anything Goes
No. 19 — Borrowing Realtor's Commission
No. 21 — Deposits
No. 45 — Cash/Equity Combo
Features: Break-even Cash Flow

LOCATING

Bob Regula of Albuquerque was in the market for small apartment buildings. He noticed an ad in the newspaper placed by a real estate firm specializing in the type of properties he wanted. A visit to their office turned up 8 apartment buildings that seemed interesting to him. He then proceeded to make 8 offers and managed to bat 1,000 — all 8 were rejected! No problem. One of the properties was especially interesting, so he followed up on it.

SITUATION

The target property was an 8-plex in an area of downtown Albuquerque being redeveloped. The owner was asking $185,000 for the block and stucco property, with $18,000 down and the balance on a wrap at 11%. There were five underlying loans. The seller was a first-time buyer who had learned only one thing about management — he hated it. He wanted to get some relief. Relief was spelled R-E-G-U-L-A — since Bob was an expert at it and was willing to step in to solve the owner's problem.

NEGOTIATION

Bob had an out-of-state partner he was counting on to come up with the down payment. He therefore made an offer of $165,000 with $15,000 down and a wrap-around contract at 10.75%. The down payment matched that of a parallel offer being considered. Then the partner pulled the plug — he was not able to come up with the needed cash for another two or three months, too late for this deal.

Because the real estate agent had done his job in selling the owner on Bob's expertise at property development and management, Bob's offer was favored. So Bob laid the cards on the table. Yes, he very much wanted the deal to go through, but his partner had backed out. It was at that point in the negotiations that the real estate agent hinted he might be willing to take

paper for his commission in lieu of cash. Bob then said he would go to work finding another partner for less down.

He lost no time sending in the reserves: a woman investor he knew. She immediately fell in love with the property and turned over to Bob her portfolio of real estate holdings to see if perhaps an exchange might be possible. During the course of their deliberations, Bob learned that she had just sold her home and was holding a contract for $6,700 as part of the proceeds of the sale. That gave him the winning idea: would the owner of the 8-plex be willing to accept this contract as a down payment if the real estate agent would in turn accept it as commission, together with a note for the balance.

The seller agreed, as long as he could retain the renters' deposits to cover his closing costs. And that is what happened. ("Anything goes!")

CLOSING

Bob had a title company prepare all the documents, being careful to stipulate that the 12-year payout in the wrap-around contract apply only to the seller's equity. The underlying loans were to remain intact. The sketch summarizes the financing facts:

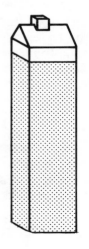

$165,000 sales price

$6,700 down in the form of a real estate contract (the Realtor accepted the Seller's note for $3,000 for the balance of the commission)

$158,300 wrap at 10.75%, 12-year payout, monthly payments to match seller's previous flow

(5 underlying loans)

The partner received 50% ownership for her contribution. Bob will take care of renovations, maintenance, and management.

OUTCOMES AND FUTURE PLANS

By completing cosmetic improvements and landscaping, Bob was able to justify raising the rents from $175 to $220 per month per unit. The income is just sufficient to cover the expenses. He figures the value of his new apartment building to be around $202,000. The instant equity is therefore $37,000.

His advice for fellow investors: "Give the seller what he is already making on his property and relieve him of the management hassles."

COMMENTARY

1. Bob Regula's story is evidence for the importance of having "partnership depth." If one partner is unable to come to the rescue when a good deal surfaces, then you can quickly turn to the next partner and not lose the opportunity for a profitable venture.
2. This case study is also a good illustration of how a number of techniques can be combined to get the job done.
3. Research among R.A.N.D. graduates shows that it takes around five creative offers to achieve one creative deal, and ten creative offers for a true "nothing down" deal. Bob clearly understood this principle when he opened this aspect of his investment program by making eight offers at once on eight different properties. Even though all eight were rejected, Bob persisted and eventually closed on the property described in this case study. Persistence is clearly an important quality in a successful investor.

DOCUMENTATION

UNIVERSAL EARNEST MONEY RECEIPT AND OFFER TO PURCHASE

"This is a legally binding contract: if not understood, seek competent advice."

1. Date and Place of Offer: November 2, 19 81; Albuquerque (city) New Mexico (state)

2. Principals: The undersigned Buyer Robert Regula agrees to buy and Seller agrees to sell, according to the indicated terms and conditions, the property described as follows:

3. Property: located at 16 Mammouth Street (street address) Albuquerque (city) New Mexico (state)

with the following legal description: to follow

including any of the following items if at present attached to the premises: plumbing, heating, and cooling equipment, including stoker and oil tanks, burners, water heaters, electric light fixtures, bathroom fixtures, roller shades, curtain rods and fixtures, draperies, venetian blinds, window and door screens, towel racks, linoleum and other attached floor coverings,

including carpeting, attached television antennas, mailboxes, all trees and shrubs, and any other fixtures EXCEPT None

The following personal property shall also be included as part of the purchase:
At the closing of the transaction, the Seller, at his expense, shall provide the Buyer with a Bill Of Sale containing a detailed inventory of the personal property included.

4. Earnest Money Deposit: Agent (or Seller) acknowledges receipt from Buyer of None dollars $ .00
in the form of ( ) cash; ( ) personal check; ( ) cashier's check; ( ) promissory note at ___% interest per annum due ___ 19 ___; or
other ___
as earnest money deposit to secure and apply on this purchase. Upon acceptance of this agreement in writing and delivery of same to Buyer, the earnest money deposit shall be assigned
to and deposited in the listing Realtor's trust account or ___, to apply on the purchase price at the time of closing.

5. Purchase Price: The total purchase price of the property shall be One Hundred Sixty-five Thousand and 00/100 dollars
$ 165,000.00

6. Payment: Purchase price is to be paid by Buyer as follows:

Aforedescribed earnest money deposit .... $ 0
Additional payment due upon acceptance of this offer .... $ --
Additional payment due at closing .... $ --

Balance to be paid as follows:
$6,700 at closing in the form of a 2nd Real Estate Contract on home located at 7649 Ginger Street.

The balance of $158,300, payable together with interest on the unpaid balance at the rate of 10 3/4% per annum in monthly installments of not less than $1,389.20 each, or more per month including interest; 1st payment is payable on the 25th day of November 1981, and subsequent payments shall be due on the 25th day of each month thereafter until twelve (12) years from the date of execution, at which time Seller's equity shall be all due and payable.

7. Title: Seller agrees to furnish good and marketable title free of all encumbrances and defects, except mortgage liens and encumbrances as set forth in this agreement, and to make

conveyance by Warranty Deed or _____. Seller shall furnish in due course to the Buyer a title insurance policy insuring the Buyer of a good and marketable title in keeping with the terms and conditions of this agreement. Prior to the closing of this transaction, the Seller, upon request, will furnish to the Buyer a preliminary title report made by a title insurance company showing the condition of the title to said property. If the Seller cannot furnish marketable title within thirty days after receipt of the notice to the Buyer containing a written statement of the defects, the earnest money deposit herein receipted shall be refunded to the Buyer and this agreement shall be null and void. The following shall not be deemed encumbrances or defects; building and use restrictions general to the area; utility easements; other easements not inconsistent with Buyer's intended use; zoning or subdivision laws, covenants, conditions, restrictions, or reservations of record; tenancies of record. In the event of sale of other than real property relating to this transaction, Seller will provide evidence of title or right to sell or lease such personal property.

8. Special Representations: Seller warrants and represents to Buyer (1) that the subject property is connected to ( ) public sewer system, ( ) cesspool or septic tank, ( ) sewer system available but not connected, ( ) city water system, ( ) private water system, and that the following special improvements are included in the sale: ( ) sidewalk, ( ) curb and gutter, ( ) special street paving, ( ) special street lighting; (2) that the Seller knows of no material structural defects; (3) that all electrical wiring, heating, cooling, and plumbing systems are free of material defects and will be in good working order at the time the Buyer is entitled to possession; (4) that the Seller has no notice from any government agency of any violation or knowledge of probable violations of the law relating to the subject property; (5) that the Seller has no notice or knowledge of planned or commenced public improvements which may result in special assessments or otherwise directly and materially affect the property; and (6) that the Seller has no notice or knowledge of any liens to be assessed against the property,

EXCEPT _____ None _____

9. Escrow Instructions: This sale shall be closed on or before _____ November 6, 19 81 by _____ or such other closing agent as mutually agreed upon by Buyer and Seller. Buyer and Seller will, immediately on demand, deposit with closing agent all instruments and monies required

to complete the purchase in accordance with the provisions of this agreement. Contract of Sale or Instrument of Conveyance to be made in the name of _____

10. Closing Costs and Pro-Ration: Seller agrees to pay for title insurance policy, preliminary title report (if requested), termite inspection as set forth below, real estate commission, cost of preparing and recording any corrective instruments, and one-half of the escrow fees. Buyer agrees to pay for recording fees for mortgages and deeds of conveyance, all costs or expenses in securing new financing or assuming existing financing, and one-half of the escrow fees. Buyer agrees to pay for recording fees for mortgages and deeds of conveyance, all costs or expenses in securing new financing or assuming existing financing, and one-half of the escrow fees. Taxes for the current year, insurance acceptable to the Buyer, rents, interest, mortgage reserves, maintenance fees, and water and other utilities constituting liens, shall be pro-rated as of closing. Renters' security deposits shall accrue to Buyer at closing. Seller to provide Buyer with all current rental or lease agreements prior to closing.

11. Termite Inspection: Seller agrees, at his expense, to provide written certification by a reputable licensed pest control firm that the property is free of termite infestation. In the event termites are found, the Seller shall have the property treated at his expense and provide acceptable certification that treatment has been rendered. If any structural repairs are required by reason of termite damage as established by acceptable certification, Seller agrees to make necessary repairs not to exceed $500. If repairs exceed $500, Buyer shall first have the right to accept the property "as is" with a credit to the Buyer at closing of $500, or the Buyer may terminate this agreement with the earnest money deposit being promptly returned to the Buyer if the Seller does not agree to pay all costs of treatment and repair.

12. Conditions of Sale: The following conditions shall also apply, and shall, if conflicting with the printed portions of this agreement, prevail and control:

None

13. Liability and Maintenance: Seller shall maintain subject property, including landscaping, in good condition until the date of transfer of title or possession by Buyer, whichever occurs first. All risk of loss and destruction of property, and all expenses of insurance, shall be borne by the seller until the date of possession. If the improvements on the property are destroyed or materially damaged prior to closing, then the Buyer shall have the right to declare this agreement null and void, and the earnest money deposit and all other sums paid by Buyer toward the purchase price shall be returned to the Buyer forthwith.

14. Possession: The Buyer shall be entitled to possession of property upon closing or _____ NA _____, 19 _____

15. Default: In the event the Buyer fails to complete the purchase as herein provided, the earnest money deposit shall be retained by the Seller as the total and entire liquidated damages. In the event the Seller fails to perform any condition of the sale as herein provided, then the Buyer may, at his option, treat the contract as terminated, and all payments made by the Buyer hereunder shall be returned to the Buyer forthwith, provided the Buyer may, at his option, treat this agreement as being in full force and effect with the right to action for specific performance and damages. In the event that either Buyer, Seller, or Agent shall institute suit to enforce any rights hereunder, the prevailing party shall be entitled to court costs and a reasonable attorney's fee.

16. Time Limit of Offer: The Seller shall have until

_____ , 19 _____ to accept this
(hour)   (date)

offer by delivering a signed copy hereof to the Buyer. If this offer is not so accepted, it shall lapse and the agent (or Seller) shall refund the earnest money deposit to the Buyer forthwith.

17. General Agreements: (1) Both parties to this purchase reserve their rights to assign and hereby otherwise agree to cooperate in effecting an Internal Revenue Code 1031 exchange or similar tax-related arrangement prior to close of escrow, upon either party's written notice of intention to do so. (2) Upon approval of this offer by the Seller, this agreement shall become a contract between Buyer and Seller and shall inure to the benefit of the heirs, administrators, executors, successors, personal representatives, and assigns of said parties. (3) Time is of the essence and an essential part of this agreement. (4) This contract constitutes the sole and entire agreement between the parties hereto and no modification of this contract shall be binding unless attached hereto and signed by all parties to the contract. No representations, promises, or inducements not included in this contract shall be binding upon any party hereto.

18. Buyer's Statement and Receipt: "I/we hereby agree to purchase the above property in accordance with the terms and conditions above stated and acknowledge receipt of a completed copy of this agreement, which I/we have fully read and understand." Dated _____ November 2, 19 81 _____, _____
(hour)

Address _____ 516 Canford Place _____ [signature] _____ Buyer

_____ Albuquerque, New Mexico _____ Buyer

Phone No: Home ___261-5191___ Business ___785-4126___

19. Seller's Statement and Response: "I/we approve and accept the above offer, which I/we have fully read and understand, and agree to the above terms and conditions this day

of _____, 19 _____, _____.

(hour)

Address _____ _____ Seller

Phone No: Home _____ Business _____ _____ Seller

20. Commission Agreement: Seller agrees to pay a commission of _____% of the gross sales price to _____ for services in this transaction, and agrees that, in the event of forfeiture of the earnest money deposit by the Buyer, said deposit shall be divided between the Seller's broker and the Seller (one half to each party), the Broker's part not to exceed the amount of the commission.

21. Buyer's Receipt for Signed Offer: The Buyer hereby acknowledges receipt of a copy of the above agreement bearing the Seller's signature in acceptance of this offer.

Dated _____, 19 _____ _____ Buyer

_____ Buyer

COMMENTARY TO DOCUMENTATION

Item 2. It is always wise to add "or Assigns" after the name of the buyer.

Item 4. No earnest money deposit shows up on this form. Two offers preceded this one from the same buyer. Perhaps the previous deposit was left in the broker's escrow on account. If so, the amount should have been recorded once more on this form.

Item 6. The contract portion is often expressed as follows: "Buyer to execute a real estate contract (land sales contract, installment land contract, contract for deed, wrap-around contract, etc.) in favor of Seller in the amount of _____." In this case, the designation wrap-around contract is appropriate since the obligation encompasses not only the seller's equity but five underlying notes as well.

A provision for rolling the balloon over for an additional period of time is always a good idea — even in a long-fuse note of this type. A prepayment provision is likewise desirable.

The buyer should consider exploring the possibility of buying out the underlying lien holders at a discount or otherwise involving them — if they are flexible — in some of the techniques that are applicable.

Item 15. The original purchase agreement used to complete our Universal Earnest Money Receipt contains a "total liquidated damages" provision — always a pro-buyer arrangement. In this case, the seller stands to receive nothing as liquidated damages since ostensibly no deposit was made.

Item 16. No time limit is imposed on the seller. This is one item not to leave blank!

Nine Techniques Net Buyer $700,000 Beach Motel

**Featuring Technique No. 19
"Borrowing The Realtor's Commission"**

In A Nutshell . . .

Type: 35-unit motel and restaurant
Price: $700,000
Source: Realtor
Means: Purchase money mortgage
Techniques: No. 4 — Contract/Wrap
                No. 5 — Raise Price, Lower Terms
                No. 6 — Balloon
                No. 8 — Defer Down/No Payments
                No. 19 — Borrowing Realtor's Commission
                No. 20 — Rents
                No. 21 — Deposits
                No. 28 — Home Equity Loan
                No. 44 — Cash/Equity Combo
Strategy: Defer payment
Features: Conversion

LOCATING

Kyle Waldon of Tampa, Florida, was on the lookout for homes or small apartment buildings in the range of $45,000 per unit. A Realtor friend in the local R.A.N.D. Group told him of a beachfront motel for sale — a promising buy for someone who might like to convert it to condos.

SITUATION

The owners, two women, were offering the 35-unit motel plus restaurant for $695,000, with $100,000 down and the balance at 10% for 29 years. That type of long-term financing appealed to Kyle, so he began to explore the waters. The location on St. Petersburg Beach was superb, just the kind of area that would appeal to potential condo buyers.

NEGOTIATION

Kyle had four major questions to begin with. First, he wanted to know from the sellers whether they wanted their Realtor to structure the deal. They said yes. Then he asked whether the Realtor would be willing to take his commission in the form of a note. Once again, the answer was yes. Third, he inquired whether the mortgage would be assignable. That affirmed, Kyle went on to his final opening question: would the sellers defer the initial payments as a means of helping with the negative cash flow? Another "Yes." With that encouragement, Kyle made his offer of $650,000.

Unfortunately, there was already another offer pending at the full price of $695,000. Kyle therefore offered an additional $5,000 for the property assuming that by raising the price to $700,000 he could count on some flexibility in finalizing the terms. His hunch

correct.

The real estate firm listing the property agreed to take the commissions in the form of paper, a $15,000 note to the listing agent and the same amount to the real estate firm's profit-sharing plan. The sellers were willing to take back an interest-free note in the amount of $6,700 to soften the blow of the first period of negative cash flows. There was to be a purchase-money first mortgage in the amount of $595,000, 10% interest for 29 years, payments of $5,251/mo. The balance of the sellers' equity, after the borrowed commissions and the front-end note, was to be in cash.

CLOSING

Kyle had an attorney draw up all the papers. One complication early on was caused by the restaurateur lessee, who got wind of the sale and intervened with the news that he had first right of refusal on the property. Sure enough, he had the papers to prove it; however, he let the 30-day option period pass without exercising his right to buy. One important factor in his acquiescing in the sale was Kyle's ability to establish himself as a desirable potential landlord.

The next problem to deal with was the $105,000 down payment. The sellers were willing to postpone a portion of the initial payments (on a note for $6,700). And $30,000 of commissions were deferred as balloons. That left $86,300 to raise. Here's how Kyle did it.

He took out a second mortgage on the equity in his own home in the amount of $30,000. Then he borrowed an additional $20,000 secured by "borrowed" stock, that is, stock owned by a partner. The remainder of the down, $18,300 (2.6% of the purchase price), was in the form of cash; $2,152 of this amount came in the form of rents and deposits at closing. The financing is indicated in the following sketch:

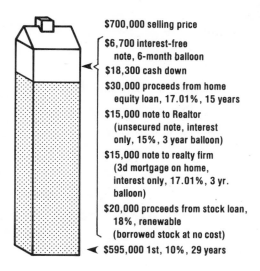

$700,000 selling price

$6,700 interest-free note, 6-month balloon

$18,300 cash down

$30,000 proceeds from home equity loan, 17.01%, 15 years

$15,000 note to Realtor (unsecured note, interest only, 15%, 3 year balloon)

$15,000 note to realty firm (3d mortgage on home, interest only, 17.01%, 3 yr. balloon)

$20,000 proceeds from stock loan, 18%, renewable (borrowed stock at no cost)

$595,000 1st, 10%, 29 years

OUTCOMES AND FUTURE PLANS

The closing took place on March 31, before the big tourist onslaught. For that reason, the initial period of ownership was marked by severe negative cash flows, around $5,000 per month. The sellers' willingness to defer the first $6,700 helped. By raising the rents and developing a promotional plan, Kyle was soon able to bring the negative under control. The sellers agreed to serve as consultants for the first few weeks as the new owner learned the motel business.

He then put his master plan into effect by converting the 35 units to condominiums. He is offering the units for around $48,500 with 5% down and the balance at 12% on a wrap, renegotiable after 5 years. At this writing, the units are going like hotcakes! The sell-out price is $1,000,000 higher than the purchase price. Down payments will generate nearly $85,000 in revenues to pay off conversion costs and meet obligations on the original down.

Looking back, Kyle thinks his success in the negotiation process was his willingness to let the listing Realtor work out the structure of the deal — to "give him the burden of figuring out how to come up with the down payment" and then just have patience. He wishes in retrospect that he had insisted on tighter warranties on the air conditioners and other maintenance aspects. It would have been useful, also, to have required a partial release clause for the condo conversion option. Moreover, Kyle wished he had tried harder to get more cash flow relief. Finally, the most important advice he could give others is this: "Spend the money necessary to hire professional management. I lost a lot learning the hard way. Also, work up plans to cover cash flow."

COMMENTARY

1. Despite the problems Kyle encountered initially with negative cash flow, he has — quite literally — made a $1,000,000 deal turn out rather successfully.

2. His strategy of putting the monkey on the backs of the agents worked well in this case. They realized that they would be better off waiting for their commissions — than missing the sale altogether.

3. This case study is a fine example of how creative techniques used in combinations can assure the success of a transaction. Oftentimes it is the person who can perceive unusual combinations and patterns of action who comes out on top.

4. The source of the lead on this property was a Realtor whom Kyle met at the R.A.N.D. Group in his local area. The R.A.N.D. Group is very frequently an excellent source of referrals of this type. However, Kyle had to be out there mingling with those in the know in order to take advantage of the opportunity. Investors who have good "antennas" — who are willing to cultivate a variety of information sources — are the ones who have the best chance to succeed.

DOCUMENTATION

UNIVERSAL EARNEST MONEY RECEIPT AND OFFER TO PURCHASE

"This is a legally binding contract: if not understood, seek competent advice."

1. Date and Place of Offer: __January 27,__ 19 __80__ ; __Redington Beach__ __Florida__
   (city) (state)

2. Principals: The undersigned Buyer __Kyle Weldon or Assigns__
   agrees to buy and Seller agrees to sell, according to the indicated terms and conditions, the property described as follows:

3. Property: located at __1218-1220 Watercrest Circle__ __St. Petersburg Bch.__ __Florida__
   (street address) (city) (state)

   with the following legal description: __Lots 1, 2, and 3. Heatherstone Beach, Block 12__

   including any of the following items if at present attached to the premises: plumbing, heating, and cooling equipment, including stoker and oil tanks, burners, water heaters, electric light fixtures, bathroom fixtures, roller shades, curtain rods and fixtures, draperies, venetian blinds, window and door screens, towel racks, linoleum and other attached floor coverings, including carpeting, attached television antennas, mailboxes, all trees and shrubs, and any other fixtures EXCEPT ___None___

The following personal property shall also be included as part of the purchase: _____
At the closing of the transaction, the Seller, at his expense, shall provide the Buyer with a Bill Of Sale containing a detailed inventory of the personal property included.

4. Earnest Money Deposit: Agent (or Seller) acknowledges receipt from Buyer of ___Five Thousand and 00/100___ dollars $ ___5,000.00___

in the form of ( ) cash; (X personal check; ( ) cashier's check; ( ) promissory note at _____% interest per annum due _____ 19 _____; or

other _____
as earnest money deposit to secure and apply on this purchase. Upon acceptance of this agreement in writing and delivery of same to Buyer, the earnest money deposit shall be assigned

to and deposited in the listing Realtor's trust account or _____, to apply on the
purchase price at the time of closing.

5. Purchase Price: The total purchase price of the property shall be ___Seven Hundred Thousand and 00/100___ dollars $ ___700,000.00___

6. Payment: Purchase price is to be paid by Buyer as follows:

Aforedescribed earnest money deposit .... $ ___5,000.00___

Additional payment due upon acceptance of this offer ___January 31, 1980___ $ ___5,000.00___

Additional payment due at closing .... $ ___95,000.00___

Balance to be paid as follows:

___$595,000 Mortgage and Note to Seller, assumable, bearing 10% interest per___
___annum, 29 years, $5,250.76 monthly payments (principal and interest). No___
___prepayment penalty.___

7. Title: Seller agrees to furnish good and marketable title free of all encumbrances and defects, except mortgage liens and encumbrances as set forth in this agreement, and to make

conveyance by Warranty Deed or _____. Seller shall furnish in due course
to the Buyer a title insurance policy insuring the Buyer of a good and marketable title in keeping with the terms and conditions of this agreement. Prior to the closing of this transaction, the Seller, upon request, will furnish to the Buyer a preliminary title report made by a title insurance company showing the condition of the title to said property. If the Seller cannot furnish marketable title within thirty days after receipt of the notice to the Buyer containing a written statement of the defects, the earnest money deposit herein receipted shall be refunded to the Buyer and this agreement shall be null and void. The following shall not be deemed encumbrances or defects; building and use restrictions general to the area; utility easements; other easements not inconsistent with Buyer's intended use; zoning or subdivision laws, covenants, conditions, restrictions, or reservations of record; tenancies of record. In the event of sale of other than real property relating to this transaction, Seller will provide evidence of title or right to sell or lease such personal property.

8. Special Representations: Seller warrants and represents to Buyer (1) that the subject property is connected to ( ) public sewer system, ( ) cesspool or septic tank, ( ) sewer system available but not connected, ( ) city water system, ( ) private water system, and that the following special improvements are included in the sale: ( ) sidewalk, ( ) curb and gutter, ( ) special street paving, ( ) special street lighting; (2) that the Seller knows of no material structural defects; (3) that all electrical wiring, heating, cooling, and plumbing systems are free of material defects and will be in good working order at the time the Buyer is entitled to possession; (4) that the Seller has no notice from any government agency of any violation or knowledge of probable violations of the law relating to the subject property; (5) that the Seller has no notice or knowledge of planned or commenced public improvements which may result in special assessments or otherwise directly and materially affect the property; and (6) that the Seller has no notice or knowledge of any liens to be assessed against the property,

EXCEPT ___None___

9. Escrow Instructions: This sale shall be closed on or before ___February 29,___ 19 ___80___ by _____
or such other closing agent as mutually agreed upon by Buyer and Seller. Buyer and Seller will, immediately on demand, deposit with closing agent all instruments and monies required

to complete the purchase in accordance with the provisions of this agreement. Contract of Sale or Instrument of Conveyance to be made in the name of _____

_____

10. Closing Costs and Pro-Ration: Seller agrees to pay for title insurance policy, preliminary title report (if requested), termite inspection as set forth below, real estate commission, cost of preparing and recording any corrective instruments, and one-half of the escrow fees. Buyer agrees to pay for recording fees for mortgages and deeds of conveyance, all costs or expenses in securing new financing or assuming existing financing, and one-half of the escrow fees. Buyer agrees to pay for recording fees for mortgages and deeds of conveyance, all costs or expenses in securing new financing or assuming existing financing, and one-half of the escrow fees. Taxes for the current year, insurance acceptable to the Buyer, rents, interest, mortgage reserves, maintenance fees, and water and other utilities constituting liens, shall be pro-rated as of closing. Renters' security deposits shall accrue to Buyer at closing. Seller to provide Buyer with all current rental or lease agreements prior to closing.

11. Termite Inspection: Seller agrees, at his expense, to provide written certification by a reputable licensed pest control firm that the property is free of termite infestation. In the event termites are found, the Seller shall have the property treated at his expense and provide acceptable certification that treatment has been rendered. If any structural repairs are required by reason of termite damage as established by acceptable certification, Seller agrees to make necessary repairs not to exceed $500. If repairs exceed $500, Buyer shall first have the right to accept the property "as is" with a credit to the Buyer at closing of $500, or the Buyer may terminate this agreement with the earnest money deposit being promptly returned to the Buyer if the Seller does not agree to pay all costs of treatment and repair.

12. Conditions of Sale: The following conditions shall also apply, and shall, if conflicting with the printed portions of this agreement, prevail and control:

___Seller presenting premises free of building code violations and safety___
___hazards that would create hardship and/or unforeseen expenses to new___
___owner. Seller to assist in rentals and advise Buyer on property manage-___
___ment during transition period (not less than 30 days).___

13. Liability and Maintenance: Seller shall maintain subject property, including landscaping, in good condition until the date of transfer of title or possession by Buyer, whichever occurs first. All risk of loss and destruction of property, and all expenses of insurance, shall be borne by the seller until the date of possession. If the improvements on the property are destroyed or materially damaged prior to closing, then the Buyer shall have the right to declare this agreement null and void, and the earnest money deposit and all other sums paid by Buyer toward the purchase price shall be returned to the Buyer forthwith.

14. Possession: The Buyer shall be entitled to possession of property upon closing or _____ , 19 _____ .

15. Default: In the event the Buyer fails to complete the purchase as herein provided, the earnest money deposit shall be retained by the Seller as the total and entire liquidated damages. In the event the Seller fails to perform any condition of the sale as herein provided, then the Buyer may, at his option, treat the contract as terminated, and all payments made by the Buyer hereunder shall be returned to the Buyer forthwith, provided the Buyer may, at his option, treat this agreement as being in full force and effect with the right to action for specific performance and damages. In the event that either Buyer, Seller, or Agent shall institute suit to enforce any rights hereunder, the prevailing party shall be entitled to court costs and a reasonable attorney's fee.

16. Time Limit of Offer: The Seller shall have until

_____ 6:00 p.m. _____ _____ January 28, _____ , 19 80 _____ to accept this
(hour)   (date)

offer by delivering a signed copy hereof to the Buyer. If this offer is not so accepted, it shall lapse and the agent (or Seller) shall refund the earnest money deposit to the Buyer forthwith.

17. General Agreements: (1) Both parties to this purchase reserve their rights to assign and hereby otherwise agree to cooperate in effecting an Internal Revenue Code 1031 exchange or similar tax-related arrangement prior to close of escrow, upon either party's written notice of intention to do so. (2) Upon approval of this offer by the Seller, this agreement shall become a contract between Buyer and Seller and shall inure to the benefit of the heirs, administrators, executors, successors, personal representatives, and assigns of said parties. (3) Time is of the essence and an essential part of this agreement. (4) This contract constitutes the sole and entire agreement between the parties hereto and no modification of this contract shall be binding unless attached hereto and signed by all parties to the contract. No representations, promises, or inducements not included in this contract shall be binding upon any party hereto.

18. Buyer's Statement and Receipt: "I/we hereby agree to purchase the above property in accordance with the terms and conditions above stated and acknowledge receipt of a completed copy of this agreement, which I/we have fully read and understand." Dated _____ January 27, _____ 19 80 _____ , _____
(hour)

Address _____ 68 Orange Grove Avenue _____   [signature] or Assigns _____ Buyer

_____ St. Petersburg, Florida _____   _____ Buyer

Phone No: Home _____ 611-1123 _____ Business _____ 591-7812 _____

19. Seller's Statement and Response: "I/we approve and accept the above offer, which I/we have fully read and understand, and agree to the above terms and conditions this day

of _____ , 19 _____ , _____
(hour)

Address _____   _____ Seller

Phone No: Home _____ Business _____   _____ Seller

20. Commission Agreement: Seller agrees to pay a commission of _____ % of the gross sales price to _____

for services in this transaction, and agrees that, in the event of forfeiture of the earnest money deposit by the Buyer, said deposit shall be divided between the Seller's broker and the Seller (one half to each party), the Broker's part not to exceed the amount of the commission.

21. Buyer's Receipt for Signed Offer: The Buyer hereby acknowledges receipt of a copy of the above agreement bearing the Seller's signature in acceptance of this offer.

Dated _____ , 19 _____   _____ Buyer

_____ Buyer

COMMENTARY TO DOCUMENTATION

On the surface, this agreement appears to be straightforward, simple, uncomplicated. But still water runs deep. The buyer put together a combination of nothing down techniques to delight the most sophisticated investor — most of them hiding underneath the entry "95,000 cash on closing." Everything worked out splendidly but not before everyone — including the sellers and the agents — chipped in their portion of the down.

Item 2. Here is one of the rare occasions where the buyer added the words "or Assigns." Great!!

Item 6. The obligation is in the form of a purchase money mortgage (technically a purchase money mortgage note secured by a purchase money mortgage),

which the buyer has wisely specified as assumable and not subject to any prepayment penalty.

Item 12. With so much at stake and so many hands in the pot, it would probably have been a good idea to insist on an exculpatory clause.

Item 15. In the original, the seller has the right to require specific performance of the buyer and sue for damages. It is always good to strike such a provision in favor of specifying that the deposit can be retained as total liquidated damages in the case of buyer default.

Item 16. Not many go to the effort of specifying an hour time limit; where it is used, it seems to give a sense of professional urgency that might impress the seller and move things along more quickly.

Buyer Wins Seller's Trust — Despite "Funny Sounding" Deal

Featuring Technique No. 19
"Borrowing The Realtor's Commission"

In A Nutshell . . .

Type: Two duplexes
Price: $92,000
Source: For Sale Sign
Means: Purchase money first mortgage
Techniques: No. 4 — Contract/Wrap
No. 10 — Supply Seller's Needs
No. 19 — Borrowing Realtor's Commission
No. 20 — Rents
No. 21 — Deposits

LOCATING

Thomas Oldroyd, a medical doctor from Homestead Florida, was in the market for SFH's and duplexes in the range of $45,000 to $50,000 per unit. He made it a practice of driving around well-located neighborhoods looking for postings that seemed "old." On one of his outings in Homestead (a small city south of Miami), he spotted a weathered For Sale sign on a pair of duplexes of the type that fit his parameters.

SITUATION

He checked with the listing agent and learned that the free and clear properties had been advertised for six months without a single offer. The owner was an older widow who was anxious to be relieved of the management hassles associated with rental properties. She was asking $92,000 for both duplexes together. Cash down payment was to be 20% ($18,400).

NEGOTIATION

Thomas opened with the customary "nothing down" inquiry: "Do you need cash now or is a regular monthly income more valuable to you?" (Note how tactful and yet penetrating his approach was.) After she had had a chance to mull this over and inquire somewhat into her buyer's background, she admitted that her needs were more in the direction of regular payments than a large cash down. As Thomas put it, "The seller trusted me on a 'funny sounding' deal because I live, work, and own other property in town."

Thomas offered full price for the duplexes — $92,000. What made the deal sound "funny" to the seller was the nature of the terms: purchase money mortgage in the amount of $86,000, reduced by specific credits (buyer to pay seller's closing costs and relinquish rents and deposits due buyer, allowance for roof repairs), buyer to pay real estate commission, balance of equity (around $500) to be paid in cash. The mortgage was to yield 12% and run for 25 years with full amortization (no

balloon payments).

The woman's attorney insisted that the roof liability be limited to $500, something Thomas readily agreed to. Otherwise, the original offer stood.

CLOSING

For his part, Thomas did not use an attorney but rather drew up all the papers himself. The commission of $5,520 was covered by a note to the listing office at 18% for one year, payable in monthly installments by the buyer. Thomas' concern for the agent paid off, as the seller's attorney tried to sabatoge the deal at the closing. It was only through the quick efforts of the agent that the seller was dissuaded from backing out at the last minute.

The figures came out this way: the $86,000 mortgage was reduced by $2,700 ($1,111.77 seller's closing costs paid by buyer, $1,088.23 in rents and deposits due buyer but turned over to seller, $500 adjustment for repairs on the roof) — final mortgage amount $83,300. After the commission was taken care of, the cash balance due the seller amounted to $480. The financing is summarized in the following sketch:

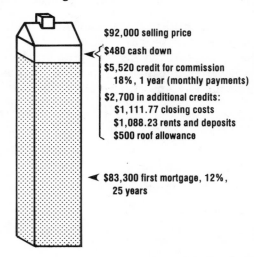

$92,000 selling price
$480 cash down
$5,520 credit for commission
18%, 1 year (monthly payments)
$2,700 in additional credits:
$1,111.77 closing costs
$1,088.23 rents and deposits
$500 roof allowance

$83,300 first mortgage, 12%, 25 years

OUTCOMES AND FUTURE PLANS

In effect, Thomas had purchased two excellent rental properties for a total cash outlay of $1,591.77 ($480 plus $1,111.77 closing costs — just what the seller needed up front). Monthly debt service of $877.34 compares with an income of $1,200, a very favorable positive cash flow situation. However, for the first year there will be a negative of $137.34 each month due to the payments on the commission note. Fortunately, the listing broker waived the 18% interest provided in the contract. Thomas plans to hold the duplexes for eight to ten years, raising the rents on a regular basis.

As he looks back on this transaction, Thomas feels that his secret strategy for successful negotiation was "to find out what the seller's real needs are and then structure my offer to those needs within my financial limitations." His advice for other investors: "Be persistent! Spend time looking. Make many offers. Don't be discouraged by attorneys and/or brokers who don't understand low or nothing down offers. Nothing down deals aren't found that way. You make them nothing down by your thoughtful offers. Read everything about real estate. Talk often with brokers and salesmen."

COMMENTARY

1. Here is your typical 20% down deal that is magically transformed into a less than 2% down deal through the power of a few questions. The secret is to get to the heart of the seller's needs. You'll never know until you ask.

2. Why would an elderly widow agree to a 25-year mortgage? Because she was concerned with a secure monthly income and came to trust the buyer. She could have required a pay-out after, say, five years. That would probably still have been acceptable to the buyer. However, he started with the 25-year provision — and the seller accepted!

3. Thomas drew up his own documents. How much would it have cost him to have a dependable attorney take care of the documentation? The cost would have been nominal in comparison to the benefits. Skilled professionals are always worth it.

4. For added flexibility in the future, Thomas should have arranged for separate mortgages on each of the properties (two purchase money mortgages and two notes). In that way he could have paved the way for the sale of just one of the duplexes should the need arise.

5. The negative cash flow for the first year may be a boon for the investor in a position to welcome the tax write-off. However, the payments could have been structured initially on an even cash flow basis by "reversing" the paper to the extent of $137.34/mo. The principal would have grown for the first 12 payments, but the impact on a 25-year amortization would have been negligible. The total savings during the first year would amount to $1,648.08, more than enough to repeat the transaction on two other duplexes!

DOCUMENTATION

UNIVERSAL EARNEST MONEY RECEIPT AND OFFER TO PURCHASE

"This is a legally binding contract: if not understood, seek competent advice."

1. Date and Place of Offer: __March 6,__ 19 __81__ ; __Homestead__ __Florida__
   (city) (state)

2. Principals: The undersigned Buyer __Thomas Oldroyd__
   agrees to buy and Seller agrees to sell, according to the indicated terms and conditions, the property described as follows:

3. Property: located at __71-73 Murdock Avenue, 61-63 Murdock Avenue__ __Homestead__ __Florida__
   (street address) (city) (state)

   with the following legal description: __to be supplied__

   including any of the following items if at present attached to the premises: plumbing, heating, and cooling equipment, including stoker and oil tanks, burners, water heaters, electric light fixtures, bathroom fixtures, roller shades, curtain rods and fixtures, draperies, venetian blinds, window and door screens, towel racks, linoleum and other attached floor coverings,

   including carpeting, attached television antennas, mailboxes, all trees and shrubs, and any other fixtures EXCEPT __None__

   The following personal property shall also be included as part of the purchase: __see inventory, attached.__
   At the closing of the transaction, the Seller, at his expense, shall provide the Buyer with a Bill Of Sale containing a detailed inventory of the personal property included.

4. Earnest Money Deposit: Agent (or Seller) acknowledges receipt from Buyer of __One Hundred and 00/100__ dollars $ __100.00__

   in the form of ( ) cash; (X) personal check; ( ) cashier's check; ( ) promissory note at _____% interest per annum due _____ 19 _____ ; or

   other _____

   as earnest money deposit to secure and apply on this purchase. Upon acceptance of this agreement in writing and delivery of same to Buyer, the earnest money deposit shall be assigned

   to and deposited in the listing Realtor's trust account or _____, to apply on the purchase price at the time of closing.

5. Purchase Price: The total purchase price of the property shall be _Ninety-two Thousand and 00/100_ dollars $ _92,000.00_.

6. Payment: Purchase price is to be paid by Buyer as follows:

Aforedescribed earnest money deposit .... $ _100.00_

Additional payment due upon acceptance of this offer .... $ _400.00_

Additional payment due at closing ___approximately___ .... $ _400.00_

Balance to be paid as follows:

Purchaser to execute a Purchase Money First Mortgage and note in favor of the Seller for approximately $86,000.00 to be adjusted by any credits due the Purchaser, payable at 12% per annum for 25 years, payable monthly at approximately $900.00 per month until paid, which includes principal and interest. The Mortgage shall also include the furnishings.

Purchaser agrees to pay all Seller's expenses to close, and to receive credit toward the Purchase Money Mortgage. Seller to pay own attorney's fees. Seller may retain all deposits (securities) and apply a credit to Purchase Money Mortgage. Seller may retain all rents collected prior to closing, and Purchaser to receive credit on a prorated basis toward Purchase Money Mortgage.

Purchaser to execute a promissory note in favor of the Real Estate Broker, Tom Burns Real Estate, for the sales commission of $5,520.00 payable at 18% per annum, payable monthly at approximately $500.00 per month until paid.

7. Title: Seller agrees to furnish good and marketable title free of all encumbrances and defects, except mortgage liens and encumbrances as set forth in this agreement, and to make conveyance by Warranty Deed or _____. Seller shall furnish in due course to the Buyer a title insurance policy insuring the Buyer of a good and marketable title in keeping with the terms and conditions of this agreement. Prior to the closing of this transaction, the Seller, upon request, will furnish to the Buyer a preliminary title report made by a title insurance company showing the condition of the title to said property. If the Seller cannot furnish marketable title within thirty days after receipt of the notice to the Buyer containing a written statement of the defects, the earnest money deposit herein receipted shall be refunded to the Buyer and this agreement shall be null and void. The following shall not be deemed encumbrances or defects; building and use restrictions general to the area; utility easements; other easements not inconsistent with Buyer's intended use; zoning or subdivision laws, covenants, conditions, restrictions, or reservations of record; tenancies of record. In the event of sale of other than real property relating to this transaction, Seller will provide evidence of title or right to sell or lease such personal property.

8. Special Representations: Seller warrants and represents to Buyer (1) that the subject property is connected to ( ) public sewer system, ( ) cesspool or septic tank, ( ) sewer system available but not connected, ( ) city water system, ( ) private water system, and that the following special improvements are included in the sale: ( ) sidewalk, ( ) curb and gutter, ( ) special street paving, ( ) special street lighting; (2) that the Seller knows of no material structural defects; (3) that all electrical wiring, heating, cooling, and plumbing systems are free of material defects and will be in good working order at the time the Buyer is entitled to possession; (4) that the Seller has no notice from any government agency of any violation or knowledge of probable violations of the law relating to the subject property; (5) that the Seller has no notice or knowledge of planned or commenced public improvements which may result in special assessments or otherwise directly and materially affect the property; and (6) that the Seller has no notice or knowledge of any liens to be assessed against the property,

EXCEPT _____None_____.

9. Escrow Instructions: This sale shall be closed on or before _April 15,_ 19 _81_ by _____ or such other closing agent as mutually agreed upon by Buyer and Seller. Buyer and Seller will, immediately on demand, deposit with closing agent all instruments and monies required to complete the purchase in accordance with the provisions of this agreement. Contract of Sale or Instrument of Conveyance to be made in the name of _____

10. Closing Costs and Pro-Ration: Seller agrees to pay for title insurance policy, preliminary title report (if requested), termite inspection as set forth below, real estate commission, cost of preparing and recording any corrective instruments, and one-half of the escrow fees. Buyer agrees to pay for recording fees for mortgages and deeds of conveyance, all costs or expenses in securing new financing or assuming existing financing, and one-half of the escrow fees. Buyer agrees to pay for recording fees for mortgages and deeds of conveyance, all costs or expenses in securing new financing or assuming existing financing, and one-half of the escrow fees. Taxes for the current year, insurance acceptable to the Buyer, rents, interest, mortgage reserves, maintenance fees, and water and other utilities constituting liens, shall be pro-rated as of closing. Renters' security deposits shall accrue to Buyer at closing. Seller to provide Buyer with all current rental or lease agreements prior to closing.

11. Termite Inspection: Seller agrees, at his expense, to provide written certification by a reputable licensed pest control firm that the property is free of termite infestation. In the event termites are found, the Seller shall have the property treated at his expense and provide acceptable certification that treatment has been rendered. If any structural repairs are required by reason of termite damage as established by acceptable certification, Seller agrees to make necessary repairs not to exceed $500. If repairs exceed $500, Buyer shall first have the right to accept the property "as is" with a credit to the Buyer at closing of $500, or the Buyer may terminate this agreement with the earnest money deposit being promptly returned to the Buyer if the Seller does not agree to pay all costs of treatment and repair.

12. Conditions of Sale: The following conditions shall also apply, and shall, if conflicting with the printed portions of this agreement, prevail and control:

Purchaser is accepting the property in "As is condition" with the exception of a roof inspection. Purchaser, at his expense, has the right to have roof inspected. Roof is to be in good condition and water-tight. Any repairs necessary shall be at the Seller's expense. In the event that the roof repairs should exceed $500.00, then and in that event _the Seller may, at her option, declare this contract to be null and void._

13. Liability and Maintenance: Seller shall maintain subject property, including landscaping, in good condition until the date of transfer of title or possession by Buyer, whichever occurs first. All risk of loss and destruction of property, and all expenses of insurance, shall be borne by the seller until the date of possession. If the improvements on the property are destroyed or materially damaged prior to closing, then the Buyer shall have the right to declare this agreement null and void, and the earnest money deposit and all other sums paid by Buyer toward the purchase price shall be returned to the Buyer forthwith.

14. Possession: The Buyer shall be entitled to possession of property upon closing or _____, 19 _____.

15. Default: In the event the Buyer fails to complete the purchase as herein provided, the earnest money deposit shall be retained by the Seller as the total and entire liquidated damages. In the event the Seller fails to perform any condition of the sale as herein provided, then the Buyer may, at his option, treat the contract as terminated, and all payments made by the Buyer hereunder shall be returned to the Buyer forthwith, provided the Buyer may, at his option, treat this agreement as being in full force and effect with the right to action for specific performance and damages. In the event that either Buyer, Seller, or Agent shall institute suit to enforce any rights hereunder, the prevailing party shall be entitled to court costs and a reasonable attorney's fee.

16. Time Limit of Offer: The Seller shall have until

_____ _____, 19 _____ to accept this
(hour) (date)

offer by delivering a signed copy hereof to the Buyer. If this offer is not so accepted, it shall lapse and the agent (or Seller) shall refund the earnest money deposit to the Buyer forthwith.

17. General Agreements: (1) Both parties to this purchase reserve their rights to assign and hereby otherwise agree to cooperate in effecting an Internal Revenue Code 1031 exchange or similar tax-related arrangement prior to close of escrow, upon either party's written notice of intention to do so. (2) Upon approval of this offer by the Seller, this agreement shall become a contract between Buyer and Seller and shall inure to the benefit of the heirs, administrators, executors, successors, personal representatives, and assigns of said parties. (3) Time is of the essence and an essential part of this agreement. (4) This contract constitutes the sole and entire agreement between the parties hereto and no modification of this contract shall be binding unless attached hereto and signed by all parties to the contract. No representations, promises, or inducements not included in this contract shall be binding upon any party hereto.

18. Buyer's Statement and Receipt: "I/we hereby agree to purchase the above property in accordance with the terms and conditions above stated and acknowledge receipt of a completed copy of this agreement, which I/we have fully read and understand." Dated ___March 6,___ 19 __81__ , _____
(hour)

Address ___212 Saratoga Street___   [signature]   Buyer

___Homestead, Florida___   Buyer

Phone No: Home _____ Business _____

19. Seller's Statement and Response: "I/we approve and accept the above offer, which I/we have fully read and understand, and agree to the above terms and conditions this day of _____, 19 _____, _____
(hour)

Address _____   Seller

Phone No: Home _____ Business _____ $5,520.00 _____ Seller
                    Buyer
20. Commission Agreement: ~~Seller~~ agrees to pay a commission of _____% of the gross sales price to ___Tom Burns Real Estate___

for services in this transaction, and agrees that, in the event of forfeiture of the earnest money deposit by the Buyer, said deposit shall be divided between the Seller's broker and the Seller (one half to each party), the Broker's part not to exceed the amount of the commission.

21. Buyer's Receipt for Signed Offer: The Buyer hereby acknowledges receipt of a copy of the above agreement bearing the Seller's signature in acceptance of this offer.

Dated _____, 19 _____   Buyer

                                                                                Buyer

COMMENTARY TO DOCUMENTATION

Item 2. Buyer should add the words "or Assigns" after his name.

Item 6. The wording was carefully chosen to admit changes in the variables. Note that in the final analysis, the figures were adjusted considerably over what is listed in the earnest money agreement. One suggestion: the usual risk-reduction clauses should have been negotiated — prepayment without penalty, assumption provision, and substitution of collateral.

Item 12. The way the roof contingency is stated, the Seller has picked up a good weasel clause. It should have been stated in such a way as to allow the buyer the option of paying for repairs beyond $500. In the event

he chose not to do so, then, and only then, would the Seller have the option of declaring the contract null and void.

Item 15. The original default clause gave the seller broader recourse than our "Universal Earnest Money Receipt." Buyers should strike out all but the "total liquidated damages" section of forms used in their area.

Item 16. Curiously, the preprinted original Deposit Receipt and Sales Purchase Contract used in this transaction did not contain an entry for imposing a time limit on the seller to accept the offer. It just goes to show you that you have to read carefully even the standard printed matter.

Part IV

The Renters

In nearly every real estate transaction involving rental property, the renters are instrumental in helping the buyer with the down payment. Of course, they are not aware of it. And few buyers are conscious ahead of time of how important the role of rents and deposits is to their success in reducing the cash down payment.

Technique No. 20   Rents

Since rents are paid in advance, a buyer who closes on the first of the month when rents are due stands to receive the gross rental income for that month. The first mortgage payment is generally not due until thirty days after closing, so the buyer has a thirty-day breather. His immediate cash down payment obligation has therefore been offset by an amount equal to the rents.

Technique No. 21   Deposits

The situation with tenant security deposits is similar. It is not uncommon for the landlord to require the tenant to pay an amount equal to the first and last month's rent as a damage deposit. If a property is sold, the deposits are passed along to the new buyer. Unless state law prohibits the co-mingling of deposit funds with the rental accounts, the buyer can effectively use the deposit funds given to him at closing as an offset to the cash down payment obligation. Of course, when a tenant moves out, all or part of the deposit must be returned. If the new buyer is a wise manager, he will require a buffer period before returning the deposit. This will give him some protection against the possibility that the tenant may have neglected to pay some bills and will allow him meanwhile to find a new tenant who can add to the deposit kitty.

Sixteen of the case studies discussed in this book include references to these two techniques. In Case No. 22, printed below under the title "A 70-Unit Trailer Park — 10 Minutes To Buy and 5% Down," rents and deposits accounted for $8,000, nearly one-third of the down payment. In Case No. 48, printed elsewhere in this volume, rents and deposits amounted to $7,000 toward the purchase of a 72-unit apartment complex.

A 70-Unit Trailer Park — 10 Minutes To Buy And 5% Down

Featuring Techniques 20 and 21
"Rents" and "Deposits"

In A Nutshell. . .

Type: Mobile Home Park and Trailers
Price: $325,000
Source: Buyer's ad
Means: Wrap around contract, assumption
Techniques: No. 1 — Ultimate Paper Out (Trailers)
No. 4 — Contract/Wrap
No. 20 — Rents
No. 21 — Deposits
Features: $2,700/mo. positive cash flow

LOCATING

George Ambrose, an attorney from Cheyenne, Wyoming, made it a practice of advertising in the newspaper for properties of various kinds. One of the respondents was an out-of-state owner of a large mobile home park in Cheyenne.

SITUATION

Management hassles and tenant problems had made the owner flexible. He had bought the property in the name of his corporation from the original owner on a contract. The current asking price was $400,000 with $100,000 down. Included were seven mobile homes being financed at 11%. The owner was willing to let them go on an assumption as part of the package. The space rental was then $60 per unit, considerably below the market. Demand for mobile home space in the area was high.

NEGOTIATION

George felt that the price was too high; and he knew that he did not have $100,000 to put down. But he also knew that the seller was anxious to divest himself of long-distance management problems. Therefore, he agreed to the asking price subject to an appraisal and inspection. The whole affair was concluded in the first ten minutes of a 20 minute long-distance telephone conversation.

To prepare the seller for a lower offer, George retained the services of a conservative appraiser friend to inspect the property. The unofficial appraisal came in at $325,000, nearly 20% below the asking figure. So George went back to the seller and offered the lower amount. He also reduced the down payment from $100,000 to $25,000, using an approach something like this: "Mr. Seller, I know you don't want to get this property back after you sell it. Our inspection revealed the need for a considerable amount of work to be done on the property. I will need capital to pour back into the

improvements. Therefore, rather than giving you $100,000 down, I will give you only $25,000 and free up some resources to invest in upgrading the property. What do you say?"

The seller said yes. Only the terms remained at issue. George offered 9% on the balance with a 20-year amortization, payout after 9 years. The seller countered with 13%. The deal was struck at 11%. The seven mobile homes, valued at $5,500 each, were to be assumed by the buyer using the existing 11% financing, nothing down — an ultimate paper out of the most generous kind.

CLOSING

George arranged the closing date to fall on the first of the month, thereby picking up around $8,000 in rents and deposits. The out-of-pocket down payment was therefore effectively reduce to $17,000 (around 5%). The following sketch shows the financing:

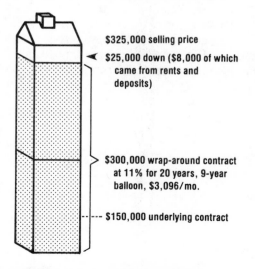

$325,000 selling price

$25,000 down ($8,000 of which came from rents and deposits)

$300,000 wrap-around contract at 11% for 20 years, 9-year balloon, $3,096/mo.

$150,000 underlying contract

OUTCOMES AND FUTURE PLANS

At take over, the monthly income from the mobile

home park was $5,500. George immediately raised the rents from $60 to $90 per month, thereby increasing the income (including the mobile home rentals) to $6,500. With debt service on the note just over $3,000, plus monthly expenses of around $800, the positive cash flow for the operation came to $2,700/mo.!

Although the seller required a clause committing George to a fixed amount of capital improvements within 12 months, he (the seller) did not choose to enforce the requirement. Therefore, George carried out only the necessary upgrading of wells, roads, and landscaping.

In retrospect, George feels that the most important aspect of his handling of the transaction was his use of the appraisal to establish a basis for the price reduction.

COMMENTARY

1. This transaction goes to show that a positive cash flow in today's economy is still possible. The mobile home sector of the housing industry presents its own set of problems and limitations — the clientele circle is relatively smaller than the single family home market and the appreciation may not be as great. However, for the person who can solve the management problems, the well-located mobile home park can be a gold mine. Where can you invest $17,000 and get a cash return of $2,700 per month or $32,400 per year (191% for the first year!)?

DOCUMENTATION

Documentation for this case study consists of the following Contract for Deed, rather than the usual Earnest Money Receipt and Offer to Purchase:

CONTRACT FOR DEED

THIS AGREEMENT made this 1st day of March, 1980, between [name], hereinafter referred to as "Seller," and [name], hereinafter referred to as "Buyer."

The seller for and in consideration of the payments and the performance of the conditions and agreements on the part of the Buyer agrees to sell and convey by good and sufficient Warranty Deed that said property described in Attachment "A" which is incorporated herein by this reference.

The purchase price of said property shall be the sum of Three Hundred Twenty-Five Thousand Dollars ($325,000.00) which shall be paid as follows: The sum of Twenty-Five Thousand Dollars ($25,000.00) shall be paid on or before March 1, 1980 and the balance of the Three Hundred Thousand Dollars ($300,000.00) shall be paid in equal monthly installments consisting of Three Thousand Ninety-Six Dollars and Sixty Cents ($3,096.60) amortized over a Twenty (20) year period. Each of the installments shall become due and payable on the first day of each calendar month, commencing April 1, 1980. Each installment shall be credited first to interest at eleven percent (11%) per annum on the unpaid balance of principal, and the remainder to principal. Buyer reserves the right to make greater payments or pay in full the amount owing at any time with no penalty of interest after the first year. Buyer shall make a payment in full of the principal remaining unpaid at the end of nine (9) years, a balloon payment.

Buyer agrees to pay all taxes and other assessments and impositions levied against the property before the same become delinquent. Taxes and rents shall be pro-rated as of March 1, 1980. Buyer shall keep the premises insured against loss or damage by fire and extended coverage perils in the sum of not less than Three Hundred Twenty-Five Thousand Dollars ($325,000.00) for the benefit of Seller and prior mortgage holders and Buyer as their respective interests appear.

Buyer shall keep all buildings in good and proper repair and permit no labor or mechanic's liens to attach to the premises. Seller is hereby authorized to pay any liens, charges, claims, insurance premiums, or taxes or to keep the premises in good repair. Said sums so expended shall be added to the balance of the price agreed to herein.

If any monthly installment is not made by Buyer when the same is due or Buyer violates any of the provisions of this Agreement, the Seller shall notify the Buyer of such default in writing addressed to 1521 McKlendon Avenue, Cheyenne, Wyoming 82001 and Buyer shall have forty-five (45) days within which to cure the same, failing in which the whole unpaid balance of the purchase price with interest at the option of the Seller shall become due at once and payable without further notice. Buyer shall pay any late charge assessed by the mortgage holder in the event of late payment.

In case the Buyer shall fail to pay the said purchase money or interest or money advanced or to keep or perform any other agreement or provisions contained herein, the Seller may terminate this Agreement, subject to the notice requirements above, and sell said property by advertising once a week for two consecutive weeks in a newspaper of general circulation in Cheyenne, Wyoming, such sale to be at public auction at a time and place in Cheyenne, Wyoming, as stated in such advertisement.

The Seller shall have the right to bid at such sale. From the proceeds of such sale, the Seller shall first receive the balance of principal owed to them under this Contract plus accrued interest, and Buyer shall receive the balance minus all expenses of sale including a reasonable attorney's fee if the Seller shall retain counsel in connection with such sale. Seller may, however, in the event of default by the Buyer, elect to affirm this contract and pursue any remedy they may have at law or in equity by reason of such default.

The Buyer shall be entitled to possession of the premises on March 1, 1980, and so long thereafter as Buyer shall comply with the terms of this Agreement. Otherwise, after the required notice, Buyer shall immediately surrender possession of said premises to the Seller. Thereafter, Seller shall be entitled to receive rents arising from the premises.

In the event this Contract has been placed on record, it shall not be construed to be or held to be a lien or cause any cloud upon the title of Seller if the Seller shall record an Affidavit showing the default of Buyer in its performance of or compliance with this Contract.

Seller agrees to furnish at his expense a policy of title insurance showing good and merchantable title in Buyer once the terms of the contract are complied with.

In case of any litigation arising out of any breach of this Agreement, the Court having jurisdiction thereof may award reasonable attorney's fees to the successful party.

No modification of this agreement in any of its particulars shall be binding upon the Seller unless the same is duly approved in writing by the Seller, nor shall Buyer assign this Contract without the written consent of the Seller first had and obtained, which consent shall not be unreasonably withheld. Said Consent will not be withheld if, at the time of the proposed Assignment, Buyer is in complete compliance with the terms and conditions contained herein.

The parties agree that this Agreement shall be placed in Escrow with the ABC Federal Savings and Loan Association, Cheyenne, Wyoming, as Escrow Agent under appropriate instructions, as to the disposition of the sums paid pursuant hereto, the Buyer to pay the cost of establishing such Escrow, and the Seller to pay the Escrow Agent's monthly service charge.

The Seller hereby certifies to the Buyer that to its knowledge, there are no major structural or mechanical defects relating to the property being conveyed with the exception of the well which had previously been hit by a truck and some minor damage has been found which includes a broken pipe to the well which needs repair and that there has been some settling of the retainer tank. It is understood that these items need repair and the current manager of the Mobile Home Park is fully aware of the problems and procedures required to repair the same. It is estimated that the total cost to repair to be approximately $1,200.00. It is further agreed, that with the exception of the foregoing, the Buyer is hereby purchasing the subject matter property in an "AS IS" condition.

It is further mutually agreed by and between the parties hereto that time of payment and the faithful performance of all other conditions, herein contained shall be the essence of this contract, and that all other terms, conditions and agreements herein contained shall apply to and bind the heirs, executors, assigns, and successors of the respective parties hereto.

IN WITNESS WHEREOF, the parties hereto have executed this Contract for Deed the day and year first above written.

[notarized signatures]

COMMENTARY TO DOCUMENTATION

It is instructive that this contract for deed does not enjoin the Buyer from putting his appreciated equity to use (except in the case of mechanic's or labor liens), unlike the contract described in Case No. 13.

Part V

The Property

The fifth source of down payment capital is the property itself. The buyer who is on his toes learns to recognize aspects of a given property that might be sold off to raise funds for the purchase. The variations are endless — everything from fixtures to parts of the land itself. There are two techniques that belong to this category.

Technique No. 22　Splitting Off Furniture and Other Items

Two years ago, one of the Nothing Down graduates in Florida was $5,000 short of funds needed to purchase an option on a valuable tract of land near Orlando. While wandering over the property one day pondering how he might come up with the necessary capital, he noticed a large area overgrown with beautiful ferns of the type one finds offered for sale in florists shops. Since problems often lead to creative solutions, he put two and two together and arranged to split off the ferns to raise enough money to bring the deal together. Today, the property is being developed into a multi-million dollar recreational park, all because of a patch of ferns —

and a creative mind.

Technique No. 23　Splitting Off Part of the Property

In some cases a given property is structured so that parts of it — extra lots or individual buildings — can be split off and sold to raise funds for the acquisition. As the next case study (No. 23) shows, splitting techniques often cause splitting headaches, but the benefits can be significant. In this case, the sale of two lots split off from the property raised $25,000 towards the cash down payment, nearly two-thirds of the required down. (Readers will rejoice to learn that the remainder was borrowed.)

23

"Splitting Headaches" Can Pay Off

**Featuring Technique No. 23
"Splitting Off Part of the Property"**

In A Nutshell. . .

Type: SFH on multiple lots
Price: $90,000
Source: For sale sign
Techniques: No. 6 — Balloon
No. 23 — Splitting Off Property
No. 32 — Second Mortgage Crank
No. 36 — Moving the Mortgage
No. 37 — Creative Refinance
No. 50 — Lease Option
Features: Leads into technique no. 34 — Buy Low, Refinance High

LOCATING

Bud Winston of West Bend, Wisconsin, was looking for properties in the $100,000 range. He made it a practice to tour the most desirable areas of the community on a regular basis looking for new opportunities. One day he spotted what looked like the perfect property.

SITUATION

The target property was a single home located on a large tract of land — in effect four lots. The package was being offered for sale as part of an estate settlement. The terms were "all cash at closing." What made the deal attractive was the discount — a $98,000 price with an appraisal of $150,000.

NEGOTIATION

The administrator of the estate was the vice-president of the local First National Bank. He did not balk at Bud's offer of $90,000, but the nothing down terms Bud wanted to negotiate did not fit in with the parameters of an estate sale. It was all cash or nothing!

Undaunted, Bud agreed to come up with $40,000 at closing. Not to be outdone, the banker himself offered to loan Bud the remaining $50,000 on a one-year note at 10% (semi-annual interest payment only). So far so good.

CLOSING

The only problem was raising the $40,000 by the time of closing. The seller (having passed away) was in no position to help with the down payment, so Bud turned to the property. The house was located on two of the four lots in the package. Over a period of three months Bud arranged for the lots to be resurveyed so that three lots were created out of the original four. The splitting process was a headache (and expensive — $400), but sometimes splitting headaches can pay off. The sketch shows how the restructuring was accomplished:

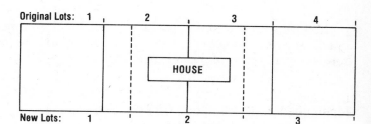

The next task was to sell off two of the three new lots. This was left up to the Realtor, who came through with flying colors. By the time of the closing, she had sold lot No. 1 for $15,000 and lot No. 3 for $10,000, the dates of closing to coincide with Bud's closing. He was, therefore, $25,000 closer to the required $40,000.

Next, he turned to his own equity resources. He owned an old house appraised at $53,000 with a first mortgage of $16,000. By refinancing the house for $35,000, he was able to pull out $19,000 in equity to apply to his estate purchase. Thus he had pulled together more than enough to consummate the deal.

However, it was not your usual run-of-the-mill refinance. Bud needed to plan for the future because he had a $50,000 balloon note coming due at the bank! He therefore arranged to refinance the older house in a creative and special way. To begin with, he explained to the lender what his needs and ideas were: if he could "definance" the older home (clear it of liens), and then sell it as a free and clear property, he would have enough to pay off his balloon at the other bank. But to do this, he needed the cooperation of the bank in substituting collateral for their refinanced loan by moving the mortgage to the estate property he was in the process of buying. Why would they agree to do this? Because their $35,000 would have even more security there than on the older home.

The banker not only saw the light, he facilitated the refinance by arranging for Bud to get a "weighted" mortgage — sometimes called a "blended yield

134

approach" — so that the new interest rate was below market levels. It worked this way: the bank averaged the 8½% interest rate on the prevailing loan of $16,000 and the current rate on the $19,000 additional extended credit to arrive at a more acceptable 13½% loan rate. Bud was therefore able to "crank" $19,000 out of the older home to apply to his down payment on the estate home and still not have excessive payments to cover. Thus the stage was set for the triple escrow (estate sale, lot sales, and refinance).

Everything went without a hitch. The banker came through with his $50,000 contribution. Bud added the proceeds of the lot sales and the creative refinance. And everyone came away happy, especially Bud, who had just picked up a property valued at $150,000 for nothing down — with all the future obligations covered from the beginning.

OUTCOMES AND FUTURE PLANS

But that was not the end of the story. Shortly after the close of escrow on the estate sale, Bud sold his older home for $60,000 on a one-year lease-purchase arrangement. Because the home was free and clear (the $35,000 mortgage having been moved meanwhile to the estate home), his proceeds from the contract were $2,500 cash down and the full balance of $57,500 in one year — precisely when the $50,000 note will fall due. The down payment will pay for taxes, insurance, and other miscellaneous expenses. The $350/mo. lease payments will go toward the interest on the $50,000 note. In effect, Bud had "cranked" all of his obligations out of the older home and he could now see his way clear to relax. He had made a truly remarkable nothing down deal. The sketch summarizes the various steps:

LEASE OPTION ON OLDER HOME

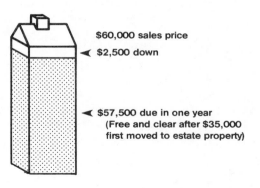

$60,000 sales price
$2,500 down

$57,500 due in one year
(Free and clear after $35,000
first moved to estate property)

Meanwhile, his payments on the estate property are only $407 per month. Therefore, he plans to live in the place for a few years, then sell it for profit or pull money out of it for future investment purchases ("Buy Low, Refinance High").

His advice to others getting started in investments: "You have to look! There are deals out there, but you have to look and then buy. Now is the time to buy, so hurry up! Don't wait." His opinion about the Nothing Down Seminar: "Best money I ever spent." He plans to retire on December 18, 1988, his 45th birthday.

COMMENTARY

1. Looking at this transaction after the fact, one gets the impression that everything fell together easily, that it was a fairly straightforward deal. Every creative act of problem solving seems simple — in retrospect. The observer thinks, "Now, why didn't I think of that?" In truth, however, it takes a certain kind of attitude, specialized knowledge, and a great deal of experience to piece together the kind of transaction described above. A willingness to explore alternative approaches to old problems is essential. As Bud described it, he had to lead the bankers and brokers through the transaction every step of the way — it was new terrain for them. They had never thought of doing it his way — but they saw that it would work, so they had the common sense to approve the solutions he was suggesting.

2. What is there about this transaction that demonstrates a new way of looking at things? First of all, the estate property consisted of four lots. To think of the property in terms of three restructured lots required the ability to visualize an adjusted use for things. Not everyone has the innate ability to look at something and be able to transform it mentally into something else — a change that might solve an existing problem. However, with practice, most people can learn this skill, especially if it brings them enormous benefits.

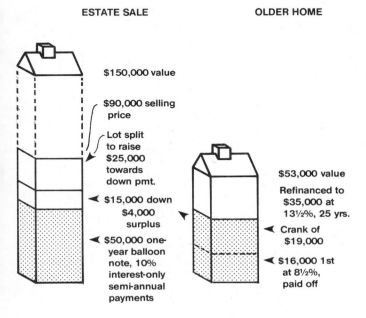

ESTATE SALE   OLDER HOME

$150,000 value

$90,000 selling
price

Lot split
to raise
$25,000
towards
down pmt.

$15,000 down
$4,000
surplus

$50,000 one-
year balloon
note, 10%
interest-only
semi-annual
payments

$53,000 value
Refinanced to
$35,000 at
13½%, 25 yrs.

Crank of
$19,000

$16,000 1st
at 8½%,
paid off

Second, the idea of moving a mortgage is a leap into a new dimension. We are conditioned to think of a mortgage as something fixed and immutable: it's locked in place until the debt is paid off, and then it is released. It takes a new perspective to understand that a mortgage is just a security agreement for a financial obligation. It makes no difference which property is used to secure a debt, just as long as the lender is happy. If he is willing to substitute collateral for his debt (move the mortgage to another property), then he opens up significant possibilities for the borrower to generate capital by borrowing against the property that has now been freed of liens — to "crank" money out of the property, as the exchangors call it.

Finally, there is the ability to see things in a larger context — to bring a number of properties together and view them as parts of a greater package. Most people are conditioned to see things in units — this property, then that property, then this one over here. A significant factor in the success of creative real estate investments is the ability to see all the units together and ask how they might be packaged for the greatest yield. Can this ability be learned? Certainly, with practice, singleness of purpose, and courage.

DOCUMENTATION

UNIVERSAL EARNEST MONEY RECEIPT
AND OFFER TO PURCHASE

"This is a legally binding contract: if not understood, seek competent advice."

1. Date and Place of Offer: __April 15,__ 19 __81__ ; __West Bend__ (city) __Wisconsin__ (state)

2. Principals: The undersigned Buyer __Bud Winston__
agrees to buy and Seller agrees to sell, according to the indicated terms and conditions, the property described as follows:

3. Property: located at __149 East Bawden Street__ (street address) __West Bend__ (city) __Wisconsin__ (state)

with the following legal description: __to be supplied__

including any of the following items if at present attached to the premises: plumbing, heating, and cooling equipment, including stoker and oil tanks, burners, water heaters, electric light fixtures, bathroom fixtures, roller shades, curtain rods and fixtures, draperies, venetian blinds, window and door screens, towel racks, linoleum and other attached floor coverings,

including carpeting, attached television antennas, mailboxes, all trees and shrubs, and any other fixtures EXCEPT _____

The following personal property shall also be included as part of the purchase: _____
At the closing of the transaction, the Seller, at his expense, shall provide the Buyer with a Bill Of Sale containing a detailed inventory of the personal property included.

4. Earnest Money Deposit: Agent (or Seller) acknowledges receipt from Buyer of __None__ dollars $ __.00__

in the form of ( ) cash; ( ) personal check; ( ) cashier's check; ( ) promissory note at _____% interest per annum due _____ 19 _____ ; or

other _____
as earnest money deposit to secure and apply on this purchase. Upon acceptance of this agreement in writing and delivery of same to Buyer, the earnest money deposit shall be assigned

to and deposited in the listing Realtor's trust account or _____ , to apply on the
purchase price at the time of closing.

5. Purchase Price: The total purchase price of the property shall be __Ninety Thousand and 00/100__ dollars $ __90,000.00__

6. Payment: Purchase price is to be paid by Buyer as follows:

Aforedescribed earnest money deposit .... $ __.00__

Additional payment due upon acceptance of this offer .... $ __1,000.00__

Additional payment due at closing .... $ __39,000.00__

Balance to be paid as follows:

__1. Subject to rear lot being sold at time of closing at acceptable price to Buyer.__

__2. Seller to accept a note for $50,000 for 1 year at 10% per annum interest with prepayment privileges.__

7. Title: Seller agrees to furnish good and marketable title free of all encumbrances and defects, except mortgage liens and encumbrances as set forth in this agreement, and to make

conveyance by Warranty Deed or _____ Seller shall furnish in due course to the Buyer a title insurance policy insuring the Buyer of a good and marketable title in keeping with the terms and conditions of this agreement. Prior to the closing of this transaction, the Seller, upon request, will furnish to the Buyer a preliminary title report made by a title insurance company showing the condition of the title to said property. If the Seller cannot furnish marketable title within thirty days after receipt of the notice to the Buyer containing a written statement of the defects, the earnest money deposit herein receipted shall be refunded to the Buyer and this agreement shall be null and void. The following shall not be deemed encumbrances or defects; building and use restrictions general to the area; utility easements; other easements not inconsistent with Buyer's intended use; zoning or subdivision laws, covenants, conditions, restrictions, or reservations of record; tenancies of record. In the event of sale of other than real property relating to this transaction, Seller will provide evidence of title or right to sell or lease such personal property.

8. Special Representations: Seller warrants and represents to Buyer (1) that the subject property is connected to ( ) public sewer system, ( ) cesspool or septic tank, ( ) sewer system available but not connected, ( ) city water system, ( ) private water system, and that the following special improvements are included in the sale: ( ) sidewalk, ( ) curb and gutter, ( ) special street paving, ( ) special street lighting; (2) that the Seller knows of no material structural defects; (3) that all electrical wiring, heating, cooling, and plumbing systems are free of material defects and will be in good working order at the time the Buyer is entitled to possession; (4) that the Seller has no notice from any government agency of any violation or knowledge of probable violations of the law relating to the subject property; (5) that the Seller has no notice or knowledge of planned or commenced public improvements which may result in special assessments or otherwise directly and materially affect the property; and (6) that the Seller has no notice or knowledge of any liens to be assessed against the property,

EXCEPT _____ None _____

9. Escrow Instructions: This sale shall be closed on or before ____ May 22, ____ 19 81 by ____ Henninger Realty Company ____ or such other closing agent as mutually agreed upon by Buyer and Seller. Buyer and Seller will, immediately on demand, deposit with closing agent all instruments and monies required

to complete the purchase in accordance with the provisions of this agreement. Contract of Sale or Instrument of Conveyance to be made in the name of _____

10. Closing Costs and Pro-Ration: Seller agrees to pay for title insurance policy, preliminary title report (if requested), termite inspection as set forth below, real estate commission, cost of preparing and recording any corrective instruments, and one-half of the escrow fees. Buyer agrees to pay for recording fees for mortgages and deeds of conveyance, all costs or expenses in securing new financing or assuming existing financing, and one-half of the escrow fees. Buyer agrees to pay for recording fees for mortgages and deeds of conveyance, all costs or expenses in securing new financing or assuming existing financing, and one-half of the escrow fees. Taxes for the current year, insurance acceptable to the Buyer, rents, interest, mortgage reserves, maintenance fees, and water and other utilities constituting liens, shall be pro-rated as of closing. Renters' security deposits shall accrue to Buyer at closing. Seller to provide Buyer with all current rental or lease agreements prior to closing.

11. Termite Inspection: Seller agrees, at his expense, to provide written certification by a reputable licensed pest control firm that the property is free of termite infestation. In the event termites are found, the Seller shall have the property treated at his expense and provide acceptable certification that treatment has been rendered. If any structural repairs are required by reason of termite damage as established by acceptable certification, Seller agrees to make necessary repairs not to exceed $500. If repairs exceed $500, Buyer shall first have the right to accept the property "as is" with a credit to the Buyer at closing of $500, or the Buyer may terminate this agreement with the earnest money deposit being promptly returned to the Buyer if the Seller does not agree to pay all costs of treatment and repair.

12. Conditions of Sale: The following conditions shall also apply, and shall, if conflicting with the printed portions of this agreement, prevail and control:

____ Buyer to inspect property before closing. _____

13. Liability and Maintenance: Seller shall maintain subject property, including landscaping, in good condition until the date of transfer of title or possession by Buyer, whichever occurs first. All risk of loss and destruction of property, and all expenses of insurance, shall be borne by the seller until the date of possession. If the improvements on the property are destroyed or materially damaged prior to closing, then the Buyer shall have the right to declare this agreement null and void, and the earnest money deposit and all other sums paid by Buyer toward the purchase price shall be returned to the Buyer forthwith.

14. Possession: The Buyer shall be entitled to possession of property upon closing or _____ , 19 _____ .

15. Default: In the event the Buyer fails to complete the purchase as herein provided, the earnest money deposit shall be retained by the Seller as the total and entire liquidated damages. In the event the Seller fails to perform any condition of the sale as herein provided, then the Buyer may, at his option, treat the contract as terminated, and all payments made by the Buyer hereunder shall be returned to the Buyer forthwith, provided the Buyer may, at his option, treat this agreement as being in full force and effect with the right to action for specific performance and damages. In the event that either Buyer, Seller, or Agent shall institute suit to enforce any rights hereunder, the prevailing party shall be entitled to court costs and a reasonable attorney's fee.

16. Time Limit of Offer: The Seller shall have until

_____ ____ April 22, _____ , 19 81 ____ to accept this
(hour)   (date)

offer by delivering a signed copy hereof to the Buyer. If this offer is not so accepted, it shall lapse and the agent (or Seller) shall refund the earnest money deposit to the Buyer forthwith.

17. General Agreements: (1) Both parties to this purchase reserve their rights to assign and hereby otherwise agree to cooperate in effecting an Internal Revenue Code 1031 exchange or similar tax-related arrangement prior to close of escrow, upon either party's written notice of intention to do so. (2) Upon approval of this offer by the Seller, this agreement shall become a contract between Buyer and Seller and shall inure to the benefit of the heirs, administrators, executors, successors, personal representatives, and assigns of said parties. (3) Time is of the essence and an essential part of this agreement. (4) This contract constitutes the sole and entire agreement between the parties hereto and no modification of this contract shall be binding unless attached hereto and signed by all parties to the contract. No representations, promises, or inducements not included in this contract shall be binding upon any party hereto.

18. Buyer's Statement and Receipt: "I/we hereby agree to purchase the above property in accordance with the terms and conditions above stated and acknowledge receipt of a

completed copy of this agreement, which I/we have fully read and understand." Dated ____ April 15, ____ 19 81 ____ , _____
                                                                                                                        (hour)

Address ____ 12 Harrison Avenue S.W. _____ [signature] _____ Buyer

____ West Bend, Wisconsin _____ Buyer

Phone No: Home ____ 211-2156 ____ Business ____ 372-9280 ____

19. Seller's Statement and Response: "I/we approve and accept the above offer, which I/we have fully read and understand, and agree to the above terms and conditions this day

of _____ , 19 _____ , _____
                                                                        (hour)

Address _____ _____ Seller

Phone No: Home _____ Business _____ _____ Seller

20. Commission Agreement: Seller agrees to pay a commission of _____% of the gross sales price to _____ for services in this transaction, and agrees that, in the event of forfeiture of the earnest money deposit by the Buyer, said deposit shall be divided between the Seller's broker and the Seller (one half to each party), the Broker's part not to exceed the amount of the commission.

21. Buyer's Receipt for Signed Offer: The Buyer hereby acknowledges receipt of a copy of the above agreement bearing the Seller's signature in acceptance of this offer.

Dated _____, 19 _____   _____ Buyer

                                                                     _____ Buyer

COMMENTARY TO DOCUMENTATION

Item 2. Buyer should add the words "or Assigns" after his name.

Item 4. The fact that the sellers did not require any deposit until the time of acceptance is indicative of the fact that Bud did his trust-building thoroughly.

Item 6. The language of provision No. 2 is rather imprecise. As it stands, the note seems as though it were unsecured. The manner of payment is also unclear (in fact the loan was interest only every 6 months). Still, the transaction took place without complication.

Part VI

Hard-Money Lenders

Hard money refers to funds borrowed from banks under strict conditions of qualifying and repayment, generally at market interest rates. Soft money from sources like sellers comes more cheaply, with terms that are generally much more flexible. For that reason, creative buyers tend to exhaust soft money sources before turning to the banking industry. Nevertheless, hard-money lenders are an important if not indispensible source of down payment capital to which buyers, sooner or later, must turn.

This section outlines eleven techniques for using hard-money funds in creative ways. Thirteen of the fifty case studies covered fall into this category. The following outline gives the organization of this section:

Technique No. 24 Small Amounts of Money From Different Banks

Investors getting started are well-advised to cultivate their credit at several banks in their area. Often credit can be built up quickly by borrowing small amounts from different banks and lending institutions and then repaying the loans promptly, even ahead of time. The strategy is to build up credit in sufficient amounts so that funds will be available when that promising deal suddenly surfaces and cash is needed quickly.

Five of the case studies discussed in this book depended, in part, on the availability of hard-money funds for the down payment. In Case No. 24, which is outlined below, the buyer depended on a credit union loan for the greater part of the down payment. Four other illustrative cases are listed in the cross-reference matrix in the appendix.

Technique No. 25 Cash-By-Mail Companies

Certain specialized lending institutions and finance companies appeal to executives and other well-qualified borrowers through ads in flight magazines and professional journals. The advantages are privacy and speed. Though none of the cases in this book depended on such hard-money sources, this technique is good to keep in mind.

Technique No. 26 Credit Cards

Two of the case studies in this book depended on the use of the buyer's credit cards to raise all or part of the down payment: Case No. 25 concerns a mobile home purchased by a young buyer whose only cash investment was $500 borrowed against his VISA/MC account; Case No. 26, also concerning a mobile home, was put together using funds borrowed through the buyer's revolving credit account. Except in unusual cases where the investor has acquired dozens of credit cards and uses them in a strategic and coordinated way, the amounts of cash generated by this technique are not generally large. However, where the buyer comes up a few hundred (or even a few thousand) dollars short, credit cards can make the difference.

Technique No. 27 Home Improvement Loans

Often hard-money funds borrowed to complete improvements to a property can relieve the pressures on cash-poor buyers and rejuvenate accounts set aside for down payments and fix-up. Allocation of home improvement funds has to comply with the lender's policy, of course. In Case No. 27, printed below, a $6,000 long-term Title I Home Improvement loan was an important ingredient in the over-all acquisitions process of a single family house.

Technique No. 28 Home Equity Loans

Even in tight-money times, there are mortgage and finance companies willing to make second-mortgage loans secured by the equity in a buyer's home. Often the beginning investor will get his or her start in this way. Case No. 28 describes how a couple in Arizona used a $20,000 home equity loan to acquire two single family rental homes and get their investment ball rolling.

Technique No. 29 Refinance Boat, Car, Stereo, or Other Personal Property

Hard-money lenders are often willing to loan money secured against valuable personal property. In a counseling session recently, a client was asking how to come up with the last $2,000 needed to consummate a deal on an excellent condo. He had no family, no partners to turn to, and no more money in savings that he could use, but he did not want to pass up the deal. I asked whether he owned a car or truck. He replied that he owned a new Datsun pickup free and clear. "Why don't you try to refinance the truck for $2,000?" I suggested. A light went on, and he headed for the banks to see what could be done. Not all lenders will welcome him with open arms, but he will eventually find one that will.

None of the fifty case studies in this book were dependent on this technique, but it is a good one to keep track of, especially for new investors just getting started.

Technique No. 30 VA Loans

For the buyer who qualifies for a Veterans Administration loan, the down payment on a property is quite manageable — zero! VA loans are also possible even if the qualifying borrower is buying a duplex or 4-plex with the idea of living in one of the units. Anyone can assume a VA loan with a minimum of hassle and cost (around $50). That leaves energy to spare for dealing creatively with the down payment challenge.

Technique No. 31 FHA Loans

Buyers who want to acquire their own residence for little down will find a loan guaranteed by the Federal Housing Administration to their liking. Down payments can be as low as 5%, although the FHA, like the VA, is particular about the quality of home they will accept. FHA loans are always readily assumable with a minimum of hassle and cost (around $50).

Techniques No. 30 and 31 are common approaches to low down transactions and are not featured in this volume. However, investors who are sensitive to the modern problems of negative cash flow will keep their eyes open for properties with assumable FHA and VA loans. Due-on-sale clauses are never a worry with such loans, and the interest rates are usually somewhat lower.

Technique No. 32 The Second Mortgage Crank

This technique is one of the foundation stones of

creative finance. Named by Robert G. Allen, the second mortgage crank is a strategy that will work equally well with fussy sellers as well as don't wanters. The term "crank" is an old exchangor's term that refers to the process of generating hard-money funds by originating new loans against a property. One speaks of "cranking" money out of the property in this way. Here's how the technique works.

The buyer looks for properties that are free and clear or have relatively low loan-to-value ratios. A new hard-money first (or second) is obtained in order to generate enough money to satisfy the seller's needs. The remainder of the seller's equity is carried back on terms that are mutually agreeable. None of the cash comes out of the buyer's pocket. Naturally, the hard-money lender's policies and requirements will have to be satisfied. It may be that the carry back will have to be secured by another property in the buyer's portfolio in order that the subject property will have no secondary financing (anathema to most hard-money lenders who are asked for refinance funds of this type).

Because of the importance of this technique, we are including four case studies to illustrate how it works. Case No. 29 describes how one buyer acquired a package of four single family homes for $159,000 by obtaining a new hard-money second for $55,000 and having the seller carry back a substantial amount of his equity secured against another property. A similar approach was used in Case No. 30 involving a small single family house. In Case No. 31, the buyer assigned his interest in a property to a partner, who then sold it back to the buyer with a credit of the down payment. A new hard-money second was then obtained in order to complete the circle of transactions. Finally, in Case No. 32, a seller deeded two free and clear houses to a buyer, who obtained a new 80% first mortgage, most of which went to the seller. Meanwhile, the seller agreed to carry the remainder of the equity on a carry-back second.

The cross-reference matrix in the appendix identifies nine additional case studies that use the second mortgage crank technique.

Technique No. 33 Variation of the Crank: Seller Refinance

In some instances it might be difficult to persuade conservative lending institutions to refinance a property or provide secondary financing as part of a "crank" purchase. They may regard the substitution of collateral on the owner carry back as too complicated. To them, it might seem as though the owner carry back still looks suspiciously like an encumbrance against the subject property (even though the mortgage has been moved to another property).

One variation of the second mortgage crank technique calls for the seller to refinance his own property and then pass the new loan on to the buyer. No one at the bank is going to object to his refinancing his own property or putting on a new second mortgage. In this way the seller's needs for cash can be taken care of, the balance of the equity being carried back in the form of a second or third mortgage.

Case No. 33 is a good example of this alternative approach to the second mortgage crank. The seller agreed to obtain a $12,000 hard-money second to generate needed capital before the property was passed on to the buyer, who in turn gave the seller a third mortgage for the remaining equity.

Technique No. 34 Buy Low, Refinance High

This is the old "buy low, sell high" strategy transferred from the stock market to creative real estate. The basic strategy is to locate a property discounted substantially below market levels and then refinance it with a new hard-money first in order to achieve higher leverage or generate funds to satisfy the needs of the seller (and buyer as well). This technique is particularly suited to tight-money times where negative cash flows can be a deterrent to investing.

Three case studies in this section illustrate the important technique of "Buy Low, Refinance High." In Case No. 34, a young woman investor stands to make around $1,500,000 using this technique on a package of 180 discounted townhomes. In Case No. 35, a buyer was able to pick up $10,000 in instant equity by refinancing a discounted duplex acquired in a nothing down deal. In Case No. 36, the buyers of three duplexes put $30,000 into their pocket by refinancing the discounted properties.

How The IRS Can Help Swing A Nothing Down Deal

Featuring Technique No. 24
"Small Amounts of Money From Different Banks"

In A Nutshell. . .

Type: SFH
Price: $28,500
Source: Realtor
Means: Contract
Techniques: No. 4 — Contract/Wrap
No. 6 — Balloon
No. 24 — Small Amounts From Banks
Strategies: Graduated payments

LOCATING

Syd LaMotte is a naval officer stationed in the Seattle area. Shortly after taking the Nothing Down Seminar, he purchased his first rental property using a partner's money and his own time and expertise. When a Realtor drew his attention to another property for sale on the same street in Bremerton, he decided to look into the matter.

SITUATION

It was a small but cozy single family home occupied by a man who had retired and was about to move from the area. The asking price was $28,500 with $5,000 down and the balance on a 20-year contract at 12%, ballooned out after three years.

NEGOTIATION

Syd's first line of questioning centered around tax matters. He asked the seller whether he had thought through the tax ramifications of accepting such a large cash down payment? Being retired, the man was sensitive about protecting his hard-earned assets; he quickly realized that the IRS would be looking over his shoulder to take a big bite out of any cash proceeds from the sale of his home.

With that little assist from the IRS, Syd was able to negotiate a deal yielding no cash at all to the seller. The first offer gave the seller his asking price of $28,500, payable with a cash down payment of $2,565 ($2,000 for the commission plus $565 for closing costs) and the balance of $25,935 on a contract at 12% for 20 years, with a ten-year balloon and graduated payments as follows: $200/mo. for the first year, $225/mo. for the second, $250/mo. for the third, and $267/mo. thereafter. Since the property could rent for no more than $250/mo., the graduated payments were designed to keep the negative cash flow under control.

The seller countered with a 7-year balloon and $225/mo. for the first year. The buyer agreed, contingent on his being able to obtain financing for $2,000 of the down payment. The $250 in earnest money was itself not in the form of cash but rather a note payable to the seller.

CLOSING

Syd had wisely cultivated his friendships at the lending institutions in his area. It was, therefore, no problem to go to the credit union and take out a small loan of $2,000 at 11.25% for two years to put down on the deal. Payments were $93 per month. His own cash contribution at closing was only $565. The details of the transaction, which was handled by a local title company, are shown in the following sketch:

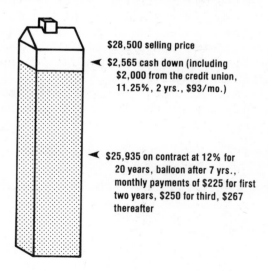

$28,500 selling price

$2,565 cash down (including $2,000 from the credit union, 11.25%, 2 yrs., $93/mo.)

$25,935 on contract at 12% for 20 years, balloon after 7 yrs., monthly payments of $225 for first two years, $250 for third, $267 thereafter

OUTCOMES AND FUTURE PLANS

With rent at $250 per month and payments on both notes of $318, the negative cash flow after monthly expenses of around $50 is over $100. The situation will wash after retirement of the credit union loan in two years.

Looking back on his second transaction, Syd feels that the most important factor in the negotiation was bringing the IRS into the picture. His advice to others getting started is this: "Keep looking. The don't wanters are out there. Every seller wants cash down, but some change their mind when the taxes are explained." His opinion about the Nothing Down Seminar: "The best thing since sliced bread! My friends can't believe I bought two houses in two months."

COMMENTARY

1. Some deals require only a small amount of cash down to fall in place. Thus the importance of having access to hard-money lenders for that small loan when it is needed. Beginning investors should cultivate their credit at several banks by meticulously and strategically turning over several small loans at these institutions. Credit unions are also a good source of ready capital. Serious investors will have developed lines of credit at their banks consonant with the dimensions of their real estate program. A line of credit in the amount of $25,000, $50,000, or more is not unusual for some individuals.

2. Syd was clever to insist on a staggered payment schedule for the monthly obligations on the note. Even though the note will grow slightly — the actual payments would have exceeded the $225 agreed to by around $58 — Syd has kept the alligator in check, at least to a certain extent.

3. What could Syd have done to cage the alligator altogether? One approach might have been to ask the Realtor to take the $2,000 commission in the form of paper — preferably interest free — for one year. The note could have been secured by a deed of

trust in second position. Another approach might have been to insist that the payments on the contract be structured to eliminate negative cash flow altogether. To meet the objections of the seller, Syd might have had to offer slightly more interest on the note.

4. The seven-year balloon is a great improvement on the three-year call at first requested by the seller. Even so, every contract with a balloon should include provisions for deferring payment by at least one additional year just in case things don't fall in place as planned. The rollover provision might cost the buyer a little cash paydown on the principal or perhaps a hike in the interest rate when the time comes, but the insurance is well worth it.

5. Syd would have been wise to insist on a substitution of collateral clause in his contract. By moving the mortgage off his house in the future, he would have a powerful tool for raising more investment capital through hard-money refinancing.

6. Note that the earnest money was paid in the form of a note, rather than cash. This is perhaps a small matter, especially when the earnest money is as manageable as $250. However, if an investor has many deals going at one time, a considerable amount of cash can be tied up in escrow accounts. The solution is, therefore, to offer notes in lieu of cash. The amount of earnest money can even be increased in this way, as long as risk is reduced through appropriate contingency clauses. One Nothing Down investor in Los Angeles regularly uses $5,000 earnest money notes in making offers on multi-unit apartment buildings.

DOCUMENTATION (INITIAL OFFER)

UNIVERSAL EARNEST MONEY RECEIPT AND OFFER TO PURCHASE

"This is a legally binding contract: if not understood, seek competent advice."

1. Date and Place of Offer: __August 19,__ 19 __81__ ; __Port Orchard__ (city) __Washington__ (state)

2. Principals: The undersigned Buyer __Syd LaMotte and Shirley LaMotte (H & W) or Assigns__
agrees to buy and Seller agrees to sell, according to the indicated terms and conditions, the property described as follows:

3. Property: located at __157 Charles Avenue__ (street address) __Bremerton__ (city) __Washington__ (state)

with the following legal description: __Clearwater Point Addition, Block 2, Lot 15, Kitsap County__

including any of the following items if at present attached to the premises: plumbing, heating, and cooling equipment, including stoker and oil tanks, burners, water heaters, electric light fixtures, bathroom fixtures, roller shades, curtain rods and fixtures, draperies, venetian blinds, window and door screens, towel racks, linoleum and other attached floor coverings,

including carpeting, attached television antennas, mailboxes, all trees and shrubs, and any other fixtures EXCEPT __None__

The following personal property shall also be included as part of the purchase: __refrigerator, stove, lawnmower__

At the closing of the transaction, the Seller, at his expense, shall provide the Buyer with a Bill Of Sale containing a detailed inventory of the personal property included.

4. Earnest Money Deposit: Agent (or Seller) acknowledges receipt from Buyer of <u>Two Hundred Fifty and 00/100</u> dollars $ <u>250.00</u>

in the form of ( ) cash; ( ) personal check; ( ) cashier's check; ( ) promissory note at <u>0</u> % interest per annum due <u>at closing</u> 19 <u>   </u> ; or

other <u>   </u>
as earnest money deposit to secure and apply on this purchase. Upon acceptance of this agreement in writing and delivery of same to Buyer, the earnest money deposit shall be assigned

to and deposited in the listing Realtor's trust account or <u>   </u>, to apply on the
purchase price at the time of closing.

5. Purchase Price: The total purchase price of the property shall be <u>Twenty-eight Thousand Five Hundred and 00/100</u> dollars

$ <u>28,500.00</u>

6. Payment: Purchase price is to be paid by Buyer as follows:

Aforedescribed earnest money deposit . . . . $ <u>250.00</u>

Additional payment due upon acceptance of this offer . . . . $ <u>--</u>

Additional payment due at closing . . . . $ <u>2,315.00</u>

Balance to be paid as follows:

Purchaser agrees to sign a promissory note, secured by a Deed of Trust Form A, a blank copy of which is attached for information and terms of which are incorporated by reference, in the amount of $25,935 more or less, with interest at 12% per annum computed on the diminishing principal balances. The monthly payments shall be: $200 per month during the first year, $225 per month during the second year, $250 per month during the third year, and $266.77 per month thereafter. On or before the tenth anniversary of the signing of the note, Purchaser agrees to pay to the Seller the remaining principal balance of the promissory note and all payments in arrears as a result of the above described graduated payment schedule, total sum of $25,731.62, more or less. Interest to commence on closing, first payment due 30 days after closing.

This offer is subject to purchaser obtaining suitable financing in the sum of $2,000.00. Purchaser agrees to make application for the same within five business days after notification of Seller's acceptance. If financing is not obtained within twenty days, the earnest money shall be refunded to the Purchaser.

7. Title: Seller agrees to furnish good and marketable title free of all encumbrances and defects, except mortgage liens and encumbrances as set forth in this agreement, and to make

conveyance by Warranty Deed or <u>   </u>. Seller shall furnish in due course
to the Buyer a title insurance policy insuring the Buyer of a good and marketable title in keeping with the terms and conditions of this agreement. Prior to the closing of this transaction, the Seller, upon request, will furnish to the Buyer a preliminary title report made by a title insurance company showing the condition of the title to said property. If the Seller cannot furnish marketable title within thirty days after receipt of the notice to the Buyer containing a written statement of the defects, the earnest money deposit herein receipted shall be refunded to the Buyer and this agreement shall be null and void. The following shall not be deemed encumbrances or defects; building and use restrictions general to the area; utility easements; other easements not inconsistent with Buyer's intended use; zoning or subdivision laws, covenants, conditions, restrictions, or reservations of record; tenancies of record. In the event of sale of other than real property relating to this transaction, Seller will provide evidence of title or right to sell or lease such personal property.

8. Special Representations: Seller warrants and represents to Buyer (1) that the subject property is connected to ( ) public sewer system, ( ) cesspool or septic tank, ( ) sewer system available but not connected, ( ) city water system, ( ) private water system, and that the following special improvements are included in the sale: ( ) sidewalk, ( ) curb and gutter, ( ) special street paving, ( ) special street lighting; (2) that the Seller knows of no material structural defects; (3) that all electrical wiring, heating, cooling, and plumbing systems are free of material defects and will be in good working order at the time the Buyer is entitled to possession; (4) that the Seller has no notice from any government agency of any violation or knowledge of probable violations of the law relating to the subject property; (5) that the Seller has no notice or knowledge of planned or commenced public improvements which may result in special assessments or otherwise directly and materially affect the property; and (6) that the Seller has no notice or knowledge of any liens to be assessed against the property,

EXCEPT <u>None</u>

9. Escrow Instructions: This sale shall be closed on or before <u>September 17</u>, 19 <u>81</u> by <u>Puget Title Company</u>
or such other closing agent as mutually agreed upon by Buyer and Seller. Buyer and Seller will, immediately on demand, deposit with closing agent all instruments and monies required

to complete the purchase in accordance with the provisions of this agreement. Contract of Sale or Instrument of Conveyance to be made in the name of <u>   </u>

10. Closing Costs and Pro-Ration: Seller agrees to pay for title insurance policy, preliminary title report (if requested), termite inspection as set forth below, real estate commission, cost of preparing and recording any corrective instruments, and one-half of the escrow fees. Buyer agrees to pay for recording fees for mortgages and deeds of conveyance, all costs or expenses in securing new financing or assuming existing financing, and one-half of the escrow fees. Buyer agrees to pay for recording fees for mortgages and deeds of conveyance, all costs or expenses in securing new financing or assuming existing financing, and one-half of the escrow fees. Taxes for the current year, insurance acceptable to the Buyer, rents, interest, mortgage reserves, maintenance fees, and water and other utilities constituting liens, shall be pro-rated as of closing. Renters' security deposits shall accrue to Buyer at closing. Seller to provide Buyer with all current rental or lease agreements prior to closing.

11. Termite Inspection: Seller agrees, at his expense, to provide written certification by a reputable licensed pest control firm that the property is free of termite infestation. In the event termites are found, the Seller shall have the property treated at his expense and provide acceptable certification that treatment has been rendered. If any structural repairs are required by reason of termite damage as established by acceptable certification, Seller agrees to make necessary repairs not to exceed $500. If repairs exceed $500, Buyer shall first have the right to accept the property "as is" with a credit to the Buyer at closing of $500, or the Buyer may terminate this agreement with the earnest money deposit being promptly returned to the Buyer if the Seller does not agree to pay all costs of treatment and repair.

12. Conditions of Sale: The following conditions shall also apply, and shall, if conflicting with the printed portions of this agreement, prevail and control:

Seller agrees to have all utilities paid to date of closing. Seller agrees to remove all personal property, equipment, supplies, and other extraneous matter from the premises prior to vacating the property. Seller agrees to restore the premises to a clean and orderly condition.

This sale is subject to a building inspection at Purchaser's expense to be conducted within seven days of the acceptance of this agreement and evidence that such inspection has been made and is acceptable to Purchaser shall be noted by initialing Hereon   Dated   .

This offer subject to a termite inspection at Purchaser's expense. Seller agrees to pay for repairs not to exceed $200.00.

This offer is subject to Seller providing a health inspection for the septic tank provided by the Kitsap County Department of Health. If the inspection stipulates that the septic tank be pumped, the Purchaser agrees to share one half of the expense.

Purchaser will not be responsible for paying prior owner's utility bills and shall not be responsible for Assessments not disclosed prior to closing.

13. Liability and Maintenance: Seller shall maintain subject property, including landscaping, in good condition until the date of transfer of title or possession by Buyer, whichever occurs first. All risk of loss and destruction of property, and all expenses of insurance, shall be borne by the seller until the date of possession. If the improvements on the property are destroyed or materially damaged prior to closing, then the Buyer shall have the right to declare this agreement null and void, and the earnest money deposit and all other sums paid by Buyer toward the purchase price shall be returned to the Buyer forthwith.

14. Possession: The Buyer shall be entitled to possession of property upon closing or _____ NA _____, 19 _____.

15. Default: In the event the Buyer fails to complete the purchase as herein provided, the earnest money deposit shall be retained by the Seller as the total and entire liquidated damages. In the event the Seller fails to perform any condition of the sale as herein provided, then the Buyer may, at his option, treat the contract as terminated, and all payments made by the Buyer hereunder shall be returned to the Buyer forthwith, provided the Buyer may, at his option, treat this agreement as being in full force and effect with the right to action for specific performance and damages. In the event that either Buyer, Seller, or Agent shall institute suit to enforce any rights hereunder, the prevailing party shall be entitled to court costs and a reasonable attorney's fee.

16. Time Limit of Offer: The Seller shall have until

_____ August 20, _____, 19 81 to accept this
(hour)   (date)

offer by delivering a signed copy hereof to the Buyer. If this offer is not so accepted, it shall lapse and the agent (or Seller) shall refund the earnest money deposit to the Buyer forthwith.

17. General Agreements: (1) Both parties to this purchase reserve their rights to assign and hereby otherwise agree to cooperate in effecting an Internal Revenue Code 1031 exchange or similar tax-related arrangement prior to close of escrow, upon either party's written notice of intention to do so. (2) Upon approval of this offer by the Seller, this agreement shall become a contract between Buyer and Seller and shall inure to the benefit of the heirs, administrators, executors, successors, personal representatives, and assigns of said parties. (3) Time is of the essence and an essential part of this agreement. (4) This contract constitutes the sole and entire agreement between the parties hereto and no modification of this contract shall be binding unless attached hereto and signed by all parties to the contract. No representations, promises, or inducements not included in this contract shall be binding upon any party hereto.

18. Buyer's Statement and Receipt: "I/we hereby agree to purchase the above property in accordance with the terms and conditions above stated and acknowledge receipt of a completed copy of this agreement, which I/we have fully read and understand." Dated _____ August 19, _____, 19 81 , _____
(hour)

Address _____ 1515 Beach Drive _____   [signature] or Assigns _____ Buyer

_____ Port Orchard, Washington _____   [signature] _____ Buyer

Phone No: Home _____ 225-3700 _____ Business _____ 225-1416

19. Seller's Statement and Response: "I/we approve and accept the above offer, which I/we have fully read and understand, and agree to the above terms and conditions this day of _____, 19 _____, _____
(hour)

Address _____ Seller

Phone No: Home _____ Business _____ Seller

20. Commission Agreement: Seller agrees to pay a commission of _____ 7 _____% of the gross sales price to Harvey Radcliff Realty, Co. for services in this transaction, and agrees that, in the event of forfeiture of the earnest money deposit by the Buyer, said deposit shall be divided between the Seller's broker and the Seller (one half to each party), the Broker's part not to exceed the amount of the commission.

21. Buyer's Receipt for Signed Offer: The Buyer hereby acknowledges receipt of a copy of the above agreement bearing the Seller's signature in acceptance of this offer.

Dated _____, 19 _____   _____ Buyer

   _____ Buyer

COMMENTARY TO DOCUMENTATION

Item 2. Buyer wisely added "or Assigns" after the names on this line.

Item 4. Rarely does a Buyer use the excellent option of paying the deposit in the form of a promissory note. In this case, the note is redeemable in cash at time of closing. Even though a relatively small amount of money is involved, the closing was set for 30 days away, and the note keeps that amount of money out of circulation and in the hands of the buyer for that period of time.

Item 6. The amortization period is, in fact, 20 years; the agent evidently neglected to add this condition. In the negotiations, the seller stepped up the graduated payments somewhat.

It would have been prudent to add the following explicit provisions concerning the note: substitution of collateral, rollover on the balloon, prepayment without penalty, assumption provision, and first right of refusal. The text does provide for the payment of the balloon "on or before" the tenth anniversary, but no waiver of penalty is mentioned.

Item 12. The buyer wisely adds clauses concerning building inspection and health inspection. The cost is minimal for enormous risk-reduction benefits.

The termite clause overrides what is printed under Item No. 11 and obligates the buyer to proceed with the purchase regardless of the eventual costs of repairs beyond $200. It would have been safer to provide for the buyer the option of proceeding in the event the costs exceeded a fixed amount.

There are two references to the seller paying utility bills up to the time of closing (even though this is covered under Item No. 10). Perhaps the buyer knows something about the seller's habits, or perhaps he is just being prudent and cautious.

Item 15. The original gives the seller the right to institute suit to enforce any rights he has under the agreement. This should be crossed out by buyer in favor of what is written in our "Universal Earnest Money Receipt" concerning the deposit constituting the "total and entire liquidated damages."

Reprinted by permission from the *Nothing Down Advisor.*

Creative Finance In Miniature: Even Little Deals Can Pay Off

Featuring Technique No. 26
''Credit Cards''

In A Nutshell. . .

Type: Mobile Home
Price: $3,000
Source: Property manager
Terms: Contract
Techniques: No. 4 — Contract/Wrap
No. 11 — Assume Seller's Obligations
No. 12 — Use Talents
No. 26 — Credit Cards
No. 40 — Selling Notes
Features: Yields $3,000 in equity and $137/mo. cash flow

The principles of creative finance are operative independent of the size of the deal — whether it involves a large multi-unit apartment complex or one mobile home. Often times, however, the small deal provides more insight into the way creative finance works because the amounts of money are somehow less intimidating. The following nothing down transaction involves hundreds rather than millions of dollars; however, the outcomes are still very impressive.

LOCATING

Jack Slade of Casselberry, Florida (a small community north of Orlando), was on the lookout for small homes for less than $30,000. He was also willing to consider mobile homes. That's why his ears perked up when his father, who was landlord for a mobile home park in the area, mentioned that one of the tenants was in arrears with the rent and had inquired about the ways to solve the problem. She had offered to pay off at least a portion of the debt and was even strongly considering selling her mobile home to relieve the financial pressures.

SITUATION

What was involved was a 12' × 60' 1972 Flamingo in good condition worth approximately $6,000. The couple still owed $1,600 on it to a local finance company, with monthly payments of $88. Besides the $700 in back lot rent they owed Jack's father, they had debts of around $800 to satisfy in order to get a fresh start. A mobile home dealer had offered them $2,500 cash for their Flamingo if they could be out in 48 hours. This would give them $900 in walking money but would leave them with the back rent and put them in a time bind. They were, therefore, amenable to other suggestions.

NEGOTIATION

After learning what the couple needed, Jack verified the underlying financing with their creditor and offered them $3,000 cash and consideration for their mobile home. He also permitted them longer to arrange their affairs and leave. The problem was that Jack didn't have any cash whatsoever to consummate the deal. What he had was enough knowledge of creative finance to put together the following schedule of buyer credits:

$ 500 cash borrowed through VISA/MC account
$ 100 promissory note due in 31 days (no interest)
$ 100 promissory note due in 61 days (no interest)
$ 700 in assumed debts (arrears lot payments of $700)

$1,400 Total down payment (all borrowed)
$1,600 assumption of mortgage against the mobile home
$3,000 Total price, including porch and utility building

The transaction was handled by means of a simple contract of sale.

CLOSING

As it turned out, the finance company would not permit assumption of the note. Therefore, Jack got power of attorney from the sellers and makes the payments for them. He had the contract of sale recorded. The financing is summarized in the following sketch:

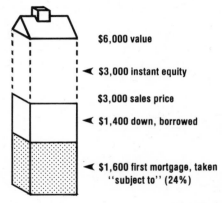

$6,000 value

◄ $3,000 instant equity

$3,000 sales price

◄ $1,400 down, borrowed

◄ $1,600 first mortgage, taken ''subject to'' (24%)

OUTCOMES AND FUTURE PLANS

The couple left the mobile home in clean condition, and Jack has rented it out for $225 per month. His payments are $88/mo. The $700 back payments owed for lot rent, together with the $60/mo. accumulating lot rent payments, are being carried interest free by the father until the investment pays off. Meanwhile, Jack is working off some of the debt by providing services at the mobile home park. His positive cash flow on the unit is therefore $137/mo. The nothing down deal also provided him with $3,000 equity in the mobile home.

Three weeks after the deal was closed, the couple approached Jack and offered to discount the two notes they were holding as part of the down payment. He redeemed the notes for $140 cash, an additional $60 in savings. He plans to hold on to the property long term and benefit from the tax benefits.

He sums up his philosophy of creative real estate investing as follows: "Try for win/win and work fast. It doesn't have to be a jazzy place to make money."

COMMENTARY

1. Just about everyone can relate to the modest amounts of money being handled in this deal. The comfort zone is broad when a few hundred dollars are involved. Essentially, Jack put down $500 in cash (borrowed), arranged for a carry-back of $200, assumed debts of $700, and took over financing of $1,600. But what if the property were not priced at $3,000 but rather $300,000. Would it take more courage to put down $50,000 (borrowed), arrange for a carry-back of $20,000, assume debts of $70,000, and take over an encumbrance of $160,000? Certainly! But the principles are the same, and as long as the resources were carefully programmed (no doubt with longer terms on the carry-back), the outcome would likewise be magnified by a very large factor. Elsewhere in this volume several very large deals are described (in the millions of dollars). The principles are the same even if the amounts differ.

2. The mobile home was discounted 50% by the sellers simply because they were desperate to get out of a tight situation. Jack might have arranged to borrow all $3,000 in needed funds (perhaps with a partner's or co-signer's help), paid off the sellers directly, then borrowed $3,000 against a free and clear property in order to roll his starter money over into another similar deal and so on ("Buy Low/Refinance High" technique).

DOCUMENTATION

No Earnest Money Agreement was used in this transaction. However, the following Bill of Sale, which the buyer had recorded, was used to complete the deal. If the buyer's obligation to pay for arrears lot payments was per oral agreement only, the sellers were trusting souls. They no doubt figured the buyer and the creditor (his father) would work things out!

Know All Men by These Presents, that Rosco Lundt and Dee Lundt of the City of Casselberry, in the County of Seminole and State of Florida, parties of the first part, for and in consideration of the sum of TEN and no/100 Dollars ($10.00) lawful money of the United States, to them paid by Jack Slade of P.O. Box 112, Casselberry, Florida, party of the second part, the receipt whereof is hereby acknowledged, have granted, bargained, sold, transferred and delivered, and by these presents do grant, bargain, sell, transfer and deliver unto the said party of the second part, and his executors, administrators and assigns, the following goods and chattels:

Mobile home at 151 Ninth Street, Casselberry, Florida, 12 × 60 1972 Flamingo, I.D. No. 6615234 and appurtenances connected to the mobile home including porch and utility shed and appliances and furniture.

To have and to hold the same unto the said party of the second part, executors, administrators and assigns forever.

AND we do, for us and our heirs, executors and administrators, convenant to and with the said party of the second part, his executors, administrators and assigns, that we are the lawful owners of the said goods and chattels; that they are free from all encumbrances; that we have good right to sell the same aforesaid, and that we will warrant and defend the sale of the said property, goods and chattels hereby made, unto the said party of the second part and his executors, administrators and assigns against the lawful claims and demands of all persons whomsoever.

In Witness Whereof, we have hereunto set our hand and seal this 2nd day of July, one thousand nine hundred and eighty-one.

[notarized signatures]

Luxury Mobile Home For $140 Bucks

**Featuring Technique No. 26
"Credit Cards"**

In A Nutshell. . .

Type: Mobile Home
Price: $14,400
Source: Acquaintance
Terms: Contract
Techniques: No. 4 — Contract/Wrap
No. 11 — Assume Seller's Obligations
No. 24 — Small Amounts From Banks
No. 26 — Credit Cards
Features: Even cash flow

LOCATING

Blanche Rirey of Phoenix was scouting for single family homes in the $30,000 to $40,000 range when an acquaintance happened to mention that he was anxious to sell his mobile home. She had not considered mobile homes for her portfolio, but, having an open mind, she looked into the details and learned the following:

SITUATION

The friend had been advised by his doctor that for health reaons he should not be living alone. Dutifully — this is the way the story was told to us — he decided to get married and move to a new location. Things had been financially tight in the past little while, and the friend was now one payment behind on his spotless 14' × 60' two-bedroom Schultz mobile home. In addition, he had not been able to make the lot rent payment for the current month. The combination of poor health, bills, and the new marriage had induced him to sell out. The loan balance on the home amounted to $12,400, with monthly payments of $177.38. Lot rent was $95/mo. The home was furnished luxuriously and located in an attractive area with a park, swimming pool, and laundromat nearby.

NEGOTIATION

Blanche asked her friend what he needed in order to make a fresh start. He asked for $2,000 above the loan, including the arrears payments, with closing in 30 days. Knowing where she could borrow the money, Blanche readily agreed. Her secret for negotiating success: "We met his immediate needs."

CLOSING

A simple contract was drawn up to cover the sale. Blanche paid the arrears payments of $272.38 and put the balance of the down payment ($1,727.62) on her revolving charge account at the local credit union for 15% interest. She arranged for the monthly payments on

the revolving account to be the same as they had been before the new loan amount was added. When she inquired about assuming the original loan, she found out that the finance company had a policy prohibiting assumptions. Refinancing the mobile home would have cost over $200 in closing fees. Blanche therefore decided to finance the total amount at her credit union for 15% and avoid all such charges. At closing she received a payoff amount of $132.06, so that the net out-of-pocket was $272.38 less $132.06, or $140.32. The financing arrangement is summarized in the following sketch:

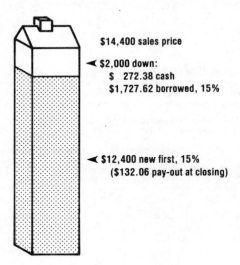

$14,400 sales price

$2,000 down:
$ 272.38 cash
$1,727.62 borrowed, 15%

$12,400 new first, 15%
($132.06 pay-out at closing)

OUTLOOK AND FUTURE PLANS

Payments on the mobile home now come to $210.00/mo., with an additional $95 for lot rent and $25 for insurance per month. Total payment is therefore $330.00, with rent income of $335.00. Blanche plans to hold her new mobile unit long term and raise the rents as quickly as possible.

COMMENTARY:

1. Blanche might have negotiated part of the down

payment in the form of an owner carry back for a more attractive interest rate than 15%.

2. She should have obtained a reliable appraisal on the unit before proceeding with the purchase.

3. Currently single family homes and small apartment buildings hold out the best promise for future appreciation. Mobile homes are less attractive because of their shorter life and the smaller circle of potential renters attracted to them. However, with the acute housing shortage expected to get worse, excellent mobile homes in superior locations may prove to be a profitable supplement to the portfolio of interested investors.

DOCUMENTATION

No Earnest Money Agreement was used to complete the transaction. The following simple contract of sale was sufficient. If the buyer was prudent, he would have had it recorded.

July 2, 1981

Sellers: Barker Selmon
           1715 Cliffton Drive
           Phoenix, Arizona 85021

Buyers: Thomas Rirey
           Blanche Rirey
           21 Manfred Ct.
           Phoenix, Arizona 85041

We, Thomas Rirey and Blanche Rirey, do agree to purchase the property, namely a 1979 2-bedroom Schultz mobile home, located at 751 West Pulman Drive, #62, from Barker Selmon, for the price of $2,000 down and assuming the loan balance of Loan #6-215-36.

The down payment of $2,000 will be paid as follows: $272.38 paid by check tonight, and the balance of $1,727.62 due on August 1, 1981, or sooner; when this can be received from lender.

[signatures]

A Fixer Upper Method For People Who Hate Fixer Uppers

Featuring Technique No. 27
"Home Improvement Loans"

In A Nutshell. . .

Type: SFH
Price: $34,632
Source: Classified ad
Means: Purchase Money Mortgage
Techniques: No. 4 — Contract/Wrap
No. 27 — Home Improvement Loan
No. 45 — Partner's Cash/Your Expertise
Features: 37% discount

LOCATING

Bert Maxwell, an engineer from Kansas City, Missouri, was having some success using the Nothing Down System. With six single family houses and a 4-plex under his belt, he was hardly ready to quit. The following ad caught his eye one day:

> WOODED LAKE FRONT—Prime location, owner finance. 3 bedrooms, 2 baths, large country kitchen, wood-burning fireplace, large yard, minor repairs, $45,000, $8,000 down, 10% interest. 578-3296.

SITUATION

Upon inspection, Bert found that the property was located on two lake front lots in a pleasant, mostly owner-occupied neighborhood not too far from the city. The setting was impressive, with many large oak trees giving shade to the house. Some repairs would be needed to bring the property up to snuff. The only encumbrance was a privately-held first of $4,632.

NEGOTIATION

Bert began with the logical questions: "Why are you selling?" "What will you be doing with the down payment?" The owner was a woman who needed money to pay for some personal debts, including back taxes and back car payments. She had neither the knowledge nor the ability to handle the needed repairs. The solution seemed clear enough to her: she wanted out. The neighborhood association was after her to clean up the property and arrange for the improvements. Her preference was to move into an apartment and get out from under home ownership responsibilities for good.

Similar homes in the neighborhood were selling for around $55,000, so Bert was interested in this house despite the fixer-upper problem. He first went to the holder of the underlying mortgage and arranged to assume the loan. Next, he offered to put $5,000 down and pay the seller $25,000 on a purchase money

mortgage (contract) at 8% for 25 years. In effect, he was offering to buy the house for $34,632. The seller grabbed it!

CLOSING

But a funny thing happened on the way to the closing. The holder of the underlying mortgage decided he did not want his note assumed after all. He would prefer cash instead. Undaunted, Bert reached into his store of partners and pulled out one with $8,000 and the ability to repair houses. Because Bert had gained control of a property with over $20,000 in potential instant equity, the partner was very pleased to put in his bit of cash and do half of the fix up in exchange for half of the equity. The arrangements were handled by a title company and turned out this way:

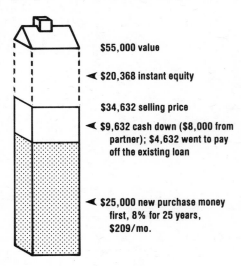

$55,000 value

◀ $20,368 instant equity

$34,632 selling price

◀ $9,632 cash down ($8,000 from partner); $4,632 went to pay off the existing loan

◀ $25,000 new purchase money first, 8% for 25 years, $209/mo.

OUTCOMES AND FUTURE PLANS

Everyone won. The seller got the creditors and the neighborhood association off her back and is now enjoying the peace of apartment living. With the help of a $6,000 long-term, low-interest Title I Home Improvement Loan and a little sweat equity (much of it done by the partner), the new owners completed the first wave of improvements and rented the house for $450 per month to a tenant who is delighted with the rustic setting. Payments on the Title I loan are only $147/mo. After servicing this obligation and debt service on the contract, there is a monthly surplus of nearly $100 for expenses and profit. Since long-range renovations can be completed over time, the home improvement loan took pressure off the entry cash situation (Bert had to put down $1,632 of his own money to get the House — still only 5%).

COMMENTARY

1. Once more, the guiding principle in creative buying is to know the needs of the seller and begin negotiating at a level that will solve those needs while maximizing the benefits to the buyer. Bert offered a price nearly 37% below the market and 23% below the asking price. He would have been willing to go higher, but the offer was already within the comfort zone of the seller, who accepted it and ran.

2. How might Bert have acquired the property without a partner? Since one of the hot buttons of the seller was to get out from under the pressure of back debts and other personal obligations, he might have arranged to take over that portion of her payables that could be paid in installments. Doing it this way, Bert might possibly have had sufficient capital to retire the underlying note and pick up all the equity in the property without having to share it with a partner. Another approach might have been to split

off one of the two lots and sell it to raise capital for the deal. Still another solution would be to put a hard-money second on the property and crank out enough money for the transaction. Bert wisely negotiated a subordination agreement with the seller, permitting him to add financing at a later date and lift the contract into second position.

3. Another smart move by Bert was to insist on a substitution of collateral clause in the contract. By moving the mortgage to another property in the future, Bert could crank a great deal of money out of the house through a new first mortgage. Alternately, if the property were freed of encumbrances through definancing (moving the mortgage), Bert could create paper against it or trade the equity into other properties.

4. With the contract running for 25 years at a rather modest rate of interest, Bert can look forward to discounting the note for cash in the future. The seller would probably be most happy to cash out at some point in time, particularly since the payments of $209/mo. will look less and less attractive under the impact of inflation. Note that Bert also exacted an agreement from the seller permitting him to assign the obligation at a later time if he should decide to sell.

5. Bert shared half the fix-up labor with a partner. For those who hate fix-up, one way to divest oneself of all the sweat equity might be to find a partner willing to do the whole job himself. The challenge is to find one with this ability who still has some cash to put into the deal! All things are possible.

DOCUMENTATION (INITIAL OFFER)

UNIVERSAL EARNEST MONEY RECEIPT
AND OFFER TO PURCHASE

"This is a legally binding contract: if not understood, seek competent advice."

1. Date and Place of Offer: **July 22,** 19 **81** ; **Houston Lake** (city) **Missouri** (state)

2. Principals: The undersigned Buyer **Bert Maxwell**
agrees to buy and Seller agrees to sell, according to the indicated terms and conditions, the property described as follows:

3. Property: located at **6219 Aquabell Circle** (street address) **Houston Lake** (city) **Missouri** (state)

with the following legal description: **to be supplied**

including any of the following items if at present attached to the premises: plumbing, heating, and cooling equipment, including stoker and oil tanks, burners, water heaters, electric light fixtures, bathroom fixtures, roller shades, curtain rods and fixtures, draperies, venetian blinds, window and door screens, towel racks, linoleum and other attached floor coverings,

including carpeting, attached television antennas, mailboxes, all trees and shrubs, and any other fixtures EXCEPT **None**

The following personal property shall also be included as part of the purchase: _____
At the closing of the transaction, the Seller, at his expense, shall provide the Buyer with a Bill Of Sale containing a detailed inventory of the personal property included.

4. Earnest Money Deposit: Agent (or Seller) acknowledges receipt from Buyer of ___One Hundred and 00/100___ dollars $ ___100.00___

in the form of ( ) cash; (X) personal check; ( ) cashier's check; ( ) promissory note at _____% interest per annum due _____ 19 _____; or

other _____
as earnest money deposit to secure and apply on this purchase. Upon acceptance of this agreement in writing and delivery of same to Buyer, the earnest money deposit shall be assigned

to and deposited in the listing Realtor's trust account or _____, to apply on the
purchase price at the time of closing.

5. Purchase Price: The total purchase price of the property shall be ___Thirty-four Thousand Six Hundred Thirty-two and___

___81/100___ dollars $ ___34,632.81___

6. Payment: Purchase price is to be paid by Buyer as follows:

Aforedescribed earnest money deposit .... $ ___100.00___

Additional payment due upon acceptance of this offer .... $ ___--___

Additional payment due at closing .... $ ___9,532.81___

Balance to be paid as follows:

Buyer to give a note securing a deed of trust on the property in favor of
the seller in the amount of $25,000.00 payable at $209.11 per month, or
more, including interest at 8 percent per annum. The cash down payment of
$9,632.81 includes $4,632.81 to pay off existing mortgage.

Buyer has the right to substitute collateral of equal or greater equity
value for the mortgage balance. Buyer has the right to assign the mortgage.
Seller agrees to allow subordination of the mortgage.

Subject to the Buyer securing a loan in the amount of $5,000 being
obtained at Buyer's expense for a period of 5 years, with interest not to
exceed 18% per annum. Buyer agrees to make application for said loan within
5 days from the date of this contract. If said loan cannot be obtained,
the earnest money deposit will be returned to Buyer.

7. Title: Seller agrees to furnish good and marketable title free of all encumbrances and defects, except mortgage liens and encumbrances as set forth in this agreement, and to make

conveyance by Warranty Deed or _____. Seller shall furnish in due course
to the Buyer a title insurance policy insuring the Buyer of a good and marketable title in keeping with the terms and conditions of this agreement. Prior to the closing of this transaction, the Seller, upon request, will furnish to the Buyer a preliminary title report made by a title insurance company showing the condition of the title to said property. If the Seller cannot furnish marketable title within thirty days after receipt of the notice to the Buyer containing a written statement of the defects, the earnest money deposit herein receipted shall be refunded to the Buyer and this agreement shall be null and void. The following shall not be deemed encumbrances or defects; building and use restrictions general to the area; utility easements; other easements not inconsistent with Buyer's intended use; zoning or subdivision laws, covenants, conditions, restrictions, or reservations of record; tenancies of record. In the event of sale of other than real property relating to this transaction, Seller will provide evidence of title or right to sell or lease such personal property.

8. Special Representations: Seller warrants and represents to Buyer (1) that the subject property is connected to ( ) public sewer system, ( ) cesspool or septic tank, ( ) sewer system available but not connected, ( ) city water system, ( ) private water system, and that the following special improvements are included in the sale: ( ) sidewalk, ( ) curb and gutter, ( ) special street paving, ( ) special street lighting; (2) that the Seller knows of no material structural defects; (3) that all electrical wiring, heating, cooling, and plumbing systems are free of material defects and will be in good working order at the time the Buyer is entitled to possession; (4) that the Seller has no notice from any government agency of any violation or knowledge of probable violations of the law relating to the subject property; (5) that the Seller has no notice or knowledge of planned or commenced public improvements which may result in special assessments or otherwise directly and materially affect the property; and (6) that the Seller has no notice or knowledge of any liens to be assessed against the property,

EXCEPT ___None___

9. Escrow Instructions: This sale shall be closed on or before ___August 1,___ 19 ___81___ by _____
or such other closing agent as mutually agreed upon by Buyer and Seller. Buyer and Seller will, immediately on demand, deposit with closing agent all instruments and monies required

to complete the purchase in accordance with the provisions of this agreement. Contract of Sale or Instrument of Conveyance to be made in the name of _____

___to be supplied___

10. Closing Costs and Pro-Ration: Seller agrees to pay for title insurance policy, preliminary title report (if requested), termite inspection as set forth below, real estate commission, cost of preparing and recording any corrective instruments, and one-half of the escrow fees. Buyer agrees to pay for recording fees for mortgages and deeds of conveyance, all costs or expenses in securing new financing or assuming existing financing, and one-half of the escrow fees. Buyer agrees to pay for recording fees for mortgages and deeds of conveyance, all costs or expenses in securing new financing or assuming existing financing, and one-half of the escrow fees. Taxes for the current year, insurance acceptable to the Buyer, rents, interest, mortgage reserves, maintenance fees, and water and other utilities constituting liens, shall be pro-rated as of closing. Renters' security deposits shall accrue to Buyer at closing. Seller to provide Buyer with all current rental or lease agreements prior to closing.

11. Termite Inspection: Seller agrees, at his expense, to provide written certification by a reputable licensed pest control firm that the property is free of termite infestation. In the event termites are found, the Seller shall have the property treated at his expense and provide acceptable certification that treatment has been rendered. If any structural repairs are required by reason of termite damage as established by acceptable certification, Seller agrees to make necessary repairs not to exceed $500. If repairs exceed $500, Buyer shall first have the right to accept the property "as is" with a credit to the Buyer at closing of $500, or the Buyer may terminate this agreement with the earnest money deposit being promptly returned to the Buyer if the Seller does not agree to pay all costs of treatment and repair.

12. Conditions of Sale: The following conditions shall also apply, and shall, if conflicting with the printed portions of this agreement, prevail and control:

___None___

13. Liability and Maintenance: Seller shall maintain subject property, including landscaping, in good condition until the date of transfer of title or possession by Buyer, whichever occurs first. All risk of loss and destruction of property, and all expenses of insurance, shall be borne by the seller until the date of possession. If the improvements on the property are destroyed or materially damaged prior to closing, then the Buyer shall have the right to declare this agreement null and void, and the earnest money deposit and all other sums paid by Buyer toward the purchase price shall be returned to the Buyer forthwith.

14. Possession: The Buyer shall be entitled to possession of property upon closing or _____, 19 _____.

15. Default: In the event the Buyer fails to complete the purchase as herein provided, the earnest money deposit shall be retained by the Seller as the total and entire liquidated damages. In the event the Seller fails to perform any condition of the sale as herein provided, then the Buyer may, at his option, treat the contract as terminated, and all payments made by the Buyer hereunder shall be returned to the Buyer forthwith, provided the Buyer may, at his option, treat this agreement as being in full force and effect with the right to action for specific performance and damages. In the event that either Buyer, Seller, or Agent shall institute suit to enforce any rights hereunder, the prevailing party shall be entitled to court costs and a reasonable attorney's fee.

16. Time Limit of Offer: The Seller shall have until

_____ _____, 19 _____ to accept this
(hour) (date)

offer by delivering a signed copy hereof to the Buyer. If this offer is not so accepted, it shall lapse and the agent (or Seller) shall refund the earnest money deposit to the Buyer forthwith.

17. General Agreements: (1) Both parties to this purchase reserve their rights to assign and hereby otherwise agree to cooperate in effecting an Internal Revenue Code 1031 exchange or similar tax-related arrangement prior to close of escrow, upon either party's written notice of intention to do so. (2) Upon approval of this offer by the Seller, this agreement shall become a contract between Buyer and Seller and shall inure to the benefit of the heirs, administrators, executors, successors, personal representatives, and assigns of said parties. (3) Time is of the essence and an essential part of this agreement. (4) This contract constitutes the sole and entire agreement between the parties hereto and no modification of this contract shall be binding unless attached hereto and signed by all parties to the contract. No representations, promises, or inducements not included in this contract shall be binding upon any party hereto.

18. Buyer's Statement and Receipt: "I/we hereby agree to purchase the above property in accordance with the terms and conditions above stated and acknowledge receipt of a completed copy of this agreement, which I/we have fully read and understand." Dated _____ 19 _____, _____
(hour)

Address _____ 412 Bluebird Avenue _____   [signature] _____ Buyer

_____ Kansas City, Missouri _____   _____ Buyer

Phone No: Home ___ 221-4419 ___ Business ___ 345-2217 ___

19. Seller's Statement and Response: "I/we approve and accept the above offer, which I/we have fully read and understand, and agree to the above terms and conditions this day

of _____, 19 _____, _____
(hour)

Address _____   _____ Seller

Phone No: Home _____ Business _____   _____ Seller

20. Commission Agreement: Seller agrees to pay a commission of ___ NA ___ % of the gross sales price to _____ for services in this transaction, and agrees that, in the event of forfeiture of the earnest money deposit by the Buyer, said deposit shall be divided between the Seller's broker and the Seller (one half to each party), the Broker's part not to exceed the amount of the commission.

21. Buyer's Receipt for Signed Offer: The Buyer hereby acknowledges receipt of a copy of the above agreement bearing the Seller's signature in acceptance of this offer.

Dated _____, 19 _____   _____ Buyer

_____ Buyer

COMMENTARY TO DOCUMENTATION

Item 2. Buyer should add the words "or Assigns" after his name.

Item 6. The technical language is "deed of trust securing a note," not the other way around. (It worked out all right in the long run anyway!) The buyer was wise to stipulate provisions for substitution of collateral, assignment (assumption), and subordination. Prepayment provisions without penalty should also have been included.

Interest at 10% per annum may well be imputed by the IRS on payments made and payments received.

As it turned out, the buyer did not need to obtain a bank loan; however, the condition stipulated permitted him leeway for the partnership.

Item 16. No time limit is imposed by the buyer, a risky venture.

Using Hidden Assets To Buy Rental Homes

**Featuring Technique No. 28
''Home Equity Loans''**

In A Nutshell. . .

Type: 2 SFH's
Price: $52,900, $53,900
Source: Realtor
Means: Assumption, carry back
Techniques: No. 4 — Contract/Wrap
　　　　　　 No. 6 — Balloon
　　　　　　 No. 9 — Savings and Inheritances
　　　　　　 No. 19 — Borrowing Realtor's Commission
　　　　　　 No. 28 — Home Equity Loans
Features: Positive cash flow

Jay and Mary Cameron of Scottsdale, Arizona, sold their veterinary practice for health reasons and turned to other strategies for building a retirement program. After taking the Nothing Down Seminar in January, 1981, they decided to develop a portfolio of residential real estate. The goal was two properties per year. They did not wait long to meet the first year's goal.

LOCATING

A Realtor graduate of the same seminar knew a man in his church who had two houses for sale. At one of the monthly R.A.N.D. meetings, the Realtor passed the lead on to the Camerons, who lost no time investigating the deal.

SITUATION

The properties were located in Tempe. Both were of brick construction, about twenty years old. One of them contained an efficiency apartment in addition to the main unit. The owner was occupying one of the houses. Since he was in the process of building a new house in the area, he needed to generate enough cash from the sale to cover expenses at the other end of his move. Around 25% down was required.

NEGOTIATION

The Camerons had some savings set aside to begin their investment program, but not enough to satisfy the needs of the seller. However, their home had an equity of around $60,000 that was available as a venture asset.

They offered the seller $23,000 in cash for the package if he would be willing to take back a note for the balance of his equity on the one house at an interest rate of 10%, with monthly payments of $226 and a balloon payment after four years. The existing first mortgages would be assumed. The seller agreed.

CLOSING

The first order of business was to arrange for an equity loan to supplement the $3,000 cash available from the Cameron's savings. Jay approached the bank he had been dealing with ever since he was fourteen years old and got his first loan of $300 to buy a steer in the 4-H program. Even though he had established an excellent credit record over the years, he was told by the loan officer, "We don't make equity loans here." No amount of negotiating could change their mind.

Jay turned to other sources. He had met the manager of another bank at a Y.M.C.A. fitness program and followed up, this time with better results. The banker quickly arranged for a $20,000 loan at 15% for nine years, payments of $340 per month, secured by the Camerons' personal residence.

The sketch shows the financing arrangements as handled by a local title company:

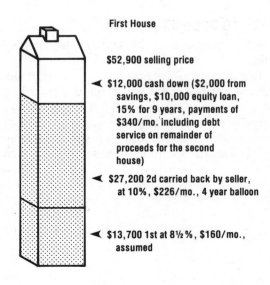

First House

$52,900 selling price

◀ $12,000 cash down ($2,000 from savings, $10,000 equity loan, 15% for 9 years, payments of $340/mo. including debt service on remainder of proceeds for the second house)

◀ $27,200 2d carried back by seller, at 10%, $226/mo., 4 year balloon

◀ $13,700 1st at 8½%, $160/mo., assumed

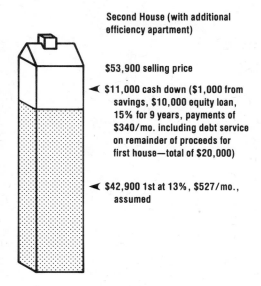

Second House (with additional efficiency apartment)

$53,900 selling price

◄ $11,000 cash down ($1,000 from savings, $10,000 equity loan, 15% for 9 years, payments of $340/mo. including debt service on remainder of proceeds for first house—total of $20,000)

◄ $42,900 1st at 13%, $527/mo., assumed

As an added bonus, the Realtor credited the Camerons with $900 at closing, an amount equal to one-half of his share of the commissions. Forgiving a portion of the commission was certainly a cut above taking it back in the form of a note.

OUTCOMES AND FUTURE PLANS

Monthly payments and expenses on the two properties, including debt service for the equity loan, actually amount to $25 less than the income, a relatively pleasant state of affairs. The seller, incidentally, remained as a tenant in his former home for a period of five months.

Looking back at his first real estate investment, Jay felt his success in negotiating was due to the win/win attitude: being reasonable and showing he wanted to help the seller. His advice to others: "Don't be afraid to get started as soon as possible . . . . Once you start, it's easy."

COMMENTARY

1. There is little to compare with the excitement of being involved in one's first income real estate transaction. A frequent approach for first-time investors is to use the hidden equity assets of a personal residence. Like the use of personal savings, this technique naturally has its limits. As the saying goes: "You always run out of money before you run out of good deals." Still, there is nothing wrong with investing cash and equity assets astutely in income-producing real estate where the yields are far higher than in savings accounts or money market certificates. The Camerons are particularly wise to have structured the financing for a positive cash flow so that the tenants are gradually paying off the encumbrances. That way, the equity loan never has the effect of a drag on family finances.

2. What other alternatives are available in cases where the seller needs a considerable amount of money down? Rather than taking out an equity loan, the Camerons might have brought in a partner to contribute cash in exchange for part interest in the properties. Another approach might have been to look for "wholesale" properties where the seller would be offering a hefty discount for cash-to-mortgage offers. The buyers could then use borrowed funds to buy out the seller completely and refinance the property to recapture the funds in time for the next deal. This technique is known as "Buy Low, Refinance High." Still another approach might have been to use a "creative refinance" strategy, particularly on the first of the two houses described above. If the lender had sold the first to Fannie Mae (The Federal National Mortgage Association), there is a current program available through Fannie Mae that permits buyers to refinance low interest loans at rates below market levels. If that were applicable in this case, the Camerons could have "cranked" enough money out of the first house to pay the seller his just dues and still avoided a negative cash flow.

3. The experience Jay had with the first banker underscores the need for investors to cultivate multiple credit sources among the hard-money lenders. An instant credit line should be available for the moment in time where the good deal comes along.

4. One way to have softened the cash down obligation might have been to require the seller-tenant to credit his monthly rent payments toward the down. It never hurts to ask.

5. The four-year balloon is on the fringes of acceptable risk. Since the seller was receiving $23,000 in cash, he should have been induced to carry back the paper for at least five years. Five years is considered a minimum fuse in these days of uncertainty when it comes to real property appreciation. We are going through an adjustment in the economy that will cause some markets to remain flat for a period of time, and perhaps even decline temporarily. To be safe, the investor should avoid anything shorter than a five-year balloon. At the very least, the contract should provide for at least a one-year rollover in case of difficulty at the end of the balloon period. The seller may have to be induced through higher interest rates or a pay-down of the principal when the time comes.

6. An important consideration for the first-time investor is to get in the habit of requiring a substitution of collateral clause in the documentation. The $27,200 carry back arranged by the Camerons should have been tied to the privilege of moving the mortgage in the future — at the buyers' option and with the seller's approval. Such an arrangement assures maximum flexibility for future investment strategies.

UNIVERSAL EARNEST MONEY RECEIPT
AND OFFER TO PURCHASE

"This is a legally binding contract: if not understood, seek competent advice."

1. Date and Place of Offer: ___March 1,___ 19 81 ; ___Tempe___ ___Arizona___
                                                                    (city)   (state)

2. Principals: The undersigned Buyer ___Jay Cameron and Mary Cameron or Assigns___
agrees to buy and Seller agrees to sell, according to the indicated terms and conditions, the property described as follows:

3. Property: located at ___674 Bickford Circle___ ___Tempe___ ___Arizona___
                                    (street address)   (city)   (state)

with the following legal description: ___to be supplied___

including any of the following items if at present attached to the premises: plumbing, heating, and cooling equipment, including stoker and oil tanks, burners, water heaters, electric light fixtures, bathroom fixtures, roller shades, curtain rods and fixtures, draperies, venetian blinds, window and door screens, towel racks, linoleum and other attached floor coverings,

including carpeting, attached television antennas, mailboxes, all trees and shrubs, and any other fixtures EXCEPT ___None___

The following personal property shall also be included as part of the purchase: ___refrigerator___
At the closing of the transaction, the Seller, at his expense, shall provide the Buyer with a Bill Of Sale containing a detailed inventory of the personal property included.

4. Earnest Money Deposit: Agent (or Seller) acknowledges receipt from Buyer of ___One Hundred and 00/100___ dollars $ ___100.00___

in the form of ( ) cash; (X) personal check; ( ) cashier's check; ( ) promissory note at _____% interest per annum due _____ 19 _____; or

other _____
as earnest money deposit to secure and apply on this purchase. Upon acceptance of this agreement in writing and delivery of same to Buyer, the earnest money deposit shall be assigned

to and deposited in the listing Realtor's trust account or _____, to apply on the
purchase price at the time of closing.

5. Purchase Price: The total purchase price of the property shall be ___Fifty-two Thousand Nine Hundred and 00/100___

dollars $ ___52,900.00___

6. Payment: Purchase price is to be paid by Buyer as follows:

Aforedescribed earnest money deposit .... $ ___100.00___

Additional payment due upon acceptance of this offer .... $ ___--___

Additional payment due at closing .... $ ___11,900.00___

Balance to be paid as follows:

This purchase is subject to Buyer assuming and paying Seller's current first trust deed and note held by American Mortgage Company with monthly payments on the approximate balance of $13,700 payable approximately $160.00 per month including interest not in excess of 8 1/2% per annum PITI.

This purchase is subject to Buyer obtaining a new loan, secured by second trust deed against Buyer's home at 884 Park Street, Scottsdale, in the amount of $20,000 payable in monthly installments of $340.00, including interest of not more than 15% per annum. $10,000 of the proceeds from this loan to apply to the purchase of 696 Bickford Circle being closed simultaneously. Buyer agrees to make application for loan within five days of acceptance of this offer by Seller.

Balance of payment to be evidenced in the form of a note and second trust deed executed by Buyer in favor of Seller in the amount of $27,200 payable $226 per month, including 10% interest per annum all due and payable four years from date of execution. Interest to accrue as of close of escrow. First payment due 30 days from close of escrow.

This purchase contingent upon the concurrent close of escrow on the property located at 696 Bickford Circle.

7. Title: Seller agrees to furnish good and marketable title free of all encumbrances and defects, except mortgage liens and encumbrances as set forth in this agreement, and to make conveyance by Warranty Deed or _____. Seller shall furnish in due course to the Buyer a title insurance policy insuring the Buyer of a good and marketable title in keeping with the terms and conditions of this agreement. Prior to the closing of this transaction, the Seller, upon request, will furnish to the Buyer a preliminary title report made by a title insurance company showing the condition of the title to said property. If the Seller cannot furnish marketable title within thirty days after receipt of the notice to the Buyer containing a written statement of the defects, the earnest money deposit herein receipted shall be refunded to the Buyer and this agreement shall be null and void. The following shall not be deemed encumbrances or defects; building and use restrictions general to the area; utility easements; other easements not inconsistent with Buyer's intended use; zoning or subdivision laws, covenants, conditions, restrictions, or reservations of record; tenancies of record. In the event of sale of other than real property relating to this transaction, Seller will provide evidence of title or right to sell or lease such personal property.

8. Special Representations: Seller warrants and represents to Buyer (1) that the subject property is connected to ( ) public sewer system, ( ) cesspool or septic tank, ( ) sewer system available but not connected, ( ) city water system, ( ) private water system, and that the following special improvements are included in the sale: ( ) sidewalk, ( ) curb and gutter, ( ) special street paving, ( ) special street lighting; (2) that the Seller knows of no material structural defects; (3) that all electrical wiring, heating, cooling, and plumbing systems are free of material defects and will be in good working order at the time the Buyer is entitled to possession; (4) that the Seller has no notice from any government agency of any violation or knowledge of probable violations of the law relating to the subject property; (5) that the Seller has no notice or knowledge of planned or commenced public improvements which may result in special assessments or otherwise directly and materially affect the property; and (6) that the Seller has no notice or knowledge of any liens to be assessed against the property,

EXCEPT _____ None

9. Escrow Instructions: This sale shall be closed on or before __March 13,__ 19 81 by __Arizona Escrow Company__ or such other closing agent as mutually agreed upon by Buyer and Seller. Buyer and Seller will, immediately on demand, deposit with closing agent all instruments and monies required to complete the purchase in accordance with the provisions of this agreement. Contract of Sale or Instrument of Conveyance to be made in the name of _____

__to be supplied__

10. Closing Costs and Pro-Ration: Seller agrees to pay for title insurance policy, preliminary title report (if requested), termite inspection as set forth below, real estate commission, cost of preparing and recording any corrective instruments, and one-half of the escrow fees. Buyer agrees to pay for recording fees for mortgages and deeds of conveyance, all costs or expenses in securing new financing or assuming existing financing, and one-half of the escrow fees. Buyer agrees to pay for recording fees for mortgages and deeds of conveyance, all costs or expenses in securing new financing or assuming existing financing, and one-half of the escrow fees. Taxes for the current year, insurance acceptable to the Buyer, rents, interest, mortgage reserves, maintenance fees, and water and other utilities constituting liens, shall be pro-rated as of closing. Renters' security deposits shall accrue to Buyer at closing. Seller to provide Buyer with all current rental or lease agreements prior to closing.

11. Termite Inspection: Seller agrees, at his expense, to provide written certification by a reputable licensed pest control firm that the property is free of termite infestation. In the event termites are found, the Seller shall have the property treated at his expense and provide acceptable certification that treatment has been rendered. If any structural repairs are required by reason of termite damage as established by acceptable certification, Seller agrees to make necessary repairs not to exceed $500. If repairs exceed $500, Buyer shall first have the right to accept the property "as is" with a credit to the Buyer at closing of $500, or the Buyer may terminate this agreement with the earnest money deposit being promptly returned to the Buyer if the Seller does not agree to pay all costs of treatment and repair.

12. Conditions of Sale: The following conditions shall also apply, and shall, if conflicting with the printed portions of this agreement, prevail and control:

_____ None

13. Liability and Maintenance: Seller shall maintain subject property, including landscaping, in good condition until the date of transfer of title or possession by Buyer, whichever occurs first. All risk of loss and destruction of property, and all expenses of insurance, shall be borne by the seller until the date of possession. If the improvements on the property are destroyed or materially damaged prior to closing, then the Buyer shall have the right to declare this agreement null and void, and the earnest money deposit and all other sums paid by Buyer toward the purchase price shall be returned to the Buyer forthwith.

14. Possession: The Buyer shall be entitled to possession of property upon closing or _____, 19 ____.

15. Default: In the event the Buyer fails to complete the purchase as herein provided, the earnest money deposit shall be retained by the Seller as the total and entire liquidated damages. In the event the Seller fails to perform any condition of the sale as herein provided, then the Buyer may, at his option, treat the contract as terminated, and all payments made by the Buyer hereunder shall be returned to the Buyer forthwith, provided the Buyer may, at his option, treat this agreement as being in full force and effect with the right to action for specific performance and damages. In the event that either Buyer, Seller, or Agent shall institute suit to enforce any rights hereunder, the prevailing party shall be entitled to court costs and a reasonable attorney's fee.

16. Time Limit of Offer: The Seller shall have until _____ __March 5,__ _____ 19 __81__ to accept this
(hour)   (date)
offer by delivering a signed copy hereof to the Buyer. If this offer is not so accepted, it shall lapse and the agent (or Seller) shall refund the earnest money deposit to the Buyer forthwith.

17. General Agreements: (1) Both parties to this purchase reserve their rights to assign and hereby otherwise agree to cooperate in effecting an Internal Revenue Code 1031 exchange or similar tax-related arrangement prior to close of escrow, upon either party's written notice of intention to do so. (2) Upon approval of this offer by the Seller, this agreement shall become a contract between Buyer and Seller and shall inure to the benefit of the heirs, administrators, executors, successors, personal representatives, and assigns of said parties. (3) Time is of the essence and an essential part of this agreement. (4) This contract constitutes the sole and entire agreement between the parties hereto and no modification of this contract shall be binding unless attached hereto and signed by all parties to the contract. No representations, promises, or inducements not included in this contract shall be binding upon any party hereto.

18. Buyer's Statement and Receipt: "I/we hereby agree to purchase the above property in accordance with the terms and conditions above stated and acknowledge receipt of a completed copy of this agreement, which I/we have fully read and understand." Dated __March 1,__ 19 __81__, _____
(hour)

Address __884 Park Street__   [signature] or Assigns ___ Buyer
__Scottsdale, Arizona__   [signature] ___ Buyer
Phone No: Home __216-1211__ Business __217-5817__

19. Seller's Statement and Response: "I/we approve and accept the above offer, which I/we have fully read and understand, and agree to the above terms and conditions this day

of _____, 19 _____, _____.

(hour)

Address _____ _____ Seller

Phone No: Home _____ Business _____ _____ Seller

20. Commission Agreement: Seller agrees to pay a commission of ___6___ % of the gross sales price to ___John Abner Realty___ for services in this transaction, and agrees that, in the event of forfeiture of the earnest money deposit by the Buyer, said deposit shall be divided between the Seller's broker and the Seller (one half to each party), the Broker's part not to exceed the amount of the commission.

21. Buyer's Receipt for Signed Offer: The Buyer hereby acknowledges receipt of a copy of the above agreement bearing the Seller's signature in acceptance of this offer.

Dated _____, 19 _____ _____ Buyer

_____ Buyer

COMMENTARY TO DOCUMENTATION

Item 6. The carry-back note should have contained provisions for rolling the balloon over for an additional year, as well as provisions for prepayment without penalty, assumption, first right of refusal, and substitution of collateral. Making one purchase contingent on the close of the other was a wise move.

Note: The earnest money arrangement for the other property was identical except for the amounts of money involved.

Reprinted by permission from the *Nothing Down Advisor.*

"Did you say, 'Yes!!!'?"

What Can Happen When The ''Crank'' Becomes A Habit?

**Featuring Technique No. 32
''The Second Mortgage Crank''**

In A Nutshell. . .

Type: 4 SFH's
Price: $159,000
Source: Classified ad
Means: ''Subject to,'' new 2d, carry back
Techniques: No. 2 — Blanket Mortgage (Addendum)
No. 4 — Contract/Wrap
No. 15 — Creation of Paper
No. 32 — Second Mortgage Crank
No. 36 — Moving the Mortgage
Features: Rebate fund for negatives

California investor Ned Crandall of Chico has purchased $1,238,000 worth of real estate in the last 13 months — all with nothing down. His strategy is simple: use a formula that works over and over again, i.e., the second mortgage crank.

His story is not of the ordinary kind. As he tells it in his own words: ''What makes my case different is that seven years ago I went through personal bankruptcy. The only thing I had left was my family and $20,000 equity in my homesteaded home. I had no job and no savings. Even my fight desire had waned as I was drug through a personally humiliating experience. Whoever says that bankruptcy solves your problems is nuts!''

After several years of struggle to get back on their feet, Ned and his wife were transferred to the Chico area. They bought a rundown almond ranch for $189,000 with $7,500 down. ''Everyone thought we were nuts. However, we dug in — refurbished and remodeled the house from top to bottom. We poured everything we had into the property. Today it has a value in excess of $860,000, with $400,000 equity.''

By refinancing the ranch, Ned raised enough cash to buy an eleven-unit apartment building requiring 22% down. Then in December of 1980 he took the Nothing Down Seminar in Sacramento and — bingo — he was off and running. In just a little over a year he had purchased a duplex, a tri-plex, and nine single family homes, all for nothing down. As of this writing, he has an additional $400,000 worth of real estate in escrow. The following case study on one of Ned's transactions will illustrate his approach:

LOCATING

As in most of Ned's deals, this one came to light through a classified ad placed by a real estate office.

SITUATION

The seller was offering four single family homes as a package — all located on a 1¼ acre parcel of land. The asking price was $200,000, with $50,000 down. The only lien consisted of a $64,000 first mortgage against the package.

NEGOTIATION

Convinced that the seller was above market, Ned offered $159,000 for the property with $30,000 down, the transaction to be carried out subject to the existing mortgage. Not only did Ned convince the seller to carry back the balance, he also persuaded him to agree to a substitution of collateral arrangement. The $65,000 balance was to be carried back as a fourth against Ned's 11-plex, leaving the 4-house package with no secondary financing. Investors with equity growth in their portfolio soon learn to ''create paper'' in this way.

CLOSING

The only problem now was to come up with the $30,000 down payment Ned had agreed to. After obtaining an appraisal of the property — it came in at $175,000 — Ned went to a finance company and put on a new second for $55,000. After paying points and closing costs, the cash proceeds to the buyer were $18,000. The sketch outlines the essentials of the deal:

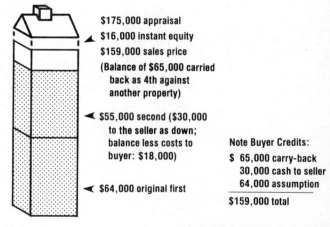

$175,000 appraisal
$16,000 instant equity
$159,000 sales price
(Balance of $65,000 carried back as 4th against another property)

$55,000 second ($30,000 to the seller as down; balance less costs to buyer: $18,000)

$64,000 original first

Note Buyer Credits:

$ 65,000 carry-back
30,000 cash to seller
64,000 assumption
$159,000 total

OUTCOMES AND FUTURE PLANS

The negative cash flows on the four houses total $850 per month, not a rosy outcome until you consider the $18,000 kitty set up for just that purpose. If the negative remained constant, the purchase would wash for 21 payments — nearly two years. With rent increases, the period is extended even further. Ned plans to do a four-way split, then hold the houses for several years, since SFH's are in more demand in his area than rental units.

ADDENDUM

Ned has used the second mortgage crank formula on several other properties since the above transaction. For example, he paid $132,500 for a tri-plex, took it subject to a first of $43,500, had the seller secure the carry back of $52,000 as a third against the 4-house package, then put a new second on the tri-plex for $49,000 ($37,000 to the seller as down, the rest for closing costs and points, with $4,600 back to the buyer). The tri-plex is a Victorian manor house near Chico State University with 5,500 square feet of space — twelve large bedrooms and five baths. The negative is $400 per month.

In another transaction, Ned bought a duplex for $120,000, subject to an existing first of $38,000. With $5,200 down, the seller allowed Ned to put a second on the property for $37,000 (all of which went to the seller). The balance of $45,000 was carried back as a third for 5 years at 12%. In retrospect, Ned wishes he had increased the loan to cover the $5,200 (his points in the deal). The negative is $450 per month, but the duplex is also near the university and has an excellent rental potential.

Here's how the crank technique worked on another single family home in Ned's portfolio: The sellers of a nice four-bedroom, three-bath home were asking $75,000. The 1,650 square foot home had a $2,500 first mortgage against it. They allowed Ned to put a new $40,000 first on the property, provided he would give them $20,000 as a down. They also agreed to move their remaining equity of $35,000 to a fifth position on Ned's 11-plex. In exchange for this, Ned granted them a blanket mortgage that also included equity in one of his other rental houses. The buyer's proceeds at closing, after all expenses and points were deducted, amounted to nearly $15,000 — an adequate kitty to cover the $50/mo. negative cash flow for this property as well as that of several other SFH's he subsequently acquired with the crank technique.

Looking back on his 13-month buying program, Ned made these comments: "As you can see, my negatives are considerable. I am almost to the point where the only house that interests me is one that I can crank. Property values are going up at a good rate, and in another year I'll have enough property with sufficient equity that staying ahead should become easier.

"I am also looking for equity-sharing partners who will pay my negatives for 50% ownership. This should also help my negatives considerably.

"I'm sure that the last 13 months are not for every-one — worrying about cash flow, how I am going to pay mortgages, etc. Given an opportunity, I'd certainly do it again. I guess flirting with disaster and winning is exhilarating."

COMMENTARY

1. The winning situation to look for with the second mortgage crank is a relatively low mortgage and a seller willing to carry back against another property (substitution of collateral). Ned seems to have had a good nose for such situations. Many buyers would note the seller demands for large down payments and immediately get discouraged — without even taking note of the most important fact: the low mortgages that lead into the cranking formula.

2. In one of Ned's deals, he had to grant the seller a blanket mortgage in order to be able to crank the property. In any blanket arrangement, the buyer should stipulate that the blanket is temporary, lasting only until an appraisal can verify appreciation growth to a specified level. Alternately, the blanket can be linked to the buyer's performance in meeting his obligations for a specified period of time. The buyer should require release upon satisfaction of the performance.

3. Is Ned acting with propriety by pulling so much cash out of his deals? As long as the seller is made fully aware of the financing arrangement and concurs, Ned is within the bounds of propriety. Some sellers might insist that the cranked proceeds be placed in an escrow account to service negative cash flow and maintenance. Utmost care should be taken to avoid over-financing a property, i.e., encumbering it beyond its fair market value. Such a procedure, though not necessarily illegal if agreed to by the seller, might be wrongly construed. Much of the negative publicity being heaped on creative finance in recent months stems from cases where unscrupulous investors have over-financed properties, cranked out a goodly portion of cash, and disappeared, leaving the unsuspecting seller holding a bag full of new and heavier mortgages. Such practices are totally out of keeping with the Nothing Down System of win/win creative finance. The moral: buyer and seller should be fully aware of all the details of the transaction. Full disclosure should be in evidence in all the documentation.

4. Here is an example where an investor has specialized in a community of less than 50,000 population. It just goes to show that success is possible — perhaps even easier — outside of the large metropolitan areas where the rate of appreciation may have slowed down (as in the large California cities).

UNIVERSAL EARNEST MONEY RECEIPT
AND OFFER TO PURCHASE

"This is a legally binding contract: if not understood, seek competent advice."

1. Date and Place of Offer: _____ January 7, _____ 19 81 ; _____ Chico _____ California
                                                                   (city)   (state)

2. Principals: The undersigned Buyer _____ Ned Crandall _____
agrees to buy and Seller agrees to sell, according to the indicated terms and conditions, the property described as follows:

3. Property: located at _____ 45106 Mexicana Street _____ Chico _____ California
                                       (street address)   (city)   (state)

with the following legal description: _____ consisting of four houses, legal description to follow

including any of the following items if at present attached to the premises: plumbing, heating, and cooling equipment, including stoker and oil tanks, burners, water heaters, electric light fixtures, bathroom fixtures, roller shades, curtain rods and fixtures, draperies, venetian blinds, window and door screens, towel racks, linoleum and other attached floor coverings,

including carpeting, attached television antennas, mailboxes, all trees and shrubs, and any other fixtures EXCEPT _____ None

The following personal property shall also be included as part of the purchase: _____
At the closing of the transaction, the Seller, at his expense, shall provide the Buyer with a Bill Of Sale containing a detailed inventory of the personal property included.

4. Earnest Money Deposit: Agent (or Seller) acknowledges receipt from Buyer of _____ Five Hundred and 00/100 _____ dollars $ _____ 500.00

in the form of ( ) cash; (X) personal check; ( ) cashier's check; ( ) promissory note at _____ % interest per annum due _____ 19 _____ ; or

other _____
as earnest money deposit to secure and apply on this purchase. Upon acceptance of this agreement in writing and delivery of same to Buyer, the earnest money deposit shall be assigned

to and deposited in the listing Realtor's trust account or _____ , to apply on the
purchase price at the time of closing.

5. Purchase Price: The total purchase price of the property shall be _____ One Hundred Fifty-nine Thousand and 00/100

dollars $ _____ 159,000.00

6. Payment: Purchase price is to be paid by Buyer as follows:

Aforedescribed earnest money deposit .... $ _____ 500.00

Additional payment due upon acceptance of this offer .... $ _____ --

Additional payment due at closing .... $ _____ 29,500.00

Balance to be paid as follows:

    The cash down of approximately $30,000 contingent on loan from Harvey
Mortgage Company being negotiated by Buyer herein: contingency expires
January 25, 1981.

    Buyer to accept title subject to existing Note bearing interest at an
annual rate of 9 1/2%, said Note having an approximate principal balance
of $63,900.00 dollars and is to be repaid in monthly installments of $850.00
dollars, principal and interest according to the same tenure of said Note,
which Note is secured by a Trust Deed on subject property. The buyer
acknowledges having been provided a copy of said Note and Trust Deed by the
broker, Justin Black.

    Buyer agrees to execute a Note for the principal sum of sixty-five
thousand dollars ($65,000.00) said note to be secured by a Deed of Trust
on a property located on the south east corner of James and Tulip Avenues,
Chico, Butte County, California (improvements consisting of eleven apartments). Said Note to bear interest at an annual rate of twelve percent
and shall be paid in monthly installments of interest only at six-hundred
and fifty dollars ($650.00) for fifty four (54) months, at which time the

entire sum of sixty-five thousand dollars principal, together with the
final interest payment shall be due in full. This Trust Deed is to be Junior
to encumbrances of no more than an aggregate of two-hundred and forty-five
thousand dollars, said sum being a prior encumbrance presently owing to
J.L. Thompson on a wrap-around Trust Deed. Seller to be provided with a
"Loan Endorsement" by Valley Escrow, the cost of which to be paid by Buyer
herein.

7. Title: Seller agrees to furnish good and marketable title free of all encumbrances and defects, except mortgage liens and encumbrances as set forth in this agreement, and to make

conveyance by Warranty Deed or _____. Seller shall furnish in due course to the Buyer a title insurance policy insuring the Buyer of a good and marketable title in keeping with the terms and conditions of this agreement. Prior to the closing of this transaction, the Seller, upon request, will furnish to the Buyer a preliminary title report made by a title insurance company showing the condition of the title to said property. If the Seller cannot furnish marketable title within thirty days after receipt of the notice to the Buyer containing a written statement of the defects, the earnest money deposit herein receipted shall be refunded to the Buyer and this agreement shall be null and void. The following shall not be deemed encumbrances or defects; building and use restrictions general to the area; utility easements; other easements not inconsistent with Buyer's intended use; zoning or subdivision laws, covenants, conditions, restrictions, or reservations of record; tenancies of record. In the event of sale of other than real property relating to this transaction, Seller will provide evidence of title or right to sell or lease such personal property.

8. Special Representations: Seller warrants and represents to Buyer (1) that the subject property is connected to ( ) public sewer system, ( ) cesspool or septic tank, ( ) sewer system available but not connected, ( ) city water system, ( ) private water system, and that the following special improvements are included in the sale: ( ) sidewalk, ( ) curb and gutter, ( ) special street paving, ( ) special street lighting; (2) that the Seller knows of no material structural defects; (3) that all electrical wiring, heating, cooling, and plumbing systems are free of material defects and will be in good working order at the time the Buyer is entitled to possession; (4) that the Seller has no notice from any government agency of any violation or knowledge of probable violations of the law relating to the subject property; (5) that the Seller has no notice or knowledge of planned or commenced public improvements which may result in special assessments or otherwise directly and materially affect the property; and (6) that the Seller has no notice or knowledge of any liens to be assessed against the property,

EXCEPT _____ None

9. Escrow Instructions: This sale shall be closed on or before March 1, 19 81 by Valley Escrow or such other closing agent as mutually agreed upon by Buyer and Seller. Buyer and Seller will, immediately on demand, deposit with closing agent all instruments and monies required

to complete the purchase in accordance with the provisions of this agreement. Contract of Sale or Instrument of Conveyance to be made in the name of _____

Ned Crandall and Marsha Crandall, husband and wife, as community property.

10. Closing Costs and Pro-Ration: Seller agrees to pay for title insurance policy, preliminary title report (if requested), termite inspection as set forth below, real estate commission, cost of preparing and recording any corrective instruments, and one-half of the escrow fees. Buyer agrees to pay for recording fees for mortgages and deeds of conveyance, all costs or expenses in securing new financing or assuming existing financing, and one-half of the escrow fees. Buyer agrees to pay for recording fees for mortgages and deeds of conveyance, all costs or expenses in securing new financing or assuming existing financing, and one-half of the escrow fees. Taxes for the current year, insurance acceptable to the Buyer, rents, interest, mortgage reserves, maintenance fees, and water and other utilities constituting liens, shall be pro-rated as of closing. Renters' security deposits shall accrue to Buyer at closing. Seller to provide Buyer with all current rental or lease agreements prior to closing.

11. Termite Inspection: Seller agrees, at his expense, to provide written certification by a reputable licensed pest control firm that the property is free of termite infestation. In the event termites are found, the Seller shall have the property treated at his expense and provide acceptable certification that treatment has been rendered. If any structural repairs are required by reason of termite damage as established by acceptable certification, Seller agrees to make necessary repairs not to exceed $500. If repairs exceed $500, Buyer shall first have the right to accept the property "as is" with a credit to the Buyer at closing of $500, or the Buyer may terminate this agreement with the earnest money deposit being promptly returned to the Buyer if the Seller does not agree to pay all costs of treatment and repair.

12. Conditions of Sale: The following conditions shall also apply, and shall, if conflicting with the printed portions of this agreement, prevail and control:

Seller to rent Building, plus 150' x 180' land on Mexicana Street, for one
year at $300.00 per month.

13. Liability and Maintenance: Seller shall maintain subject property, including landscaping, in good condition until the date of transfer of title or possession by Buyer, whichever occurs first. All risk of loss and destruction of property, and all expenses of insurance, shall be borne by the seller until the date of possession. If the improvements on the property are destroyed or materially damaged prior to closing, then the Buyer shall have the right to declare this agreement null and void, and the earnest money deposit and all other sums paid by Buyer toward the purchase price shall be returned to the Buyer forthwith.

14. Possession: The Buyer shall be entitled to possession of property upon closing or _____ -- _____, 19 _____

15. Default: In the event the Buyer fails to complete the purchase as herein provided, the earnest money deposit shall be retained by the Seller as the total and entire liquidated damages. In the event the Seller fails to perform any condition of the sale as herein provided, then the Buyer may, at his option, treat the contract as terminated, and all payments made by the Buyer hereunder shall be returned to the Buyer forthwith, provided the Buyer may, at his option, treat this agreement as being in full force and effect with the right to action for specific performance and damages. In the event that either Buyer, Seller, or Agent shall institute suit to enforce any rights hereunder, the prevailing party shall be entitled to court costs and a reasonable attorney's fee.

16. Time Limit of Offer: The Seller shall have until

_____ January 12, _____, 19 81 to accept this
        (hour)   (date)

offer by delivering a signed copy hereof to the Buyer. If this offer is not so accepted, it shall lapse and the agent (or Seller) shall refund the earnest money deposit to the Buyer forthwith.

17. General Agreements: (1) Both parties to this purchase reserve their rights to assign and hereby otherwise agree to cooperate in effecting an Internal Revenue Code 1031 exchange or similar tax-related arrangement prior to close of escrow, upon either party's written notice of intention to do so. (2) Upon approval of this offer by the Seller, this agreement shall become a contract between Buyer and Seller and shall inure to the benefit of the heirs, administrators, executors, successors, personal representatives, and assigns of said parties. (3) Time is of the essence and an essential part of this agreement. (4) This contract constitutes the sole and entire agreement between the parties hereto and no modification of this contract shall be binding unless attached hereto and signed by all parties to the contract. No representations, promises, or inducements not included in this contract shall be binding upon any party hereto.

18. Buyer's Statement and Receipt: "I/we hereby agree to purchase the above property in accordance with the terms and conditions above stated and acknowledge receipt of a completed copy of this agreement, which I/we have fully read and understand." Dated ___January 7,___ 19 _81_ , _____
(hour)

Address ___6169 Brooks Avenue___   _____[signature]_____ Buyer

___Chico, California___   _____ Buyer

Phone No: Home ___226-1131___ Business ___889-4136___

19. Seller's Statement and Response: "I/we approve and accept the above offer, which I/we have fully read and understand, and agree to the above terms and conditions this day

of _____, 19 _____ , _____.
(hour)

Address _____   _____ Seller

Phone No: Home _____ Business _____   _____ Seller

20. Commission Agreement: Seller agrees to pay a commission of _____% of the gross sales price to _____ for services in this transaction, and agrees that, in the event of forfeiture of the earnest money deposit by the Buyer, said deposit shall be divided between the Seller's broker and the Seller (one half to each party), the Broker's part not to exceed the amount of the commission.

21. Buyer's Receipt for Signed Offer: The Buyer hereby acknowledges receipt of a copy of the above agreement bearing the Seller's signature in acceptance of this offer.

Dated _____, 19 _____   _____ Buyer

_____ Buyer

COMMENTARY TO DOCUMENTATION

Item 2. "Or Assigns" should always be added after the name of the buyer.

Item 6. The carry-back second secured against the buyer's 11-plex should have contained as many of the following provisions as the seller would allow: substitu-tion of collateral, rollover on the balloon, prepayment without penalty, assumption, first right of refusal.

Item 15. The buyer elected to grant the seller broader recourse than specified in our "Universal Earnest Money Receipt."

"Miss Smedley. . . . A memo for all directors of this bank. . . . Blast it! . . . Tell them if 'Nothing Down' really worked I would have thought of it years ago!"

30

Creative Buyers Crank Their Way Into Small Rancher

Featuring Technique No. 32 "The Second Mortgage Crank"

In A Nutshell . . .

Type:	SFH
Price:	$41,000
Source:	Agent
Means:	Assumption, 2d mortgage
Techniques:	No. 4 — Contract/Wrap
	No. 15 — Creation of Paper
	No. 32 — Second Mortgage Crank
	No. 36 — Moving the Mortgage
Strategies:	Stepped payments

LOCATING

Since taking the Nothing Down Seminar, Jill and Jerry McKendrick of Aloha, Oregon, had used the principles of creative financing to buy their own home and one rental. "However, the ball didn't start to roll," as Jerry put it, "until I ran into a sharp real estate salesperson who was unafraid of presenting 'nothing down' deals." It was through this agent that they located their second rental house, an attractive three-bedroom rancher.

SITUATION

The house, which had been listed for six months without any action, was now sitting vacant. The owners were ready to deal. The list price was $44,000, and the listing agent felt that the owners would settle for $6,000 to $8,000 down, with the balance on a contract. The existing financing was an Oregon State G.I. Loan with a balance of $15,000. If assumed by a non-G.I., the 8½% loan was supposed to go to 13%, resulting in a hike of nearly $100 per month in the payment.

NEGOTIATION

The McKendricks did a little research on the underlying loan and found out that the present owner had already assumed the G.I. loan three years earlier. Since he was a non-G.I., the current 8½% rate of interest was in fact locked in and couldn't be bumped up again. That gave them courage!

Therefore, they made the following offer: $41,000 for the house, with $6,000 down (which they planned to borrow creatively), the balance of the equity ($20,000) being carried back as a second at 11% with stepped payments as follows: 1st year, $120/mo.; 2d year, $145/mo.; 3rd year, $170/mo.; 4th year, $195/mo.; 5th year, $220/mo. According to their rent projection of $350 per month, the stepped payments would give them an even cash flow. The balance after five years would be ballooned out.

The clever part of their offer was the stipulation that the second would be secured by their own home, rather than the rental house they were buying. "Creating paper" in this way is a powerful tool often overlooked by people with equities to apply to a transaction. The owners had no problem with the substitution of collateral but insisted on a down payment of $8,000 (as they found out they had to pay off a $2,000 weatherization loan at the time of the sale). To this the McKendricks gave their approval.

CLOSING

Jill and Jerry had accomplished the following: upon closing they were the owners of an attractive rental unit with only one encumbrance — the G.I. first of $15,000. They had the house appraised and found it to be worth $46,750, $5,750 more than they had paid. The sketch shows the details:

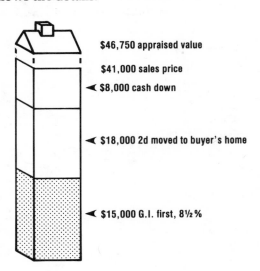

$46,750 appraised value

$41,000 sales price

◄ $8,000 cash down

◄ $18,000 2d moved to buyer's home

◄ $15,000 G.I. first, 8½%

OUTCOMES AND FUTURE PLANS

We have seen the way the second mortgage was moved to the McKendricks' home (financing it, incidentally at 100% of value). Now comes the crank. They immediately put a commercial second mortgage against the rental and pulled ("cranked") $15,075 out of it at 18%, with payments of $243 per month, with a 15-year amortization. Instead of the expected $350/mo. rent, they found some excellent tenants willing to pay $375/mo. Six months later they raised the rent to $395/mo. The total payment on the first and second is $368. With expenses, the cash flow is even. After deducting the $8,000 down payment, their proceeds from the crank are $7,075, a nice kitty to use in their next investment deal, described elsewhere in this volume in the section on Moving the Mortgage.

COMMENTARY

1. Jerry makes the point that a creative real estate agent is an invaluable professional to have on your team. The stepped payments and substitution of collateral, while not complicated, are innovative procedures that not every seller can understand without getting nervous. An excellent agent can build trust in accomplishing such techniques. On the other hand, it is not unusual to find agents who are themselves unfamiliar with creative financing and who therefore turn out to be "deal killers." Jill and Jerry are fortunate to have struck it rich with their man.

2. The McKendricks might have considered sparing themselves part of the down payment by inducing the agent to take back his commission in the form of a note (thus reducing pressure on the sellers to come up with so much cash at closing).

3. What if the McKendricks had not had the credentials to qualify for the commercial second mortgage? Would the "crank" have failed to materialize? Not necessarily. The next alternative would have been to have the seller add the second (Technique No. 33 — Variation of the Crank) and then the buyers would take title subject to the new financing.

DOCUMENTATION (INITIAL OFFER)

UNIVERSAL EARNEST MONEY RECEIPT AND OFFER TO PURCHASE

"This is a legally binding contract: if not understood, seek competent advice."

1. Date and Place of Offer: December 21, 19 81 ; Portland (city) Oregon (state)

2. Principals: The undersigned Buyer Jerry McKendrick
agrees to buy and Seller agrees to sell, according to the indicated terms and conditions, the property described as follows:

3. Property: located at 101 Black Walnut Drive (street address) Portland (city) Oregon (state)

with the following legal description: Lot 12 and 13, Block 7, West Palm Addition

including any of the following items if at present attached to the premises: plumbing, heating, and cooling equipment, including stoker and oil tanks, burners, water heaters, electric light fixtures, bathroom fixtures, roller shades, curtain rods and fixtures, draperies, venetian blinds, window and door screens, towel racks, linoleum and other attached floor coverings,

including carpeting, attached television antennas, mailboxes, all trees and shrubs, and any other fixtures EXCEPT None

The following personal property shall also be included as part of the purchase: refrigerator and kitchen range
At the closing of the transaction, the Seller, at his expense, shall provide the Buyer with a Bill Of Sale containing a detailed inventory of the personal property included.

4. Earnest Money Deposit: Agent (or Seller) acknowledges receipt from Buyer of One Thousand and 00/100 dollars $ 1,000.00

in the form of ( ) cash; ( ) personal check; ( ) cashier's check; (X) promissory note at 0 % interest per annum due Dec. 31, 19 81 ; or

other --

as earnest money deposit to secure and apply on this purchase. Upon acceptance of this agreement in writing and delivery of same to Buyer, the earnest money deposit shall be assigned

to and deposited in the listing Realtor's trust account or _____, to apply on the purchase price at the time of closing.

5. Purchase Price: The total purchase price of the property shall be Forty-one Thousand and 00/100 dollars $ 41,000.00

6. Payment: Purchase price is to be paid by Buyer as follows:

Aforedescribed earnest money deposit .... $ 1,000.00

Additional payment due upon acceptance of this offer .... $ --

Additional payment due at closing .... $ 5,000.00

Balance to be paid as follows:

Purchaser to take title subject to Seller's mortgage of record. Approximate balance of $14,000.00 payable at $196.00 per month approximately, including principal and interest at 13% per annum.

Balance of sales price of approximately $21,000.00 to be secured by a second trust deed on the purchaser's personal residence, payable as follows: $50 per month the first year, $75.00/month, second year, $100.00/month, third year, $125.00/month, fourth year, $150.00/month, fifth year. Balance of principal and remaining interest at 11% per annum due on the 60th month.

7. Title: Seller agrees to furnish good and marketable title free of all encumbrances and defects, except mortgage liens and encumbrances as set forth in this agreement, and to make conveyance by Warranty Deed or ___ __ ___. Seller shall furnish in due course to the Buyer a title insurance policy insuring the Buyer of a good and marketable title in keeping with the terms and conditions of this agreement. Prior to the closing of this transaction, the Seller, upon request, will furnish to the Buyer a preliminary title report made by a title insurance company showing the condition of the title to said property. If the Seller cannot furnish marketable title within thirty days after receipt of the notice to the Buyer containing a written statement of the defects, the earnest money deposit herein receipted shall be refunded to the Buyer and this agreement shall be null and void. The following shall not be deemed encumbrances or defects; building and use restrictions general to the area; utility easements; other easements not inconsistent with Buyer's intended use; zoning or subdivision laws, covenants, conditions, restrictions, or reservations of record; tenancies of record. In the event of sale of other than real property relating to this transaction, Seller will provide evidence of title or right to sell or lease such personal property.

8. Special Representations: Seller warrants and represents to Buyer (1) that the subject property is connected to ( ) public sewer system, ( ) cesspool or septic tank, ( ) sewer system available but not connected, ( ) city water system, ( ) private water system, and that the following special improvements are included in the sale: ( ) sidewalk, ( ) curb and gutter, ( ) special street paving, ( ) special street lighting; (2) that the Seller knows of no material structural defects; (3) that all electrical wiring, heating, cooling, and plumbing systems are free of material defects and will be in good working order at the time the Buyer is entitled to possession; (4) that the Seller has no notice from any government agency of any violation or knowledge of probable violations of the law relating to the subject property; (5) that the Seller has no notice or knowledge of planned or commenced public improvements which may result in special assessments or otherwise directly and materially affect the property; and (6) that the Seller has no notice or knowledge of any liens to be assessed against the property,

EXCEPT   None

9. Escrow Instructions: This sale shall be closed on or before January 15, 19 81 by _____ or such other closing agent as mutually agreed upon by Buyer and Seller. Buyer and Seller will, immediately on demand, deposit with closing agent all instruments and monies required to complete the purchase in accordance with the provisions of this agreement. Contract of Sale or Instrument of Conveyance to be made in the name of _____

to be supplied

10. Closing Costs and Pro-Ration: Seller agrees to pay for title insurance policy, preliminary title report (if requested), termite inspection as set forth below, real estate commission, cost of preparing and recording any corrective instruments, and one-half of the escrow fees. Buyer agrees to pay for recording fees for mortgages and deeds of conveyance, all costs or expenses in securing new financing or assuming existing financing, and one-half of the escrow fees. Buyer agrees to pay for recording fees for mortgages and deeds of conveyance, all costs or expenses in securing new financing or assuming existing financing, and one-half of the escrow fees. Taxes for the current year, insurance acceptable to the Buyer, rents, interest, mortgage reserves, maintenance fees, and water and other utilities constituting liens, shall be pro-rated as of closing. Renters' security deposits shall accrue to Buyer at closing. Seller to provide Buyer with all current rental or lease agreements prior to closing.

11. Termite Inspection: Seller agrees, at his expense, to provide written certification by a reputable licensed pest control firm that the property is free of termite infestation. In the event termites are found, the Seller shall have the property treated at his expense and provide acceptable certification that treatment has been rendered. If any structural repairs are required by reason of termite damage as established by acceptable certification, Seller agrees to make necessary repairs not to exceed $500. If repairs exceed $500, Buyer shall first have the right to accept the property "as is" with a credit to the Buyer at closing of $500, or the Buyer may terminate this agreement with the earnest money deposit being promptly returned to the Buyer if the Seller does not agree to pay all costs of treatment and repair.

12. Conditions of Sale: The following conditions shall also apply, and shall, if conflicting with the printed portions of this agreement, prevail and control:

None

13. Liability and Maintenance: Seller shall maintain subject property, including landscaping, in good condition until the date of transfer of title or possession by Buyer, whichever occurs first. All risk of loss and destruction of property, and all expenses of insurance, shall be borne by the seller until the date of possession. If the improvements on the property are destroyed or materially damaged prior to closing, then the Buyer shall have the right to declare this agreement null and void, and the earnest money deposit and all other sums paid by Buyer toward the purchase price shall be returned to the Buyer forthwith.

14. Possession: The Buyer shall be entitled to possession of property upon closing or ___ __ ___, 19 ___.

15. Default: In the event the Buyer fails to complete the purchase as herein provided, the earnest money deposit shall be retained by the Seller as the total and entire liquidated damages. In the event the Seller fails to perform any condition of the sale as herein provided, then the Buyer may, at his option, treat the contract as terminated, and all payments made by the Buyer hereunder shall be returned to the Buyer forthwith, provided the Buyer may, at his option, treat this agreement as being in full force and effect with the right to action for specific performance and damages. In the event that either Buyer, Seller, or Agent shall institute suit to enforce any rights hereunder, the prevailing party shall be entitled to court costs and a reasonable attorney's fee.

16. Time Limit of Offer: The Seller shall have until

_____, 19 ___ to accept this
(hour)   (date)
offer by delivering a signed copy hereof to the Buyer. If this offer is not so accepted, it shall lapse and the agent (or Seller) shall refund the earnest money deposit to the Buyer forthwith.

17. General Agreements: (1) Both parties to this purchase reserve their rights to assign and hereby otherwise agree to cooperate in effecting an Internal Revenue Code 1031 exchange or similar tax-related arrangement prior to close of escrow, upon either party's written notice of intention to do so. (2) Upon approval of this offer by the Seller, this agreement shall become a contract between Buyer and Seller and shall inure to the benefit of the heirs, administrators, executors, successors, personal representatives, and assigns of said parties. (3) Time is of the essence and an essential part of this agreement. (4) This contract constitutes the sole and entire agreement between the parties hereto and no modification of this contract shall be binding unless attached hereto and signed by all parties to the contract. No representations, promises, or inducements not included in this contract shall be binding upon any party hereto.

18. Buyer's Statement and Receipt: "I/we hereby agree to purchase the above property in accordance with the terms and conditions above stated and acknowledge receipt of a completed copy of this agreement, which I/we have fully read and understand." Dated ___December 21,___ 19 _81_ , _____
(hour)

Address ___14 Crestview___   [signature]

___Aloha, Oregon___   _____ Buyer

Phone No: Home ___271-1508___ Business ___432-1421___   _____ Buyer

19. Seller's Statement and Response: "I/we approve and accept the above offer, which I/we have fully read and understand, and agree to the above terms and conditions this day

of _____, 19 _____, _____.
(hour)

Address _____   _____ Seller

Phone No: Home _____ Business _____   _____ Seller

20. Commission Agreement: Seller agrees to pay a commission of _____% of the gross sales price to _____ for services in this transaction, and agrees that, in the event of forfeiture of the earnest money deposit by the Buyer, said deposit shall be divided between the Seller's broker and the Seller (one half to each party), the Broker's part not to exceed the amount of the commission.

21. Buyer's Receipt for Signed Offer: The Buyer hereby acknowledges receipt of a copy of the above agreement bearing the Seller's signature in acceptance of this offer.

Dated _____, 19 _____   _____ Buyer

                                                           _____ Buyer

COMMENTARY TO DOCUMENTATION

In counteroffers by the seller, the graduated payments were raised to the levels indicated in the narrative of the case study. Also, the interest rate on the underlying mortgage was specified as 8½%, and the down was increased to $8,000. The seller added this condition: "If the Buyer sells personal residence encumbered by second trust deed, he will pay seller in full for balance owing at time of closing. Purchaser to provide copy of financial statement to seller. Contingent upon verification of market value of purchaser's property of at least $82,000.00. Purchase price does not include refrigerator, swing set."

Item 2. Buyer should add the words "or Assigns" after his name.

Item 6. The seller refused to grant assumption or assignment privileges for the carry-back note. However, the buyer should have attempted to secure provisions for substitution of collateral (even after the trust deed was moved), rollover on the balloon, prepayment without penalty, and first right of refusal.

It is unusual that a seller would ask for a financial statement or ask for verification of property value on the collateral. If the seller had asked the proper question, he would have asked for a verification of the buyer's liens, as well as fair market value (to assure that the collateral would be sufficient).

Item 15. The original contained a strong preprinted "total liquidated damages" clause similar to the one shown in our "Universal Earnest Money Receipt."

Item 16. The buyer failed to specify a time limit for the seller's response.

The Second Mortgage Crank With A Touch Of Matrimony

**Featuring Technique No. 32
"The Second Mortgage Crank"**

In A Nutshell. . .

Type: SFH
Price: $52,000
Source: MLS Book
Means: Assumption, carry back
Techniques: No. 4 — Contract/Wrap
No. 6 — Balloon
No. 32 — Second Mortgage Crank
No. 43 — Partner's Money Till Your Money Comes

Vic Campanella is a buyer for a large department store in Dallas. His hobby, after putting in his hours buying fashionable clothes for the store, is to buy real estate using the techniques of creative finance. The approach that seems to work best for him is the "Second Mortgage Crank," which he has used in recent months to acquire seven single family homes. The following case study deals with his inaugural purchase, but the same formula, with minor variations, has continued to serve him well right up to the present time.

LOCATING

Vic was scouting the Multiple Listing Service books looking for homes in the $45,000 to $50,000 range when he noticed an interesting entry for a property in Lancaster, a suburb of Dallas to the south.

SITUATION

It was a three-bedroom, two-bath home with a single garage and a list price of $54,000. The owner wanted cash-to-loan in the amount of $34,000. When Vic inquired why the owner was selling, he was told that the owner was being transferred out of the city.

NEGOTIATION

Vic guessed what the owner wanted the cash for — sure enough, the man had bought a house in another city and needed the capital to complete the transaction. Was the time of closing therefore a factor of importance? Yes, it was. Would the seller take some cash now and some later? Yes, he would. The preliminaries out of the way, Vic could get down to brass tacks.

He began with a full-price offer of $54,000 as follows: $17,000 cash down, $17,000 carried back at 10% in a five-year balloon, and the first of $20,000 assumed (the interest rate on the first was 8.9%). The owner countered that he needed at least $20,000 down, plus 11% on the carry back, which was now to be adjusted to

$14,000.

Vic compromised this way: he granted the larger down but offered 10½% on a carry back of $12,000 (thus lowering the price to $52,000). The owner accepted. Not having $20,000 to put down, Vic had to go to work. Since the first mortgage against the property amounted to less than half the property value, Vic's strategy was to "crank" the down payment out of the property itself. Here is how he did it:

CLOSING

The accepted offer was written in the name of Vic's girl friend, with the addition of the phrase "or assigns," meaning that she could subsequently assign her interest in the property to another person or persons before the closing. Essentially the offer included financing as indicated in the sketch:

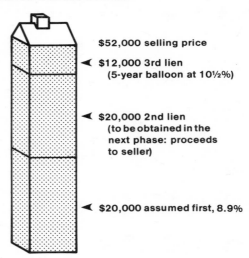

$52,000 selling price

$12,000 3rd lien
(5-year balloon at 10½%)

$20,000 2nd lien
(to be obtained in the next phase: proceeds to seller)

$20,000 assumed first, 8.9%

Then the girl friend, acting as Vic's partner, turned around and assigned the interest over to Vic. This time, the financing looked like this:

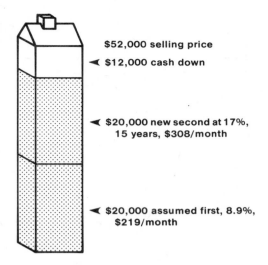

$52,000 selling price

◄ $12,000 cash down

◄ $20,000 new second at 17%,
15 years, $308/month

◄ $20,000 assumed first, 8.9%,
$219/month

It was the second "sale" that they took to the bank in order to obtain secondary financing. In effect, Vic's girl friend had "loaned" him the $12,000 as down payment, or, more accurately, had credited him with that amount in the transaction until such time as his money might come. Did he give her part interest in the property for her assistance? No, but he subsequently married her, so the issue became moot. That is the "Second Mortgage Crank" with a touch of matrimony. (Incidentally, it will only work once this way with the same partner.)

OUTCOMES AND FUTURE PLANS

The double escrow went as planned. Payments on the first are $219/month and $308/month on the second, for a total of $527. The negative cash flow is only $27/month, something that can readily be cured next time the rent is raised.

Since Vic wisely induced the seller to accept a substitution of collateral clause, he intends in three years to move the $12,000 lien from the home to another property and then crank out enough additional money to pay off the seller entirely.

COMMENTARY

1. The substitution of collateral clause is of fundamental importance in any real estate transaction involving owner financing. It is best to reach agreement on this point as part of the original negotiations, since sellers frequently balk at it after the fact. Sometimes it is necessary to "sweeten" the deal by agreeing to raise the interest rate if the mortgage is in fact moved or providing for paydown of the principal by a certain amount in order to persuade the seller to accept the clause. Be that as it may, it is well worth it to write these provisions into the documentation because of the potential value in freeing the property of liens for the purpose of cranking out more money or creating paper for down payments, etc.

2. Nothing down investors often bypass high down deals in favor of those where the owner expressly sanctions very high leverage approaches. This is a mistake. Many high down deals can be nothing down to the investor, either through the use of partners or through techniques like the "Second Mortgage Crank." The clue to look for is a situation where the property is either free and clear or has a low loan-to-value ratio (perhaps a third or less encumbered). This technique works best in times where money is plentiful and interest rates less severe than at present. However, as Vic's case study shows, it will work even in difficult economic times if done carefully (watching the numbers and cash flow).

3. Does the double-escrow approach used in this case study (seller to partner, partner to Vic) constitute a slight distortion of the facts as far as the bank is concerned? From our perspective, it seems problematic. However, Vic, who followed legal advice, does not seem to think so. The seller has his cash and goes away happy. The bank has a new second mortgage from a qualified buyer and is happy. The partner has a new husband, and she is happy. And the buyer has an excellent rental property, which, by virtue of the marriage, he now shares with his new wife on a fifty-fifty basis. So he is happy. Everyone wins. Still, competent legal advice is always essential in complex real estate transactions.

How else might this deal have worked without using the double escrow approach? The bank might have been satisfied that a down payment had been made if the seller had simply stated that it had been in the form of an exchange — a note of value secured by another property being used as down payment. Of course, in this case Vic would have to have other equities to use in creating this note, either his own or a partner's. Looking at it in another way, the seller would agree to "move the mortgage" (for his carry back portion) to another property so that the bank could grant a second mortgage (or refinance of the first) on the subject property.

One thing that would not work in Texas (or other states with similar "homestead" laws) is to move the mortgage to one's own residence. Lenders do not have recourse to personal residences under provisions of that law. Consequently, it is not possible to secure secondary loans using one's home as collateral. How do investors overcome this barrier to raising needed capital? According to Vic, once you have established your credit, you don't have any trouble borrowing needed funds in other ways. The more you owe, the easier it is to borrow more. Strange, but true.

DOCUMENTATION (INITIAL OFFER)

UNIVERSAL EARNEST MONEY RECEIPT
AND OFFER TO PURCHASE

"This is a legally binding contract: if not understood, seek competent advice."

1. Date and Place of Offer: ___ May 10, ___ 19 81 ; ___ Dallas ___ Texas
   (city)   (state)

2. Principals: The undersigned Buyer ___ Carla Evans and Assigns
   agrees to buy and Seller agrees to sell, according to the indicated terms and conditions, the property described as follows:

3. Property: located at ___ 4758 Winchester Drive ___ Lancaster ___ Texas
   (street address)   (city)   (state)

   with the following legal description: ___ Lot 41, Block 12, Plain Estates Addition, Lancaster

including any of the following items if at present attached to the premises: plumbing, heating, and cooling equipment, including stoker and oil tanks, burners, water heaters, electric light fixtures, bathroom fixtures, roller shades, curtain rods and fixtures, draperies, venetian blinds, window and door screens, towel racks, linoleum and other attached floor coverings,

including carpeting, attached television antennas, mailboxes, all trees and shrubs, and any other fixtures EXCEPT ___ None

The following personal property shall also be included as part of the purchase: ___
At the closing of the transaction, the Seller, at his expense, shall provide the Buyer with a Bill Of Sale containing a detailed inventory of the personal property included.

4. Earnest Money Deposit: Agent (or Seller) acknowledges receipt from Buyer of One Hundred and 00/100 ___ dollars $ ___ 100.00

in the form of ( ) cash; (X) personal check; ( ) cashier's check; ( ) promissory note at ___ % interest per annum due ___ 19 ___ ; or

other ___

as earnest money deposit to secure and apply on this purchase. Upon acceptance of this agreement in writing and delivery of same to Buyer, the earnest money deposit shall be assigned

to and deposited in the listing Realtor's trust account or ___ , to apply on the
purchase price at the time of closing.

5. Purchase Price: The total purchase price of the property shall be Fifty-Three Thousand Nine Hundred Ninety-Five and

00/100 ___ dollars $ ___ 53,995.00

6. Payment: Purchase price is to be paid by Buyer as follows:

   Aforedescribed earnest money deposit .... $ ___ 100.00

   Additional payment due upon acceptance of this offer .... $ ___ --

   Additional payment due at closing .... $ ___ 16,900.00

   Balance to be paid as follows:

   1. Buyer's assumption of the unpaid balance of a promissory note payable
      in present monthly installments of $230, including principal and in-
      terest and any reserve deposits, with Buyer's first installment payable
      to Federal Mortgage Company on 1st month after closing, the assumed
      principal balance of which at closing (allowing for an agreed variance
      of $250) will be $20,000. If Noteholder on assumption requires Buyer
      to pay an assumption fee in excess of $50 and Seller declines to pay
      such excess, or raises the existing interest rate above 8.89% or re-
      quires approval of Buyer, or can accelerate the note and Buyer does not
      receive from Noteholder written approval and acceleration waiver prior
      to closing date, Buyer may terminate this contract and the earnest money
      deposit shall be refunded. Buyer shall apply for the approval and waiver
      within 7 days from the effective date hereof and shall make every rea-
      sonable effort to obtain same.

   2. The balance of the sales price, $16,995, to be evidenced by a 3rd lien
      note payable to Seller, bearing interest rate of 10% per annum, in one

lump sum on or before 5 years from date of closing. Buyer has the right to substitute collateral of equal or greater value on the third lien with the Seller having the right of approval.

3. Seller agrees that the second lien amount shown above may be for substantially more or substantially less depending on the credit capability of the Buyer or her Assigns.

4. Total of cash due Seller at closing to be at least $17,000.

5. Buyer to have right to sell property without payoff penalty.

6. Offer is subject to Buyer obtaining suitable and adequate financing.

7. Title: Seller agrees to furnish good and marketable title free of all encumbrances and defects, except mortgage liens and encumbrances as set forth in this agreement, and to make conveyance by Warranty Deed or _____. Seller shall furnish in due course to the Buyer a title insurance policy insuring the Buyer of a good and marketable title in keeping with the terms and conditions of this agreement. Prior to the closing of this transaction, the Seller, upon request, will furnish to the Buyer a preliminary title report made by a title insurance company showing the condition of the title to said property. If the Seller cannot furnish marketable title within thirty days after receipt of the notice to the Buyer containing a written statement of the defects, the earnest money deposit herein receipted shall be refunded to the Buyer and this agreement shall be null and void. The following shall not be deemed encumbrances or defects; building and use restrictions general to the area; utility easements; other easements not inconsistent with Buyer's intended use; zoning or subdivision laws, covenants, conditions, restrictions, or reservations of record; tenancies of record. In the event of sale of other than real property relating to this transaction, Seller will provide evidence of title or right to sell or lease such personal property.

8. Special Representations: Seller warrants and represents to Buyer (1) that the subject property is connected to ( ) public sewer system, ( ) cesspool or septic tank, ( ) sewer system available but not connected, ( ) city water system, ( ) private water system, and that the following special improvements are included in the sale: ( ) sidewalk, ( ) curb and gutter, ( ) special street paving, ( ) special street lighting; (2) that the Seller knows of no material structural defects; (3) that all electrical wiring, heating, cooling, and plumbing systems are free of material defects and will be in good working order at the time the Buyer is entitled to possession; (4) that the Seller has no notice from any government agency of any violation or knowledge of probable violations of the law relating to the subject property; (5) that the Seller has no notice or knowledge of planned or commenced public improvements which may result in special assessments or otherwise directly and materially affect the property; and (6) that the Seller has no notice or knowledge of any liens to be assessed against the property,

EXCEPT   None _____

9. Escrow Instructions: This sale shall be closed on or before ____May 22,____ 19 81 by ____Gulf States Escrow____ or such other closing agent as mutually agreed upon by Buyer and Seller. Buyer and Seller will, immediately on demand, deposit with closing agent all instruments and monies required to complete the purchase in accordance with the provisions of this agreement. Contract of Sale or Instrument of Conveyance to be made in the name of _____

to be supplied later

10. Closing Costs and Pro-Ration: Seller agrees to pay for title insurance policy, preliminary title report (if requested), termite inspection as set forth below, real estate commission, cost of preparing and recording any corrective instruments, and one-half of the escrow fees. Buyer agrees to pay for recording fees for mortgages and deeds of conveyance, all costs or expenses in securing new financing or assuming existing financing, and one-half of the escrow fees. Buyer agrees to pay for recording fees for mortgages and deeds of conveyance, all costs or expenses in securing new financing or assuming existing financing, and one-half of the escrow fees. Taxes for the current year, insurance acceptable to the Buyer, rents, interest, mortgage reserves, maintenance fees, and water and other utilities constituting liens, shall be pro-rated as of closing. Renters' security deposits shall accrue to Buyer at closing. Seller to provide Buyer with all current rental or lease agreements prior to closing.

11. Termite Inspection: Seller agrees, at his expense, to provide written certification by a reputable licensed pest control firm that the property is free of termite infestation. In the event termites are found, the Seller shall have the property treated at his expense and provide acceptable certification that treatment has been rendered. If any structural repairs are required by reason of termite damage as established by acceptable certification, Seller agrees to make necessary repairs not to exceed $500. If repairs exceed $500, Buyer shall first have the right to accept the property "as is" with a credit to the Buyer at closing of $500, or the Buyer may terminate this agreement with the earnest money deposit being promptly returned to the Buyer if the Seller does not agree to pay all costs of treatment and repair.

12. Conditions of Sale: The following conditions shall also apply, and shall, if conflicting with the printed portions of this agreement, prevail and control:

None

13. Liability and Maintenance: Seller shall maintain subject property, including landscaping, in good condition until the date of transfer of title or possession by Buyer, whichever occurs first. All risk of loss and destruction of property, and all expenses of insurance, shall be borne by the seller until the date of possession. If the improvements on the property are destroyed or materially damaged prior to closing, then the Buyer shall have the right to declare this agreement null and void, and the earnest money deposit and all other sums paid by Buyer toward the purchase price shall be returned to the Buyer forthwith.

14. Possession: The Buyer shall be entitled to possession of property upon closing or _____--_____, 19 _____.

15. Default: In the event the Buyer fails to complete the purchase as herein provided, the earnest money deposit shall be retained by the Seller as the total and entire liquidated damages. In the event the Seller fails to perform any condition of the sale as herein provided, then the Buyer may, at his option, treat the contract as terminated, and all payments made by the Buyer hereunder shall be returned to the Buyer forthwith, provided the Buyer may, at his option, treat this agreement as being in full force and effect with the right to action for specific performance and damages. In the event that either Buyer, Seller, or Agent shall institute suit to enforce any rights hereunder, the prevailing party shall be entitled to court costs and a reasonable attorney's fee.

16. Time Limit of Offer: The Seller shall have until

_____ ____May 12,_____, 19 __81__ to accept this
(hour)   (date)

offer by delivering a signed copy hereof to the Buyer. If this offer is not so accepted, it shall lapse and the agent (or Seller) shall refund the earnest money deposit to the Buyer forthwith.

17. General Agreements: (1) Both parties to this purchase reserve their rights to assign and hereby otherwise agree to cooperate in effecting an Internal Revenue Code 1031 exchange or similar tax-related arrangement prior to close of escrow, upon either party's written notice of intention to do so. (2) Upon approval of this offer by the Seller, this agreement shall become a contract between Buyer and Seller and shall inure to the benefit of the heirs, administrators, executors, successors, personal representatives, and assigns of said parties. (3) Time is of the essence and an essential part of this agreement. (4) This contract constitutes the sole and entire agreement between the parties hereto and no modification of this contract shall be binding unless attached hereto and signed by all parties to the contract. No representations, promises, or inducements not included in this contract shall be binding upon any party hereto.

18. Buyer's Statement and Receipt: "I/we hereby agree to purchase the above property in accordance with the terms and conditions above stated and acknowledge receipt of a completed copy of this agreement, which I/we have fully read and understand." Dated _____ May 10, 19 81 _____

(hour)

Address _____ 14 Beachclub Street _____ [signature] and Assigns _____ Buyer

_____ Dallas, Texas _____ _____ Buyer

Phone No: Home 531-1211 Business 896-1818

19. Seller's Statement and Response: "I/we approve and accept the above offer, which I/we have fully read and understand, and agree to the above terms and conditions this day of _____ , 19 _____ , _____ .

(hour)

Address _____ _____ Seller

Phone No: Home _____ Business _____ _____ Seller

20. Commission Agreement: Seller agrees to pay a commission of _____% of the gross sales price to _____ for services in this transaction, and agrees that, in the event of forfeiture of the earnest money deposit by the Buyer, said deposit shall be divided between the Seller's broker and the Seller (one half to each party), the Broker's part not to exceed the amount of the commission.

21. Buyer's Receipt for Signed Offer: The Buyer hereby acknowledges receipt of a copy of the above agreement bearing the Seller's signature in acceptance of this offer.

Dated _____ , 19 _____ _____ Buyer

_____ Buyer

ADDENDUM

On the basis of a counteroffer from the Seller, which occasioned more negotiation, the figures were juggled a bit as follows: down payment to be $20,000, carry back of $12,000 at 10.5%, assumption of $20,000, for a total price of $52,000 (as in the narrative to the case study).

Then the buyer turned around and assigned interest in the property to Vic Campanella (her boyfriend), with figures as follows: cash down payment of $12,000, assumption of $20,000, and the balance of $20,000 evidenced by a second lien payable to a third party (i.e., a commercial lender). It was this final offer that was the basis for obtaining secondary financing necessary to satisfy the original seller's needs.

COMMENTARY TO DOCUMENTATION

Item 2. Here is one case where the phrase "or Assigns" was essential to what the buyer did.

Item 6. The buyer was wise to add a substitution of collateral clause and a provision of prepayment. Also important would have been provisions for rolling the balloon payment over for another year when due and retaining first right of refusal on the note. The offer contained the following sentence, typed in: "$100 earnest money deposit will be retained by Seller as total liquidated damages in case of a default by Buyer." This is an important clause that few people insist on. In this case even the amount of the deposit is made explicit.

Note: As indicated in the commentary to the narrative, this double-escrow arrangement worked but seems unnecessarily complex. Certainly the buyer was prudent to work with legal counsel in order that everything remained above board. Our recommendation would be to use the more direct approach of making a down payment in the form of a note secured against another property acceptable to the seller. The seller could then represent to any lender that consideration had been made for the down payment.

"Gloria! I found a don't wanter!
Quick — look in the book to see what the next step is . . ."

Reprinted by permission from the *Nothing Down Advisor*.

The Notorious "Overfinance" — Can It Ever Be Legitimate?

**Featuring Technique No. 32
"The Second Mortgage Crank"**

In A Nutshell . . .

Type: Two SFHs
Price: $16,400
Source: Realtor
Means: New first, carry back
Techniques: No. 4 — Contract/Wrap
No. 6 — Balloon
No. 32 — Second Mortgage Crank
Features: Positive cash flow

Connie Braniff is a part-time secretary to a tax consultant in Oklahoma City. Since taking the Nothing Down Seminar, she has occupied her spare time buying real estate using creative finance. Within a year's time she acquired seven single family homes with less than $15,000 total cash outlay. The following case study illustrates her approach.

LOCATING

Connie works with a Realtor who is conversant with the techniques of creative finance. His instructions are to locate properties that have a potential of returning cash to the buyer. The two houses described below came to his attention, and he passed the opportunity along to Connie.

SITUATION

Both of the small, free-and-clear houses were located on the same corner lot with detached garage and fenced yard. One house had two bedrooms; the other had one. The total rent generated by them was around $200, half the market potential. The owner was an older widow who was asking $16,400 for the package, with $10,000 down. Even for Oklahoma, where real estate prices are generally still moderate, such a price level was unusually low.

NEGOTIATION

Connie asked the owner why she wanted the cash and learned that the need for security was paramount. Since the properties were free and clear, Connie's strategy was to seek permission from the seller to use the properties as collateral for hard-money funds and have the seller take back the remainder in the form of a second mortgage.

The seller agreed to carry back $6,400 at 12% for 20 years, with monthly payments of $70 and a balloon after five years.

CLOSING

The seller executed a deed for the properties in favor of the buyer, who then obtained an appraisal and made application for a bank loan on a one year's note at 18%. Since the appraisal came in at $26,000, the bank was pleased to fund the purchase to the extent of $13,000 (80% of the sales price). Meanwhile, the buyer executed a "cross deed" back to the seller to secure the buyer's performance under the contract. The Realtor, who did the legwork on the bank financing, also served as escrow agent for the cross deed. The following sketch shows how the "crank" worked. Note that the encumbrances on the properties exceeded the selling price by $3,000 upon closing:

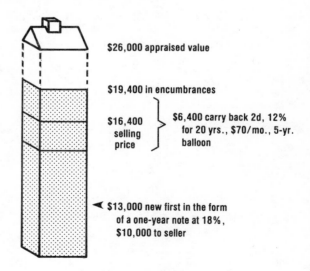

$26,000 appraised value

$19,400 in encumbrances

$16,400 selling price

$6,400 carry back 2d, 12% for 20 yrs., $70/mo., 5-yr. balloon

$13,000 new first in the form of a one-year note at 18%, $10,000 to seller

OUTCOMES AND FUTURE PLANS

The $3,000 rebate was used to cover closing costs and complete over $2,000 worth of repairs (ceiling tiles, paneling, improvements to bathroom, carpeting, etc.). The rents were immediately raised to $400 for the two homes, leaving over $300 in positive cash flow after expenses and debt service on the second mortgage.

Looking back at the deal, Connie herself is still pleasantly surprised that she was able to get in for no cash and still have a rebate for repairs. However, as she put it: "The seller agreed to it," so it was a win/win proposition with mutually-beneficial outcomes.

COMMENTARY

1. In an era where $100,000 bread-and-butter homes are not uncommon in many areas, stories like this one have the ring of yesteryear. Still, if a package of well-located homes totalling $16,400 brings in $400 per month, who is going to knock it? Precisely such small homes will be in the vanguard of demand for young couples taking the step upward from apartments or retiring persons taking a step down into something more manageable.

2. What will Connie do when her balloon falls due at the bank? She can refinance with a long-term first (something she might have done at the outset), obtain secondary financing against her other equity (or equities), split off one of the houses to pay off the first entirely, or bring in a cash partner. Some $3,600 in positive cash flow could be contributed toward the note, leaving less than $10,000 to cure.

3. Why did Connie not attempt to get the seller to agree to a substitution of collateral clause in the documentation? Such a precaution might be very useful after a year's time in order to pave the way for a refinance large enough to generate down payment funds for other transactions.

4. The encumbrances secured by Connie against the properties exceed the selling price by $3,000. Is Connie involved in fraud? The answer in this case is no. With the recent emergence of creative finance as a new way of life for more and more property buyers and sellers, the attention of the public is not infrequently directed to a variety of notorious real estate transactions where wily investors will persuade unsuspecting sellers to encumber properties far beyond reasonable and value-related levels.

The buyers then pocket large amounts of cash at closing and disappear into the sunset, leaving the sellers holding a bag full of mortgages. It is this type of con-artistry that has given a bad connotation to the term "over finance," a term now scrupulously avoided by most purveyors of creative finance education and counsel.

What did Connie do, then, if not an "over finance?" There are at least three redeeming aspects to her deal: 1. The property appraised at $26,000, meaning that the encumbrances of $19,400 were entirely secure — in fact, at 75% of appraised value, they even fell within most bank loan guidelines; 2. The rebate was applied to improvements, adding to the security for the bank and the seller; and 3. The transaction was accomplished with full disclosure to the seller, who concurred with all that was done. Connie was acting with total propriety. She was just smart enough to pick up two properties that were discounted nearly 40%.

The situation to guard against is the case where a property is financed beyond its market value, especially in cash-to-buyer deals without full disclosure. The door of fraud is wide open in such cases, and only the foolish will enter. Investors who have any doubts about where their deals fall in the range of appropriate to fraudulent should (as always) consult competent professionals.

5. In this case, Connie chose to leave the "cross deed" in the hands of the Realtor. It is customarily more advisable to use a neutral escrow agent rather than the Realtor, who (except in the case of a buyer's broker) represents the interests of the seller.

6. Most of the cases discussed in this book involve male investors; this one, however, shows what a woman investor can do in her spare time. As she put it: "I've really used the ideas from the seminar. This is our retirement, and since my husband earns the living, I can devote most of my time to this investment. Thanks!" Who says marriage isn't a partnership?

DOCUMENTATION

UNIVERSAL EARNEST MONEY RECEIPT
AND OFFER TO PURCHASE

"This is a legally binding contract: if not understood, seek competent advice."

1. Date and Place of Offer: ___August 26,___ 19 _81_ ; ___Oklahoma City___ ___Oklahoma___
(city) (state)

2. Principals: The undersigned Buyer ___Carel Braniff and Connie Braniff___
agrees to buy and Seller agrees to sell, according to the indicated terms and conditions, the property described as follows:

3. Property: located at ___12 and 14 Hickory Street___ ___Oklahoma City___ ___Oklahoma___
(street address) (city) (state)

with the following legal description: _____ to be supplied _____

including any of the following items if at present attached to the premises: plumbing, heating, and cooling equipment, including stoker and oil tanks, burners, water heaters, electric light fixtures, bathroom fixtures, roller shades, curtain rods and fixtures, draperies, venetian blinds, window and door screens, towel racks, linoleum and other attached floor coverings,

including carpeting, attached television antennas, mailboxes, all trees and shrubs, and any other fixtures EXCEPT _____ None _____

The following personal property shall also be included as part of the purchase: _____
At the closing of the transaction, the Seller, at his expense, shall provide the Buyer with a Bill Of Sale containing a detailed inventory of the personal property included.

4. Earnest Money Deposit: Agent (or Seller) acknowledges receipt from Buyer of _____ Three Hundred and 00/100 _____ dollars $ _____ 300.00 _____

in the form of ( ) cash; (X) personal check; ( ) cashier's check; ( ) promissory note at _____% interest per annum due _____ 19 _____; or

other _____
as earnest money deposit to secure and apply on this purchase. Upon acceptance of this agreement in writing and delivery of same to Buyer, the earnest money deposit shall be assigned

to and deposited in the listing Realtor's trust account or _____, to apply on the purchase price at the time of closing.

5. Purchase Price: The total purchase price of the property shall be _____ Sixteen Thousand Four Hundred and 00/100 _____

dollars $ _____ 16,400.00 _____

6. Payment: Purchase price is to be paid by Buyer as follows:

Aforedescribed earnest money deposit .... $ _____ 300.00 _____

Additional payment due upon acceptance of this offer .... $ _____ -- _____

Additional payment due at closing .... $ _____ 9,700.00 _____

Balance to be paid as follows:

> Seller to carry a second mortgage for $6,400.00 at 12% interest, payable at $70.48 per month for 20 years, principal and interest. Said second mortgage to balloon in 5 years in the amount of $5,941.26. Buyer to have the privilege of paying all or any additional amount at any time without paying unearned interest. Second mortgage to have due on sale clause.
> Within 10 days from acceptance hereof, Seller is to execute a Deed to buyer for the purpose of allowing Buyer to secure financing on subject property. Buyer to execute a Cross-Deed back to Seller to secure Buyer's performance under this contract. Seller's agent to hold said Cross-Deed in escrow.

7. Title: Seller agrees to furnish good and marketable title free of all encumbrances and defects, except mortgage liens and encumbrances as set forth in this agreement, and to make

conveyance by Warranty Deed or _____. Seller shall furnish in due course to the Buyer a title insurance policy insuring the Buyer of a good and marketable title in keeping with the terms and conditions of this agreement. Prior to the closing of this transaction, the Seller, upon request, will furnish to the Buyer a preliminary title report made by a title insurance company showing the condition of the title to said property. If the Seller cannot furnish marketable title within thirty days after receipt of the notice to the Buyer containing a written statement of the defects, the earnest money deposit herein receipted shall be refunded to the Buyer and this agreement shall be null and void. The following shall not be deemed encumbrances or defects; building and use restrictions general to the area; utility easements; other easements not inconsistent with Buyer's intended use; zoning or subdivision laws, covenants, conditions, restrictions, or reservations of record; tenancies of record. In the event of sale of other than real property relating to this transaction, Seller will provide evidence of title or right to sell or lease such personal property.

8. Special Representations: Seller warrants and represents to Buyer (1) that the subject property is connected to ( ) public sewer system, ( ) cesspool or septic tank, ( ) sewer system available but not connected, ( ) city water system, ( ) private water system, and that the following special improvements are included in the sale: ( ) sidewalk, ( ) curb and gutter, ( ) special street paving, ( ) special street lighting; (2) that the Seller knows of no material structural defects; (3) that all electrical wiring, heating, cooling, and plumbing systems are free of material defects and will be in good working order at the time the Buyer is entitled to possession; (4) that the Seller has no notice from any government agency of any violation or knowledge of probable violations of the law relating to the subject property; (5) that the Seller has no notice or knowledge of planned or commenced public improvements which may result in special assessments or otherwise directly and materially affect the property; and (6) that the Seller has no notice or knowledge of any liens to be assessed against the property,

EXCEPT _____ None _____

9. Escrow Instructions: This sale shall be closed on or before _____ Sept. 25, _____ 19 81 by _____ Calero Escrow Company _____
or such other closing agent as mutually agreed upon by Buyer and Seller. Buyer and Seller will, immediately on demand, deposit with closing agent all instruments and monies required

to complete the purchase in accordance with the provisions of this agreement. Contract of Sale or Instrument of Conveyance to be made in the name of _____

10. Closing Costs and Pro-Ration: Seller agrees to pay for title insurance policy, preliminary title report (if requested), termite inspection as set forth below, real estate commission, cost of preparing and recording any corrective instruments, and one-half of the escrow fees. Buyer agrees to pay for recording fees for mortgages and deeds of conveyance, all costs or expenses in securing new financing or assuming existing financing, and one-half of the escrow fees. Buyer agrees to pay for recording fees for mortgages and deeds of conveyance, all costs or expenses in securing new financing or assuming existing financing, and one-half of the escrow fees. Taxes for the current year, insurance acceptable to the Buyer, rents, interest, mortgage reserves, maintenance fees, and water and other utilities constituting liens, shall be pro-rated as of closing. Renters' security deposits shall accrue to Buyer at closing. Seller to provide Buyer with all current rental or lease agreements prior to closing.

11. Termite Inspection: Seller agrees, at his expense, to provide written certification by a reputable licensed pest control firm that the property is free of termite infestation. In the event termites are found, the Seller shall have the property treated at his expense and provide acceptable certification that treatment has been rendered. If any structural repairs are required by reason of termite damage as established by acceptable certification, Seller agrees to make necessary repairs not to exceed $500. If repairs exceed $500, Buyer shall first have the right to accept the property "as is" with a credit to the Buyer at closing of $500, or the Buyer may terminate this agreement with the earnest money deposit being promptly returned to the Buyer if the Seller does not agree to pay all costs of treatment and repair.

12. Conditions of Sale: The following conditions shall also apply, and shall, if conflicting with the printed portions of this agreement, prevail and control:

Buyers to pay their own taxes and insurance.

Said property to be free of all liens and encumbrances. Seller to furnish Buyer with a termite certificate that is current. Property is to be sold in "as is" condition, except that Buyer is to pay for electrical inspection and Seller to make necessary repairs.

13. Liability and Maintenance: Seller shall maintain subject property, including landscaping, in good condition until the date of transfer of title or possession by Buyer, whichever occurs first. All risk of loss and destruction of property, and all expenses of insurance, shall be borne by the seller until the date of possession. If the improvements on the property are destroyed or materially damaged prior to closing, then the Buyer shall have the right to declare this agreement null and void, and the earnest money deposit and all other sums paid by Buyer toward the purchase price shall be returned to the Buyer forthwith.

14. Possession: The Buyer shall be entitled to possession of property upon closing or _____, 19____.

15. Default: In the event the Buyer fails to complete the purchase as herein provided, the earnest money deposit shall be retained by the Seller as the total and entire liquidated damages. In the event the Seller fails to perform any condition of the sale as herein provided, then the Buyer may, at his option, treat the contract as terminated, and all payments made by the Buyer hereunder shall be returned to the Buyer forthwith, provided the Buyer may, at his option, treat this agreement as being in full force and effect with the right to action for specific performance and damages. In the event that either Buyer, Seller, or Agent shall institute suit to enforce any rights hereunder, the prevailing party shall be entitled to court costs and a reasonable attorney's fee.

16. Time Limit of Offer: The Seller shall have until

_____6:00 p.m._____ _____August 28,_____ 19 __81__ to accept this
      (hour)   (date)

offer by delivering a signed copy hereof to the Buyer. If this offer is not so accepted, it shall lapse and the agent (or Seller) shall refund the earnest money deposit to the Buyer forthwith.

17. General Agreements: (1) Both parties to this purchase reserve their rights to assign and hereby otherwise agree to cooperate in effecting an Internal Revenue Code 1031 exchange or similar tax-related arrangement prior to close of escrow, upon either party's written notice of intention to do so. (2) Upon approval of this offer by the Seller, this agreement shall become a contract between Buyer and Seller and shall inure to the benefit of the heirs, administrators, executors, successors, personal representatives, and assigns of said parties. (3) Time is of the essence and an essential part of this agreement. (4) This contract constitutes the sole and entire agreement between the parties hereto and no modification of this contract shall be binding unless attached hereto and signed by all parties to the contract. No representations, promises, or inducements not included in this contract shall be binding upon any party hereto.

18. Buyer's Statement and Receipt: "I/we hereby agree to purchase the above property in accordance with the terms and conditions above stated and acknowledge receipt of a completed copy of this agreement, which I/we have fully read and understand." Dated _____August 26,_____ 19 __81__ , _____
                                                                    (hour)

Address _____198 Pilgrim Circle_____ [signature] _____ Buyer

_____Oklahoma City, Oklahoma_____ [signature] _____ Buyer

Phone No: Home __211-2115__ Business __518-1414__

19. Seller's Statement and Response: "I/we approve and accept the above offer, which I/we have fully read and understand, and agree to the above terms and conditions this day of _____, 19____, _____
                                                   (hour)

Address _____ Seller

Phone No: Home _____ Business _____ Seller

20. Commission Agreement: Seller agrees to pay a commission of _____% of the gross sales price to _____ for services in this transaction, and agrees that, in the event of forfeiture of the earnest money deposit by the Buyer, said deposit shall be divided between the Seller's broker and the Seller (one half to each party), the Broker's part not to exceed the amount of the commission.

21. Buyer's Receipt for Signed Offer: The Buyer hereby acknowledges receipt of a copy of the above agreement bearing the Seller's signature in acceptance of this offer.

Dated _____, 19____ _____ Buyer

_____ Buyer

COMMENTARY TO DOCUMENTATION

Item 2. Connie found the property and arranged for the financing, but she closed on it along with her husband. Neither one thought to add the words "or Assigns" to the offer.

Item 6. Unfortunately, the seller insisted on an acceleration clause in the carry-back note. The buyer should have insisted on a trade-off: provisions for substi-tution of collateral, rollover of the balloon, and first right of refusal on the note.

It appears as though the seller deeded the property over to the buyer in order for a new loan to be applied; in the escrow, the second was then attached to the property and most of the proceeds of the first disbursed to the seller. In such situations, it is doubly necessary to have the close scrutiny and assistance of competent legal professionals to make sure all regulations and laws are observed, and everyone emerges a winner.

One alternative to the method used would have been for the seller to carry all the equity back against another property belonging to the buyer (or a partner of the buyer). That would have left the subject property free and clear for a first mortgage crank, part of which could then have been paid to the seller under conditions stipulated in the carry-back note. In any complex real estate transaction, the help of excellent professional tax people and attorneys is vital.

Item 15. The original contained a preprinted clause giving the seller broader recourse than in our "total liquidated damages clause." Buyers are always well advised to strike out what seems contrary to their interest.

Reprinted by permission from the *Nothing Down Advisor*.

"It's all right . . . he was strictly win/win."

The Ideal Creative Approach For Our Day

Featuring Technique No. 33
"Variation of the Crank: Seller Refinance"

In A Nutshell . . .

Type: SFH
Price: $49,900
Source: MLS Book
Means: Assumption, Carry Back
Techniques: No. 4 — Contract/Wrap
No. 6 — Balloon
No. 32 — Second Mortgage Crank
No. 33 — Seller Refinance
Features: Even cash flow

When Tucson investors Morris and Eva Painter took the Nothing Down Seminar, they were, in their own words, "flat broke." They made a commitment to themselves that weekend to acquire $1,000,000 in real estate during the ensuing year. Not only did they meet their goal, they exceeded it by 50%, then went on during the first fifteen months of their program to build up a portfolio of single family homes worth some $2,000,000. Their success is all the more remarkable because of the fact that their properties have minimal negative cash flows despite the nothing down character of the transactions.

The Painters have specialized in the second mortgage crank, especially a variation of the crank in which the seller first puts a second on his property and pulls out some cash before it is passed on to the buyers. They look for excellent, well-located properties with low-interest assumable loans. The following example is typical of their pattern. In this case the acquisition was made through an agent friend.

LOCATING

Most of the Painters' deals are located through the Multiple Listing Service publications. The clues are easy to spot: price range of $50,000 to $75,000, low loan-to-value ratio, low interest assumable first, willingness of seller to consider creative offers. In the case described here, the listing was not all that inviting: "CTM, Submit on FHA or VA depending on points." Cash to mortgage would have required over $23,000, but the Painters' Realtor colleague followed up anyway. Fortunately so.

SITUATION

The house and grounds were exceptionally clean and appealing. It was a 3 to 4 bedroom "bread and butter" dwelling with an assumable FHA loan of $26,800 at 8½%. The owner was moving from the area and needed a hefty cash down payment to make a start elsewhere.

NEGOTIATION

Because there was to be cash involved on the front end, the agent did not have difficulty with the agreement. The Painters instructed him to arrange for the following full-price offer: the seller was to put a hard-money second of $12,000 on the property, which, along with the first of $26,800, would be taken over by the buyers. The proceeds of the new second would go to the seller, who would also take back a third for the balance of his equity — $11,100 — at 10% interest for seven years. Payments on the third would not commence until the third year, and even then they would be restricted to $100 per month, going up only $25/mo. for each succeeding year.

The owner countered by insisting on 11% for the carry back, rather than the 10% initially offered. He also shortened the balloon from seven to five years. Apart from these changes, all of the conditions remained the same.

CLOSING

In accordance with the plan, the seller took out a second from Citicorp Person to Person Financial Center in the amount of $12,000 at 18.96% for fifteen years. The Citicorp package was attractive because there was no balloon involved and because the loan was fully assumable, with no prepayment penalties. The payments amounted to $205/mo. This loan satisfied the cash needs of the seller without overextending the buyers relative to rental income on the property. The sketch shows what was done:

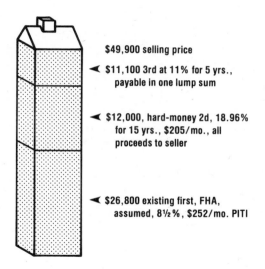

$49,900 selling price

◄ $11,100 3rd at 11% for 5 yrs.,
payable in one lump sum

◄ $12,000, hard-money 2d, 18.96%
for 15 yrs., $205/mo., all
proceeds to seller

◄ $26,800 existing first, FHA,
assumed, 8½%, $252/mo. PITI

OUTCOMES AND FUTURE PLANS

The agent involved deeded the property over to the Painters immediately after the closing. The payments on the first and second total $457 per month, only $100 shy of the rental income performance of the property. The Painters had "cranked" themselves into an excellent property without incurring an excessive negative cash flow. While the market level of rents in the area is $25 to $35 above what they are charging, the Painters prefer to charge less in order to retain the tenants in their properties longer. With vacancy rates in Tucson above the national average, they feel rent moderation will pay off in the long term. In practice, they use a rental agreement that gives the tenants a discount for paying on time, provided they take care of minor maintenance on their own.

COMMENTARY

1. Why is this approach "ideal" for our day? First of all, the subject property belongs to the "bread and butter" category that will remain virtually immune to economic aberrations. Acceptable homes at the bottom of the broad spectrum of American real estate will be most heavily in demand by the greatest percentage of the people. Such homes are at the cutting edge of the market where apartment dwellers enter the home-ownership sector. Such homes are also ideal for the retired who leave larger homes in quest of relief from big mortgage payments.

Next, at a time when money is tight, the owner-refinance approach gets around the cashless nothing down deal and also relieves the buyer of going to the banker with all sorts of gimmicks to prove there is no "secondary financing" to worry about if he refinances in his own name. When the seller adds the second, the issue of secondary financing is moot. The ease of generating front-end cash in this way broadens the number of potential sellers whose problems the creative buyer is in a position to solve. Only 5% of the sellers are amenable to truly cashless or nearly cashless deals. A much larger percentage of sellers can be served with the second mortgage crank approach, especially if they can qualify for a seller refinance as in this variation. And no one is happier than the agent in such cases, for there is nearly always money for the commission.

Finally, the Painters' formula calls for balloons of seven years on the carry back (five years at the earliest). In an age where economic uncertainties have slowed real estate appreciation in certain areas, or even flattened or depressed it in others, short-term balloons are risky. Five years is the shortest fuse one should accept. It is to the Painters' credit that they are able to negotiate terms such as these and still come out with an even cash flow.

2. In the hands of an expert, the second mortgage crank becomes what Bob Allen and Barney Zick — independent of each other — call a "cookie cutter." By this they mean a creative approach that works over and over again. Once the guidelines are established and the operational pattern perfected, such a "cookie cutter" stamps out deal after deal. The investor, while remaining flexible, does not have to lay a new foundation for every transaction; he has his pattern of success, his unique configuration of creative techniques, to carry him to his goal time after time.

3. The existing financing in this case was an FHA-insured first mortgage. In an era where due-on-sale controversies abound, buyers are well instructed to look for the fully-assumable FHA and VA mortgages, which generally also have lower interest rates. The assumption fee is generally less than $50 — a bargain if there ever was one!

DOCUMENTATION

UNIVERSAL EARNEST MONEY RECEIPT
AND OFFER TO PURCHASE

"This is a legally binding contract: if not understood, seek competent advice."

1. Date and Place of Offer: _____ September 19, __ 19 __ 81 __ ; _____ Tucson _____ Arizona _____
                                                     (city)   (state)

Slade Austrian and/or assigns

2. Principals: The undersigned Buyer _____
agrees to buy and Seller agrees to sell, according to the indicated terms and conditions, the property described as follows:

3. Property: located at ___142 Simon Blvd.___ ___Tucson___ ___Arizona___
(street address)   (city)   (state)

with the following legal description: ___Lot 15, Forrest Bluff Terrace, Pima County, Arizona___

including any of the following items if at present attached to the premises: plumbing, heating, and cooling equipment, including stoker and oil tanks, burners, water heaters, electric light fixtures, bathroom fixtures, roller shades, curtain rods and fixtures, draperies, venetian blinds, window and door screens, towel racks, linoleum and other attached floor coverings,

including carpeting, attached television antennas, mailboxes, all trees and shrubs, and any other fixtures EXCEPT ___None___

The following personal property shall also be included as part of the purchase: ___range, refrigerator, dishwasher___

At the closing of the transaction, the Seller, at his expense, shall provide the Buyer with a Bill Of Sale containing a detailed inventory of the personal property included.

4. Earnest Money Deposit: Agent (or Seller) acknowledges receipt from Buyer of ___Two Hundred and 00/100___ dollars $ ___200.00___

in the form of ( ) cash; (X) personal check; ( ) cashier's check; ( ) promissory note at _____% interest per annum due _____ 19 _____; or

other _____

as earnest money deposit to secure and apply on this purchase. Upon acceptance of this agreement in writing and delivery of same to Buyer, the earnest money deposit shall be assigned

to and deposited in the listing Realtor's trust account or _____, to apply on the purchase price at the time of closing.

5. Purchase Price: The total purchase price of the property shall be ___Forty Nine Thousand Nine Hundred and 00/100___

dollars $ ___49,900.00___

6. Payment: Purchase price is to be paid by Buyer as follows:

Aforedescribed earnest money deposit .... $ ___200.00___

Additional payment due upon acceptance of this offer .... $ ___--___

Additional payment due at closing .... $ ___11,800.00___

Balance to be paid as follows:

1. Seller to obtain a loan with Buyer's assistance for said down payment totaling $12,000. Said loan to be secured by a Note and 2nd Deed of Trust on the property, to be assumed by Buyer. All cash proceeds to Seller.

2. Buyer agrees to assume and pay the 1st Note and Deed of Trust in the approximate amount of $26,800 currently payable at $252.00 per month including principal and interest at the rate of 8 1/2% per annum and also including taxes and insurance.

3. Buyer will execute a 3rd Note and Deed of Trust on the property in favor of the Seller in the amount of approximately $11,100 at 10% interest per annum all due and payable seven (7) years from close of escrow. Payments of $100 per month to commence after 3rd year, and payments to increase $25.00 per year until due date.

Seller is aware that Slade Austrian is a licensed real estate agent in the State of Arizona.

7. Title: Seller agrees to furnish good and marketable title free of all encumbrances and defects, except mortgage liens and encumbrances as set forth in this agreement, and to make

conveyance by Warranty Deed or _____. Seller shall furnish in due course to the Buyer a title insurance policy insuring the Buyer of a good and marketable title in keeping with the terms and conditions of this agreement. Prior to the closing of this transaction, the Seller, upon request, will furnish to the Buyer a preliminary title report made by a title insurance company showing the condition of the title to said property. If the Seller cannot furnish marketable title within thirty days after receipt of the notice to the Buyer containing a written statement of the defects, the earnest money deposit herein receipted shall be refunded to the Buyer and this agreement shall be null and void. The following shall not be deemed encumbrances or defects; building and use restrictions general to the area; utility easements; other easements not inconsistent with Buyer's intended use; zoning or subdivision laws, covenants, conditions, restrictions, or reservations of record; tenancies of record. In the event of sale of other than real property relating to this transaction, Seller will provide evidence of title or right to sell or lease such personal property.

8. Special Representations: Seller warrants and represents to Buyer (1) that the subject property is connected to ( ) public sewer system, ( ) cesspool or septic tank, ( ) sewer system available but not connected, ( ) city water system, ( ) private water system, and that the following special improvements are included in the sale: ( ) sidewalk, ( ) curb and gutter, ( ) special street paving, ( ) special street lighting; (2) that the Seller knows of no material structural defects; (3) that all electrical wiring, heating, cooling, and plumbing systems are free of material defects and will be in good working order at the time the Buyer is entitled to possession; (4) that the Seller has no notice from any government agency of any violation or knowledge of probable violations of the law relating to the subject property; (5) that the Seller has no notice or knowledge of planned or commenced public improvements which may result in special assessments or otherwise directly and materially affect the property; and (6) that the Seller has no notice or knowledge of any liens to be assessed against the property,

EXCEPT ___None___

9. Escrow Instructions: This sale shall be closed on or before ___November 4,___ 19 _81_ by ___Strong title and Escrow, Co.___ or such other closing agent as mutually agreed upon by Buyer and Seller. Buyer and Seller will, immediately on demand, deposit with closing agent all instruments and monies required to complete the purchase in accordance with the provisions of this agreement. Contract of Sale or Instrument of Conveyance to be made in the name of _____

___to be supplied___

10. Closing Costs and Pro-Ration: Seller agrees to pay for title insurance policy, preliminary title report (if requested), termite inspection as set forth below, real estate commission, cost of preparing and recording any corrective instruments, and one-half of the escrow fees. Buyer agrees to pay for recording fees for mortgages and deeds of conveyance, all costs or expenses in securing new financing or assuming existing financing, and one-half of the escrow fees. Buyer agrees to pay for recording fees for mortgages and deeds of conveyance, all costs or expenses in securing new financing or assuming existing financing, and one-half of the escrow fees. Taxes for the current year, insurance acceptable to the Buyer, rents, interest, mortgage reserves, maintenance fees, and water and other utilities constituting liens, shall be pro-rated as of closing. Renters' security deposits shall accrue to Buyer at closing. Seller to provide Buyer with all current rental or lease agreements prior to closing.

11. Termite Inspection: Seller agrees, at his expense, to provide written certification by a reputable licensed pest control firm that the property is free of termite infestation. In the event termites are found, the Seller shall have the property treated at his expense and provide acceptable certification that treatment has been rendered. If any structural repairs are required by reason of termite damage as established by acceptable certification, Seller agrees to make necessary repairs not to exceed $500. If repairs exceed $500, Buyer shall first have the right to accept the property "as is" with a credit to the Buyer at closing of $500, or the Buyer may terminate this agreement with the earnest money deposit being promptly returned to the Buyer if the Seller does not agree to pay all costs of treatment and repair.

12. Conditions of Sale: The following conditions shall also apply, and shall, if conflicting with the printed portions of this agreement, prevail and control:

1. Subject to Seller furnishing a pest inspection and clearance and a roof inspection by a licensed contractor.

2. Seller to warrant all plumbing, electrical, heating, cooling and appliances to be in safe and proper working order at close of escrow.

3. Subject to Buyer's inspection and approval of property within 72 hours of Seller's acceptance. Seller to accompany Buyer through inspection of property. A list of repairs is to be prepared and provided to escrow, signed by both parties as to who does what work. Said repairs are to be accomplished within five (5) days before close of escrow evidenced by final clearance provided to escrow. If repairs are not completed, $1,000 shall be held back in escrow to pay for repairs.

4. Seller will deliver home clean, vacant, and landscaping well maintained to Buyer at close of escrow. All debris to be removed from the yard and property to be free of any broken windows.

5. Buyer reserves the right to a walk through inspection and approval 24 hours before close of escrow. All utilities are to be on at time of final inspection, paid for by the Seller.

6. There shall be no prepayment penalty on the 3rd Note and Deed of Trust.

7. Impound account to be assigned to Buyer at no cost.

8. Seller to furnish Home Warranty on home for one full year.

13. Liability and Maintenance: Seller shall maintain subject property, including landscaping, in good condition until the date of transfer of title or possession by Buyer, whichever occurs first. All risk of loss and destruction of property, and all expenses of insurance, shall be borne by the seller until the date of possession. If the improvements on the property are destroyed or materially damaged prior to closing, then the Buyer shall have the right to declare this agreement null and void, and the earnest money deposit and all other sums paid by Buyer toward the purchase price shall be returned to the Buyer forthwith.

14. Possession: The Buyer shall be entitled to possession of property upon closing or _____, 19 _____.

15. Default: In the event the Buyer fails to complete the purchase as herein provided, the earnest money deposit shall be retained by the Seller as the total and entire liquidated damages. In the event the Seller fails to perform any condition of the sale as herein provided, then the Buyer may, at his option, treat the contract as terminated, and all payments made by the Buyer hereunder shall be returned to the Buyer forthwith, provided the Buyer may, at his option, treat this agreement as being in full force and effect with the right to action for specific performance and damages. In the event that either Buyer, Seller, or Agent shall institute suit to enforce any rights hereunder, the prevailing party shall be entitled to court costs and a reasonable attorney's fee.

16. Time Limit of Offer: The Seller shall have until

_____ ___September 21,___ _____, 19 _81_ to accept this
(hour) (date)

offer by delivering a signed copy hereof to the Buyer. If this offer is not so accepted, it shall lapse and the agent (or Seller) shall refund the earnest money deposit to the Buyer forthwith.

17. General Agreements: (1) Both parties to this purchase reserve their rights to assign and hereby otherwise agree to cooperate in effecting an Internal Revenue Code 1031 exchange or similar tax-related arrangement prior to close of escrow, upon either party's written notice of intention to do so. (2) Upon approval of this offer by the Seller, this agreement shall become a contract between Buyer and Seller and shall inure to the benefit of the heirs, administrators, executors, successors, personal representatives, and assigns of said parties. (3) Time is of the essence and an essential part of this agreement. (4) This contract constitutes the sole and entire agreement between the parties hereto and no modification of this contract shall be binding unless attached hereto and signed by all parties to the contract. No representations, promises, or inducements not included in this contract shall be binding upon any party hereto.

18. Buyer's Statement and Receipt: "I/we hereby agree to purchase the above property in accordance with the terms and conditions above stated and acknowledge receipt of a completed copy of this agreement, which I/we have fully read and understand." Dated ___September 19,___ 19 __81__ , _____
(hour)

Address ___14 Jessup Drive___   [signature] and/or Assigns _____ Buyer

_____Tucson, Arizona_____   _____ Buyer

Phone No: Home ___141-1211___ Business ___671-3584___

19. Seller's Statement and Response: "I/we approve and accept the above offer, which I/we have fully read and understand, and agree to the above terms and conditions this day

of _____ , 19 _____ , _____
(hour)

Address _____   _____ Seller

Phone No: Home _____ Business _____   _____ Seller

20. Commission Agreement: Seller agrees to pay a commission of ___7___ % of the gross sales price to ___Jones Realty___ for services in this transaction, and agrees that, in the event of forfeiture of the earnest money deposit by the Buyer, said deposit shall be divided between the Seller's broker and the Seller (one half to each party), the Broker's part not to exceed the amount of the commission.

21. Buyer's Receipt for Signed Offer: The Buyer hereby acknowledges receipt of a copy of the above agreement bearing the Seller's signature in acceptance of this offer.

Dated _____ , 19 _____   _____ Buyer

                                                                _____ Buyer

COMMENTARY TO DOCUMENTATION

Item 2. The interest in the purchase agreement was assigned by Slade Austrian to the ultimate buyers, Morris and Eva Painter, as part of the escrow. A good illustration of the importance of adding "or Assigns" to the agreement!

Item 6. The buyer wisely retained the right to prepay the carry-back note without penalty. Other provisions that would have been desirable: rollover of the balloon, assumption, first right of refusal on the note. In the counter offer, the seller bumped the interest to 11% and insisted on a five-year balloon. That would have been the point in time to insist on a rollover provision for the balloon.

Item 12. The inspection provision is well structured to reduce risk to the buyers — a model of contingency planning.

Reprinted by permission from the *Nothing Down Advisor*.

"Mabel, perhaps we should have started out
asking for a somewhat *smaller* unsecured loan."

Woman Investor Stands To Make $1,500,000 In A Single Creative Deal

**Featuring Technique No. 34
"Buy Low, Refinance High"**

In A Nutshell. . .

Type: 180 townhomes plus adjoining land
Price: $2,950,000; $375,000
Source: Classified ad
Means: Refinance and assumption
Techniques: No. 4 — Contract/Wrap
No. 5 — Raise Price/Lower Terms
No. 6 — Balloon
No. 34 — Buy Low, Refinance High
Strategies: Reserve fund; delayed payments

LOCATING

Gina Decker of Orange County, California, is an experienced investor. Using the techniques taught in the Nothing Down Seminar she has acquired a fairly extensive real estate portfolio of SFH's, condos, and small apartment buildings. Despite her youth, unassuming demeanor, and petite size, she has developed a shrewd market sense and a keen understanding of how to apply the techniques of creative finance in the real estate world.

Among her many talents is the ability to "sniff" out deals where owner flexibility might lead to creative solutions. It was that talent that drew her attention to an ad in the *Wall Street Journal* advertising the property that was to become the subject of this case study.

The ad invited offers on a package of 180 new townhomes in a major Arizona city. The asking price was $3,400,000 on an appraisal of $5,700,000 — a rather good clue for owner flexibility.

SITUATION

Gina immediately called the owner to verify the offer. As she suspected, he was desperate to liquidate his interest in the property. Partnership difficulties were making life miserable, and he wanted to be freed of his troubles — quickly. The townhomes were all two and three-bedroom units with one, one-and-half, or two baths. She made an appointment and flew out, accompanied by an associate, to inspect the properties and negotiate a nothing down transaction.

NEGOTIATION

After inspecting the units and verifying the appraisal, Gina was satisfied that she was on to something big. Her first offer, accompanied by deeds of trust worth $30,000, was as follows: selling price of $3,700,000, new first of $2,700,000 ($700,000 of which was to go into a reserve and trust account for the buyer), the balance of $1,000,000 to be in the form of a carry back at 12%,

payable in monthly payments at 1% for 42 periods (to start 100 days after closing). Her strategy was to raise the price and lower the terms (Technique No. 5). The 100 days leeway would give her time to start the marketing process for the individual units (each of which was to have its own second trust deed for the pro rata amount of the secondary obligation).

It was a good plan, but the owner would not buy it. He wanted all of his money up front. With such a discount on the property, no carry back would be acceptable. (One can't blame Gina for trying!)

Her next offer, the one that was accepted, called for the following price and terms: selling price of $2,950,000, with a new first of not less than $3,600,000 and not more than $4,275,000. Any amount of financing above the $2,950,000 was to go into a special reserve and trust account for use by the buyer in servicing the property through its disposition and resale period. The discount, according to this offer, would therefore be $2,750,000 (appraisal of $5,700,000 less the selling price of $2,950,000), a rather attractive 48%!

In addition to the townhome package, the seller was offering a parcel of adjacent development land consisting of six acres. Gina offered $375,000 for this, with $75,000 down and the balance of $300,000 carried back at 10%, no payments for the first three years, and then monthly payments the fourth and fifth years on a balance of $399,300. The seller agreed to this as well and granted subordination rights in order that Gina might develop the property.

CLOSING

As of this writing, the deal is still pending finalization of the financing package. To date, Gina has been able to secure tentative approval for a loan of $4,200,000 against the Arizona property at 18% for 25 years, with a seven-year balloon. The lenders were so impressed with the low loan-to-value ratio that they immediately arranged for a site inspection and began the process of final approval.

What would the consummation of the deal mean for Gina? With a loan of $4,200,000, the reserve and trust account would amount to $1,250,000. The potential profit after resale would be $1,500,000 ($5,700,000 appraisal less the financed amount of $4,200,000), to say nothing of the six-acre development project. The sketch shows the scale of the transaction:

$5,700,000 appraisal value

$1,500,000 profit

$4,200,000 first trust deed, 18% for 25 years, 7-year balloon

$1,250,000 reserve and trust account

$2,950,000 actual selling price

OUTCOMES AND FUTURE PLANS

If the deal should come together successfully, Gina plans to sell off the individual units at market value, around $31,700 each, with a small down payment and a wrap-around contract. Separation of the various units from the blanket mortgage is provided for in the loan agreement.

What of the negative cash flow? Payments on the first would amount to $62,790 per month, not a small sum. However, after anticipated closing costs of $100,000, there would still be $1,150,000 in the reserve account — enough for 18 full months of campaigning to sell off the townhomes, all of which are vacant and in the final stages of being completed.

COMMENTARY

1. Gina has courage! It doesn't take many deals of this type to catapult someone into financial independence. It is instructive that only one other person called on the ad in the *Wall Street Journal*, despite its extensive circulation. Don't wanters are out there in abundance — but it takes a responsive and creative person to solve their problems.

2. Bank financing in this case exceeded the sales price by a wide margin. Does this constitute an over finance of the property? No, because the deal was transacted with full disclosure to all parties and because the appraisal showed that the value was there to secure the loan. Moreover, the excess proceeds beyond the loan amount were trust funds designated for use in servicing the property. The bank was willing to pursue the deal precisely because of the low loan-to-value ratio.

On the other hand, one reads occasionally about situations where unsuspecting sellers will permit fast-buck artists to over encumber their properties (so that the loan obligations actually exceed the value of the collateral) and walk away with the excess cash in their pockets — in some cases never to be seen again. Practices of this kind are totally antithetical to the principles of win/win creative finance.

3. The concept of using a note or trust deeds as earnest money is a valuable one, especially on larger deals calling for a larger deposit. Using a note secured by other property can quickly build trust because the face value can be large. The benefit to the buyer is that he or she does not need to tie large amounts of money up in the broker's escrow accounts.

4. Will Gina have any difficulty marketing the townhome units with such a high rate of interest (18% underlying)? Perhaps, but the low down will be an offsetting benefit to the resale buyer. There may be leeway, also, for Gina to "buy down" the interest on the wrap for the first six months or a year as an incentive for prospective buyers. Perhaps the lender ultimately will participate in creative resale procedures.

DOCUMENTATION

The following contains the wording of the original offer to purchase:

UNIVERSAL EARNEST MONEY RECEIPT AND OFFER TO PURCHASE

"This is a legally binding contract: if not understood, seek competent advice."

1. Date and Place of Offer: September 8, 19 81 ; Tucson Arizona
(city) (state)

2. Principals: The undersigned Buyer Cooperative Investments, Inc. and/or Assigns
agrees to buy and Seller agrees to sell, according to the indicated terms and conditions, the property described as follows:

3. Property: located at Desert Flower Development, West Alameda Highway Tucson Arizona
(street address) (city) (state)

with the following legal description: ___ 180 townhomes, legal description to be supplied ___

including any of the following items if at present attached to the premises: plumbing, heating, and cooling equipment, including stoker and oil tanks, burners, water heaters, electric light fixtures, bathroom fixtures, roller shades, curtain rods and fixtures, draperies, venetian blinds, window and door screens, towel racks, linoleum and other attached floor coverings,

including carpeting, attached television antennas, mailboxes, all trees and shrubs, and any other fixtures EXCEPT ___ None ___

The following personal property shall also be included as part of the purchase: _____
At the closing of the transaction, the Seller, at his expense, shall provide the Buyer with a Bill Of Sale containing a detailed inventory of the personal property included.

4. Earnest Money Deposit: Agent (or Seller) acknowledges receipt from Buyer of ___ Thirty Thousand and 00/100 ___ dollars $ ___ 30,000 .00 ___

in the form of ( ) cash; ( ) personal check; ( ) cashier's check; ( ) promissory note at _____% interest per annum due _____ 19 _____ ; or

other ___ Deeds of Trust payable to Crawford Investments or designates to be held uncashed until acceptance of this offer. ___

as earnest money deposit to secure and apply on this purchase. Upon acceptance of this agreement in writing and delivery of same to Buyer, the earnest money deposit shall be assigned

to and deposited in the listing Realtor's trust account or _____, to apply on the purchase price at the time of closing.

5. Purchase Price: The total purchase price of the property shall be ___ Three Million Seven Hundred Thousand and 00/100 ___

dollars $ ___ 3,700,000 .00 ___

6. Payment: Purchase price is to be paid by Buyer as follows:

Aforedescribed earnest money deposit . . . . $ _____

Additional payment due upon acceptance of this offer . . . . $ _____

Additional payment due at closing . . . . $ _____

Balance to be paid as follows:

Property and Sellers to qualify and obtain a new first trust deed in the amount of $2,700,000.00 at best rates/terms available. Buyers to subsequently assume subject-to said loan.

Sellers to authorize payment of $700,000 approximately to Buyers from escrow proceeds as a reserve and trust account for the property.

Buyers to execute for Sellers 180 separate second trust deeds totaling the amount of $1,000,000.00 at 12% interest per annum payable at 1% per month for 42 months. First payment is due 100 days after close of escrow. Said notes to contain a 10% late fee penalty, subordination, and substitution of collateral clauses.

Buyers to pay for all refinancing or new loan costs incurred, and will assist Sellers in the successful sale of second trust deeds at a reasonable discount.

Upon verification of Buyer's lender's loan capabilities and disclosure to Seller of Buyer's lending source, any other offers accepted will be considered and construed as breach of contract by Seller and shall immediately cancel escrow. Buyer's deposit shall be refunded on demand and in addition, shall require Seller to compensate Buyer with an amount equitable to Buyer's deposit.

7. Title: Seller agrees to furnish good and marketable title free of all encumbrances and defects, except mortgage liens and encumbrances as set forth in this agreement, and to make

conveyance by Warranty Deed or ___ to be provided later ___. Seller shall furnish in due course to the Buyer a title insurance policy insuring the Buyer of a good and marketable title in keeping with the terms and conditions of this agreement. Prior to the closing of this transaction, the Seller, upon request, will furnish to the Buyer a preliminary title report made by a title insurance company showing the condition of the title to said property. If the Seller cannot furnish marketable title within thirty days after receipt of the notice to the Buyer containing a written statement of the defects, the earnest money deposit herein receipted shall be refunded to the Buyer and this agreement shall be null and void. The following shall not be deemed encumbrances or defects; building and use restrictions general to the area; utility easements; other easements not inconsistent with Buyer's intended use; zoning or subdivision laws, covenants, conditions, restrictions, or reservations of record; tenancies of record. In the event of sale of other than real property relating to this transaction, Seller will provide evidence of title or right to sell or lease such personal property.

Seller to provide preliminary title report to Buyer's at Seller's expense for approval.

8. Special Representations: Seller warrants and represents to Buyer (1) that the subject property is connected to ( ) public sewer system, ( ) cesspool or septic tank, ( ) sewer system available but not connected, ( ) city water system, ( ) private water system, and that the following special improvements are included in the sale: ( ) sidewalk, ( ) curb and gutter, ( ) special street paving, ( ) special street lighting; (2) that the Seller knows of no material structural defects; (3) that all electrical wiring, heating, cooling, and plumbing systems are free of

material defects and will be in good working order at the time the Buyer is entitled to possession; (4) that the Seller has no notice from any government agency of any violation or knowledge of probable violations of the law relating to the subject property; (5) that the Seller has no notice or knowledge of planned or commenced public improvements which may result in special assessments or otherwise directly and materially affect the property; and (6) that the Seller has no notice or knowledge of any liens to be assessed against the property,

EXCEPT _____ None _____

9. Escrow Instructions: This sale shall be closed on or before within 60 days of Seller's acceptance by any reliable company or such other closing agent as mutually agreed upon by Buyer and Seller. Buyer and Seller will, immediately on demand, deposit with closing agent all instruments and monies required to complete the purchase in accordance with the provisions of this agreement. Contract of Sale or Instrument of Conveyance to be made in the name of

_____ to be provided prior to closing _____

10. Closing Costs and Pro-Ration: Seller agrees to pay for title insurance policy, preliminary title report (if requested), termite inspection as set forth below, real estate commission, cost of preparing and recording any corrective instruments, and one-half of the escrow fees. Buyer agrees to pay for recording fees for mortgages and deeds of conveyance, all costs or expenses in securing new financing or assuming existing financing, and one-half of the escrow fees. Buyer agrees to pay for recording fees for mortgages and deeds of conveyance, all costs or expenses in securing new financing or assuming existing financing, and one-half of the escrow fees. Taxes for the current year, insurance acceptable to the Buyer, rents, interest, mortgage reserves, maintenance fees, and water and other utilities constituting liens, shall be pro-rated as of closing. Renters' security deposits shall accrue to Buyer at closing. Seller to provide Buyer with all current rental or lease agreements prior to closing.

11. Termite Inspection: Seller agrees, at his expense, to provide written certification by a reputable licensed pest control firm that the property is free of termite infestation. In the event termites are found, the Seller shall have the property treated at his expense and provide acceptable certification that treatment has been rendered. If any structural repairs are required by reason of termite damage as established by acceptable certification, Seller agrees to make necessary repairs not to exceed $500. If repairs exceed $500, Buyer shall first have the right to accept the property "as is" with a credit to the Buyer at closing of $500, or the Buyer may terminate this agreement with the earnest money deposit being promptly returned to the Buyer if the Seller does not agree to pay all costs of treatment and repair.

12. Conditions of Sale: The following conditions shall also apply, and shall, if conflicting with the printed portions of this agreement, prevail and control:

Exterior to all units to be painted and all uncarpeted units to be fully carpeted prior to close of escrow as per Seller's original plans for upgrading.

Seller to successfully subdivide adjoining six acres of land during and/or prior to close of escrow.

13. Liability and Maintenance: Seller shall maintain subject property, including landscaping, in good condition until the date of transfer of title or possession by Buyer, whichever occurs first. All risk of loss and destruction of property, and all expenses of insurance, shall be borne by the seller until the date of possession. If the improvements on the property are destroyed or materially damaged prior to closing, then the Buyer shall have the right to declare this agreement null and void, and the earnest money deposit and all other sums paid by Buyer toward the purchase price shall be returned to the Buyer forthwith.

14. Possession: The Buyer shall be entitled to possession of property upon closing or not later than 3 days after close of escrow

15. Default: In the event the Buyer fails to complete the purchase as herein provided, the earnest money deposit shall be retained by the Seller as the total and entire liquidated damages. In the event the Seller fails to perform any condition of the sale as herein provided, then the Buyer may, at his option, treat the contract as terminated, and all payments made by the Buyer hereunder shall be returned to the Buyer forthwith, provided the Buyer may, at his option, treat this agreement as being in full force and effect with the right to action for specific performance and damages. In the event that either Buyer, Seller, or Agent shall institute suit to enforce any rights hereunder, the prevailing party shall be entitled to court costs and a reasonable attorney's fee.

16. Time Limit of Offer: The Seller shall have until

_____ Within 24 hours after presentation _____, 19 _____ to accept this
(hour)   (date)

offer by delivering a signed copy hereof to the Buyer. If this offer is not so accepted, it shall lapse and the agent (or Seller) shall refund the earnest money deposit to the Buyer forthwith.

17. General Agreements: (1) Both parties to this purchase reserve their rights to assign and hereby otherwise agree to cooperate in effecting an Internal Revenue Code 1031 exchange or similar tax-related arrangement prior to close of escrow, upon either party's written notice of intention to do so. (2) Upon approval of this offer by the Seller, this agreement shall become a contract between Buyer and Seller and shall inure to the benefit of the heirs, administrators, executors, successors, personal representatives, and assigns of said parties. (3) Time is of the essence and an essential part of this agreement. (4) This contract constitutes the sole and entire agreement between the parties hereto and no modification of this contract shall be binding unless attached hereto and signed by all parties to the contract. No representations, promises, or inducements not included in this contract shall be binding upon any party hereto.

18. Buyer's Statement and Receipt: "I/we hereby agree to purchase the above property in accordance with the terms and conditions above stated and acknowledge receipt of a completed copy of this agreement, which I/we have fully read and understand." Dated September 8, 19 81, _____
(hour)

Address ____ 4714 Lagoon Circle _____   ____ [signature] and/or Assigns ____ Buyer

____ Lakewood California ____   _____ Buyer

Phone No: Home 271-5161 Business 283-4897

19. Seller's Statement and Response: "I/we approve and accept the above offer, which I/we have fully read and understand, and agree to the above terms and conditions this day

of _____, 19 _____, _____
(hour)

Address _____   _____ Seller

Phone No: Home _____ Business _____   _____ Seller

20. Commission Agreement: Seller agrees to pay a commission of _____ % of the gross sales price to _____
for services in this transaction, and agrees that, in the event of forfeiture of the earnest money deposit by the Buyer, said deposit shall be divided between the Seller's broker and the Seller (one half to each party), the Broker's part not to exceed the amount of the commission.

21. Buyer's Receipt for Signed Offer: The Buyer hereby acknowledges receipt of a copy of the above agreement bearing the Seller's signature in acceptance of this offer.

Dated _____, 19 _____   _____ Buyer

    _____ Buyer

COMMENTARY TO DOCUMENTATION

The above offer was not accepted by the seller. After continued negotiation, the following offer was accepted by all parties. (This is the entire offer — only the names have been changed.):

REAL ESTATE PURCHASE CONTRACT AND RECEIPT FOR DEPOSIT

This is more than a receipt for money. It is intended to be a legally binding contract. Read it carefully.

Tucson, Arizona, September 8, 1981.

Received from COOPERATIVE INVESTMENTS, INC. and/or assigns herein called Buyer, the sum of thirty-thousand and no/100 Dollars ($30,000.00) evidenced by deeds of trust payable to CRAWFORD INVESTMENTS or designates, to be held uncashed until acceptance of this offer, as deposit on account of purchase price of Two-million nine-hundred-fifty-thousand and no/100 Dollars ($2,950,000.00) for the purchase of property, situated in Tucson, Arizona, County of Pima, described as follows: Desert Flower Development on West Alameda Highway.

1. Buyer will deposit in escrow with buyer's choice of services the balance of purchase price as follows:

   a. Property and sellers to qualify and obtain a new first trust deed in the amount of not more than $4,275,000.00 and not less than $3,600,000.00 at best rates/terms available. Buyers to subsequently assume subject-to said loan.

   b. Sellers to authorize payment of amount in excess of $2,950,000.00 to buyers from escrow proceeds as a reserve and trust account for the property.

   c. Buyers to pay for all refinancing or new loan costs incurred.

   d. Exterior of all units to be painted and all uncarpeted units to be fully carpeted prior to close of escrow as per sellers' original plans for upgrading.

   e. Upon verification of buyers' lender's loan capabilities and disclosure to seller of buyers' lending source, any other offers accepted will be considered and construed as breach of contract by seller and shall immediately cancel escrow. Buyers' deposit shall be refunded on demand. Seller has right to sell or obtain loan commitment on the property until Buyer's lender is ready to issue a formal, unconditional loan commitment and buyer puts up loan fees.

   f. Seller to successfully subdivide adjoining six acres of land during and/or prior to close of escrow. (See 3)

2. Buyer and Seller shall deliver signed instructions to the escrow holder within 5 days from Seller's acceptance which shall provide for closing within 60 or sooner days from Seller's acceptance. Escrow fees to be paid as follows:

   Buyer and seller to pay for own escrow costs.

3. PROPERTY: 6 acres of land adjoining Desert Flower Development in Tucson, Arizona.

   Sales Price: $375,000.

   Down Payment: $75,000.

   Balance on a note and deed of trust for $300,000 at 10% interest. Interest shall accrue for the first three years, and then shall be paid monthly for years four and five. The face amount of the loan at the beginning of year four shall be $399,300. The note shall be all due and payable at the end of year five. Seller agrees to subordinate to a construction loan.

(Signatures)

The curious thing about this offer is the insight it gives to the onlooker: it is just as easy to fill out an earnest money receipt and offer to purchase for $3,000,000 as it is for $3,000. The principles are the same, if the amounts differ somewhat.

When you are flying high, you remember all the little rules — like "and/or Assigns."

Using Trust Deeds as earnest money is a brilliant way to avoid putting cash on the barrell. Upon the acceptance of the offer, the deeds (or rather the equities they covered) would accrue to the seller and be held pending completion of the transaction. It is a way of exchanging equities into a larger package but calling it earnest money.

The two offers yield similar results for the buyers, but the change from the first to the second is a fundamental one. It is worth studying closely as an example of how a creative thinker can go full circle and come up with a totally different way of viewing things. Consider this analogy:

A seller has a home worth $57,000, which he is anxious to sell. A buyer says to him, "Hey, I'll give you $37,000 for your home. You go and put on a new first for $27,000, give me $7,000 of that as a kitty, and I'll give you a note for the other $10,000 at 1% per month for 42 months. Then I'll balloon you out." The seller doesn't buy that because he is not anxious to carry any paper and because he wants more like $30,000 cash. He just wants out altogether. So the buyer puts on his thinking cap. He somehow has to get about the same size kitty for himself no matter what. The only place to get it is from a bank — so he says to the seller, "Okay. You go and put on a new first of between $36,000 and $42,750. Take your $29,500 and run but leave me everything above that. I'll just assume the new lien and have my kitty. Sure, the note is higher, and the payments are higher, but I don't have any second to worry about meanwhile." So the seller thinks about it and says, "Okay." And that's how deals are made when everyone wins.

A final thought: note how the buyer arranged for separate trust deeds in the carry-back portion of the obligation, each with its own subordination and substitution of collateral clause. That permits smooth sailing when it comes to selling off the units. (Prepayment, assumption, and first right of refusal clauses would also be of interest.) A partial collateral release capability would need to be built into the new first in the case of the final offer.

"Technique 51 — after you've done your homework,
sometimes it's just necessary to jump off the cliff."

Reprinted by permission from the *Nothing Down Advisor.*

$10,000 Instant Equity In Duplex

**Featuring Technique No. 34
"Buy Low, Refinance High"**

In A Nutshell. . .

Type: Duplex
Price: $25,000
Source: Classified ad
Means: Conventional 1st
Techniques: No. 32 — Second Mortgage Crank
No. 34 — Buy Low, Refinance High
Features: $10,000 under market, positive cash flow,
$3,000 back at closing

LOCATING

Harvey Epsom of Wallingford, Pennsylvania, was looking for a duplex in the range $35,000 to $40,000. He was sytematically using the scouting techniques taught in the Nothing Down Seminar, emphasizing especially the real estate classified ads of the local newspaper. It was there that he spotted an ad that looked promising.

SITUATION

A woman in Yeadon (a community within the greater Philadelphia metropolitan area) was offering a modest duplex for $35,900 "cash or conventional financing." Her price was near the market level for properties in the area. Since the duplex was free and clear, Harvey knew that there might be room for creative financing in the deal, especially in view of the fact that the woman seemed very anxious to generate some cash up front.

NEGOTIATION

Harvey's strategy is to ask probing questions "politely but assertively." So he began where few conventional buyers and most Nothing Down investors begin — by asking why the seller needed the cash. As it turned out, the woman needed it desperately to offset the convalescent costs incurred by her father. It would take approximately six months for him to qualify for social security benefits to pay for his health care; until then the woman needed around $1,500 per month on his behalf. Since she didn't have the cash, she was forced to sell her duplex. It was essential for her that the sale go quickly.

Harvey offered her $25,000 all cash, to be generated through a conventional first mortgage against the property, provided that he could have $3,000 of the proceeds to take care of settlement costs. In essence, he was using the second mortgage crank technique but with a first mortgage rather than a second. She agreed to his plan.

CLOSING

The sketch will clarify the nature of Harvey's purchase:

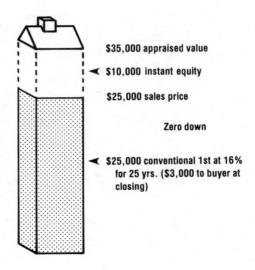

$35,000 appraised value

← $10,000 instant equity

$25,000 sales price

Zero down

← $25,000 conventional 1st at 16% for 25 yrs. ($3,000 to buyer at closing)

OUTCOMES AND FUTURE PLANS

Debt service for the duplex is $335/mo. After expenses, the units produce a positive cash flow of around $100/mo. Harvey plans to hold the property for long-term appreciation. His instant equity of $10,000 will be used to good advantage in acquiring additional properties creatively.

Looking back on the transaction, Harvey feels he should have arranged for a higher mortgage, with a greater return to the buyer on closing. He also feels he should have arranged with the Realtor to take back his commission in the form of paper. This would have relieved the seller of some of her cash pressures up front and perhaps permitted Harvey to pocket more money at closing.

Obviously Harvey enjoys creative real estate

investing. He summarizes his philosophy and approach this way: "Question the seller, be sincere, and love what you are doing."

COMMENTARY

1. This case study is a good example of a "wholesale" transaction. Frequently sellers will discount properties where they insist on lots of cash up front. It took courage for Harvey to ask for such a large discount, but he clearly understood the wholesale principle, seized the opportunity, and wound up — like the seller — in a winning posture.

2. Note that the settlement costs for this transaction were rather high — $3,000. Harvey was wise to prepare for the costs by insisting on a portion of the loan proceeds. Settlement costs vary widely from area to area. Investors, especially those just getting started with their portfolio, need to be familiar with the costs involved.

3. Harvey now has $10,000 in equity against which he can create notes to use as down payments on future properties. Alternately, he has a place to move mortgages to, especially as his equity grows.

DOCUMENTATION

UNIVERSAL EARNEST MONEY RECEIPT AND OFFER TO PURCHASE

"This is a legally binding contract: if not understood, seek competent advice."

1. Date and Place of Offer: __July 28,__ 19 __81__ ; __Glenolden__ __Pennsylvania__
   (city)   (state)

2. Principals: The undersigned Buyer __Harvey Epsom__
   agrees to buy and Seller agrees to sell, according to the indicated terms and conditions, the property described as follows:

3. Property: located at __143 Southwick Place__ __Yeadon__ __Pennsylvania__
   (street address)   (city)   (state)

   with the following legal description: __to be supplied__

including any of the following items if at present attached to the premises: plumbing, heating, and cooling equipment, including stoker and oil tanks, burners, water heaters, electric light fixtures, bathroom fixtures, roller shades, curtain rods and fixtures, draperies, venetian blinds, window and door screens, towel racks, linoleum and other attached floor coverings,

including carpeting, attached television antennas, mailboxes, all trees and shrubs, and any other fixtures EXCEPT __None__

The following personal property shall also be included as part of the purchase: _____
At the closing of the transaction, the Seller, at his expense, shall provide the Buyer with a Bill Of Sale containing a detailed inventory of the personal property included.

4. Earnest Money Deposit: Agent (or Seller) acknowledges receipt from Buyer of __Five Hundred and 00/100__ dollars $ __500.00__

in the form of ( ) cash; X) personal check; ( ) cashier's check; ( ) promissory note at _____% interest per annum due _____ 19 _____ ; or

other _____
as earnest money deposit to secure and apply on this purchase. Upon acceptance of this agreement in writing and delivery of same to Buyer, the earnest money deposit shall be assigned

to and deposited in the listing Realtor's trust account or _____, to apply on the
purchase price at the time of closing.

5. Purchase Price: The total purchase price of the property shall be __Twenty-Five Thousand and 00/100__ dollars $ __25,000.00__

6. Payment: Purchase price is to be paid by Buyer as follows:

   Aforedescribed earnest money deposit .... $ __500.00__

   Additional payment due upon acceptance of this offer __August 8, 1981__ .... $ __2,000.00__

   Additional payment due at closing .... $ __--__

   Balance to be paid as follows:
   Purchase is subject to Buyer obtaining a new conventional first mortgage in the amount of $25,000 for 25 years, payable in monthly payments at an interest rate of 16 1/2% per annum. However, Buyer agrees to accept the interest rate as may be committed by the mortgage lender. Commitment date for approval of the mortgage: August 25, 1981. If said commitment cannot be obtained, this offer shall be null and void.

   It is understood and agreed that at the time of final settlement, the Seller will give the Buyer a credit of $3,000 toward settlement cost.

7. Title: Seller agrees to furnish good and marketable title free of all encumbrances and defects, except mortgage liens and encumbrances as set forth in this agreement, and to make

conveyance by Warranty Deed or _____ Seller shall furnish in due course to the Buyer a title insurance policy insuring the Buyer of a good and marketable title in keeping with the terms and conditions of this agreement. Prior to the closing of this transaction, the Seller, upon request, will furnish to the Buyer a preliminary title report made by a title insurance company showing the condition of the title to said property. If the Seller cannot furnish marketable title within thirty days after receipt of the notice to the Buyer containing a written statement of the defects, the earnest money deposit herein receipted shall be refunded to the Buyer and this agreement shall be null and void. The following shall not be deemed encumbrances or defects; building and use restrictions general to the area; utility easements; other easements not inconsistent with Buyer's intended use; zoning or subdivision laws, covenants, conditions, restrictions, or reservations of record; tenancies of record. In the event of sale of other than real property relating to this transaction, Seller will provide evidence of title or right to sell or lease such personal property.

8. Special Representations: Seller warrants and represents to Buyer (1) that the subject property is connected to ( ) public sewer system, ( ) cesspool or septic tank, ( ) sewer system available but not connected, ( ) city water system, ( ) private water system, and that the following special improvements are included in the sale: ( ) sidewalk, ( ) curb and gutter, ( ) special street paving, ( ) special street lighting; (2) that the Seller knows of no material structural defects; (3) that all electrical wiring, heating, cooling, and plumbing systems are free of material defects and will be in good working order at the time the Buyer is entitled to possession; (4) that the Seller has no notice from any government agency of any violation or knowledge of probable violations of the law relating to the subject property; (5) that the Seller has no notice or knowledge of planned or commenced public improvements which may result in special assessments or otherwise directly and materially affect the property; and (6) that the Seller has no notice or knowledge of any liens to be assessed against the property,

EXCEPT   None _____

9. Escrow Instructions: This sale shall be closed on or before ___ Sept. 1, ___19__81__ by ___--___ or such other closing agent as mutually agreed upon by Buyer and Seller. Buyer and Seller will, immediately on demand, deposit with closing agent all instruments and monies required

to complete the purchase in accordance with the provisions of this agreement. Contract of Sale or Instrument of Conveyance to be made in the name of _____

   to be supplied

10. Closing Costs and Pro-Ration: Seller agrees to pay for title insurance policy, preliminary title report (if requested), termite inspection as set forth below, real estate commission, cost of preparing and recording any corrective instruments, and one-half of the escrow fees. Buyer agrees to pay for recording fees for mortgages and deeds of conveyance, all costs or expenses in securing new financing or assuming existing financing, and one-half of the escrow fees. Buyer agrees to pay for recording fees for mortgages and deeds of conveyance, all costs or expenses in securing new financing or assuming existing financing, and one-half of the escrow fees. Taxes for the current year, insurance acceptable to the Buyer, rents, interest, mortgage reserves, maintenance fees, and water and other utilities constituting liens, shall be pro-rated as of closing. Renters' security deposits shall accrue to Buyer at closing. Seller to provide Buyer with all current rental or lease agreements prior to closing.

11. Termite Inspection: Seller agrees, at his expense, to provide written certification by a reputable licensed pest control firm that the property is free of termite infestation. In the event termites are found, the Seller shall have the property treated at his expense and provide acceptable certification that treatment has been rendered. If any structural repairs are required by reason of termite damage as established by acceptable certification, Seller agrees to make necessary repairs not to exceed $500. If repairs exceed $500, Buyer shall first have the right to accept the property "as is" with a credit to the Buyer at closing of $500, or the Buyer may terminate this agreement with the earnest money deposit being promptly returned to the Buyer if the Seller does not agree to pay all costs of treatment and repair.

12. Conditions of Sale: The following conditions shall also apply, and shall, if conflicting with the printed portions of this agreement, prevail and control:

   It is understood that the Buyers are accepting said property in "as is"
   condition.

13. Liability and Maintenance: Seller shall maintain subject property, including landscaping, in good condition until the date of transfer of title or possession by Buyer, whichever occurs first. All risk of loss and destruction of property, and all expenses of insurance, shall be borne by the seller until the date of possession. If the improvements on the property are destroyed or materially damaged prior to closing, then the Buyer shall have the right to declare this agreement null and void, and the earnest money deposit and all other sums paid by Buyer toward the purchase price shall be returned to the Buyer forthwith.

14. Possession: The Buyer shall be entitled to possession of property upon closing or _____--_____, 19_____.

15. Default: In the event the Buyer fails to complete the purchase as herein provided, the earnest money deposit shall be retained by the Seller as the total and entire liquidated damages. In the event the Seller fails to perform any condition of the sale as herein provided, then the Buyer may, at his option, treat the contract as terminated, and all payments made by the Buyer hereunder shall be returned to the Buyer forthwith, provided the Buyer may, at his option, treat this agreement as being in full force and effect with the right to action for specific performance and damages. In the event that either Buyer, Seller, or Agent shall institute suit to enforce any rights hereunder, the prevailing party shall be entitled to court costs and a reasonable attorney's fee.

16. Time Limit of Offer: The Seller shall have until

_____ ___ August 1, ___ , 19__81__ to accept this
     (hour)   (date)
offer by delivering a signed copy hereof to the Buyer. If this offer is not so accepted, it shall lapse and the agent (or Seller) shall refund the earnest money deposit to the Buyer forthwith.

17. General Agreements: (1) Both parties to this purchase reserve their rights to assign and hereby otherwise agree to cooperate in effecting an Internal Revenue Code 1031 exchange or similar tax-related arrangement prior to close of escrow, upon either party's written notice of intention to do so. (2) Upon approval of this offer by the Seller, this agreement shall become a contract between Buyer and Seller and shall inure to the benefit of the heirs, administrators, executors, successors, personal representatives, and assigns of said parties. (3) Time is of the essence and an essential part of this agreement. (4) This contract constitutes the sole and entire agreement between the parties hereto and no modification of this contract shall be binding unless attached hereto and signed by all parties to the contract. No representations, promises, or inducements not included in this contract shall be binding upon any party hereto.

18. Buyer's Statement and Receipt: "I/we hereby agree to purchase the above property in accordance with the terms and conditions above stated and acknowledge receipt of a

completed copy of this agreement, which I/we have fully read and understand." Dated ___ July 28, ___ 19__81__ , _____
                                                                                                                    (hour)

Address ___ 714 Baltimore Avenue ___   [signature] _____ Buyer

         ___ Wallingford, Pennsylvania ___   _____ Buyer

Phone No: Home ___ 678-4131 ___ Business ___ 794-1181 ___

19. Seller's Statement and Response: "I/we approve and accept the above offer, which I/we have fully read and understand, and agree to the above terms and conditions this day

of _____ , 19_____ , _____
                                                          (hour)

Address _____ Seller

Phone No: Home _____ Business _____   _____ Seller

20. Commission Agreement: Seller agrees to pay a commission of _____% of the gross sales price to _____
for services in this transaction, and agrees that, in the event of forfeiture of the earnest money deposit by the Buyer, said deposit shall be divided between the Seller's broker and the Seller (one half to each party), the Broker's part not to exceed the amount of the commission.

21. Buyer's Receipt for Signed Offer: The Buyer hereby acknowledges receipt of a copy of the above agreement bearing the Seller's signature in acceptance of this offer.

Dated _____, 19 _____   _____ Buyer

                                                             _____ Buyer

COMMENTARY TO DOCUMENTATION

Item 2. Once again, the litany about adding the words "or Assigns" after the buyer's name. It is a small thing but potentially of immense importance.

Item 6. If our arithmetic is correct, the buyer puts up $2,500 cash ahead of time. The bank chips in $25,000, of which $22,000 goes to the seller. This means that the excess is $5,500. Of this, the buyer takes the $2,500 and puts it back into his pocket. The rest ($3,000) goes, as planned, to pay for the buyer's settlement costs. Everyone wins! The secret ingredient is the fact that the property is heavily discounted and free and clear.

How To Succeed By Giving The Seller A Range Of Choices

**Featuring Technique No. 34
"Buy Low, Refinance High"**

In A Nutshell. . .

Type: 3 Duplexes
Price: $165,000
Source: Classified ad
Means: Refinance
Techniques: No. 32 — Second Mortgage Crank
No. 34 — Buy Low, Refinance High
Features: Positive cash flow

LOCATING

Keith Dutton has had some experience in rental properties. When he began looking for the property described below, he had already acquired a 15-unit apartment building, two duplexes, and a commercial building. He began his search by studying the ads in the local paper. Not finding any promising leads in the For Sale columns, he turned to the section on apartments for rent and spotted an ad with the following wording:

"Looking for good tenant—last one a bummer. Must have good references. Fix up needed—will trade your efforts for part of rent."

Acting on the hunch that the owner might be a don't wanter, Keith called on the ad. His suspicions were confirmed.

SITUATION

The property involved was a duplex unit in Bixby, Oklahoma (southeast of Tulsa). There were two other duplexes on the same lot, one of which had been converted to a single family residence presently occupied by the owner. He was tired of the units and needed to raise capital to start a new business. All three buildings were free and clear of any encumbrances. An appraisal two years previous to that had evaluated the duplexes at $68,000 each.

NEGOTIATION

Keith learned that the owner was willing to sell the duplexes for $65,000 with the right terms. The problem for Keith was to structure the offer so that the seller could not say "No." He hit on the strategy of making not one, but four different offers at the same time. He reasoned that it might make good sense to ask the seller to choose among alternative offers rather than between a "Yea" and a "Nay."

After mulling things over for a day, Keith met with the owner and laid the following offers before him:

1. $65,000 per building, with $5,000 down and balance at 10%;
2. $65,000 per building, with $10,000 down and balance at 9%;
3. $65,000 per building, with $15,000 down and balance at 8%;
4. $53,500 per building, all cash in thirty days.

The cash offer was too tempting for the owner, so he countered with $55,000 per building, and Keith quickly accepted. The agreement was drawn up and secured with an earnest money note.

CLOSING

Keith had jumped off a cliff. He needed to raise $165,000 in a hurry. Since his wife worked as a teller in one of the local banks, they started their search by going to her supervisor, who happened to be a loan officer. When they explained the situation, he seemed interested and asked for a current appraisal. Keith arranged for the bank appraiser to inspect the properties. Imagine their excitement when his appraisal came in at $79,800!

By borrowing $66,500 on each duplex, Keith and his wife generated $199,500 for the package — $34,500 more than the $165,000 they had promised the seller. In effect, they had used the Second Mortgage Crank technique but with a first mortgage instead of a second. After closing costs, the transaction netted the buyers around $30,000 in cash. The sketch summarizes the figures:

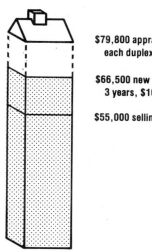

$79,800 appraised value, each duplex

$66,500 new first at 15%, 3 years, $1000/mo.

$55,000 selling price

OUTCOMES AND FUTURE PLANS

Keith converted the one building back to its former duplex status. He raised the rents across the board and now realizes a monthly gross income of $1,400, nearly $400 per month in excess of the expenses. He plans to split the lot into three separate lots and eventually refinance the duplexes when they appreciate more in value.

What does he plan to do with the $30,000 cash proceeds from the closing? Buy more real estate! His advice for others getting into the creative real estate field: "Jump in! If the numbers are there and you make the move, you'll find yourself thinking, analyzing, working, etc., to make it all work out. Then you can't wait for the next one."

COMMENTARY

1. There are many cash-to-buyer deals being closed these days in the name of "creative finance." Some of them are "over finance" transactions where the owner is asked to carry back paper that exceeds the value of the property and paves the way for the buyer to walk away with cash in his pocket. Such transactions are risky — especially for the seller — and can lead to abuse.

The cash-to-buyer deal completed by Keith Dutton in this case study is an example of a totally above-board transaction where the seller is willing to discount his property in exchange for cash on the barrel. The "Buy Low, Refinance High" technique is one of the best ways to generate cash for future deals, improvements, or covering negative cash flows. Note who wins: the seller takes his cash and goes away happy, the buyer gets in for nothing down and has extra operating or investment funds, and the banker has placed a good loan that will generate profits. Why should the buyer get the extra cash? Because he has the expertise to generate the good deal in the first place; think of his benefits as being consideration for an outstanding job of problem-solving! But can't he just walk away with his $30,000 and leave the bank holding the properties? Sure, but the bank is not dumb — they have made a judgment about the quality of this buyer and are satisfied that their investment is secure. Besides, the buyer realizes that the greatest benefit to him will be in the form of long-term appreciation and tax advantages. He'll stay around to harvest his real estate money crop.

2. Note how Keith was willing to jump off a cliff into what might be called the "valley of creative thinking." By committing himself to a course of action, he triggered the thought power and energy needed to find the solutions to the problem. It is to people of action that the greatest benefits accrue. Of course, he did his homework carefully and protected himself with contingencies on the issue of raising the needed funds. But he took action. So many refuse to take action — even with contingencies to protect them — and as a result never move forward.

DOCUMENTATION

UNIVERSAL EARNEST MONEY RECEIPT AND OFFER TO PURCHASE

"This is a legally binding contract: if not understood, seek competent advice."

1. Date and Place of Offer: __August 6,__ 19 __80__; __Tulsa__ (city) __Oklahoma__ (state)

2. Principals: The undersigned Buyer __Keith Dutton and Jackie Lynn Dutton__
agrees to buy and Seller agrees to sell, according to the indicated terms and conditions, the property described as follows:

3. Property: located at __605 New Haven Road__ (street address) __Bixby__ (city) __Oklahoma__ (state)
with the following legal description: __Lot 7, Block 14, Bixby original town (3 buildings)__
__property used in connection with operating above properties.__

including any of the following items if at present attached to the premises: plumbing, heating, and cooling equipment, including stoker and oil tanks, burners, water heaters, electric light fixtures, bathroom fixtures, roller shades, curtain rods and fixtures, draperies, venetian blinds, window and door screens, towel racks, linoleum and other attached floor coverings,

including carpeting, attached television antennas, mailboxes, all trees and shrubs, and any other fixtures EXCEPT _____ None

The following personal property shall also be included as part of the purchase: _____ appliances, furniture, and other personal
At the closing of the transaction, the Seller, at his expense, shall provide the Buyer with a Bill Of Sale containing a detailed inventory of the personal property included.

4. Earnest Money Deposit: Agent (or Seller) acknowledges receipt from Buyer of _____ Three Hundred and 00/100 dollars $ 300.00

in the form of ( ) cash; (X personal check; ( ) cashier's check; ( ) promissory note at _____% interest per annum due _____ 19 _____; or

other _____

as earnest money deposit to secure and apply on this purchase. Upon acceptance of this agreement in writing and delivery of same to Buyer, the earnest money deposit shall be assigned

to and deposited in the listing Realtor's trust account or _____, to apply on the purchase price at the time of closing.

5. Purchase Price: The total purchase price of the property shall be _____ Fifty-Five Thousand and 00/100 dollars $ 55,000.00

6. Payment: Purchase price is to be paid by Buyer as follows:

Aforedescribed earnest money deposit .... $ 300.00

Additional payment due upon acceptance of this offer .... $ --

Additional payment due at closing .... $ --

Balance to be paid as follows:

1.   This contract contingent upon Buyer obtaining FHA loan or other financing.
2.   Seller warrants that property has not been flooded.
3.   In the event a loan cannot be found for the above property by closing, earnest money will be refunded.

7. Title: Seller agrees to furnish good and marketable title free of all encumbrances and defects, except mortgage liens and encumbrances as set forth in this agreement, and to make

conveyance by Warranty Deed or _____ Seller shall furnish in due course to the Buyer a title insurance policy insuring the Buyer of a good and marketable title in keeping with the terms and conditions of this agreement. Prior to the closing of this transaction, the Seller, upon request, will furnish to the Buyer a preliminary title report made by a title insurance company showing the condition of the title to said property. If the Seller cannot furnish marketable title within thirty days after receipt of the notice to the Buyer containing a written statement of the defects, the earnest money deposit herein receipted shall be refunded to the Buyer and this agreement shall be null and void. The following shall not be deemed encumbrances or defects; building and use restrictions general to the area; utility easements; other easements not inconsistent with Buyer's intended use; zoning or subdivision laws, covenants, conditions, restrictions, or reservations of record; tenancies of record. In the event of sale of other than real property relating to this transaction, Seller will provide evidence of title or right to sell or lease such personal property.

8. Special Representations: Seller warrants and represents to Buyer (1) that the subject property is connected to ( ) public sewer system, ( ) cesspool or septic tank, ( ) sewer system available but not connected, ( ) city water system, ( ) private water system, and that the following special improvements are included in the sale: ( ) sidewalk, ( ) curb and gutter, ( ) special street paving, ( ) special street lighting; (2) that the Seller knows of no material structural defects; (3) that all electrical wiring, heating, cooling, and plumbing systems are free of material defects and will be in good working order at the time the Buyer is entitled to possession; (4) that the Seller has no notice from any government agency of any violation or knowledge of probable violations of the law relating to the subject property; (5) that the Seller has no notice or knowledge of planned or commenced public improvements which may result in special assessments or otherwise directly and materially affect the property; and (6) that the Seller has no notice or knowledge of any liens to be assessed against the property,

EXCEPT _____ None

9. Escrow Instructions: This sale shall be closed on or before _____ Sept. 5, 19 81 by _____ --
or such other closing agent as mutually agreed upon by Buyer and Seller. Buyer and Seller will, immediately on demand, deposit with closing agent all instruments and monies required

to complete the purchase in accordance with the provisions of this agreement. Contract of Sale or Instrument of Conveyance to be made in the name of _____

10. Closing Costs and Pro-Ration: Seller agrees to pay for title insurance policy, preliminary title report (if requested), termite inspection as set forth below, real estate commission, cost of preparing and recording any corrective instruments, and one-half of the escrow fees. Buyer agrees to pay for recording fees for mortgages and deeds of conveyance, all costs or expenses in securing new financing or assuming existing financing, and one-half of the escrow fees. Buyer agrees to pay for recording fees for mortgages and deeds of conveyance, all costs or expenses in securing new financing or assuming existing financing, and one-half of the escrow fees. Taxes for the current year, insurance acceptable to the Buyer, rents, interest, mortgage reserves, maintenance fees, and water and other utilities constituting liens, shall be pro-rated as of closing. Renters' security deposits shall accrue to Buyer at closing. Seller to provide Buyer with all current rental or lease agreements prior to closing.

11. Termite Inspection: Seller agrees, at his expense, to provide written certification by a reputable licensed pest control firm that the property is free of termite infestation. In the event termites are found, the Seller shall have the property treated at his expense and provide acceptable certification that treatment has been rendered. If any structural repairs are required by reason of termite damage as established by acceptable certification, Seller agrees to make necessary repairs not to exceed $500. If repairs exceed $500, Buyer shall first have the right to accept the property "as is" with a credit to the Buyer at closing of $500, or the Buyer may terminate this agreement with the earnest money deposit being promptly returned to the Buyer if the Seller does not agree to pay all costs of treatment and repair.

12. Conditions of Sale: The following conditions shall also apply, and shall, if conflicting with the printed portions of this agreement, prevail and control:
None

13. Liability and Maintenance: Seller shall maintain subject property, including landscaping, in good condition until the date of transfer of title or possession by Buyer, whichever occurs first. All risk of loss and destruction of property, and all expenses of insurance, shall be borne by the seller until the date of possession. If the improvements on the property are destroyed or materially damaged prior to closing, then the Buyer shall have the right to declare this agreement null and void, and the earnest money deposit and all other sums paid by Buyer toward the purchase price shall be returned to the Buyer forthwith.

14. Possession: The Buyer shall be entitled to possession of property upon closing or _____ -- _____, 19 _____.

15. Default: In the event the Buyer fails to complete the purchase as herein provided, the earnest money deposit shall be retained by the Seller as the total and entire liquidated damages. In the event the Seller fails to perform any condition of the sale as herein provided, then the Buyer may, at his option, treat the contract as terminated, and all payments made by the Buyer hereunder shall be returned to the Buyer forthwith, provided the Buyer may, at his option, treat this agreement as being in full force and effect with the right to action for specific performance and damages. In the event that either Buyer, Seller, or Agent shall institute suit to enforce any rights hereunder, the prevailing party shall be entitled to court costs and a reasonable attorney's fee.

16. Time Limit of Offer: The Seller shall have until

_____ Upon presentation _____, 19 _____ to accept this
(hour)   (date)

offer by delivering a signed copy hereof to the Buyer. If this offer is not so accepted, it shall lapse and the agent (or Seller) shall refund the earnest money deposit to the Buyer forthwith.

17. General Agreements: (1) Both parties to this purchase reserve their rights to assign and hereby otherwise agree to cooperate in effecting an Internal Revenue Code 1031 exchange or similar tax-related arrangement prior to close of escrow, upon either party's written notice of intention to do so. (2) Upon approval of this offer by the Seller, this agreement shall become a contract between Buyer and Seller and shall inure to the benefit of the heirs, administrators, executors, successors, personal representatives, and assigns of said parties. (3) Time is of the essence and an essential part of this agreement. (4) This contract constitutes the sole and entire agreement between the parties hereto and no modification of this contract shall be binding unless attached hereto and signed by all parties to the contract. No representations, promises, or inducements not included in this contract shall be binding upon any party hereto.

18. Buyer's Statement and Receipt: "I/we hereby agree to purchase the above property in accordance with the terms and conditions above stated and acknowledge receipt of a completed copy of this agreement, which I/we have fully read and understand." Dated _____ August 6, _____ 19 _81_ , _____
                                                                                                                                                              (hour)

Address _____ 6165 North Hillen Way _____   [signature] _____ Buyer

_____ Tulsa, Oklahoma _____   [signature] _____ Buyer

Phone No: Home _516-1113_   Business _851-7152_

19. Seller's Statement and Response: "I/we approve and accept the above offer, which I/we have fully read and understand, and agree to the above terms and conditions this day

of _____, 19 _____, _____.
                                                                          (hour)

Address _____   _____ Seller

Phone No: Home _____ Business _____   _____ Seller

20. Commission Agreement: Seller agrees to pay a commission of _____ % of the gross sales price to _____ for services in this transaction, and agrees that, in the event of forfeiture of the earnest money deposit by the Buyer, said deposit shall be divided between the Seller's broker and the Seller (one half to each party), the Broker's part not to exceed the amount of the commission.

21. Buyer's Receipt for Signed Offer: The Buyer hereby acknowledges receipt of a copy of the above agreement bearing the Seller's signature in acceptance of this offer.

Dated _____, 19 _____   _____ Buyer

_____ Buyer

COMMENTARY TO DOCUMENTATION

Each of the three duplexes was handled on a separate form as a separate purchase (wisely so). The offers were all similar.

Item 2. The words "or Assigns" should always be added after the buyer's name.

Item 6. This one is played fairly loosely! The balance is to be covered through a new loan. No contingencies are given as to the terms or tenure of the loan. But there is a good escape: no loan, no sale. That's when the buyers got the ball rolling and found out they could borrow $66,500 against each of the duplexes. Not all the news is bad these days.

The flood warranty has no teeth. What is needed is a contingency based on damages to be tested through a qualified building inspection. The seller should be made liable for any damages, and the sale contingent on satisfaction.

Part VII

Underlying Mortgages

The seventh area of flexibility in acquiring property for nothing down is the area of underlying mortgages. Three vital questions for the analysis phase are: What mortgages (trust deeds, liens) are there against the property? Who holds them? Would these holders of underlying mortgages be flexible with their assets? In most cases the mortgagees are banks; for that reason conventional wisdom assumes that there will be no flexibility whatsoever. Hard-money lenders, after all, are "tightwads" who never yield on the terms of their loans. Conventional wisdom is usually correct in this, and yet even hard-money lenders can soften up if it is in their best interests to do so. The unprecedented rise in interest rates in the last few years has caused some agencies and institutions to develop flexibilities with their mortgage holdings that can benefit real estate investors.

With private mortgage holders, the opportunities for creative finance techniques are even greater. The mortgagees may be sellers who have accepted paper back for part of their equity when they sold the property. Now they are receiving payments over time, sometimes at interest rates far below the current market. Often such private mortgage holders realize that their assets are not well invested in relation to current investment opportunities and yields, so they become open to suggestions from creative buyers who present more beneficial solutions to the problem.

This section outlines five techniques and five case studies from this area of flexibility. The following summary gives an overview:

Technique No. 35 — Use Discounts From Holders Of Mortgages
    Case No. 37: American Real Estate Through The Eyes Of An Immigrant: "Pure Gold!"

Technique No. 36 — Moving The Mortgage
    Case No. 38: Creative Exchange Puts Couple Into 10-Plex
    Case No. 39: Trust-Building Is Key To Win/Win Deal On Duplex

Technique No. 37 — Creative Refinance Of Underlying Mortgage
    Case No. 40: How To Get Your Feet Wet In Real Estate Without Taking A Bath

Technique No. 38 — Pulling Cash Out Of Buildings You Own But Don't Want To Sell

Technique No. 39 — Making A Partner Of The Holder Of An Underlying Mortgage
    Case No. 41: "Just Let Yourself In. . .The Key's Under The Mortgage"

Technique No. 35   Use Discounts from Holders of Mortgages

The basic approach to the private holders of underlying financing is this: "Mr. Mortgagee, you are receiving monthly payments on this note at a moderate rate of interest, and you must wait patiently until the note is paid off. Would you not rather have this mortgage redeemed for cash right away?" If the holder of the mortgage is willing to discount his note for cash, the buyer can look for new financing to put on the property in order to pay off the existing private mortgage. The strategy is to have enough refinance funds to pay off the private mortgagee and still have sufficient funds to take care of part or all of the down payment needed to acquire the property in the first place. It might turn out that the private mortgage holder will be willing to discount only a part of his note for cash. Perhaps he would respond to the idea of taking part in cash (at a discount) and the rest in new secondary financing above the refinance mortgage, possibly with an improvement in his interest rate or other terms.

There are many variations to this technique, but the basic idea is to redeem the underlying mortgage at a discount for cash (using borrowed funds), with the balance being applied to the down payment. Case No. 37 provides an illustration of how the technique works. The buyer of a rental home had induced a seller to take back a single-payment second of $11,000 for three years. After the closing, the buyer approached the seller and offered to buy back the second for $7,000 cash. When the seller agreed, the buyer borrowed $10,000, paid off the note, and had $3,000 to offset the small cash down payment he had made to get into the property.

Technique No. 36   Moving the Mortgage

A mortgage consists of two basic documents: one is a note setting forth the terms for paying back funds that are borrowed; the other is a security agreement that provides collateral for the loan in case of default. The security agreement promises, in essence, to back up the performance of the borrower in repaying the note. If the buyer fails to live up to his commitments, then the lender is entitled to the collateral (property) pledged as security for the loan.

What conventional wisdom fails to grasp is the idea that while the terms of the note are fixed, there may be dozens of ways to satisfy the security needs of the seller other than using the subject property itself as collateral. As the procedures of Technique No. 36, "Moving the Mortgage," will make clear, it is always wise in negotiating a real estate purchase to include a "substitution of collateral" clause in the purchase agreement. Such a clause allows the buyer to substitute other collateral as security for the note in the future, subject to the approval of the seller. It is sometimes possible, even after the fact, to induce a seller or the holder of an underlying mortgage to "move the mortgage" to another property (substitute other collateral). Frequently sweeteners are needed to get the job done — an increase in the interest rate or the principal amount, an improvement in the position of the note (e.g., from third to second or from second to first), an increase in the amount or quality of the collateral, etc.).

Why is it beneficial to move a mortgage? The key is

this: if property owned by a buyer can be definanced (freed of encumbrances, in this case by having the existing mortgages moved to other properties), then the buyer will be free to put new financing on the property and "crank" out funds that can be used, for example, as down payments. Alternately, the definanced property can be sold to raise capital for the same purposes. Now here is the twist that boggles conventional wisdom: What if the down payment funds generated in this way are used to acquire the very property to which the mortgages we have been talking about are to be moved? Is it possible to arrange for a simultaneous escrow involving both properties? Certainly!

One of the case studies that apply to this technique shows how it is done. In Case No. 38, a brilliant investor acquired a 10-plex in the following way: using funds he had cranked out of an earlier investment property, he bought a SFH whose owners were willing to accept security for their carry back against the 10-plex our investor wanted to acquire. He then traded the definanced SFH to the owners of the 10-plex, who in turn put new financing against the SFH to get capital they needed. Brilliant! Readers will want to study the details of this case study very carefully.

In Case No. 39, the problem was not one of generating cash for the down payment but rather in assuming a first mortgage without violating the policy of the lender prohibiting secondary financing on the property. The buyer simply induced the seller to carry back the difference on a note secured against other properties. By moving the mortgage off the subject property, the buyer prepared the way for a future refinance or sale to raise capital for the next big deal. The cross-reference matrix in the appendix lists five other case studies where the "Moving of the Mortgage" technique is used.

Technique No. 37   Creative Refinance of Underlying Mortgage

In general, the only flexible holders of underlying mortgages are private parties. Hard-money mortgagees are for the most part not cooperative when it comes to techniques discussed in this section. However, there is one aspect of underlying financing where even the hard-money people are beginning to show flexibility: refinance. The unprecedented flight of interest rates in recent years has left financial institutions holding large portfolios of undesirable low-interest mortgages. With the advent of high-yield money market funds, deposits in savings and loan associations have been withdrawn in record amounts, making the situation even worse. The result is that the lenders are desperate to rid their holdings of the older, low interest loans made in yesteryear. A symptom of the malaise is the aggressiveness of many banks in upholding the due-on-sale provisions of conventional loans made during the last decade. They want those loans paid off or assumed at higher interest rates.

The current situation will bring about a softening of

hard-money hearts in the interests of institutional solvency. One major example of this has already become policy. The Federal National Mortgage Association, which holds a vast portfolio of home mortgages acquired from lenders around the country, is offering to refinance their own mortgages at rates below the market for both owner-occupied as well as investment situations. Since they will go as high as 90% for owner-occupants and 80% for investors, the program offers interesting possibilities for the creative buyer. FNMA calculates the new interest rate on the refinanced loan by averaging the yield on the old amount with the yield on the added amount according to an internal formula. The combination is always lower than the market rate. Although FNMA guidelines must be met, buyers should consider taking advantage of the opportunities the refinance program offers to raise funds.

The Fannie Mae program is not the only "creative refinance" opportunity available. Many primary lending institutions around the country are devising innovative ways to divest themselves of unprofitable low-interest loans in ways that might be beneficial to investors. One prominent S&L in the St. Louis area, for example, refinances low interest loans in its own portfolio (loans at 11% or less) for up to double the old loan amount at 12.31% interest for 30 years (adjustable interest rate factored in every six months with monthly payments adjusted every five years). Another lender in Cleveland is discounting its older mortgages by 25%. Investors should explore opportunities for working creative deals with lenders in their own areas. The next period of time will be marked with increased hard-money flexibilities that could lead to win/win deals for everyone involved.

Of special interest also are the R.E.O.'s—"Real Estate Owned" properties that the lending institutions have had to take back through foreclosure and now want to get rid of. Foreclosure activity increases during tight-money times, and investors should cultivate relationships with lenders who might be very anxious to sell R.E.O.'s to them on soft terms.

Case No. 40 shows how one buyer used the program to generate $15,000 toward the down payment on a condo. The existing FNMA first at $41,000 was refinanced at $56,000, with the excess proceeds going to the seller. The new interest rate was 12.25%, far below market levels. Two other case studies among the fifty also show how the creative refinance technique can be used to good advantage. (See the cross-reference matrix in the appendix.)

Technique No. 38   Pulling Cash Out of Buildings You Own But Don't Want To Sell

Many variations in the basic approach of dealing creatively with holders of underlying mortgages are possible. Here is one other example — not reflected in any of the case studies in this book — of how a creative investor might pull investment funds out of a property without actually selling it. Let's suppose that a private party holds a mortgage against a property our investor wants to keep. He needs to raise investment capital, but a refinance of the property would not net a large amount of cash because most of the proceeds, let's suppose, would go to pay off the existing private mortgage. What can he do? Perhaps the private mortgagee would agree to share the proceeds of the new loan with the investor and take back the balance in the form of a new second mortgage against the property. The investor may have to sweeten the deal (perhaps in the form of a higher interest rate, higher monthly payments, or a shorter pay-out period), but at least he gets to keep his property and achieve his goal of raising capital.

Technique No. 39   Making A Partner of the Holder of an Underlying Mortgage

What other ways are there to induce a private mortgage holder to cooperate in creative arrangements such as moving the mortgage? One could offer to give the party one-half interest in the property if he would release his mortgage so that a refinance could take place. Out of the refinance would come the funds to buy the property from its owner.

Short of an equity position, one might offer the holder of an underlying mortgage a higher interest rate in exchange for certain concessions that would facilitate the purchase. In Case No. 41, printed in this section, one buyer came up against a non-assumable private mortgage on the property he wanted to buy. By giving the holder a three point interest increase, he eliminated the hurdle and bought the property. In effect, the holder became an investment partner who said, "Help me make more money and I will see to it that you get the property." The variations are endless.

American Real Estate Through The Eyes Of An Immigrant: "Pure Gold"!

Featuring Technique No. 35
"Use Discounts From Holders of
Underlying Mortgages"

In A Nutshell. . .

Type: SFH
Price: $110,000
Source: Realtor
Means: New first, carry back
Techniques: No. 4 — Contract/Wrap
No. 6 — Balloon
No. 19 — Borrowing Realtor's Commission
No. 35 — Holders' Discounts
No. 42 — Partners' Money for Down
Features: From $620 negative to $200 positive in 11 months

Enos Karov is a mechanical engineer who came to the United States recently as an immigrant. His work took him to Los Angeles where he had the opportunity to attend the Nothing Down Seminar and learn the techniques of creative finance. He became fascinated with the idea of attaining financial independence through real estate investments. His perspective as an immigrant gave him insights into the value of American real estate that few Americans enjoy. "Why do you suppose people from foreign countries are buying so much property here? Because they know that American real estate is pure gold! Why are Americans so slow to realize this?"

LOCATING

With the help of a real estate agent, Enos began looking for single family homes in the range of $100,000 to $150,000. His target was the don't wanter seller who would be flexible with terms. Before long, the agent had located a home in the Los Angeles suburbs that seemed to fill the bill.

SITUATION

The fairly spacious home was listed at $129,000, free and clear. The owner was desperate to sell the property and seemed willing to entertain all offers.

NEGOTIATION

Enos' initial offer was for $100,000, with $5,000 down and the balance of the equity carried back for five years at 10%. However, the owner insisted on a price of at least $110,000, with $11,000 cash down and no more than $11,000 carried back, a new first to be obtained. The terms on the second were to be 12% for three years (payments of $115/month, balloon in three years). Enos agreed; his challenge now was to come up with the $11,000 cash down payment.

CLOSING

With $2,500 of his own money to put down, Enos first turned to the Realtor and asked him to take $3,500 of the commission in the form of paper at 10% for one year. The Realtor agreed. That left $5,000 yet to be raised. Enos then did a very interesting thing. He began asking his friends and associates at every opportunity how much money they were earning on their savings. Many reported that they had money lying around in passbook accounts at around 5½%. He then asked them, "If I can show you how you can earn 10% to 12% on that same money and have instant access to it anytime in the future, would you be interested?" Many said that they would. So he arranged to borrow small sums of money from them for six to twelve months at interest rates in the range quoted. Before long, he had put together a little kitty that he was able to apply to this real estate deal. Initially, $5,000 of this kitty went toward the down payment. He had thus put together the $11,000 needed. As we shall see, this same kitty was to come in handy once more after the closing.

As the title company pulled together the documents needed for closing, two interesting facts came to light. First, the seller was two months behind in his mortgage payments; as a result, the foreclosure process was about to begin. Second, at $110,000, the property was undervalued by $15,000. The first fact explained the seller's desperation to get rid of his property; the second fact confirmed the smile on Enos' face. He was going to get a rather good deal for $2,500 of his own money down.

Despite the buyer's anxieties over a first-time transaction using terminology he was still getting used to, the closing went without a hitch. He was the proud owner of an excellent piece of American real estate. The sketch summarizes the terms:

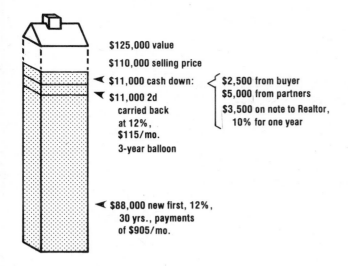

$125,000 value

$110,000 selling price

◀ $11,000 cash down: ⎧ $2,500 from buyer
⎨ $5,000 from partners
⎩ $3,500 on note to Realtor, 10% for one year

◀ $11,000 2d carried back at 12%, $115/mo. 3-year balloon

◀ $88,000 new first, 12%, 30 yrs., payments of $905/mo.

OUTCOMES AND FUTURE PLANS

Immediately after the closing, Enos went to the seller and offered to buy back the second for $7,000 cash. Because of the seller's financial difficulties, this sounded like music from heaven. He concurred on the spot.

Enos then turned to his kitty of "partnership funds" and made sure that he had $10,000 set aside to carry out the transaction. Why $10,000 for a $7,000 purchase? Because he had borrowed from his friends with the promise that they could have access to their "investment" funds anytime they wanted. Sure enough, soon after he had bought back his $11,000 note for $7,000, one of the friends came to Enos and said, "I have to have my $2,000 back tomorrow. A problem has come up, and I need the money."

With a twinkle in his eye that the friend evidently missed, Enos replied, "I am very sorry. You cannot have your money back tomorrow." At this, the friend flew into a rage and reminded Enos of the agreement. He was adamant that his $2,000 had to be returned to him without delay, in fact the very next day. "You cannot have your money tomorrow," Enos replied with a smile. "You shall have it within 45 minutes!" Whereupon he went to the bank and returned shortly with the funds. The friend had learned two things about his private "investment banker": Enos was scrupulously honest and had a good sense of humor.

As a matter of fact, Enos needed that sense of humor from the very beginning of his property management career. With payments of nearly $1,020/mo. and rents of only $400/mo., there was a painful $620 negative cash flow to be reckoned with. Enos improved the house by painting it and installing new appliances and furnishings. He then systematically raised the rents and upgraded the tenants so that within five months the cash flow was even, and six months after that he had the place rented for $1,200/mo. (nearly $200 per month positive)! He plans eventually to trade into a 4-plex or 6-plex after

his first SFH has had a chance to appreciate for a while.

In his own words, the best strategy for real estate investments is as follows: "Be friendly and cooperative with the seller. Use nothing down concepts to buy. Be very precise. Provide reserve money to offset the unpredictable. To be active in investments, apply: 1. knowledge, 2. experience, 3. ability to manage, 4. money, and 5. time is essential." According to Enos, there are "no limitations." Anything can be accomplished using this system. It is a matter of what he calls "the metaphysics of the subconscious mind" — the ability to release the mental blocks and tell yourself you are going to succeed.

COMMENTARY

1. Enos' point about the attraction of American real estate for foreign capital is a good one. The Germans, the Canadians, the Japanese, the Saudis, and many other foreign nationals are investing billions in land and income property in the United States. By and large, the average American is either oblivious to the value of such investments or ignorant of the techniques needed to get started. The mission of the Robert Allen Nothing Down System is to acquaint Americans of all types and in all socio-economic brackets with the methodology of creative real estate investments. The purpose of this present book is to demonstrate the effectiveness of the system in the lives of many of its practitioners with the hope that others will have the sense and the courage to take some positive steps in their own best interest. Sometimes it takes the example of an immigrant who has now become a part of the American "melting pot" to show the way to others whose lineage in this country may go back a little longer.

2. The system Enos developed for raising down payment funds is an interesting variation on the partnership techniques. His friends are pleased to have doubled their yield, and Enos is happy to give them their higher interest rates because he knows the yields in real estate will be much higher for him. Clearly he will have no difficulty when it comes to raising more substantial amounts from partners who may in the future insist on having a share in the equity as well.

3. Balloons with fuses shorter than 5 years are not recommended in this period of tight money and uncertainty. The three-year balloon discussed in this case study was for a relatively small sum, hence less problematic. However, the solution that Enos came up with to buy it back himself at a discount is a technique that has merit and should not be neglected even in the case of larger balloons. The secret is to have alternative solutions ready in the sidelines.

DOCUMENTATION (INITIAL OFFER)

UNIVERSAL EARNEST MONEY RECEIPT
AND OFFER TO PURCHASE

"This is a legally binding contract: if not understood, seek competent advice."

1. Date and Place of Offer: __June 18,__ 19 __81__ ; __Los Angeles__ __California__

(city)   (state)

2. Principals: The undersigned Buyer __Enos Karov and Anna Karov, husband and wife__

agrees to buy and Seller agrees to sell, according to the indicated terms and conditions, the property described as follows:

3. Property: located at __61 Crystal Avenue__ __Culver City__ __California__

(street address)   (city)   (state)

with the following legal description: __to be supplied__

including any of the following items if at present attached to the premises: plumbing, heating, and cooling equipment, including stoker and oil tanks, burners, water heaters, electric light fixtures, bathroom fixtures, roller shades, curtain rods and fixtures, draperies, venetian blinds, window and door screens, towel racks, linoleum and other attached floor coverings,

including carpeting, attached television antennas, mailboxes, all trees and shrubs, and any other fixtures EXCEPT __None__

The following personal property shall also be included as part of the purchase: _____

At the closing of the transaction, the Seller, at his expense, shall provide the Buyer with a Bill Of Sale containing a detailed inventory of the personal property included.

4. Earnest Money Deposit: Agent (or Seller) acknowledges receipt from Buyer of __Three Thousand and 00/100__ dollars $ __3,000.00__

in the form of ( ) cash; (X) personal check; ( ) cashier's check; ( ) promissory note at _____% interest per annum due _____ 19 _____ ; or

other _____

as earnest money deposit to secure and apply on this purchase. Upon acceptance of this agreement in writing and delivery of same to Buyer, the earnest money deposit shall be assigned

to and deposited in the listing Realtor's trust account or _____, to apply on the

purchase price at the time of closing.

5. Purchase Price: The total purchase price of the property shall be __One Hundred-Five Thousand and 00/100__

dollars $ __105,000.00__

6. Payment: Purchase price is to be paid by Buyer as follows:

Aforedescribed earnest money deposit .... $ __3,000.00__

Additional payment due upon acceptance of this offer .... $ __--__

Additional payment due at closing .... $ __7,500.00__

Balance to be paid as follows:

> $84,000.00 Note secured by First Trust Deed at an annual interest rate, fixed, not to exceed 12.50% per annum for a period of 30 years, payable in substantially equal monthly installments of not more than $877.00 principal and interest, with the payment by the Buyer of not more than 1.5% of the loan as a loan fee plus other normal lender's charges to obtain said loan. This offer contingent upon Buyer being able to obtain said loan within 30 business days of date of escrow instructions. Prepayment penalty on existing financing, if any, shall be paid by Seller. Loan shall be obtained from Mutual Mortgage Company and applied for within 5 days of acceptance.

> $10,500.00 Note secured by Second Trust Deed in favor of Seller payable $105.00, or more, per month including interest at the annual rate of 10% per annum all due and payable five years from the close of escrow.

7. Title: Seller agrees to furnish good and marketable title free of all encumbrances and defects, except mortgage liens and encumbrances as set forth in this agreement, and to make

conveyance by Warranty Deed or _____. Seller shall furnish in due course to the Buyer a title insurance policy insuring the Buyer of a good and marketable title in keeping with the terms and conditions of this agreement. Prior to the closing of this transaction, the Seller, upon request, will furnish to the Buyer a preliminary title report made by a title insurance company showing the condition of the title to said property. If the Seller cannot furnish marketable title within thirty days after receipt of the notice to the Buyer containing a written statement of the defects, the earnest money deposit herein receipted shall be refunded to the Buyer and this agreement shall be null and void. The following shall not be deemed encumbrances or defects; building and use restrictions general to the area; utility easements; other easements not inconsistent with Buyer's intended use; zoning or subdivision laws, covenants, conditions, restrictions, or reservations of record; tenancies of record. In the event of sale of other than real property relating to this transaction, Seller will provide evidence of title or right to sell or lease such personal property.

8. Special Representations: Seller warrants and represents to Buyer (1) that the subject property is connected to ( ) public sewer system, ( ) cesspool or septic tank, ( ) sewer system available but not connected, ( ) city water system, ( ) private water system, and that the following special improvements are included in the sale: ( ) sidewalk, ( ) curb and gutter, ( ) special street paving, ( ) special street lighting; (2) that the Seller knows of no material structural defects; (3) that all electrical wiring, heating, cooling, and plumbing systems are free of material defects and will be in good working order at the time the Buyer is entitled to possession; (4) that the Seller has no notice from any government agency of any violation or knowledge of probable violations of the law relating to the subject property; (5) that the Seller has no notice or knowledge of planned or commenced public improvements which may result in special assessments or otherwise directly and materially affect the property; and (6) that the Seller has no notice or knowledge of any liens to be assessed against the property,

EXCEPT _____ None _____

9. Escrow Instructions: This sale shall be closed on or before __August 1,__ 19 __81__ by __Thompson Escrow, Co.__ or such other closing agent as mutually agreed upon by Buyer and Seller. Buyer and Seller will, immediately on demand, deposit with closing agent all instruments and monies required

to complete the purchase in accordance with the provisions of this agreement. Contract of Sale or Instrument of Conveyance to be made in the name of _____

__to be supplied__

10. Closing Costs and Pro-Ration: Seller agrees to pay for title insurance policy, preliminary title report (if requested), termite inspection as set forth below, real estate commission, cost of preparing and recording any corrective instruments, and one-half of the escrow fees. Buyer agrees to pay for recording fees for mortgages and deeds of conveyance, all costs or expenses in securing new financing or assuming existing financing, and one-half of the escrow fees. Buyer agrees to pay for recording fees for mortgages and deeds of conveyance, all costs or expenses in securing new financing or assuming existing financing, and one-half of the escrow fees. Taxes for the current year, insurance acceptable to the Buyer, rents, interest, mortgage reserves, maintenance fees, and water and other utilities constituting liens, shall be pro-rated as of closing. Renters' security deposits shall accrue to Buyer at closing. Seller to provide Buyer with all current rental or lease agreements prior to closing.

11. Termite Inspection: Seller agrees, at his expense, to provide written certification by a reputable licensed pest control firm that the property is free of termite infestation. In the event termites are found, the Seller shall have the property treated at his expense and provide acceptable certification that treatment has been rendered. If any structural repairs are required by reason of termite damage as established by acceptable certification, Seller agrees to make necessary repairs not to exceed $500. If repairs exceed $500, Buyer shall first have the right to accept the property "as is" with a credit to the Buyer at closing of $500, or the Buyer may terminate this agreement with the earnest money deposit being promptly returned to the Buyer if the Seller does not agree to pay all costs of treatment and repair.

12. Conditions of Sale: The following conditions shall also apply, and shall, if conflicting with the printed portions of this agreement, prevail and control:

1. Seller to notify tenant to vacate 30 days prior to close of escrow. Possession to be one day after close of escrow or Seller to pay Buyer $30.00 per day until possession is possible.

2. Buyer is aware roof may need repair.

3. This offer contingent upon Buyer's inspection and approval after offer is accepted.

13. Liability and Maintenance: Seller shall maintain subject property, including landscaping, in good condition until the date of transfer of title or possession by Buyer, whichever occurs first. All risk of loss and destruction of property, and all expenses of insurance, shall be borne by the seller until the date of possession. If the improvements on the property are destroyed or materially damaged prior to closing, then the Buyer shall have the right to declare this agreement null and void, and the earnest money deposit and all other sums paid by Buyer toward the purchase price shall be returned to the Buyer forthwith.

14. Possession: The Buyer shall be entitled to possession of property upon closing or __One day thereafter__ , 19 ____

15. Default: In the event the Buyer fails to complete the purchase as herein provided, the earnest money deposit shall be retained by the Seller as the total and entire liquidated damages. In the event the Seller fails to perform any condition of the sale as herein provided, then the Buyer may, at his option, treat the contract as terminated, and all payments made by the Buyer hereunder shall be returned to the Buyer forthwith, provided the Buyer may, at his option, treat this agreement as being in full force and effect with the right to action for specific performance and damages. In the event that either Buyer, Seller, or Agent shall institute suit to enforce any rights hereunder, the prevailing party shall be entitled to court costs and a reasonable attorney's fee.

16. Time Limit of Offer: The Seller shall have until

____6:00 p.m.____ ____June 20,____ , 19 __81__ to accept this
(hour)   (date)

offer by delivering a signed copy hereof to the Buyer. If this offer is not so accepted, it shall lapse and the agent (or Seller) shall refund the earnest money deposit to the Buyer forthwith.

17. General Agreements: (1) Both parties to this purchase reserve their rights to assign and hereby otherwise agree to cooperate in effecting an Internal Revenue Code 1031 exchange or similar tax-related arrangement prior to close of escrow, upon either party's written notice of intention to do so. (2) Upon approval of this offer by the Seller, this agreement shall become a contract between Buyer and Seller and shall inure to the benefit of the heirs, administrators, executors, successors, personal representatives, and assigns of said parties. (3) Time is of the essence and an essential part of this agreement. (4) This contract constitutes the sole and entire agreement between the parties hereto and no modification of this contract shall be binding unless attached hereto and signed by all parties to the contract. No representations, promises, or inducements not included in this contract shall be binding upon any party hereto.

18. Buyer's Statement and Receipt: "I/we hereby agree to purchase the above property in accordance with the terms and conditions above stated and acknowledge receipt of a

completed copy of this agreement, which I/we have fully read and understand." Dated __June 18,__ 19 __81__ , _____
(hour)

Address ___1498 Lotus Street___   [signature] _____ Buyer

___Culver City, California___   [signature] _____ Buyer

Phone No: Home __617-3398__   Business __456-6894__

19. Seller's Statement and Response: "I/we approve and accept the above offer, which I/we have fully read and understand, and agree to the above terms and conditions this day

of _____ , 19 _____ , _____ .

                                                     (hour)

Address _____   _____ Seller

Phone No: Home _____ Business _____   _____ Seller

20. Commission Agreement: Seller agrees to pay a commission of _____% of the gross sales price to _____

for services in this transaction, and agrees that, in the event of forfeiture of the earnest money deposit by the Buyer, said deposit shall be divided between the Seller's broker and the Seller (one half to each party), the Broker's part not to exceed the amount of the commission.

21. Buyer's Receipt for Signed Offer: The Buyer hereby acknowledges receipt of a copy of the above agreement bearing the Seller's signature in acceptance of this offer.

Dated _____ , 19 _____   _____ Buyer

     _____ Buyer

COMMENTARY TO DOCUMENTATION

In a counter offer of June 18, 1980, the seller made the following amendments: Price to be $110,000.00; $10,500 note to be secured by second trust deed in favor of seller, payable $105.00 or more per month including interest at the annual rate of 12%, all due and payable three years from the close of escrow.

The counter to the counter provided the following: the carry-back note to be $11,000, with monthly payments of $115.00; cash down payment, including deposit of $3,000 to be $11,000; 1st trust deed balance to be $88,000.00; buyer has inspected and approved property.

Item 2. "Or Assigns" belongs after the names of the buyers.

Item 4. $3,000 is a rather hefty deposit — the seller and agent were probably very impressed. The buyer might have achieved the same impact with a promissory note for that amount — and spared himself the pain of losing the use of that money in the meantime.

Item 6. The carry-back note should have contained a provision for prepayment without penalty, also rollover on the balloon, assumption privileges, first right of refusal, and substitution of collateral. As it turned out, the issues were for the most part moot, as the note was bought back for $7,000 soon after close of escrow.

Here is a situation where the leverage was fairly high, but the cash flow, with considerable massaging, still turned out to be positive.

Reprinted by permission from the *Nothing Down Advisor.*

"We can't get Gort to come back with us . . . Something
about a 'far out' earthling investment system
he has stumbled onto . . ."

Creative Exchange Puts Couple Into 10-Plex

Featuring Technique No. 36
"Moving The Mortgage"

In A Nutshell . . .

Type: 10-Plex, SFH
Price: $141,500, $57,500
Source: Agent, MLS Book
Means: Equity Exchange, Assumption
Techniques: No. 4 — Contract/Wrap
No. 16 — 2-Way Exchange
No. 32 — Second Mortgage Crank
No. 36 — Moving the Mortgage
Strategies: Defer payments 90 days
Features: No balloons, positive cash flow

We have already seen how Jill and Jerry McKendrick of Aloha, Oregon, used the second mortgage crank technique to acquire a three-bedroom rental house with an even cash flow ("Creative Buyers Crank Their Way into Small Rancher"). That transaction became the springboard to the following remarkable exchange.

LOCATING

The McKendricks were looking for a multi-unit in the $100,000 to $400,000 range. Their real estate agent helped them located a 10-plex that happened to be very near the place where Jerry had grown up. He knew the building well.

SITUATION

It was a two-story solid concrete building — 53 years old — with seven studio apartments and three one-bedroom apartments. The structure had not been painted in nearly thirty years. The interiors likewise showed much evidence of deferred maintenance.

The owners were five members of the same family who had made the purchase less than one year earlier from an estate sale. They had bought the free-and-clear building with the intention of rehabilitating it and selling it for a large profit. Things did not go as planned.

The partners consisted of a set of parents, two sons, and a daughter-in-law. The sons were doing all of the renovation work on a part-time basis in addition to their regular jobs. Because of the noise and confusion of the work — or perhaps in anticipation of higher rents — all the tenants left. Not several — all! The owners were left with no income for the building. They had ten alligators and no alligator food.

Overworked and financially strapped, they did what any desperate landlord would be tempted to do but shouldn't do. They lowered their standards and started to rent to anyone who showed up. This resulted in a house full of undesirable tenants who began to destroy the units as quickly as the owners could renovate

them. It all added up to a severe case of don't wanteritis. The McKendricks had come on the scene at a propitious moment.

NEGOTIATION

The sellers were asking $155,000, with $55,000 cash or trade. They were excluding an adjacent commercially-zoned lot they had acquired from the estate at the same time. Jill and Jerry were not intimidated by the high down. Armed with some knowledge of creative finance and a little cash from an earlier 3-bedroom "cranker," they began the negotiating process.

Their first offer (let's call it O-1) was for $120,000, including the extra lot, with $15,000 down (suspiciously like the amount of their previous crank). They had already investigated the possibility of splitting off the lot to help with the down payment and found that it would not be feasible; the lot, however, would be a nice addition to their portfolio anyway. As part of their offer, they were to assume the first mortgage of $100,000 at 9% interest, payments of $750/mo., balance to be worked out.

The owners came back with their first counter-offer (CO-1): price of $142,500 for the 10-plex and extra lot, with $52,500 down. At this stage of the negotiation, the McKendricks learned that the owners were facing a balloon of $10,000 in about three months, with a second balloon — also for $10,000 — one year after the first came due. The owners were willing to pay the first balloon — leaving a loan balance of $90,000 to be assumed — but expected the buyers to pick up the second balloon.

Now here came O-2. Jill and Jerry offered $141,500, with $15,000 down (there is that figure again), provided the holder of the underlying first mortgage would not require either of the balloons. The balance of $26,500 would be amortized over twenty years at 10% to keep the payments in line with projected cash flows.

The owners came back with CO-2 (which sounds like a lot of gas): $141,500, with $30,000 down and the balance of $11,500 to be paid off in three years. They were certain the underlying mortgagee would adjust the loan to eliminate the balloons.

At this point it was clear to Jill and Jerry that two recurring problems had to be solved. The sellers wanted too much down in cash. They also wanted their balance too quickly, conjuring up the spectre of negative cash flow. Moreover, even though the holder of the underlying mortgage was willing to forego the second balloon, he absolutely needed the first to satisfy a note coming due at the same time.

What could be done? The McKendricks started their creative juices flowing. They recalled that the owners had asked for their equity in cash OR trade. Jill and Jerry certainly did not have that much cash. Still, the deal might go through just as well if they could come up with an equivalent amount of equity. Problem: they didn't have that much equity. Solution: get it!

Jerry went straight to the MLS book in search of a piece of free-and-clear property valued at around $51,500. He soon located one listed at $62,500 for which the owners would accept a long-term contract. Since the property was overpriced, Jerry offered $51,500. They wanted $15,000 down at that price, but Jerry offered $10,000. They wanted payments structured over 20 years with a balloon in 10 years; Jerry offered them a straight 15-year amortization with no balloon, interest at 10%.

Now comes the creative twist. Since Jerry needed a free-and-clear property to offer to his 10-plex sellers, he had to figure out a way to satisfy the owners of the MLS rental home without encumbering it at all. Therefore, he stipulated that his contract with them be secured by another property. You can almost hear him saying it: "Mr. Sellers, how would you like this note to be secured by a valuable 10-plex with a positive cash flow?"

In other words, Jerry wanted to move the mortgage he was creating on the MLS rental home to the 10-plex he was about to buy. And his ability to buy the 10-plex in the first place was predicated on his getting permission to move that mortgage. Nice bit of circular reasoning that happens to take him straight to his goal. Moreover, he asked the owners of the MLS rental home to subordinate their mortgage at his option. What would go on the 10-plex as a second mortgage would then become a third behind a future second that Jerry might want to put on. Why was he thinking of putting on another second? So that he could raise money to complete the rehabilitation of the building. He also made both offers contingent upon all parties agreeing to all the terms of the exchange.

Meanwhile, the owners of the MLS rental home countered back with another price, $57,500, and a down payment of $15,000 (there is that number again), all else remaining as before. The McKendricks promptly accepted. The stage was set for success.

Now Jill and Jerry presented their final offer to the 10-plex owners (O-3 if you are keeping score): price of $141,500, with the free-and-clear MLS rental home given in exchange. The sellers were to pay the first balloon, leaving a balance of $90,000 to be assumed by the buyers. In response, the owners inspected the home and fell in love with it. It was a desirable piece of property in a desirable area of town. No fix-up. No management hassles. No destructive tenants. And its value ($57,500) even exceeded their equity after the first balloon ($51,500) by $6,000. There was only one problem — they needed cash to pay that $10,000 balloon and the closing costs and commissions.

Solution: They got a loan commitment from their banker and pulled enough cash out of the property to cover their expenses. Since Jerry had moved the mortgage from the home to the 10-plex, it was totally unencumbered; the new owners could crank out of it what they needed.

There was one last dimension of the deal that needed to be finalized. The McKendricks had bought themselves a solid building, but they needed a little breathing room to get it ready for the new tenants. They asked the holders of the first and second mortgages to defer any payments for 90 days. Their request was granted. ("You never know until you ask.")

CLOSING

The ultimate financing is summarized in the sketch:

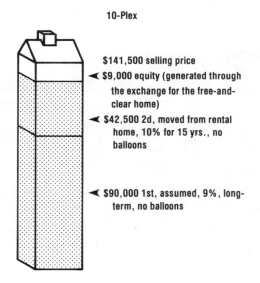

10-Plex

$141,500 selling price

◄ $9,000 equity (generated through the exchange for the free-and-clear home)

◄ $42,500 2d, moved from rental home, 10% for 15 yrs., no balloons

◄ $90,000 1st, assumed, 9%, long-term, no balloons

In case you have lost track, here are the initial two steps once more:

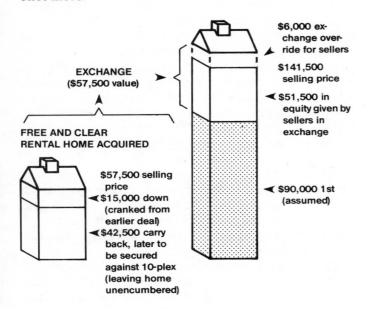

EXCHANGE ($57,500 value)

FREE AND CLEAR RENTAL HOME ACQUIRED

$57,500 selling price
$15,000 down (cranked from earlier deal)
$42,500 carry back, later to be secured against 10-plex (leaving home unencumbered)

$6,000 exchange override for sellers
$141,500 selling price
$51,500 in equity given by sellers in exchange
$90,000 1st (assumed)

OUTCOMES AND FUTURE PLANS

The cash flow situation looks like this: payments on the first and second are $885 and $457, respectively, for a total of $1,342. Projected rental income is $1,900, leaving enough rough for a modest positive flow after expenses.

Jim characterizes the transaction in these words: "This was not a win/win situation; it was a win/win/win situation where everyone was happy with the end solution. The Nothing Down win/win approach definitely works for us."

Since this creative exchange purchase, Jill and Jerry have added another rental home to their portfolio — a "cranker" out of which they were able to pull $12,500 with no negative cash flow. As this book is being written, they are actively working on another 10-plex. Are they crusty investors in their senior years? Hardly. Jill is 28, Jerry 29. Old age has no monopoly on creativity.

COMMENTARY

1. The McKendricks have the ability to think ahead—so rare in the ordinary investor. They are careful about their analysis, e.g., determining ahead of time whether the extra lot could be split off, conferring with the holder of the underlying mortgage (actually trust deed) concerning the balloons, etc.

2. They also have courage — courage to stick out the negotiation, courage to ask for a deferral of their initial payments, courage to ask the sellers of the MLS rental home to subordinate.

3. Above all, they have the ability to look for alternative solutions when it seems that they have come to a dead end. That's the essence of creativity, and it is an admirable trait.

4. It is remarkable that they were able to structure their financing without balloon payments and still come out with a positive cash flow. They will be able to sleep well at night — deservedly so.

DOCUMENTATION (INITIAL OFFER)

UNIVERSAL EARNEST MONEY RECEIPT AND OFFER TO PURCHASE

"This is a legally binding contract: if not understood, seek competent advice."

1. Date and Place of Offer: December 29, 19 80 ; Portland (city) Oregon (state)

2. Principals: The undersigned Buyer Jerry McKendrick and Jill McKendrick
agrees to buy and Seller agrees to sell, according to the indicated terms and conditions, the property described as follows:

3. Property: located at 719 Harward Circle (street address) Portland (city) Oregon (state)
with the following legal description: Lot 15 and 16, Block 47, Roberts Addition to St. Johns

including any of the following items if at present attached to the premises: plumbing, heating, and cooling equipment, including stoker and oil tanks, burners, water heaters, electric light fixtures, bathroom fixtures, roller shades, curtain rods and fixtures, draperies, venetian blinds, window and door screens, towel racks, linoleum and other attached floor coverings,

including carpeting, attached television antennas, mailboxes, all trees and shrubs, and any other fixtures EXCEPT None

The following personal property shall also be included as part of the purchase: 10 ranges, 10 refrigerators, window coverings
At the closing of the transaction, the Seller, at his expense, shall provide the Buyer with a Bill Of Sale containing a detailed inventory of the personal property included.

4. Earnest Money Deposit: Agent (or Seller) acknowledges receipt from Buyer of Five Thousand and 00/100 dollars $ 5,000.00

in the form of ( ) cash; ( ) personal check; ( ) cashier's check; (X) promissory note at 0 % interest per annum due * 19 ; or

other * after meeting special conditions
as earnest money deposit to secure and apply on this purchase. Upon acceptance of this agreement in writing and delivery of same to Buyer, the earnest money deposit shall be assigned

to and deposited in the listing Realtor's trust account or _____, to apply on the purchase price at the time of closing.

5. Purchase Price: The total purchase price of the property shall be _____ One Hundred-Twenty Thousand and 00/100 _____

dollars $ __120,000 .00__

6. Payment: Purchase price is to be paid by Buyer as follows:

Aforedescribed earnest money deposit .... $ __5,000 .00__

Additional payment due upon acceptance of this offer .... $ __--__

Additional payment due at closing .... $ __15,000 .00__

Balance to be paid as follows:

> Purchaser to assume and agree to pay existing note secured by Deed of record. Approximate balance $100,000.00 payable at not less than $750.00 per month including principal and interest at 9% per annum. Balance of sales price to be paid in cash upon delivery of deed.

7. Title: Seller agrees to furnish good and marketable title free of all encumbrances and defects, except mortgage liens and encumbrances as set forth in this agreement, and to make

conveyance by Warranty Deed or _____. Seller shall furnish in due course to the Buyer a title insurance policy insuring the Buyer of a good and marketable title in keeping with the terms and conditions of this agreement. Prior to the closing of this transaction, the Seller, upon request, will furnish to the Buyer a preliminary title report made by a title insurance company showing the condition of the title to said property. If the Seller cannot furnish marketable title within thirty days after receipt of the notice to the Buyer containing a written statement of the defects, the earnest money deposit herein receipted shall be refunded to the Buyer and this agreement shall be null and void. The following shall not be deemed encumbrances or defects; building and use restrictions general to the area; utility easements; other easements not inconsistent with Buyer's intended use; zoning or subdivision laws, covenants, conditions, restrictions, or reservations of record; tenancies of record. In the event of sale of other than real property relating to this transaction, Seller will provide evidence of title or right to sell or lease such personal property.

8. Special Representations: Seller warrants and represents to Buyer (1) that the subject property is connected to ( ) public sewer system, ( ) cesspool or septic tank, ( ) sewer system available but not connected, ( ) city water system, ( ) private water system, and that the following special improvements are included in the sale: ( ) sidewalk, ( ) curb and gutter, ( ) special street paving, ( ) special street lighting; (2) that the Seller knows of no material structural defects; (3) that all electrical wiring, heating, cooling, and plumbing systems are free of material defects and will be in good working order at the time the Buyer is entitled to possession; (4) that the Seller has no notice from any government agency of any violation or knowledge of probable violations of the law relating to the subject property; (5) that the Seller has no notice or knowledge of planned or commenced public improvements which may result in special assessments or otherwise directly and materially affect the property; and (6) that the Seller has no notice or knowledge of any liens to be assessed against the property,

EXCEPT _____ None _____

9. Escrow Instructions: This sale shall be closed on or before ___ February 15, 19 81 ___ by _____ or such other closing agent as mutually agreed upon by Buyer and Seller. Buyer and Seller will, immediately on demand, deposit with closing agent all instruments and monies required

to complete the purchase in accordance with the provisions of this agreement. Contract of Sale or Instrument of Conveyance to be made in the name of _____

10. Closing Costs and Pro-Ration: Seller agrees to pay for title insurance policy, preliminary title report (if requested), termite inspection as set forth below, real estate commission, cost of preparing and recording any corrective instruments, and one-half of the escrow fees. Buyer agrees to pay for recording fees for mortgages and deeds of conveyance, all costs or expenses in securing new financing or assuming existing financing, and one-half of the escrow fees. Buyer agrees to pay for recording fees for mortgages and deeds of conveyance, all costs or expenses in securing new financing or assuming existing financing, and one-half of the escrow fees. Taxes for the current year, insurance acceptable to the Buyer, rents, interest, mortgage reserves, maintenance fees, and water and other utilities constituting liens, shall be pro-rated as of closing. Renters' security deposits shall accrue to Buyer at closing. Seller to provide Buyer with all current rental or lease agreements prior to closing.

11. Termite Inspection: Seller agrees, at his expense, to provide written certification by a reputable licensed pest control firm that the property is free of termite infestation. In the event termites are found, the Seller shall have the property treated at his expense and provide acceptable certification that treatment has been rendered. If any structural repairs are required by reason of termite damage as established by acceptable certification, Seller agrees to make necessary repairs not to exceed $500. If repairs exceed $500, Buyer shall first have the right to accept the property "as is" with a credit to the Buyer at closing of $500, or the Buyer may terminate this agreement with the earnest money deposit being promptly returned to the Buyer if the Seller does not agree to pay all costs of treatment and repair.

12. Conditions of Sale: The following conditions shall also apply, and shall, if conflicting with the printed portions of this agreement, prevail and control:

> Sale subject to the following conditions: Interior inspection, proof of certification of Boiler, electrical and heating inspection, pest and dry rot inspection.

13. Liability and Maintenance: Seller shall maintain subject property, including landscaping, in good condition until the date of transfer of title or possession by Buyer, whichever occurs first. All risk of loss and destruction of property, and all expenses of insurance, shall be borne by the seller until the date of possession. If the improvements on the property are destroyed or materially damaged prior to closing, then the Buyer shall have the right to declare this agreement null and void, and the earnest money deposit and all other sums paid by Buyer toward the purchase price shall be returned to the Buyer forthwith.

14. Possession: The Buyer shall be entitled to possession of property upon closing or ___ one day later ___, 19 ___.

15. Default: In the event the Buyer fails to complete the purchase as herein provided, the earnest money deposit shall be retained by the Seller as the total and entire liquidated damages. In the event the Seller fails to perform any condition of the sale as herein provided, then the Buyer may, at his option, treat the contract as terminated, and all payments made by the Buyer hereunder shall be returned to the Buyer forthwith, provided the Buyer may, at his option, treat this agreement as being in full force and effect with the right to action for specific performance and damages. In the event that either Buyer, Seller, or Agent shall institute suit to enforce any rights hereunder, the prevailing party shall be entitled to court costs and a reasonable attorney's fee.

16. Time Limit of Offer: The Seller shall have until

Three days after time of Purchaser's signature. ____, 19 _____ to accept this
<u>(hour)</u>   <u>(date)</u>

offer by delivering a signed copy hereof to the Buyer. If this offer is not so accepted, it shall lapse and the agent (or Seller) shall refund the earnest money deposit to the Buyer forthwith.

17. General Agreements: (1) Both parties to this purchase reserve their rights to assign and hereby otherwise agree to cooperate in effecting an Internal Revenue Code 1031 exchange or similar tax-related arrangement prior to close of escrow, upon either party's written notice of intention to do so. (2) Upon approval of this offer by the Seller, this agreement shall become a contract between Buyer and Seller and shall inure to the benefit of the heirs, administrators, executors, successors, personal representatives, and assigns of said parties. (3) Time is of the essence and an essential part of this agreement. (4) This contract constitutes the sole and entire agreement between the parties hereto and no modification of this contract shall be binding unless attached hereto and signed by all parties to the contract. No representations, promises, or inducements not included in this contract shall be binding upon any party hereto.

18. Buyer's Statement and Receipt: "I/we hereby agree to purchase the above property in accordance with the terms and conditions above stated and acknowledge receipt of a completed copy of this agreement, which I/we have fully read and understand." Dated ___**December 29,**___ 19 **80** , _____
                                                                         (hour)

Address ___**14 Crestview**___   [signature] _____ Buyer

___**Aloha, Oregon**___   [signature] _____ Buyer

Phone No: Home ___**271-1508**___ Business ___**432-1421**___

19. Seller's Statement and Response: "I/we approve and accept the above offer, which I/we have fully read and understand, and agree to the above terms and conditions this day

of _____, 19 _____, _____.
                                                 (hour)

Address _____ Seller

Phone No: Home _____ Business _____ Seller

20. Commission Agreement: Seller agrees to pay a commission of _____% of the gross sales price to _____
for services in this transaction, and agrees that, in the event of forfeiture of the earnest money deposit by the Buyer, said deposit shall be divided between the Seller's broker and the Seller (one half to each party), the Broker's part not to exceed the amount of the commission.

21. Buyer's Receipt for Signed Offer: The Buyer hereby acknowledges receipt of a copy of the above agreement bearing the Seller's signature in acceptance of this offer.

Dated _____, 19 _____ _____ Buyer

_____ Buyer

MEMORANDUM OF AGREEMENT PERTAINING TO SUBORDINATION

Heber Markham and Severna Markham and Jerry McKendrick and Jill McKendrick have executed an Agreement whereby Heber Markham and Severna Markham have agreed to subordinate their interest in the following described property for a loan not to exceed $20,000. This real property is situated in the City of Portland, County of Multnomah, State of Oregon, described as:

[Legal Description]

This Agreement is dated March 31, 1981, which terms are by reference, incorporated herein and made a part hereof. This Memorandum is executed and recorded pursuant to ORS 93,640(1).

The true consideration for this Agreement is $-0-; however, the actual consideration consists of other value given or promised which is the whole of the consideration.

DATED this 31st day of March, 1981.

[Notarized Signatures]

COMMENTARY TO DOCUMENTATION

After much negotiating back and forth, the following addendum to the above offer emerged, setting forth the terms under which the transaction closed:

(1) Sales price of $141,500.00.

(2) Earnest money of $5,000.00 to be transferred to the property located at 56 Gregory Street (i.e., the free and clear rental home) and applied to the down payment and purchase price.

(3) Sellers agree to accept 56 Gregory Street for their entire equity in 719 Harward Circle.

(4) Sellers agree to reduce the balance on 719 Harward Circle to $90,000.00.

(5) Purchaser to assume the existing Trust Deed in the amount of $90,000.00.

(6) Sale not to close before February 20, 1981.

(7) Buyers to deliver free and clear title to 56 Gregory Street.

(8) Sale contingent upon Sellers obtaining satisfactory terms for financing on 56 Gregory Street.

(9) All contingencies of original Earnest Money Agreement to be removed or renegotiated no later than February 14, 1981.

(10) All parties to agree to above conditions by February 14, 1981.

In retrospect, the following points seem pertinent:

Item 2 (Of the Earnest Money Receipt). The words "or Assigns" belong after the names of the buyers.

Item 4. Using a note as earnest money is an idea too seldom applied. In this case, the close of escrow did not take place until March 25, 1981, nearly three months after the date of the original offer. By using a note, the buyer has the luxury of making a large and impressive down payment without having to tie up these funds for long periods of time.

Item 12. The word "inspection" as the heart of a contingency is not sufficient. What is intended is "inspection and approval." That is what should be stated.

Finally, this case illustrates how far different from the original offer a final outcome can be. What happens in between is a lesson in skillful problem-solving and creative finance.

Trust-Building Is Key To Win/Win Deal On Duplex

**Featuring Technique No. 36
"Moving The Mortgage"**

In A Nutshell

Type: Duplex
Price: $110,000
Source: Classified Ad—FSBO
Means: Contract, assumption
Techniques: No. 4 — Contract/Wrap
No. 6 — Balloon
No. 15 — Creation of Paper
No. 36 — Moving the Mortgage
Strategies: Reverse paper, stepped payments

LOCATION

Investor Dale Porterhouse from Evergreen, Colorado, wanted to add a SFH or duplex to his growing real estate portfolio in the range of $70,000 to $100,000. He spotted a for-sale-by-owner ad in the classified section of the local newspaper and followed up.

SITUATION

The owner was asking $110,000 for his property, with terms to be established by the buyer — a flexible situation if there ever was one. Dale had checked into comparable sales on that particular street and knew the asking price was in line. The owner was anxious for relief from management headaches. In the past year he had gone through eight turnovers and could not understand why. But Dale knew why — poor management! Exactly the problem he was in a position to rectify.

NEGOTIATION

Prior to getting down to serious talk, Dale checked with the mortgage company on the status of the seller's first mortgage. The $82,000 12.9% loan was assumable without qualifying. However, the lender would not permit carry-back financing on the property. A wraparound contract was likewise proscribed. As it turned out, this situation played into Dale's hands because he was hoping to transact the duplex deal by leveraging other properties he already owned.

His basic questions to the seller were these: "Do you need cash going into the deal?" and "How can the monthly payments be kept in line?" The owner responded that he did not need much cash down and offered to carry back all but $1,000 of his equity himself.

That hurdle out of the way, Dale's next task was to find a way to provide the seller with security for the $27,000 carry-back amount. So he invited the seller to join him in a tour around town to visit and inspect the other properties in the Porterhouse portfolio. Two properties were selected as acceptable collateral for the carry-back.

Dale then offered the owner full price for his duplex with $1,000 down — just what the owner was asking for. As Dale put it, "He suggested an offer far better than I would have — the one who goes first loses!"

However, there was one problem that remained to be solved: the negative cash flow. Dale persuaded the seller to secure $17,000 of his carry back as a third against Property A, a SFH valued at $80,000 with an existing first mortgage of $45,000 and a second mortgage of $10,000. The third would yield 12% simple interest — no payments — all due and payable in 10 years! The rest of the carry-back amount, $10,000, would be secured as a second against Dale's Property B, a SFH valued at $70,000, with an existing first mortgage of $50,000. Monthly payments on this new second with interest at 12% for 10 years would have amounted to $143. However, Dale negotiated an interesting alternative schedule involving 10 separate notes of $1,000 each, bearing 12% interest as follows:

Note no.	Amount	APR	Interest to be added to prin. 1 month prior to first pmt. date	Monthly payment amount	Date mo. payment to commence	Maturity date
1	$ 1,000	12%	$ 0	$ 88.85	7/1/81	6/1/82
2	$ 1,000	12%	$ 120	$ 99.51	7/1/82	6/1/83
3	$ 1,000	12%	$ 240	$110.17	7/1/83	6/1/84
4	$ 1,000	12%	$ 360	$120.83	7/1/84	6/1/85
5	$ 1,000	12%	$ 480	$131.50	7/1/85	6/1/86
6	$ 1,000	12%	$ 600	$142.16	7/1/86	6/1/87
7	$ 1,000	12%	$ 720	$152.82	7/1/87	6/1/88
8	$ 1,000	12%	$ 840	$163.48	7/1/88	6/1/89
9	$ 1,000	12%	$ 960	$174.14	7/1/89	6/1/90
10	$ 1,000	12%	$1,080	$184.81	7/1/90	6/1/91
	$10,000 total					

By stepping the payments according to the above schedule, Dale was able to reduce the negative cash flow on the duplex during the early years of the note when the rents were relatively lower.

CLOSING

Prior to closing, Dale repainted one of the units and rented it out with the payment credited to the seller. This project was beneficial to both parties. The actual closing was delayed one week to permit the seller to clear up a collection problem with the tenant in the other unit. The financing is summarized in the following sketch:

The title company didn't want to have a thing to do with my problem. So I called the seller and explained how I had talked the title company into doing the closing wrong and lost $1,000. He studied the settlement sheet for a day and then agreed he owed me $1,000. Two days later I got a check! He, of course, had every legal right to tell me to eat it. I think this is the ultimate example of win/win!"

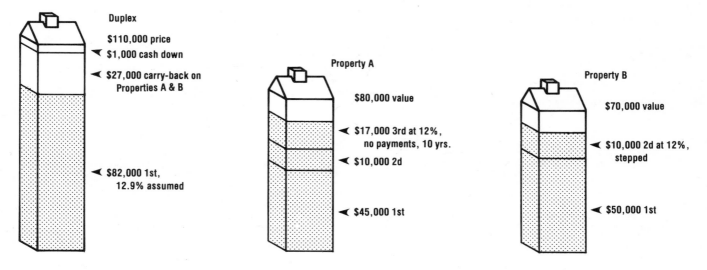

OUTCOMES AND FUTURE PLANS

In effect, Dale had moved the secondary financing from the duplex to two of his other properties, achieving a loan-to-value ratio of 90% on Property A and 86% on Property B. The mortgage company was pleased because there was no financing above their first mortgage on the duplex. The owner was happy because he was at last free of his management hassles and had his equity invested in a secure place.

With payments on the first mortgage at $1,012 PITI and rental income at $900, there is a negative cash flow of $112 on the duplex, not including the payment on the $10,000 second. Dale's plan is to increase the rents by $50 per unit within one year to offset the negative.

In an interesting sidelight to the closing, Dale mistakenly persuaded a clerk at the title company to enter the $1,000 down payment as a debit on the purchaser's settlement statement. It should have been entered as a credit to the purchaser. As Dale tells it: "Don't ask how I figured that one! How embarrassing. She didn't understand but assumed that a big time investor like me must know what I'm doing! Two weeks after the closing I realized how stupid I had been.

In retrospect, Dale puts his finger on the secret of his negotiation strategy: "I gained his trust, convinced him I was looking for a win/win solution."

COMMENTARY

1. What would Dale have done in the absence of other properties for use as collateral? The case would have been a classic partnership deal where the contribution would not have been cash down but rather "equity space" for moving the mortgage to.
2. What is particularly impressive about this case study is the success of the buyer in extending the repayment span of the major part of the secondary financing to ten years. In an era of the big short-term balloon, Dale will be able to sleep well at night.
3. The no-payment second and the "reverse paper" third with stepped payments protected Dale against oppressive negative cash flow. How would it have been to try to negotiate no payments or interest only payments on the $10,000 third as well? Perhaps he tried and could not make it work.

UNIVERSAL EARNEST MONEY RECEIPT
AND OFFER TO PURCHASE

"This is a legally binding contract: if not understood, seek competent advice."

1. Date and Place of Offer: _____ May 12, _____ 19 81 _____ ; _____ Evergreen _____ Colorado
   (city)   (state)

2. Principals: The undersigned Buyer _____ Dale Porterhouse   (a single man) _____
   agrees to buy and Seller agrees to sell, according to the indicated terms and conditions, the property described as follows:

3. Property: located at _____ 882-84 Park Avenue _____ Kittredge _____ Colorado
   (street address)   (city)   (state)

   with the following legal description: _____ Lots 51-52, City of Kittredge, Colorado _____

including any of the following items if at present attached to the premises: plumbing, heating, and cooling equipment, including stoker and oil tanks, burners, water heaters, electric light fixtures, bathroom fixtures, roller shades, curtain rods and fixtures, draperies, venetian blinds, window and door screens, towel racks, linoleum and other attached floor coverings,

including carpeting, attached television antennas, mailboxes, all trees and shrubs, and any other fixtures EXCEPT _____ None

The following personal property shall also be included as part of the purchase: _____
At the closing of the transaction, the Seller, at his expense, shall provide the Buyer with a Bill Of Sale containing a detailed inventory of the personal property included.

4. Earnest Money Deposit: Agent (or Seller) acknowledges receipt from Buyer of _____ Five Hundred and 00/100 _____ dollars $ _____ 500.00

in the form of ( ) cash; (X) personal check; ( ) cashier's check; ( ) promissory note at _____ % interest per annum due _____ 19 _____ ; or

other _____
as earnest money deposit to secure and apply on this purchase. Upon acceptance of this agreement in writing and delivery of same to Buyer, the earnest money deposit shall be assigned

to and deposited in the listing Realtor's trust account or _____ , to apply on the
purchase price at the time of closing.

5. Purchase Price: The total purchase price of the property shall be _____ One Hundred-Ten Thousand and 00/100 _____
   dollars $ _____ 110,000.00

6. Payment: Purchase price is to be paid by Buyer as follows:

   Aforedescribed earnest money deposit . . . . $ _____ 500.00

   Additional payment due upon acceptance of this offer . . . . $ _____ --

   Additional payment due at closing . . . . $ _____ 500.00

   Balance to be paid as follows:
   Purchaser shall assume the promissory note secured by trust deed in favor
   of Pacific Mortgage Company in the approximate amount of $81,715.00. The
   balance of approximately $27,285.00 shall be evidenced by promissory notes
   secured by trust deeds executed by Purchaser in favor of Sellers as
   scheduled in Exhibit A attached hereto.

   The Purchaser agrees to pay a loan transfer fee not to exceed $125.00 and
   it is a condition of this contract that the Purchaser may assume such encumbrance without change in its terms or conditions.

7. Title: Seller agrees to furnish good and marketable title free of all encumbrances and defects, except mortgage liens and encumbrances as set forth in this agreement, and to make

conveyance by Warranty Deed or _____ . Seller shall furnish in due course to the Buyer a title insurance policy insuring the Buyer of a good and marketable title in keeping with the terms and conditions of this agreement. Prior to the closing of this transaction, the Seller, upon request, will furnish to the Buyer a preliminary title report made by a title insurance company showing the condition of the title to said property. If the Seller cannot furnish marketable title within thirty days after receipt of the notice to the Buyer containing a written statement of the defects, the earnest money deposit herein receipted shall be refunded to the Buyer and this agreement shall be null and void. The following shall not be deemed encumbrances or defects; building and use restrictions general to the area; utility easements; other easements not inconsistent with Buyer's intended use; zoning or subdivision laws, covenants, conditions, restrictions, or reservations of record; tenancies of record. In the event of sale of other than real property relating to this transaction, Seller will provide evidence of title or right to sell or lease such personal property.

8. Special Representations: Seller warrants and represents to Buyer (1) that the subject property is connected to ( ) public sewer system, ( ) cesspool or septic tank, (·) sewer system available but not connected, ( ) city water system, ( ) private water system, and that the following special improvements are included in the sale: ( ) sidewalk, ( ) curb and gutter, ( ) special street paving, ( ) special street lighting; (2) that the Seller knows of no material structural defects; (3) that all electrical wiring, heating, cooling, and plumbing systems are free of material defects and will be in good working order at the time the Buyer is entitled to possession; (4) that the Seller has no notice from any government agency of any violation or knowledge of probable violations of the law relating to the subject property; (5) that the Seller has no notice or knowledge of planned or commenced public improvements which may result in special assessments or otherwise directly and materially affect the property; and (6) that the Seller has no notice or knowledge of any liens to be assessed against the property,

EXCEPT _____ None

9. Escrow Instructions: This sale shall be closed on or before _____ 19 _____ by _____
or such other closing agent as mutually agreed upon by Buyer and Seller. Buyer and Seller will, immediately on demand, deposit with closing agent all instruments and monies required

to complete the purchase in accordance with the provisions of this agreement. Contract of Sale or Instrument of Conveyance to be made in the name of _____

10. Closing Costs and Pro-Ration: Seller agrees to pay for title insurance policy, preliminary title report (if requested), termite inspection as set forth below, real estate commission, cost of preparing and recording any corrective instruments, and one-half of the escrow fees. Buyer agrees to pay for recording fees for mortgages and deeds of conveyance, all costs or expenses in securing new financing or assuming existing financing, and one-half of the escrow fees. Buyer agrees to pay for recording fees for mortgages and deeds of conveyance, all costs or expenses in securing new financing or assuming existing financing, and one-half of the escrow fees. Taxes for the current year, insurance acceptable to the Buyer, rents, interest, mortgage reserves, maintenance fees, and water and other utilities constituting liens, shall be pro-rated as of closing. Renters' security deposits shall accrue to Buyer at closing. Seller to provide Buyer with all current rental or lease agreements prior to closing.

11. Termite Inspection: Seller agrees, at his expense, to provide written certification by a reputable licensed pest control firm that the property is free of termite infestation. In the event termites are found, the Seller shall have the property treated at his expense and provide acceptable certification that treatment has been rendered. If any structural repairs are required by reason of termite damage as established by acceptable certification, Seller agrees to make necessary repairs not to exceed $500. If repairs exceed $500, Buyer shall first have the right to accept the property "as is" with a credit to the Buyer at closing of $500, or the Buyer may terminate this agreement with the earnest money deposit being promptly returned to the Buyer if the Seller does not agree to pay all costs of treatment and repair.

12. Conditions of Sale: The following conditions shall also apply, and shall, if conflicting with the printed portions of this agreement, prevail and control:

Additional provisions:

a. Sellers warrant that plumbing and heating systems and appliances are in good working order.

b. Purchaser reserves the right to inspect the plumbing and heating systems and appliances on or before the date and hour of transfer of deed for the express purpose of satisfying himself that they are in good working order.

c. Sellers agree that Purchaser shall have no personal liability to satisfy the promissory notes to be executed in favor of Sellers as scheduled in Exhibit A. That is, Sellers may look only to the property securing such notes for recourse in the event of default by Purchaser.

d. Sellers agree to accept prepayments of principal from Purchaser on promissory notes schedules in Exhibit A attached at any time and from time to time without prepayment penalty.

e. Current commitments for title insurance policies in an amount of $10,000 on 16 Bradstreet Avenue and $17,285 on 48 Clover Street at Purchaser's expense, shall be furnished the Sellers on or before May 20, 1981. Purchaser will deliver the title insurance policies to Sellers after closing and pay the premium thereon.

f. Purchaser warrants to Sellers that the properties to be used as security in this transaction as identified in Exhibit A are free and clear of all liens and encumbrances except utility easements, and except existing deeds of trust as follows:

Lender	Approximate Note Balance	Loan Number
16 Bradstreet Avenue		
Jenkins Pacific Mortgage	$50,000.00	123
48 Clover Street		
Boston Mortgage	$45,500.00	456
Horizon Savings and Loan	9,700.00	789

g. Any tenant security deposits held by Sellers shall be transferred to Purchaser at date of delivery of deed. Sellers are currently holding

_____ $350.00 as a security deposit from Joseph Grant. _____

13. Liability and Maintenance: Seller shall maintain subject property, including landscaping, in good condition until the date of transfer of title or possession by Buyer, whichever occurs first. All risk of loss and destruction of property, and all expenses of insurance, shall be borne by the seller until the date of possession. If the improvements on the property are destroyed or materially damaged prior to closing, then the Buyer shall have the right to declare this agreement null and void, and the earnest money deposit and all other sums paid by Buyer toward the purchase price shall be returned to the Buyer forthwith.

14. Possession: The Buyer shall be entitled to possession of property upon closing or _____ date of delivery _____, 19 ____.

If Seller fails to deliver possession on the date herein specified, the
Seller shall be subject to eviction and shall be liable for a daily rental
of $30.00 until possession is delivered.

15. Default: In the event the Buyer fails to complete the purchase as herein provided, the earnest money deposit shall be retained by the Seller as the total and entire liquidated damages. In the event the Seller fails to perform any condition of the sale as herein provided, then the Buyer may, at his option, treat the contract as terminated, and all payments made by the Buyer hereunder shall be returned to the Buyer forthwith, provided the Buyer may, at his option, treat this agreement as being in full force and effect with the right to action for specific performance and damages. In the event that either Buyer, Seller, or Agent shall institute suit to enforce any rights hereunder, the prevailing party shall be entitled to court costs and a reasonable attorney's fee.

16. Time Limit of Offer: The Seller shall have until _____ May 15, _____, 19 81 _____ to accept this
(hour)   (date)

offer by delivering a signed copy hereof to the Buyer. If this offer is not so accepted, it shall lapse and the agent (or Seller) shall refund the earnest money deposit to the Buyer forthwith.

17. General Agreements: (1) Both parties to this purchase reserve their rights to assign and hereby otherwise agree to cooperate in effecting an Internal Revenue Code 1031 exchange or similar tax-related arrangement prior to close of escrow, upon either party's written notice of intention to do so. (2) Upon approval of this offer by the Seller, this agreement shall become a contract between Buyer and Seller and shall inure to the benefit of the heirs, administrators, executors, successors, personal representatives, and assigns of said parties. (3) Time is of the essence and an essential part of this agreement. (4) This contract constitutes the sole and entire agreement between the parties hereto and no modification of this contract shall be binding unless attached hereto and signed by all parties to the contract. No representations, promises, or inducements not included in this contract shall be binding upon any party hereto.

18. Buyer's Statement and Receipt: "I/we hereby agree to purchase the above property in accordance with the terms and conditions above stated and acknowledge receipt of a completed copy of this agreement, which I/we have fully read and understand." Dated _____ May 12, _____ 19 81 _____, _____
(hour)

Address _____ 251 Quebec Street _____   [signature] _____ Buyer

_____ Evergreen, Colorado _____   _____ Buyer

Phone No: Home _____ 512-1135 _____ Business _____ 225-3167 _____

19. Seller's Statement and Response: "I/we approve and accept the above offer, which I/we have fully read and understand, and agree to the above terms and conditions this day of _____ May 14, _____, 19 81 _____, _____.
(hour)

Address _____ P.O. Box 61, Evergreen, CO _____   [signature] _____ Seller

Phone No: Home _____ 215-1161 _____ Business _____ 216-1897 _____   _____ Seller

20. Commission Agreement: Seller agrees to pay a commission of _____ 0 _____ % of the gross sales price to _____ NA _____ for services in this transaction, and agrees that, in the event of forfeiture of the earnest money deposit by the Buyer, said deposit shall be divided between the Seller's broker and the Seller (one half to each party), the Broker's part not to exceed the amount of the commission.

21. Buyer's Receipt for Signed Offer: The Buyer hereby acknowledges receipt of a copy of the above agreement bearing the Seller's signature in acceptance of this offer.

Dated _____, 19 _____   _____ Buyer

_____ Buyer

COMMENTARY TO DOCUMENTATION

Item 2. Once again, the old bugaboo "or Assigns" has escaped notice. It should always be present after the buyer's name.

Item 6. The process of moving a mortgage is a thing of beauty in the eyes of the beholder if he or she digs creative finance! The carry-back notes, however, should have had provisions for assumption, first right of refusal, and rollover of the balloon (in the case of the 3rd trust note).

Item 12. The buyer has a strong exculpatory clause in place.

Item 15. The original contains a strong preprinted "total liquidated damages clause" of the type used in our "Universal Earnest Money Receipt" form.

Reprinted by permission from the *Nothing Down Advisor*.

"I want a soccer ball. Suzy wants a new dress. And Daddy
wants someone to take care of his balloon payment on January 31st."

How To Get Your Feet Wet In Real Estate Without Taking A Bath

**Featuring Technique No. 37
''Creative Refinance of
Underlying Mortgage'**

In A Nutshell. . .

Type: Condo
Price: $72,000
Source: Classified ad
Means: Refinance, carry back
Techniques: No. 4 — Contract/Wrap
No. 6 — Balloon
No. 24 — Small Amounts from Banks
No. 37 — Creative Refinance
No. 39 — Holder As Partner
Strategies: Tenant equity participation

LOCATING

Takio Fujikawa of Fremont, California, a recent graduate of the Nothing Down Seminar, was anxious to get his feet wet in the world of creative acquisition techniques. In poring over the ads one day he spotted a condo entry that seemed to suggest owner flexibility:

> ''72,950. CTL, OWC, FNMA, 1 yr. home warranty, sellers will carry ½ equity on saleable 2d.''

A little practice had taught him to decipher the ad jargon: CTL — cash to loan, OWC — owner will carry back a second, FNMA — the first had been sold by the lender to Federal National Mortgage Association and could therefore be refinanced at below market rates. These options seemed attractive, so Takio made a stop at the listing office.

SITUATION

The subject property was in a pleasant location in Union City (north of Fremont). It was a clean two-bedroom, one-bath condo with a two-car garage. Encumbrances consisted of a $41,000 FNMA first and a $4,000 second held by the owner's mother. As it turned out, the real estate broker and his father (the founder of the real estate company) were good friends of the seller. It gave Takio some sense of trust that both father and son had been active in the ministry for many years. He, therefore, did not seek personal contact with the seller but let the brokerage handle the communications.

NEGOTIATION

Takio's first offer was for $70,000, with $7,000 down, a carry back of $7,000 (12%, no payments, balloon in three years), and a FNMA refinance for $56,000. The seller countered with $73,900 with $7,400 down, a carry back of $7,390 (18%, interest-only payments monthly, balloon in three years), FNMA refinance for $59,160.

Takio responded that the bank would go no higher than $56,000 on the FNMA refinance, so the seller sent back word that he would accept $72,000, with $7,600 down and a carry back of $8,400 (18% for 3 years, $126/mo.). There was a verbal agreement that the second would be adjusted after closing to a no-payment note ballooning after 3 years. Takio accepted, provided the seller would pay the closing costs.

CLOSING

In preparation for closing, Takio transferred $13,000 to a money market account yielding 17% as an offset to a loan he took out at his credit union ($5,000, 18%, 3 years) to pay most of the down. His cash outlay at closing was therefore $2,600 (3.6% of the selling price). The agreement he had on the carry back was in effect a partnership arrangement with the holder of an underlying loan: the seller's mother was going to continue (and increase the amount) on her existing second. The facts are summarized in the following sketch:

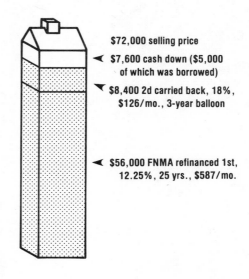

$72,000 selling price

$7,600 cash down ($5,000 of which was borrowed)

$8,400 2d carried back, 18%, $126/mo., 3-year balloon

$56,000 FNMA refinanced 1st, 12.25%, 25 yrs., $587/mo.

OUTCOMES AND FUTURE PLANS

With rents at $440 per month, the condo would have shown a negative cash flow of $194/mo., including escrow expenses, if the arrangement had worked out as planned. Unfortunately, the verbal agreement to convert the $8,400 second to a non-payment balloon following the close of escrow was not honored by the party involved. The negative was therefore increased by $126/mo. In response, Takio raised the rents on a 5-plex he owns in order to recover most of the lost ground.

In addition, he plans to work out a tenant equity sharing plan for the condo in order to eliminate the rest of the negative cash flow. Fortunately the current occupants have a flair for upkeep and repair. His plan is to refinance the condo again in one to 2½ years, then sell it on a contract.

Looking back on his first creative finance deal, Takio feels he would have changed things by insisting on a selling price around 5% lower than he paid. He would also have required a written side-agreement on adjusting the terms for the carry-back second (lower than 18%, longer period on the balloon).

Takio was asked to formulate the most important advice he could give to other investors. He responded with typical Oriental charm: "There is an old Japanese poem — 'Old fish pond, frog jumps in, the sound of water.' I needed to get my feet wet."

COMMENTARY

1. Takio raised $15,000 of his down payment through the creative refinance technique. At a time when high interest rates are depressing the real estate market throughout the country, investors are wise to look for properties with mortgages that have been sold by the lenders to FNMA. The FNMA refinance program provides for new firsts at interest rates below the current market, as long as the existing financing falls within certain guidelines. The program applies also to non-owner-occupied situations. Investors should check with local lending institutions for current details. Even better than the FNMA program is any situation where the property has a fully assumable FHA or VA loan.

2. Takio left it to the real estate agent to deal with the seller. Wherever possible, the buyer should have personal contact with the seller to learn his or her needs and find out what the "hot buttons" are. Problem-solving is much easier if one knows, for example, why the seller is selling and what he intends to do with the cash down payment. Frequently the agent refuses to allow the buyer and seller to come together on the theory that the chemistry will be bad and the deal (commission) jeopardized. Agents often lack an understanding of the way creative finance works as a problem-solving approach to buying. Buyers must first build trust with the agents in such cases in order to gain access to the seller. If the buyer insists that the deal depends on buyer-seller contact, the agent will usually agree, provided he or she can be present. Where the agent refuses, the buyer can always walk away or speak with the seller directly. According to their professional code of practice, however, agents must present all offers to the seller.

3. Since the father-and-son broker team were able to create trust with Takio, he should have asked whether they would be willing to take their commissions in the form of a note (all due and payable in one or two years, or even with monthly payments). This would have tested their own ability to trust others! Takio might then have accomplished a true nothing down deal.

4. A further option for dealing with the negative cash flow in this situation might have been a lease-option agreement with the tenant. The $194/mo. negative carried by the tenant could have been applied toward a future purchase at a specified price. In many ways, the long-term lease-option arrangement is simpler and less open to legal complications than a tenant equity-sharing plan. Since Takio was planning to sell the property in one to 2½ years anyway, the lease-option approach has merit. Should the tenants fail to exercise their option, he would have avoided the negative cash flow for the interim period and be much further ahead.

5. This case study is a classic example of a situation where a cash partner could have been brought in to solve the problems (cash down and negative flow) at one fell swoop. If Takio felt uneasy about borrowing the down payment and handling the negative cash flow, he could have found a cash partner and offered half interest in the property. In any case, he should begin to cultivate partnership funds for future nothing down transactions. It is interesting, also, that Takio borrowed from the credit union at 18% rather than using a portion of his money market funds (at 17%) for the down payment.

6. The unfortunate outcome of the verbal agreement to adjust the $8,400 second after the closing is another illustration of the age-old dictum: "Get it in writing." Takio felt that he could give extra credence to the word of the brokers because they had a background in the ministry. Perhaps there is logic to his reasoning. Perhaps the brokers simply found that the holder of the underlying second backed out on her verbal commitment. In any case, such agreements need to be worked out carefully in written form, preferably with the help of a competent professional (attorney, escrow officer, etc.). At the very least, Takio should have insisted on a contingency clause covering the terms of the second.

UNIVERSAL EARNEST MONEY RECEIPT
AND OFFER TO PURCHASE

"This is a legally binding contract: if not understood, seek competent advice."

1. Date and Place of Offer: _____ June 6, _____ 19 81 _____ ; _____ Union City _____ California
   (city)   (state)

2. Principals: The undersigned Buyer _____ Takio Fujikawa _____ (a married man) _____
agrees to buy and Seller agrees to sell, according to the indicated terms and conditions, the property described as follows:

3. Property: located at _____ 361 Vista Blvd. _____ Union City _____ California
   (street address)   (city)   (state)

with the following legal description: _____ to be supplied _____

including any of the following items if at present attached to the premises: plumbing, heating, and cooling equipment, including stoker and oil tanks, burners, water heaters, electric light fixtures, bathroom fixtures, roller shades, curtain rods and fixtures, draperies, venetian blinds, window and door screens, towel racks, linoleum and other attached floor coverings,

including carpeting, attached television antennas, mailboxes, all trees and shrubs, and any other fixtures EXCEPT _____ None _____

The following personal property shall also be included as part of the purchase: _____
At the closing of the transaction, the Seller, at his expense, shall provide the Buyer with a Bill Of Sale containing a detailed inventory of the personal property included.

4. Earnest Money Deposit: Agent (or Seller) acknowledges receipt from Buyer of _____ Five Hundred and 00/100 _____ dollars $ _____ 500.00 _____

in the form of ( ) cash; ( ) personal check; (X) cashier's check; ( ) promissory note at _____% interest per annum due _____ 19 _____ ; or

other _____

as earnest money deposit to secure and apply on this purchase. Upon acceptance of this agreement in writing and delivery of same to Buyer, the earnest money deposit shall be assigned

to and deposited in the listing Realtor's trust account or _____ -- _____, to apply on the purchase price at the time of closing.

5. Purchase Price: The total purchase price of the property shall be _____ Seventy Thousand and 00/100 _____ dollars $ _____ 70,000.00 _____

6. Payment: Purchase price is to be paid by Buyer as follows:

Aforedescribed earnest money deposit .... $ _____ 500.00 _____

Additional payment due upon acceptance of this offer .... $ _____ -- _____

Additional payment due at closing .... $ _____ -- _____

Balance to be paid as follows:

1. Buyer to pay exactly seven thousand dollars cash down including the above deposit, plus secondary financing as noted below.

2. Subject to Buyer applying for, qualifying for and receiving a new conventional FNMA loan in the amount of $56,000.00.

3. Seller to pay all closing costs with the exception of the first months payment (PITI), which is usually collected in escrow.

4. Buyer to be lender-qualified within 15 working days.

5. Balance of the purchase price in the amount of $7,000.00 shall be a Note secured by a Deed of Trust executed by the Buyer in favor of the Seller. Said Note and Deed of Trust shall bear interest at 12% per annum, be payable at the rate of $0.00 per month, contain an acceleration clause, and shall be all due and payable in 3 years.

7. Title: Seller agrees to furnish good and marketable title free of all encumbrances and defects, except mortgage liens and encumbrances as set forth in this agreement, and to make

conveyance by Warranty Deed or _____. Seller shall furnish in due course to the Buyer a title insurance policy insuring the Buyer of a good and marketable title in keeping with the terms and conditions of this agreement. Prior to the closing of this transaction, the Seller, upon request, will furnish to the Buyer a preliminary title report made by a title insurance company showing the condition of the title to said property. If the Seller cannot furnish marketable title within thirty days after receipt of the notice to the Buyer containing a written statement of the defects, the earnest money deposit herein receipted shall be refunded to the Buyer and this agreement shall be null and void. The following shall not be deemed encumbrances or defects: building and use restrictions general to the area; utility easements; other easements not inconsistent with Buyer's intended use; zoning or subdivision laws, covenants, conditions, restrictions, or reservations of record; tenancies of record. In the event of sale of other than real property relating to this transaction, Seller will provide evidence of title or right to sell or lease such personal property.

8. Special Representations: Seller warrants and represents to Buyer (1) that the subject property is connected to ( ) public sewer system, ( ) cesspool or septic tank, ( ) sewer system available but not connected, ( ) city water system, ( ) private water system, and that the following special improvements are included in the sale: ( ) sidewalk, ( ) curb and gutter, ( ) special street paving, ( ) special street lighting; (2) that the Seller knows of no material structural defects; (3) that all electrical wiring, heating, cooling, and plumbing systems are free of material defects and will be in good working order at the time the Buyer is entitled to possession; (4) that the Seller has no notice from any government agency of any violation or knowledge of probable violations of the law relating to the subject property; (5) that the Seller has no notice or knowledge of planned or commenced public improvements which may result in special assessments or otherwise directly and materially affect the property; and (6) that the Seller has no notice or knowledge of any liens to be assessed against the property,

EXCEPT _____ None _____

9. Escrow Instructions: This sale shall be closed on or before _____ within 60 days after date of acceptance _____

or such other closing agent as mutually agreed upon by Buyer and Seller. Buyer and Seller will, immediately on demand, deposit with closing agent all instruments and monies required

to complete the purchase in accordance with the provisions of this agreement. Contract of Sale or Instrument of Conveyance to be made in the name of _____

to be supplied

10. Closing Costs and Pro-Ration: Seller agrees to pay for title insurance policy, preliminary title report (if requested), termite inspection as set forth below, real estate commission, cost of preparing and recording any corrective instruments, and one-half of the escrow fees. Buyer agrees to pay for recording fees for mortgages and deeds of conveyance, all costs or expenses in securing new financing or assuming existing financing, and one-half of the escrow fees. Buyer agrees to pay for recording fees for mortgages and deeds of conveyance, all costs or expenses in securing new financing or assuming existing financing, and one-half of the escrow fees. Taxes for the current year, insurance acceptable to the Buyer, rents, interest, mortgage reserves, maintenance fees, and water and other utilities constituting liens, shall be pro-rated as of closing. Renters' security deposits shall accrue to Buyer at closing. Seller to provide Buyer with all current rental or lease agreements prior to closing.

11. Termite Inspection: Seller agrees, at his expense, to provide written certification by a reputable licensed pest control firm that the property is free of termite infestation. In the event termites are found, the Seller shall have the property treated at his expense and provide acceptable certification that treatment has been rendered. If any structural repairs are required by reason of termite damage as established by acceptable certification, Seller agrees to make necessary repairs not to exceed $500. If repairs exceed $500, Buyer shall first have the right to accept the property "as is" with a credit to the Buyer at closing of $500, or the Buyer may terminate this agreement with the earnest money deposit being promptly returned to the Buyer if the Seller does not agree to pay all costs of treatment and repair.

12. Conditions of Sale: The following conditions shall also apply, and shall, if conflicting with the printed portions of this agreement, prevail and control:

None

13. Liability and Maintenance: Seller shall maintain subject property, including landscaping, in good condition until the date of transfer of title or possession by Buyer, whichever occurs first. All risk of loss and destruction of property, and all expenses of insurance, shall be borne by the seller until the date of possession. If the improvements on the property are destroyed or materially damaged prior to closing, then the Buyer shall have the right to declare this agreement null and void, and the earnest money deposit and all other sums paid by Buyer toward the purchase price shall be returned to the Buyer forthwith.

14. Possession: The Buyer shall be entitled to possession of property upon closing or _____ within 30 days after close of escrow _____

15. Default: In the event the Buyer fails to complete the purchase as herein provided, the earnest money deposit shall be retained by the Seller as the total and entire liquidated damages. In the event the Seller fails to perform any condition of the sale as herein provided, then the Buyer may, at his option, treat the contract as terminated, and all payments made by the Buyer hereunder shall be returned to the Buyer forthwith, provided the Buyer may, at his option, treat this agreement as being in full force and effect with the right to action for specific performance and damages. In the event that either Buyer, Seller, or Agent shall institute suit to enforce any rights hereunder, the prevailing party shall be entitled to court costs and a reasonable attorney's fee.

16. Time Limit of Offer: The Seller shall have until

_____ June 8, _____ , 19 _81_ to accept this
(hour)   (date)

offer by delivering a signed copy hereof to the Buyer. If this offer is not so accepted, it shall lapse and the agent (or Seller) shall refund the earnest money deposit to the Buyer forthwith.

17. General Agreements: (1) Both parties to this purchase reserve their rights to assign and hereby otherwise agree to cooperate in effecting an Internal Revenue Code 1031 exchange or similar tax-related arrangement prior to close of escrow, upon either party's written notice of intention to do so. (2) Upon approval of this offer by the Seller, this agreement shall become a contract between Buyer and Seller and shall inure to the benefit of the heirs, administrators, executors, successors, personal representatives, and assigns of said parties. (3) Time is of the essence and an essential part of this agreement. (4) This contract constitutes the sole and entire agreement between the parties hereto and no modification of this contract shall be binding unless attached hereto and signed by all parties to the contract. No representations, promises, or inducements not included in this contract shall be binding upon any party hereto.

18. Buyer's Statement and Receipt: "I/we hereby agree to purchase the above property in accordance with the terms and conditions above stated and acknowledge receipt of a completed copy of this agreement, which I/we have fully read and understand." Dated _____ June 6, _____ , 19 _81_ , _____
(hour)

Address _____ 8513 Rose Avenue _____   [signature] _____ Buyer

_____ Fremont, California _____   _____ Buyer

Phone No: Home _612-7156_ Business _847-1193_

19. Seller's Statement and Response: "I/we approve and accept the above offer, which I/we have fully read and understand, and agree to the above terms and conditions this day of _____ , 19 _____ , _____
(hour)

Address _____   _____ Seller

Phone No: Home _____ Business _____   _____ Seller

20. Commission Agreement: Seller agrees to pay a commission of _6_ % of the gross sales price to _Blake Real Estate, Co._ for services in this transaction, and agrees that, in the event of forfeiture of the earnest money deposit by the Buyer, said deposit shall be divided between the Seller's broker and the Seller (one half to each party), the Broker's part not to exceed the amount of the commission.

21. Buyer's Receipt for Signed Offer: The Buyer hereby acknowledges receipt of a copy of the above agreement bearing the Seller's signature in acceptance of this offer.

Dated _____ , 19 _____   _____ Buyer

_____ Buyer

COMMENTARY TO DOCUMENTATION

Item 2. "Or Assigns" should be written after the name of the buyer.

Item 6. Everything is straightforward enough; however, the carry-back note should have included provisions for rollover of the balloon, assumption, and first right of refusal (in the unlikely event a seller would want to discount a short-fuse note such as this).

The following counter arrangements were finally agreed upon:

1. Sale price to be exactly $72,000.00.
2. Amount of FNMA rewrite to be exactly $56,000.00 (the seller had wanted more).
3. Buyer to pay exactly $7,600.00 cash down, including deposit.
4. Seller to carry back a Second Note secured by a Deed of Trust in the amount of exactly $8,400.00 with 18% annual interest. Said note to be amortized for 30 years but all due and payable in 3 years with monthly payments of $126.60. Said note to contain standard acceleration clause and prepayment penalty and late charge.
5. Seller to pay $980.00 of Buyer's closing costs.

It was unfortunate that the seller insisted on the non-assumption clause and the prepayment with penalty. The $980 of subsidy to the buyer was a pleasant consolation.

Item 15. The original preprinted boilerplate was initialed so as to permit the seller recourse only to the deposit as liquidated damages (or up to 3% of the sales price). The buyer should have struck the 3% clause.

Reprinted by permission from the *Nothing Down Advisor.*

"Let's play 'get rich.' I'll be the creative investor. You be the don't wanter. And I'll pick up your place on a wrap with nothing down."

"Just Let Yourself In . . . The Key's Under The Mortgage"

Featuring Technique No. 39
"Making A Partner of the Holder of An Underlying Mortgage"

In A Nutshell . . .

Type: 5-Plex
Price: $60,000
Source: Realtor
Means: Assumption, carry back
Techniques: No. 4 — Contract/Wrap
No. 6 — Balloon
No. 19 — Borrowing Realtor's Commission
No. 39 — Holder As Partner
No. 42 — Partner's Money for Down

LOCATING

Bob Martinez of Sante Fe, New Mexico, is a Realtor who makes use of creative finance techniques every day. As a R.A.N.D. graduate, he is always on the lookout for promising deals to pass along to his colleagues in the R.A.N.D. network. One of his own listings struck him as meeting the specifications given to him by a woman investor, also a R.A.N.D. graduate, who had come to him for leads.

SITUATION

The subject property was a home in Las Vegas, a community east of Sante Fe. It had been converted to a five-plex. The owner was asking $68,000, with $30,000 down and the rest on a real estate contract at 12% for 20 years. Bob asked the seller the universal question: "Why do you want so much money down?" The seller told him that he had made a verbal commitment to the holder of the underlying mortgage to pay off the note if the property should subsequently be sold. Therefore, he needed a good part of the down payment, nearly $11,000, to honor his agreement.

NEGOTIATION

Since Bob knew that his buyer would be interested in the property only if it could be highly leveraged, he immediately contacted the holder of the underlying mortgage and explored the possibility of an assumption. Contrary to the seller's opinion, the underlying mortgagee was quite willing to be flexible. All he wanted was to realize an advantage for his cooperation. In this case, the "sweetener" was a higher interest rate — 15% instead of the 12% he had been getting. Bob knew he had found the key to a nothing down transaction — right where so few think to look: under the mortgage! Or rather, in the hands of the holder of the underlying mortgage. Sometimes that is the key for getting into a creative deal.

He went to the seller and asked whether a payment of $5,000 down would be sufficient provided the underlying note could be assumed by the buyer. The seller thought about it, then agreed on the condition that the broker take his share of the commission in the form of a no-interest note for four months. Since there was no problem with that, they went on to negotiate an acceptable selling price of $60,000, and all the pieces of the puzzle were in place for the closing.

CLOSING

Bob's buyer was delighted with the arrangements, except for one slight problem. She did not have the $5,000 down payment. However, she had a friend who was willing to loan her the money on a personal note at a mutually acceptable rate of interest. In this case, the partner was not an equity participant in the deal but only a bystanding investor.

The sketch shows the details of the financing:

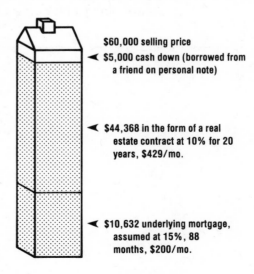

$60,000 selling price

$5,000 cash down (borrowed from a friend on personal note)

$44,368 in the form of a real estate contract at 10% for 20 years, $429/mo.

$10,632 underlying mortgage, assumed at 15%, 88 months, $200/mo.

OUTCOMES AND FUTURE PLANS

One-half of the commission ($3,128) was deferred for

four months. However, the seller was able to pay it off after only seven weeks. The five-plex rents were such that the cash flow after debt service and expenses was only slightly negative. The next round of rent raises will correct that.

Looking back on the deal, Bob wished that he had decided to buy the property himself! However, his gains were still considerable — a welcome commission and the satisfaction of having got a R.A.N.D. colleague into a solid nothing down deal.

COMMENTARY

1. This case study puts two prevailing myths to rest: first the notion — cultivated by fearful and unknowledgeable agents — that nothing down deals send commissions flying out the window. And second, the notion among beginning investors that agents siphon off all the good deals before they ever reach the public.

   Nothing down does not necessarily mean that no cash is involved, but only that the cash does not come from the buyer's pocket. Furthermore, agents who are willing to be flexible with their commissions by taking them in the form of paper where necessary to cement a deal, find that the seasonal ups and downs of the real estate business are dispelled. Instead, the agent can look forward to a steadier income based on predictable cash flows from commission notes. Better to consummate sales creatively with notes than not to sell at all.

   As to the superstition that agents buy up all the good deals: like everyone else, agents must put bread on the table. Real estate as a long-range investment venture does not always generate cash flow income, particularly where high leverage is used on the front end. It takes sales to keep the family in shoes. Moreover, even if the agent has a nest egg to use for investments, he — again like everyone else — will run out of money before he runs out of good deals. Bob Martinez could have bought his own listing, but he didn't. Just as in the case of thousands of other agents, he has to operate within certain cash-flow guidelines. So, like his colleagues in the real estate industry, he passes along deal after deal (including this five-plex) to his buyers. That's the name of the game.

2. In this case, the deferred commission was handled by the seller. If the buyer had wanted to reduce the $5,000 cash down payment by the same amount, she could have negotiated to assume responsibility herself for payment of the note. This would have given her more leeway to come up with the needed money without incurring any interest charges.

3. It is instructive that the seller in this case structured his asking terms around a $30,000 cash down payment. Such a large amount of money (nearly half of his asking price) is enough to frighten away most investors. If he had only thought to check with the holder of the underlying mortgage, he might have laid the groundwork for a far more attractive financing package and sold the property more quickly. Fortunately, the agent he selected knew the ins and outs of creative financing. Very few sellers realize the full power of creative financing as a tool for selling real estate in today's sluggish economy.

4. Note the strategy followed by the agent in this case: the seller threw up a barrier by declaring the underlying note non-assumable. Rather than accepting this as policy, the agent went to the source to check things out. Creative investors always go to the source of information before they consider a lead exhausted. There is no substitute for person-to-person fact-finding and negotiations at the source. The universal rule in this business is: "You never know until you ask." The corollary to this is: "When you ask, always ask the right person."

5. There are many ways to facilitate deals using the flexibility of underlying mortgagees. The buyer in this case might well consider offering to cash out the mortgagee by discounting the $10,632 note for, say $7,000. If the seller had been induced to accept a substitution of collateral clause as part of the transaction, the second (the real estate contract) could have been moved off the five-plex to make room for a new first mortgage. The new mortgage would have wiped out the existing first by paying it off at the discounted price of $7,000, leaving $3,632 extra (some of which would go for loans costs). The buyer could decide how large the new first would be according to rental income restraints. Probably $30,000 could be cranked out of the property in this way.

UNIVERSAL EARNEST MONEY RECEIPT
AND OFFER TO PURCHASE

"This is a legally binding contract: if not understood, seek competent advice."

1. Date and Place of Offer: __April 16,__ 19 __81__ ; __Las Vegas__ __New Mexico__
(city) (state)

2. Principals: The undersigned Buyer __Estelle Montrose or Assigns__
agrees to buy and Seller agrees to sell, according to the indicated terms and conditions, the property described as follows:

3. Property: located at __4816 Huntington Street__ __Las Vegas__ __New Mexico__
(street address) (city) (state)

with the following legal description: __to be supplied__

including any of the following items if at present attached to the premises: plumbing, heating, and cooling equipment, including stoker and oil tanks, burners, water heaters, electric light fixtures, bathroom fixtures, roller shades, curtain rods and fixtures, draperies, venetian blinds, window and door screens, towel racks, linoleum and other attached floor coverings,

including carpeting, attached television antennas, mailboxes, all trees and shrubs, and any other fixtures EXCEPT __None__

The following personal property shall also be included as part of the purchase: _____
At the closing of the transaction, the Seller, at his expense, shall provide the Buyer with a Bill Of Sale containing a detailed inventory of the personal property included.

4. Earnest Money Deposit: Agent (or Seller) acknowledges receipt from Buyer of __Five Hundred and 00/100__ dollars $ __500.00__

in the form of ( ) cash; (X) personal check; ( ) cashier's check; ( ) promissory note at _____% interest per annum due _____ 19 _____ ; or

other _____
as earnest money deposit to secure and apply on this purchase. Upon acceptance of this agreement in writing and delivery of same to Buyer, the earnest money deposit shall be assigned

to and deposited in the listing Realtor's trust account or _____, to apply on the
purchase price at the time of closing.

5. Purchase Price: The total purchase price of the property shall be __Sixty Thousand and 00/100__ dollars $ __60,000.00__

6. Payment: Purchase price is to be paid by Buyer as follows:

Aforedescribed earnest money deposit .... $ __500.00__

Additional payment due upon acceptance of this offer .... $ __--__

Additional payment due at closing .... $ __4,500.00__

Balance to be paid as follows:

Assume existing mortgage of $10,632.36 at 15% for 88 months, payments $199.88. Sale is contingent upon Buyer's ability to assume.

A real estate contract for $44,367.64 at 10% for 20 years, payments $428.59. Real estate contract is not assignable or assumable. It must be paid off in case of resale.

Seller's mortgage shall be subordinate and inferior to the existing prior mortgage and to any extension, replacement or renewal thereof.

Liability of this contract shall be limited to the property itself and not extend beyond this.

No prepayment penalty.

7. Title: Seller agrees to furnish good and marketable title free of all encumbrances and defects, except mortgage liens and encumbrances as set forth in this agreement, and to make

conveyance by Warranty Deed or _____. Seller shall furnish in due course to the Buyer a title insurance policy insuring the Buyer of a good and marketable title in keeping with the terms and conditions of this agreement. Prior to the closing of this transaction, the Seller, upon request, will furnish to the Buyer a preliminary title report made by a title insurance company showing the condition of the title to said property. If the Seller cannot furnish marketable title within thirty days after receipt of the notice to the Buyer containing a written statement of the defects, the earnest money deposit herein receipted shall be refunded to the Buyer and this agreement shall be null and void. The following shall not be deemed encumbrances or defects; building and use restrictions general to the area; utility easements; other easements not inconsistent with Buyer's intended use; zoning or subdivision laws, covenants, conditions, restrictions, or reservations of record; tenancies of record. In the event of sale of other than real property relating to this transaction, Seller will provide evidence of title or right to sell or lease such personal property.

8. Special Representations: Seller warrants and represents to Buyer (1) that the subject property is connected to ( ) public sewer system, ( ) cesspool or septic tank, ( ) sewer system available but not connected, ( ) city water system, ( ) private water system, and that the following special improvements are included in the sale: ( ) sidewalk, ( ) curb and gutter, ( ) special street paving, ( ) special street lighting; (2) that the Seller knows of no material structural defects; (3) that all electrical wiring, heating, cooling, and plumbing systems are free of material defects and will be in good working order at the time the Buyer is entitled to possession; (4) that the Seller has no notice from any government agency of any violation or knowledge of probable violations of the law relating to the subject property; (5) that the Seller has no notice or knowledge of planned or commenced public improvements which may result in special assessments or otherwise directly and materially affect the property; and (6) that the Seller has no notice or knowledge of any liens to be assessed against the property,

EXCEPT _____ None _____

9. Escrow Instructions: This sale shall be closed on or before _____ June 1, __ 19 81 by _____
or such other closing agent as mutually agreed upon by Buyer and Seller. Buyer and Seller will, immediately on demand, deposit with closing agent all instruments and monies required

to complete the purchase in accordance with the provisions of this agreement. Contract of Sale or Instrument of Conveyance to be made in the name of _____
__ to be supplied _____

10. Closing Costs and Pro-Ration: Seller agrees to pay for title insurance policy, preliminary title report (if requested), termite inspection as set forth below, real estate commission, cost of preparing and recording any corrective instruments, and one-half of the escrow fees. Buyer agrees to pay for recording fees for mortgages and deeds of conveyance, all costs or expenses in securing new financing or assuming existing financing, and one-half of the escrow fees. Buyer agrees to pay for recording fees for mortgages and deeds of conveyance, all costs or expenses in securing new financing or assuming existing financing, and one-half of the escrow fees. Taxes for the current year, insurance acceptable to the Buyer, rents, interest, mortgage reserves, maintenance fees, and water and other utilities constituting liens, shall be pro-rated as of closing. Renters' security deposits shall accrue to Buyer at closing. Seller to provide Buyer with all current rental or lease agreements prior to closing.

11. Termite Inspection: Seller agrees, at his expense, to provide written certification by a reputable licensed pest control firm that the property is free of termite infestation. In the event termites are found, the Seller shall have the property treated at his expense and provide acceptable certification that treatment has been rendered. If any structural repairs are required by reason of termite damage as established by acceptable certification, Seller agrees to make necessary repairs not to exceed $500. If repairs exceed $500, Buyer shall first have the right to accept the property "as is" with a credit to the Buyer at closing of $500, or the Buyer may terminate this agreement with the earnest money deposit being promptly returned to the Buyer if the Seller does not agree to pay all costs of treatment and repair.

12. Conditions of Sale: The following conditions shall also apply, and shall, if conflicting with the printed portions of this agreement, prevail and control:

Buyer and Seller to share equally in title company fees.

Seller will pay for setting up of escrow. Buyer to pay for monthly escrow fee ($2.00 document or $4.00 total).

Rental deposits to be advanced to Buyer and advance rents to be pro-rated to date of closing.

Contingent upon complete inspection of premises by Buyer's partner within 14 days of acceptance.

Buyer will pay one-half title insurance fee.

Liability of this contract shall be limited to the property itself and not extend beyond this.

Seller to furnish copies of any agreements made with tenants.

13. Liability and Maintenance: Seller shall maintain subject property, including landscaping, in good condition until the date of transfer of title or possession by Buyer, whichever occurs first. All risk of loss and destruction of property, and all expenses of insurance, shall be borne by the seller until the date of possession. If the improvements on the property are destroyed or materially damaged prior to closing, then the Buyer shall have the right to declare this agreement null and void, and the earnest money deposit and all other sums paid by Buyer toward the purchase price shall be returned to the Buyer forthwith.

14. Possession: The Buyer shall be entitled to possession of property upon closing or _____ -- _____, 19____

15. Default: In the event the Buyer fails to complete the purchase as herein provided, the earnest money deposit shall be retained by the Seller as the total and entire liquidated damages. In the event the Seller fails to perform any condition of the sale as herein provided, then the Buyer may, at his option, treat the contract as terminated, and all payments made by the Buyer hereunder shall be returned to the Buyer forthwith, provided the Buyer may, at his option, treat this agreement as being in full force and effect with the right to action for specific performance and damages. In the event that either Buyer, Seller, or Agent shall institute suit to enforce any rights hereunder, the prevailing party shall be entitled to court costs and a reasonable attorney's fee.

16. Time Limit of Offer: The Seller shall have until

_____ April 17, _____, 19 __81__ to accept this
(hour)   (date)
offer by delivering a signed copy hereof to the Buyer. If this offer is not so accepted, it shall lapse and the agent (or Seller) shall refund the earnest money deposit to the Buyer forthwith.

17. General Agreements: (1) Both parties to this purchase reserve their rights to assign and hereby otherwise agree to cooperate in effecting an Internal Revenue Code 1031 exchange or similar tax-related arrangement prior to close of escrow, upon either party's written notice of intention to do so. (2) Upon approval of this offer by the Seller, this agreement shall become a contract between Buyer and Seller and shall inure to the benefit of the heirs, administrators, executors, successors, personal representatives, and assigns of said parties. (3) Time is of the essence and an essential part of this agreement. (4) This contract constitutes the sole and entire agreement between the parties hereto and no modification of this contract shall be binding unless attached hereto and signed by all parties to the contract. No representations, promises, or inducements not included in this contract shall be binding upon any party hereto.

18. Buyer's Statement and Receipt: "I/we hereby agree to purchase the above property in accordance with the terms and conditions above stated and acknowledge receipt of a

completed copy of this agreement, which I/we have fully read and understand." Dated _____ April 16, _____ 19 __81__, _____
(hour)

Address ____ 4689 Cactus Flower Drive _____   [signature] or Assigns _____ Buyer

____ Santa Fe, New Mexico _____   _____ Buyer

Phone No: Home ____ 216-3511 ____ Business ____ 489-5197 ____

19. Seller's Statement and Response: "I/we approve and accept the above offer, which I/we have fully read and understand, and agree to the above terms and conditions this day

of _____, 19 _____, _____.

(hour)

Address _____ _____ Seller

Phone No: Home _____ Business _____ _____ Seller

20. Commission Agreement: Seller agrees to pay a commission of ____10____ % of the gross sales price to   George Epland Realty

for services in this transaction, and agrees that, in the event of forfeiture of the earnest money deposit by the Buyer, said deposit shall be divided between the Seller's broker and the Seller (one half to each party), the Broker's part not to exceed the amount of the commission.

21. Buyer's Receipt for Signed Offer: The Buyer hereby acknowledges receipt of a copy of the above agreement bearing the Seller's signature in acceptance of this offer.

Dated _____, 19 _____   _____ Buyer

_____ Buyer

COMMENTARY TO DOCUMENTATION

Item 2. "Or Assigns" was properly entered in after the buyer's name.

Item 6. The buyer is using her head to insist on subordination and prepayment provisions. The seller evidently refused to grant an assumption (or assignment clause).

Item 12. The exculpatory clause limiting liability to the subject property is an excellent idea. Technically the inspection contingency is worthless unless the partner is also given the right to approve the property (not just inspect it).

Item 15. The original stated it this way in print: "Buyers understand and agree that the earnest money deposit paid by Buyers shall be forfeited if Buyers fail to comply with the terms of this agreement."

Part VIII

Investors

In the eighth area of creative financing flexibility, we turn to investors for help with down payments. Our interest is in a particular kind of investor — the kind specializing in buying and selling second trust notes. When a note is created, it tends to have a life of its own. It can move from master to master as it continues to generate monthly payments in accordance with the terms its originators gave to it. The person to whom it is first given — as for example in a real estate transaction where the seller carries back paper on his equity — can turn around and sell it in the marketplace for cash. In order to convert it to cash, he will have to sell it at a discount, anywhere from, say, twenty to fifty percent, depending on the nature of the note, how "seasoned" it might be, its collateral, etc. But the seller is willing to do this for the privilege of having at least a major part of the face value of the note in the form of immediate cash.

It is the marketability of the note, as well as the difference between its face value and its cash value, that makes it interesting to real estate buyers. There are two major possibilities to keep in mind. If a buyer can acquire second trust notes in the marketplace at a discount, and then use them at face value as down payments on real estate, he has effectively picked up the difference between the discounted value (cash value) and the face value. That difference has now been converted to equity in the property he has purchased. And since the note traded into the subject property is secured by another piece of property altogether, he can "crank" funds out of his newly acquired real estate to take care of buying the note in the first place. It is a remarkable chain of events that can yield handsome rewards.

The other major role for second trust notes in creative real estate is generating cash for the seller who needs more down payment than the buyer can provide. The following technique illustrates the approach:

Technique No. 40   Selling of Second Trust Notes

If a buyer cannot supply the seller with a large enough cash down payment, he can give the seller a note — fully secured by the property — with a face value just large enough to yield the required cash proceeds when sold to an investor in the marketplace. Of course, the buyer has to make payments on the note according to the terms agreed upon, no matter who holds the note. Alternately, the buyer can give the seller a note secured by another property in the buyer's portfolio. The same process of selling the note at a discount can be used to generate the cash needed by the seller. By moving the mortgage, however, the buyer has the advantage of fully leveraging other assets that may have already been encumbered beyond the threshold tolerated by commercial lenders. He also can now "crank" funds out of the newly-acquired property more readily since it is left with less secondary financing or none at all.

An example of how this process works in the real world is given in Case No. 42, "Working Miracles With A Discounted Note" (printed below). The buyer gave the seller two notes for his equity, one of which was sold by the seller at a discount to raise the needed cash. The other note remained as a third with a single-payment balloon after three years.

Working Miracles With A Discounted Second

Featuring Technique No. 40
"Selling of Second Trust Notes"

In A Nutshell. . .

Type: SFH
Price: $64,900
Source: Realtor
Means: Trust deed combo (Purchase Money Mortgages)
Techniques: No. 1 — Ultimate Paper Out
No. 4 — Contract/Wrap
No. 5 — Raise Price, Lower Terms
No. 6 — Balloon
No. 8 — Defer Down, No Payments
No. 40 — Selling Notes
Features: Even cash flow

LOCATING

Julian Calb of Phoenix was looking for a single family home to add to his growing portfolio of over $500,000 worth of real estate — all purchased using nothing down techniques. A Realtor acquaintance drew his attention to a property with an unusually good potential for creative finance.

SITUATION

The home was offered for sale by an owner-occupant, a woman in her senior years who was planning sometime in the near future to move into a rest home. She was advertising with the following kind of wording: "Want $64,500. Submit offers. Seller to approve points. Will not carry."

That kind of language is not bristling with clues of seller flexibility. However, Julian probed a little further and learned that the property was free and clear of any liens. And that gave him some ideas.

NEGOTIATION

His first order of business was to apply Calb's Rule No. 1 for Negotiating — "Find out what motivates the seller." In further conversations he learned that the woman really did not need a cash down payment. Her primary concern was to be in a position of flexibility when her waiting list application was finally approved for residency in a rest home. The waiting period could go as long as three years. She wanted a place to stay in the meantime but was afraid to stay alone in a large home. Her present location would be perfect if the right buyer could be found. What she wanted was a secure future, with arrangements for finishing out her life free of concerns about real estate. Above all, she did not want to have to take her house back after it was sold.

Julian's first (and only) offer was as follows: he raised the price of the home by $400 to $64,900, then suggested the equity be paid out using three separate notes — a 1st for $20,930 at 10% with payments of $200/mo. ballooned in three years, a 2nd for $25,000 at 14% with payments of $296/mo. ballooned in 5 years, and a 3rd of $18,970 at 10% with payments of $25/mo. ballooned in 3 years.

Julian then agreed to rent the home back to the woman for an amount equal to the payments on the second plus 1/12th of the annual taxes and insurance per month. In turn, the woman was to sell the second at a discount in order to raise cash for the commission and other purposes.

As it turned out, she was so satisfied with this arrangement that she agreed to forego payments on the first and third trust deeds until after she moved. The "installment" down payment was therefore entirely deferred.

CLOSING

The papers were drawn up by a title company. The seller did in fact sell the second at a discount for $20,200, which went in part to pay the commissions of $4,543. Everything went without a hitch — Julian had bought an excellent rental home with nothing down, a true "ultimate paper out" on a free and clear property. The sketch summarizes the details of the financing:

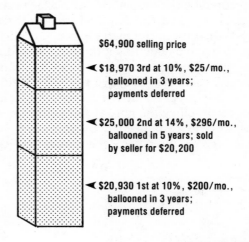

$64,900 selling price

◀ $18,970 3rd at 10%, $25/mo.,
balloond in 3 years;
payments deferred

◀ $25,000 2nd at 14%, $296/mo.,
balloond in 5 years; sold
by seller for $20,200

◀ $20,930 1st at 10%, $200/mo.,
balloond in 3 years;
payments deferred

OUTCOMES AND FUTURE PLANS

Julian's payments on the second are exactly offset by the rental income from the seller-tenant. Since the payments on the 1st and 3rd trust notes are deferred, his cash flow is even. At the same time, depreciation on the property amounts to nearly $4,000 per year — an attractive write off. When the woman moves into her rest home, Julian will rent the property for a small positive cash flow. No major improvements to the property are necessary.

What was the secret to his success? In Julian's own words: "Find out the seller's needs." That insight, coupled with a knowledge of how to combine applicable creative financing techniques and work a little miracle with the discounted second, resulted in a successful win/win transaction.

COMMENTARY

1. At the outset, the seller insisted she "would not carry." But as it turned out, she "carried" the whole thing. What made the difference? The buyer was able to build trust by solving the seller's problems in creative ways. He did not dicker over the price but instead created a climate for trust by raising the price and showing how his terms could be mutually helpful. Instead of getting discouraged by the seller's initial stance of inflexibility, he quietly went about his work getting the facts — especially the fact that the property was free and clear — then formulated a winning strategy.

2. Realtors who may not understand creative finance thoroughly are often mislead into thinking that "nothing down" inevitably means "no commission." This case study is a good illustration of how a buyer can get into a property with none of his own money down and still make sure the real estate agent is assured of getting his commission.

3. Julian put together a transaction involving three balloons, two of which came due after three years, and another after five years. Given the current economic climate, anything shorter than a five-year balloon might present some difficulties. In retrospect, Julian has stated that if he had it to do over again, he would "try harder to extend the notes." To prepare for handling the balloons, he should have written into the documentation a clause permitting substitution of collateral at the option of the buyer and with the approval of the seller. This would have given Julian more flexibility to maneuver when it came time to solve the balloon situation. He should also have negotiated the rollover of the balloons for at least one more year in exchange for some added sweetener if necessary. Possible sweeteners might be a paydown of the principal by a specified amount or an increase in the interest rate.

DOCUMENTATION

UNIVERSAL EARNEST MONEY RECEIPT AND OFFER TO PURCHASE

"This is a legally binding contract: if not understood, seek competent advice."

1. Date and Place of Offer: _____ October 1, _____ 19 81 _____ ; _____ Phoenix _____ Arizona _____
                                                                        (city)   (state)

2. Principals: The undersigned Buyer _____ Julian Calb and/or Nominee _____
agrees to buy and Seller agrees to sell, according to the indicated terms and conditions, the property described as follows:

3. Property: located at _____ 887 Jackson Street _____ Phoenix _____ Arizona _____
                                              (street address)   (city)   (state)

with the following legal description: _____ Lot 512, Star Development _____

including any of the following items if at present attached to the premises: plumbing, heating, and cooling equipment, including stoker and oil tanks, burners, water heaters, electric light fixtures, bathroom fixtures, roller shades, curtain rods and fixtures, draperies, venetian blinds, window and door screens, towel racks, linoleum and other attached floor coverings,

including carpeting, attached television antennas, mailboxes, all trees and shrubs, and any other fixtures EXCEPT _____ None _____

The following personal property shall also be included as part of the purchase: _____
At the closing of the transaction, the Seller, at his expense, shall provide the Buyer with a Bill Of Sale containing a detailed inventory of the personal property included.

4. Earnest Money Deposit: Agent (or Seller) acknowledges receipt from Buyer of _____ One Hundred and 00/100 _____ dollars $ _____ 100.00 _____

in the form of ( ) cash; ( ) personal check; ( ) cashier's check; (X) promissory note at _____ 0 _____ % interest per annum due _____ * _____ 19 _____ -- _____ ; or

other _____ *close of escrow _____

as earnest money deposit to secure and apply on this purchase. Upon acceptance of this agreement in writing and delivery of same to Buyer, the earnest money deposit shall be assigned

to and deposited in the listing Realtor's trust account or _____, to apply on the purchase price at the time of closing.

5. Purchase Price: The total purchase price of the property shall be <u>Sixty-four Thousand Nine Hundred and 00/100</u> dollars

$ <u>64,900.00</u>

6. Payment: Purchase price is to be paid by Buyer as follows:

Aforedescribed earnest money deposit . . . . $ <u>100.00</u>

Additional payment due upon acceptance of this offer . . . . $ <u>--</u>

Additional payment due at closing . . . . $ <u>--</u>

Balance to be paid as follows:

$20,930 by a first Deed of Trust in favor of the Seller payable $200.00 per month or more including 10% interest per annum all due and payable in 3 years from the close of escrow.

$25,000 by a second Deed of Trust in favor of the Seller payable at 14% interest of $296.22 per month or more. All due and payable five years from the close of escrow.

$18,970 by a third Deed of Trust in favor of the Seller payable at $25.00 per month or more including 10% interest all due and payable in three years from close of escrow. Both payments to be sent to American Title and Escrow who will act as collection agent.

Note due Seller to start 30 days after possession by Buyer.

7. Title: Seller agrees to furnish good and marketable title free of all encumbrances and defects, except mortgage liens and encumbrances as set forth in this agreement, and to make

conveyance by Warranty Deed or _____. Seller shall furnish in due course to the Buyer a title insurance policy insuring the Buyer of a good and marketable title in keeping with the terms and conditions of this agreement. Prior to the closing of this transaction, the Seller, upon request, will furnish to the Buyer a preliminary title report made by a title insurance company showing the condition of the title to said property. If the Seller cannot furnish marketable title within thirty days after receipt of the notice to the Buyer containing a written statement of the defects, the earnest money deposit herein receipted shall be refunded to the Buyer and this agreement shall be null and void. The following shall not be deemed encumbrances or defects; building and use restrictions general to the area; utility easements; other easements not inconsistent with Buyer's intended use; zoning or subdivision laws, covenants, conditions, restrictions, or reservations of record; tenancies of record. In the event of sale of other than real property relating to this transaction, Seller will provide evidence of title or right to sell or lease such personal property.

8. Special Representations: Seller warrants and represents to Buyer (1) that the subject property is connected to ( ) public sewer system, ( ) cesspool or septic tank, ( ) sewer system available but not connected, ( ) city water system, ( ) private water system, and that the following special improvements are included in the sale: ( ) sidewalk, ( ) curb and gutter, ( ) special street paving, ( ) special street lighting; (2) that the Seller knows of no material structural defects; (3) that all electrical wiring, heating, cooling, and plumbing systems are free of material defects and will be in good working order at the time the Buyer is entitled to possession; (4) that the Seller has no notice from any government agency of any violation or knowledge of probable violations of the law relating to the subject property; (5) that the Seller has no notice or knowledge of planned or commenced public improvements which may result in special assessments or otherwise directly and materially affect the property; and (6) that the Seller has no notice or knowledge of any liens to be assessed against the property,

EXCEPT <u>None</u>

9. Escrow Instructions: This sale shall be closed on or before _____ 19 ____ by <u>American Title and Escrow</u> or such other closing agent as mutually agreed upon by Buyer and Seller. Buyer and Seller will, immediately on demand, deposit with closing agent all instruments and monies required

to complete the purchase in accordance with the provisions of this agreement. Contract of Sale or Instrument of Conveyance to be made in the name of _____

<u>to be supplied</u>

10. Closing Costs and Pro-Ration: Seller agrees to pay for title insurance policy, preliminary title report (if requested), termite inspection as set forth below, real estate commission, cost of preparing and recording any corrective instruments, and one-half of the escrow fees. Buyer agrees to pay for recording fees for mortgages and deeds of conveyance, all costs or expenses in securing new financing or assuming existing financing, and one-half of the escrow fees. Buyer agrees to pay for recording fees for mortgages and deeds of conveyance, all costs or expenses in securing new financing or assuming existing financing, and one-half of the escrow fees. Taxes for the current year, insurance acceptable to the Buyer, rents, interest, mortgage reserves, maintenance fees, and water and other utilities constituting liens, shall be pro-rated as of closing. Renters' security deposits shall accrue to Buyer at closing. Seller to provide Buyer with all current rental or lease agreements prior to closing.

11. Termite Inspection: Seller agrees, at his expense, to provide written certification by a reputable licensed pest control firm that the property is free of termite infestation. In the event termites are found, the Seller shall have the property treated at his expense and provide acceptable certification that treatment has been rendered. If any structural repairs are required by reason of termite damage as established by acceptable certification, Seller agrees to make necessary repairs not to exceed $500. If repairs exceed $500, Buyer shall first have the right to accept the property "as is" with a credit to the Buyer at closing of $500, or the Buyer may terminate this agreement with the earnest money deposit being promptly returned to the Buyer if the Seller does not agree to pay all costs of treatment and repair.

12. Conditions of Sale: The following conditions shall also apply, and shall, if conflicting with the printed portions of this agreement, prevail and control:

<u>Fire/Hazard insurance to be in the principal amount due Seller at all times.</u>

<u>Buyer to approve preliminary title report.</u>

Buyer agrees to rent property back to Seller for payments due plus 1/12 taxes and insurance per month.

13. **Liability and Maintenance:** Seller shall maintain subject property, including landscaping, in good condition until the date of transfer of title or possession by Buyer, whichever occurs first. All risk of loss and destruction of property, and all expenses of insurance, shall be borne by the seller until the date of possession. If the improvements on the property are destroyed or materially damaged prior to closing, then the Buyer shall have the right to declare this agreement null and void, and the earnest money deposit and all other sums paid by Buyer toward the purchase price shall be returned to the Buyer forthwith.

14. **Possession:** The Buyer shall be entitled to possession of property upon closing or _____, 19 _____.

15. **Default:** In the event the Buyer fails to complete the purchase as herein provided, the earnest money deposit shall be retained by the Seller as the total and entire liquidated damages. In the event the Seller fails to perform any condition of the sale as herein provided, then the Buyer may, at his option, treat the contract as terminated, and all payments made by the Buyer hereunder shall be returned to the Buyer forthwith, provided the Buyer may, at his option, treat this agreement as being in full force and effect with the right to action for specific performance and damages. In the event that either Buyer, Seller, or Agent shall institute suit to enforce any rights hereunder, the prevailing party shall be entitled to court costs and a reasonable attorney's fee.

16. **Time Limit of Offer:** The Seller shall have until

Upon presentation _____, 19 _____ to accept this
(hour)   (date)

offer by delivering a signed copy hereof to the Buyer. If this offer is not so accepted, it shall lapse and the agent (or Seller) shall refund the earnest money deposit to the Buyer forthwith.

17. **General Agreements:** (1) Both parties to this purchase reserve their rights to assign and hereby otherwise agree to cooperate in effecting an Internal Revenue Code 1031 exchange or similar tax-related arrangement prior to close of escrow, upon either party's written notice of intention to do so. (2) Upon approval of this offer by the Seller, this agreement shall become a contract between Buyer and Seller and shall inure to the benefit of the heirs, administrators, executors, successors, personal representatives, and assigns of said parties. (3) Time is of the essence and an essential part of this agreement. (4) This contract constitutes the sole and entire agreement between the parties hereto and no modification of this contract shall be binding unless attached hereto and signed by all parties to the contract. No representations, promises, or inducements not included in this contract shall be binding upon any party hereto.

18. **Buyer's Statement and Receipt:** "I/we hereby agree to purchase the above property in accordance with the terms and conditions above stated and acknowledge receipt of a completed copy of this agreement, which I/we have fully read and understand." Dated _October 1,_ 19 _81_ , _____ (hour)

Address _68 Winchester Blvd._   _[signature] and/or Nominee_ _____ Buyer

Phoenix, Arizona   _____ Buyer

Phone No: Home _611-3339_ Business _593-1852_

19. **Seller's Statement and Response:** "I/we approve and accept the above offer, which I/we have fully read and understand, and agree to the above terms and conditions this day of _____, 19 _____ , _____ (hour)

Address _____ Seller

Phone No: Home _____ Business _____ _____ Seller

20. **Commission Agreement:** Seller agrees to pay a commission of _7_ % of the gross sales price to _Mann Realty_ for services in this transaction, and agrees that, in the event of forfeiture of the earnest money deposit by the Buyer, said deposit shall be divided between the Seller's broker and the Seller (one half to each party), the Broker's part not to exceed the amount of the commission.

21. **Buyer's Receipt for Signed Offer:** The Buyer hereby acknowledges receipt of a copy of the above agreement bearing the Seller's signature in acceptance of this offer.

Dated _____, 19 _____   _____ Buyer

_____ Buyer

COMMENTARY TO DOCUMENTATION

Item 2. "And/or Nominee" is equivalent to "and/or Assigns." One or the other is an essential addition.

Item 4. Even though the deposit was relatively modest, this buyer used a note rather than cash. Why not! It kept money (always in short supply) out of the seller's hands until closing.

Item 6. As mentioned in the commentary to the narrative of the case study, the notes should have clauses providing for rollover of the balloon and substitution of collateral. Three other clauses to have gone for are: prepayment without penalty, assumption, and first right of refusal. Sellers will not always accept all of these conditions, but it never hurts to ask.

Item 9. No date is given for closing. This blank should always be filled in as a control for the proceedings, even if it is only a target to aim at. Frequently the date of closing is so important to the buyer that it becomes a contingency for the agreement, as for example in a multi-chain exchange.

Part IX

Partners

The final area of flexibility in creative finance is the use of partners. For those who rationalize their investment inactivity on the basis of having no money, no credit, no financial statement, no equity, etc., Robert Allen has the following response: "If you don't have it, someone else does." The strategy is to make that someone your partner if you cannot bring the deal off in any other legitimate way. Assuming that the buyer has exhausted all other areas of flexibility, there are any number of quid-pro-quo arrangements he might use to involve a partner. Five of them are covered in this section, with six case studies as illustrations of the major approaches. An outline follows:

Technique No. 41 Borrow Partner's Financial Statement

Many investors without strong financial statements feel they must approach sellers with fear and trembling. Not necessarily. If the deal requires partnership support in this area, a successful investor will add to his team the strength he needs and go into the marketplace with confidence.

In Case No. 41, a creative buyer induced a seller to discount an 11-plex by over 20% and carry most of his equity on a wrap, largely on the strength of his partners' financial statements. Both of the buyer's partners happened to be millionaires, not bad company to keep when facing an experienced seller.

Technique No. 42 Borrow Partner's Money for Down Payment

Frequently an investment partner can be persuaded to loan the buyer all or part of a down payment. The loan may or may not be secured by a trust deed on the property. In any case, the buyer who is just short on funds for the down payment is probably better off to avoid giving the partner an equity position in the property unless absolutely necessary. Equity sharing partnerships are costly when calculated over the entire life of the investment.

Two case studies in this section show how investment partnerships can contribute to the success of real estate purchases. In Case No. 44, an equity sharing partner on a 4-plex deal was able to raise $5,000 of his contribution by borrowing it from his mother. The buyer in Case No. 45 did a similar thing. His mother came up with $10,000 as an investment to help him buy a 6-plex. (It was not just a case of maternal support — the women were shrewd investors who received a good return on their money.)

Technique No. 43   Borrow Partner's Money for Down Payment Until Your Money Comes

In this variation, the partner does not have to leave his cash investment tied up in the property in exchange for an equity position: he gets it all back plus interest as soon as the buyer can put together the cash. The partner puts his money to good use and still comes out with part interest in the property. None of the fifty case studies in this book feature this approach, although something similar to it played a role in Case No. 31, "The Second Mortgage Crank With A Touch of Matrimony."

Technique No. 44   Your Cash Flow/My Equity Or Some Combination

Often the partner provides something other than cash to make the deal fall together. Two earlier case studies illustrate the possibilities. In Case No. 16, "Creative Mortgaging: A Very 'Moving' Experience," the partner provided a property to which a created second mortgage was moved. In Case No. 20, "Nine Techniques Net Buyer $700,000 Beach Motel," a partner provided stock that was used as collateral to borrow $20,000 essential to the deal. Like Bob says: "If you don't have it, someone else does."

Technique No. 45   You Put Up the Cash; I Put Up the Time and Expertise

This is the most common partnership arrangement. In exchange for cash needed at the front end, and sometimes cash to offset negative cash flows and balloons, the partner receives an equity position in the property.

Three case studies feature this approach. In Case No. 46, a beginning investor with only $100 rent money in his pocket was able to close his first deal using $2,000 from a partner. In Case No. 47, a father and son team located a partner with the $7,000 needed to get into a condo. Somewhat bigger stakes were played for in Case No. 48, where the buyer lined up several partners to provide the cash needed ($148,000) to close on a 72-unit property. Regardless of the amount invested by partners, the principles are always the same. The cross-reference matrix in the appendix will guide the reader to seven additional case studies where this technique was used.

Reprinted by permission from the *Nothing Down Advisor*.

"This just arrived — it's an offer from some don't wanter."

43

$900 Positive Cash Flow On Nothing Down 11-Plex

Featuring Technique No. 41
"Borrow Partner's Financial Statement"

In A Nutshell . . .

Type: 11-Plex
Price: $145,000
Source: Classified Ad
Means: Wrap
Techniques: No. 4 — Contract/Wrap
No. 6 — Balloon
No. 41 — Partner's Financial Statement
No. 45 — Partner's Cash/Your Expertise
Features: $900/mo. positive cash flow

James Judd is a building designer from Albuquerque. We have seen elsewhere in this volume how successful he has been with the "Ultimate Paper Out" as described in the case study "Four Houses for the Price of Two." The next two case studies illustrate his abilities with the wrap-around mortgage on multi-unit properties.

LOCATING

James noticed a classified ad for an 11-plex in a low-cost redevelopment area of the city. Because of his skill in building design and construction, he decided to take a look at the possibilities.

SITUATION

The seller was asking $185,000 for the frame-and-stucco structure, with $25,000 down. Each of the eight units was renting for $140/mo. Why was the seller anxious to get out of the property? Management hassles. He was an executive whose time was sorely taxed already, and he hated the management headaches associated with a multi-unit apartment building, particularly in that part of town. The building carried a $45,000 first mortgage held by a private party.

NEGOTIATION

After numerous offers and counteroffers, James got the seller to agree to the following terms: $145,000 price, with $12,500 down and the balance on a wrap-around contract at 10%, ballooned out after 10 years.

A major factor in persuading the seller to reduce his price by $40,000 and cut his down payment requirement in half was the strength of James' partnership situation. James had described the 11-plex to an associate whose brother in Ohio was looking for properties in Albuquerque. The woman and her brother were both millionaires whose financial statements impressed the seller of the 11-plex and induced him to soften his terms.

But another factor was equally important. The listing agent for the property was familiar with James' expertise in the area of renovation and management. Therefore, he actually sold James to the seller as much as the property to James. The seller's primary hot button was management — so he responded to a buyer with the needed strength and experience.

CLOSING

The transaction was handled by means of a wrap-around contract of sale. James and his two partners each took one-third ownership. He provided the management follow-through, while they came up with the $12,500 down payment and the financial strength. The sketch shows the arrangement:

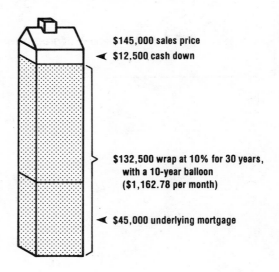

$145,000 sales price
$12,500 cash down

$132,500 wrap at 10% for 30 years, with a 10-year balloon ($1,162.78 per month)

$45,000 underlying mortgage

It is instructive that James writes into his wrap documents a stipulation that the payout applies only to the seller's equity above the underlying loans. That way the low-interest first mortgage on the property is always left intact. The paperwork was handled by a title company.

246   How To Write A Nothing Down Offer

OUTCOMES AND FUTURE PLANS

James' strategy was to create the most comfortable units in that area of town. He, therefore, completed cosmetic improvements in all the units and landscaped the surrounding grounds. Within three month's time he was able to achieve 100% occupancy and raise the rents sufficiently to obtain a positive cash flow of $900 per month. An MAI appraisal on the property shows that it now has a value of $237,500, fully $92,500 above the $145,000 price he paid!

ADDENDUM

A note on James' success in getting partners: while he was negotiating for the 11-plex described above, he was also working out a deal for a 19-plex in the same area of town. The seller was asking $225,000 for the property, which had appraised two years earlier for $237,500. It took three weeks to negotiate down to a price of $220,000. The seller agreed to accept a $55,000 note on other properties in James' portfolio as the down payment. He was then going to sell the note at a discount to raise the cash he needed. Meanwhile, James became distracted with the 11-plex, which he realized was going to take most of his time for the next few months. He therefore turned over his interest in the 19-plex to a friend, for whom he renegotiated the terms at $220,000 with $12,100 down.

While James lost this property, he gained a potential partner. He could have benefited from his skillful negotiation with the 19-plex by selling his interest in it (Technique No. 49 – "Earnest Money Option"). However, he chose to give the deal away. It was more important to him to lay the groundwork for future cash deals with this partner. That's what you call win/win planning.

COMMENTARY

1. This is a splendid example of partnership development. Here is an investor who has a handle on the "big picture." Rather than complain about lack of personal funds, he goes ahead and lines up willing partners who are anxious to put their funds to work in the hands of a skillful property expert. Rather than go after $5,000 or more on an earnest money option with the 19-plex, he has the foresight to know that his friend will probably be ready to put $20,000 or more into a future deal that will net both of them ten times the profit.

2. It would be profitable for James to investigate the flexibility of the private holder of the underlying mortgage. Creative things can be done to generate down payment money when such private mortgagees are willing to cooperate in mutually beneficial deals.

DOCUMENTATION

[The following illustrative document was completed on the basis of data supplied by the buyer.]

UNIVERSAL EARNEST MONEY RECEIPT AND OFFER TO PURCHASE

"This is a legally binding contract: if not understood, seek competent advice."

1. Date and Place of Offer: __July 1,__ 19 __81__ ; __Albuquerque__ (city) __New Mexico__ (state)

2. Principals: The undersigned Buyer __James Judd or Assigns__
agrees to buy and Seller agrees to sell, according to the indicated terms and conditions, the property described as follows:

3. Property: located at __61 Benedict Avenue__ (street address) __Albuquerque__ (city) __New Mexico__ (state)

with the following legal description: __to be supplied__

including any of the following items if at present attached to the premises: plumbing, heating, and cooling equipment, including stoker and oil tanks, burners, water heaters, electric light fixtures, bathroom fixtures, roller shades, curtain rods and fixtures, draperies, venetian blinds, window and door screens, towel racks, linoleum and other attached floor coverings,

including carpeting, attached television antennas, mailboxes, all trees and shrubs, and any other fixtures EXCEPT __None__

The following personal property shall also be included as part of the purchase: _____
At the closing of the transaction, the Seller, at his expense, shall provide the Buyer with a Bill Of Sale containing a detailed inventory of the personal property included.

4. Earnest Money Deposit: Agent (or Seller) acknowledges receipt from Buyer of __Five Hundred and 00/100__ dollars $ __500.00__

in the form of ( ) cash; (X) personal check; ( ) cashier's check; ( ) promissory note at _____% interest per annum due _____ 19 _____ ; or

other _____
as earnest money deposit to secure and apply on this purchase. Upon acceptance of this agreement in writing and delivery of same to Buyer, the earnest money deposit shall be assigned

to and deposited in the listing Realtor's trust account or _____ , to apply on the purchase price at the time of closing.

5. Purchase Price: The total purchase price of the property shall be ___One Hundred Forty-Five Thousand and 00/100___ dollars

$ __145,000.00__

6. Payment: Purchase price is to be paid by Buyer as follows:

Aforedescribed earnest money deposit .... $ ___500.00___

Additional payment due upon acceptance of this offer .... $ ___--___

Additional payment due at closing .... $ __12,000.00__

Balance to be paid as follows:

> Buyer to execute a real estate contract in favor of the Seller in the amount of $132,500.00 payable $1,162.78 per month, including 10% interest per annum, amortized over a period of 30 years, principal and interest all due and payable 10 years from the date of execution.
>
> Payout after 10 years applies only to the Seller's equity. Seller agrees to leave preexisting first mortgage intact.
>
> Buyer may at any time and without penalty pay in full all amounts owing to Seller under conditions and terms of this agreement.

7. Title: Seller agrees to furnish good and marketable title free of all encumbrances and defects, except mortgage liens and encumbrances as set forth in this agreement, and to make conveyance by Warranty Deed or _____. Seller shall furnish in due course to the Buyer a title insurance policy insuring the Buyer of a good and marketable title in keeping with the terms and conditions of this agreement. Prior to the closing of this transaction, the Seller, upon request, will furnish to the Buyer a preliminary title report made by a title insurance company showing the condition of the title to said property. If the Seller cannot furnish marketable title within thirty days after receipt of the notice to the Buyer containing a written statement of the defects, the earnest money deposit herein receipted shall be refunded to the Buyer and this agreement shall be null and void. The following shall not be deemed encumbrances or defects; building and use restrictions general to the area; utility easements; other easements not inconsistent with Buyer's intended use; zoning or subdivision laws, covenants, conditions, restrictions, or reservations of record; tenancies of record. In the event of sale of other than real property relating to this transaction, Seller will provide evidence of title or right to sell or lease such personal property.

8. Special Representations: Seller warrants and represents to Buyer (1) that the subject property is connected to ( ) public sewer system, ( ) cesspool or septic tank, ( ) sewer system available but not connected, ( ) city water system, ( ) private water system, and that the following special improvements are included in the sale: ( ) sidewalk, ( ) curb and gutter, ( ) special street paving, ( ) special street lighting; (2) that the Seller knows of no material structural defects; (3) that all electrical wiring, heating, cooling, and plumbing systems are free of material defects and will be in good working order at the time the Buyer is entitled to possession; (4) that the Seller has no notice from any government agency of any violation or knowledge of probable violations of the law relating to the subject property; (5) that the Seller has no notice or knowledge of planned or commenced public improvements which may result in special assessments or otherwise directly and materially affect the property; and (6) that the Seller has no notice or knowledge of any liens to be assessed against the property,

EXCEPT ___None___.

9. Escrow Instructions: This sale shall be closed on or before ___July 31,___ 19 _81_ by ___Jenkins Escrow and Trust___ or such other closing agent as mutually agreed upon by Buyer and Seller. Buyer and Seller will, immediately on demand, deposit with closing agent all instruments and monies required to complete the purchase in accordance with the provisions of this agreement. Contract of Sale or Instrument of Conveyance to be made in the name of _____

> to be supplied

10. Closing Costs and Pro-Ration: Seller agrees to pay for title insurance policy, preliminary title report (if requested), termite inspection as set forth below, real estate commission, cost of preparing and recording any corrective instruments, and one-half of the escrow fees. Buyer agrees to pay for recording fees for mortgages and deeds of conveyance, all costs or expenses in securing new financing or assuming existing financing, and one-half of the escrow fees. Buyer agrees to pay for recording fees for mortgages and deeds of conveyance, all costs or expenses in securing new financing or assuming existing financing, and one-half of the escrow fees. Taxes for the current year, insurance acceptable to the Buyer, rents, interest, mortgage reserves, maintenance fees, and water and other utilities constituting liens, shall be pro-rated as of closing. Renters' security deposits shall accrue to Buyer at closing. Seller to provide Buyer with all current rental or lease agreements prior to closing.

11. Termite Inspection: Seller agrees, at his expense, to provide written certification by a reputable licensed pest control firm that the property is free of termite infestation. In the event termites are found, the Seller shall have the property treated at his expense and provide acceptable certification that treatment has been rendered. If any structural repairs are required by reason of termite damage as established by acceptable certification, Seller agrees to make necessary repairs not to exceed $500. If repairs exceed $500, Buyer shall first have the right to accept the property "as is" with a credit to the Buyer at closing of $500, or the Buyer may terminate this agreement with the earnest money deposit being promptly returned to the Buyer if the Seller does not agree to pay all costs of treatment and repair.

12. Conditions of Sale: The following conditions shall also apply, and shall, if conflicting with the printed portions of this agreement, prevail and control:

> Subject to inspection and approval by partner within 72 hours of acceptance of this offer.

13. Liability and Maintenance: Seller shall maintain subject property, including landscaping, in good condition until the date of transfer of title or possession by Buyer, whichever occurs first. All risk of loss and destruction of property, and all expenses of insurance, shall be borne by the seller until the date of possession. If the improvements on the property are destroyed or materially damaged prior to closing, then the Buyer shall have the right to declare this agreement null and void, and the earnest money deposit and all other sums paid by Buyer toward the purchase price shall be returned to the Buyer forthwith.

14. Possession: The Buyer shall be entitled to possession of property upon closing or ___--___, 19 ____.

15. Default: In the event the Buyer fails to complete the purchase as herein provided, the earnest money deposit shall be retained by the Seller as the total and entire liquidated damages. In the event the Seller fails to perform any condition of the sale as herein provided, then the Buyer may, at his option, treat the contract as terminated, and all payments made by the Buyer hereunder shall be returned to the Buyer forthwith, provided the Buyer may, at his option, treat this agreement as being in full force and effect with the right to action for specific performance and damages. In the event that either Buyer, Seller, or Agent shall institute suit to enforce any rights hereunder, the prevailing party shall be entitled to court costs and a reasonable attorney's fee.

16. Time Limit of Offer: The Seller shall have until

_____ July 3, _____, 19 __81__ to accept this
(hour)   (date)

offer by delivering a signed copy hereof to the Buyer. If this offer is not so accepted, it shall lapse and the agent (or Seller) shall refund the earnest money deposit to the Buyer forthwith.

17. General Agreements: (1) Both parties to this purchase reserve their rights to assign and hereby otherwise agree to cooperate in effecting an Internal Revenue Code 1031 exchange or similar tax-related arrangement prior to close of escrow, upon either party's written notice of intention to do so. (2) Upon approval of this offer by the Seller, this agreement shall become a contract between Buyer and Seller and shall inure to the benefit of the heirs, administrators, executors, successors, personal representatives, and assigns of said parties. (3) Time is of the essence and an essential part of this agreement. (4) This contract constitutes the sole and entire agreement between the parties hereto and no modification of this contract shall be binding unless attached hereto and signed by all parties to the contract. No representations, promises, or inducements not included in this contract shall be binding upon any party hereto.

18. Buyer's Statement and Receipt: "I/we hereby agree to purchase the above property in accordance with the terms and conditions above stated and acknowledge receipt of a completed copy of this agreement, which I/we have fully read and understand." Dated _____ July 1, _____ 19 __81__ , _____
(hour)

Address _____ 1643 Falcrest Court _____   [signature] or Assigns _____ Buyer

_____ Albuquerque, New Mexico _____   _____ Buyer

Phone No: Home __555-3343__ Business __555-3343__

19. Seller's Statement and Response: "I/we approve and accept the above offer, which I/we have fully read and understand, and agree to the above terms and conditions this day of _____, 19 _____, _____
(hour)

Address _____   _____ Seller

Phone No: Home _____ Business _____   _____ Seller

20. Commission Agreement: Seller agrees to pay a commission of __7__ % of the gross sales price to ____ Eagle Real Estate, Co. ____ for services in this transaction, and agrees that, in the event of forfeiture of the earnest money deposit by the Buyer, said deposit shall be divided between the Seller's broker and the Seller (one half to each party), the Broker's part not to exceed the amount of the commission.

21. Buyer's Receipt for Signed Offer: The Buyer hereby acknowledges receipt of a copy of the above agreement bearing the Seller's signature in acceptance of this offer.

Dated _____, 19 _____   _____ Buyer

         _____ Buyer

COMMENTARY TO DOCUMENTATION

Item 6. The provision for prepayment is wise. Another provision that would have been useful is a rollover clause for the balloon. Buyers in similar situations would do well to follow the example of this investor in limiting the amount of the balloon payoff to the seller's equity.

Into A Knotty-Pine Four-Plex — For $500 Down

Featuring Technique No. 42
''Borrow Partner's Money for Down Payment''

In A Nutshell. . .

Type: 4-plex
Price: $56,900
Source: Classified Ads
Terms: Contract
Means: Purchase Money Trust Deed
Techniques: No. 4 — Contract/Wrap
No. 6 — Balloon
No. 42 — Partner's Money for Down
No. 45 — Partner's Cash/Your Expertise
Strategies: Double rents
Features: Even cash flow

Insurance agent Bill Williamson, of St. Charles, Missouri, was out looking for a 4-plex that he could purchase for nothing down. He was concerned that the price and financing be right, since this was to be his first purchase after taking the seminar. As it turned out, the transaction was (in his words) ''a smooth closing, no surprises, great opportunity!''

LOCATING

He spotted a new listing in the classified ads, one that he hadn't seen before. Without delay he called and learned that he was the first to inquire. (Clearly the responsive buyer has an advantage over the slower competition.)

SITUATION

The seller, a retired carpenter, was offering the 25-year-old 4-plex of 1-bedroom units for $56,900. The building was owned free and clear. While it was generally in excellent condition — a new roof had been installed in 1979 — there was some external cosmetic work on windows and gutters that needed to be done. The interior, however, was exceptionally clean, with around $12,000 worth of knotty pine on the walls and ceilings.

The rents were far below market because the seller had been protective of the somewhat older tenants in his building and because fix-up had been deferred. Even at that, the rents had not been raised in a long while.

NEGOTIATION

At $56,900, the property was **below** market — both Bill and the seller knew that. Moreover, Bill knew that he could raise the rents significantly as soon as he had closed the transaction. In addition, he had done his homework on the location and had learned that a new General Motors manufacturing plant was going to be built just a few miles away. Therefore, he offered full asking price, with $2,000 down. Unfortunately, the seller needed $6,000 down. Bill agreed, knowing that he could find a partner to come up with most of the cash. For his part, the seller agreed to carry all the rest at 12%, with a $20,000 balloon in 10 years, and the balance due in 14 years.

CLOSING

Bill persuaded a partner to invest $5,500 in the deal for half interest in the property. This amount, together with $500 from Bill (less than 1% out of pocket), took care of the down payment. The partner, incidentally, raised $5,000 of his share by borrowing it on a note from his mother with monthly payments of about $100. Because no bank was involved in financing the 4-plex, the closing took place quickly. The sketch summarizes the financing:

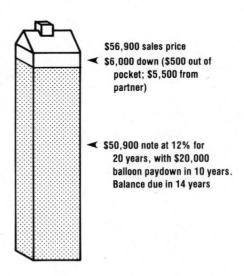

$56,900 sales price
$6,000 down ($500 out of pocket; $5,500 from partner)

$50,900 note at 12% for 20 years, with $20,000 balloon paydown in 10 years. Balance due in 14 years

OUTCOMES AND FUTURE PLANS

Bill immediately **doubled** the rents from $100 to $200 per month. The tenants agreed, knowing that the new landlord would take care of fix-up concerns and other problems that had been ignored. Payments on the $50,900 are $560 per month, leaving a comfortable portion of the rental income for utilities, payments on the $5,000 note, and other expenses, including fix-up. According to the initial cash flow analysis, the property would be around $200 per month negative. As it turned out, the flow was basically even. He anticipates a modest positive cash flow sometime during the second year.

As soon as a vacancy occurs, Bill plans to move into one of the units himself. While he lives there, he will take out a Title I Home Improvement loan in order to install new showers and change the heating system from oil to individually metered heating units for each tenant. This will lower expenses and make the property much more marketable and valuable when sold in the future.

Bill's advice for other investors: "Look at a variety of properties before purchasing. Don't be afraid to make the first offer. You can protect yourself with a contingency clause (subject to inspection and verification of expenses). You **can** buy don't wanters! Incredible! Finally, be realistic about your goals. I plan to buy one house each year for the next ten years."

COMMENTARY

1. The secret of Nothing Down buying is to be creative in acquisitions but highly conservative in analysis. Bill did his homework in analyzing the property and the potential commercial growth in the immediate area. He was conservative in penciling out the annual property operating data schedule. By expecting the worst ($200 per month negative), he was prepared to bite the bullet and move ahead doggedly toward better times. As it turned out, the cash flow was even! Far better to project conservatively and be pleasantly surprised than rationalize the analysis and wind up with an unmanageable negative.

2. It is impressive that Bill entered the negotiations with a partner in his pocket. When the seller insisted on a higher down payment than anticipated, Bill was immediately prepared to turn to a contingent source of capital.

3. As an alternative approach: Bill might have "cranked" the free-and-clear property for, say, $10,000 in order to provide the seller needed capital. The remainder might have been carried back by the seller with payments adjusted to preserve the even cash flow. In this way, Bill might have concluded the deal without recourse to a partner.

DOCUMENTATION

UNIVERSAL EARNEST MONEY RECEIPT AND OFFER TO PURCHASE

"This is a legally binding contract: if not understood, seek competent advice."

1. Date and Place of Offer: ___May 30,___ 19 _81_ ; ___St. Charles___ ___Missouri___
   (city) (state)

2. Principals: The undersigned Buyer ___William Williamson, single and Stanley Considine, single___
   agrees to buy and Seller agrees to sell, according to the indicated terms and conditions, the property described as follows:

3. Property: located at ___1621 41st Street S.W.___ ___St. Charles___ ___Missouri___
   (street address) (city) (state)

   with the following legal description: ___Lots 11 and 12 in Block 16 of Tidewater Addition, Plot___ ___Book 62 Page 12 of the St. Charles County records___

including any of the following items if at present attached to the premises: plumbing, heating, and cooling equipment, including stoker and oil tanks, burners, water heaters, electric light fixtures, bathroom fixtures, roller shades, curtain rods and fixtures, draperies, venetian blinds, window and door screens, towel racks, linoleum and other attached floor coverings,

including carpeting, attached television antennas, mailboxes, all trees and shrubs, and any other fixtures EXCEPT ___None___

The following personal property shall also be included as part of the purchase: _____
At the closing of the transaction, the Seller, at his expense, shall provide the Buyer with a Bill Of Sale containing a detailed inventory of the personal property included.

4. Earnest Money Deposit: Agent (or Seller) acknowledges receipt from Buyer of ___One Hundred and 00/100___ dollars $ ___100.00___

in the form of ( ) cash; ( ) personal check; ( ) cashier's check; ( ) promissory note at _____ % interest per annum due _____ 19 _____ ; or

other _____
as earnest money deposit to secure and apply on this purchase. Upon acceptance of this agreement in writing and delivery of same to Buyer, the earnest money deposit shall be assigned

to and deposited in the listing Realtor's trust account or _____ , to apply on the purchase price at the time of closing.

5. Purchase Price: The total purchase price of the property shall be ___Fifty-six Thousand Nine Hundred and 00/100___ dollars
$ _56,900.00_

6. Payment: Purchase price is to be paid by Buyer as follows:

Aforedescribed earnest money deposit .... $ ___100.00___

Additional payment due upon acceptance of this offer .... $ ___--___

Additional payment due at closing .... $ ___5,900.00___

Balance to be paid as follows:

The Seller shall hold a first Deed of Trust in the amount of $50,900 to be amortized for a period of 20 years with a monthly payment of principal and interest to be $560.46. In addition to the monthly payment, $20,000 shall become due and payable in 10 years from inception of Deed of Trust. Monthly payments shall continue until the 14th year and any outstanding principal payments shall be paid in full at that time. The first payment will be due on August 1, 1981.

7. Title: Seller agrees to furnish good and marketable title free of all encumbrances and defects, except mortgage liens and encumbrances as set forth in this agreement, and to make conveyance by Warranty Deed or _____. Seller shall furnish in due course to the Buyer a title insurance policy insuring the Buyer of a good and marketable title in keeping with the terms and conditions of this agreement. Prior to the closing of this transaction, the Seller, upon request, will furnish to the Buyer a preliminary title report made by a title insurance company showing the condition of the title to said property. If the Seller cannot furnish marketable title within thirty days after receipt of the notice to the Buyer containing a written statement of the defects, the earnest money deposit herein receipted shall be refunded to the Buyer and this agreement shall be null and void. The following shall not be deemed encumbrances or defects; building and use restrictions general to the area; utility easements; other easements not inconsistent with Buyer's intended use; zoning or subdivision laws, covenants, conditions, restrictions, or reservations of record; tenancies of record. In the event of sale of other than real property relating to this transaction, Seller will provide evidence of title or right to sell or lease such personal property.

8. Special Representations: Seller warrants and represents to Buyer (1) that the subject property is connected to ( ) public sewer system, ( ) cesspool or septic tank, ( ) sewer system available but not connected, ( ) city water system, ( ) private water system, and that the following special improvements are included in the sale: ( ) sidewalk, ( ) curb and gutter, ( ) special street paving, ( ) special street lighting; (2) that the Seller knows of no material structural defects; (3) that all electrical wiring, heating, cooling, and plumbing systems are free of material defects and will be in good working order at the time the Buyer is entitled to possession; (4) that the Seller has no notice from any government agency of any violation or knowledge of probable violations of the law relating to the subject property; (5) that the Seller has no notice or knowledge of planned or commenced public improvements which may result in special assessments or otherwise directly and materially affect the property; and (6) that the Seller has no notice or knowledge of any liens to be assessed against the property,

EXCEPT ___None___

9. Escrow Instructions: This sale shall be closed on or before ___July 1,___ 19_81_ by ___Heavenly Realty___ or such other closing agent as mutually agreed upon by Buyer and Seller. Buyer and Seller will, immediately on demand, deposit with closing agent all instruments and monies required to complete the purchase in accordance with the provisions of this agreement. Contract of Sale or Instrument of Conveyance to be made in the name of _____

to be supplied

10. Closing Costs and Pro-Ration: Seller agrees to pay for title insurance policy, preliminary title report (if requested), termite inspection as set forth below, real estate commission, cost of preparing and recording any corrective instruments, and one-half of the escrow fees. Buyer agrees to pay for recording fees for mortgages and deeds of conveyance, all costs or expenses in securing new financing or assuming existing financing, and one-half of the escrow fees. Buyer agrees to pay for recording fees for mortgages and deeds of conveyance, all costs or expenses in securing new financing or assuming existing financing, and one-half of the escrow fees. Taxes for the current year, insurance acceptable to the Buyer, rents, interest, mortgage reserves, maintenance fees, and water and other utilities constituting liens, shall be pro-rated as of closing. Renters' security deposits shall accrue to Buyer at closing. Seller to provide Buyer with all current rental or lease agreements prior to closing.

11. Termite Inspection: Seller agrees, at his expense, to provide written certification by a reputable licensed pest control firm that the property is free of termite infestation. In the event termites are found, the Seller shall have the property treated at his expense and provide acceptable certification that treatment has been rendered. If any structural repairs are required by reason of termite damage as established by acceptable certification, Seller agrees to make necessary repairs not to exceed $500. If repairs exceed $500, Buyer shall first have the right to accept the property "as is" with a credit to the Buyer at closing of $500, or the Buyer may terminate this agreement with the earnest money deposit being promptly returned to the Buyer if the Seller does not agree to pay all costs of treatment and repair.

12. Conditions of Sale: The following conditions shall also apply, and shall, if conflicting with the printed portions of this agreement, prevail and control:

This contract is contingent upon inspection of units 3 and 4 being in similar condition as units 1 and 2. Also subject to verification by Seller as to annual real estate taxes, gas, water, and trash, oil and insurance costs.

13. Liability and Maintenance: Seller shall maintain subject property, including landscaping, in good condition until the date of transfer of title or possession by Buyer, whichever occurs first. All risk of loss and destruction of property, and all expenses of insurance, shall be borne by the seller until the date of possession. If the improvements on the property are destroyed or materially damaged prior to closing, then the Buyer shall have the right to declare this agreement null and void, and the earnest money deposit and all other sums paid by Buyer toward the purchase price shall be returned to the Buyer forthwith.

14. Possession: The Buyer shall be entitled to possession of property upon closing or ___--___, 19___.

15. Default: In the event the Buyer fails to complete the purchase as herein provided, the earnest money deposit shall be retained by the Seller as the total and entire liquidated damages. In the event the Seller fails to perform any condition of the sale as herein provided, then the Buyer may, at his option, treat the contract as terminated, and all payments made by the Buyer hereunder shall be returned to the Buyer forthwith, provided the Buyer may, at his option, treat this agreement as being in full force and effect with the right to action for specific performance and damages. In the event that either Buyer, Seller, or Agent shall institute suit to enforce any rights hereunder, the prevailing party shall be entitled to court costs and a reasonable attorney's fee.

16. Time Limit of Offer: The Seller shall have until

<u>12:00 noon</u>   <u>June 1,</u>   , 19 <u>81</u>   to accept this
    (hour)   (date)

offer by delivering a signed copy hereof to the Buyer. If this offer is not so accepted, it shall lapse and the agent (or Seller) shall refund the earnest money deposit to the Buyer forthwith.

17. General Agreements: (1) Both parties to this purchase reserve their rights to assign and hereby otherwise agree to cooperate in effecting an Internal Revenue Code 1031 exchange or similar tax-related arrangement prior to close of escrow, upon either party's written notice of intention to do so. (2) Upon approval of this offer by the Seller, this agreement shall become a contract between Buyer and Seller and shall inure to the benefit of the heirs, administrators, executors, successors, personal representatives, and assigns of said parties. (3) Time is of the essence and an essential part of this agreement. (4) This contract constitutes the sole and entire agreement between the parties hereto and no modification of this contract shall be binding unless attached hereto and signed by all parties to the contract. No representations, promises, or inducements not included in this contract shall be binding upon any party hereto.

18. Buyer's Statement and Receipt: "I/we hereby agree to purchase the above property in accordance with the terms and conditions above stated and acknowledge receipt of a

completed copy of this agreement, which I/we have fully read and understand." Dated <u>May 30,</u>   19 <u>81</u> , _____
                              (hour)

Address   <u>316 Benton Square</u>   <u>[signature]</u>   Buyer

<u>St. Charles, Missouri</u>   <u>[signature]</u>   Buyer

Phone No: Home <u>221-1561</u> Business <u>893-1452</u>

19. Seller's Statement and Response: "I/we approve and accept the above offer, which I/we have fully read and understand, and agree to the above terms and conditions this day

of _____, 19 _____, _____
                                        (hour)

Address _____ _____ Seller

Phone No: Home _____ Business _____ _____ Seller

20. Commission Agreement: Seller agrees to pay a commission of <u>6</u> % of the gross sales price to <u>Heavenly Realty, Co.</u>

for services in this transaction, and agrees that, in the event of forfeiture of the earnest money deposit by the Buyer, said deposit shall be divided between the Seller's broker and the Seller (one half to each party), the Broker's part not to exceed the amount of the commission.

21. Buyer's Receipt for Signed Offer: The Buyer hereby acknowledges receipt of a copy of the above agreement bearing the Seller's signature in acceptance of this offer.

Dated _____, 19 _____ _____ Buyer

_____ Buyer

NOTE

<u>$50,900.00</u>   <u>July 1, 1981</u>

For Value Received, the undersigned jointly and severally as principals promise to pay to the order of

[Seller]

Fifty Thousand Nine Hundred and 00/100 . . . .($50,900.00)

with interest thereon from date at the rate of 12 percent per annum, said principal and interest to be paid as follows:

1)   Monthly installments of Five Hundred Sixty and 46/100 Dollars-------------($560.46) on the 1st day of August, 1981, and a like amount on the same day of each succeeding month thereafter, for 166 months, the balance of principal and interest to be paid on the 1st day of July, 1995, each of such payments to be applied first in payment of interest due on the entire unpaid principal and the remainder in reduction of the principal, with interest after maturity at the rate of * percent per annum on principal.

2)   One installment of Twenty Thousand and 00/100----------($20,000.00) due on the 1st day of July, 1991.

If default be made in the payment of any of said installments when due, the holder of this note may at the option of said holder declare all unpaid indebtness evidenced by this note immediately due and payable, and thereupon the undersigned agree to pay all costs of collection, including a reasonable attorney's fee. Failure at times to exercise such option shall not constitute a waiver of the right to exercise it later.

In the event default be made in the payment of any installment, when due, and the holder of this note does not exercise its option to declare all unpaid indebtedness due and payable, the undersigned agree to pay, during the period of delinquency, interest on the unpaid balance of the loan at the rate of * percent per annum on principal.

The holder may rearrange, adjust, and extend the times and amounts of payments of interest or principal of this note by agreement with the present or subsequent owner of the real estate securing the same, without notice to or consent of and without releasing any party liable hereon.

*The highest rate allowable by law.

PAYABLE AT:

Secured by Deed of Trust

[Signatures]

ANALYSIS PREPARED BY BUYER PRIOR TO SALE

Analysis
Personal Reconstruction Projection

4 unit apartment building
Price: $56,900
Loans: -0-
Equity: $56,900

Assessed Appraised Values
Land: $11,380   20%
Improvement: $45,520   80%
Personal Property: -0-   0%
NOTE: $45,520 ÷ 4 = $11,380/unit
With stoves ($560), Fridges ($560), A/C ($300), Conversion ($700)
New Worth: $47,640/4 = $11,910/unit
Total New Value: $59,020

Financing:
Existing: None
Potential: 1st $46,900-$51,900
Monthly payments: $516.83 to $571.94
Interest Rate: 12% per annum
Notes: Loan period amortized over twenty years with balloon payments negotiated by the owner.

Gross Scheduled Rental Income	$9,600	
Other Income	0	(potential laundry)
Total Gross Income	$9,600	
Less Vacancy Losses	384	(4%)
Gross Operating Income	$9,216	

Operating Expenses:
Accounting and legal	100	
Advertising and Licenses	0	
Property Insurance	241	
Property Management	0	
Payroll	0	
Personal Property Taxes	0	(no furnishings included)
Real Estate Taxes	465	
Repairs and Maintenance	768	(8%)
Lawn Maintenance	55	($50 mower, $5 gas)
Garbage and water	285	
Supplies	75	(paint, wood treatment)

Utilities:
Electricity	0	
Gas	90	(water heater)
Oil	1,800	

Other Possible Expenses:
A. 4 Refrigerators	$560-1,396	(at $140/at $349)
B. 4 Stoves	$560-2,196	(at $140/at $549)
Air Conditioners*	$300-1,192	(at $75/at $298)
Furnace Conversion*	$700	
*Possible Combination w/Williams type unit	$2677	per news add one unit
Total Other Expenses:	$2120-6,269	

Total Operating Expenses Including A&B	4,999	
Net Operating Income	4,217	
Less Total Annual Debt Service	6,522	at $543.50 × 12
Cash Flow Before Taxes	(2,305)	

COMMENTARY TO DOCUMENTATION

Item 2. Buyers should add words "or Assigns" after their names.

Item 6. The obligation described is sometimes referred to as a purchase money deed of trust (technically a purchase money note secured by a purchase money deed of trust) because there is no commercial lender involved.

The buyers should have attempted to secure the following provisions: rollover clause for the ultimate payout, prepayment without penalty, and assumption (especially since the term of the loan is rather long).

Item 12. A contingency for verification of expenses is a good idea, especially where the buyer feels the data supplied to him are a bit suspicious.

Item 15. The default clause in the original permitted the seller recourse to specific performance besides retention of the deposit. Our "Universal Earnest Money Receipt," with its "total damages" clause, is more favorable to the buyer.

Reprinted by permission from the *Nothing Down Advisor*.

Creative 6-Plex Buyer Lets Money Do The Talking

Featuring Technique No. 42
"Borrow Partner's Money for Down Payment"

In A Nutshell. . .

Type: 6-plex
Price: $160,000
Source: Realtor
Terms: A.I.T.D.
Techniques: No. 4 — Contract/Wrap
No. 6 — Balloon
No. 13 — Borrow Against Insurance
No. 42 — Partners' Money for Down
No. 45 — Partner's Cash/Your Expertise
Strategies: Borrowed fund for negatives
Features: Excellent location

Matthew Hansen, by profession a boy scout comptroller/accountant, attended the Nothing Down Seminar in Seattle in January, 1981. He immediately began to line up his credit and keep watch for promising apartment houses. The creative purchase outlined below was Matthew's first venture into real estate other than his own home.

LOCATING

One real estate agent Matthew contacted in response to a classified ad in the newspaper took him under her wing. He told her that he had $50,000 in equity in his own home to work with. After looking at several pieces of property to no avail, he received a call from her one day with the news that she had found a "real buy." A seller had six different apartment houses he wanted to sell at "minimum terms." One of them was in the price range Matthew wanted.

SITUATION

Immediately Matthew made an inspection. The location was excellent — in an area of big homes, good shopping opportunities, bus service one block away, and — best of all — within one-half block of an exclusive school of art that attracts students from all over the country. Five of the six units were being rented by students because of the convenience. Since the owner was anxious to sell, he had already defined his terms as "the lowest best he would accept." In the case of the 6-plex, he wanted $160,000, with $25,000 down and the rest on a contract at 12% interest with a balloon after five years.

NEGOTIATION

Matthew realized that he would have to be creative to work the terms set by the seller. He immediately went to the realty company to prepare an earnest money offer. Much to his chagrin, he learned that a couple had just submitted an offer before him. His

became the second, and there were two others delivered to the seller that afternoon. Matthew had to wait five days for the first couple to decide to withdraw their offer.

Matthew's position was not negotiated; he simply granted the seller his wishes. It was the buyer's ability to come up with the front-end funds that made the deal succeed. Sometimes money is the best negotiator.

Matthew's offer was accompanied by an earnest money deposit in the form of a note for $2,500 to be converted to cash upon acceptance. As Matthew put it, "I had a sleepless night before signing the papers. Now I had committed myself for $25,000 cash." Unfortunately, the seller would not accept a trust deed on Matthew's house because he was raising cash for a bigger complex.

CLOSING

Where could he come up with the down payment? His own account of the process confirms the wisdom of lining up credit ahead of time: "After I took the Nothing Down Seminar I applied for a loan on my G. I. Insurance (to handle closing costs, etc., on my future purchases). So I got $5,500 at 5% just in time for this purchase. When I did my mother's taxes, I saw that she was keeping most of her money in savings, so I borrowed $10,000 from her at 10%. Then I talked to one of my associates about the great opportunity [for buying the 6-plex]. We decided to buy it together with each putting in $15,000. Thus we had the $25,000 down plus $5,000 for the negative cash flow ($252/mo.) and money for capital improvements." In addition, there was a $500 amount left over to reimburse Matthew for the seminar expenses he had incurred a few months earlier! The benefits of the purchase were to be split 50/50.

The sketch will summarize the financing:

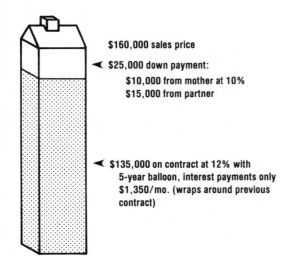

$160,000 sales price

◀ $25,000 down payment:
$10,000 from mother at 10%
$15,000 from partner

◀ $135,000 on contract at 12% with
5-year balloon, interest payments only
$1,350/mo. (wraps around previous
contract)

OUTCOMES AND FUTURE PLANS

Matthew and his partner immediately raised the rents to $1,500 to reduce the negative cash flow from $252 to only $100/mo. They allocated $1,750 for painting and remodeling projects. The balance of their "kitty" was invested in a flexifund at 16% until needed. They plan to hold the property for two years and then sell.

How does he feel about his first income-property acquisition? "This is probably thrilling only to me. But as of January 15 of this year [1981], I had no indication that it would ever be possible for me to think of investing in real estate. The Nothing Down Seminar changed all of that. Now my only restriction has been time enough to follow up on other deals. I feel I can buy **anything** I set my mind to . . . Anything is possible when you see something you really want . . . For the first time, I feel great!"

COMMENTARY:

1. The importance of an effective Realtor cannot be stressed too much. Note how Matthew made it a point of acting on the Realtor's suggestions "immediately." Not only did that put him in a better position in the earnest money order, it demonstrated to the Realtor that she could count on his cooperation.
2. The use of a note as earnest money is an effective way of keeping large sums of the buyer's money from being tied up in the broker's escrow account; in addition, a note for a relatively large sum of money sounds better to the seller than a small cash deposit. It is possible, of course, to convert only part of the note to cash upon acceptance of the offer, leaving until closing the task of coming up with the full amount of cash. Everything is negotiable.
3. Matthew was smart to line up his partnership funds, at least in part, ahead of time. It was a simple matter after locating the deal to go to an associate for the rest.
4. Our only question is this — what about the other five properties being offered by the seller? Why did Matthew not pursue them as well?
5. We note also that this one deal made it possible for Matthew to recover, as he later did, all of the seminar expenses he incurred at the Nothing Down Seminar!
6. Since the contract wraps around an existing private encumbrance, it would have been, and might still be, of interest to negotiate with the holder of the note in regard to the applicable creative techniques (Nos. 35-39). One approach that Matthew should not overlook in the future is the possibility of discounting the underlying note out for cash.

DOCUMENTATION

UNIVERSAL EARNEST MONEY RECEIPT
AND OFFER TO PURCHASE

"This is a legally binding contract: if not understood, seek competent advice."

1. Date and Place of Offer: ____ April 3, ____ 19 81 ; ____ Seattle (city) ____ Washington (state)

2. Principals: The undersigned Buyer ____ Matthew Hansen and Charlene Hansen, husband and wife ____
agrees to buy and Seller agrees to sell, according to the indicated terms and conditions, the property described as follows:

3. Property: located at ____ 12 Hopkins Blvd. (street address) ____ Seattle (city) ____ Washington (state)

with the following legal description: ____ to be supplied

including any of the following items if at present attached to the premises: plumbing, heating, and cooling equipment, including stoker and oil tanks, burners, water heaters, electric light fixtures, bathroom fixtures, roller shades, curtain rods and fixtures, draperies, venetian blinds, window and door screens, towel racks, linoleum and other attached floor coverings,

including carpeting, attached television antennas, mailboxes, all trees and shrubs, and any other fixtures EXCEPT ____ None

The following personal property shall also be included as part of the purchase: _____

At the closing of the transaction, the Seller, at his expense, shall provide the Buyer with a Bill Of Sale containing a detailed inventory of the personal property included.

4. Earnest Money Deposit: Agent (or Seller) acknowledges receipt from Buyer of _____ Two Thousand Five Hundred and 00/100 _____ dollars

$ __2,500.00__

in the form of ( ) cash; ( ) personal check; ( ) cashier's check; (X promissory note at __0__ % interest per annum due _____ * _____ 19 _____ ; or

other ___*upon removal of contingencies___

as earnest money deposit to secure and apply on this purchase. Upon acceptance of this agreement in writing and delivery of same to Buyer, the earnest money deposit shall be assigned

to and deposited in the listing Realtor's trust account or _____, to apply on the purchase price at the time of closing.

5. Purchase Price: The total purchase price of the property shall be _____ One Hundred Sixty Thousand and 00/100 _____ dollars

$ __160,000.00__

6. Payment: Purchase price is to be paid by Buyer as follows:

Aforedescribed earnest money deposit .... $ 2,500.00

Additional payment due upon acceptance of this offer .... $ --

Additional payment due at closing .... $ 22,500.00

Balance to be paid as follows:

$135,000.00 by the Purchaser executing to Seller a Note for the Balance of the Purchase Price, secured by a standard form all-inclusive Deed of Trust on subject property, and payable at the rate of $1,350.00 per month or more at the Purchaser's option including interest at the rate of 12% per annum, computed on the diminishing principal balance. First payment due 30 days from date of closing. Cash out to underlying balance in five years.

This offer is in 2nd position to earnest money dated April 3, 1981 between Horace and Mary Spencer, Buyers, and George Henry, Seller.

7. Title: Seller agrees to furnish good and marketable title free of all encumbrances and defects, except mortgage liens and encumbrances as set forth in this agreement, and to make conveyance by Warranty Deed or _____. Seller shall furnish in due course to the Buyer a title insurance policy insuring the Buyer of a good and marketable title in keeping with the terms and conditions of this agreement. Prior to the closing of this transaction, the Seller, upon request, will furnish to the Buyer a preliminary title report made by a title insurance company showing the condition of the title to said property. If the Seller cannot furnish marketable title within thirty days after receipt of the notice to the Buyer containing a written statement of the defects, the earnest money deposit herein receipted shall be refunded to the Buyer and this agreement shall be null and void. The following shall not be deemed encumbrances or defects; building and use restrictions general to the area; utility easements; other easements not inconsistent with Buyer's intended use; zoning or subdivision laws, covenants, conditions, restrictions, or reservations of record; tenancies of record. In the event of sale of other than real property relating to this transaction, Seller will provide evidence of title or right to sell or lease such personal property.

8. Special Representations: Seller warrants and represents to Buyer (1) that the subject property is connected to ( ) public sewer system, ( ) cesspool or septic tank, ( ) sewer system available but not connected, ( ) city water system, ( ) private water system, and that the following special improvements are included in the sale: ( ) sidewalk, ( ) curb and gutter, ( ) special street paving, ( ) special street lighting; (2) that the Seller knows of no material structural defects; (3) that all electrical wiring, heating, cooling, and plumbing systems are free of material defects and will be in good working order at the time the Buyer is entitled to possession; (4) that the Seller has no notice from any government agency of any violation or knowledge of probable violations of the law relating to the subject property; (5) that the Seller has no notice or knowledge of planned or commenced public improvements which may result in special assessments or otherwise directly and materially affect the property; and (6) that the Seller has no notice or knowledge of any liens to be assessed against the property,

EXCEPT ___None___

9. Escrow Instructions: This sale shall be closed on or before _____ May 15, _____ 19 81 by _____ or such other closing agent as mutually agreed upon by Buyer and Seller. Buyer and Seller will, immediately on demand, deposit with closing agent all instruments and monies required

to complete the purchase in accordance with the provisions of this agreement. Contract of Sale or Instrument of Conveyance to be made in the name of _____

___to be supplied___

10. Closing Costs and Pro-Ration: Seller agrees to pay for title insurance policy, preliminary title report (if requested), termite inspection as set forth below, real estate commission, cost of preparing and recording any corrective instruments, and one-half of the escrow fees. Buyer agrees to pay for recording fees for mortgages and deeds of conveyance, all costs or expenses in securing new financing or assuming existing financing, and one-half of the escrow fees. Buyer agrees to pay for recording fees for mortgages and deeds of conveyance, all costs or expenses in securing new financing or assuming existing financing, and one-half of the escrow fees. Taxes for the current year, insurance acceptable to the Buyer, rents, interest, mortgage reserves, maintenance fees, and water and other utilities constituting liens, shall be pro-rated as of closing. Renters' security deposits shall accrue to Buyer at closing. Seller to provide Buyer with all current rental or lease agreements prior to closing.

11. Termite Inspection: Seller agrees, at his expense, to provide written certification by a reputable licensed pest control firm that the property is free of termite infestation. In the event termites are found, the Seller shall have the property treated at his expense and provide acceptable certification that treatment has been rendered. If any structural repairs are required by reason of termite damage as established by acceptable certification, Seller agrees to make necessary repairs not to exceed $500. If repairs exceed $500, Buyer shall first have the right to accept the property "as is" with a credit to the Buyer at closing of $500, or the Buyer may terminate this agreement with the earnest money deposit being promptly returned to the Buyer if the Seller does not agree to pay all costs of treatment and repair.

12. Conditions of Sale: The following conditions shall also apply, and shall, if conflicting with the printed portions of this agreement, prevail and control:

This agreement is made subject to and contingent upon Purchaser's inspection and written approval of the Property, Income and Expense of operations within 5 days of Seller's acceptance of this offer. Seller agrees to make information and the property available to the Purchaser and failure of the Purchaser to give approval in writing within said time period will render this Agreement null and void.

13. Liability and Maintenance: Seller shall maintain subject property, including landscaping, in good condition until the date of transfer of title or possession by Buyer, whichever occurs first. All risk of loss and destruction of property, and all expenses of insurance, shall be borne by the seller until the date of possession. If the improvements on the property are destroyed or materially damaged prior to closing, then the Buyer shall have the right to declare this agreement null and void, and the earnest money deposit and all other sums paid by Buyer toward the purchase price shall be returned to the Buyer forthwith.

14. Possession: The Buyer shall be entitled to possession of property upon closing or _____ -- _____, 19 _____.

15. Default: In the event the Buyer fails to complete the purchase as herein provided, the earnest money deposit shall be retained by the Seller as the total and entire liquidated damages. In the event the Seller fails to perform any condition of the sale as herein provided, then the Buyer may, at his option, treat the contract as terminated, and all payments made by the Buyer hereunder shall be returned to the Buyer forthwith, provided the Buyer may, at his option, treat this agreement as being in full force and effect with the right to action for specific performance and damages. In the event that either Buyer, Seller, or Agent shall institute suit to enforce any rights hereunder, the prevailing party shall be entitled to court costs and a reasonable attorney's fee.

16. Time Limit of Offer: The Seller shall have until

_____ 12:00 midnight _____ April 8, _____, 19 __81__ to accept this
(hour) (date)

offer by delivering a signed copy hereof to the Buyer. If this offer is not so accepted, it shall lapse and the agent (or Seller) shall refund the earnest money deposit to the Buyer forthwith.

17. General Agreements: (1) Both parties to this purchase reserve their rights to assign and hereby otherwise agree to cooperate in effecting an Internal Revenue Code 1031 exchange or similar tax-related arrangement prior to close of escrow, upon either party's written notice of intention to do so. (2) Upon approval of this offer by the Seller, this agreement shall become a contract between Buyer and Seller and shall inure to the benefit of the heirs, administrators, executors, successors, personal representatives, and assigns of said parties. (3) Time is of the essence and an essential part of this agreement. (4) This contract constitutes the sole and entire agreement between the parties hereto and no modification of this contract shall be binding unless attached hereto and signed by all parties to the contract. No representations, promises, or inducements not included in this contract shall be binding upon any party hereto.

18. Buyer's Statement and Receipt: "I/we hereby agree to purchase the above property in accordance with the terms and conditions above stated and acknowledge receipt of a completed copy of this agreement, which I/we have fully read and understand." Dated _____ April 3, _____ 19 __81__, _____
(hour)

Address _____ 47 Park Avenue _____ [signature] _____ Buyer

_____ Seattle, Washington _____ [signature] _____ Buyer

Phone No: Home __611-4321__ Business __812-5507__

19. Seller's Statement and Response: "I/we approve and accept the above offer, which I/we have fully read and understand, and agree to the above terms and conditions this day

of _____, 19 _____, _____
(hour)

Address _____ Seller

Phone No: Home _____ Business _____ Seller

20. Commission Agreement: Seller agrees to pay a commission of _____ $590.00 _____ to _____ Banner Realty _____

for services in this transaction, and agrees that, in the event of forfeiture of the earnest money deposit by the Buyer, said deposit shall be divided between the Seller's broker and the Seller (one half to each party), the Broker's part not to exceed the amount of the commission.

21. Buyer's Receipt for Signed Offer: The Buyer hereby acknowledges receipt of a copy of the above agreement bearing the Seller's signature in acceptance of this offer.

Dated _____, 19 _____ _____ Buyer

_____ Buyer

Promissory Note

(INTEREST INCLUDED — DUE DATE)

$135,000.00   May 5, 1981

For value received, Matthew Hansen and Claudette Hansen, husband and wife and Frank Hardy and Lois Hardy, husband and wife, promise to pay to Jules Denton, an unmarried person, or order, at Agency of Beneficiary's choice, the sum of one hundred thirty-five thousand and no/100 DOLLARS, with interest from May 15, 1981 on unpaid principal at the rate of 12 percent per annum; principal and interest payable in installments of one thousand three hundred fifty and no/100 ($1,350.00) Dollars or more on the 15th day of each calendar month, beginning on the 15th day of June, 1981 and continuing until the 15th day of May, 1986 at which time the Beneficiary's equity shall be cashed out to the then balance of the underlying Real Estate Contract in favor of Sarah Benson as recorded under Auditor's File No. 6606135, which contract the Grantors herein will assume and agree to pay according to its terms and conditions.

Each payment shall be credited first on interest then due and the remainder on principal; and interest shall thereupon cease upon the principal so credited. Should default be made in payment of any installment when due the whole sum of principal and interest shall become immediately due at the option of the holder of this note. Principal and interest payable in lawful money of the United States. If action be instituted on this note, I promise to pay such sum as the Court may fix as attorney's fees. This note is secured by a Deed of Trust of even date.

_____
Matthew Hansen

_____
Claudette Hansen

_____
Frank Hardy

_____
Lois Hardy

The following partnership agreement was used in the transaction:

Statement of Understanding and Agreement for Holding Real Estate by "Tenancy in Common"

This agreement is between Matthew Hansen and Claudette Hansen, husband and wife, and Frank Hardy and Lois Hardy, husband and wife, for the ownership and operation of the income property at 615 Bertha Ave., Seattle, WN. The legal description of the property is [as given].

1. **Term.** This agreement shall start as of May 15, 1981, the date of acquisition of the property, and shall continue until, by mutual agreement, the property is sold.

2. **Capital.** It is agreed that each of the two families will put $15,000.00 into a common pool to make the down payment and to pay expenses in excess of income and for capital improvements as needed and agreed upon.

3. **Profit and Loss.** Each family shall own 50% interest in the property, and will share net profits or net losses at the same ratio. Profit from the sale of the property will also be shared at the 50% ratio. Exception to this item is contained in item #4.

4. **Operation.** It is agreed that the work load of operating this income property shall be shared on an equal basis between the families. In the event that one family shall be unable to continue sharing the work load because of moving or death, a management fee of 10% of the monthly rents will be paid for services rendered by the remaining family, until property is sold. Fee shall commence on the first day of such event.

5. **Compensation.** No compensation for services by the families will be paid to any member of this agreement, except as stated in #4.

6. **Management.** All members of this agreement shall have equal rights in the operation of this property, but Matthew Hansen is hereby appointed and designated as general manager to act for and on behalf of the members in the ordinary course of operation of the property (on a non-fee basis).

7. **Banking.** Banking will be done through ABC Mutual Savings Bank. Authorized check signers will be Matthew Hansen and Frank Hardy. All monies received from operation of the property will be deposited to the account, or at such other bank, from time to time as designated by members. All expenditures will be paid by check. Any member shall be reimbursed for expenses on behalf of the property by submitting receipts to the manager.

8. **Books.** The books will be maintained by Matthew Hansen and each member shall at all times have access thereto. Books shall be kept on a calendar year basis and shall be closed at year end. A financial statement shall be issued to each family for inclusion on personal tax reports.

9. **Termination.** It is agreed that this property shall be held for one year and one day, and that it shall be sold by May 31, 1983, and this agreement to be terminated on date of sale. Each family shall have the opportunity to buy the other 50% share of the property, based on the fair market value at that time.

10. **Death.** In the event of the death of one member, the surviving spouse shall continue to hold the family share, per clause 3 & 4. In the event of death of both members of a family, the estate of that family shall continue a share per clause 4. If such event happens after May 16, 1982, property will be sold as soon as possible and final disposition of funds be made. Surviving family shall have first right to buy the other 50%, based on fair market value at that time.

11. **Assignment.** No member, without the written consent of the other members, shall have any right to sell, assign, pledge or mortgage his or her interest in the property, prior to May 16, 1982.

In witness Where of, all members have signed this agreement on this _____ day of _____, 1981.

[signatures]

COMMENTARY TO DOCUMENTATION

Item 2. "Or Assigns" is an essential addition to this line.

Item 4. The use of a note as earnest money permits a larger amount to be involved. The liability to the buyer is greater with larger amounts, since the note will have to be honored just as if it were cash. However, the buyer has the use of the cash in the meantime, and the seller is psychologically tuned into greater trust because a larger amount is used.

Item 12. This item was preprinted in the original and is phrased to put the greater pressure on the buyer. However, the contingency of access to expense records is an excellent idea that deserves consideration by other investors.

Reprinted by permission from the *Nothing Down Advisor*.

"Every month I collect your rent . . . and every month I have to remind you —
NO PETS!"

Young Investor Finds Discounted Properties — On Foot!

**Featuring Technique No. 45
"You Put Up The Cash; I Put Up
The Time and Expertise"**

In A Nutshell . . .

Type: SFH
Price: $10,000
Source: Agent
Means: Purchase Money Mortgage
Techniques: No. 4 — Contract/Wrap
No. 6 — Balloon
No. 45 — Partner's Cash/Your Expertise
Strategies: Delay payments for 60 days
Features: Discounted 33⅓%, positive cash flow

Brent Markham of Atlanta is an investor with a unique set of resources. As he puts it in his own words: "I'm a student without a job, money, car, or credit. But I have confidence and persistence — and a lot of personal debt. Incidently, my roommate is kicking me out of the apartment because I used my half of the rent as earnest money on the house, which I'll occupy to fix up, with no payment for 60 days."

The house he is referring to is his very first real estate transaction as a graduate of the Nothing Down Seminar. The details are given below.

LOCATING

Brent had been spending his days on foot looking around promising neighborhoods for real estate opportunities. His target was a SFH in the range of $20,000. After a few days of sore feet and no luck, he asked a real estate agent if she had any properties in that range that had been listed longer than three or four months. In response, she sent him over to the property that became his first nothing down success story.

SITUATION

It was a small 30-year-old, free and clear single family home with two bedrooms and two baths. Under the heading "financing," the listing indicated the following invitation: "Any." That was flexible enough. The asking price was $15,000 with $2,500 down and the balance at 14% for 20 years. Considerable cosmetic work was needed.

NEGOTIATION

In the initial data-gathering phase, Brent asked the following questions: Why was she selling? Did she really need the money? Why had the property not sold before? From these questions he learned that her husband had suffered a stroke. Her time did not permit her to worry about this rental property as well as their own home. She did not really need the money asked as down payment in the listing. As to why the property had not sold — the tenants who were there before had been "hellacious." They even went so far as to paint the inside walls dark blue and the ceilings black. After they left, no one at the real estate office really made an effort to show the house. No one seemed interested.

But Brent was interested. He saw in this little SFH the opportunity he was looking for to pull himself up by his bootstraps. So he offered the woman $10,000, with $1,000 down and the balance at 9% for 15 years. The earnest money document asked for a six weeks interim before closing (a fairly long wait on a purchase money mortgage). But Brent had his reasons.

It took the seller two hours to respond affirmatively. Brent was ecstatic. His approach to the agent had paid off. He had told the agent that it would cost almost $4,000 to repair the house and that if the seller would knock $5,000 off the asking price, he would buy the house. In fact, the seller wound up reducing her price by $5,500. That is flexibility.

CLOSING

Brent figured that by doing the work himself, he could get by with $1,000 in cosmetic improvements to the house to start with. And he needed $1,000 for the down payment. The problem was that he had only his rent money of $100, which he had used for the earnest money. The solution to his problem was easy — he found an investor who was willing to put $2,000 into the deal in exchange for half interest. He had left himself plenty of time until closing to accomplish this task.

The financing is summarized in the following sketch:

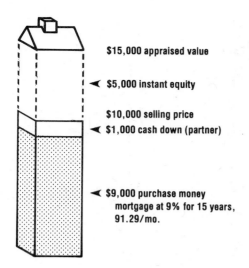

$15,000 appraised value

◄ $5,000 instant equity

$10,000 selling price
◄ $1,000 cash down (partner)

◄ $9,000 purchase money
mortgage at 9% for 15 years,
91.29/mo.

By getting the seller to delay the first payment for 60 days, Brent left himself enough time to take care of the cosmetic improvements (using the partner's money).

OUTCOMES AND FUTURE PLANS

The property, when improved, will rent for $150 to $200 per month. The new owner's plans include selling the house in order to pay his debts to his roommate and others (around $800) and have enough money to get his portfolio rolling. "I have no job, no savings, and one pair of worn out shoes after walking through several neighborhoods looking for houses."

He feels the house will sell for around $20,000 to $22,000 with $4,000 down and a wrap at 13½ to 14½%. The partner will get half of the down (which constitutes his entire investment) plus half of the equity. They may then sell the mortgage at a discount to raise investment capital.

In retrospect, Brent feels that he should have made a lower offer with a lower interest rate. "I should have asked the seller to pay the closing costs of $85.00. They were the original owners of the house when it was built and had never sold it — so I just continued the abstract and went to the court house and checked the title myself." As it was, the down payment went mostly for the commission ($700); the sale was practically an "Ultimate Paper Out."

His advice to others getting started in the real estate investment world: "Get a multiple listing service book, a newspaper, and a phone. Look at back issues of the MLS book and find slow selling lower priced properties. Every one here is looking for the $35,000 to $65,000 houses. They pass up the $15,000 to $30,000 bargains, many of which can be bought for less and sold for more with low down payments and lots of paper to other investors or young couples looking for a home."

COMMENTARY

1. Here is a young man with pluck. Beginning with nothing but $100 rent money and a pair of shank's ponies, he has started his investment program with a minimum of risk and a maximum of benefits. His case is symbolic of the plight of so many bright and eager people who have been locked in a renter's world. Most continue to pour their rent money down the drain. Here is a person who — with a little knowledge of creative finance and a lot of courage — catapults his $100 rent money into $5,000 equity and a monthly cash flow of $50 to $100. There is no stopping him now. He was hurting — and did something about it. The small $10,000 SFH is not much, but wait till you see Brent Markham five years from now.

2. Brent was smart enough to identify for himself a real estate domain that fit his current program — the neglected "bread and butter" house that could lead into a fairly large discount. The discount serves as the catapult to get the buyer off to a flying leap.

3. Brent also has a strategy in mind for disposing of his cosmetically improved properties — he has his eye on the young couples who want a home but cannot afford one in the middle range of prices. It is a simple but effective plan: buy discounted houses for low or no down and resell them for low or no down at a higher price. There is no faster way for the beginner to raise assets for getting into the bigger deals.

4. The use of partners is perhaps the most neglected tool of the nothing down investor. One does not rush into partnerships, particulary because they are expensive, costing as much as half the benefits. However, when a partner is absolutely essential, there is no better solution. Brent has learned this lesson early in his career. He is aware, also, of little twists and creative practices like asking the seller to delay the first payment for 60 days in order to avoid negative cash flow prior to renting out the property. What prompted him to ask for this concession? The fact that he had absolutely no money! Most of the techniques of creative finance and creative negotiation were developed to fill a need on the part of the investor. Creativity is nothing more than finding alternative solutions to problems that occur every day.

UNIVERSAL EARNEST MONEY RECEIPT
AND OFFER TO PURCHASE

"This is a legally binding contract: if not understood, seek competent advice."

1. Date and Place of Offer: __July 15,__ 19 __81__ ; __Atlanta__ __Georgia__
(city) (state)

2. Principals: The undersigned Buyer __Brent Markham__
agrees to buy and Seller agrees to sell, according to the indicated terms and conditions, the property described as follows:

3. Property: located at __1412 Elm Street__ __Atlanta__ __Georgia__
(street address) (city) (state)

with the following legal description: __Land Lot 12 of the 20th District of Fulton County, Georgia,__
__being Lot 18, South Atlanta Subdivision__

including any of the following items if at present attached to the premises: plumbing, heating, and cooling equipment, including stoker and oil tanks, burners, water heaters, electric light fixtures, bathroom fixtures, roller shades, curtain rods and fixtures, draperies, venetian blinds, window and door screens, towel racks, linoleum and other attached floor coverings,

including carpeting, attached television antennas, mailboxes, all trees and shrubs, and any other fixtures EXCEPT __None__

The following personal property shall also be included as part of the purchase: _____
At the closing of the transaction, the Seller, at his expense, shall provide the Buyer with a Bill Of Sale containing a detailed inventory of the personal property included.

4. Earnest Money Deposit: Agent (or Seller) acknowledges receipt from Buyer of __One Hundred and 00/100__ dollars $ __100.00__

in the form of ( ) cash; (X) personal check; ( ) cashier's check; ( ) promissory note at _____% interest per annum due _____ 19 _____ ; or

other _____
as earnest money deposit to secure and apply on this purchase. Upon acceptance of this agreement in writing and delivery of same to Buyer, the earnest money deposit shall be assigned

to and deposited in the listing Realtor's trust account or _____, to apply on the
purchase price at the time of closing.

5. Purchase Price: The total purchase price of the property shall be __Ten Thousand and 00/100__ dollars $ __10,000.00__

6. Payment: Purchase price is to be paid by Buyer as follows:

Aforedescribed earnest money deposit .... $ __100.00__

Additional payment due upon acceptance of this offer .... $ __--__

Additional payment due at closing .... $ __900.00__

Balance to be paid as follows:
__Seller will accept from Purchaser one note secured by a purchase money__
__security deed, secured by said property, in the principal amount of__
__$9,000.00 bearing interest at the rate of 9% per annum and amortized over__
__180 equal monthly payments of $91.29 each, including principal and interest.__

__Payments on purchase money mortgage shall not begin and interest shall not__
__accrue until 60 days after closing.__

7. Title: Seller agrees to furnish good and marketable title free of all encumbrances and defects, except mortgage liens and encumbrances as set forth in this agreement, and to make

conveyance by Warranty Deed or _____ Seller shall furnish in due course
to the Buyer a title insurance policy insuring the Buyer of a good and marketable title in keeping with the terms and conditions of this agreement. Prior to the closing of this transaction, the Seller, upon request, will furnish to the Buyer a preliminary title report made by a title insurance company showing the condition of the title to said property. If the Seller cannot furnish marketable title within thirty days after receipt of the notice to the Buyer containing a written statement of the defects, the earnest money deposit herein receipted shall be refunded to the Buyer and this agreement shall be null and void. The following shall not be deemed encumbrances or defects; building and use restrictions general to the area; utility easements; other easements not inconsistent with Buyer's intended use; zoning or subdivision laws, covenants, conditions, restrictions, or reservations of record; tenancies of record. In the event of sale of other than real property relating to this transaction, Seller will provide evidence of title or right to sell or lease such personal property.

8. Special Representations: Seller warrants and represents to Buyer (1) that the subject property is connected to ( ) public sewer system, ( ) cesspool or septic tank, ( ) sewer system available but not connected, ( ) city water system, ( ) private water system, and that the following special improvements are included in the sale: ( ) sidewalk, ( ) curb and gutter, ( ) special street paving, ( ) special street lighting; (2) that the Seller knows of no material structural defects; (3) that all electrical wiring, heating, cooling, and plumbing systems are free of material defects and will be in good working order at the time the Buyer is entitled to possession; (4) that the Seller has no notice from any government agency of any violation or knowledge of probable violations of the law relating to the subject property; (5) that the Seller has no notice or knowledge of planned or commenced public improvements which may result in special assessments or otherwise directly and materially affect the property; and (6) that the Seller has no notice or knowledge of any liens to be assessed against the property,

EXCEPT __None__

9. Escrow Instructions: This sale shall be closed on or before __August 28,__ 19 __81__ by _____

or such other closing agent as mutually agreed upon by Buyer and Seller. Buyer and Seller will, immediately on demand, deposit with closing agent all instruments and monies required

to complete the purchase in accordance with the provisions of this agreement. Contract of Sale or Instrument of Conveyance to be made in the name of _____

10. **Closing Costs and Pro-Ration:** Seller agrees to pay for title insurance policy, preliminary title report (if requested), termite inspection as set forth below, real estate commission, cost of preparing and recording any corrective instruments, and one-half of the escrow fees. Buyer agrees to pay for recording fees for mortgages and deeds of conveyance, all costs or expenses in securing new financing or assuming existing financing, and one-half of the escrow fees. Buyer agrees to pay for recording fees for mortgages and deeds of conveyance, all costs or expenses in securing new financing or assuming existing financing, and one-half of the escrow fees. Taxes for the current year, insurance acceptable to the Buyer, rents, interest, mortgage reserves, maintenance fees, and water and other utilities constituting liens, shall be pro-rated as of closing. Renters' security deposits shall accrue to Buyer at closing. Seller to provide Buyer with all current rental or lease agreements prior to closing.

11. **Termite Inspection:** Seller agrees, at his expense, to provide written certification by a reputable licensed pest control firm that the property is free of termite infestation. In the event termites are found, the Seller shall have the property treated at his expense and provide acceptable certification that treatment has been rendered. If any structural repairs are required by reason of termite damage as established by acceptable certification, Seller agrees to make necessary repairs not to exceed $500. If repairs exceed $500, Buyer shall first have the right to accept the property "as is" with a credit to the Buyer at closing of $500, or the Buyer may terminate this agreement with the earnest money deposit being promptly returned to the Buyer if the Seller does not agree to pay all costs of treatment and repair.

12. **Conditions of Sale:** The following conditions shall also apply, and shall, if conflicting with the printed portions of this agreement, prevail and control:

Purchaser to pay closing costs.

Purchaser agrees to accept property in its "as is" condition.

This contract shall survive the closing, execution, and delivery of warranty deed, as agreed herein by the undersigned.

13. **Liability and Maintenance:** Seller shall maintain subject property, including landscaping, in good condition until the date of transfer of title or possession by Buyer, whichever occurs first. All risk of loss and destruction of property, and all expenses of insurance, shall be borne by the seller until the date of possession. If the improvements on the property are destroyed or materially damaged prior to closing, then the Buyer shall have the right to declare this agreement null and void, and the earnest money deposit and all other sums paid by Buyer toward the purchase price shall be returned to the Buyer forthwith.

14. **Possession:** The Buyer shall be entitled to possession of property upon closing or _____, 19_____.

15. **Default:** In the event the Buyer fails to complete the purchase as herein provided, the earnest money deposit shall be retained by the Seller as the total and entire liquidated damages. In the event the Seller fails to perform any condition of the sale as herein provided, then the Buyer may, at his option, treat the contract as terminated, and all payments made by the Buyer hereunder shall be returned to the Buyer forthwith, provided the Buyer may, at his option, treat this agreement as being in full force and effect with the right to action for specific performance and damages. In the event that either Buyer, Seller, or Agent shall institute suit to enforce any rights hereunder, the prevailing party shall be entitled to court costs and a reasonable attorney's fee.

16. **Time Limit of Offer:** The Seller shall have until

_____, 19_____ to accept this
(hour)   (date)

offer by delivering a signed copy hereof to the Buyer. If this offer is not so accepted, it shall lapse and the agent (or Seller) shall refund the earnest money deposit to the Buyer forthwith.

17. **General Agreements:** (1) Both parties to this purchase reserve their rights to assign and hereby otherwise agree to cooperate in effecting an Internal Revenue Code 1031 exchange or similar tax-related arrangement prior to close of escrow, upon either party's written notice of intention to do so. (2) Upon approval of this offer by the Seller, this agreement shall become a contract between Buyer and Seller and shall inure to the benefit of the heirs, administrators, executors, successors, personal representatives, and assigns of said parties. (3) Time is of the essence and an essential part of this agreement. (4) This contract constitutes the sole and entire agreement between the parties hereto and no modification of this contract shall be binding unless attached hereto and signed by all parties to the contract. No representations, promises, or inducements not included in this contract shall be binding upon any party hereto.

18. **Buyer's Statement and Receipt:** "I/we hereby agree to purchase the above property in accordance with the terms and conditions above stated and acknowledge receipt of a completed copy of this agreement, which I/we have fully read and understand." Dated ___July 15,_____ 19__81__, _____
                                                                                                                              (hour)

Address _____126 4th Avenue South_____   [signature] _____ Buyer

_____Atlanta, Georgia_____   _____ Buyer

Phone No: Home ____555-1516____ Business ___678-5555___

19. **Seller's Statement and Response:** "I/we approve and accept the above offer, which I/we have fully read and understand, and agree to the above terms and conditions this day

of _____, 19_____, _____
                                                              (hour)

Address _____   _____ Seller

Phone No: Home _____ Business _____   _____ Seller

20. **Commission Agreement:** Seller agrees to pay a commission of ___7___ % of the gross sales price to ___Hansen Realty_____
for services in this transaction, and agrees that, in the event of forfeiture of the earnest money deposit by the Buyer, said deposit shall be divided between the Seller's broker and the Seller (one half to each party), the Broker's part not to exceed the amount of the commission.

21. **Buyer's Receipt for Signed Offer:** The Buyer hereby acknowledges receipt of a copy of the above agreement bearing the Seller's signature in acceptance of this offer.

Dated _____, 19_____   _____ Buyer

                                                              _____ Buyer

COMMENTARY TO DOCUMENTATION

Item 2. The buyer should write "or Assigns" after his name.

Item 5. Provisions in the purchase money note should have included: substitution of collateral, prepayment provisions without penalty, and assumption.

It is possible that the IRS will impute 10% interest on the payments made in fulfilling the contract (both to seller and buyer). That is, even though the stated interest is 9%, the IRS will likely insist that the amount of money paid and received be allocated such that the interest portion is 10%, rather than 9%. The IRS is interested in making sure that sellers are not attempting to shift too much into the long-term capital gains area, rather than the interest (ordinary income) area.

Item 12. According to the provisions of the note, payments and interest accrual are not to begin until 60 days after closing. Does this imply that the first payment (on the 60th day) will be a principal-only payment? Since interest is paid in arrears, the second payment (after 90 days) would be the first one to contain interest. This condition is unclear — but it seems to be a bonus for the buyer.

Item 14. No date is given for possession. Here is one line not to leave blank in the earnest money form!

Item 16. No time limit is given for the seller's acceptance of the offer. Unless the offer is accepted on the spot (as the offer is filled out with all parties present), a specific time limit for acceptance should always be given.

Reprinted by permission from the *Nothing Down Advisor.*

Father/Son Team Perfect Nothing Down Partnership System

Featuring Technique No. 45
''You Put Up The Cash; I Put Up
The Time and Expertise''

In A Nutshell. . .

Type: Condo
Price: $70,000
Source: Finder referral
Terms: Assumption and carry back
Techniques: No. 4 — Contract/Wrap
No. 13 — Borrow Against Insurance
No. 45 — Partner's Cash/Your Expertise
Strategies: Partner covers negative
Features: System can be used repeatedly

LOCATING

Jim Davis of San Diego was in the market for condos in the $60,000 to $90,000 price range. He made arrangements with the manager of a large condo project in a desirable part of town to scout for good opportunities. For a small finder's fee conditioned on a consummated purchase, the manager was to inform Jim of any situation where an owner was anxious to sell. The arrangement soon paid off.

SITUATION

Jim learned from the condo manager that one of the occupants was anxious to sell. He was a judge with cardiac problems. Since he was near retirement and had recently remarried, he was planning to move to larger quarters. The unit, which was not yet listed with a Realtor, had an assumable first trust deed of $32,300 at 9¾% interest. Except for minor cosmetic touch-up needs, the property was in excellent condition.

NEGOTIATION

The owner opened with his offer to sell the unit for $75,000, with an earnest money deposit of $1,000, a down payment of $10,000, and a carry back on the balance in the form of a second trust deed at 14% for 25 years. Jim put his philosophy of negotiation into effect, i.e., to get to know the seller's problems, investment needs, and attitudes in order to arrive as soon as possible at a mutually beneficial arrangement.

Jim asked what the seller intended to do with the down payment. Upon learning that the judge did not need the money but was planning to invest it locally in a certificate of deposit, Jim explained that the tax liability would be lessened if the down payment were lowered. He was also able to persuade the seller that a steady 12% on the carry back would be a dependable source of monthly income.

Since the seller was unfamiliar with comparable sales in his development, Jim took the time to bring together figures from recent transactions. The figures indicated that the $75,000 sales price was around $5,000 too high. Therefore, Jim offered to pay $70,000, with $500 deposit and $7,000 down, the balance to be paid over 25 years at 12%. The seller accepted, the whole process having taken less than two hours.

CLOSING

Drawing up the Real Estate Purchase Contract and Receipt for Deposit was no problem. Jim had a Realtor friend check the wording and figures. The only problem was to come up with the down payment. That's where the father/son combination came into play. Jim's son was an insurance agent who kept a file of contacts with sums of money invested for small returns like 5 or 6% — as in the cash value of whole-life insurance policies. Together, they selected a partner who could provide assets for the condo transaction, including the down payment and coverage for negatives and expenses.

The arrangement was generous for the partner — 60% ownership in the condo, naturally with 60% of the tax benefits. The other 40% was split between Jim and his son, the father retaining the partnership management rights. The financial arrangement is summarized in the sketch:

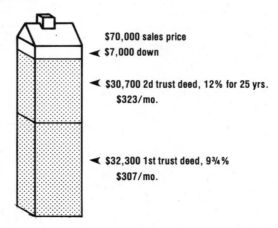

$70,000 sales price
$7,000 down
$30,700 2d trust deed, 12% for 25 yrs. $323/mo.
$32,300 1st trust deed, 9¾% $307/mo.

OUTCOMES AND FUTURE PLANS

Debt service on the condo totals $630/month. This, together with the condo association fee of $69 and miscellaneous expenses of $50, brings the monthly outlay to $749 as compared with a rental income of $525. The negative cash flow is therefore $224 per month, all of which is covered by the partner.

As part of the transaction, the seller cleaned and repainted the unit, putting it into top condition for renting. Jim plans to hold the condo long term. His projections show that rent increases will eliminate the negative cash flow in 3 to 5 years. In retrospect, Jim feels that he might have been able to solve the creative financing for the condo on his own, perhaps by putting a second on his home to raise the down payment. That way he would have had 100% of the benefits of ownership. His advice to others in the investment business: "Don't wait for opportunities to come to you. Plant seeds all over with many concerned people. Some are bound to flower. Know the seller's needs. Listen to what he says and read between the lines as you listen."

COMMENTARY:

1. It would be prudent to check on the legality of paying a finder's fee in your area. In some states, only licensed agents can be engaged where a fee is involved.
2. The ownership share given to the partner seems rather generous; however, it is better to be on the generous side and have a happy partner than to scrimp and create future ill will.
3. The system for finding partners is ingenious. It is amazing that there would be people willing to leave their funds in cash value insurance when they could be getting so much higher yields — and yet many people do it simply because no one puts a better deal under their noses. That's where the creative investor can succeed — by showing prospective partners (and sellers) a better way.
4. In an era where the carry-back arrangement typically involves a balloon payment — something with a dangerously short fuse — it is refreshing to find a buyer who was successful in negotiating a fully-amortized seller second. Jim will sleep better at night knowing that a large lump-sum payment is not stalking him just around the corner. Of course, the price he and his partner have to pay for this peace of mind is the $224/month negative cash flow.

Could he have reduced or eliminated the negative without the use of a partner? Possibly. The payments on the second might have been structured in a graduated fashion to begin with, say, $200/month for the first year, $225/month for the second, and so on. Alternately, Jim might have elected to accept the risk of a balloon payment, say seven years, no monthly payments, all due and payable in one lump sum. He might have had to offer a higher interest rate to induce the seller to cooperate. Perhaps the seller would have required interest-only monthly payments or an annual pay-down of principal. In any case, the way it stands, Jim has given up 60% of ownership to his partner; perhaps a way could have been found to structure the carry-back financing to eliminate both the negative cash flow **and** the need for a partner.

DOCUMENTATION

UNIVERSAL EARNEST MONEY RECEIPT AND OFFER TO PURCHASE

"This is a legally binding contract: if not understood, seek competent advice."

1. Date and Place of Offer: June 28, 19 81; San Diego (city) California (state)

2. Principals: The undersigned Buyer Jim Davis and his Nominees
agrees to buy and Seller agrees to sell, according to the indicated terms and conditions, the property described as follows:

3. Property: located at Unit number 17 at 158 Anaconda Road San Diego (city) California (state) (street address)

with the following legal description: to be supplied

including any of the following items if at present attached to the premises: plumbing, heating, and cooling equipment, including stoker and oil tanks, burners, water heaters, electric light fixtures, bathroom fixtures, roller shades, curtain rods and fixtures, draperies, venetian blinds, window and door screens, towel racks, linoleum and other attached floor coverings,

including carpeting, attached television antennas, mailboxes, all trees and shrubs, and any other fixtures EXCEPT None

The following personal property shall also be included as part of the purchase: installed refrigerator

At the closing of the transaction, the Seller, at his expense, shall provide the Buyer with a Bill Of Sale containing a detailed inventory of the personal property included.

4. Earnest Money Deposit: Agent (or Seller) acknowledges receipt from Buyer of ___ Five Hundred and 00/100 ___ dollars $ __500.00__

in the form of ( ) cash; (X) personal check; ( ) cashier's check; ( ) promissory note at _____% interest per annum due _____ 19 _____; or

other _____

as earnest money deposit to secure and apply on this purchase. Upon acceptance of this agreement in writing and delivery of same to Buyer, the earnest money deposit shall be assigned

to and deposited in the listing Realtor's trust account or _____, to apply on the purchase price at the time of closing.

5. Purchase Price: The total purchase price of the property shall be ___ Seventy Thousand and 00/100 ___ dollars $ __70,000.00__

6. Payment: Purchase price is to be paid by Buyer as follows:

Aforedescribed earnest money deposit .... $ __500.00__

Additional payment due upon acceptance of this offer .... $ __--__

Additional payment due at closing .... $ __6,500.00__

Balance to be paid as follows:

  1. Assumption of 1st Trust Deed with Pacific American Savings and Loan
      Association, in the approximate amount of $32,300 and not to exceed
      9 3/4% interest payable monthly at $307 or more including principal,
      interest, taxes, and insurance.

  2. Buyer to execute through escrow a 2nd Trust Deed and Note in favor of
      Seller in the approximate amount of $30,700 at 12% interest payable
      including interest at $323.00 or more per month for 300 months or 25
      years.

  3. Trust Deed and Note to include a request for notice.

7. Title: Seller agrees to furnish good and marketable title free of all encumbrances and defects, except mortgage liens and encumbrances as set forth in this agreement, and to make

conveyance by Warranty Deed or ___--_____. Seller shall furnish in due course to the Buyer a title insurance policy insuring the Buyer of a good and marketable title in keeping with the terms and conditions of this agreement. Prior to the closing of this transaction, the Seller, upon request, will furnish to the Buyer a preliminary title report made by a title insurance company showing the condition of the title to said property. If the Seller cannot furnish marketable title within thirty days after receipt of the notice to the Buyer containing a written statement of the defects, the earnest money deposit herein receipted shall be refunded to the Buyer and this agreement shall be null and void. The following shall not be deemed encumbrances or defects; building and use restrictions general to the area; utility easements; other easements not inconsistent with Buyer's intended use; zoning or subdivision laws, covenants, conditions, restrictions, or reservations of record; tenancies of record. In the event of sale of other than real property relating to this transaction, Seller will provide evidence of title or right to sell or lease such personal property.

8. Special Representations: Seller warrants and represents to Buyer (1) that the subject property is connected to ( ) public sewer system, ( ) cesspool or septic tank, ( ) sewer system available but not connected, ( ) city water system, ( ) private water system, and that the following special improvements are included in the sale: ( ) sidewalk, ( ) curb and gutter, ( ) special street paving, ( ) special street lighting; (2) that the Seller knows of no material structural defects; (3) that all electrical wiring, heating, cooling, and plumbing systems are free of material defects and will be in good working order at the time the Buyer is entitled to possession; (4) that the Seller has no notice from any government agency of any violation or knowledge of probable violations of the law relating to the subject property; (5) that the Seller has no notice or knowledge of planned or commenced public improvements which may result in special assessments or otherwise directly and materially affect the property; and (6) that the Seller has no notice or knowledge of any liens to be assessed against the property,

EXCEPT ___ None _____.

9. Escrow Instructions: This sale shall be closed on or before ___ 45 days after opening of escrow ___

or such other closing agent as mutually agreed upon by Buyer and Seller. Buyer and Seller will, immediately on demand, deposit with closing agent all instruments and monies required

to complete the purchase in accordance with the provisions of this agreement. Contract of Sale or Instrument of Conveyance to be made in the name of _____

  to be provided by August 1, 1981

  Escrow instructions signed by Buyer and Seller shall be delivered to the
  escrow holder within 5 days of the Seller's acceptance.

10. Closing Costs and Pro-Ration: Seller agrees to pay for title insurance policy, preliminary title report (if requested), termite inspection as set forth below, real estate commission, cost of preparing and recording any corrective instruments, and one-half of the escrow fees. Buyer agrees to pay for recording fees for mortgages and deeds of conveyance, all costs or expenses in securing new financing or assuming existing financing, and one-half of the escrow fees. Buyer agrees to pay for recording fees for mortgages and deeds of conveyance, all costs or expenses in securing new financing or assuming existing financing, and one-half of the escrow fees. Taxes for the current year, insurance acceptable to the Buyer, rents, interest, mortgage reserves, maintenance fees, and water and other utilities constituting liens, shall be pro-rated as of closing. Renters' security deposits shall accrue to Buyer at closing. Seller to provide Buyer with all current rental or lease agreements prior to closing.

  Condo association fee also to be prorated.

11. Termite Inspection: Seller agrees, at his expense, to provide written certification by a reputable licensed pest control firm that the property is free of termite infestation. In the event termites are found, the Seller shall have the property treated at his expense and provide acceptable certification that treatment has been rendered. If any structural repairs are required by reason of termite damage as established by acceptable certification, Seller agrees to make necessary repairs not to exceed $500. If repairs exceed $500, Buyer shall first have the right to accept the property "as is" with a credit to the Buyer at closing of $500, or the Buyer may terminate this agreement with the earnest money deposit being promptly returned to the Buyer if the Seller does not agree to pay all costs of treatment and repair.

12. Conditions of Sale: The following conditions shall also apply, and shall, if conflicting with the printed portions of this agreement, prevail and control:

  1. Seller agrees to furnish a structural pest control certificate by a
      licensed operator and to pay for all recommended work and include

report to Buyer's prior to close of escrow.

2. Installed refrigerator to be included in purchase price and to be in good working order.

3. All plumbing, heating, and air conditioning, electrical and installed equipment to be in proper working order prior to C.O.E. Buyer to have an inspection and approval walk-thru 5 days before close of escrow.

4. Seller to offer a one-year home-owners warranty on all items included above contracted through Majesty Home Improvement Company or its equivalent.

5. All carpeting, drapes and fixtures now attached to the property to stay in the unit.

6. Buyers to inspect and approve condominium C.C. and R's.

7. Seller to paint interior and shampoo carpets before C.O.E.

13. Liability and Maintenance: Seller shall maintain subject property, including landscaping, in good condition until the date of transfer of title or possession by Buyer, whichever occurs first. All risk of loss and destruction of property, and all expenses of insurance, shall be borne by the seller until the date of possession. If the improvements on the property are destroyed or materially damaged prior to closing, then the Buyer shall have the right to declare this agreement null and void, and the earnest money deposit and all other sums paid by Buyer toward the purchase price shall be returned to the Buyer forthwith.

14. Possession: The Buyer shall be entitled to possession of property upon closing or _____ -- _____, 19 ____.

15. Default: In the event the Buyer fails to complete the purchase as herein provided, the earnest money deposit shall be retained by the Seller as the total and entire liquidated damages. In the event the Seller fails to perform any condition of the sale as herein provided, then the Buyer may, at his option, treat the contract as terminated, and all payments made by the Buyer hereunder shall be returned to the Buyer forthwith, provided the Buyer may, at his option, treat this agreement as being in full force and effect with the right to action for specific performance and damages. In the event that either Buyer, Seller, or Agent shall institute suit to enforce any rights hereunder, the prevailing party shall be entitled to court costs and a reasonable attorney's fee.

16. Time Limit of Offer: The Seller shall have until

_____ Upon presentation _____, 19 ____ to accept this
(hour)   (date)

offer by delivering a signed copy hereof to the Buyer. If this offer is not so accepted, it shall lapse and the agent (or Seller) shall refund the earnest money deposit to the Buyer forthwith.

17. General Agreements: (1) Both parties to this purchase reserve their rights to assign and hereby otherwise agree to cooperate in effecting an Internal Revenue Code 1031 exchange or similar tax-related arrangement prior to close of escrow, upon either party's written notice of intention to do so. (2) Upon approval of this offer by the Seller, this agreement shall become a contract between Buyer and Seller and shall inure to the benefit of the heirs, administrators, executors, successors, personal representatives, and assigns of said parties. (3) Time is of the essence and an essential part of this agreement. (4) This contract constitutes the sole and entire agreement between the parties hereto and no modification of this contract shall be binding unless attached hereto and signed by all parties to the contract. No representations, promises, or inducements not included in this contract shall be binding upon any party hereto.

18. Buyer's Statement and Receipt: "I/we hereby agree to purchase the above property in accordance with the terms and conditions above stated and acknowledge receipt of a completed copy of this agreement, which I/we have fully read and understand." Dated __ June 28, __ 19 81 __,
                                                                                                                                    (hour)

Address _____ 800 Baldwin Avenue _____   [signature] and Nominees _____ Buyer

_____ San Diego, California _____   _____ Buyer

Phone No: Home __ 461-1218 __ Business __ 461-1218 __

19. Seller's Statement and Response: "I/we approve and accept the above offer, which I/we have fully read and understand, and agree to the above terms and conditions this day

of _____, 19 ____, _____.
                                              (hour)

Address _____   _____ Seller

Phone No: Home _____ Business _____   _____ Seller

20. Commission Agreement: Seller agrees to pay a commission of __ NA __ % of the gross sales price to _____ for services in this transaction, and agrees that, in the event of forfeiture of the earnest money deposit by the Buyer, said deposit shall be divided between the Seller's broker and the Seller (one half to each party), the Broker's part not to exceed the amount of the commission.

21. Buyer's Receipt for Signed Offer: The Buyer hereby acknowledges receipt of a copy of the above agreement bearing the Seller's signature in acceptance of this offer.

Dated _____, 19 ____   _____ Buyer

                                                        _____ Buyer

COMMENTARY TO DOCUMENTATION

Item 2. Buyer is wise to add "and Nominees" after his name. This provides for the addition of partners to the transaction without change of documentation.

Item 6. Generally it is wise to add a contingency to the assumption statement providing for limits to the amount of assumption costs the buyer may be asked to pay by the lender. Occasionally the buyer will stipulate that the sale is contingent on his being able to assume the existing loan without any change in the terms of the loan whatsoever.

The carry-back note should contain certain buyer-oriented provisions, i.e., substitution of collateral, subordination, prepayment without penalty, assumption (or assignment), and first right of refusal. It is prudent to get as many of these approved by the seller as he will tolerate.

Item 12. The addition of a pre-closing walk-through and inspection may sound like a nuisance, but it is a prudent contingency that may save the buyer considerable agony. Very few sellers will stick around after closing to see if there isn't anything else they might be able to do to make things nicer for the buyer. The time to get the seller to do his job is before the closing, not after.

Reprinted by permission from the *Nothing Down Advisor.*

Into A 72-Plex For $2,000

**Featuring Technique No. 45
"You Put Up The Cash; I Put Up
The Time and Expertise"**

In A Nutshell . . .

Type: 72-Plex
Price: $929,000
Source: Classified Ad
Means: Assumption, Carry Back
Techniques: No. 4 — Contract/Wrap
No. 9 — Savings and Inheritances
No. 20 — Rents
No. 21 — Deposits
No. 32 — Second Mortgage Crank
No. 45 — Partner's Cash/Your Expertise
Features: $20,000/yr. positive cash flow

LOCATING

Everett Carson, a Los Angeles investor specializing in larger properties, located the 72-unit complex described in this case study by reading through the classified ads.

SITUATION

The two buildings — 35 units in the one and 37 in the other — were favorably located and needed only cosmetic improvements. Each was encumbered with a first mortgage at 14¼%, 19 years to go ($284,000 and $273,000 respectively, for a total of $557,000). In addition, there was a blanket second of $137,000 at 10% ballooned in 8 years. The owner wanted $950,000, with $256,000 down to cover his equity.

NEGOTIATION

Everett's first offer was to pay $1,080,000 for the property by putting $5,000 down, assuming the firsts and the second, creating a new owner carry back third for $381,000, and rounding out the deal by selling the new third (at the buyer's expense) at a discount to raise $225,000 for the seller. This approach would essentially correspond to the creative technique of raising the price and lowering the terms. The only serious problem with this approach (apart from the two-year balloon) was the fact that the seller did not like it. He countered instead with a price of $929,000, his equity of $235,000 to be cashed out at closing. He liked his down payment in the form of cold, hard cash on the line. Everett accepted, provided the seller would place $12,000 of the proceeds from the closing at the disposal of the buyer for use in repairs and improvements. The seller agreed.

Everett's problem now was how to raise $235,000 without resorting to the sale of discounted paper.

CLOSING

The outcome of his financing program was this: he provided $2,000 towards the down payment from his own pocket, then raised an additional $148,000 through

a partnership arrangement involving six people, and placed a new hard-money third of $85,000 on the property at 24%, ballooned in two years (in effect the second mortgage crank technique in third position). The total cash generated amounted to $235,000, just what the seller wanted.

Approximately $7,000 in rents and deposits accrued to the buyer at closing. After the dust had settled, Everett received $18,000 back, including the $12,000 repair fund. The sketch summarizes the financing:

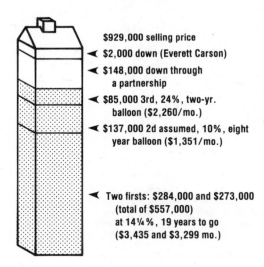

$929,000 selling price
◄ $2,000 down (Everett Carson)
◄ $148,000 down through a partnership
◄ $85,000 3rd, 24%, two-yr. balloon ($2,260/mo.)
◄ $137,000 2d assumed, 10%, eight year balloon ($1,351/mo.)
◄ Two firsts: $284,000 and $273,000 (total of $557,000) at 14¼%, 19 years to go ($3,435 and $3,299 mo.)

OUTCOMES AND FUTURE PLANS

After five months of ownership, the cash flow analysis showed the following annual figures: Gross operating income — $207,480, Total operating expenses — $145,516, Net operating income — $61,964, Debt service — $125,340, Cash flow before taxes — $20,176.

An appraisal at the time of closing evaluated the property at $1,140,000. Everett and his associates were therefore picking up $211,000 in instant equity. Not bad for the time and energy invested in one deal. The most recent appraisal shows a value of $1,400,000. After one year of ownership, the projected value is $1,638,000. The current plan is to sell the property after one year for a profit of around $709,000.

COMMENTARY

1. Everett has courage! The cash flow situation seems very favorable, but there is that $85,000 balloon coming up fast. Is there provision in the hard-money 3rd to extend the balloon in case resale does not work out as planned? Are there other partners in the wings ready to step in with more cash should the need arise?

2. Limited partnerships bring with them their own set of problems and challenges, not the least of which is the need to keep many minds and pocketbooks satisfied. Then there are potential legal and regulatory hurdles to cross (e.g., approvals and registrations — or the problem of proving that these are not applicable). All in all, this is the domain of the sophisticated investor with access to very competent legal and tax counsel.

3. Which is best: large multi-unit complexes or a portfolio of smaller properties (SFH's and small apartment buildings)? It depends on one's goals and views of the future. Management of a 72-unit complex is almost certainly easier than management of 72 single family homes. And if this one deal works for the buyer, the one-time rewards are very high. Still, the risk of putting all one's eggs in a single basket is not small. If a buyer with many SFH's gets into financial straits, he can readily sell off enough of the units to solve an interim problem. If the owner of a large complex gets pinched, he may have to sell his one property and take a beating. For most real estate investors, especially those who are just beginning, the advantages of having many smaller properties rather than one big one seem irresistible. Flexibility in the next few years seems strongly indicated — and there is more flexibility in smaller properties. Still, Everett and those like him with considerable experience can do very well in the big properties — but it takes know-how and courage.

DOCUMENTATION

[The following illustrative document was completed on the basis of data supplied by the buyer.]

UNIVERSAL EARNEST MONEY RECEIPT
AND OFFER TO PURCHASE

"This is a legally binding contract: if not understood, seek competent advice."

1. Date and Place of Offer: __February 27,__ 19 __81__ ; __Los Angeles__ (city) __California__ (state)

2. Principals: The undersigned Buyer __Everett Carson and/or Assigns, but in no event shall the failure to select an assignee relieve the Buyer from the obligations of this contract.__

agrees to buy and Seller agrees to sell, according to the indicated terms and conditions, the property described as follows:

3. Property: located at __14217 and 14221 Broderick Avenue__ (street address) __Los Angeles__ (city) __California__ (state)

with the following legal description: __to be supplied in escrow__

including any of the following items if at present attached to the premises: plumbing, heating, and cooling equipment, including stoker and oil tanks, burners, water heaters, electric light fixtures, bathroom fixtures, roller shades, curtain rods and fixtures, draperies, venetian blinds, window and door screens, towel racks, linoleum and other attached floor coverings,

including carpeting, attached television antennas, mailboxes, all trees and shrubs, and any other fixtures EXCEPT __None__

The following personal property shall also be included as part of the purchase: ____
At the closing of the transaction, the Seller, at his expense, shall provide the Buyer with a Bill Of Sale containing a detailed inventory of the personal property included.

4. Earnest Money Deposit: Agent (or Seller) acknowledges receipt from Buyer of __Five Thousand and 00/100__ dollars $ __5,000.00__

in the form of ( ) cash; (X) personal check; ( ) cashier's check; ( ) promissory note at ____% interest per annum due ____ 19 ____; or

other ____
as earnest money deposit to secure and apply on this purchase. Upon acceptance of this agreement in writing and delivery of same to Buyer, the earnest money deposit shall be assigned

to and deposited in the listing Realtor's trust account or __--__ , to apply on the purchase price at the time of closing.

5. Purchase Price: The total purchase price of the property shall be __Nine Hundred Twenty-Nine Thousand and 00/100__ dollars
$ __929,000.00__

6. Payment: Purchase price is to be paid by Buyer as follows:

Aforedescribed earnest money deposit .... $ 5,000.00

Additional payment due upon acceptance of this offer .... $ --

Additional payment due at closing .... $ 145,000.00

Balance to be paid as follows:

    Buyer shall assume First Trust Deed of record with an approximate unpaid balance of $557,000, payable $6,734 per month, including 14.25% interest per annum, plus prevailing processing fees for subject to.

    Buyer shall assume Second Trust Deed of record with an approximate unpaid balance of $137,000, payable $1,351 per month, including 10% interest per annum.

    Buyer to secure a new loan on subject property secured by a Third Trust Deed in the amount of $85,000, payable $2,260 or more per month, including 24% interest, all due and payable in 2 years. Proceeds to the Seller. This offer is contingent on Buyer being able to obtain the loan with the terms indicated.

7. Title: Seller agrees to furnish good and marketable title free of all encumbrances and defects, except mortgage liens and encumbrances as set forth in this agreement, and to make

conveyance by Warranty Deed or _____. Seller shall furnish in due course to the Buyer a title insurance policy insuring the Buyer of a good and marketable title in keeping with the terms and conditions of this agreement. Prior to the closing of this transaction, the Seller, upon request, will furnish to the Buyer a preliminary title report made by a title insurance company showing the condition of the title to said property. If the Seller cannot furnish marketable title within thirty days after receipt of the notice to the Buyer containing a written statement of the defects, the earnest money deposit herein receipted shall be refunded to the Buyer and this agreement shall be null and void. The following shall not be deemed encumbrances or defects: building and use restrictions general to the area; utility easements; other easements not inconsistent with Buyer's intended use; zoning or subdivision laws, covenants, conditions, restrictions, or reservations of record; tenancies of record. In the event of sale of other than real property relating to this transaction, Seller will provide evidence of title or right to sell or lease such personal property.

8. Special Representations: Seller warrants and represents to Buyer (1) that the subject property is connected to ( ) public sewer system, ( ) cesspool or septic tank, ( ) sewer system available but not connected, ( ) city water system, ( ) private water system, and that the following special improvements are included in the sale: ( ) sidewalk, ( ) curb and gutter, ( ) special street paving, ( ) special street lighting; (2) that the Seller knows of no material structural defects; (3) that all electrical wiring, heating, cooling, and plumbing systems are free of material defects and will be in good working order at the time the Buyer is entitled to possession; (4) that the Seller has no notice from any government agency of any violation or knowledge of probable violations of the law relating to the subject property; (5) that the Seller has no notice or knowledge of planned or commenced public improvements which may result in special assessments or otherwise directly and materially affect the property; and (6) that the Seller has no notice or knowledge of any liens to be assessed against the property,

EXCEPT _____ None

9. Escrow Instructions: This sale shall be closed on or before _____ * _____ 19 __ by Fidelity Escrow _____ or such other closing agent as mutually agreed upon by Buyer and Seller. Buyer and Seller will, immediately on demand, deposit with closing agent all instruments and monies required

to complete the purchase in accordance with the provisions of this agreement. Contract of Sale or Instrument of Conveyance to be made in the name of _____

    *Escrow shall be opened within 2 days from date of Buyer's physical inspection and approval of subject property and escrow shall be for a period of 30 days, but no sooner than March 3, 1981.

10. Closing Costs and Pro-Ration: Seller agrees to pay for title insurance policy, preliminary title report (if requested), termite inspection as set forth below, real estate commission, cost of preparing and recording any corrective instruments, and one-half of the escrow fees. Buyer agrees to pay for recording fees for mortgages and deeds of conveyance, all costs or expenses in securing new financing or assuming existing financing, and one-half of the escrow fees. Buyer agrees to pay for recording fees for mortgages and deeds of conveyance, all costs or expenses in securing new financing or assuming existing financing, and one-half of the escrow fees. Taxes for the current year, insurance acceptable to the Buyer, rents, interest, mortgage reserves, maintenance fees, and water and other utilities constituting liens, shall be pro-rated as of closing. Renters' security deposits shall accrue to Buyer at closing. Seller to provide Buyer with all current rental or lease agreements prior to closing.

11. ~~Termite Inspection: Seller agrees, at his expense, to provide written certification by a reputable licensed pest control firm that the property is free of termite infestation. In the event termites are found, the Seller shall have the property treated at his expense and provide acceptable certification that treatment has been rendered. If any structural repairs are required by reason of termite damage as established by acceptable certification, Seller agrees to make necessary repairs not to exceed $500. If repairs exceed $500, Buyer shall first have the right to accept the property "as is" with a credit to the Buyer at closing of $500, or the Buyer may terminate this agreement with the earnest money deposit being promptly returned to the Buyer if the Seller does not agree to pay all costs of treatment and repair.~~

12. Conditions of Sale: The following conditions shall also apply, and shall, if conflicting with the printed portions of this agreement, prevail and control:

1. Property sold "as is".

2. Buyers will accomodate Seller if Seller elects a 1031 exchange.

3. Buyers will procure 3rd mortgage financing at no costs borne to Seller.

4. Seller to credit $12,000 to Buyers in cash at the close of escrow for refurbishing and maintenance, etc.

5. Buyers request that there be no more than 6 vacancies at the close of escrow.

6. Seller to cooperate with Buyers with renting vacancies during the escrow period.

7. Buyer is a licensed Real Estate Agent buying property for investment only.

8. Smoke detectors to be installed at the close of escrow.

9. Existing rental agreements and rental books to be assigned to Buyers at close of escrow.

10. Seller shall furnish to Buyer a rent statement concerning subject real property. Seller agrees that he will not enter into or renew any contracts or leases concerning subject property without the Buyer's approval. Seller warrants the following concerning subject property: (a) the scheduled monthly income when fully occupied is no less than $15,716.68; (b) 1980-1981 property taxes were no more than $6,841; (c) utility expenses for the 12-month period ended October 1980 were $18,432 est.

11. This agreement subject to Buyer's physical inspection and approval of subject property on or before 5:00 p.m. on the 5th day after Seller's acceptance herein, or the 5th day after Buyer's approval of Seller's counter-offer.

13. Liability and Maintenance: Seller shall maintain subject property, including landscaping, in good condition until the date of transfer of title or possession by Buyer, whichever occurs first. All risk of loss and destruction of property, and all expenses of insurance, shall be borne by the seller until the date of possession. If the improvements on the property are destroyed or materially damaged prior to closing, then the Buyer shall have the right to declare this agreement null and void, and the earnest money deposit and all other sums paid by Buyer toward the purchase price shall be returned to the Buyer forthwith.

14. Possession: The Buyer shall be entitled to possession of property upon closing or _____, 19 _____.

15. Default: In the event the Buyer fails to complete the purchase as herein provided, the earnest money deposit shall be retained by the Seller as the total and entire liquidated damages. In the event the Seller fails to perform any condition of the sale as herein provided, then the Buyer may, at his option, treat the contract as terminated, and all payments made by the Buyer hereunder shall be returned to the Buyer forthwith, provided the Buyer may, at his option, treat this agreement as being in full force and effect with the right to action for specific performance and damages. In the event that either Buyer, Seller, or Agent shall institute suit to enforce any rights hereunder, the prevailing party shall be entitled to court costs and a reasonable attorney's fee.

16. Time Limit of Offer: The Seller shall have until

within 6 days after date hereof _____, 19 _____ to accept this
(hour)   (date)

offer by delivering a signed copy hereof to the Buyer. If this offer is not so accepted, it shall lapse and the agent (or Seller) shall refund the earnest money deposit to the Buyer forthwith.

17. General Agreements: (1) Both parties to this purchase reserve their rights to assign and hereby otherwise agree to cooperate in effecting an Internal Revenue Code 1031 exchange or similar tax-related arrangement prior to close of escrow, upon either party's written notice of intention to do so. (2) Upon approval of this offer by the Seller, this agreement shall become a contract between Buyer and Seller and shall inure to the benefit of the heirs, administrators, executors, successors, personal representatives, and assigns of said parties. (3) Time is of the essence and an essential part of this agreement. (4) This contract constitutes the sole and entire agreement between the parties hereto and no modification of this contract shall be binding unless attached hereto and signed by all parties to the contract. No representations, promises, or inducements not included in this contract shall be binding upon any party hereto.

18. Buyer's Statement and Receipt: "I/we hereby agree to purchase the above property in accordance with the terms and conditions above stated and acknowledge receipt of a completed copy of this agreement, which I/we have fully read and understand." Dated __February 27,__ 19 __81__, _____
(hour)

Address __616 Packer Street__ [signature] and/or Assigns _____ Buyer

__Los Angeles, California__ _____ Buyer

Phone No: Home __661-1418__ Business __741-1336__

19. Seller's Statement and Response: "I/we approve and accept the above offer, which I/we have fully read and understand, and agree to the above terms and conditions this day

of _____, 19 _____, _____
(hour)

Address _____ _____ Seller

Phone No: Home _____ Business _____ _____ Seller

20. Commission Agreement: Seller agrees to pay a commission of _____% of the gross sales price to _____

for services in this transaction, and agrees that, in the event of forfeiture of the earnest money deposit by the Buyer, said deposit shall be divided between the Seller's broker and the Seller (one half to each party), the Broker's part not to exceed the amount of the commission.

21. Buyer's Receipt for Signed Offer: The Buyer hereby acknowledges receipt of a copy of the above agreement bearing the Seller's signature in acceptance of this offer.

Dated _____, 19 _____ _____ Buyer

COMMENTARY TO DOCUMENTATION

Item 2. The presence of the wording "and/or Assignee" permits the buyer to collaborate with a partner or partners in the performance of the contract. The added contingency is a gesture to the seller. The message is, "I'm not putting in a weasel clause by writing 'and/or assignee.' I really want to go through with the deal."

Item 4. Here is perhaps a case where a note would have been useful rather than cash. The note could have been for an even larger sum.

Item 6. The third is a hard-money loan — not much one can do here in providing flexible provisions. With a two-year fuse, this note is almost in the form of cash anyway.

Item 12. The "request" that there be no more than 6 vacancies seems to indicate that the seller may be holding the cards. He has already refused to carry a penny back. Now the buyer is walking a bit carefully through the contingencies. If the buyer had total control, he would not "request" but rather make the offer subject to and contingent on the vacancy situation being such and so. The seller could be obligated to pay a penalty on the vacancies in excess of a stipulated number. As it stands, the "request" for no fewer than 6 vacancies seems to be a way of putting on record that the buyer wants the seller to do his best.

The contingency that the seller warrant certain facts about the property (gross scheduled income, taxes, utilities) is an excellent practice, one designed to get at the truth very quickly.

Item 15. The original contained a preprinted clause where initialing of the parties would invoke a "total liquidated damages" clause like the one in our "Universal Earnest Money Receipt and Offer to Purchase." The buyer had initialed this part, of course, and wisely so.

Final note, the procedures involved in setting up a limited partnership are not simple. It is imperative that persons involved in such arrangements retain legal counsel to make certain all laws and regulations are accommodated.

Part X

Options

This final section treats a group of special creative finance techniques that permit a buyer to gain control of significant amounts of real estate with little down, even though ownership may be months or years away—if ever. The principle is simple: the person buying the option gives the seller a sum of money in exchange for the right to buy the property at a given price within a defined period of time. The buyer benefits by locking in the price and gaining control of the property without a large investment. The seller benefits by retaining the tax advantages of ownership while locking in the sale at an acceptable price or picking up the option money in the event the buyer decides to back out.

The Nothing Down System includes five variations of the option approach, the last of which is illustrated in this volume by means of two feature case studies:

Technique No. 46 — The Rolling Option

Technique No. 47 — Equity For Options

Technique No. 48 — Sale Option Back

Technique No. 49 — The Earnest Money Option

Technique No. 50 — Lease With An Option To Purchase
    Case No. 49:   Lease Option Is Key To Win/Win Deal On 14-Plex
    Case No. 50:   Nashville Investor Buys Home Near Johnny Cash—For $1,000 Down

---

Technique No. 46   The Rolling Option

In this approach, a large tract of land is optioned piecemeal by the buyer. Rather than taking control of the whole package at once, which would be very expensive, the buyer purchases a segment for development or resale while at the same time buying an option on the next segment. The option can then be rolled from segment to segment until the whole package is developed or the option dropped.

Technique No. 47   Equity for Options

Other assets besides cash can be used as an option payment. Personal property (cars, trucks, equipment, collectibles), equity resources, and even services can work just as well.

Technique No. 48   Sale Option Back

What if a property owner needs to sell a piece of property now in order to raise capital but wishes he could eventually have it back to take advantage of predicted appreciation and future growth? What can be done for him? The "Sale Option Back" technique is cut to order: the seller disposes of his property at a moderate discount but with the option to buy it back within a specified time frame at a price fixed now. Whether or not the option is exercised, the buyer wins;

and the seller has the choice of getting his property back if future conditions develop as planned.

Technique No. 49   The Earnest Money Option

Every Earnest Money Agreement is an option. For a short period of time, the potential buyer has control of the disposition of the property. If he fails to follow through as agreed, he loses the earnest money (option payment) as liquidated damages. Meanwhile, if he has executed the offer to purchase in his own name with the additional phrase "Or Assigns," he can choose to sell his interest in the property to whomever he will. If he has struck a good bargain, it is possible the assignment of the earnest money rights to some other investor could be very profitable.

Many of the earnest money agreements used in the case studies of this book were filled out appropriately with the phrase "Or Assigns." One of the cases, No. 31, involved an actual assignment under this arrangement.

Technique No. 50   Lease With An Option To Purchase

This is the most common form of the option. Buyers who don't have enough cash for a down payment or who wish to build up a portfolio of properties using this technique can use their available funds as option money and then maneuver for purchase later on. Meanwhile, if monthly payments have been carefully structured, the buyer (optioner) might be able to pick up a little extra cash on sub-lease payments.

Two case studies in the current volume illustrate this technique. In Case No. 49, the buyer of a 14-plex initiated his program with a six-month lease option. The reason? He did not yet have the down payment funds, and besides, the seller needed to hold the property a little longer to qualify for long-term capital gains. In Case No. 50, a home buyer picked up an estate property for $1,000 on a six-month lease option. The breathing room permitted him to get together the down payment needed for closing.

Reprinted by permission from the *Nothing Down Advisor*.

"We've detected a peculiar pattern in our progress for last year."

Lease-Option Is Key To Win/Win Deal On 14-Plex

Featuring Technique No. 50
"Lease With An Option To Purchase"

In A Nutshell. . .

Type: 14-plex
Price: $140,000
Source: Classified ad
Means: Lease Option, Contract
Techniques: No. 4 — Contract/Wrap
No. 9 — Savings and Inheritances
No. 50 — Lease with Option
Features: Sizeable cash flow

LOCATING

Bruce Mitchell of Bremerton, Washington, had spotted a 14-plex in the classified ads late in 1980. At the time he found that the property needed too much work to be attractive to him; however, he kept his eye on it after it sold for $130,000 and watched as the new owner proceeded to fix the place up. A few months later the property was put back on the market. That's when Bruce made his move.

SITUATION

The owner was offering the property for $140,000 with $10,000 down, balance on a contract. Included were two buildings: a one-bedroom single family home and a two-story multi-unit apartment complex with 8 studio units and 5 one-bedroom units. The rents ranged from $155 to $225 per unit.

NEGOTIATION

Bruce inquired why the owner was selling so soon after he had purchased the property. The owner told him that he was tired of the management hassles caused by the 14-plex and was about to move out of state. The problem was that he had held the property less than a year; for that reason he was facing the unpleasant tax consequences occasioned by a short-term gain.

For his part (although he did not say so), Bruce did not have the money for a down payment and was therefore delighted with the owner's situation. The logical technique for the transaction was a lease with option. Such an arrangement would give Bruce the time he needed to raise the money for the down payment, stabilize the rents, and complete some needed improvements. The owner welcomed a lease-option arrangement because he could then complete his year's holding period and let his profit be taxed as a long-term gain. He could also have the benefit of the depreciation for a longer period of time.

They settled on the following terms: Price of

$140,000, with $3,600 down and the balance of the owner's equity, $11,400, carried back at 12% per annum payable yearly until paid off. The remaining encumbrances — four underlying contracts and a first deed of trust — were to be carried on an offsetting contract. The sketch summarizes the details:

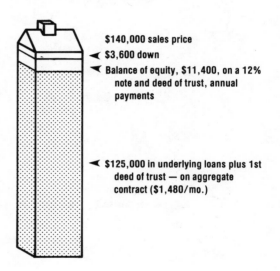

$140,000 sales price
$3,600 down
Balance of equity, $11,400, on a 12% note and deed of trust, annual payments

$125,000 in underlying loans plus 1st deed of trust — on aggregate contract ($1,480/mo.)

CLOSING

Bruce and his seller made an appointment immediately to have a title company prepare the papers. The whole agreement was signed, sealed, and delivered five days after the initial contact. Bruce attributes the success of the project to his willingness to "spend time with the seller and listen."

OUTLOOK AND PLANS FOR THE FUTURE

Soon after the closing, Bruce hired a property manager to look after the affairs of his newly-acquired 14-plex. Then he arranged for improvements to be completed on the units — painting, remodeling, upgrading. The quality of tenants was also raised.

Monthly rental income totals $2,365, with monthly lease payments during the first year of $1,480 and expenses of $580/mo. The positive cash flow is, therefore, $305 each month or a total of $3,660 for the year, nearly enough to equal the cash down.

Bruce's advice to other investors is: "Listen to the seller and learn what he or she is not verbalizing. Work closely with an escrow agent who is helpful."

Since entering into the 14-plex lease-option agreement, Bruce has purchased a triplex that yielded $30,000 cash on a refinance but generated a sizeable negative cash flow. The 14-plex positive flow will be used over the long haul to offset the negative on the triplex. In addition, he has purchased four other properties since taking the Nothing Down Seminar in August of 1980.

Listen to his report on current plans to enlarge his portfolio: "At this time I am negotiating for three more properties — two 4-plexes and a 5-unit apartment. One of the 4-plexes is valued at $100,000 with good terms except for $20,000 cash the seller wants down. It may require a creative house purchase to generate the funds.

"The 5-unit will cost around $90,000 — an assumption of $65,000 at $700 per month and a couple of notes for his equity. The newer 4-plex should be interesting. It is three years old, and the seller has an $86,000 note due in 3 months. He wants to get $155,000 — equal to last year's appraisal. The seller also wants $20,000 cash plus clearing a $30,000 obligation. We are currently negotiating the possibility of a $110,000 VA loan, an equity trade for one house which the seller will use to partially satisfy the $30,000 obligation, and negotiating new terms for the balance, which will be about $15,000 — if I obtain a second on the house before the trade. Another $20,000 will come from an equity trade for another house which I will lease and buy back in a few years (giving him tax advantages), the balance being negotiated on a deed of trust (about $15,000)."

COMMENTARY

1. Judging from Bruce's past successes and current plans, he has mastered the art of win/win creative investing. He listens to the seller, determines what is needed, then finds the solutions that will bring satisfaction to all parties. Even though his sellers might require sizeable down payments, Bruce does not get discouraged and throw in the towel but plunges into the fray and finds ways to generate the needed capital creatively. His talents and procedures are impressive.

2. Bruce did not mention the size of the rental deposit accounts that were turned over to him as part of the lease agreement. However, if the deposits equaled one month's rent on the units, and the laws of his state permit comingling of funds, he would have taken control of around $2,400 in deposit assets which could be used for remodeling, taking care of the down payment when it came time to exercise the option in a year, etc.

3. We note also that Bruce arranged for a one month's extension of the purchase on the lease option just in case he needed a breather a year hence to get his affairs in order. We would have tried for a full year's rollover on the option just for security (maybe he did and the seller would not grant it).

DOCUMENTATION

UNIVERSAL EARNEST MONEY RECEIPT AND OFFER TO PURCHASE

"This is a legally binding contract: if not understood, seek competent advice."

1. Date and Place of Offer: __July 31,__ 19 __81__ ; __Bremerton__ (city) __Washington__ (state)

2. Principals: The undersigned Buyer __Bruce Mitchell and Joan Messina, single persons__
agrees to buy and Seller agrees to sell, according to the indicated terms and conditions, the property described as follows:

3. Property: located at __5120 Clement Street__ (street address) __Bremerton__ (city) __Washington__ (state)

with the following legal description: __Lot 2 and 4, Block 17, Town of Bremerton as per plat__

__recorded Volume 4 of Plats, P. 14; Kitsap County__

including any of the following items if at present attached to the premises: plumbing, heating, and cooling equipment, including stoker and oil tanks, burners, water heaters, electric light fixtures, bathroom fixtures, roller shades, curtain rods and fixtures, draperies, venetian blinds, window and door screens, towel racks, linoleum and other attached floor coverings,

including carpeting, attached television antennas, mailboxes, all trees and shrubs, and any other fixtures EXCEPT __None__

The following personal property shall also be included as part of the purchase: _____
At the closing of the transaction, the Seller, at his expense, shall provide the Buyer with a Bill Of Sale containing a detailed inventory of the personal property included.

4. Earnest Money Deposit: Agent (or Seller) acknowledges receipt from Buyer of ___option monies___ dollars $ ___—___

in the form of ( ) cash; ( ) personal check; ( ) cashier's check; ( ) promissory note at _____% interest per annum due _____ 19 _____; or

other _____

as earnest money deposit to secure and apply on this purchase. Upon acceptance of this agreement in writing and delivery of same to Buyer, the earnest money deposit shall be assigned

to and deposited in the listing Realtor's trust account or _____, to apply on the purchase price at the time of closing.

5. Purchase Price: The total purchase price of the property shall be ___One Hundred Forty Thousand and 00/100___ dollars

$ _140,000.00_

6. Payment: Purchase price is to be paid by Buyer as follows:

Aforedescribed earnest money deposit .... $ ___—___

Additional payment due upon acceptance of this offer .... $ ___—___

Additional payment due at closing .... $ ___—___

Balance to be paid as follows:

___(See Lease Option to Purchase Agreement attached, dated July 31, 1981.___
___Both purchasers are licensed Realtors in the State of Washington.)___

7. Title: Seller agrees to furnish good and marketable title free of all encumbrances and defects, except mortgage liens and encumbrances as set forth in this agreement, and to make

conveyance by Warranty Deed or _____ Seller shall furnish in due course to the Buyer a title insurance policy insuring the Buyer of a good and marketable title in keeping with the terms and conditions of this agreement. Prior to the closing of this transaction, the Seller, upon request, will furnish to the Buyer a preliminary title report made by a title insurance company showing the condition of the title to said property. If the Seller cannot furnish marketable title within thirty days after receipt of the notice to the Buyer containing a written statement of the defects, the earnest money deposit herein receipted shall be refunded to the Buyer and this agreement shall be null and void. The following shall not be deemed encumbrances or defects; building and use restrictions general to the area; utility easements; other easements not inconsistent with Buyer's intended use; zoning or subdivision laws, covenants, conditions, restrictions, or reservations of record; tenancies of record. In the event of sale of other than real property relating to this transaction, Seller will provide evidence of title or right to sell or lease such personal property.

8. Special Representations: Seller warrants and represents to Buyer (1) that the subject property is connected to ( ) public sewer system, ( ) cesspool or septic tank, ( ) sewer system available but not connected, ( ) city water system, ( ) private water system, and that the following special improvements are included in the sale: ( ) sidewalk, ( ) curb and gutter, ( ) special street paving, ( ) special street lighting; (2) that the Seller knows of no material structural defects; (3) that all electrical wiring, heating, cooling, and plumbing systems are free of material defects and will be in good working order at the time the Buyer is entitled to possession; (4) that the Seller has no notice from any government agency of any violation or knowledge of probable violations of the law relating to the subject property; (5) that the Seller has no notice or knowledge of planned or commenced public improvements which may result in special assessments or otherwise directly and materially affect the property; and (6) that the Seller has no notice or knowledge of any liens to be assessed against the property,

EXCEPT ___None___

9. Escrow Instructions: This sale shall be closed on or before ___January 7,___ 19 _82_ by ___Washington Pacific Escrow___ or such other closing agent as mutually agreed upon by Buyer and Seller. Buyer and Seller will, immediately on demand, deposit with closing agent all instruments and monies required

to complete the purchase in accordance with the provisions of this agreement. Contract of Sale or Instrument of Conveyance to be made in the name of _____

___to be supplied___

10. Closing Costs and Pro-Ration: Seller agrees to pay for title insurance policy, preliminary title report (if requested), termite inspection as set forth below, real estate commission, cost of preparing and recording any corrective instruments, and one-half of the escrow fees. Buyer agrees to pay for recording fees for mortgages and deeds of conveyance, all costs or expenses in securing new financing or assuming existing financing, and one-half of the escrow fees. Buyer agrees to pay for recording fees for mortgages and deeds of conveyance, all costs or expenses in securing new financing or assuming existing financing, and one-half of the escrow fees. Taxes for the current year, insurance acceptable to the Buyer, rents, interest, mortgage reserves, maintenance fees, and water and other utilities constituting liens, shall be pro-rated as of closing. Renters' security deposits shall accrue to Buyer at closing. Seller to provide Buyer with all current rental or lease agreements prior to closing.

11. Termite Inspection: Seller agrees, at his expense, to provide written certification by a reputable licensed pest control firm that the property is free of termite infestation. In the event termites are found, the Seller shall have the property treated at his expense and provide acceptable certification that treatment has been rendered. If any structural repairs are required by reason of termite damage as established by acceptable certification, Seller agrees to make necessary repairs not to exceed $500. If repairs exceed $500, Buyer shall first have the right to accept the property "as is" with a credit to the Buyer at closing of $500, or the Buyer may terminate this agreement with the earnest money deposit being promptly returned to the Buyer if the Seller does not agree to pay all costs of treatment and repair.

12. Conditions of Sale: The following conditions shall also apply, and shall, if conflicting with the printed portions of this agreement, prevail and control:

___None___

13. Liability and Maintenance: Seller shall maintain subject property, including landscaping, in good condition until the date of transfer of title or possession by Buyer, whichever occurs first. All risk of loss and destruction of property, and all expenses of insurance, shall be borne by the seller until the date of possession. If the improvements on the property are destroyed or materially damaged prior to closing, then the Buyer shall have the right to declare this agreement null and void, and the earnest money deposit and all other sums paid by Buyer toward the purchase price shall be returned to the Buyer forthwith.

14. Possession: The Buyer shall be entitled to possession of property upon closing or ___see lease option attached___, 19 _____.

15. Default: In the event the Buyer fails to complete the purchase as herein provided, the earnest money deposit shall be retained by the Seller as the total and entire liquidated damages. In the event the Seller fails to perform any condition of the sale as herein provided, then the Buyer may, at his option, treat the contract as terminated, and all payments made by the Buyer hereunder shall be returned to the Buyer forthwith, provided the Buyer may, at his option, treat this agreement as being in full force and effect with the right to action for specific performance and damages. In the event that either Buyer, Seller, or Agent shall institute suit to enforce any rights hereunder, the prevailing party shall be entitled to court costs and a reasonable attorney's fee.

16. Time Limit of Offer: The Seller shall have until

_____ _____, 19 _____ to accept this
      (hour)   (date)

offer by delivering a signed copy hereof to the Buyer. If this offer is not so accepted, it shall lapse and the agent (or Seller) shall refund the earnest money deposit to the Buyer forthwith.

17. **General Agreements:** (1) Both parties to this purchase reserve their rights to assign and hereby otherwise agree to cooperate in effecting an Internal Revenue Code 1031 exchange or similar tax-related arrangement prior to close of escrow, upon either party's written notice of intention to do so. (2) Upon approval of this offer by the Seller, this agreement shall become a contract between Buyer and Seller and shall inure to the benefit of the heirs, administrators, executors, successors, personal representatives, and assigns of said parties. (3) Time is of the essence and an essential part of this agreement. (4) This contract constitutes the sole and entire agreement between the parties hereto and no modification of this contract shall be binding unless attached hereto and signed by all parties to the contract. No representations, promises, or inducements not included in this contract shall be binding upon any party hereto.

18. **Buyer's Statement and Receipt:** "I/we hereby agree to purchase the above property in accordance with the terms and conditions above stated and acknowledge receipt of a completed copy of this agreement, which I/we have fully read and understand." Dated ___July 31,_____ 19 _81__, _____
                                                                          (hour)

Address   __P.O. Box 471_____ [signature] _____ Buyer

            __Bremerton, Washington_____ [signature] _____ Buyer

Phone No: Home __671-1418__ Business __671-1597__

19. **Seller's Statement and Response:** "I/we approve and accept the above offer, which I/we have fully read and understand, and agree to the above terms and conditions this day

of _____, 19 _____, _____
                                                               (hour)

Address _____ Seller

Phone No: Home _____ Business _____ _____ Seller

20. **Commission Agreement:** Seller agrees to pay a commission of ___NA___ % of the gross sales price to _____ for services in this transaction, and agrees that, in the event of forfeiture of the earnest money deposit by the Buyer, said deposit shall be divided between the Seller's broker and the Seller (one half to each party), the Broker's part not to exceed the amount of the commission.

21. **Buyer's Receipt for Signed Offer:** The Buyer hereby acknowledges receipt of a copy of the above agreement bearing the Seller's signature in acceptance of this offer.

Dated _____, 19 _____ _____ Buyer

                                                                     _____ Buyer

LEASE WITH AN OPTION TO PURCHASE

Samual Consap and Veronica Consap, husband and wife hereafter referred to as "lessors"; and Bruce Mitchell, a single person, and Denise Jones, a single person, hereafter referred to as "lessee" agree to enter into a lease agreement with an option to purchase the Georgian Apartments, 5120 Clement St., Bremerton, Washington, legal description:

[as given]

The aforementioned lease agreement will commence August 1, 1981 with the payment of One thousand four hundred eighty and no/100 ($1,480.00) and the assumption of the oil liabilities in the amount of $1,011.23 and also all other utilities bearing appropriately on the property. All current 1981 property taxes are to be paid by the lessor. Insurance presently with ABC Casualty will be negotiated between the lessor and lessee to present the most favorable position to each with the lessee acquiring the liability for payment.

Deposits now in trust will be transferred to the new lessee prior to thirty (30) days from the execution of this agreement. This lease agreement will run until January 7, 1982 at which time a purchase agreement will be executed upon at the following terms and conditions:

Purchase price will be One hundred forty thousand and no/100 ($140,000.00) with credit allowed for oil assumption in the amount of $1,011.23. Purchaser will assume all underlying contracts, deed of trust and other encumbrances at their current balance. Purchaser will pay Thirty six hundred and no/100 ($3,600.00) down with the remainder on a note and Deed of Trust at 12% per annum payable yearly until paid in full. Interest will be included in the $3,600.00 yearly payment, interest calculated on the diminishing balance. Penalty for late payment will be five (5%) percent of the total payment due if unpaid sixty (60) days from the date due.

The lessee agrees to maintain the premises, collect and disburse all revenues when due and payable, and in no way encumber the present property:

The Lessee has the option of extending this agreement for a period of thirty (30) days from January 7, 1981 if requested in writing and accompanied by an irrevocable fifty dollars ($50.00).

The aforementioned Lessor enters into this agreement 31 July 1981 for the valuable consideration ten ($10.00) and other valuable consideration granting unto the lessee the rights and privileges of this instrument.

[notarized signatures]

COMMENTARY TO DOCUMENTATION

The earnest money agreement in this case serves mainly as a vehicle for the approval of the lease-option agreement, the heart of the deal. Still, the addition of the words "or Assigns" could have been used profitably, as well as Item 16: stipulating a time limit for response. The terms of the lease option might have been strengthened somewhat in favor of the buyers: the carry-back note could have contained a substitution of collateral provision, as well as a prepayment and assumption clause — also first right of refusal. The rollover provision for exercise of the option is a wise insertion. All in all, the lease-option arrangement seems ideal for this situation.

Nashville Investor Buys Home Near Johnny Cash—For $1,000 Down

**Featuring Technique No. 50
"Lease With An Option To Purchase"**

In A Nutshell . . .

Type: SFH
Price: $112,000
Source: Classified ad
Means: Lease option, contract
Techniques: No. 4 — Contract/Wrap
 No. 6 — Balloon
 No. 9 — Savings and Inheritances
 No. 50 — Lease Option

When Russell Smith moved from Arizona to Nashville, Tennessee, his first real estate project was to buy a home for his family to live in.

LOCATING

A thorough search of the MLS books over a period of weeks proved fruitless. Nothing struck his fancy until he was glancing one day through a neighborhood classified ad booklet of the type distributed through supermarkets. There he found a listing for a home northeast of Nashville in the lake area close to the estates of Johnny Cash and Barbara Mandrell.

SITUATION

The owner had purchased the home at an auction using money he had borrowed at 18% interest. He had not been able to find a tenant or buyer since January of 1981. The asking price for the attractive home was $155,000. The only encumbrance was a $68,000 first mortgage.

When Russell explored some creative offers with the listing agent, she told him to forget it, that no one would be willing to accept a down payment of as little as $1,000—which was what he had. He explained to her that her professional responsibility required her to present all offers to the seller. With great reluctance she approached the seller with the following offer.

NEGOTIATION

Russell offered the seller $112,000 for the property on a lease-option arrangement for six months. The rent, at $900 per month for the lease period, was to be prepaid. The option amount was $1,000—in effect, a down payment. The seller expressed an interest as long as the carry-back involved 18% in order to offset the terms of his own acquisition note.

Russell refused, offering instead to provide a balloon of $6,000 in March of 1982, with 12% on the carry-back, interest-only payments annually with an open-ended

amortization on the personal, unsecured note. Did the owner accept such terms? Absolutely, because he was a don't wanter who was tired of the property and knew that Russell would take care of it as his own personal residence.

CLOSING

Because the arrangement was a lease option, matters were simple. The financing looked like this:

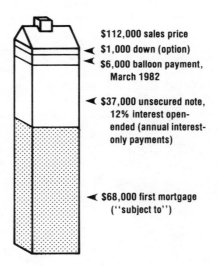

$112,000 sales price
$1,000 down (option)
$6,000 balloon payment, March 1982
$37,000 unsecured note, 12% interest open-ended (annual interest-only payments)
$68,000 first mortgage ("subject to")

ADDENDUM

After Russell had got his family squared away in their new nothing down residence, he began looking for more property, preferably property that would provide immediate income while he was building up his rental portfolio. He noticed a listing for a commercial property being offered for sale by a local music celebrity. The business (a club) reputedly generated a monthly income of over $6,000, with a free and clear building listed at $110,000. Russell offered $90,000 for the package with the requested $30,000 down as follows: $10,000 in an escrow account to be released after four months provided the business generated the claimed income, the balance to be paid out of monthly proceeds at $5,000 per month, once again contingent on the claimed success of the business. The $60,000 balance was to be paid off in a balloon sum after eight years—no interest!

The seller agreed, because she wanted to be free of the property due to partnership headaches. Russell had negotiated a risk-free nothing down deal—everything would be paid out of income from the property itself or else the deal would be suspended. Since part of the deal involved a management contract for the business, he was able to use existing permits to operate it—important for a newcomer to the area.

As it turned out, the commercial venture did **not** perform as claimed. Therefore, Russell was able to get out without any losses. We mention this added transaction as an illustration of creative buying. Followers of the Nothing Down Program are not encouraged to buy commercial property because of the added risks involved in today's economy. However, Russell had brought considerable experience to the venture, and it is instructive to see how he was able to use creative principles to achieve his goals.

COMMENTARY

1. The most important thing that this buyer did was to find a motivated seller. Once you find a motivated don't wanter, everything is easy. The next best thing that the buyer did was to have the seller carry his equity in the form of an unsecured note for $37,000. This means that when the $6,000 balloon payment comes due, our creative buyer can go down to his bank and put on a small $6,000 second mortgage secured by the property and give him enough cash to pay the balloon note off. He could also go in and borrow an extra amount of cash in the form of a new second mortgage and take the extra cash and use it in a very creative way to expand his real estate portfolio. This is buying a property and getting both the price and the terms.

DOCUMENTATION

[The following illustrative document was completed on the basis of data supplied by the buyer.]

UNIVERSAL EARNEST MONEY RECEIPT
AND OFFER TO PURCHASE

"This is a legally binding contract: if not understood, seek competent advice."

1. Date and Place of Offer: __August 15,__ 19 __81__ ; __Nashville__ (city) __Tennessee__ (state)

2. Principals: The undersigned Buyer __Russell Smith or Assigns__
agrees to buy and Seller agrees to sell, according to the indicated terms and conditions, the property described as follows:

3. Property: located at __461 Lake Avenue__ (street address) __Nashville__ (city) __Tennessee__ (state)
with the following legal description: __to be supplied__

including any of the following items if at present attached to the premises: plumbing, heating, and cooling equipment, including stoker and oil tanks, burners, water heaters, electric light fixtures, bathroom fixtures, roller shades, curtain rods and fixtures, draperies, venetian blinds, window and door screens, towel racks, linoleum and other attached floor coverings,

including carpeting, attached television antennas, mailboxes, all trees and shrubs, and any other fixtures EXCEPT __None__

The following personal property shall also be included as part of the purchase: _____
At the closing of the transaction, the Seller, at his expense, shall provide the Buyer with a Bill Of Sale containing a detailed inventory of the personal property included.

4. ~~Earnest Money Deposit~~ Option Deposit: Agent (or Seller) acknowledges receipt from Buyer of __One Thousand and 00/100__ dollars $ __1,000.00__

in the form of ( ) cash; (X) personal check; ( ) cashier's check; ( ) promissory note at _____% interest per annum due _____ 19 _____ ; or

other _____
as ~~earnest~~ money deposit to secure and apply on this purchase. Upon acceptance of this agreement in writing and delivery of same to Buyer, the ~~earnest~~ money deposit shall be assigned

to and ~~deposited in the listing Realtor's trust account or~~ __accrue to seller__ , to apply on the
purchase price at the time of closing.

5. Purchase Price: The total purchase price of the property shall be __One Hundred Twelve and 00/100__ dollars $ __112,000.00__

6. Payment: Purchase price is to be paid by Buyer as follows:

Aforedescribed earnest money deposit .... $ __1,000.00__

Additional payment due upon acceptance of this offer .... $ __--__

Additional payment due at closing __Upon exercise of Option, March 1, 1982__ .... $ __6,000.00__

Balance to be paid as follows:

Upon the exercise of the option, Buyer to execute note in favor of Seller in the amount of $37,000.00, unsecured, payable at 12% interest per annum in annual payments of interest only. Payment of principal to be left open-ended and subject to mutual agreement of the parties.

Upon the exercise of the option, Buyer will purchase subject to the existing first mortgage of approximately $68,000 and agrees to pay the mortgage in accordance with the currently prevailing terms and conditions of said mortgage. Seller to provide Buyer with copies of loan documents for approval within five days of acceptance of this offer.

Buyer to execute lease agreement acceptable to Buyer and Seller, with lease period to commence September 1, 1981, and run for a period of six months, the monthly rental payments being $900.00.

All conditions of the earnest money form to apply as of March 1, 1982, when option period expires and purchase must be completed by Buyer. Should Buyer not exercise the option to purchase the subject property by March 1, 1982, the option deposit is forfeited, Seller is released from all obligations hereunder, and all of Buyer's rights hereunder, legal or equitable, shall cease.

7. Title: Seller agrees to furnish good and marketable title free of all encumbrances and defects, except mortgage liens and encumbrances as set forth in this agreement, and to make conveyance by Warranty Deed or _____. Seller shall furnish in due course to the Buyer a title insurance policy insuring the Buyer of a good and marketable title in keeping with the terms and conditions of this agreement. Prior to the closing of this transaction, the Seller, upon request, will furnish to the Buyer a preliminary title report made by a title insurance company showing the condition of the title to said property. If the Seller cannot furnish marketable title within thirty days after receipt of the notice to the Buyer containing a written statement of the defects, the earnest money deposit herein receipted shall be refunded to the Buyer and this agreement shall be null and void. The following shall not be deemed encumbrances or defects; building and use restrictions general to the area; utility easements; other easements not inconsistent with Buyer's intended use; zoning or subdivision laws, covenants, conditions, restrictions, or reservations of record; tenancies of record. In the event of sale of other than real property relating to this transaction, Seller will provide evidence of title or right to sell or lease such personal property.

8. Special Representations: Seller warrants and represents to Buyer (1) that the subject property is connected to ( ) public sewer system, ( ) cesspool or septic tank, ( ) sewer system available but not connected, ( ) city water system, ( ) private water system, and that the following special improvements are included in the sale: ( ) sidewalk, ( ) curb and gutter, ( ) special street paving, ( ) special street lighting; (2) that the Seller knows of no material structural defects; (3) that all electrical wiring, heating, cooling, and plumbing systems are free of material defects and will be in good working order at the time the Buyer is entitled to possession; (4) that the Seller has no notice from any government agency of any violation or knowledge of probable violations of the law relating to the subject property; (5) that the Seller has no notice or knowledge of planned or commenced public improvements which may result in special assessments or otherwise directly and materially affect the property; and (6) that the Seller has no notice or knowledge of any liens to be assessed against the property,

EXCEPT _____ None _____.

9. Escrow Instructions: This sale shall be closed on or before March 1, 19 82 by American Escrow & Trust or such other closing agent as mutually agreed upon by Buyer and Seller. Buyer and Seller will, immediately on demand, deposit with closing agent all instruments and monies required to complete the purchase in accordance with the provisions of this agreement. Contract of Sale or Instrument of Conveyance to be made in the name of _____

to be supplied

10. Closing Costs and Pro-Ration: Seller agrees to pay for title insurance policy, preliminary title report (if requested), termite inspection as set forth below, real estate commission, cost of preparing and recording any corrective instruments, and one-half of the escrow fees. Buyer agrees to pay for recording fees for mortgages and deeds of conveyance, all costs or expenses in securing new financing or assuming existing financing, and one-half of the escrow fees. Buyer agrees to pay for recording fees for mortgages and deeds of conveyance, all costs or expenses in securing new financing or assuming existing financing, and one-half of the escrow fees. Taxes for the current year, insurance acceptable to the Buyer, rents, interest, mortgage reserves, maintenance fees, and water and other utilities constituting liens, shall be pro-rated as of closing. Renters' security deposits shall accrue to Buyer at closing. Seller to provide Buyer with all current rental or lease agreements prior to closing.

11. Termite Inspection: Seller agrees, at his expense, to provide written certification by a reputable licensed pest control firm that the property is free of termite infestation. In the event termites are found, the Seller shall have the property treated at his expense and provide acceptable certification that treatment has been rendered. If any structural repairs are required by reason of termite damage as established by acceptable certification, Seller agrees to make necessary repairs not to exceed $500. If repairs exceed $500, Buyer shall first have the right to accept the property "as is" with a credit to the Buyer at closing of $500, or the Buyer may terminate this agreement with the earnest money deposit being promptly returned to the Buyer if the Seller does not agree to pay all costs of treatment and repair.

12. Conditions of Sale: The following conditions shall also apply, and shall, if conflicting with the printed portions of this agreement, prevail and control:

None

13. Liability and Maintenance: Seller shall maintain subject property, including landscaping, in good condition until the date of transfer of title or possession by Buyer, whichever occurs first. All risk of loss and destruction of property, and all expenses of insurance, shall be borne by the seller until the date of possession. If the improvements on the property are destroyed or materially damaged prior to closing, then the Buyer shall have the right to declare this agreement null and void, and the earnest money deposit and all other sums paid by Buyer toward the purchase price shall be returned to the Buyer forthwith.

14. Possession: The Buyer shall be entitled to possession of property upon closing or _____, 19 ___.

15. Default: In the event the Buyer fails to complete the purchase as herein provided, the earnest money deposit shall be retained by the Seller as the total and entire liquidated damages. In the event the Seller fails to perform any condition of the sale as herein provided, then the Buyer may, at his option, treat the contract as terminated, and all payments made by the Buyer hereunder shall be returned to the Buyer forthwith, provided the Buyer may, at his option, treat this agreement as being in full force and effect with the right to action for specific performance

and damages. In the event that either Buyer, Seller, or Agent shall institute suit to enforce any rights hereunder, the prevailing party shall be entitled to court costs and a reasonable attorney's fee.

16. Time Limit of Offer: The Seller shall have until

_____ August 17, _____ , 19 __81__ to accept this
(hour)   (date)

offer by delivering a signed copy hereof to the Buyer. If this offer is not so accepted, it shall lapse and the agent (or Seller) shall refund the ~~earnest money~~ deposit to the Buyer forthwith.

17. General Agreements: (1) Both parties to this purchase reserve their rights to assign and hereby otherwise agree to cooperate in effecting an Internal Revenue Code 1031 exchange or similar tax-related arrangement prior to close of escrow, upon either party's written notice of intention to do so. (2) Upon approval of this offer by the Seller, this agreement shall become a contract between Buyer and Seller and shall inure to the benefit of the heirs, administrators, executors, successors, personal representatives, and assigns of said parties. (3) Time is of the essence and an essential part of this agreement. (4) This contract constitutes the sole and entire agreement between the parties hereto and no modification of this contract shall be binding unless attached hereto and signed by all parties to the contract. No representations, promises, or inducements not included in this contract shall be binding upon any party hereto.

18. Buyer's Statement and Receipt: "I/we hereby agree to purchase the above property in accordance with the terms and conditions above stated and acknowledge receipt of a

completed copy of this agreement, which I/we have fully read and understand." Dated _____ August 15, _____ 19 __81__ , _____
(hour)

Address _____ 314 Brook Avenue _____   _____ [signature] or Assigns _____ Buyer

_____ Nashville, Tennessee _____   _____ Buyer

Phone No: Home __321-1492__   Business __865-4135__

19. Seller's Statement and Response: "I/we approve and accept the above offer, which I/we have fully read and understand, and agree to the above terms and conditions this day

of _____ , 19 _____ , _____ .
(hour)

Address _____   _____ Seller

Phone No: Home _____ Business _____   _____ Seller

20. Commission Agreement: Seller agrees to pay a commission of __NA__ % of the gross sales price to _____

for services in this transaction, and agrees that, in the event of forfeiture of the earnest money deposit by the Buyer, said deposit shall be divided between the Seller's broker and the Seller (one half to each party), the Broker's part not to exceed the amount of the commission.

21. Buyer's Receipt for Signed Offer: The Buyer hereby acknowledges receipt of a copy of the above agreement bearing the Seller's signature in acceptance of this offer.

Dated _____ , 19 _____   _____ Buyer

_____ Buyer

COMMENTARY TO DOCUMENTATION

In this instance, the "Universal Earnest Receipt and Offer to Purchase" has been adjusted to serve as the basis for a Lease Option. The agreement calls for the execution of a lease contract between buyer (Tenant) and seller. Most large office supply stores carry standard "Lease With Option to Purchase" forms in which the lease (rental) agreement is combined with the offer to purchase.

Item 6. The terms of the purchase are unusual in that the bulk of the seller's equity is being carried back in the form of a personal, unsecured note with open-ended amortization. The explanation for this is simply that the seller is extremely anxious to sell. There is no other way to account for his willingness to accept a note without collateral.

The earnest money form does not state the terms and conditions of the underlying first mortgage. However, there is a contingency of approval by the buyer — a safety clause in case there is any problem with the "subject to" arrangement.

Summing Up

"Education is the acquisition of the art of the utilization of knowledge."
—Alfred North Whitehead

"Without doubt, the highest privilege of wealth is the opportunity it affords for doing good, without giving up one's fortune."
—Cicero

What have you learned from this book? How can it continue to be of help to you in the future? Each reader will have a different answer to these questions depending on the factors that go to define his or her unique situation: present level of competence in real estate investing, personal goals, the location and type of property sought, financial situation, access to resources, and so on. These are the obvious variables. Then there is a host of significant additional factors, including how we relate to risk, how successfully we cultivate a win/win philosophy of dealing with others, and how we define "wealth" — that mysterious intangible that reveals what is ultimately of importance to us.

Each person is different; each will bring different expectations to a book of this type. As author, I can only speculate how my own "hidden agenda" of goals for readers might have been fulfilled through these pages. There are four goals that I hope might have been realized by the majority:

(1) **The Formation of a New Gestalt.**

At the outset, we wrote about the "Great Divide" that we all encounter at significant moments in our lives. If you are one who has reached that point in life (whether you are young or old) where you sense the need to seize the initiative in behalf of your own financial independence, then I would hope this book might have proved this one thing: "You can do it!" It is still possible in our day to exercise the qualities of vision, independence, creativity, trust, optimism, and educated risk—taking and coming out on top. There is no better opportunity to do this than with American income property. As one of the case contributors put it: "Why do you suppose people from foreign countries are buying so much property here? Because they know that American real estate is pure gold! Why are Americans so slow to realize this?"

This book is intended to help people gain a new perspective on their possibilities—a new gestalt of "pure gold." Another contributor stated it this way:

"This is probably thrilling only to me. But as of January 15 of this year [1981], I had no indication that it would ever be possible for me to think of investing in real estate. The Nothing Down Seminar changed all of that. Now my only restriction has been time enough to follow up on other deals. I feel I can buy anything I set my mind to . . . Anything is possible when you see something you really want . . . For the first time, I feel great!"

(2) New Action Knowledge

The cliché has it that education is the acquisition of *knowledge.* Whitehead knew better; his quote above makes it clear that education is learning how to *use* knowledge. The goal of this book has been to supply knowledge of the type that can be used—new action knowledge. The objectives can be expressed in "How To's": How to locate desirable properties, how to analyze the deals, how to negotiate with the sellers, how to apply appropriate alternative financing techniques, how to build a team of professionals and partners, how to structure the offers and documentation to minimize risk, how to manage the cash flows, how to close on the transaction, and how to plan for future usage. Above all, the variety of approaches illustrated in this book make it possible for anyone to adapt the material to the realization of personal goals. Here is how one of the case contributors expressed his feelings concerning the type of action knowledge the Nothing Down System provided him:

"Look at a variety of properties before purchasing. Don't be afraid to make the first offer. You can protect yourself with a contingency clause (subject to inspection and verification of expenses). You can buy don't wanters! Incredible! Finally, be realistic about your goals. I plan to buy one house each year for the next ten years."

(3) Understanding the System

If this book has been successful, the reader should come away with a stronger sense of the coherence and logic of the Robert Allen Nothing Down System of real estate investing. Too often creative finance becomes a token banner flying above a hodge podge of miscellaneous techniques. What is needed is a step-by-step program that "hangs together." That is not to say that the practitioner must be caught up in a lock-step system that dictates every move. Quite to the contrary. To be successful, the Nothing Down System depends on flexibility, creative use of options, alternative approaches to solving problems.

However, the investor must have a way to organize the options available to him in such a way that he or she is ever in control of the next move. That is why the system used in this book categorizes the flexible sources of down payments according to the *people* you meet "on the way to the closing"—the sellers, the buyers, the Realtors, the renters, the property itself (a kind of person, if you look at it that way!), the hard-money lenders, the holders of underlying mortgages, the investors, and the partners. These categories, together with option opportunities, form one major dimension of the "system." The other two dimensions comprise, in the first place, the fifty creative finance techniques of the Nothing Down Program, and in the second place, the major action steps of the actual purchase—locating, analyzing the situation, negotiating, closing (including preparing the offer and the documentation), and following through with management and future plans. Review the flow chart at the beginning of the book and note how everything fits together. Get this plan in mind—it's your roadmap to success. The following statements from two of the case contributors show that they are imbued—like all the others featured in this book—with a sense of the "win/win system" we are describing:

"This was not a win/win situation; it was a win/win/win situation where everyone was happy with the end solution. The Nothing Down win/win approach definitely works for us."

"Don't wait for opportunities to come to you. Plant seeds all over with many concerned people. Some are bound to flower. Know the seller's needs. Listen to what he says and read between the lines as you listen."

(4) Taking Action

Above all, this book is intended to persuade the reader to take action—to set goals, form alliances with competent professionals, learn the system, and act! No one can say it better than the contributors to this book. Here is how one of them put it:

"Jump in! If the numbers are there and you make the move, you'll find yourself thinking, analyzing, working, etc., to make it all work out. Then you can't wait for the next one."

New gestalt, new action knowledge, understanding the system, taking action—these four major items constitute the thrust of the book *How to Write a Nothing Down Offer.* To make it easier for the reader to use the material in a practical way, we conclude with a series of a "finder's indexes" that provide cross-referencing to the case studies from the point of view of the most important parameters of investing.

Finder's Indexes

Index A
Location Index

The numbers following the names of the cities refer to case studies.

SEATTLE 45

BREMERTON 24 49

PORTLAND 30 38

EUGENE 13

WEST BEND 23

SPRINGFIELD, MA 6

CHEYENNE 22

MILWAUKEE 1 2 8 17

CHICO 29

CLEVELAND 11

PHILADELPHIA 35

SACRAMENTO 15

PALO ALTO 10 18

FREMONT 40

DENVER 39

ST. LOUIS 44

KANSAS CITY, MO 27

FLAGSTAFF 12

SANTA FE 41

BIXBY 36

NASHVILLE 50

LOS ANGELES 37 48

OKLAHOMA CITY 32

ORANGE COUNTY 34

ALBUQUERQUE 4 5 19 43

ATLANTA 46

SAN DIEGO 14 47

PHOENIX 26 28 42

TUCSON 33

DALLAS 31

JACKSONVILLE 7

ORLANDO 25

ST. PETERSBURG 20

WEST PALM BEACH 3 9 16

HOMESTEAD 21

Index B
Source Index

source of lead	total number	case study
1. Classified Ad	21	3, 5, 9, 10, 11, 13, 17, 19, 22, 27, 29, 34, 35, 36, 39, 40, 43, 44, 48, 49, 50 (including two buyer's ads: 17 and 22)
2. Real Estate Agent	17	1, 2, 6, 7, 8, 15, 20, 24, 28, 30, 32, 37, 38, 41, 42, 45, 46
3. MLS Book	7	12, 13, 14, 16, 31, 33, 38
4. Colleague or Friend	5	4, 13, 25, 26, 47
5. For Sale Sign	3	21, 23, 4*
6. Exchange Broker	1	18

Conclusion: Classified ads are the most important source of leads. Agents come next, followed by the grouping of miscellaneous sources. Best advice: use *all* sources simultaneously — you never know when you will hit a gold mine.

Indicates transaction discussed in case study addendum.

Index C
Property-Type Index

TOTAL: 543 Rental Units
256 Buildings

57 Transactions in 50 Case Studies
Average number of rental units per transaction: 9.5
Median = Single Family Home

Indicates transaction discussed in case study addendum.

Index D
Price Range Index

selling price in thousands	case study	selling price in thousands	case study	selling price in thousands	case study	selling price in thousands	case study
$2,950	34	$140	49	$70	47	$49.9	33
929	48	132.5	29*	69.3	5	48	1
700	20	120	29*	66.5	3	43.2	11
375	34	112	50	64.9	42	42.5	16
325	22	110	39	64	13	41.0	30
280	17	110	37	60	41	38	2
245	9	102.1	18	60	13	35	8
220	43*	92	21	57.5	38	35	4
195	14	92	18	57.5	12	34.6	27
165	36	90	23	56.9	44	28.5	24
165	19	80	7	56	15	25	35
160	45	80	6	53.9	28	16.4	32
159	29	77.6	18	52.9	28	14.4	26
155	10	75	29*	52	31	10	46
145	43	72	40	50	4*	3	25
141.5	38						

Total $10,014,600 (61 transactions in 50 case studies)
Average Price Per Transaction: $164,174
Median Price: $72,000

Indicates transaction discussed in a case study addendum.

Index E
Techniques Index

Master List of the Fifty Robert Allen Nothing Down Techniques
Brief vignettes describing each technique can be found on the indicated pages.

Which Are The Most Popular Techniques?

RANK	FREQ. (No. of Ref.)	%		TECHNIQUES
1	39	19.4%	No. 4	Contract/Wrap
2	27	13.4%	No. 6	Balloon
3	13	6.5%	No. 32	Second Mortgage Crank
4	10	5.0%	No. 19	Borrowing Realtor's Commission
			No. 45	Partner's Cash/Your Expertise
5	9	4.5%	No. 21	Deposits
6	7	3.5%	No. 1	Ultimate Paper Out
			No. 20	Rents
			No. 36	Moving the Mortgage
7	5	2.5%	No. 13	Borrow Against Insurance
			No. 15	Creation of Paper
			No. 24	Small Amounts from Banks
			No. 42	Partner's Money for Down
8	4	2.0%	No. 5	Raise Price/Lower Terms
			No. 9	Savings and Inheritances
			No. 10	Supply Seller's Needs
			No. 11	Assume Seller's Obligations
			No. 34	Buy Low, Refinance High
9	3	1.5%	No. 8	Defer Down/No Payments
			No. 37	Creative Refinance
			No. 50	Lease Option
10	2	1.0%	No. 14	Anything Goes
			No. 16	Two-Way Exchange
			No. 26	Credit Cards
			No. 28	Home Equity Loans
			No. 39	Holder as Partner
			No. 40	Selling Notes
			No. 44	Cash/Equity Combo

RANK	FREQ. (No. of Ref.)	%		TECHNIQUES
11	1	0.5%	No. 2	Blanket
			No. 12	Using Talents
			No. 17	Three-Way Exchange
			No. 23	Splitting Off Property
			No. 27	Home Improvement Loans
			No. 33	Seller Refinance
			No. 35	Holders' Discounts
			No. 41	Partner's Financial Statement
			No. 43	Partner's Money Till Your Money Comes
12	0	0.0%	No. 3	Insurance Policy
			No. 7	High Monthly Down
			No. 18	Lemonading
			No. 22	Splitting off Furniture
			No. 25	Cash-By-Mail Companies
			No. 29	Refinance Personal Property
			No. 30	VA Loans
			No. 31	FHA Loans
			No. 38	Pulling Cash Out of Own Buildings
			No. 46	Rolling Option
			No. 47	Equity for Options
			No. 48	Sale Option Back
			No. 49	Earnest Money Option

Total of 201 References

Techniques Matrix

Cases	\ Techniques	1	2	3	4	5	6	7	8	9	10	11	12	13	14	15	16	17	18	19	20	21	22	23	24	25
	1	1			4		6																			
	2	1			4		6					11								19						
	3	1			4		6														20	21				
	4	1			4																					
	5				4															19		21				
	6				4																					
	7				4	5					10				14											
	8						6				10															
	9						6		8												20	21				
	10				4		6				10															
	11											11													24	
	12						6							13												
	13	1			4									13												
	14														14											
	15						6									15				19					24	
	16						6									15										
	17																16			19	20	21				
	18				4													17								
	19				4									13						19		21				
	20				4	5	6		8											19	20	21				
	21				4						10									19	20	21				
	22	1			4																20	21				
	23						6																	23		
	24				4		6																		24	
	25				4							11	12													
	26				4							11													24	
	27				4																					
	28				4		6			9										19						
	29		2		4											15										
	30				4											15										
	31				4		6																			
	32				4		6																			
	33				4		6																			
	34				4	5	6																			
	35																									
	36																									
	37				4		6													19						
	38				4												16									
	39				4		6									15										
	40				4		6																		24	
	41				4		6													19						
	42	1			4	5	6		8																	
	43				4		6																			
	44				4		6																			
	45				4		6							13												
	46				4		6																			
	47				4									13												
	48				4					9											20	21				
	49				4					9																
	50				4		6			9																
Technique		1	2	3	4	5	6	7	8	9	10	11	12	13	14	15	16	17	18	19	20	21	22	23	24	25
Total References		7	1	0	39	4	27	0	3	4	4	4	1	5	2	5	2	1	0	10	7	9	0	1	5	0

Cases	Techniques	26	27	28	29	30	31	32	33	34	35	36	37	38	39	40	41	42	43	44	45	46	47	48	49	50
	1												37													
	2																									
	3							32																		
	4																									
	5																									
	6																									
	7																				45					
	8									34																
	9																				45					
	10																									
	11																	42								
	12							32																		
	13																									
	14																									
	15							32				36														
	16											36								44						
	17																									
	18																									
	19																				45					
	20			28																						
	21																									
	22																									
	23							32				36	37													50
	24																									
	25	26														40										
	26	26																								
	27		27																		45					
	28			28																						
	29							32				36														
	30							32				36														
	31							32											43							
	32							32																		
	33							32	33																	
	34									34																
	35							32		34																
	36							32		34																
	37										35							42								
	38							32				36														
	39											36														
	40												37		39											
	41														39			42								
	42															40										
	43																41				45					
	44																	42			45					
	45																	42			45					
	46																				45					
	47																				45					
	48							32													45					
	49																									50
	50																									50
Technique		26	27	28	29	30	31	32	33	34	35	36	37	38	39	40	41	42	43	44	45	46	47	48	49	50
Total References		2	1	2	0	0	0	13	1	4	1	7	3	0	2	2	1	5	1	2	10	0	0	0	0	3

Index F

Financing Index

TYPE OF FINANCING USED AS BASIS OF TRANSACTION	TOTAL NUMBER	%	CASE STUDY
1. Assumption	12	22%	9, 11, 12, 22, 28, 30, 31, 33, 38, 41, 47, 48
2. Contract/Wrap	11	20%	2, 5, 13, 19, 22, 24, 25, 26, 38, 39, 43
3. Purchase Money Mortgage (or Trust Deed)	9	16%	6, 7, 16, 20, 21, 27, 42, 44, 46
4. Refinance	7	13%	1, 3, 14, 23, 34, 36, 40
5. New First Mortgage (or Trust Deed)	5	9%	8, 29*, 32, 35, 37
6. Exchange	3	5%	17, 18, 38
7. "Subject To" Purchase	3	5%	15, 29, 29*, 29*
8. A.I.T.D.	2	4%	10, 45
9. Lease Option	2	4%	49, 50
10. Personal Unsecured Note	1	2%	4
	55 Transactions in 50 Deals	100%	

Indicates transaction discussed in a case study addendum.

Index G
Index of Clauses

Index G

The following listing of clauses gives the text location where the originals are used in the documentation for the cases. Readers should also consult the commentary to each case for additional advice on the clauses. See also the section on filling out the Universal Earnest Money Receipt and Offer to Purchase, pages 7-15.

1. INSTRUMENTS OF PURCHASE
All-inclusive purchase money trust note and deed, 65-66
All-inclusive trust deed, 258
Assumption, 11, 13, 30, 56, 74, 78, 158, 174, 186, 192, 217, 222, 234, 270, 276
Contract, 144, 234
Exchange agreement, 99-100
Land contract, 29, 78
Lease option, 285, 287-88
Note, unsecured, 288
Owner carry back, 26, 52, 56, 105, 111, 158, 174, 180, 186, 192, 210, 228, 270, 276
Owner carry back on another property (moving the mortgage), 90, 158, 164, 170
Purchase money first mortgage (or deed of trust), 44, 48, 50, 122, 124, 154, 240, 252, 264
Purchase money second mortgage (or deed of trust), 34, 95, 107, 240
Purchase money third mortgage (or deed of trust), 240
Refinance (or new loan), 26, 34, 51, 84, 95, 105, 136, 180, 192, 197, 202, 210, 228
Second note and deed of trust, 74, 186
"Subject to," 11-12, 78, 90, 107, 109, 111, 164, 170, 288
Third note and deed of trust, 74
Wrap, 39-40, 117-18, 248

2. CONTINGENCIES
Absence of divorce judgment, 70
Absence of flooding effects, 202
Acceleration (due-on-sale), 67, 180, 228, 234
Acceleration, adjustments in case of, 78-79, 174
Agent disclosure, 85, 186, 277
Agreements with tenants, seller to furnish copies of, 235, 277

Approval of interim tenants by buyer, 277
Approval of loan, 34
Approval of loan documents, 107, 109, 288
Approval of preliminary title report, 74, 84, 192, 240
Approval of termite report, 34
"As is" purchase, 48, 91, 126, 181
Assignment, right of, 154
Assignment prohibition, 34, 234
Assumability of first, 70, 107, 111, 222
Assumption of note, 90
Closing costs, 30, 228, 265
Closing costs, seller to pay buyer's, 96
Commission carried back, 126
Completion of construction, 193
Condition, general contingency on cleanliness, 187
Condo fee prorated, 270
Contingent sale, 108, 110, 112, 159
Contract used as down payment, 117
Credits toward principal, 126
"Cross deed," 180
Debris removed, 70
Deed in anticipation of financing, 180
Default, 15, 57, 92
Delayed payments, 90, 264
Delivery of property, 224
Deposit increase upon removal of contingencies, 105
Escrow fund for repairs, 112, 187
Eviction of tenants, 112, 211
Exchange, accommodating, 276
Exchange disclosure, 105
Exclusion of other offers, 192
Exculpatory clause, 14, 223, 234, 235
Financial statement, buyer to provide, 171

Index H
Documents

The following sample documents and schedules are reproduced on the indicated pages:

Bibliography

The following titles will provide information on real estate investing in all its dimensions. Most titles can be obtained conveniently by mail through The Allen Group, Inc., 145 East Center Street, Provo, Utah 84601. Credit-card orders: Call toll-free (800) 453-1364. Please call or write for a current price list.

Guarantee: You must be completely satisfied with your purchase. If not, return the book or tape — in saleable condition — postage paid within thirty days. You will receive a prompt refund of the full purchase price.

Books, Tapes, and Newsletters

The American Congress on Real Estate (ACRE) *ACRE Highlights.* Tapes of general sessions and selected workshops featuring today's leading experts on real estate investing. Recorded at national conferences of The American Congress on Real Estate. 16 tapes.

The American Congress on Real Estate (ACRE) *The Complete ACRE.* Tapes of general sessions and all workshops featuring today's leading experts on real estate investing. Recorded at national conferences of The American Congress on Real Estate. 32 tapes.

Allen, Richard J. *How to Write a Nothing Down Offer So That Everyone Wins.* A casebook based on Robert G. Allen's Nothing Down System of creative real estate investing. Features 50 actual case studies.

Allen, Robert G. *Nothing Down: How to Buy Real Estate With Little or No Money Down.* The classic handbook for nothing-down buyers.

Allen, Robert G. *Creating Wealth.* Shows exactly how to create a wealth-building program tailored to suit individual situations.

Allen, Robert G. *Creating Wealth With Little or Nothing Down.* Eight hours of instruction. Six tapes and workbook.

Allen, Robert G. *Real Estate Cookie Cutters.* Twelve unique real estate investing techniques. Six tapes.

Allen, Robert G. *Tape-of-the-Month Subscription.* Monthly update and instructions from Mr. Allen and other leading real estate authorities. One year.

Allen, Robert G. *Special Reports.* A set of three special reports by Mr. Allen: *Launching Yourself Into Financial Self-Reliance, Recession Tactics: Specific Ways of Making Money In a Sluggish or Declining Real Estate Market,* and *The Great San Francisco Real Estate Adventure: The Ultimate Test for "Nothing Down."*

Allen, Robert G. *How to Buy a Home.* One-hour video-cassette giving step-by-step instructions for beginning investors. Specify VHS or Beta.

The Allen Group *The Real Estate Advisor: The Action Newsletter of Creative Real Estate Investing.* Richard J. Allen, Editor. Monthly 12-page newsletter; one-year subscription.

The Allen Group *Combination Offer.* Includes *Creating Wealth, The Real Estate Advisor, Creating Wealth With Little or Nothing Down,* and *How to Write a Nothing Down Offer* by Richard J. Allen.

The Allen Group *Robert G. Allen's Creating Wealth Conference.* Full proceedings. Twelve tapes and workbook.

Beck, John *Forced Sale Workbook.* Learn how to buy distressed real estate at bargain prices.

Beck, John *Big Money in Forced Sales.* Two tapes.

Beck, John *Forced Sale Package.* Book and two tapes.

Beck, John *How to Get Rich Giving Away Real Estate.* Book and tape.

Beck, John *How to Get Rich Package.* Book and tape.

Beck, John *Partnership Package.* Two tapes and 20-page pamphlet with 60 pages of forms.

Beck, John *Options Package.* Two tapes and 24-page pamphlet with contract forms.

Beck, John *Purchasing Forced-Sale Property.* Eight tapes and workbook.

Beck, John *How to Cash Out of Forced-Sale Property and Make Big Money.* Six tapes.

Beck, John *Combination Offer.* Includes all of the above items by Mr. Beck (no duplicates).

Behle, John *The Paper Game: How to Profit Through Buying, Selling, Trading, Creating, and Improving Real Estate Paper.* Instruction manual plus glossary of terms used in the acquisition of discounted mortgages.

Behle, John *The Paper Game Tape Package.* Eight tapes which enlarge upon the material in the book.

Behle, John *Combination Offer.* Book and tapes.

Berman, Donald M. *The Owners' System: Small Property Management and Control.* Instructions and all forms necessary for managing three properties for three years.

Berman, Donald M. *Managing for Success.* Six tapes and 65-page workbook.

Berman, Donald M. *The Success Package.* Book and tapes.

Bruss, Robert *The Smart Investor's Guide to Real Estate: Big Profits from Small Investments.* Basic real estate investing.

Bruss, Robert *How to Avoid the Due-on-Sale Clause.*

Childers, John *Steps to Building Wealth.* Includes *The Lazy Way to Buy Real Estate* (six tapes plus two *Creative Amortization Schedule Handbooks*) and *The ABZs of Buying Property: Steps to Building Wealth* (six tapes and workbook).

Chodack, David A. *Fortune Builders.* Success stories of 21 successful real estate investors.

Cohen, Herb *You Can Negotiate Anything: How to Get What You Want.*

Cook, Wade B. *How to Build a Real Estate Money Machine.* How to buy and sell real estate on contract.

Cook, Wade B. *How to Build a Real Estate Money Machine Tape Package.* Two tapes.

Cook, Wade B. *Pay No Taxes With Real Estate.* Use recent real estate tax changes to maximize your tax benefits.

Cook, Wade B. *Things Your CPA Never Told You.* Companion to *Pay No Taxes.* Two tapes.

Cook, Wade B. *How to Pick Up Foreclosures.* Step-by-step procedures for acquiring property from distressed sellers.

Cook, Wade B. *Cook's Book on Creative Real Estate.* A casebook of creative real estate transactions.

Cook, Wade B. *Owner Financing.*

Cook, Wade B. *Real Estate: The Best Game in Town.*

Cook, Wade B. *The Three Entity Approach to Investing in Real Estate.* Pension, profit-sharing, and trusts as investment vehicles.

Cook, Wade B. *Big Bucks by Selling Your Property.* The art of making money by selling property.

Cook, Wade B. *The First National Bank of Real Estate Clauses.*

Cook, Wade B. *Wade Cook's Real Estate Newsletter.* Monthly; one-year subscription.

Cook, Wade B. *Super Pack.* Includes all of the above items by Mr. Cook, plus *Legal Forms* and *Record Keeping System,* described in the "Forms" section.

Cook, Wade B. *A Day with Wade Cook.* Eight tapes.

Cook, Wade B. *The Complete Foreclosure System.* Four tapes, workbook, and forms.

Drummond, Phil *Control Without Ownership.* Lease options. Four tapes and workbook.

Drummond, Phil *How to Make the Ultimate Purchase Offer.* Clauses and techniques. Six tapes and workbook.

Drummond, Phil *How to Get Start-Up Funds.* Tape and workbook.

Drummond, Phil *How to Write a Firm But Fair Lease/ Rental Agreement.* Tape and workbook.

Drummond, Phil *Complete Real Estate Investor's Training Portfolio.* Includes all of the above items by Mr. Drummond, plus *How to Get Started in Real Estate Investing* (five tapes and workbook, $139 value), and a one-year subscription to *Phil Drummond's Investor Alert* newsletter ($36 value), packaged in an attractive attaché case ($40 value).

Dykes, James M. *How to Find Real Estate Bargains.* Four tapes.

Dykes, James M. *Recycling Your Properties: Advanced Techniques and Advantages.* Six tapes and workbook.

Fox, Claire R. *Syndicating Single-Family Homes: How to Form Group Investment Partnerships Using Other People's Money.*

Glubetich, David *How to Grow a Money Tree: Earn 20 to 30 Percent and More By Investing in Safe, Hi-Yield Second Mortgages and Trust Deeds.*

Glubetich, David *Double Your Money in Real Estate Every Two Years.* How to turn inflation to your advantage.

Glubetich, David *The Monopoly Game: The "How-To" Book of Making Big Money with Rental Homes.* Buying and managing the single-family rental home.

Hall, Sam F. *Positive Solutions to Negative Cash Flows.* Dealing with balloon notes, lease options, shared appreciation, discounted mortgages, refinancing, seasonal demand properties, and others.

Hall, Sam F. *Positive Solutions to Negative Cash Flows Tape Package.* Two tapes.

Hall, Sam F. *Positive Solutions Combination Offer.* Book and tapes.

Hall, Sam F. *How to Find Real Estate Bargains.* Identifying and analyzing potential real estate investments.

Kessler, A.D. *A Fortune at Your Feet: How You Can Get Rich, Stay Rich, and Enjoy Being Rich With Creative Real Estate.*

Koon, Nick *How to Become a Millionaire Buying Single-Family Homes.*

Koon, Nick *How to Get Started.* Six tapes and workbook.

Koon, Nick *Structuring Cash Flow.* Six tapes and workbook.

Koon, Nick *Hard-Nosed Management.* Six tapes and workbook.

Lee, Dick *How to Pay Zero Income Tax — Legally.* Tax benefits of owning income property.

Land, Joe *Paper: The Ultimate Tool for the Real Estate Investor.* Purchasing real estate using discounted mortgages, trust deeds, corporate bonds, etc. Eight tapes and workbook.

Land, Joe *Tax Strategies for the Real Estate Investor.* Eight tapes and workbook.

Land, Joe *Real Estate Tax Update.* Monthly newsletter; one-year subscription.

Land, Joe *Combination Offer.* Includes all of the above items by Mr. Land.

Milin, Mike and Irene *Landlording Made Easy.* Sixteen tapes and workbook.

Milin, Mike and Irene *Cash Flow, Cash Flow, Cash Flow.* Six tapes and workbook.

Milin, Mike and Irene *Money-Making Clauses That Get Results.* Two tapes and workbook.

Milin, Mike and Irene *Real Estate Investor Analysis.* Bi-monthly newsletter; one-year subscription

Milin, Mike and Irene *Combination Offer.* Includes all of the above items by Mr. and Mrs. Milin.

Mitton, Jay *Keeping It! A Tax Program for the Eighties.* Workbook with sample trusts and estate plans, and four tapes.

Morris, Hal *Crisis Real Estate Investing.* Low-risk guide for protecting assets and avoiding disaster.

Morris, Hal *How to Stop Foreclosure.* How to save your home and property.

Morris, Hal *Foreclosure Systems.* Eight tapes, workbook, and bank/savings and loan computer printout.

Morris, Hal *Equity Sharing: An Answer for the '80s.* Six tapes and five contracts.

Morris, Hal *Combination Offer.* Includes all of the above items by Mr. Morris, plus a nine-tape album, *Money-Making Ideas* ($73.95 value).

Murdock, Clint *The Bucks Stop Here: How to Win With Your Banker.*

Murdock, Clint *A Comprehensive Guide to Financing Options for Real Estate.* Expandable loose-leaf format. Learn about loan sources for financing single and multiple residences, etc.

Napier, Jimmy *Invest in Debt.* Investing in discounted mortgages.

Napier, Jimmy *Combination Offer.* Includes *Invest in Debt* described above, plus *Money Maker: 2-Day Home Study Course* (eight tapes), *Money Maker Report* newsletter (18-month subscription), and *Live at Caesar's Palace: Guest Appearance with Jack Miller* (eight tapes).

Nickerson, William *How I Turned $1,000 Into Five Million in Real Estate.* Fixing-up investment property to build equity.

Phillips, Wayne *How to Get Government Loans.* Finding and using low-interest loans for qualified investment properties.

Robinson, Leigh *Landlording.* One of the best books available on property management.

Santucci, Danny *Successful Estate Planning: It's Your Money — How to Keep It Now That You Made It.* Eight tapes and workbook.

Santucci, Danny *Real Estate and the IRS: How to Keep the IRS Out of Your Pocket.* Eight tapes and workbook.

Santucci, Danny *Tactics for Tough Times.* Eight tapes.

Santucci, Danny *Concepts and Mechanics of Exchanges.* Six tapes and book.

Santucci, Danny *Combination Offer.* Includes all of the above items by Mr. Santucci.

Santucci, Danny *Estate Planning Combination Offer.* Includes the above *Combination Offer,* plus *Investment Vehicles for Real Estate Investors* (manual, $65 value), *Tax Planning for Closely-Held Businesses* (six tapes, $115 value), and *Wills and Trusts* (manual, $50 value).

Schaub, John *Investing for Success: How to Creatively Acquire and Manage Single-Family Houses for Your Investment Portfolio.* Six tapes and workbook.

Steele, Robert *Creative Real Estate: Problem-Solving Formulas.*

Steele, Robert *Creative Real Estate Tapes.* Ten tapes.

Steele, Robert *Fifteen Ways to Buy, Sell, and Exchange Real Estate Without Using Cash.*

Steele, Robert *Fifty Ways to Acquire Real Estate.*

Steele, Robert *An Extra House as an Investment.*

Steele, Robert *The Real Exchange Market and How It Operates.*

Steele, Robert *Mortgage Investments: Principles and Methods.*

Southard, Jim *Real Estate Wealth-Seeker's Guide.* Eight tapes and workbook.

Tauscher, Don *Creative Banking Techniques.* Developing banking relationships — how to bank when others cannot. Twelve tapes and workbook.

Tauscher, Don *Paper Magic.* The creative use of paper formulas to acquire investment real estate. Four tapes and booklet.

Tauscher, Don *Combination Offer.* Includes the above items by Mr. Tauscher.

Forms and Investor Aids

Consumer Guide to Mortgage Payments. Financial Publishing Company.

Creative Real Estate Forms by Robert Steele.

Earnest Money Receipt and Offer to Purchase Form. The Allen Group, Inc. Developed by Richard J. Allen. Package of 30 four-part carbonless forms.

Financial I Calculator. Full-function amortizing calculator. Easy to use.

Leasehold Document Forms by Robert Steele.

Legal Forms by Wade B. Cook. Sample contracts, forms, and agreements.

Professional Planner: The Forced-Focus System for Time Management by Wm. Rolf Kerr.

Property Management Forms by Donald M. Berman

1. Package of 25 each of *Residential Occupancy Agreement* and *Notice of Intent to Vacate* forms, and ten each of *Residential Occupancy Agreement* (rent increase), *Pet Addendum, Waterbed Addendum,* and *Past-Due Notice* forms.

2. Package of 50 *Rental Unit Resident Application* forms.

3. Package of 25 *Residential Occupancy Agreement* forms.

Real Estate Bluebook by Robert DeHeer. A daily reference tool for use in every phase of real estate.

Record Keeping System by Wade B. Cook.

Screening Sellers by Phone by Sam F. Hall. Questions designed to glean information necessary to analyze potential investment property. Includes 50 analysis forms.

Who's Who in Creative Real Estate by William R. Broadbent.

Your New Home and How to Take Care of It National Association of Home Builders.

Additional Recommended Reading

Available in leading bookstores nationwide.

Bockl, George *How Real Estate Fortunes are Made.* Englewood Cliffs, NJ: Prentice–Hall, Inc., 1972.

Campbell, David *Take the Road to Creativity and Get Off Your Dead End.* Niles, IL: Argus Communications, 1977.

Carnegie, Dale *How to Win Friends and Influence People.* New York, NY: Pocket Books, Inc., 1982.

Clason, George *Richest Man in Babylon.* New York, NY: E.P. Dutton, 1955.

Conwell, Russell *Acres of Diamonds.* New York, NY: Jove Publications, 1982.

Edwards, David D. *How to Be More Creative.* Los Gatos, CA: Occasional Productions, 1978.

Greene, Bill *Think Like a Tycoon: Inflation Can Make You Rich Through Taxes and Real Estate.* San Francisco, CA: Harbor Publishing, Inc., 1980.

Haroldsen, Mark O. *Financial Genius.* Salt Lake City, UT: Mark O. Haroldsen, Inc., 1983.

Hill, Napoleon *Think and Grow Rich.* New York, NY: Fawcett Publications, 1979.

Kiplinger, Austin *The Exciting '80s: A Kiplinger Forecast for the Next Decade.* Washington, DC: The Kiplinger Washington Editors, Inc., 1979.

Lakein, Alan *How to Get Control of Your Time and Your Life.* New York, NY: New American Library, 1974.

Lowry, Albert *How You Can Become Financially Independent by Investing in Real Estate.* New York, NY: Simon and Schuster, 1982.

Lowry, Albert *How to Manage Real Estate Successfully — In Your Spare Time.* New York, NY: Simon and Schuster, 1977.

Linkletter, Art *Yes, You Can!* New York, NY: Jove Publications, 1980.

Maltz, Maxwell *Psycho-Cybernetics.* New York, NY: Pocket Books, Inc., 1960.

Mandino, Og *The Greatest Salesman in the World.* New York, NY: Fell, 1968.

Miller, Jack *Commonwealth Letters* newsletter. Available through P.O. Box 24837, Tampa, FL 33623.

Nierenberg, Gerard *The Art of Negotiating.* New York, NY: Cornerstone Library, Inc., 1981.

Ringer, Robert J. *Winning Through Intimidation.* New York, NY: Fawcett Publications, 1979.

Ruff, Howard *How to Prosper During the Coming Bad Years.* New York, NY: Warner Books, 1980.

Schwartz, David J. *The Magic of Thinking Big.* New York, NY: Cornerstone Library, Inc., 1980.

Ziglar, Zig *See You at the Top.* Gretna, LA: Pelican, 1982.

Alphabetical Index